DATE DUE

NOV 1 5 1996	DEC - 5 1995
	JAN - 4 2000
JAN 2 6 1997	MAR 0 3 2000
MAR - 6 1997	MAR 2 0 2000
MAR 2 9 1997	
MAY - 8 1997	JUN - 7 2000
OCT 1 0 1997	
	NOV 0 6 2000
OCT 2 4 1997	MAR 2 7 20
Nov 6, 1997	OCT 1 5 2003
OCT 1 2 1998	
	NOV 1 8 2003
OCT 2 7 1998	
NOV - 9 1998	
NOV 2 4 1998	
SEP 2 1 1999	
NOV - 1999	
NOV - 4 1999	

FETAL DEVELOPMENT
A Psychobiological Perspective

FETAL DEVELOPMENT
A Psychobiological Perspective

Edited by

Jean-Pierre Lecanuet
Centre National de la Recherche Scientifique
Ecole Pratique des Hautes Etudes

William P. Fifer
Columbia College of Physicians and Surgeons

Norman A. Krasnegor
National Institute of Child Health and Human
Development, National Institutes of Health

William P. Smotherman
Binghamton University

LAWRENCE ERLBAUM ASSOCIATES, PUBLISHERS
1995   Hillsdale, New Jersey   Hove, UK

Lawrence Erlbaum Associates, Inc., Publishers
365 Broadway
Hillsdale, New Jersey 07642

Cover design by Kate Dusza

Library of Congress Cataloging-in-Publication Data

Fetal development : a psychobiological perspective / edited by Jean-
  Pierre Lecanuet . . . [et al.].
        p.   cm.
     Includes bibliographical references and index.
     ISBN 0-8058-1485-X (alk. paper)
     1. Fetal behavior. 2. Developmental psychobiology.
  3. Psychology, Comparative. 4. Comparative neurobiology.
  I. Lecanuet, Jean-Pierre.
     [DNLM: 1. Fetal Development. 2. Embryo—physiology. WQ 210
  F4187 1995]
  RG622.F48   1995
  612.6'47—dc20
  DNLM/DLC
  for Library of Congress   94-44324
                                                                 CIP

Books published by Lawrence Erlbaum Associates are printed
on acid-free paper, and their bindings are chosen for strength
and durability.

Printed in the United States of America
10 9 8 7 6 5 4 3 2 1

To my mother, Julia Krasnegor

—*Norman A. Krasnegor*

Contents

Preface

This volume consists of 24 chapters that focus on prenatal behavioral development. This work is set apart from others by its emphasis on a psychobiological analysis of fetal behavior. The chapters provide a discussion of new methodologies and data that elucidate the normative behavioral repertoire of human and animal fetuses and how the expression of behavior by the fetus relates to the postnatal adaptation of the newborn. A second feature of the book is the emphasis on a comparative developmental approach. Results are provided from studies of embryonic/fetal and newborn behavior in chicks, rats, sheep, primates, and humans. The book also affords the reader an overview of perspectives, hypotheses, and experimental results from a group of basic scientists and clinicians who conduct research to elucidate the role of fetal behavior in development.

This book should be of interest to developmental psychologists, developmental neurobiologists, and those researchers interested in sensory capacity, learning, motor development, and state development. Clinicians and researchers working in the fields of obstetrics, fetomaternal medicine, and neonatology should similarly find the book of interest. Many chapters have implications for understanding linkages between behavioral and biological mechanisms that may be relevant to the diagnosis of fetal well-being and treatment of the premature infant. The work is also of direct relevance to the emerging field of behavioral perinatology. The book could be of immediate use in medical school curricula in obstetrics and pediatrics and doctoral level courses such as behavioral pediatrics, behavioral medicine, developmental psychobiology, and developmental psychology.

The book was inspired by a conference jointly sponsored by the Human

Learning and Behavior Branch of the National Institute of Child Health and Human Development (NICHD) of the National Institutes of Health (NIH) and the Laboratoire De Psycho-Biologie du Developpement of the Centre Nationale de la Recherche Scientifique (CNRS), Unité de Recherche Associée (URA) and École Practique des Haute Etudes (EPHE) held in Paris, France, in September 1992. However, the contents were written and submitted independently of the meeting. The contributions are original manuscripts presented in the form of peer-reviewed scholarly chapters. The book may thus be viewed as a useful new addition to the growing literature of developmental psychobiology.

ACKNOWLEDGMENT

The editors wish thank Ms. Jackie Corby and Ms. Judith Rothenberg for their valuable assistance in assembling this volume.

Jean-Pierre Lecanuet
William P. Fifer
Norman A. Krasnegor
William P. Smotherman

Part I

HISTORICAL OVERVIEW

1

Behavioral Development of the Fetus

Norman A. Krasnegor
National Institute of Child Health and Human Development,
National Institutes of Health

Jean-Pierre Lecanuet
Centre National de la Recherche Scientifique
Ecole Pratique des Hautes Etudes

HISTORICAL OVERVIEW

During this century, with few exceptions, studies of the earliest ontogenetic period of behavioral development focused on observations of the newborn animal or human neonate. Yet, as recently as the 1960s, developmentalists, pediatricians, and behavioral scientists still believed the newborn to be a *tabula rasa* (James, 1890). The conclusion, based on this belief, was that human newborns were considered incapable of doing, learning or knowing anything until sufficient time (some thought as much as 6 months) had elapsed and sensory and perceptual capacity developed enough for them to begin to adapt behaviorally and psychologically to their terrestrial environment. During the past 3 decades, research findings have dramatically altered this conceptualization of the ontogeny of behavioral development.

We now know that human babies are sentient beings who are aware of their surroundings, can learn within hours of birth, and are responsive to their environment at sensory, behavioral, and psychological levels. Research has convincingly documented that newborn human babies are

3

capable of adaptation, of identifying their caregivers, and of eliciting behavior from them (Gandelman, 1992; Rovee-Collier & Lipsitt, 1993). This revolution in our understanding of the newborn's psychobiological capacity raises questions concerning the origins of the observed behavior and the capacity to adapt after birth.

Birth is clearly a dramatic event in the life of all placental organisms, because it demarcates the change from an aquatic to a terrestrial existence. However, the behavioral repertoire of newborns is so sophisticated that one must ask, should the roots of behavior be sought before birth? A group of leading scientists who study prenatal behavior have argued that the fetus is vitally involved in its own development (Smotherman & Robinson, 1988). This process entails two tasks. The first of these is to learn about and adapt to its uterine environment. The second is to prepare for postnatal life.

Research on fetal behavioral development is still a relatively new enterprise. Although historically there have been studies of prenatal development by behavioral embryologists (Smotherman & Robinson, 1988), the modern era of systematic fetal behavior investigation has been under way only since the late 1970s. Prior to this time the field of scientific inquiry concerning fetal behavioral development was not unlike that described already for the human newborn. The inability to directly observe and quantify fetal behavior during gestation led to much speculation by clinicians, scientists and parents-to-be concerning the development of fetal state, movement, and sensory capacity. Some of this speculation was based on cultural and religious traditions derived, in part, from basic texts such as the Old Testament, the Mahrabata, and so on. Technological innovations such as ultrasonography changed the rules of the game. Direct visualization allowed clinicians to see and describe the fetus and its behavior in real time. Scientific advances, based on the use of model animal systems, provided methods for directly observing and quantifying fetal movement, sensory capacity, and learning in utero.

In 1984, the Human Learning and Behavior Branch of the National Institute of Child Health and Human Development (NICHD) hosted a workshop to assess the approaches for measuring fetal behavioral development. A group of scientists who pioneered research on fetal behavioral capacities outlined methodological advances made and problems associated with studying development during gestation (Kolata, 1984). In 1985, the NICHD hosted a conference on perinatal development. At that gathering was a group of leading U.S. psychobiologists who conduct research on behavior during the period of development that includes the last trimester through the first month of postnatal life. Several participating scientists presented research findings that demonstrated linkages between prenatal and postnatal behavioral development (Krasnegor, Blass, Hofer, & Smotherman, 1987).

Much has been learned concerning the capacities of the human fetus. For example, systematic observation of human fetuses, through the use of ultrasonography, has led to the characterization of four behavioral states (see Nijhuis, chapter 5, and Arduini, Rizzo, & Romanini, chapter 6, this volume). Data reveal that the human fetus has the capacity to habituate. Knowledge of this capability allowed scientists to employ a behavioral paradigm to ask questions of the developing fetus. For example, the human fetus was challenged to distinguish between speech stimuli and was found able to make such discriminations. Human neonates, within 2 days of birth, were able to distinguish between auditory stimuli (rhyming children's stories) that they were exposed to or not exposed to during the last trimester of gestation (DeCasper & Spence, 1986).

Based on acoustical measurements made, three naturally occurring, high-fidelity, auditory stimuli are continuously available to the developing fetus. These are maternal heart sounds, maternal bowel sounds, and maternal voice. Research results have demonstrated that these naturally occurring sounds are functionally important for the newborn. For example, maternal heart sounds have been used in neonatal intensive care nurseries to calm premature infants. Studies have also shown that on the first day of life, human newborns exhibit a preference for their mother's voice compared to that of another woman (Decasper & Fifer, 1980). How can human neonates so quickly identify their mother's voice and distinguish it from that of another female? Developmental psychobiologists, who made these important observations, assert that preference for and, by implication, recognition of maternal voice just after birth are based on the neonate's exposure to voice sounds during fetal development. Accurate discrimination of maternal voice is a behavior that, among others, is important for establishing the psychological attachment between the mother and her offspring.

Because research on behavioral development of human fetuses is so expensive, labor-intensive, and difficult to carry out and interpret, the vast majority of fetal behavioral studies have been conducted using animal models. Such model systems are of great scientific value because they provide the opportunity to establish reliable methods to directly observe and quantify fetal behaviors of interest. Such tactics are the hallmark of good science. These approaches have enabled developmental psychobiologists to discover and describe the ontogeny of embryonic/fetal and newborn behavior patterns (motor, sensory, and learning) in several species (e.g., chick, rat, and sheep) and ascertain mechanisms that underlie such development.

For example, rigorous and highly reliable methods have been established to systematically observe, manipulate, and quantify behavior in the fetal rat. The developmental trajectory of normative motor patterns in fetal rats has been studied and classified in terms of their frequency and sequence of appearance from day 16 to parturition (Smotherman & Robinson,

1987). Such data have been used to establish baselines for assessing prenatal learning. The data reveal that rat fetuses have the capacity for associative conditioning (a form of learning). Other studies demonstrate that such learning is retained for up to 2 weeks after birth in neonatal rat pups that were conditioned as fetuses. More recent work has revealed the role of endogenous peptides in the acquisition of in utero conditioned behavior in fetal rats (see Robinson & Smotherman, chapter 16, this volume). Fetal lambs have also been studied to gain an understanding of fetal motor and sensory development and learning. Significant advances have been made in elucidating the capacity of the fetal lamb to habituate and dishabituate. Recent work has evaluated the possible deleterious effects of vibroacoustic stimulation (VAS) on the behavior of fetal lambs. This work is important due to the use made by obstetricians of VAS to assess human fetal well-being (see Gagnon, chapter 8, Kisilevsky, chapter 14, Leader, chapter 21, and Abrams, Gerhardt, & Peters, chapter 17, this volume).

As evidenced by the contents of this volume, developmental psychobiologists have been instrumental in providing reliable and valid methods to study fetal development of humans and animal models. Future progress necessitates that multiple disciplines become involved in the context of an interdisciplinary effort to gain a comprehensive understanding of the role fetal behavior plays in development. Basic scientists and clinicians should ally themselves with developmental psychobiologists to study behavioral development during gestation. There is a need for input from the disciplines of developmental neurobiology, fetal medicine, and neonatology to pose and answer questions concerning the origins and effects of prenatal behavior on the whole organism. In the future, questions should be raised and research conducted to determine:

1. How is prenatal behavioral development involved in sculpting of the central nervous system?
2. How can fetal-medicine practitioners best establish and then employ behavioral baselines to assess the well-being of normally developing fetuses and those who are diagnosed as being ill?
3. How can psychologists and neonatologists best apply knowledge of fetal behavioral development to enhance the design of environments and treatment regimens for the premature infant?

Answers to these and other questions will greatly enrich our basic understanding of prenatal behavioral development and will demonstrate the value of such scientifically based knowledge for the betterment of the health of our future generations of children.

The volume is divided into six sections: Part I: Historical Overview, Part II: Introduction: Basic Concepts, Part III: Behavioral States of the Fetus,

Part IV: Motor and Sensory Development of the Fetus, Part V: Fetal Experience: Basic Studies, and Part VI: Clinical Evaluation of Perinatal Experience.

The ideas, methods, and data set forth in this book represent cutting-edge work in the field of fetal behavioral development. The international participation reflects the interest, worldwide, in the topic for both scientists and clinicians.

CHAPTER THEMES

Part I: Historical Overview

This provides a historical perspective on fetal behavioral development research and a description of the central theme(s) for each chapter.

Part II: Introduction: Basic Concepts

This section provides an overview of some basic concepts that govern fetal behavioral development and the linkages from the prenatal period to postnatal behavior of the newborn.

The work is by William P. Smotherman and Scott R. Robinson. Smotherman and Robinson are developmental psychobiologists who are acknowledged pioneers in the field of fetal behavioral development research. They and their colleagues have developed procedures, using an animal model (fetal rat), to directly observe and quantify fetal behavior. In their chapter, Smotherman and Robinson give an overview of fetal behavioral development and its contribution to gaining a deep understanding of the roots of postnatal behavioral development. They provide examples from their own research on the control and development of behavioral patterns that become functionally relevant after birth.

Part III: Behavioral States of the Fetus

This section contains seven chapters that focus on experimental and clinical investigations of state development in the fetal animal and human.

The first chapter is by Michael M. Myers, Karl F. Schulze, William P. Fifer, and Raymond I. Stark, a team of developmental psychobiologists and neonatologists, who employ a comparative strategy to investigate transitions from fetal to newborn life. The authors elucidate a quantitative method for classifying patterns of electroencephalographic (EEG) activity in the fetal baboon. This approach permits systematic and detailed analysis of the emergence in a primate model of fetal states such as quiet sleep and active sleep which are believed to be homologous with patterns observed in the human fetus and newborn.

The next chapter is by Raymond I. Stark and Michael M. Myers, a neonatologist and developmental psychobiologist, whose research focus is on perinatal physiology. They employ animal models (fetal lamb and fetal baboon) to monitor longitudinal development of fetal behavior and physiology. Stark and Myers describe their research to characterize and quantify patterns of breathing activity in the fetal baboon. Their results demonstrate how such patterns develop and their similarity to patterns observed in the human fetus.

The third chapter is by Jan G. Nijhuis, an obstetrician, who works in the field of perinatology and ultrasonography. He and his colleagues have defined four fetal behavioral states that have gained wide acceptance among clinicians and researchers. His chapter provides an overview of the insights given, through the use of ultrasonographic recordings, of fetal behavioral state development. He elucidates the cyclic nature of behavioral states that are best observed during the last weeks of pregnancy.

Next, Domenico Arduini, Giuseppe Rizzo, and Carlo Romanini, who are obstetricians, present an overview of their investigation of the ontogeny of fetal state. Arduini and his colleagues discuss the development of fetal behavioral state in terms of fetal behaviors. They detail data from their own research on how transitions between measured states and their duration and organization can be employed to characterize the health status of the human fetus.

The next chapter is by David James, Mary Pillai, and John Smoleniec, specialists in fetomaternal medicine, who study the neurobehavioral development of the human fetus. James and his colleagues provide an overview of their research on the neurodevelopmental assessment of human fetuses with a view toward making their findings relevant to the practicing obstetrician.

The following chapter is by Robert Gagnon, an obstetrician, who investigates behavioral states in the fetal lamb and fetal human. Gagnon discusses the advantages and disadvantages of employing VAS to assess fetal well being. VAS, a procedure that is increasingly being used by obstetricians, when delivered to the fetus can induce a change in behavioral state from quiet sleep to active sleep and thereby provide clues about health of the fetus. The author argues in favor of employing undisturbed observations of the fetus, without VAS, to assess the fetus's health status.

The final chapter in this section is by Karl F. Schulze, Sudha Kashyap, Rakesh Sahni, William P. Fifer, and Michael M. Myers, a team of neonatologists and developmental psycholobiologists, who review their work on the development of behavioral states in the premature infant. Schulze and his colleagues describe their prospective, longitudinal research designed to elucidate relationships between diet (protein and energy intake) and state development in a group of low-birthweight babies. They show how dietary intake is specifically related to states of wakefulness and sleep. The authors discuss their findings for management of the premature infant and, by implication, the fetus in terms of dietary effects on state development.

Part IV: Motor and Sensory Development of the Fetus

This section of the volume consists of five chapters that explore the motor capacity of the fetus and its responsivity to olfactory, tactile, and auditory stimulation.

The first chapter is authored by Steven S. Robertson and Leigh Foster Bacher, developmental psychologists, who are interested in the cyclical organization of motor behavior in fetal and newborn mammals. The authors describe approaches for mathematically modeling the ontogeny of cyclic motor activity in the developing fetal lamb. They explicate the use of dynamical systems (chaos theory) analysis for gaining an understanding of how motor behavior develops in this model animal system.

The next chapter is by Anne Bekoff, a behavioral embryologist, who utilizes avian models to investigate the neural basis of embryonic motor behavior. Bekoff provides an overview of her research on the relationships between embryonic leg motility in chicks and species specific postnatal behaviors. Her work details how sensory inputs help control the shift from one stable motor pattern to another during development.

The next chapter is by Benoist Schaal, Pierre Orgeur, and Christian Rognon, developmental ethologists, whose major interests are in the ontogeny of olfaction and its involvement in early maternal–infant recognition. Schaal and his colleagues review the evidence concerning prenatal olfaction in the rat fetus. They discuss experimental evidence and new methodological procedures that could extend their inquiries to the fetal lamb and human. More specifically, they describe their studies on the placental transfer of food flavors designed to assess the possible effects of prenatal odor exposure on neonatal preference behaviors in ovine and human neonates.

The fourth chapter in this section is by Jean-Pierre Lecanuet, Carolyn Granier-Deferre, and Marie-Claire Busnel, developmental psychobiologists interested in characterizing fetal auditory discrimination, the transmission of sound in the sheep uterus, and fetal reactivity to external stimulation. Lecanuet and colleagues provide an historical overview of the methodological approaches to ascertain fetal auditory capacity. They describe studies from their laboratory on habituation and dishabituation responses of human fetuses to auditory stimuli and how heart-rate deceleration can be used to reliably quantify the fetus's capacity to perceive speech and nonspeech auditory stimulation.

The final chapter in this section is by Barbara Kisilevsky, a developmental psychologist, who investigates sensory development of the human fetus and neonate. Her work involves studies of stimulus and subject variables on fetal responses to sound and vibration during the transition from prenatal to postnatal life. She provides an overview of her research on these topics and discusses the utility of evoking fetal behavior to assess fetal well-being.

Part V: Fetal Experience: Basic Studies

This section consists of five chapters that describe basic experimental research to evaluate the capacity of human and animal fetuses and human newborns to habituate, to exhibit classical conditioning, and to be responsive to speech sounds and the human voice.

The first chapter is by Robert Lickliter, a developmental psychobiologist, who utilizes avian models to investigate interaction among different sensory systems in early auditory learning. Lickliter describes his research to explore the idea that the sequential emergence of function in the various sensory systems has an important influence in determining the nature of intersensory relationships during perinatal development. In particular, he evaluates the hypothesis that limited sensory functioning during prenatal development serves to reduce available sensory input or experience from particular modalities at particular times, thereby decreasing potential competition between emerging sensory systems.

The next chapter is by Scott R. Robinson and William P. Smotherman, developmental psychobiologists, who employ a rodent model to study the expression and development of behavioral organization in the fetus. Robinson and Smotherman describe their empirical research on in utero classical conditioning of the fetal rat. They provide important evidence that links the endogenous opioids to learning in the fetus and newborn.

The third chapter in this section is by Robert M. Abrams, Kenneth J. Gerhardt, and Aemil J. M. Peters, who specialize in studying the fetal sound environment and the effects of sound and vibration on brain function in the fetal sheep. Abrams and colleagues describe research that evaluates the adequacy of externally produced auditory stimuli generated by vibroacoustic stimulators or loudspeakers to affect change in the fetal sheep auditory system. They discuss their research, which demonstrates that these two sources produce quite different sound pressure levels in the uterus. Their investigations point to some of the potential hazards of using vibroacoustic stimulation for assessing fetal well-being due to the intraabdominal pressure increases in frequencies below 100 Hz (see also chapter 8 by Gagnon).

In the next chapter April E. Ronca and Jeffery R. Alberts, both developmental psychobiologists, describe their research on the development of sensory systems of fetal and neonatal rodents. They review their elegant studies of the effects of tactile stimulation provided by the dam on the developing fetus. Ronca and Alberts provide data on autonomic and behavioral reactions of the perinatal rat to such naturally occurring stimuli. They consider the role of maternally produced stimuli in the fetus's adaptation to intrauterine life and preparation for postnatal adaptation.

The final chapter in this section is by William P. Fifer and Christine M. Moon, developmental psychobiologists, interested in fetal and neonatal sensory, perceptual, and behavioral development. Fifer and Moon review evidence from their research on the role of in utero auditory experience on the postnatal preference shown for voices and speech patterns by the newborn human. They also describe evidence from their laboratory concerning the autonomic response of the newborn to speech sound stimulation. In the last part of their chapter, Fifer and Moon describe studies on the acute response of the fetus to an array of stimuli including vibroacoustic, speech sounds, and mother's voice.

Part VI: Clinical Evaluation of Perinatal Experience

This section is composed of five chapters that provide experimental data on the analysis of perinatal experience as a means of evaluating clinical status.

The first chapter is by Peter W. Nathanielsz. Nathanielsz is an obstetrician and reproductive physiologist who employs chronically instrumented fetal lambs to study maternal and fetal regulation of labor and delivery. The author discusses his research contributions on maternal contractures as afferent stimulation that affects the organization and development of the fetal brain.

The next chapter is by Leo R. Leader, an obstetrician/gynecologist, who studies the responses of human fetuses to acoustic stimulation. He employs habituation procedures as an approach for assessing the well-being of the fetus. Dr. Leader describes his experimental research to characterize human fetal habituation to the presentation of repeated vibroacoustic stimulation. He relates his work to clinical situations in which a behavioral response or lack thereof could be employed by an obstetrician as an aid to decide whether to induce delivery.

In the next chapter, Peter G. Hepper, a comparative psychologist who employs animal and human models to investigate fetal learning and its underlying neural substrates, discusses his observations of human fetal behavior. Hepper evaluates fetal behavior that can, he asserts, be used to predict abnormality in neural functioning. He describes and discusses data derived from his investigations of fetal learning. These investigations are conducted to characterize normal and abnormal behavioral development, assess neural organization, and predict the well-being of the fetus.

In the fourth chapter of this section, Juan Carlos Molina, Maria Gabriela Chotro, and Hector Daniel Dominguez, developmental psychobiologists who employ rodent models to investigate the effects ethanol exposure has on perinatal learning, describe their extensive studies of rat pups that have been exposed prenatally to ethanol. They discuss the implications of their findings for identifying behavioral mechanisms that may be responsible for the observed ethanol preferences that rat pups exhibit given their history of prenatal exposure.

The last chapter in this section is by Heidelise Als, a developmental psychologist, who has focused her research on the neurobehavioral development of the premature baby. Als provides an overview and implications of her hypothesis that there exists a mismatch in the brain's expectancy and its environmental input. This mismatch, she believes, may lead to a form of active inhibition of certain pathways. The resulting suppression may induce an overactivation that relates to changes in the environmental niche and thereby the sensory experience of the premature baby.

REFERENCES

DeCasper, A. J., & Fifer, W. P. (1980). Of human bonding: Newborns prefer their mothers' voices. *Science, 208*, 1174–1176.

DeCasper, A. J., & Spence, M. J. (1986). Newborns prefer a familiar story over an unfamiliar one. *Infant Behavior & Development, 9*, 133–150.

Gandelman, R. (1992). *The psychobiology of behavioral development.* New York: Oxford University Press.

James, W. (1890). *The principles of psychology* (p. 488). New York: Henry Holt.

Kolata, G. (1984). Studying learning in the womb. *Science, 225*, 302–303.

Krasnegor, N. A., Blass, E. M., Hofer, M. A., & Smotherman, W. P. (Eds.). (1987). *Perinatal development: A psychobiological perspective.* Orlando, Fl: Academic Press.

Rovee-Collier, C., & Lipsitt, L. P. (Eds.). (1993). *Advances in infancy research.* Norwood, NJ: Ablex.

Smotherman, W. P., & Robinson, S. R. (1987). Psychobiology of fetal rat experience. In N. A. Krasnegor, E. M. Blass, M. A. Hofer, & W. P. Smotherman (Eds.), *Perinatal development: A psychobiological perspective* (pp. 39–60). Orlando, FL: Academic Press.

Smotherman, W. P., & Robinson, S. R. (Eds.). (1988). *Behavior of the fetus.* Caldwell, NJ: Telford.

Part II

INTRODUCTION:
BASIC CONCEPTS

2

Tracing Developmental Trajectories into the Prenatal Period

William P. Smotherman
Scott R. Robinson
Binghamton University

One of the clear implications of psychobiological research is the importance of early events in shaping subsequent development. Techniques that provide access to the fetus in utero permit investigation of the process, not merely the description, of prenatal behavioral development. Investigation of the behavior expressed by fetuses in utero traces developmental trajectories to their origin in the prenatal period. The fetal rodent model provides direct experimental access to fetal subjects, permitting visual observation and videotape recording of behavior for detailed analysis of movement patterns. Prenatal sensory experience can be manipulated by presentation of chemosensory or tactile stimuli to individual fetal subjects against a relatively stable sensory background. Contingencies between different stimuli also can be controlled, providing a range of experimental techniques for assessing habituation, classical conditioning, and appetitive learning during the prenatal period. The use of ecologically relevant and developmentally appropriate sensory manipulations to evoke species-typical behavior in the fetus provides a means for quantitative assessment of the integrated output of the developing nervous system. Study of the rodent fetus thus permits experimental investigation of motor control, sensorimotor integration, and learning in a simple mammalian system that comprises an incomplete nervous system that undergoes constant and rapid change during early ontogeny. Recent research on animal and human fetuses has suggested a number of questions that are relevant to both the basic developmental scientist and the clinician interested in the health and well-being of the human perinate.

WHY STUDY BEHAVIORAL DEVELOPMENT DURING THE PRENATAL PERIOD?

Research conducted since the 1960s has confirmed repeatedly the crucial role of early sensory experience in behavioral and cognitive development. The importance of interaction between a young animal and its surroundings in activating, guiding, and shaping developmental processes also extends to the domain of neurobiology; early functional activity promotes the normal development of motor and sensory systems and cognitive abilities (Coopersmith & Leon, 1988; Hofer, 1988). The recent research interest in prenatal development has begun to provide parallel information about sensory and behavioral development before birth. Fetuses develop within a complex environment, the uterus, that provides sensory stimulation in many modalities (Smotherman & Robinson, 1988). Further, different sensory systems begin to exhibit function before birth (Fifer & Moon, 1988; Smotherman & Robinson, 1990). The implication of recent behavioral and fetal research, therefore, is that sensory experience is a potentially important determinant of behavioral development before birth. To fully appreciate subsequent sensory and behavioral development, it is essential to begin inquiry at the time when ontogenetic trajectories are initiated—during the prenatal period.

The prediction that sensory experience is an important determinant of prenatal development has only begun to be explored empirically. In our laboratory, studies of behavioral biology in the rodent fetus have contributed to the recognition of prenatal sensory capacities and behavioral adaptation. The repertoire of behavior expressed spontaneously by the fetus (i.e., in the absence of explicit stimulation by the experimenter) expands in diversity and exhibits increasing temporal, serial, and spatial organization as gestation proceeds (Robinson & Smotherman, 1992a). The ability of the fetus to detect and process sensory information also emerges during gestation. Associations formed in utero can alter subsequent fetal behavior and be retained into postnatal life (Robinson & Smotherman, 1991; Smotherman & Robinson, 1987a). Expression of species-typical action patterns before birth foreshadows important behavioral capacities of newborn and adult animals, and argues for behavioral continuity between prenatal and postnatal life (Smotherman & Robinson, 1989). Fetal behavior is plastic and responsive, reflecting continuing adaptation of the fetus to changing and occasionally suboptimal environmental conditions in utero. These discoveries reveal the fetus as substantially different than once thought. The fetus bears more than the potential for future behavioral and cognitive complexity; it is behaviorally sophisticated in utero. Further, sensory experience and behavior are not trivial aspects of fetal life, but are essential for normal morphological and behavioral development (Smotherman & Robinson, 1987b).

Fetal study offers advantages over study of neonates that depend on maternal behavior for survival. Many recent studies have documented how behavioral interactions between mother and infant control the exchange of information, energy, and matter within the dyad (Alberts, 1986). For example, maternal contact with newborn rats varies cyclically as the mother periodically leaves the nest to dissipate heat, and salt and fluid balance is regulated by the coupled processes of pup micturition stimulated by maternal licking. Measurement of neonatal motor and sensory abilities often necessitates separation of the infant from the mother, which removes the pup from the regulatory mechanisms of thermal, tactile, and olfactory stimulation and the rhythmicity of its interaction with the mother, all of which contribute to maintaining physiological homeostasis of the pup (Hofer, 1991). Study of the rodent fetus can circumvent some of these difficulties. The fetus is dependent on the mother for life support, but is directly connected to maternal physiology and does not require active behavioral care by the mother. The fetus can be studied in experimental preparations that prevent active interference by the mother while preserving the physiological system that sustains the fetus (Smotherman & Robinson, 1991). The prenatal period thus provides a unique testing ground for investigating the development of behavior.

Although amniotic fluid, embryonic membranes, uterus, and maternal abdomen provide a concentric series of barriers that buffer the fetus from disturbances in the outside world, the fetus nevertheless is exposed to a variety of sensory stimuli in utero. Mechanical stimuli, such as sound, vibration, and vestibular changes, are abundant in the uterine environment (Fifer & Moon, 1988). Many chemical compounds can be transported across the placenta to be incorporated in amniotic fluid, providing the fetus with taste, odor, and/or trigeminal stimulation before birth. The amniotic fluid that surrounds the fetus bathes the oral, nasal, and pharyngeal cavities and is ingested and respired by the fetus, permitting direct access of chemical cues to the receptors of many chemosensory systems (lingual taste buds, pharyngeal and epiglottal taste buds, main olfactory epithelia, vomeronasal system, trigeminal system). Moreover, blood-borne chemical cues may gain direct access to the capillary beds of olfactory receptors and evoke sensory potentials. The fetus therefore is potentially exposed to a wide variety of chemosensory stimuli in amniotic fluid (Robinson & Smotherman, 1991), some of which also may be present after birth at the nipple or in the nest environment (Blass, 1990).

Across a broad range of mammals, the perinatal period is associated with rapid growth of neural structures involved in chemosensation. Histological and neurophysiological evidence indicates that fetal rats possess functional taste and olfactory systems prior to birth (Brunjes & Frazier, 1986; Mistretta & Bradley, 1986). Experiments involving early chemical stimulation have demonstrated that at least one mode of chemosensation, the olfactory system, exhibits considerable plasticity in both morphological development and involvement in lasting behavioral changes (Coopersmith & Leon, 1988). Chemical signals play a crucial, adaptive role in regulating maternal–infant interactions and infant feeding immediately after birth. Thus, neurophysiological and ecological perspectives both suggest that chemosensation is an ideal sensory modality to investigate during the prenatal period.

Despite the richness of the sensory environment in utero, the fetus lacks specific experience with many complex stimuli that will become crucial for survival and growth after birth. Because chemical cues are transmitted to the fetus by way of maternal circulation, changes in the intrauterine chemical environment are effected over a relatively long time scale (minutes or hours). The fetus thus lacks experience with temporally delimited chemical stimulation—stimuli that appear suddenly, persist for only a brief time, and disappear from the fetal environment. In contrast, experimental study of the fetus permits specific chemical stimuli to be presented directly to the fetal tongue (or other areas within the oral cavity) in a precisely controlled pulse that lasts for only a few seconds, which more closely approximates the conditions of olfactory or taste exposure in the postnatal environment. The combination of a maternally modulated chemical environment in utero and precise experimental control over parameters of stimulus presentation ensures that (a) the fetal subject lacks specific experience with pulsatile cues of the same intensity, temporal pattern, and chemical quality as the test stimulus, and (b) the test stimulus will be presented against a relatively stable, nonfluctuating background of chemical noise. The slowly changing chemical environment of the fetus contrasts with the relatively high, fluctuating levels of background noise in the acoustic and somatosensory modalities, improving the ability of the experimenter to accurately detect and characterize changes in fetal responsiveness to stimulation.

HOW CAN ANIMAL MODELS CONTRIBUTE TO UNDERSTANDING FETAL BEHAVIORAL BIOLOGY?

Concern for the healthy development of the fetus and the premature infant continues to spawn academic, institutional, and popular interest in human prenatal development. Yet in spite of technological advances, methodological problems and ethical considerations have limited the study of the human fetus to indirect monitoring, ultrasound imaging, and retrospective inference. Although these technologies have been fruitfully exploited by a few elegant studies of human fetuses (Robertson, 1988), the ability to employ true experimental designs, manipulate behavioral and neural systems, and measure dependent variables of behavioral importance during the prenatal period is generally possible only with nonhuman animal subjects. Techniques that allow direct manipulation and observation of rat fetuses in vivo circumvent these limitations. Methods that provide access to fetal subjects were originally pioneered by behavioral embryologists in the 1920s. Following irreversible blockade of neural transmission in the spinal cord at the low thoracic level, pregnant rats are immersed in a temperature-regulated saline bath that provides a supportive environment for fetuses externalized from the uterus. Individual fetal subjects retain intact umbilical connections to the placenta and remain healthy through extended observation periods. This method of accessing rodent fetuses permits observation of fetal behavior without the activity-suppressing effects of general maternal anesthesia (Smotherman & Robinson, 1991).

The rationale for using animal models is not to duplicate the human condition, but to provide simpler systems that can be probed with analytic experiments to identify general principles and processes of development (Hofer, 1987). Animal studies can suggest hypotheses that can be tested in more complex systems, including the human. Studies of infant rats have provided a focus for psychobiological research for nearly three decades. The infant rat has come to be viewed as a sophisticated organism that contributes to its own maintenance and development within a specialized niche (Alberts & Cramer, 1988; Hall & Oppenheim, 1987). One of the emerging perspectives of this research is that behavioral development reflects the close adaptation of the infant to the sequence of environments encountered during early life—ontogenetic adaptations—as well as the emergence of new behavioral capacities that are antecedents of later functional behavior (Oppenheim, 1980, 1982). Invasive procedures in animals facilitate identification of causal mechanisms of both adaptation to immediate circumstances and behavioral change during development. Recognition of behavioral sophistication in infant rats and other mammals has promoted similar inquiries into the behavioral biology of human infants, realizing the broad objective of comparative research.

The rat fetus satisfies the necessary criteria to provide an equally useful animal model of prenatal behavioral development. Research in our laboratory has built a foundation of information about the emergence and organization of behavior during the prenatal period. Applying quantitative techniques to nonevoked fetal movements has revealed evidence for cyclic motor activity and motor synchrony in the rat fetus (Robertson, 1988; Robinson & Smotherman, 1992b). Behavioral organization emerges from a background of random motor activity during gestation and is influenced, in both quantity and quality, by features of the environment at the time of measurement. Quantitative methods of measuring the normal develop- ment of fetal motor behavior have provided important baseline informa- tion essential in evaluating the results of experiments employing chemosensory stimulation. Some of these analytic techniques recently have been applied to human fetuses and neonates (Hayes, Plante, Kumar, & Delivoria-Papadopoulos, 1993; Robertson, 1993), suggesting that the findings obtained from rat fetuses may be generally relevant for a broad range of mammals.

Comparative study of fetal development utilizing rodent models pro- vides advantages for experimental analysis (Smotherman & Robinson, 1994a). The production of multiple offspring in rats permits experimental designs in which all experimental and control groups are represented within the same pregnancy. Study of fetal behavior in rats can eliminate much of the variability between pregnancies evident in research on human fetuses. Moreover, the concepts underlying experimental study of rodent fetuses can suggest new analytic approaches that can be addressed in studies of the human fetus. Animal research can contribute to an under- standing of human concerns by identifying common causal mechanisms and novel ways of thinking about the complexity of behavioral develop- ment.

WHY UNDERTAKE DETAILED ANALYSIS OF FETAL BEHAVIOR?

The majority of studies of fetal behavior have inferred fetal responses from measures of gross motor activity or changes in heart rate. Studies of fetal rats have confirmed that fetuses can exhibit pronounced increases or decreases in motor activity or heart rate in response to certain forms of stimulation (Smotherman, Robinson, Hepper, Ronca, & Alberts, 1991]. For instance, infusion of a small volume of lemon odor extract into the mouth of the fetal rat results in a four- to fivefold increase in fetal movements and a bradycardia amounting to 20%–25% of basal heart rate. These responses are evident within a few seconds of stimulus presentation and are ex- pressed over a 30- to 60-sec period. However, fetuses often exhibit very specific behavioral responses to different sensory stimuli that may not be reflected in general response measures such as overall activity or heart rate. The responses evoked by intraoral infusion of milk provide a clear example of the importance of examining the details of fetal behavior (Smotherman & Robinson, 1992a).

Milk is a biologically important fluid that fulfills vital functions in the neonatal period. Because newborn mammals must attach to the nipple and actively extract milk within minutes or hours of birth, one may expect the

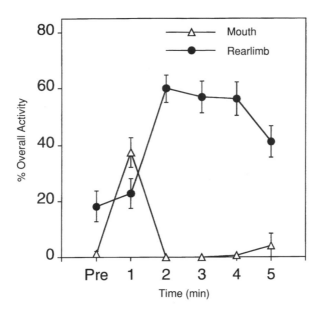

FIG. 2.1.   Changes in mouthing and rearlimb activity, expressed as a percentage of overall motor activity, in E20 rat fetuses during the 1 min before (Pre) and 5 min following intraoral infusion of milk. Time-dependent changes in behavior, which include a brief period of mouth activity followed by a more protracted period of elevated rearlimb movements, are evident upon the fetus's first experimental exposure to milk. Points represent mean percentage of movement in each minute of observation; vertical bars show SEM.

ability to recognize and respond to milk should develop during the prenatal period. Delivery of a small volume of milk into the mouth of the fetal rat results in little or no obvious change in overall motor activity or heart rate during a 60-sec period after infusion. Closer inspection of fetal responses, however, reveals that the first exposure to milk evokes a cascade of behavioral effects and engages several important neurochemical systems. Immediately after infusion, rat fetuses exhibit an increase in mouthing activity that is not elicited by other chemosensory stimuli (Fig. 2.1). Mouthing behavior gradually is replaced by other movements as fetal motor activity is reorganized over the next 1–4 min. This change in motor organization consists of a proportional increase in rearlimb activity, which eventually constitutes 75%–80% of all fetal movements (compared to the 25%–30% before infusion). Although average heart rate shows little change from preinfusion levels, variability in heart rate from one 5-sec interval to the next is sharply reduced after milk infusion. This reduction in heart-rate variability persists for several minutes, after which the fetus exhibits a transient episode of bradycardia. As heart rate returns to baseline levels after this bradycardia, the fetus exhibits a stereotypic motor pattern—the stretch response—which resembles the behavior expressed by newborn rats during milk letdown at the nipple. The fetal stretch response involves elongation and dorsal flexion of the body trunk, often associated with caudal extension of the rearlimbs. The delayed expression of the stretch response in the fetus—which typically occurs 3–5 min after infusion of milk—contrasts starkly with the nearly immediate expression of stretching after milk letdown at the nipple in neonatal rats (Drewett, Statham, & Wakerley, 1974). The unusually long delay between the moment of milk infusion and the stretch in the fetus has permitted experimental investigation of the sequence of neural and behavioral changes that appear necessary in the control of this behavior (Andersen, Robinson, & Smotherman, 1993; Smotherman & Robinson, 1992b). Following the stretch response, milk continues to exert effects on the spatial and temporal organization of fetal activity for up to 30 min (Robinson & Smotherman, 1992b; Smotherman & Robinson, 1992a).

Changes in the overt behavior of fetal rats following milk infusion are accompanied by changes in fetal responsiveness to other forms of stimulation. For example, application of a cutaneous tactile stimulus to the perioral region of the fetal rat reliably evokes a facial wiping response in otherwise unmanipulated subjects. Facial wiping is a distinctive motor pattern that involves placement of one or both forepaws in contact with the side of the head and sliding the paws over the face, toward the nose. The same perioral stimulus administered 60 s after infusion of milk evokes little or no fetal response and fails to elicit facial wiping behavior. Pretreatment of fetal subjects with pharmacological antagonists of neurotransmitter systems has demonstrated that milk-induced changes in fetal responsiveness are mediated by changes in the endogenous opioid and dopamine systems of the fetus. Administration of naloxone, which blocks opioid activity, or of more selective antagonists of opioid (kappa) or dopamine (D1) receptor subtypes, reverses the effects of milk and reinstates the wiping response to a perioral cutaneous stimulus. Pharmacological manipulations, in conjunction with sensory stimulation, thus have provided evidence of interactions between neurotransmitter systems and the ability of milk to promote changes in the neurochemical substrates of fetal behavior (Smotherman & Robinson, 1992a). Experimental findings such as these have been possible only by attending to the details of fetal behavior.

WHAT FACTORS CONTRIBUTE TO THE EXPRESSION OF FETAL BEHAVIOR?

Fetuses behave in the absence of explicit stimulation, and information can be gleaned from detailed examination of spontaneous fetal movements (Robinson & Smotherman, 1988). However, much of the behavioral repertoire of the fetus is expressed rarely during nonevoked activity, and is revealed only by manipulating sensory experience, environmental context, or the internal state of the fetus (Smotherman & Robinson, 1990). Hidden behavioral capacities may be unveiled by presentation of experimental stimuli that mimic important features of the postnatal environment. For example, fetal rats exhibit an assortment of specific behavioral responses that are not otherwise expressed upon exposure to an artificial vinyl nipple. Tactile contact with the artificial nipple elicits licking, mouthing, and orientational movements of the head. On the last 3 days of gestation (E19–E21), fetal rats exhibit a directed grasping response in which the nipple is seized and firmly held by the mouth. Grasping results in an increase in compression pressure on the nipple (biting) as well as negative pressure exerted on the tip (sucking). After establishing oral contact, fetuses show responses such as rhythmic mouthing, forelimb treadling, and rejection behavior, including facial wiping and head aversion, which often terminates oral contact with the nipple. Younger fetuses (E18) also respond to the artificial nipple, but fail to exhibit a grasping response. Instead, side-to-side head movements are expressed that eventually lead to oral capture of the nipple, producing a sequence that resembles the rooting behavior of newborn human infants (Robinson et al., 1992). Responses to an artificial nipple are just one example of organized behavior evoked by specific sensory stimuli in the rat fetus.

Fetal behavior expressed during nonevoked activity or in response to explicit stimulation also may be modified by context. Both the level of overall motor activity and the tendency of fetuses to exhibit synchronized movements are influenced by the conditions of observation, namely, whether fetuses remain inside (in utero) or outside (ex utero) of the uterus during behavioral observation. On E20 and E21 of gestation, fetal rats reliably perform a flurry of facial wiping strokes in response to intraoral lemon infusion. This response is reduced on E21 if fetuses are placed on a submerged surface, which promotes maintenance of a prone posture requiring forelimb contact with the substrate, and interferes with the paw–face contact necessary for facial wiping (Smotherman & Robinson, 1989). Conversely, E19 fetuses observed ex utero rarely express the wiping response, but perform facial wiping when tested within the amniotic sac, which inhibits head movement and promotes paw–face contact (Robinson & Smotherman, 1992a). A different form of contextual influence is evident in fetal responses to different sensory stimuli presented sequentially. In the context of postnatal maternal–infant interactions, rat pups grasp and attach to the nipple, exhibit rhythmic mouthing movements on the nipple, and then swallow after milk letdown by the mother. The tendency for fetal rats to exhibit appropriate responses to an artificial nipple or milk is contingent on the order of presentation of these two stimuli. Intraoral infusion of milk consistently evokes mouthing activity, but presentation of

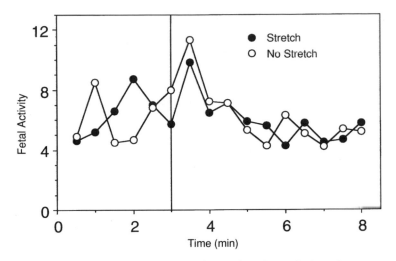

FIG. 2.2.   Phase of fetal activity in E20 rat fetuses that ultimately do or do not express the stretch response after intraoral infusion of milk. Activity is represented for 3 min before milk infusion (vertical line) and 5 min after infusion. Note that fetuses that exhibited the stretch response showed decreasing levels of spontaneous motor activity at the time of infusion, whereas fetuses that did not stretch showed increasing activity.

an artificial nipple 15 sec before milk delivery results in an enhanced mouthing response to milk. Although presentation of these two stimuli in a species-typical sequence increases fetal responses to milk, presentation in the reverse sequence reduces responsiveness to the nipple. Fewer fetuses exhibit a grasping response when presented with the nipple subsequent to milk infusion, compared to fetuses exposed to the nipple alone. These studies suggest that environmental context and relationships between different stimuli are important determinants of fetal behavior.

Pharmacological treatments can have profound effects on the responsiveness of fetuses to sensory stimulation, providing one source of evidence that conditions internal to the fetus play an important role in regulating fetal behavior. Variation in internal conditions also is reflected in measures of cyclic motor activity and behavioral states in the fetus. Fetal movements are not generated as a steady-state process, but vary cyclically with a relatively short time period, typically 0.5–2.0 min. Cyclic activity has been reported across a range of species and ages before and after birth and appears to be a fundamental aspect of spontaneous motor organization during the perinatal period (Robertson, 1988). Evidence from fetal rats suggests that specific behavioral responses to sensory stimuli are influenced by cyclic motor organization prior to stimulus presentation. In a large sample of fetal subjects, a single infusion of milk produces two subpopulations comprising fetuses that exhibit the stretch response and fetuses that do not. Subjects in these two groups show few differences in behavior immediately after infusion that are predictive of their performance of the stretch response 3–5 min later. Examination of fetal activity during the 3 min before infusion, however, suggests systematic differences in the "phase" of cyclic activity between fetuses that do or do not stretch. One group of fetuses exhibited decreasing levels of motor activity during the 1-min interval before milk infusion, whereas a second group exhibited increasing activity before infusion. Although the two groups did not differ in their initial responses to milk infusion, fetuses that showed decreasing activity at the time of milk presentation ultimately exhibited the stretch response, whereas fetuses that showed increasing activity failed to stretch (Fig. 2.2). This example illustrates how conditions internal to the subject existing at the time of stimulus presentation can affect the expression of organized behavior by the fetus.

WHAT ARE THE IMPLICATIONS OF FETAL STUDY FOR CONCEPTIONS OF BEHAVIORAL DEVELOPMENT?

Patterns of development have been conceptualized in a variety of ways, as illustrated in Fig. 2.3. A common feature of conceptualizations such as these is that developmental trajectories progress uniformly from less to more. As one moves from left to right with advancing age, performance measures steadily improve. Progressive conceptions of development engender an important assumption about the conduct of developmental research. If one measures a low level of performance at one age, it is implicit that no further information will be gleaned from study at earlier ages. This assumption is called into question by the findings of recent fetal research.

A useful example is provided by the ontogeny of facial wiping in rodents. Adult rats exhibit a characteristic sequence of motor patterns during grooming sequences that includes facial wiping or "face-washing," which involves repetitive, coordinate forelimb strokes over the surface of the face. Facial wiping can be evoked by presentation of novel or aversive chemosensory stimuli in both adults and juvenile rats, but typically is not expressed by rat pups earlier than 10–12 days after birth. Research on fetal rats, however, has documented facial wiping in response to chemosensory infusion on the last 2 days of gestation, suggesting that this behavior emerges during the prenatal period. Experimental manipulations of environmental context during the neonatal period have shed light on the apparent discontinuity between fetal and adult facial wiping. Rat neonates suspended in air or immersed in a buoyant fluid medium, thereby freeing

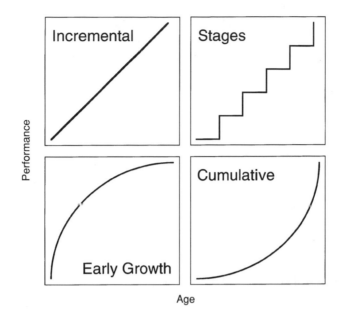

FIG. 2.3. Schematic representations of traditional views of behavioral development.

the forelimbs from a support function, express facial wiping during the first week after birth (Smotherman & Robinson, 1990). These findings indicate that mechanical constraints imposed on the forelimbs by the needs of postural maintenance interfere with the expression of facial wiping behavior. In fact, newborn rats tested on the day of birth occasionally exhibit facial wiping when they fail to maintain a prone posture. The conflict between different behavioral systems also is apparent during the reemergence of wiping behavior at the end of the second postnatal week. Eleven-day-old pups exhibit a variety of provisional postures, including support by the elbows, support by one forepaw, or leaning against a vertical surface, in order to express facial wiping. These provisional postures disappear as older pups become capable of maintaining an upright posture supported by the rearlimbs alone (Robinson & Smotherman, 1992a).

The example of facial wiping provides an example of a discontinuous developmental trajectory (Fig. 2.4). Parallel examples of early appearance, disappearance, and later reappearance of behavior have been described in a number of developmental studies of animals and human infants (Bekoff, 1992; Stehouwer, 1992; Thelen, 1988). The implication of such a developmental pattern is that characterization of behavioral capacities at a given age is contingent on the circumstances of measurement, and that different environmental conditions during development would yield a different developmental trajectory. Behavior is affected by multiple determinants, including quantity and quality of sensory stimulation, environmental context, and variables internal to the subject, including morphological and biochemical substrates, physiological conditions, and behavioral states. Some of these issues are well recognized and applied in studies of postnatal behavior, but are seldom appreciated in studies of prenatal development. The complexity inherent in behavioral control is evident shortly after fetuses first exhibit the ability to move and detect sensory stimuli. Because the position of each point along a developmental trajectory is influenced by testing conditions, any plot of developmental trajectory is relative. One should expect to find consistency in developmental pattern only as long as there is consistency in the interactions among variables that give rise to development.

The ontogenetic patterns illustrated in Fig. 2.3 also encourage certain ways of thinking about underlying neural development. Progressive changes in behavioral performance imply steady growth in number or efficacy of neural synapses (incremental pattern), an early burst of neural growth that slows with maturity (early growth), increasing connectivity between neurons or brain areas with exponential effects (cumulative), or permissive effects upon reaching thresholds in neural development (stages). Discontinuous developmental trajectories are more difficult to map to progressive changes in the nervous system and point out the need to identify the full range of factors, in addition to intrinsic changes in the

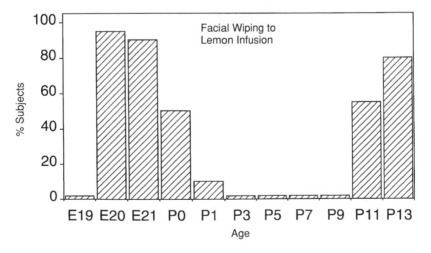

FIG. 2.4.   Appearance, disappearance, and reappearance of facial wiping behavior in response to intraoral infusion of lemon in the perinatal rat. Appropriate manipulations of the environmental context at the time of infusion can promote the expression of facial wiping on E19, P1, and P3.

nervous system such as the development of inhibitory as well as excitatory systems, that shape behavioral development (Oppenheim, 1982). This goal is inherent in the concept of epigenesis: that development emerges from the interaction of genetic, phenotypic, and environmental variables (Kuo, 1967).

The emergence of novel patterns is a fundamental problem in the study of development. One explanation of the appearance of new patterns is preformation, which assumes that a novel behavior is encoded in the genes (or in the nervous system, which is built by the genes), and unfolds in accordance with a programmed set of instructions. Paradoxically, the opposing view that pattern is imposed on the developing organism by its environment also is preformationist, differing only in the postulated source of information that dictates the developmental appearance of new patterns (Oyama, 1985). It has become a truism that neither nature nor nurture provides a satisfactory explanation and that development occurs as the product of interaction between genes and environment. However, this perspective is not completely satisfying because it merely attributes the information that dictates the course of development to two sources instead of one. The common element in all of these viewpoints is the assumption that emergent pattern depends on a preexisting plan (Thelen, 1989). The challenge for progress in developmental theory is not merely to describe trajectories or to characterize the factors involved in the control of behavior at each age or to attribute change to a preexisting set of information, but to generate a transformational or ontogenetic grammar to specify the mechanisms of how behavioral capacities change from one age to the next. Whatever framework emerges for such a transformational grammar, it will need to address the basic problem of how moment-to-moment events in "real time" contribute to age-related differences on a developmental time scale.

HOW IS FETAL STUDY RELEVANT FOR THE CLINICIAN?

Study of animal fetuses has identified important methodological, empirical, and theoretical issues in developmental research. In turn, these issues have relevance for the clinical application of fetal research findings to human infants. An interesting case in point is the preterm infant, which in essence is a fetus by postconceptional age but is asked to survive and grow in an age-atypical neonatal environment. The clinician is faced with the dual tasks of ensuring survival of the preterm infant while promoting growth, development, and adaptation to the postnatal environment. The goal of the clinician is to merge this atypical developmental trajectory with the age-typical profile of a full-term infant. It is unknown at what age such merging should occur or what strategies may be most effective to promote a merging of developmental trajectories. Current approaches to managing preterm infants range from treating the preterm infant like a full-term newborn to mimicking features of the fetal environment within the neonatal intensive care unit (NICU). Interventions aimed at promoting the precocial expression of organized behavioral responses are likely to have far-reaching consequences on future development. The implication of basic and theoretical fetal research is that alternative, nonintuitive approaches, based on understanding the mechanisms underlying developmental change instead of simply accelerating physical growth, may be more appropriate for the preterm infant. Because developmental trajectories are relative and are contingent on conditions of measuring performance, it may be inappropriate to evaluate the progress of such infants by comparison to developmental milestones based on either fetal or neonatal standards, as is routinely done in pediatric practice. Rather, it is more appropriate to identify methods of manipulating the developmental process, through early sensory or environmental events, to "nudge" the preterm trajectory into a channel that facilitates further development (Smotherman & Robinson, 1994b).

The unique circumstances of premature birth also can contribute to our understanding of the process of normal development. Experimental study of behavioral development employs artificial manipulations of sensory events or early environments to challenge the young organism. Premature birth represents a kind of natural experiment that can augment study of normal development in the fetus and full-term neonate. Because the preterm infant experiences unusual environments and behavioral challenges, it represents a potentially rich source of information about the lability of early development. Clinicians can contribute to our understanding of development and the improvement of developmental theory by incorporating theoretical and basic empirical issues into research on preterm infants. The reciprocal exchange of research findings between basic developmental scientists and clinicians will accelerate progress toward promoting the health and well-being of at-risk human infants.

ACKNOWLEDGMENTS

The fetal research reported in this paper was supported by National Institutes of Health grants HD 16102 to W. P. Smotherman, and HD 28231 and HD 28014 to W. P. Smotherman and S. R. Robinson.

REFERENCES

Alberts, J. R. (1986). New views of parent-offspring relationships. In W. T. Greenough & J. M. Juraska (Eds.), *Developmental neuropsychobiology* (pp. 450–478). Orlando, FL: Academic Press.

Alberts, J. R., & Cramer, C. P. (1988). Ecology and experience: Sources of means and meaning of developmental change. In E. M. Blass (Ed.), *Handbook of behavioral neurobiology, Vol. 9, Developmental psychobiology and behavioral ecology* (pp. 1–39). New York: Plenum.

Andersen, S. L., Robinson, S. R., & Smotherman, W. P. (1993). Ontogeny of the stretch response in the rat fetus: Kappa opioid involvement. *Behavioral Neuroscience, 107,* 370–376.

Bekoff, A. (1992). Neuroethological approaches to the study of motor development in chicks: Achievements and challenges. *Journal of Neurobiology, 23,* 1486–1505.

Blass, E. M. (1990). Suckling: Determinants, changes, mechanisms, and lasting impressions. *Developmental Psychology, 26,* 520–533.

Brunjes, P. C., & Frazier, L. L. (1986). Maturation and plasticity in the olfactory system of vertebrates. *Brain Research Reviews, 11,* 1–45.

Coopersmith, R., & Leon, M. (1988). The neurobiology of early olfactory learning. In E. M. Blass (Ed.), *Handbook of behavioral neurobiology, Vol. 9, Developmental psychobiology and behavioral ecology* (pp. 283–308). New York: Plenum.

Drewett, R. F., Statham, C., & Wakerley, J. B. (1974). A quantitative analysis of the feeding behaviour of suckling rats. *Animal Behaviour, 22,* 907–913.

Fifer, W. P., & Moon, C. (1988). Auditory experience in the fetus. In W. P. Smotherman & S. R. Robinson (Eds.), *Behavior of the fetus* (pp. 175–188). Caldwell, NJ: Telford.

Hall, W. G., & Oppenheim, R. W. (1987). Developmental psychobiology: Prenatal, perinatal, and early postnatal aspects of behavioral development. *Annual Review of Psychology, 38,* 91–128.

Hayes, M. J., Plante, L., Kumar, S. P., & Delivoria-Papadopoulos, M. (1993). Spontaneous motility in premature infants: Features of behavioral activity and rhythmic organization. *Developmental Psychobiology, 26,* 279–291.

Hofer, M. A. (1987). Early social relationships: A psychobiologist's view. *Child Development, 58,* 633–647.

Hofer, M. A. (1988). On the nature and function of prenatal behavior. In W. P. Smotherman & S. R. Robinson (Eds.), *Behavior of the fetus* (pp. 3–18). Caldwell, NJ: Telford.

Hofer, M. A. (1991). Hidden behavioral regulators in development. In B. J. Carroll & J. E. Barrett (Eds.), *Psychopathology and the brain* (pp. 113–132). New York: Raven Press.

Kuo, Z.-Y. (1967). *The dynamics of behavior development.* New York: Random House.

Mistretta, C. M., & Bradley, R. M. (1986). Development of the sense of taste. In E. M. Blass (Ed.), *Handbook of behavioral neurobiology: Vol. 8. Developmental psychobiology and developmental neurobiology* (pp. 205–236). New York: Plenum.

Oppenheim, R. W. (1980). Metamorphosis and adaptation in the behavior of developing organisms. *Developmental Psychobiology, 13,* 353–356.

Oppenheim, R. W. (1982). The neuroembryological study of behavior: Progress, problems, perspectives. In R. K. Hunt (Ed.), *Current topics in developmental biology: Vol. 17. Neural Development, Part III* (pp. 257–309). New York: Academic Press.

Oyama, S. (1985). *The ontogeny of information.* Cambridge: Cambridge University Press.

Robertson, S. S. (1988). Mechanism and function of cyclicity in spontaneous movement. In W. P. Smotherman & S. R. Robinson (Eds.), *Behavior of the fetus* (pp. 77–94). Caldwell, NJ: Telford.

Robertson, S. S. (1993). Probing the mechanism of oscillations in newborn motor activity. *Developmental Psychology, 29,* 677–685.

Robinson, S. R., Hoeltzel, T. C. M., Cooke, K. M., Umphress, S. M., Smotherman, W. P., & Murrish, D. E. (1992). Oral capture and grasping of an artificial nipple by rat fetuses. *Developmental Psychobiology, 25,* 543–555.

Robinson, S. R., & Smotherman, W. P. (1988). Chance and chunks in the ontogeny of fetal behavior. In W. P. Smotherman & S. R. Robinson (Eds.), *Behavior of the fetus* (pp. 95–115). Caldwell, NJ: Telford Press.

Robinson, S. R., & Smotherman, W. P. (1991). Fetal learning: Implications for the development of kin recognition. In P. G. Hepper (Ed.), *Kin recognition* (pp. 308–334). Cambridge: Cambridge University Press.

Robinson, S. R., & Smotherman, W. P. (1992a). Fundamental motor patterns of the mammalian fetus. *Journal of Neurobiology, 23,* 1574–1600.

Robinson, S. R., & Smotherman, W. P. (1992b). The emergence of behavioral regulation during fetal development. *Annals of the New York Academy of Science, 662,* 53–83.

Smotherman, W. P., & Robinson, S. R. (1987a). Psychobiology of fetal experience in the rat. In N. A. Krasnegor, E. M. Blass, M. A. Hofer, & W. P. Smotherman (Eds.), *Perinatal development: a psychobiological perspective* (pp. 39–60). Orlando, FL: Academic Press.

Smotherman, W. P., & Robinson, S. R. (1987b). Prenatal influences on development: Behavior is not a trivial aspect of prenatal life. *Journal of Developmental and Behavioral Pediatrics, 8,* 171–176.

Smotherman, W. P., & Robinson, S. R. (1988). The uterus as environment: The ecology of fetal behavior. In E. M. Blass (Ed.), *Handbook of behavioral neurobiology, Vol. 9, Developmental psychobiology and behavioral ecology* (pp. 149–196). New York: Plenum.

Smotherman, W. P., & Robinson, S. R. (1989). Cryptopsychobiology: The appearance, disappearance and reappearance of a species-typical action pattern during early development. *Behavioral Neuroscience, 103,* 246–253.

Smotherman, W. P., & Robinson, S. R. (1990). The prenatal origins of behavioral organization. *Psychological Science, 1,* 97–106.

Smotherman, W. P., & Robinson, S. R. (1991). Accessibility of the rat fetus for psychobiological investigation. In H. N. Shair, M. A. Hofer, & G. Barr (Eds.), *Developmental psychobiology: Current methodology and conceptual issues* (pp. 148–164). New York: Oxford University Press.

Smotherman, W. P., & Robinson, S. R. (1992a). Prenatal experience with milk: Fetal behavior and endogenous opioid systems. *Neuroscience & Biobehavioral Reviews, 16,* 351–364.

Smotherman, W. P., & Robinson, S. R. (1992b). Opioid control of the fetal stretch response: Implications for the first suckling episode. *Behavioral Neuroscience, 106,* 866–873.

Smotherman, W. P., & Robinson, S. R. (1994a). Caveats in the study of perinatal behavioral development. *Neuroscience & Biobehavioral Reviews, 18,* 347–354.

Smotherman, W. P., & Robinson, S. R. (1994b). Milk as the proximal mechanism for behavioral change in the newborn. *Acta Pædiatrica, Supplement, 397,* 64–70.

Smotherman, W. P., Robinson, S. R., Hepper, P. G., Ronca, A. E., & Alberts, J. R. (1991). Heart rate response of the rat fetus and neonate to a chemosensory stimulus. *Physiology & Behavior, 50,* 47–52.

Stehouwer, D. J. (1992). Development of anuran locomotion: Ethological and neurophysiological considerations. *Journal of Neurobiology, 23,* 1467–1485.

Thelen, E. (1988). On the nature of developing motor system and the transition from prenatal to postnatal life. In W. P. Smotherman & S. R. Robinson (Eds.), *Behavior of the fetus* (pp. 207–224). Caldwell, NJ: Telford.

Thelen, E. (1989). Self-organization in developmental processes: Can systems approaches work? In M. Gunnar (Ed.), *Systems in development: The Minnesota Symposium on Child Psychology* (Vol. 24, pp. 77–117). Hillsdale, NJ: Lawrence Erlbaum Associates.

Part III

BEHAVIORAL STATES OF THE FETUS

3

Methods for Quantifying State-Specific Patterns of EEG Activity in Fetal Baboons and Immature Human Infants

Michael M. Myers
Karl F. Schulze
William P. Fifer
Raymond I. Stark
Columbia College of Physicians & Surgeons
and
New York State Psychiatric Institute

Characterizing human fetal development poses one of the great challenges for modern biology. Scientists have long recognized the fetal period to be critical for the proper formation of organs and limb buds. However, in the past two decades, psychobiologists have stimulated an appreciation of the fact that prenatal life is not just a time of passive growth, but is also the period when developmentally diverse systems coalesce to form an organized, environmentally responsive organism. Among the first observations that contributed to this more enlightened view of the fetus were the classic studies of Nijhuis, Martin, and Prechtl (1984). These studies showed that during the later stages of fetal development there are cyclic patterns of activity within particular physiologic systems and that with maturation, these disparate activities become synchronized and behavioral states emerge. It is now widely held that the expression of these temporally organized, coherent states represents one of the earliest markers of fetal well-being and central nervous system integrity.

In the newborn, and throughout adult life, one of the primary indices for the study of sleep states is electrocortical activity. Distinctive patterns of electroencephalographic (EEG) activity have been shown to be associated with states of sleep in the newborns of many species (Guthrie, Standaert, Hodson, & Woodrum, 1980; Jouvet-Mounier, Astic, & Locote, 1970; Meier & Berger, 1965), in the ovine fetus (Dawes, Fox, Leduc, Liggins, & Richards, 1972; McNerney & Szeto, 1990; Ruckebusch, 1972; Szeto & Hinman, 1985), and in the term and preterm human infant (Anders, Ende, & Parmelee, 1971; Stefanski et al., 1984; Werner, Stockard, & Bickford, 1977). This central role of the EEG in state determination and the desire to monitor the integrity of central nervous system activity during early development make measurements of EEG highly desirable. However, even though the innovative studies of Chik, Sokol, Rosen, and Brogstedt (1976) demonstrated distinct patterns of human fetal EEG activity could be identified at the time of delivery, the developmental and state-dependent characteristics of this important index of fetal brain function remain largely unknown. Although it may never be practical to assay EEG activity of the human fetus for long periods of time, these measurements can be made in other primates, and data from these animal models can provide important insights into the processes of fetal development. The purpose of this chapter is to summarize recent studies that have demonstrated that, during late gestation, EEG activity of chronically instrumented fetal baboons exhibits discernable patterns of activity comparable to those of prematurely born human infants during active sleep (AS) and quiet sleep (QS). In particular, the presentation focuses on new quantitative methods for the analysis of EEG that appear to be appropriate for both the fetal baboon and the human infant.

THE FETAL BABOON PREPARATION

The data discussed in this chapter were obtained from the fetuses of three pregnant baboons (*Papio* sp.) over an interval of 143–153 days of gestation, with term being 175–180 days. Data collection began after at least 1 week of recovery from surgical instrumentation and discontinuation of all postoperative analgesic medications. The animals were maintained in an American Association for the Accreditation of Laboratory Animal Care (AAALAC) approved facility in accordance with the National Institutes of Health (NIH) guidelines for the care and use of laboratory animals, and all research protocols were approved after extensive review by the Committee on Animal Care and Use at the Columbia College of Physicians and Surgeons. The well-being of each of the fetuses was monitored during the study period by repeated measurements of acid–base and blood gases, which were always found to be within the normal range expected for fetal baboons (Daniel, James, MacCarter, Morishima, & Stark, 1992).

Detailed descriptions of the maintenance, breeding and preconditioning to the backpack and tether device, anesthetic, and surgical and analytical techniques have been reported previously (Stark et al., 1989; Stark, Haiken, Nordli, & Myers, 1991). Briefly, at a mean gestation of 135 days, under general anesthesia and with sterile surgical technique, the head of the fetus was delivered through a low-segment hysterotomy. After exposure of the calvarium, Teflon-coated, stainless steel wires tipped with silver solder balls were placed on the dura and fixed to the skull. There were two parietal leads (P_3, P_4) and one frontal lead (F_1) whose placement was in accordance with the standard EEG montage in human neonatal electroencephalography (Anders et al., 1971). The leads were brought out through the uterus and maternal fascia, tunneled subcutaneously to the midscapular area of the mother, and passed into a backpack secured in place by a shoulder harness. The backpack and harness system served to protect the leads, catheters, and transducers, and to provide a secure attachment point for the flexible stainless steel tether cable through which all connectors were passed to an electrical swivel outside the top of the home cage of the mother. The entire system rotated freely with movements of the mother, thus allowing continuous monitoring of electrical signals from the fetus with minimal physical restraint and no conspicuous changes in the behavior of the mother.

The EEG activity was measured between one of the two parietal leads and the frontal lead. This signal was preprocessed with a bioelectric amplifier with bandpass settings of 1.5–30 Hz and was recorded on a strip-chart recorder at a speed of 30 mm/sec for subsequent visual coding. Analog records (FM tape) of these signals along with 100-μV calibration signals at the beginning of each tape were made at the same time. For each fetus, approximately 20 hr of data, 5 hr from four different tapes, were used in the analyses.

VISUAL ASSESSMENT OF EEG PATTERNS

In the first study of EEG activity using this fetal baboon preparation, the signal was characterized by its visual appearance (Stark et al., 1991). In these analyses two types of EEG activity could be readily discriminated in the polygraph records from the fetal baboons. These two types of activity were comparable to those described in atlases of human neonatal encephalography as patterns of EEG activity associated with quiet and active states of sleep in the newborn human infant (Anders et al., 1971; Werner et al., 1977). Starting at about 30 weeks postconceptual age in preterm infants

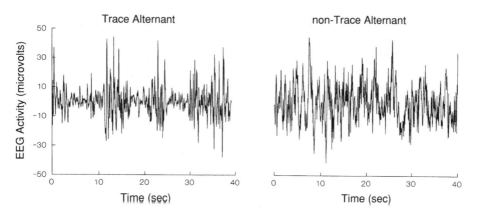

FIG. 3.1.   Tracings of EEG from a baboon fetus at 151 days of gestation. The left tracing shows 40 sec of data in which there are bursts of high-voltage activity with a frequency of approximately 6–8 bursts per minute. This segment of data was visually coded as trace alternant (TA). The panel on the right shows a segment of data with relatively lower amplitude in which these periodic bursts are absent. This segment was visually coded as non-trace alternant (non-TA).

(i.e., 0.75 gestation) and for the first 1–2 months of life in term infants, the EEG pattern associated with quiet sleep is a discontinuous bursting of activity that at later ages is called trace alternant (TA; Werner et al., 1977). Trace alternant is characterized by periodic bursts of high (>100 μV) amplitude activity alternating with low (~25 μV) amplitude activity. In the fetal baboon at 0.8 of term gestation, the TA bursts occurred on average about 6 times per minute. In contrast, the EEG records of non-trace alternant (non-TA) are characterized by more uniform activity of moderate (50–75 μV) amplitude. Representative samples of these two visually defined types of EEG activity found in the fetal baboon are depicted in Fig. 3.1.

Results from this first study indicated that epochs of TA lasted, on average, 15 min (range 1–40 min). These epochs were interspersed between periods of non-TA that had an average duration of about 25 min (range 1–60 min). Thus, when observers classified EEG activity either as TA or non-TA, approximately 40% of the time the EEG of the fetal baboon was characterized by repetitive bursts of high-voltage electrical activity that was indistinguishable from TA.

QUANTITATIVE METHODS
FOR EEG PATTERN RECOGNITION

Although discrete patterns of EEG activity that are known to be associated with states of sleep can be identified by visual analysis, many investigators have proposed strategies for computer-aided scoring of EEG (Chik et al., 1976; Goeller & Sinton, 1989; Haustein, Pilcher, Klink, & Schulz, 1986;

McNerney & Szeto, 1990; Szeto, 1990). The advantages of automated methods for coding of EEG state are increased objectivity, greater consistency of pattern recognition, and enhanced ability to resolve salient features. These methods also facilitate the processing and quantitative evaluation of large amounts of data. However, there is no automated method for the classification of EEG activity during early development when the primary distinguishing feature of the patterns is TA. The following sections summarize the results from a study recently published in which such a method was described (Myers et al., 1993).

Twelve analog tape records of the EEG signal, four from each of three animals, were digitized at 50 samples/sec using a PC-AT compatible computer with a 12-bit analog-to-digital converter. Following digitization, the EEG signal was converted from digital units to microvolts using the external calibration signal as reference.

Artifacts in EEG appeared visually on the polygraph records as pen deflections with amplitudes greater than the full range of the recorder (±250 µV). Periods of out-of-range data were generally associated with excessive maternal movements or failure of the electrical swivel. These segments of data, which comprised about 14% of the EEG activity analyzed in this study, were objectively defined as minutes in which total EEG power was 1.5 times the interquartile range above the 75% percentile and were excluded from further analyses (Wilkinson, 1988).

The initial procedure used for numerical processing of EEG was fast Fourier transformation (FFT). The FFTs, which required a power of 2 number of data points to be analyzed, were performed on the first 40.96 sec (2,048 data points) of each minute of data, and total EEG power was partitioned into five frequency bands (0–1, 1–4, 4–8, 8–12, and 12–24 Hz). Although somewhat arbitrary, these bands roughly correspond to standard EEG frequency bands (Werner et al., 1977). In addition, power was sequentially summed, starting at 1 Hz, until the frequency that corresponded to 80% of the total power was reached. This frequency was recorded as the spectral edge frequency (SEF).

A second set of procedures was developed specifically for discrimination of TA activity. First, a highpass filter was used to attenuate low-frequency components of the EEG. This step is essential because low-frequency components of the original signal interfere with the subsequent quantification of the intermittent bursts of activity that are characteristic of TA. This filtered signal was then subjected to linear full-wave rectification. Rectification is key to the recognition of the TA bursts because it emphasizes the envelope of TA bursts. Finally, to enhance graphic representation of TA activity, the rectified EEG signal was smoothed using a moving-average filter with a 0.25-sec time constant. Figure 3.2 shows the results of applying these filtering procedures to the raw data shown in Fig. 3.1. Note that the periodic bursts of activity found during periods of TA

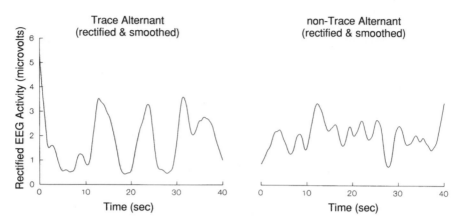

FIG. 3.2.   Effect of rectification and smoothing of EEG activity. The raw data for these panels are the same as shown in Fig. 3.1. Details of the rectification procedure are given in the text.

were transformed into low-frequency fluctuations (left panel) and that in the absence of TA these procedures yield less pronounced low-frequency activity (right panel).

To quantify the amount of TA activity, the rectified signals were subjected to FFT analysis, and power was summed over a low-frequency band (0.03–0.20 Hz), which conforms to the range of occurrence of bursts of activity during TA in both human infants and baboon fetuses (~2–12 bursts/min).

RESULTS FROM QUANTITATIVE ANALYSES

After deletion of artifact, a total of 3694 min of data was available for subsequent analysis. Of these, 1227 had been visually coded as TA, and 2467 as non-TA. The means of power, by visually coded state, for each of five frequency bands and for SEF, are presented in Table 3.1. These analyses showed consistent differences between the two types of visually coded EEG that were statistically significant for four of the six frequency bands. Most notably, in all 12 records, power in the 0–1, 8–12, and 12–24 Hz bands and SEF was lower during minutes of TA than in minutes of non-TA. Of these parameters, power in the highest frequency band (12–24 Hz) exhibited the most robust difference between the two visually coded types of EEG activity (paired $t = 16.41$, $p<.001$).

Although power in the 12–24 Hz band provided good quantitative differentiation of EEG, high-frequency activity was not the primary attribute used in our qualitative visual coding of EEG. Rather, the presence or absence of bursts of activity (TA) was the dominant feature of the signal used for visual coding of EEG (see Fig. 3.1). As described previously, TA

TABLE 3.1
Mean EEG Power (μV²) in Five Frequency Bands and SEF from Records
Visually Coded for the Presence of Trace Alternant (TA) and the Absence
of Trace Alternant (non-TA)

Frequency Bands	0–1 Hz		1–4 Hz		4–8 Hz		8–12 Hz		12–24 Hz		SEF	
Data	TA	non-TA	TA	non-TA	TA	non-TA	TA	non-TA	TA	non-TA	TA	non-TA
FFT power	15.1	24.6	16.5	16.2	5.7	5.3	2.7	4.0	2.2	3.9	8.3	10.6
Paired t	3.6		0.29		1.19		4.75		16.41		7.43	
Number of records	12		12		12		12		12		12	
p	<.005		ns		ns		<.001		<.001		<.001	

Note. Data are averages of the means from each of 12 records. There were four records from each of three animals. Also shown are the results from paired *t*-tests comparing data from the two visually coded patterns of EEG activity. The mean numbers of minutes of TA and non-TA across the 12 records were 102 and 206, respectively.

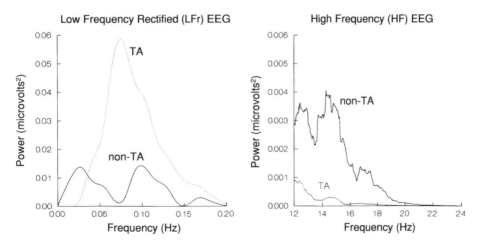

FIG. 3.3.   Results from spectral analyses of rectified (left panel) and raw (right panel) EEG activity. For rectified data only the low frequencies (0–0.20 Hz) of the spectrum are shown. Note that within this frequency band the spectrum of a segment of TA has much more power than does the segment of non-TA. In contrast, when 12–24 Hz power from the nonrectified EEG is examined, the non-TA segment has greater power than the TA segment.

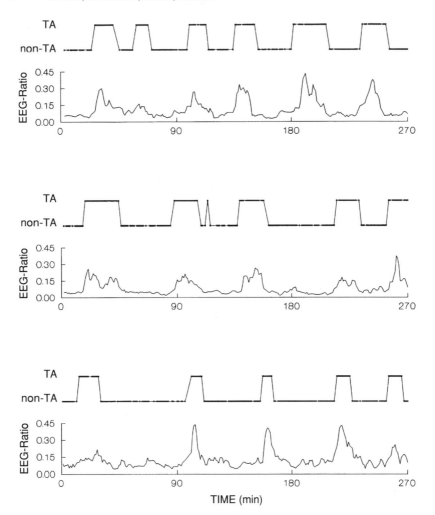

FIG. 3.4.   Three examples, from different fetuses, of the alignment between EEG coded visually as trace alternant (TA) and non-TA coded EEG with EEG-Ratio. EEG-Ratio was computed as low-frequency (0.03–0.2 Hz) power in the rectified EEG divided by high-frequency (12–24 Hz) power in the EEG and then smoothed with a 3-min moving average.

activity was quantified by summating power in the rectified EEG signal over a low-frequency band (0.03–0.20 Hz) that corresponds to the frequency of TA bursts (2–12/min). Analyses showed that power over this low-frequency band is greater during TA than non-TA. The mean value over all 12 records of this parameter during TA (mean±SE; $0.42\pm0.03~\mu V^2$) was 44.8% greater than during non-TA (mean±SE; $0.29\pm0.03~\mu V^2$). This difference held for all records, and was highly significant (paired $t = 13.48$, $p<.001$).

Thus, two parameters derived from spectral analysis of EEG were found to be strongly related to visually coded EEG. Examples of these results are depicted in Fig. 3.3. On one hand, power in the low-frequency band (0.03–0.20 Hz) in the rectified signal (LFr) was higher during periods of TA (see left panel), while power in the high-frequency band (12–24 Hz) of the nonrectified EEG (HF) was increased during periods of non-TA (see right panel). This inverse relationship suggested that a ratio computed as LFr divided by HF (EEG-Ratio) would provide a more powerful discriminator of visually coded EEG activity than either parameter alone. Indeed, in every record, LFr and HF were significant discriminators of visually coded EEG, but in each instance EEG-Ratio was a more powerful discriminator than either of the individual parameters. In subsequent analyses it was found that the ability of EEG-Ratio to distinguish patterns of EEG activity was further improved by smoothing, and thus, in all subsequent analyses, a 3-min moving average of EEG-Ratio was used as a single continuous measure of EEG activity that provided the best fit to visually coded patterns.

Figure 3.4 depicts graphically three examples, one record from each animal, of the relationship between the smoothed EEG-Ratio and visually coded EEG. Note that EEG-Ratio always increases during periods coded visually as TA.

DICHOTOMIZATION OF EEG-RATIO

The final goal of this series of analyses was to devise a statistical procedure for objective dichotomization of EEG-Ratio that would correspond with visual coding of EEG activity. K-means cluster analyses were used to accomplish this goal (Wilkinson, 1988). This procedure defines the boundaries that maximize separation between clusters of data as measured by analysis of variance (F-tests). From preliminary iterative analyses, it was found that classification was optimized by clustering the smoothed EEG-Ratio into three groups and then merging the two groups with the highest values. An example of the application of this clustering strategy is shown in Fig. 3.5. Four hours of EEG-Ratio are plotted in the top panel along with the two cutoff values defined by a three-group cluster analysis. In the middle panel, cluster 1 and the merged cluster (2 + 3) are plotted over time. Note that changes in the dichotomized EEG-Ratio are very similar to changes in visually coded patterns of EEG activity (bottom panel).

To test the reliability of this cluster strategy for classification of EEG-Ratio, analyses were run on each of the 12 records. Overall, 87.1% of the 3694 min of visually coded EEG were correctly classified by the cluster analyses of EEG-Ratio. The range of percent agreements over the 12 records was 78.2% to 91.7%, and in each of the 12 records concordance was highly

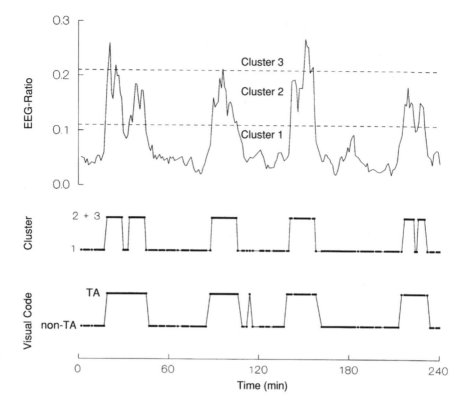

FIG. 3.5.   Representation of the statistical method for dichotomization of EEG-Ratio-3 and comparison to visual coding of EEG. Top, minute-by-minute changes in EEG-Ratio-3 over a 4-hr period. The dashed lines show the two cutoff values defined by a three-group cluster analysis of EEG-Ratio-3. Middle, dichotomous representation of EEG-Ratio-3 in which clusters 2 and 3 were merged. Bottom, the visual coding (TA vs. non-TA) of the original EEG tracing.

significant (all p values<.001). On average, 79.7% of minutes visually coded as TA were statistically assigned to the high EEG-Ratio group (clusters 2+3), and 91.3% of minutes visually coded as non-TA were in the low EEG-Ratio cluster (cluster 1).

EEG-RATIO AND SLEEP STATES IN PREMATURELY BORN HUMAN INFANTS

The last issue addressed in this chapter is the question of whether the patterns of EEG activity that are detected by cluster analysis of EEG-Ratio are those known to be associated with states of sleep. This is a difficult question to answer directly in the fetal baboon and will ultimately involve detailed analyses of the relationships among several physiologic parameters. However, this issue has been approached in an alternative way by asking whether cluster analysis of EEG-Ratio tracks behavioral coded sleep states in premature human infants. As described in a recent report (Myers, Grose-Fifer, Schulze, Fifer, & Stark, 1994), the data from 10 infants were used to answer to this question. These infants, which were on average 34 weeks postconception at the time of study, had all been observed for 6-hr periods during which time sleep states were recorded each minute. Further information about this sleep state protocol can be found in chapter 9 in this volume, by Schulze, Kashyap, Sahni, Fifer, and Myers. The EEG activity was recorded throughout this period and was analyzed in the same way as has been described for the fetal baboon. Figure 3.6 shows the results from the analysis of data from one of these infants. As can be seen in this figure, periods of behavioral coded quiet sleep are indeed aligned with periods of high EEG-Ratio. Analysis of the almost 4,000 min of data from all 10 infants showed that about 85% of the behaviorally coded active or quiet sleep minutes were correctly identified by cluster analysis of EEG-Ratio.

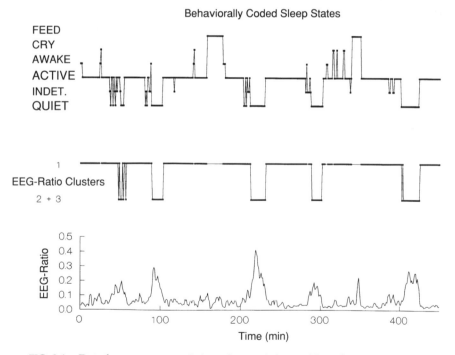

FIG. 3.6.   Data from a prematurely born human infant at 34 weeks postconception. Top, behavioral states each minute for about 7 hr. Middle, results from cluster analysis of EEG-Ratio, which is shown in continuous, minute-by-minute form in the bottom panel. Note the alignment between periods of behaviorally coded quiet sleep, high EEG-Ratio, and the 2+3 EEG-Ratio cluster.

DISCUSSION/FUTURE DIRECTIONS

In work by other investigators it has been shown that continuous low-frequency high-voltage EEG activity is the predominant pattern of activity during quiet sleep in fetal sheep (Dawes et al., 1972; Ruckebusch, 1972; Szeto & Hinman, 1985), in nonhuman primate infants (Meier & Berger, 1965), and in human infants after about 2 months of age (Werner et al., 1977). However, this type of activity was not present in the records of fetal baboon EEG over the narrow range of gestational ages studied. In the studies summarized in this chapter, two patterns of EEG activity could be visually discerned; however, the criterion for differentiation of these types of activity was the presence or absence of trace alternant (TA), not continuous high voltage. The TA, which is characterized by periodic bursts of activity, is the principal EEG correlate of quiet sleep in human preterm and term infants (Anders et al., 1971; Stefanski et al., 1984; Werner et al., 1977). Occurrences of TA have also been reported by Chik et al. (1976) in the human fetus at term. In premature *Macaca* monkeys, both TA and continuous high voltage activity have been used to visually code quiet sleep, but the relative frequency of occurrence of these two patterns of EEG activity was not reported (Guthrie et al., 1980). These studies suggest that TA is a distinct pattern of EEG activity that may be unique to primate species during early development.

The focus of this work was to derive quantitative parameters that would discriminate the visually distinct patterns of EEG activity in the fetal baboon, and then to develop a method for automated recognition of these patterns. The results demonstrate that several specific parameters derived from frequency domain analyses are significantly related to visually coded patterns. In agreement with studies of fetal sheep, it was found that high-frequency activity and spectral edge frequency (SEF) are good discriminators of EEG patterns (Szeto, 1990). However, there is another parameter, EEG-Ratio, which provides an even better correlate of the EEG patterns characteristic of the fetal baboon. EEG-Ratio is computed as power in the rectified EEG within a band corresponding to the frequency of bursts during TA (0.03–0.20 Hz) divided by power in the 12–24 Hz band of the unfiltered EEG.

In addition to deriving a new measure of fetal EEG activity, a new technique for the objective minute-by-minute dichotomization of EEG-Ratio using cluster analysis was devised. The accuracy of this technique was validated by comparing results from the cluster analysis of EEG-Ratio with visual coding of EEG. There are a number of machine coding methodologies of EEG (Chik et al., 1976; Goeller & Sinton, 1989; Haustein et al., 1986; McNerney & Szeto, 1990; Szeto, 1990), but no currently available method is tailored to the analysis of EEG patterns that are present in primates during early development. Although the methods used in this study were designed to classify only two patterns of EEG activity, other investigators have developed quantitative methods for the identification of transitions and multiple patterns of EEG activity in the fetal lamb (McNerney & Szeto, 1990). The questions of how many fetal states there are, whether the fetus is ever in an awake state, and how to best quantify these states are profoundly complex. Resolving these issues will be the focus of future studies in which the relationships between EEG patterns and other physiologic variables will be investigated in detail.

The impetus for automated classification of fetal baboon EEG activity was to facilitate the study of the ontogeny of sleep states and of the effects of various clinically relevant perturbations, such as hypoxia and drug therapies, on central nervous system function. The methods presented in this chapter describe our strategy for the quantitative analysis of fetal EEG. However, other standard physiologic criteria must be evaluated before it can be concluded with certainty that periods of high EEG-Ratio are indeed epochs of quiet sleep. In some of the animals used in these studies, eye movements (electro-oculogram, EOG), gross body movements (nuchal muscle electromyogram, EMG), heart rate, and fetal breathing activity were recorded simultaneously with EEG. In exploratory analyses of these variables it is clear that periods of high EEG-Ratio are often associated with low heart rates and heart rate variability and with reduced EOG and EMG. In a recent report, it was also possible to show that fetal breathing activity varied as a function of EEG-Ratio (Stark, Daniel, Kim, Leung, Myers, & Tropper, 1994). These finding are consistent with the conclusion that classification of EEG-Ratio, in large part, reflects fetal sleep states. However, the comprehensive analyses of these interrelationships that are currently being conducted will need to be completed before states of sleep can be definitively quantified. Nonetheless, results from the application of these techniques to EEG records obtained from human infants strongly suggest that this approach is indeed classifying the EEG into states that are highly correlated with behavioral sleep states.

Although a method for classifying fetal EEG activity into two states has been derived, it is important to point out that EEG-Ratio is not inherently dichotomous. As depicted in Fig. 3.4, EEG-Ratio, like any physiologic parameter, is continuous and expresses graded changes and intermediate values. Indeed, levels of EEG-Ratio differ among different fetuses, among different periods of TA, and among minutes within periods of TA. It is likely that this variability is not random, but rather reflects higher order complexities of brain activity. Although there are distinct changes in EEG-Ratio coincident with transitions in state, it is also clear that EEG-Ratio continues to change after the visually defined state transition has occurred. Thus, quantitation of EEG activity as a continuous parameter may provide new insights into the maturation and responsiveness of the fetal central nervous system that cannot be appreciated using dichotomized data. However, traditional descriptions of the organization of sleep states in terms of epoch durations and relative distributions of states are clearly informative. Accordingly, future studies should be directed at pursuing the developmental changes in EEG activity not only as a traditional dichotomous index of state, but also as a continuous marker of central nervous system integrity.

REFERENCES

Anders, T. F., Ende, R., & Parmelee, A. H. (1971). *A manual of standardized terminology techniques and criteria for the scoring of status of sleep and wakefulness in newborn infants.* Los Angeles: Brain Information Service.

Chik, L., Sokol, R. J., Rosen, M. G., & Brogstedt, A. D. (1976). Computer interpreted fetal electroencephalogram. *American Journal of Obstetrics and Gynecology, 125,* 537–540.

Daniel, S. S., James, L. S., MacCarter, G., Morishima, H. O., & Stark, R. I. (1992). Long-term acid-base measurement in the fetal and maternal baboon. *American Journal of Obstetrics and Gynecology, 2,* 707–712.

Dawes, G. S., Fox, H. E., Leduc, B. M., Liggins, G. C., & Richards, R. T. (1972). Respiratory movements and rapid eye movements in foetal sheep. *Journal of Physiology* (London), *220,* 119–143.

Goeller, C. J., & Sinton, C. M. (1989). A microcomputer-based sleep stage analyzer. *Computers, Methods and Programs in Biomedicine, 29,* 31–36.

Guthrie, R. D., Standaert, T. A., Hodson, W. A., & Woodrum, D. E. (1980). Sleep and maturation of eucapnic ventilation and CO_2 sensitivity in the premature primate. *Journal of Applied Physiology, 48,* 347–354.

Haustein, W., Pilcher, J., Klink, J., & Schulz, H. (1986). Automatic analysis overcomes limitations of sleep stage scoring. *Electroencephalography and Clinical Neurophysiology, 64,* 364–374.

Jouvet-Mounier, D., Astic, L., & Locote, D. (1970). Ontogenesis of the states of sleep in rat, cat and guinea pig during the first postnatal month. *Developmental Psychobiology, 2,* 216–239.

McNerney, M. E., & Szeto, H. H. (1990). Automated identification and quantification of four patterns of electrocortical activity in the near-term fetal lamb. *Pediatric Research, 28,* 106–110.

Meier, G. W., & Berger, R. J. (1965). Development of sleep and wakefulness patterns in the infant rhesus monkey. *Experimental Neurology, 12,* 257–277.

Myers, M. M., Grose-Fifer, J., Schulze, K. F., Fifer, W. P., & Stark, R. I. (1994.) *A new method for coding patterns of EEG activity in premature human infants.* Manuscript submitted for review.

Myers, M. M., Stark, R. I., Fifer, W. P., Grieve, P. G., Haiken, J., Leung, K., & Schulze, K. F. 1993. A quantitative method for classification of EEG in the fetal baboon. *American Journal of Physiology, 265,* 706–715.

Nijhuis, J. G., Martin, C. B. Jr., & Prechtl, H. F. R. (1984). Behavioral states of the human fetus. In H. F. R. Prechtl (Ed.), *Clinics in developmental medicine, No. 94: Continuity of neural functions from prenatal to postnatal life* (pp. 65–78). London: Spastics International Medical Publications.

Ruckebusch, Y. (1972). Development of sleep and wakefulness in the foetal lamb. *Electroencephalography and Clinical Neurophysiology, 32,* 119–128.

Stark, R. I., Daniel, S. S., James, L. S., MacCarter, G., Morishima, H. O., Niemann, W. H., Tropper, P .J., & Yeh, M-N. (1989). Chronic instrumentation and longterm investigation in the fetal and maternal baboon: Tether system, conditioning procedures and surgical techniques. *Laboratory Animal Sciences, 39,* 25–32.

Stark, R. I., Daniel, S. S., Kim, Y-I, Leung, K., Myers, M. M., & Tropper, P. J. (1994). Patterns of fetal breathing in the baboon vary with EEG sleep state. *Early Human Development, 38,* 11–26.

Stark, R. I., Haiken, J., Nordli, D., & Myers, M. M. (1991). Characterization of electroencephalographic state in fetal baboons. *American Journal of Physiology, 261,* R496–R500.

Stefanski, M., Schulze, K., Bateman, D., Kairam, R., Pedley, T. A. Masterson, J., & James, L. S. (1984). A scoring system for states of sleep and wakefulness in term and preterm infants. *Pediatric Research, 18,* 58–62.

Szeto, H. H. (1990). Spectral edge frequency as a simple quantitative measure of the maturation of electrocortical activity. *Pediatric Research, 27,* 289–292.

Szeto, H. H., & Hinman, D. J. (1985). Perinatal development of sleep-wake patterns in sheep. *Sleep, 8,* 347–355.

Werner, S. S., Stockard, J. E., & Bickford, R. G. (1977). *Atlas of neonatal electroencephalography.* New York: Raven.

Wilkinson, L. (1988). *SYSTAT: The system for statistics.* Evanston, IL: Systat, Inc..

4

Breathing and Hiccups in the Fetal Baboon

Raymond I. Stark
Michael M. Myers
Columbia College of Physicians & Surgeons
and
New York State Psychiatric Institute

It has been just over 20 years since the publication of a classic report by Dawes et al. (Dawes, Fox, Leduc, Liggins, & Richard, 1972) in which they provided the initial detailed description of the rapid irregular breathing movements of the chronically instrumented fetal lamb. With the advent of technology for high-resolution ultrasound shortly thereafter, it became possible to document the occurrence of breathing activity and other aspects of fetal behavior in the human fetus during the course of gestation (Pillai & James, 1990b). From studies in these and other species it became clear that under normal conditions fetal breathing movements are intermittent. Epochs of fetal breathing activity of variable duration are interspersed over time with periods of apnea that are equally variable in duration. Research suggests that mechanisms that act to generate this periodicity do so by inhibition of fetal breathing movements (Bryan, Bowes, & Maloney, 1986; Jensen & Chernick, 1991). These regulatory processes may be in part a specialized adaptation to the demands of fetal life and serve to promote conservation of oxygen and nutrient supply. On the other hand, the presence of these movements, at least for some part of the time, is essential for growth of the lungs and development of normal pulmonary architecture (Alcorn, Adamson, Maloney, & Robinson, 1986).

In addition to issues of development and respiratory control, clinical research has related the occurrence of altered patterns of fetal breathing activity to factors that may compromise fetal well-being such as maternal smoking, ethanol consumption, or premature labor (Jensen & Chernick, 1983). The response of the fetus to hypoxia is paradoxical when compared to the response of the adult. The acute effect of lowered oxygen tension on the fetus is a depression of breathing activity, in contrast to the expected stimulation that is seen in normal adults and, for that matter, infants after the immediate postpartum period (Bryan et al., 1986; Walker, 1984). In experimental animals profound fetal distress and asphyxia induce a grossly abnormal gasping pattern of breathing activity (Patrick, Dalton, & Dawes, 1976). Other common events are associated with changes in the pattern of breathing of the fetus. Prominent among these is a diminution in activity seen in the days preceding normal term delivery (Castle & Turnbull, 1983). Thus, there exists a substantial literature that relates change in the characteristics of fetal breathing to aspects of fetal well-being, lung development, and possibly for impending labor.

One striking observation related to the control of fetal breathing is the close relationship of this behavior with fetal sleep state (Dawes et al., 1972). Indeed, in the latter third of gestation, the breathing activity of the fetal lamb is found only during times of rapid eye movement and low-voltage/high-frequency electroencephalographic (EEG) activity, that is, fetal active sleep. In contrast, breathing activity is virtually absent during quiet sleep in this species. In the human infant and adult, states of sleep exert a dramatic influence not on the presence or absence of the activity, but rather on respiratory patterning and variability (Jensen & Chernick, 1983). State in the human fetus is characterized by heart rate patterns, body and eye movements (see Nijhuis, chapter 5, this volume). During the last weeks of gestation the human fetus spends a majority of time in active sleep. Episodic fetal breathing is present during active sleep and persists with a lower incidence during the quiet state (Nijhuis et al., 1983; van Vliet, Martin, Nijhuis, & Prechtl, 1985). State-dependent patterning of other characteristics of fetal breathing may occur in utero, but a detailed examination of these interactions has not been reported. Our work with the fetus of a nonhuman primate suggests that the baboon (*Papio* sp.) would be an appropriate animal for the detailed study of the linkage between fetal breathing and sleep state (Rey et al., 1989; Stark et al. 1993). A second fascinating issue related to the control of fetal breathing is the effect of time of day on the behavior. In a set of studies by Dr. John Patrick and his colleagues (Patrick, Natale, & Richardson, 1978), the fetuses of pregnant women were monitored with ultrasound for 24 consecutive hours. These studies demonstrated a circadian pattern of fetal breathing activity. This rhythm was lost when the normal diurnal variation in maternal cortisol and adrenocorticotropin (ACTH) was suppressed (Seron-Ferre, Ducsay, &

Valenzuela, 1993). These and other data suggest that there is considerable interaction between the mother and her fetus with respect to circadian rhythms. The origins and significance of the diurnal variation of fetal breathing movements are a topic of active investigation and may serve as a model to uncover the mechanism for the complex interactions between mother and fetus.

Despite an extensive literature on fetal breathing activity, other types of movements of the fetal diaphragm have received little attention. As described by Newberry (1942), clinical reports of fetal hiccups from pregnant women date back at least 100 years. More recent ultrasound studies of the human fetus have demonstrated that fetal hiccups are one of the earliest distinct movement patterns to appear, being observed as early as 9 weeks of gestation (de Vries, Visser, & Prechtl, 1982; Pillai & James, 1990b; van Woerden et al., 1989). During the early stages of development hiccups are the most common type of diaphragmatic movement. Their incidence diminishes to a stable low level at the end of the second trimester, after which fetal breaths become predominant. As in the adult, fetal hiccups remain a poorly understood behavior, although folk medicine and empirical speculation have suggested that fetal hiccups are a sign of well-being (Launois, Bizec, Whitelaw, Cabane, & Derenne, 1993). Very little has been accomplished with experimental animals to confirm or deny this speculation (Harding, Fowden, & Silver, 1992; Stark et al., in press).

We have undertaken the task of developing a nonhuman primate model to permit the chronic monitoring of fetal behavior. The model provides data for characterization of fetal sleep state (see Myers, Schulze, Fifer, & Stark, chapter 3, this volume) and recognition and quantifying fetal breathing and hiccups. Long-term recordings from these fetuses are made without major disruption of the intrauterine environment or the normal activities of the mother. In this report analyses of data from the fetal baboon have been summarized to: (a) describe fetal breathing and hiccuping activity, (b) examine the developmental patterns of these activities, (c) elucidate linkages of these activities with sleep state, and (d) demonstrate the presence of circadian rhythms in the occurrence of these activities.

METHODS

Data were summarized from the fetuses of eight pregnant baboons (*Papio* sp.) who were monitored for assessment of fetal breathing and hiccuping through changes in tracheal fluid pressure and sleep state through analysis of fetal electroencephalogram (EEG). These animals were maintained and studied with the use of a backpack and tether system in accordance with the National Institutes of Health (NIH) Guide for the Care and Use of Laboratory Animals. Research protocols were approved by the Institutional Animal Care and Use Committee of Columbia University College of Physicians and Surgeons. The development of methodology for these long-term studies has been described in detail elsewhere (Daniel, James, McCarter, Morishima, & Stark, 1992; Myers, Fifer, Haiken, & Stark, 1990; Stark, Haiken, Nordli, & Myers, 1991; Stark et al., 1989).

Prior to breeding, animals were conditioned to the tether and backpack, and intolerant animals were excluded from further study. Special attention was paid to the social dominance in organization of the colony and the behavior patterns of individual females. Breeding was done within the colony and conception defined to within ±3 days with real-time ultrasound evaluation of fetal growth (Ferine, McCarter, Timor-Tritsch, Yeh, & Stark, 1988).

Under general anesthesia, surgery was performed between 115 and 135 days postconception (term $\approx$ 175 days) for catheterization of the fetal trachea and amniotic fluid cavity with placement of ECG leads. Additional instrumentation in selected animals included maternal and fetal vascular catheters and EEG leads. After surgery the mother was refitted with her backpack, which in turn was attached to a tether system permitting continuous acquisition of data from all catheters and leads with minimal physical restraint. The mothers were returned to their home cages within the colony. Patterns of maternal behavior following recovery from surgery and discontinuation of analgesic medications were not different from those observed before the operation. The condition of the fetus was assessed metabolically by measurements of pH and arterial blood gases. Values were considered normal when pH > 7.380, $PaCO_2$ < 45 torr, and PaO_2 > 25 torr (Daniel et al., 1992). Other indices of well-being included monitoring of fetal heart rate patterns, amniotic fluid pressure change, and/or neuroendocrine parameters (Goland, Stark, & Wardlaw, 1990). Finally, sleep state was assigned by characterization of patterns of EEG using the methods described by Myers et al., this volume.

In six of the eight animals, polygraph records for the entire study period (130–164 days) were reviewed visually to determine the time of day of occurrence and duration of every bout of hiccups. These data were summarized for assessment of changes in hiccuping over gestation and ultradian properties of their occurrence. A subset of the records from these six animals and records from two additional animals was digitized at 25 Hz in 16- or 24-hr long data files and analyzed with specifically designed methods for recognition of breaths and hiccups (Stark et al., 1993). Negative deflections of tracheal minus amniotic fluid pressure of 2.0 torr or greater were recognized as fetal breaths. Within characteristic bouts, hiccups were recognized as pressure deflections of greater than 15 torr pressure. In addition to amplitude, the time interval of the deflection from the baseline to the nadir of pressure change (Ti), from the nadir to return of pressure to baseline (Te), and the interval between deflections (Ttot) were defined. Criteria were established for the definition of bouts of breathing and hiccuping based on the statistical characteristics of these intervals and their amplitude. Included in the present review are characteristics of the duration of bouts of breathing and hiccupping activity, percent of total time spent with each activity, and rate and variability of rate.

RESULTS

Breaths and Hiccups Recognition

The distinctive characteristics that permit differentiation of fetal breaths from hiccups are exemplified in the sample tracheal fluid pressure recording in Fig. 4.1. The upper panel of this figure is a 1-min segment with fetal breaths and the middle panel a segment with hiccups.

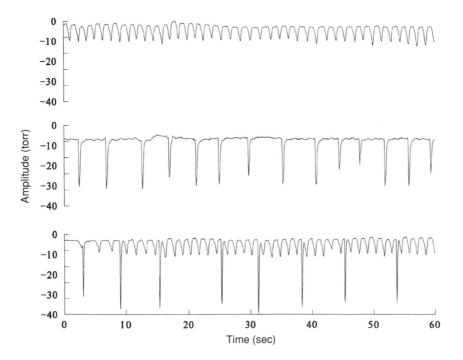

FIG. 4.1.   Segments of a tracheal fluid pressure recording from a fetal baboon at 144 days of gestation. Top, 1-min segment with fetal breathing; middle, segment with fetal hiccuping; bottom, segment with a mix of both breaths and hiccups.

TABLE 4.1
Differences in Characteristics of Hiccups and Breaths from Four
Fetal Baboons at a Mean of 151 Days Gestation.

Characteristics	Hiccups	Breaths
Ti (sec)	0.25 (0.01)	0.50 (0.02)
Te (sec)	0.24 (0.01)	0.38 (0.01)
Amplitude (torr)	25.8 (0.8)	7.3 (0.6)
Incidence (%)	1.8 (0.3)	53.3 (12.8)
Dur (sec)	303.6 (13.1)	58.2 (4.6)
Rate (min^{-1})	24.2 (2.5)	45.8 (2.1)
CV rate (%)	3.8 (0.3)	5.6 (0.1)

Note. Comparisons include mean + (SD) of inspiratory time (Ti), expiratory time (Te), amplitude, incidence as percent of total time, bout duration (Dur), rate as number of hiccups or breaths per minute (min^{-1}), and coefficient of variation (CV) of rate. All differences between hiccups and breaths are significant at $p < .05$ or better.

It can be appreciated by visual inspection of records that the two populations of deflections in tracheal fluid pressure are distinct with respect to amplitude, duration of inspiratory and expiratory intervals (Ti and Te), and rhythmicity. In the lower panel, when these two activities occur simultaneously, hiccups can begin at variable times during a breath cycle, but most frequently hiccups start during the intervals between fetal breaths. The characteristics of hiccups and breaths are summarized statistically in Table 4.1. The mean amplitude of fetal hiccups is threefold greater than that of fetal breaths, and the mean values of Ti and Te for hiccups are both shorter than these time intervals for breaths. Not apparent from the 1-min segments shown in Fig. 4.1 is the fact that these two activities occur in bouts or epochs with intervening periods of apnea. Characteristics of these epochs of hiccuping and breathing are also quite distinctive (see Table 4.1). Fetal breathing is present about half the time, although there is a wide range in variability from fetus to fetus and from day to day in an individual fetus. In contrast, hiccuping is about 25-fold less common and occurs with a lesser degree of variability in incidence both over time for an individual fetus and between different fetuses during the same portion in gestation. Although less common, bouts of fetal hiccuping last on average 5 min compared to a mean of about 1 min for the duration of epochs of breathing. On average 18% of bouts of hiccuping occur during apnea, 30% during continuous breathing, and 52% are accompanied by a mix of both breathing and apnea. Finally, other characteristics of bouts of hiccups are distinct from breathing. As summarized in Table 4.1, the rate of hiccups is about half that of breathing and the variability of rate is less. Thus, these two types of episodic diaphragmatic activities are highly differentiated.

Effects of Gestational Age

Next, the effects of maturation on these two types of diaphragmatic movement were examined. In a prior study of fetal breathing Stark et al. (1993)
found no significant change in the incidence during the latter third of
gestation. Nonetheless, a clear pattern of maturation of other aspects of the
behavior was apparent including progressive increases in amplitude, inspiratory time interval, and a decrease in rate (see Fig. 4.2).

The data summarized in Table 4.2 confirm these earlier findings. It is of
interest that over the same interval in late gestation the maturational
pattern of hiccups is different. Unlike fetal breathing, the incidence of
bouts of hiccuping decreases by about half in this 3-week interval prior to
term, whereas no apparent change is found in the inspiratory time, ampli-

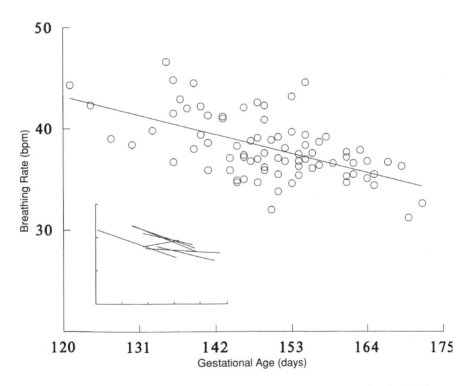

FIG. 4.2.   Mean amplitude (mm Hg) of fetal breaths from 81 records of 16–24 hr
duration over a range in gestation from 121 to 172 days and the regression line ($r = .73$,
$p < .001$). In the insert on a proportional scale the regression lines for each of seven
animals are represented to facilitate comparisons between data from individual fetuses
and the aggregate data set. The slopes of these regression lines were positive for all in
six of seven fetuses and significant ($p < .01$) in six of seven.

TABLE 4.2
Differences in Characteristics of Hiccups and Breaths by Gestational Age (GA) Interval, E = Earlier (142±0.9 Days, Mean±SD), and L = Later (159±1.1 Days)

Parameter	GA Interval	Breaths	Hiccups
Ti (sec)	E	0.47 (0.01)	0.24 (0.01)
	L	0.53 (0.2)[a]	0.25 (0.01)
Amplitude (torr)	E	6.3 (0.3)	24.7 (1.3)
	L	8.3 (0.9)[a]	26.9 (0.6)
Incidence (% time)	E	58.3 (3.9)	2.2 (0.3)
	L	48.2 (5.1)	1.3 (0.2)[a]
Rate (min⁻¹)	E	48.7 (1.3)	27.0 (2.5)
	L	43.0 (1.0)[a]	22.8 (2.5)[a]

Note. Comparisons include mean (±SEM) inspiratory time (Ti), amplitude (amp), incidence as percent total time, and rate as number of hiccups or breaths per minute (min⁻¹).
[a]Later differs from earlier, $p < .05$ or better, determined by paired analysis in five fetuses.

tude, or rate of hiccups. Thus it would seem that there are different developmental trajectories for these two types of diaphragmatic activity.

Effects of Electrocortical State

Differences between hiccuping and breathing are also apparent in analyses of the linkages between these behaviors and electrocortical (EEG) state. The method described by Myers et al. (1993; Myers et al., chapter 3, this volume) was used for state recognition, and the characteristics of breathing and hiccuping were then analyzed by state. From prior analyses Stark et al. (1991) demonstrated that the duration of a representative state cycle was 40 min with 25 min of active and 15 min of quiet state. Assuming an average hiccup bout duration of 5 min, it can be estimated that approximately 50% of hiccup bouts will occur in the active state (AS), 25% in the quiet state (QS), and 25% during transitions. We found that 50% of hiccup bouts actually occurred in AS, 30% in QS, and 20% in transition. Thus, hiccups do not appear to be preferentially distributed into one state or the other. In addition, bouts of hiccups that occurred during transitions were equally distributed between those from AS to QS and those from QS to AS. Thus, despite the vigorous nature of hiccuping behavior, bouts of hiccups did not appear to induce transitions from one state to another.

In contrast, the incidence of fetal breathing occurs about 60% of the time in AS and is about half as common during QS. As shown in Table 4.3, characteristics of hiccuping are comparable in the two states, whereas characteristics of fetal breathing are highly differentiated with respect to state. Not only were the characteristics of breaths (i.e., amplitude) and

TABLE 4.3
Comparisons of Breaths and Hiccups by Electroencephalographic
(EEG) State

	EEG State	Breaths	Hiccups
Ti (sec)	Quiet	0.50 (0.02)	0.25 (0.006)
	Active	0.47 (0.01)[a]	0.25 (0.003)
Amp (torr)	Quiet	5.9 (0.3)	24.7 (0.7)
	Active	6.9 (0.3)[a]	24.5 (0.6)
Rate (min⁻¹)	Quiet	38.7 (1.0)	23.7 (1.2)
	Active	48.0 (1.2)[a]	23.8 (1.3)

Note. Variables include mean (±SEM) of Inspiratory Time (Ti), amplitude (amp) and rate as number of breaths or hiccups per minute.

[a]Quiet differs from active, $p < .05$, determined by analysis of data from four fetuses.

breathing (i.e., rate) differentiated by state, but their variability (i.e., rate SD) was also distinct. All these features of breathing were significantly increased in AS as opposed to QS. It is apparent that the patterning of fetal breathing behavior is regulated by mechanisms governing state cyclicity whereas the more stereotypic bouts of hiccuping appear to be independent of this modulatory process.

Effects of Diurnal Processes

Finally, another aspect of the mechanisms governing these two behaviors was examined by summarization of data as hourly means over daily cycles. In preliminary studies, both breathing and hiccuping can be linked with the time of day. The incidence of fetal breathing was greater in the daylight hours than at night, whereas bouts of hiccuping were more common during the night than during the day. These initial findings are plotted in Fig. 4.3. Thus, modulators that govern circadian processes may also affect the centers regulating both breathing and hiccuping behavior.

DISCUSSION

In part because the fetus is hidden from view, the understanding of processes governing changes in behavior during the prenatal period of life is far less complete than those governing the dramatic evolution from infancy to senescence. We have used techniques of chronic instrumentation to reveal fetal behaviors to the experimenter while maintaining the maternal support system within carefully controlled bounds (Daniel et al., 1992; Goland et al., 1990; Myers et al., 1990; Stark, et al., 1989). This chapter

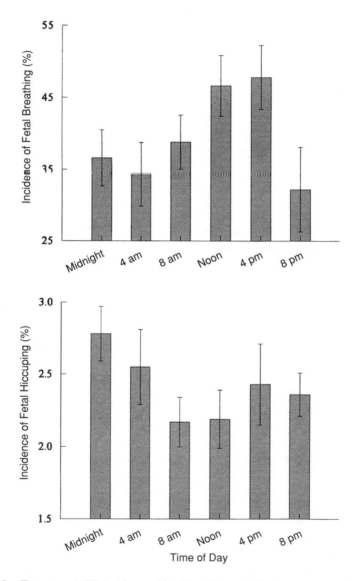

FIG. 4.3. Top, mean (±SE) incidence of fetal breathing activity in percentage of total time summarized at 4-hr intervals over 24 hr for five fetal baboons. For each fetus four records of 24 hr duration were included in the analysis. Bottom, mean (±SE) incidence of fetal hiccuping activity for the same data set.

summarizes in a quantitative fashion some aspects of the differentiation, development, and temporal organization of movements of the fetal diaphragm characterized as fetal breaths and hiccups.

These behaviors are assessed by monitoring deflections of pressure in the fetal trachea. Because the viscosity of the fluid that fills the fetal lungs is high, very little fluid is moved with a contraction of the diaphragm. Thus, changes in tracheal fluid pressure are a fairly accurate reflection of fetal diaphragmatic activity (Jensen & Chernick, 1983). It should be noted that chronic drainage of lung liquid or obstruction of normal flow can cause derangements in lung development (Alcorn et al, 1986). Thus, in chronic experiments, care must be taken to avoid both of these abnormalities in lung liquid dynamics, when deflections of tracheal pressure are used to monitor movements of the fetal diaphragm.

Two distinct behaviors, breathing and hiccuping, are recognized from analysis of the deflections in tracheal fluid pressure of the fetal baboon (see Table 4.1 and Fig. 4.1). There is evidence from many sources that fetal breathing movements are a normal and essential part of intrauterine existence (Bryan et al., 1986; Jensen & Chernick, 1991). The same cannot be said for hiccupping behavior. It is only with recent longitudinal ultrasound studies of the human that fetal hiccupping has been accepted as part of normal fetal behavior (de Vries et al., 1982; Pillai & James, 1990b; Roodenburg, Wladimiroff, Vanes, & Prechtl, 1991; van Woerden et al., 1989). The stimuli for hiccups and the mechanisms regulating their occurrence remain as poorly defined for the fetus as they are for the adult. Nonetheless, examination of this behavior in the fetus has led to an appreciation of the richness and diversity of diaphragmatic movements.

From the earliest stages of human development, when the first gross movements of the fetus can be detected, hiccups and subsequently breaths are a regular part of the emerging repertoire of fetal movements. In the human these behaviors assume distinctive developmental trajectories. Hiccups are the dominant diaphragmatic movements early in gestation and diminish to a stable low level of occurrence halfway to term. In contrast, epochs of breathing increase in frequency and duration to reach a relative plateau (about 30–40% of total time) in the last trimester (de Vries et al., 1982; Jensen & Chernick, 1991; Pillai & James, 1990b; Roodenburg et al., 1991). In the fetal baboon a highly organized and consistent pattern of development of fetal breathing activity has been found in the latter third of gestation (Stark et al., 1993). In contrast, hiccupping behavior, although equally consistent, does not follow a comparable pattern of change, but rather assumes an invariant, almost vestigial, pattern of occurrence.

The implication of these developmental differences may rest in the concept that progressive maturation of higher centers within the central nervous system permits new capacities and forms of organization to be brought to bear on a behavior. It would appear that centers governing hiccupping behavior fit into the hierarchy of organization in a less complex fashion than the centers governing the regulation of breathing. Thus, in subsequent research hiccupping behavior might be thought to represent reflexive, stereotypic activity of the diaphragm, whereas changes in fetal breathing behavior would reflect development of more advanced motor patterns. As such, assessment of fetal breathing should be useful as a means to investigate coordination of motor and sensory capacities as well as a tool to probe the influence of environmental events on fetal behavior. In support of this notion there is an extensive literature relating changes in fetal breathing behavior to various drugs and substances ingested by pregnant women or administered to pregnant animals (Jensen & Cherinck, 1983). Certainly these agents can have long-term ramifications for behavioral organization as evidenced by the delayed development of the child with fetal alcohol syndrome.

In another realm, factors such as state consciousness have also been shown to influence normal patterns of breathing (Phillipson & Bowes, 1986). The occurrence of fetal breathing behavior in the sheep is present almost exclusively during active sleep, although even in this state it is present only 50–80% of time (Dawes et al., 1972). In the baboon, as in the human, fetal breathing is present in both the active and, albeit at lower levels, the quiet state (Stark et al., 1994). As anticipated, the patterning of fetal breathing is highly distinctive in the two states. In contrast, fetal hiccups are not similarly differentiated by state. It is of interest that, even though bouts of hiccups may be the most vigorous activity performed by the fetus, hiccups are not associated with arousal from quiet sleep. Bouts of hiccups in the fetal baboon are just as likely to occur in the transition from the quiet to the active state as they are from the active to the quiet state. These data would again support the concept that bouts of hiccups are a primitive behavior governed by simple inhibitory neural pathways.

Diurnal rhythmicity in a number of physiologic processes has been described for the fetuses of both experimental animals and humans (Seron-Ferre et al., 1993). It is most likely that these fetal rhythms are not mediated by perception of light by the fetal retina and stimulation of suprachiasmatic pacemakers. Rather, these rhythms, which link the fetus to conditions in the extra uterine environment, are thought to be mediated by a variety of maternal signals that cross the placenta and provide the fetus with time-of-day cues. In the human fetus the incidence of fetal breathing activity is highest in the early morning hours. However, the situation is complicated by the superimposition of ultradian rhythms in fetal breathing associated with maternal meals and fluctuations in maternal blood glucose (Patrick et al., 1978). In the fetal baboon both hiccups and breathing appear to have a diurnal periodicity. Further exploration of the ontogeny of rhythmicity should provide insight into the mechanisms by which the mother communicates information about conditions in the environment to her fetus.

SUMMARY AND FUTURE DIRECTIONS

Many years of effort have been invested in the development of the fetal baboon preparation. It is currently the only system in which long-term studies of the physiology and behavior of the primate mother and her fetus are being performed. It is important to point out that the results presented in this chapter should not be viewed as the end product of these efforts. Indeed, the detailed analysis of sleep state, circadian, and age-dependent changes in two types of fetal diaphragmatic activity represent the normative data against which future work can be compared. It is now possible to proceed with analyses directed at determining whether changes in the characteristics of breathing and hiccuping might be used as indices of fetal well-being. In future work acute hypoxia, changes in the nutritional and endocrine environment, and repetitive auditory stimuli will be used to challenge the fetus in an attempt to discover the capabilities and limitations of the organism during this most critical phase of development.

ACKNOWLEDGMENT

This research is supported by National Institute of Child Health and Human Development grant HD-13063. The authors wish to express their gratitude to Dr. L. Stanley James for his guidance and encouragement of this research.

REFERENCES

Alcorn, D. T., Adamson, T. M., Maloney, J. E., & Robinson, P. M. (1986). Morphological effects of chronic bilateral phrenectomy or vagotomy in the fetal lamb lung. *Journal of Anatomy, 130,* 683–695.

Bryan, A. C., Bowes, G., & Maloney, J. E. (1986). Control of breathing in the fetus and newborn. In *Handbook of physiology, Section 3. The respiratory system: Vol. II. Control of Breathing* (pp. 62–647). Washington, DC: American Physiological Society.

Castle, B. M., & Turnbull, A. C. (1983). The presence or absence of fetal breathing movements predicts outcome of preterm labor. *Lancet, 2,* 471–473.

Daniel, S. S., James, L. S., MacCarter, G., Morishima, H. O., & Stark, R. I. (1992). Long-term acid-base measurements in the fetal and maternal baboon. *American Journal of Obstetrics and Gynecology, 2,* 707–712.

Dawes, G. S., Fox, H. E., Leduc, B. M., Liggins, G. C., & Richard, R. T. (1972).

Respiratory movements and rapid eye movement sleep in foetal lamb. *Journal of Physiology* (London), *220*, 119–143.

de Vries, J. I. P., Visser, G. H. A., & Prechtl, H. F. R. (1982). The emergence of fetal behavior I. Quantitative aspects. *Early Human Development, 7*, 301–322.

Ferine, D., MacCarter, G., Timor-Tritsch, I.E., Yeh, M.-N., & Stark, R. I. (1988). Real time ultrasound evaluation of baboon pregnancy. *Journal of Medical Primatology, 17*, 215–221.

Goland, R. S., Stark, R. I., & Wardlaw, S. L. (1990). Corticotropin-releasing hormone during pregnancy in the baboon. *Journal of Clinical Endocrinology & Metabolism, 70*, 925–929.

Harding, R., Fowden, A. L., & Silver, M. (1991). Respiratory and nonrespiratory movements in the fetal pig. *Journal of Developmental Physiology, 15*, 296–275.

Jensen, A. H., & Chernick, V. (1983). Development of respiratory control. *Physiological Reviews, 63*, 437–438.

Jensen, A. H., & Chernick, V. (1991). Fetal breathing and development of control of breathing. *Journal of Applied Physiology, 70*, 1431–1446.

Launois, S., Bizec, J. L., Whitelaw, W. A., Cabane, J., & Derenne, J. P. (1993). Hiccup in adults: an overview. *European Respiratory Journal, 6*, 563–575.

Myers, M. M., Fifer, W., Haiken, J., & Stark, R. I. (1990). Relationship between breathing activity and heart rate in fetal baboons. *American Journal of Physiology.* R1479–R1485.

Myers, M. M., Stark, R. I., Fifer, W. P., Grieve, P. G., Haiken, J., Leung, K., & Schulze, K. F. (1993). A quantitative method for classification of EEG in the fetal baboon. *American Journal of Physiology, 265*, R706–R714.

Newbery, H. N. (1942). Fetal hiccups. *Journal of Comparative Psychology, 34*, 65–73.

Nijhuis, J. G., Martin, C. B., Gommers, S., Brow P., Bots, R. S. G. M., & Jongsma, H. W. (1983). The rhythmicity of fetal breathing varies with behavioral state in the human fetus. *Early Human Development, 9*, 1–7.

Patrick, J. E., Dalton, K. S., & Dawes, G. S. (1976). Breathing patterns before death in fetal lambs. *American Journal of Obstetrics and Gynecology, 125*, 73–78.

Patrick, J., Natale, R., & Richardson, B. (1978). Patterns of human fetal breathing activity at 34 to 35 weeks of gestation. *American Journal of Obstetrics and Gynecology, 132*, 507–513.

Phillipson, E. A., & Bowes, G. (1986). Control of breathing during sleep. In N. S. Cherniak & J. G. Widdicombe (Eds.), *Handbook of physiology.* (Vol. 2, section 3). (pp. 649–689). Washington, DC: American Physiological Society.

Pillai, M., & James, D. (1990a). Hiccups and breathing in human fetus. *Archives of Diseases in Childhood, 65*, 1072–1075.

Pillai, M., & James, D. (1990b). Development of human fetal behavior: A review. *Fetal Diagnosis and Therapy, 5*, 15–32.

Rey, H. R., Stark, R. I., Kim, Y.-I., Daniel, S. S., MacCarter, G., & James, L. S. (1989). Method for processing of fetal breathing: Epoch analysis. *IEEE Engineering, Medicine, Biology, 8*, 30–43.

Roodenburg, P. J., Wladimiroff, W. J., Vanes, A., & Prechtl, H. F. R. (1991). Classification and quantitative aspects of fetal movements during the second half of normal pregnancy. *Early Human Development, 25*, 19–35.

Seron-Ferre, M., Ducsay C. A., & Valenzuela, J. G. (1993). Circadian rhythms during pregnancy. *Endocrinology Reviews, 14*, 594–609.

Stark, R. I., Daniel, S. S., Kim. Y. I., Leung, K., Myers, M. M., & Trooper, P. J. (1994). Patterns of fetal breathing in the baboon vary with EEG sleepstate. *Early Human Development, 38*, 11–26.

Stark, R. I., Daniel, S. S., Garland, M., Jaille-Marti, J. C., Kim., Y.-I., Leung, K., Myers, M. M., & Tropper, P. J. (in press). Fetal hiccups in the baboon. *American Journal of Physiology*.

Stark, R. I., Daniel, S. S., James, L. S., MacCarter, G., Morishima, H. O., Niemann, W. H., Tropper, P. J., & Yeh, M.-N. (1989). Chronic instrumentation and long term investigation in the fetal and maternal baboon: Tether system, conditioning procedures and surgical techniques. *Laboratory Animal Sciences, 39*, 25–32.

Stark, R. I., Daniel, S. S., Kim, Y.-I., Leung, K., Rey, H. R., & Tropper, P. J. (1993). Patterns of development in fetal breathing activity in the latter third of gestation in the baboon. *Early Human Development, 32*, 31–47.

Stark, R. I., Haiken, J., Nordli, D., & Myers, M. M. (1991). Characterization of electroencephalographic state in fetal baboons. *American Journal of Physiology, 261*, R496–R500.

van Vliet, M. T. A., Martin, C. B., Nijhuis, J. G., & Prechtl, H. F. R. (1985). The relationship between fetal activity and behavioral states and fetal breathing movements in normal and growth-retarded fetuses. *American Journal of Gynecology, 153*, 582–588.

van Woerden, E. E., van Geijn, H. P., Caron, F. J. M., Mantel, R., Swartjes, J. M., & Arts, N. F. T. (1989). Fetal hiccups; Characteristics and relation to fetal heart rate. *European Journal of Obstetrics, Gynecology and Reproductive Biology, 30*, 209–216.

Walker, D. W. (1984). Brain mechanisms, hypoxia and fetal breathing. *Journal of Developmental Physiology, 6*, 225–236.

5

Physiological and Clinical Consequences in Relation to the Development of Fetal Behavior and Fetal Behavioral States

Jan G. Nijhuis
University Hospital of Nijmegen

After all, the fetus is but a human being,
just as prone as a child or adult to get
an accident, a disease or an iatrogenic problem!

The accessibility of the human fetus changed dramatically when ultrasonography became available for both clinicians and people working in the field of fetal research. It rapidly became clear that a fetus was more than "a positive pregnancy test" or "audible heart tones." Research has shown that a fetus makes movements from 7 weeks of gestation onward and that the development of fetal behavior and movement patterns during gestation can be well defined in the first trimester (for an overview, see de Vries, 1992), the second trimester (Visser, 1992), and through to the last weeks of pregnancy (Nijhuis, 1992). It is important to emphasize that during all of gestation one tries to find tools to investigate fetal health and preferably to be able to assess the quality and the activity of the fetal central nervous system (CNS). Because the CNS itself is still inaccessible, assessment of fetal behavior is the next best possibility. Furthermore, as in the newborn, many fetal activities appear to be state dependent. As an example, one shouldn't expect a fetus or a neonate to make eye movements if it is in a quiet sleep state (non-rapid eye movements sleep [non-REM sleep]). Therefore, behavior and behavioral states should be taken into account if the fetal condition is examined. Finally, only when the normal developmental pathway is well understood is it possible to judge the fetal condition properly and to recognize the abnormally behaving fetus.

Of course, insight into fetal behavior and its development is also of great importance for those working in the fields of fetal psychology, physiology, and developmental psychobiology. Psychologists seem to have traditionally ignored the fetal period, and it is good that many of them are now focusing on this new research area.

In this chapter we first consider aspects of the development of several physiological variables and then highlight the development of association of these variables into *fetal behavior* and, near term, *fetal behavioral states*. Consequences for fetal research are discussed, and I also emphasize the influence of the knowledge of fetal behavior for clinical practice.

FETAL HEART RATE PATTERNS

The electronic monitoring of the fetal heart rate, in combination with contractions (if present), is used worldwide for the assessment of fetal condition (cardiotocography [CTG]). The technique was introduced for intrapartum use by Caldeyro-Barcia et al. in 1966, Hammacher (Hammacher & Werners, 1968), and Hon (1968). In 1969, Kubli, Kaeser, and Hinselmann (1969) introduced the technique also for antepartum use. Although the intra- and interobserver variability is still large, the specificity is such that clinicians rely on the method (Lotgering, Wallenburg, &

Fetal Behavioural States
Criteria

	FHRP	Body	Eye	(breath)
Behavioural State 1F	A	– –	– –	(regular)
Behavioural State 2F	B	++	++	(irreg.)
Behavioural State 3F	C	– –	++	(regular)
Behavioural State 4F	D	++	++	(irreg.)

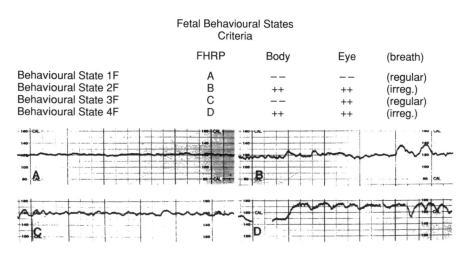

FIG. 5.1.   Schematic diagram of the definition of the four behavioral states and their relation to breathing (if present). In the lower part, an example is given of each of the fetal heart rate patterns A through D, at a recording speed of 3 cm/min.

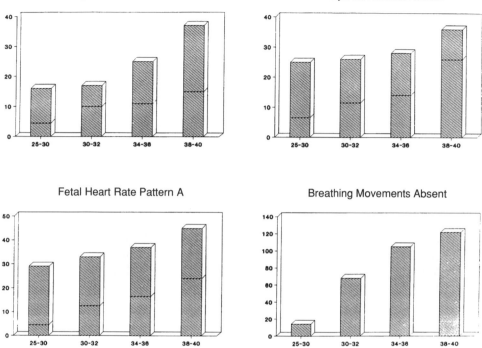

FIG. 5.2. Duration (in minutes) of fetal heart rate pattern A, and durations of periods (in minutes) that body, eye, and breathing movements can be absent at different gestational ages. In three of the four charts, the median duration is also indicated. From Tas and Nijhuis (1992). Reprinted by permission.

Schouten, 1982; Trimbos & Keirse, 1978). The sensitivity, however, is rather poor. In general, good bandwidth or (beat-to-beat) variability in the presence of accelerations is indicative of good fetal condition, whereas a silent pattern (small bandwidth, no accelerations) is indicative of fetal distress, especially in the presence of late decelerations. One of the problems is that many scores that were developed for a better interpretation of the CTG did not take the age of the fetus into account. However, Visser, Dawes and Redman (1981) showed a clear developmental trend during gestation in the amplitude and duration of the accelerations. In 1978, Timor-Tritsch, Dierker, Hertz, Deagan, and Rosen (1979) pointed out that the fetal heart rate pattern (FHRP) was dependent on the fetal behavioral state. In 1982 we defined four different fetal heart rate patterns, FHRP A through D, which could be used to define behavioral states (Nijhuis, Bots, Martin, & Prechtl, 1982; Fig. 5.1). It was also found not only that the form of the accelerations changed during gestation but also that during gestation the length of silent heart rate patterns (FHRP A) increases, without any sign of fetal distress (Fig. 5.2).

FETAL BODY MOVEMENTS

One of the very first descriptions of fetal movements can be found in the Bible (Genesis 25:22): "And the children struggled together within her." However, it was not until 1976 that Reinold was the first to show that the fetus indeed moved spontaneously in utero under normal circumstances as early as the first trimester of pregnancy. He also showed that absence of body movements may indicate impending fetal death, whereas the presence of body movements is very reassuring if the question of viability of pregnancy is raised. It is of much more interest to see the developmental pathway that can be observed. With modern ultrasound techniques the very first fetal activity that can be observed is fetal heart rate (van Heeswijk, Nijhuis, & Hollanders, 1990). The first appearance of fetal somatic activity was described by de Vries et al. (1982) based on a longitudinal study. They introduced a categorization of movement patterns and described how the individual movements were performed in terms of speed, force and amplitude. The work of De Vries et al. clearly showed that most of the movements that can be distinguished in the third trimester and after birth are present by 14 weeks of gestation.

In the second and third trimester, much attention has been paid to the presence of gross body movements, and in the last weeks of pregnancy the fetus clearly exhibits longer periods where movements are present of absent. As gestational age progresses the epochs that body movements can be absent increase dramatically. Although in the first trimester periods without movements will not be longer than 10 min, in the term period it is not unusual for body movements to be absent for up to 45 min (Nijhuis & Tas, 1991; see Fig. 5.2).

Over the past decade it has become clear that the measurement of the number of movements is, in general, not very useful: Even the mildly hypoxic, growth-retarded fetus will still make body movements. It seems to be of much more importance to look at the quality of the movements and the speed and amplitude. de Vries et al. (1982) started to use the concept of *quality* in the first trimester, and Bekedam et al. looked for this aspect in 10 intrauterine growth-retarded fetuses between 29 and 35 weeks (Bekedam, Visser, de Vries, & Prechtl, 1985), but what the clinical consequences could be certainly needs to be further elucidated. Arduini and colleagues, in chapter 6 in this volume, discuss this subject further.

FETAL EYE MOVEMENTS

It is easy to understand that "eyes open" or "eyes closed" would be very helpful to differentiate between two "states," sleep and wakefulness. In the fetus, however, it is very difficult to observe (active) opening of the eyes. Therefore, this variable cannot be used. In contrast, the presence or absence of eye movements has been used in the neonate to distinguish between rapid eye movement-sleep (REM) and non-REM sleep) (Aserinsky & Kleitman, 1955). In 1981, Bots and co-workers (Bots, Nijhuis, Martin, & Prechtl, 1981) were able to detect eye movements in utero using ultrasound. They also recorded eye movements by means of M-mode ultrasonography. Their findings were confirmed in the same year by Birnholz (1981). The possibility to observe and to record eye movements created a chance to study fetal motility in relation to a new variable.

FETAL BREATHING MOVEMENTS

It was Ahlfeld in Germany who published the first observation of fetal breathing movements in 1888. His observations were almost unanimously neglected until an avalanche of breathing research started when the issue was reintroduced by in 1970 Dawes, who described breathing movements in fetal lambs (Dawes, Leduc, Liggins, & Richardson, 1970), and by Boddy and Robinson in 1971 in the human fetus. Bots, Broeders, Farman, Haverkorn, and Stolte (1978) published a detailed analysis of human fetal breathing movements and described them as "paradoxal" because the ribcage made an inward movement during "inspiration" when the diaphragm made a downward movement. Originally it was thought that breathing movements could be used as a perfect indicator for the detection of fetal distress. It soon became apparent that breathing movements are not continuously present and are influenced by many conditions. A postprandial increase in breathing movements has been described from 20–22 weeks onward (de Vries et al., 1987), and Nijhuis, Jongsma, Crijns, de Valk, and van der Velden (1986) showed an increase after glucose-intake by the mother at 24 weeks. In contrast, smoking diminishes the incidence of fetal breathing. Furthermore, breathing is more likely to be absent during fetal rest periods (van Vliet et al., 1985) and also much more regular (Nijhuis et al., 1983; Timor-Tritsch, Dierker, Hertz, Chik, & Rosen, 1980). During the last weeks of pregnancy the incidence of fetal breathing decreases and breathing movements are absent during labor (Carmichael, Campbell, & Patrick, 1984). The duration of periods that breathing movements can be absent increases enormously during pregnancy, and near term it is not unusual for breathing movements to be absent for as long as 120 min (Patrick, Campbell, Carmichael, Natale, & Richardson, 1980; see Fig. 5.2). One might conclude that for fetal surveillance purposes fetal breathing movements did not fulfill the initial expectations (Patrick et al., 1980). In general, for behavioral studies, fetal breathing should not be studied as an independent variable but always in combination with other variables and preferably under highly standardized conditions.

FETAL MOUTH MOVEMENTS

With modern ultrasonographic equipment it is easy to visualize not only the fetal eye but also the fetal mouth region. One may observe not only movements of the tongue but also very specific sucking behaviors: During quiet periods (state 1F, discussed later) recurrent clusters of "regular mouthing movements" can be observed, whereas during state 3F "sucking movements" can be distinguished (for an overview, see van Woerden & van Geijn, 1992). Although it is rather rare, one may even observe the fetus sucking its thumb. Both activities, regular mouthing and sucking, are able to entrain a fairly specific sinusoidal heart rate pattern, which may confuse the clinicians (Nijhuis, Staisch, Martin, & Prechtl, 1984; van Woerden et al., 1988).

FETAL BEHAVIOR

In the first half of pregnancy, *fetal behavior* is similar to *fetal motility*. As already mentioned, the fetus is almost continuously active, although the periods in which no movements can be observed gradually increase. In the second half of pregnancy the observation of fetal motility can be combined with the simultaneous recording of the fetal heart rate. Such a joined recording is then called the registration of fetal behavior. In the beginning it is as if all sorts of movements occur more or less independently of one another and they do not elicit specific fetal heart rate patterns. However, when pregnancy progresses, an increasing linkage can be observed between periods with "presence of eye movements" and periods with "presence of body movements" or with a reactive heart rate pattern, fetal heart rate pattern B (FHRP B) (Nijhuis & van de Pas, 1992). This increasing linkage, which has been described by Drogtrop, Ubels, and Nijhuis (1990) at 25–30 weeks and by Visser et al. (1987) at 30–32 weeks, is crucial for the development of recognizable behavioral states.

BEHAVIORAL STATES

Behavioral states are constellations of physiological and behavioral variables (e.g., eyes closed, regular breathing, and no movements: quiet sleep) that are stable over time and recur repeatedly, not only in the same infant, but also in similar forms in all infants (definition modified from Prechtl, Weinmann, & Akiyama, 1969).

In the neonate, Prechtl defined five behavioral states: state 1 (quiet sleep, similar to non-REM sleep), state 2 (active sleep, similar to REM sleep), state 3 (quiet awake), state 4 (active awake), and state 5 (vocalization), respectively. This concept is fairly simple and therefore indeed very useful. In fact, everybody uses this concept in daily life, and everybody realizes that each state reflects a particular mode of CNS activity. As an example, nobody would consider the possibility of an interesting discussion with a person who is clearly sleeping! And everybody would be surprised if such a sleeping individual were to suddenly start talking without any other sign of wakefulness. Of course, this concept is also age dependent: A neonate and an adult are expected to behave differently within the same state. If one considers these examples, it is clear that there are three major requirements that have to be fulfilled before a behavioral state can be recognized. First, a specific combination of certain variables must occur at the same time (coincidence, linkage), such as absence of body and eye movements, FHRP A for state 1F. Second, to be able to recognize this combination, it should be stable over time (by definition at least 3 min). Third, it must be possible to see a clear change from one state into another, a state transition. For example, if a neonate changes from non-REM into REM sleep, breathing will become irregular and almost at the same time the neonate will start to make body movements while eye movements appear behind the closed eyelids. If the transitional periods become too long (i.e., longer than 3 min of "no coincidence") it is not possible anymore to distinguish clear behavioral states.

FETAL BEHAVIORAL STATES

Following the concept of behavioral states in the neonate it appeared to be possible to study the development of human fetal behavior. Fetal behavior can be adequately recorded with two ultrasound scanners and a simultaneous registration of the fetal heart rate pattern. Using this method we defined four behavioral states that have now gained worldwide acceptance (Nijhuis et al., 1982). To emphasize the similarity with the neonatal states they were called 1F (F for fetal) through 4F, respectively. We have used the following definitions (see also Fig. 5.1):

State 1F (similar to state 1 in the neonate): quiescence, which can be regularly interrupted by brief gross body movements, mostly startles. Eye movements are absent. The FHRP A is a stable pattern with a small oscillation bandwidth and no accelerations, except in combination with a startle.

State 2F (similar to state 2 in the neonate): frequent and periodic gross body movements—mainly stretches and retroflections—and movements of the extremities. Eye movements are present. FHRP B has a wider oscillation bandwidth and frequent accelerations during movements.

State 3F (similar to state 3 in the neonate): gross body movements absent. Eye movements present. FHRP C is stable but with a wider oscillation bandwidth than FHRP A and no accelerations.

State 4F (similar to state 4 in the neonate): vigorous, continual activity including many trunk rotations. Eye movements are present. FHRP D is unstable, with large and long-lasting accelerations, often fused into a sustained tachycardia.

At this point it is important to emphasize that for the analysis of the results of a longitudinal study into the development of behavioral states a *moving window* technique was introduced. This is in contrast with the more classic *epoch-analysis*. The technique has been extensively discussed else where (Nijhuis, Martin, & Prechtl, 1984), but for a proper orientation in the field of behavior it is necessary to illustrate this technique with an example. If one were to walk through a grassland and come across one or two trees, one would not say that these trees divide the grassland into two separate fields. Rather, one would say this is a grassland with one or two isolated trees. In the same way, we have measured durations of a quiet state from one transition to another, whereas epoch analysis would divide such a state in two parts: from a transition up to a single movement and from this movement up to the next transition. Therefore, if one compares results of different studies, one should be aware of this difference. Using this moving window technique, percentages of incidences of coincidence 1F through 4F could be calculated, and these are presented in Table 5.1. When clear states can be defined, which is the case near term, similar data can be given for behavioral states 1F through 4F (Table 5.2). The durations of "enclosed periods of states" (i.e., the beginning and the end of a period are being recorded) are also given in Table 5.2. As already mentioned before, states can only be defined on the basis of coincidence and stability over time and the presence of state transitions.

After the introduction of these definitions, many other research groups were able to confirm the same findings (e.g., Arduini et al., 1985; van Vliet, Martin, Nijhuis, & Prechtl, 1985a; Van Woerden et al., 1989). The introduction of the concept of states had a great influence on the research that was performed in both animal and human research. As an example, it appeared the case that breathing movements were largely absent during state 1F (van Vliet et al., 1985), but if they were present they were much more regular (Nijhuis et al., 1983). Therefore, if one studies the influence of a certain stimulus on breathing, it is now clear that such a study needs to be standardized for states. Otherwise one might think that the stimulus used abolishes breathing, whereas in fact only a state transition from 2F (with breathing) into 1F (without breathing) has been induced. The same holds of course for the interpretation of heart rate patterns: Although silent FHR

TABLE 5.1
Coincidences 1F Through 4F and "No Coincidence" from 32 to 40
Weeks of Gestation in Low-risk Fetuses

	Percentages	*Gestational age (weeks of menstrual age)*				
		32	*34*	*36*	*38*	*40*
Coincidence 1F	Median	7	18.5	15	25	36
	Q_1-Q_3	2.5–16	12–26	9–25	15.5–37	22–42.5
	Range	0–25	0–29	0–42	7–49	21–51
Coincidence 2F	Median	49	53	47.5	52	47.5
	Q_1-Q_3	41–63	45–65	31–60	39–64	39.5–56
	Range	24–76	23–66	17–65	23–74	23–80
Coincidence 3F	Median	—	—	5 Values	2 Values	3 Values
	Q_1-Q_3				(6.5, 8)	(2.5, 5.5, 5.5)
	Range			3–6		
Coincidence 4F	Median	9 Values	10 Values	6	3	4
	Q_1-Q_3			0–46	0–15	0–12
	Range	2.5–41.5	3–36	0–100	0–19	0–76
No coincidence	Median	29	20.5	19.5	15	5.5
	Q_1-Q_3	22.5–37	11–26	16–28	10–19.5	2.4–14
	Range	13–63	6–49	0–53	1–54	0–26

Note. From van Vliet, Martin, Nijhuis, and Prechtl (1985b). Reprinted by permission. Data are given as median percentages, quartiles, and ranges per age group.

patterns under certain circumstances indicate fetal distress, they may also reflect a physiologic behavioral state 1F. It is therefore of crucial importance that one considers a differential diagnosis if a silent heart rate pattern is recorded (Nijhuis, Crevels, & van Dongen, 1990; Table 5.3). We have already mentioned that a fetus makes regular mouthing movements during state 1F (van Woerden et al., 1988), whereas sucking movements can be seen during 3F (Nijhuis, Staisch, Martin, & Prechtl, 1984; van Woerden & van Geijn, 1992). Both categories of mouth movements may entrain a "sinusoidal-like" fetal heart rate pattern, a heart rate pattern that can also be recorded in combination with severe fetal anemia. For this FHRP a differential diagnosis can also be made (Table 5.4). We have only made a beginning with the understanding of the human fetus in its natural environment, but these examples make perfectly clear how important it is to be aware of these behavioral states.

Following the description of fetal behavior under normal conditions, many studies have been looking for changes in behavior in growth-retarded fetuses (Arduini, Rizzo, & Romanini, 1992; Bekedam et al., 1985; van Vliet et al., 1985), fetuses of diabetic mothers (Mulder, 1992), and fetuses of mothers who used antiepileptic drugs (van Geijn et al., 1986),

TABLE 5.2

Percentages and Durations of Behavioral States 1F Through 4F in Low-Risk Fetuses at 38 and 40 Weeks of Gestation

		Percentages		Durations (min; Enclosed Epochs)	
		38 Weeks of Gestation	40 Weeks of Gestation	38 Weeks of Gestation	40 Weeks of Gestation
State 1F ("quiet sleep")	Median	32	38	23.5	26
	Q_1–Q_3	17–40	29.5–45.5	14–26.5	19–30.5
	Range	9–53.5	24.5–52.5	8.5–37.5	12.5–36.5
State 2F ("active sleep")	Median	42.5	42.5	12	3 periods (4.5, 4.5, and 14.5 min)
	Q_1–Q_3	31.5–46.5	39.5–48.5	7.5–22	
	Range	23–64	22–73.5	4–30.5	
State 3F ("quiet awake")	Median	2 Values (6.5 and 8)	3 Values (2.5, 5.5, and 5.5)	2 periods (5 and 3 min)	4 periods (3, 3, 4, and 6.5 min)
	Q_1–Q_3				
	Range				
State 4F ("active awake")	Median	7.5	9	7.0	6.5
	Q_1–Q_3	0–18.5	0–14	5.5–8	6–9
	Range	0–25	0–32.5	3.5–16	5–20.5
No state identified	Median	11.5	5		
	Q_1–Q_3	7.5–19	0–9.5		
	Range	3–53.5	0–26.5		

Note. Durations are based on calculations of enclosed periods within a recording period of 2 hr. State 2F is the most frequently occurring state, and it is often the case that either the beginning or the end of such an epoch was not recorded. Therefore, the actual mean duration of state 2F is probably much longer. Modified from Nijhuis, Martin, and Prechtl (1984). Reprinted by permission.

TABLE 5.3
Differential Diagnosis and Proposed Management When a Silent
Heart Rate Pattern is Recorded

Differential Diagnosis	Management
State 1F	Extension of the recording time
Effect of drugs	Exclusion of use of drugs
Tachycardia	Inspection of baseline
Anomalies	Ultrasonographic examination
	Behavioral study
Hypoxia	Contraction stress test (CST)
Brain death	Cordocentesis

Note. From Nijhuis et al. (1990). Adapted by permission.

cocaine (Hume, O'Donnell, Stanger, Killam, & Gingras, 1989), or methadone (Archie, Milton, Sokol, & Norman, 1989). It is beyond the scope of
this chapter to discuss the results in detail, but more information can be
obtained chapter 6 by Arduini, Rizzo, and Romanini in this volume and in
many review articles or books (e.g., Groome & Watson, 1992; Nijhuis, 1992;
Richardson, 1992).

If one accepts that the fetus exhibits clear behavioral states, similar to
the neonate, then it becomes apparent that birth by itself does not seem to
alter the developmental pathway of this output of the CNS. Of course, at
birth breathing starts to be continuous, oxygen tension changes, and so
forth, but the organization of states does not change. If birth by itself is not
that important, then it is understandable that a great deal of neonatal
morbidity does not originate from a (hypoxic) accident during birth, but
rather from a (hypoxic) accident somewhere during gestation. The most
extreme example is *intrauterine brain death syndrome.* In such a case the
FHRP is silent over a long period of time, with a somewhat elevated
baseline, and the fetus does not move. At birth—mostly via a cesarean
section because of "fetal distress"—a floppy infant is born and artificial
ventilation will be needed. An electroencephalogram will be isoelectric
and then a diagnosis of "brain death" will finally be made (Nijhuis, Kruyt,
& van Wijck, 1988; Nijhuis et al., 1990). An accurate diagnosis would not
have prevented the disaster but perhaps the unnecessary operative intervention. The etiology must be a period of severe asphyxia, which was too
short to kill the fetus but long enough to cause definite brain damage,
"intrauterine coma." A longer period of asphyxia would have led to a case
of "sudden fetal demise" without a clear cause ("intrauterine sudden
infant death"). Milder cases will not be detected at birth but may lead to
handicaps that may later on be attributed to a difficult birth, which is
seldom the real cause (Nelson & Ellenberg, 1988). On the other hand, it
may well be that "difficult birth in itself in certain cases is merely a

TABLE 5.4
Differential Diagnosis and Proposed Management When a Sinusoidal Heart Rate Pattern is Recorded

Differential Diagnosis	Management
Fetal mouth movements	
Sucking ("major" or "marked")	
Regular mouthing ("minor")	Behavioral study
Effect of drugs	Exclusion of use of drugs
Congenital anomalies	Ultrasonographic examination
Fetal asphyxia	Biophysical profile testing
Fetal anemia	Cordocentesis

symptom of deeper effects that influenced the development of the fetus" (Freud, 1897).

To get a better insight into the condition of the fetus before birth and in particular the condition of the fetal CNS, we should pursue the research on fetal behavior in the human fetus and try to develop an intrauterine fetal neurological assessment. A beginning was made by Tas et al. (1990), who were able to evoke an intercostal to phrenic inhibitory reflex (IPIR): Compression of the fetal ribcage results in an apnea. In a second series of experiments, they were unable to find a different result in a group of growth-retarded fetuses, characterized by growth below the 10th percentile (Tas, Nijhuis, Nelen, & Willems, 1993). Furthermore, it has been noticed that fetuses with congenital anomalies may show bizarre behavior (Pillai, Garrett, & James, 1991) or dissociation of heart rate and movements (Tas & Nijhuis, 1992).

CONCLUSION

The study of fetal behavior has made the position of the fetus very clear. The fetus can no longer be regarded as a "growing organism" that will react independently of age and state. The fetus is indeed "but a human being," and if one wants to assess its condition or if one wants to learn something about its development in its intrauterine environment, then one should start to do so under standardized conditions with respect to fetal age, time of day, relation to maternal meals, and so forth. Last but not least, certainly in the last trimester one should be aware of fetal behavioral states.

FUTURE DIRECTIONS

Although knowledge of fetal behavior and fetal behavioral states is necessary for an optimal assessment of fetal condition, it is very unlikely that clinicians will increasingly use time-consuming fetal behavioral recordings in daily practice. For the near future there are two directions for which the study of fetal behavior appears to be of great importance.

1. Researchers working in the field of fetal psychology cannot do so without taking fetal behavior into account. Studies regarding fetal learning, fetal habituation, and so forth should be standardized for behavioral states. As is the case in the neonate, fetal reflexes and responses may be dependent on fetal behavioral states.

2. Although fetal monitoring has been introduced worldwide, the number of children with handicaps has not decreased. The sensitivity of fetal monitoring is up to now very disappointing. It may well be the case that the study of fetal behavior will give more insight in the activity of the central nervous system. Behavioral studies in fetuses at risk for future handicaps might give the answer to whether we may be able to detect neurological disturbances already as fetal life.

REFERENCES

Ahlfeld, F. (1888). Ueber intrauterine Athembewegungen des Kindes [About intrauterine breeding movements of the child]. *Verhandlungen der Deutschen Gesellschaft für Gynäkologie, 2,* 203–210.

Archie, C. L., Milton, I. L., Sokol, R. J., & Norman, G. (1989). The effects of Methadone treatment on the reactivity of the nonstress test. *Obstetrical and Gynecology, 74,* 254–255.

Arduini, D., Rizzo, G., Giorlandino, C. Vizzone, A., Nava, S., & Dell'Acqua, S. (1985). The fetal behavioural states: An ultrasonic study. *Prenatal Diagnosis, 5,* 269–276.

Arduini, D., Rizzo, G., & Romanini, C. (1992). Growth retardation. In J. G. Nijhuis (Ed.), *Fetal behaviour, developmental and perinatal aspects* (pp. 181–208). Oxford: Oxford University Press.

Aserinsky, E., & Kleitman, N. (1955). A motility cycle in sleeping infants as manifested by ocular and gross bodily activity. *Journal of Applied Physiology, 8,* 11–18.

Bekedam, D. J., Visser, G. H. A., de Vries, J. J., & Prechtl, H. F. R. (1985). Motor behaviour in the growth-retarded fetus. *Early Human Development, 12,* 155–165.

Birnholz, J. C. (1981). The development of human fetal eye movement patterns. *Science, 213,* 679–681.

Boddy, K., & Robinson, J. S. (1971). External method for detection of fetal breathing in utero. *Lancet, 2,* 1231–1233.

Bots, R. S. G. M., Broeders, G. H. B., Farman, D. J., Haverkorn, M. J., & Stolte, L. A. M. (1978). Fetal breathing movements in the normal and growth-retarded fetus: A multiscan/M-mode echofetographic study. *European Journal of Obstetrics and Gynecology and Reproductive Biology, 8,* 21–29.

Bots, R. S. G. M., Nijhuis, J. G., Martin, C. B., Jr., & Prechtl, H. F. R. (1981). Human fetal eye movements: Detection in utero by ultrasonography. *Early Human Development, 5,* 87–94.

Caldeyro-Barcia, R., Mendez-Bauer, C., Poseiro, J. J., Excarcena, L. A., Pose, S. V., Bieniarz, J., Arnt, I. C., Gulin, L., & Althabe, O. (1966). Control of human fetal heart rate during labor. In D. E. Cassels (Ed.), *The heart rate and circulation in the newborn and infant.* New York: Grune and Stratton.

Carmichael, L., Campbell, K., & Patrick, J. (1984). Fetal breathing, gross fetal body movements, and maternal and fetal heart rates before spontaneous labor at term. *American Journal of Obstetrics and Gynecology, 148,* 675–679.

Dawes, G. S., Leduc, H. E., Liggins, G. C., & Richards, R. T. (1970). Respiratory movements and paradoxal sleep in the foetal lamb. *Journal of Physiology, 210,* 47–48.

de Vries, J. I. P., Visser, G. H. A., & Prechtl, H. F. R. (1982). The emergence of fetal behavior I. Qualitative aspects. *Early Human Development, 7,* 301–322.

de Vries, J. I. P. (1992). The first trimester. In J. G. Nijhuis (Ed.), *Fetal behaviour, developmental and perinatal aspects* (pp. 3–16). Oxford: Oxford University Press

de Vries, J. I. P., Visser, G. H. A., Mulder, E. J. H., & Prechtl, H. F. R. (1987). Diurnal and other variations in fetal movement, and heart rate patterns at 20–22 weeks. *Early Human Development, 15,* 333–348.

Drogtrop, A. P., Ubels, R., & Nijhuis, J. G. (1990). The association between fetal body movements, eye movements, and heart rate patterns between 25 and 30 weeks of gestation. *Early Human Development, 23,* 67–73.

Freud, S. (1897). Die infantile Cerebrallämung [Cerebral palsy]. In H. Nothnagel (Ed.), *Specielle Pathologie und Therapie* (pp. 1–327). Vienna: Holder

Groome, L. J., & Watson, J. E. (1992). Assessment of in utero neurobehavioral development. I. Fetal behavioral states. *Journal of Maternal Fetal Investigation, 2,* 183–194.

Hammacher, K., & Werners, P. H. (1968). Ueber die Auswertung und Dokumentation von CTG-Ergebnissen [About the value and registration of CT6-data]. *Gynaecologia, 166,* 410–423.

Hon, E. H. (1968). *An atlas of fetal heart rate patterns.* New Haven, CT: Harty Press.

Hume, R. F., Jr., O'Donnell, K. J., Stanger, C. L., Killam, A. P., & Gingras, J. L. (1989). In utero cocaine exposure: Observations of fetal behavioral state may predict neonatal outcome. *American Journal of Obstetrics and Gynecology, 161,* 685–690.

Kubli, F. W., Kaeser, O., & Hinselmann, M. (1969). Diagnostic management of chronic placental insufficiency. In A. Pecile & C. Finzi (Eds.), *The foeto-placental unit* (pp. 323–339). Amsterdam: Excerpta Medica.

Lotgering, F. K., Wallenburg, H. C. S., & Schouten, H. J. A. (1982). Interobserver and intraobserver variation in the assessment of antepartum cardiotocograms. *American Journal of Obstetrics and Gynecology, 144,* 701–705.

Mulder, E. J. H. (1992). Diabetic pregnancy. In J. G. Nijhuis (Ed.), *Fetal behavior, developmental and perinatal aspects* (pp. 193–209). Oxford: Oxford University Press.

Nelson, K. B., & Ellenberg, J. H. (1988). Intrapartum events and cerebral palsy. In F. W. Kubli, N. Patel, W. Schmidt, & O. Linderkamp (Eds.), *Prenatal events and brain damage in surviving children* (pp. 139–148). Heidelberg: Springer Verlag,.

Nijhuis, J. G. (Ed.). (1992). *Fetal behaviour, developmental and perinatal aspects.* Oxford: Oxford University Press.

Nijhuis, J. G., Bots, R. S. G. M., Martin, C. B., Jr., & Prechtl, H. F. R. (1982). Are there behavioural states in the human fetus? *Early Human Development, 6,* 177–195.

Nijhuis, J. G., Crevels, A. J., & van Dongen, P. W. J. (1990). Fetal brain death: The definition of a fetal heart rate pattern and its clinical consequences. *Obstetrics and Gynecological Survey, 46,* 229–232.

Nijhuis, J. G., Jongsma, H. W., Crijns, I. J. M. J., de Valk, I. M. G. M., & van der Velden, J. W. H. J. (1986). Effects of maternal glucose ingestion on human fetal breathing movements at weeks 24 and 28 of gestation. *Early Human Development, 13,* 183–188.

Nijhuis, J. G., Kruyt, N., & van Wijck, J. A. M.(1988). Fetal brain death. Two case reports. *British Journal of Obstetrics and Gynaecology, 95,* 197–200.

Nijhuis, J. G., Martin, C. B., Jr., Gommers, S., Bouws, P., Bots, R. S. G. M., & Jongsma, H. W. (1983). The rhythmicity of fetal breathing varies with behavioural state in the human fetus. *Early Human Development, 9,* 1–7.

Nijhuis, J. G., Martin, C. B., Jr., & Prechtl, H. F. R. (1984). Behavioural states of the human fetus. In H. F. R. Prechtl (Ed.), *Continuity of neural functions from prenatal to postnatal life* (pp. 65–79). Clinics in developmental medicine, 94. Oxford: Blackwell.

Nijhuis, J. G., & van de Pas, M. (1992). Behavioral states and their ontogeny: Human studies. *Seminars in Perinatology, 16,* 206–210.

Nijhuis, J. G., Staisch, K. J., Martin, C. B., Jr., & Prechtl, H. F. R. (1984). A sinusoidal-like fetal heart-rate pattern in association with fetal sucking—Report of 2 cases. *European Journal of Obstetrics and Gynecology and Reproductive Biology, 16,* 353–358.

Nijhuis, J. G., & Tas, B. A. P. J. (1991). Physiological and clinical aspects of the development of fetal behaviour. In M. A. Hanson (Ed.), *The fetal and neonatal brainstem, developmental and clinical issues* (pp. 268–281). Cambridge: Cambridge University Press.

Patrick, J., Campbell, K., Carmichael, L., Natale, R., & Richardson, B. (1980). Patterns of human fetal breathing during the last 10 weeks of pregnancy. *Obstetrics and Gynecology, 56,* 24–30.

Pillai, M., Garrett, C., & James, D. (1991). Bizarre fetal behaviour associated with lethal congenital anomalies: a case report. *European Journal of Obstetrics and Gynecology and Reproductive Biology, 39,* 215–218.

Prechtl, H. F. R., Weinmann, H. M., & Akiyama, Y. (1969). Organization of physiological parameters in normal and neurologically abnormal infants. *Neuropädiatrie, 1,* 101–129.

Reinold, E. (1976). Beobachtung fetaler Aktivität in der ersten Hälfte der Gravidität mit dem Ultraschall [Observation of fetal activity in the first half of pregnancy with ultrasound]. *Pädiatrie und Pädologie, 6,* 274–279.

Richardson, B. S. (1992). Fetal behavioral states. *Seminars in Perinatology, 16,* 4.

Tas, B. A. P. J., Nijhuis, J. G., Lucas, A. J., & Folgering, H. T. M. (1990). The intercostal-to-phrenic inhibitory reflex in the human fetus near term. *Early Human Development, 22,* 145–149.

Tas, B. A. P. J., & Nijhuis, J. G. (1992). Consequences for fetal monitoring. In J. G. Nijhuis (Ed.), *Fetal behaviour, developmental and perinatal aspects* (pp. 258–269). Oxford: Oxford University Press.

Tas, B. A. P. J., Nijhuis, J. G., Nelen, W., & Willems, E. (1993). The intercostal-to-phrenic inhibitory reflex in normal and intra-uterine growth-retarded (IUGR) human fetuses from 26 to 40 weeks of gestation. *Early Human Development, 32,* 177–182.

Timor-Tritsch, I. E., Dierker, L. J., Hertz, R. H., Deagan, C., & Rosen, M. G. (1979).

Studies of antepartum behavioral states in the human fetus at term. *American Journal of Obstetrics and Gynecology, 132*, 524–528.

Timor-Tritsch, I. E., Dierker, L. J., Hertz, R. H., Chik, L., & Rosen, M. G. (1980). Regular and irregular human fetal respiratory movements. *Early Human Development, 4*, 315–324.

Trimbos, J. B., & Keirse, M. J. C. N. (1978). Observer variability in assessment of antepartum cardiotocograms. *British Journal of Obstetrics and Gynaecology, 85*, 900–906.

van Geijn, H. P., Swartjes, J. M., van Woerden, E. E., Caron, F. J. M., Brons, J. T. J., & Arts, N. F. T. (1986). Fetal behavioural states in epileptic pregnancies. *European Journal of Obstetrics and Gynecology and Reproductive Biology, 21*, 309-314.

van Heeswijk, M., Nijhuis, J. G., & Hollanders, H. M. G. (1990). Fetal heart rate in early pregnancy. *Early Human Development, 22*, 151–156.

van Vliet, M. A. T., Martin, C. B., Jr., Nijhuis, J. G., & Prechtl, H. F. R. (1985). The relationship between fetal activity, and behavioural states and fetal breathing movements in normal and growth-retarded fetuses. *American Journal of Obstetrics and Gynecology, 153*, 5, 582-588.

van Vliet, M. A. T., Martin, C. B., Jr., Nijhuis, J. G., & Prechtl, H. F. R. (1985a). Behavioural states in fetuses of nulliparous women. *Early Human Development, 12*, 121–135.

van Vliet, M. A. T., Martin, C. B., Jr., Nijhuis, J. G., & Prechtl, H. F. R. (1985b). Behavioural states in growth retarded human fetuses. *Early Human Development, 12*, 183–197.

van Woerden, E. E., van Geijn, H. P., Swartjes, J. M., Caron, F. J. M., Brons, J. T. J., & Arts, N. F. T. (1988). Fetal heart rhythms during behavioural state 1F. *European Journal of Obstetrics and Gynecology and Reproductive Biology, 28*, 29–38.

van Woerden, E. E., & van Geijn, H. P. (1992). Heart-rate patterns and fetal movements. In J. G. Nijhuis (Ed.), *Fetal behaviour, developmental and perinatal aspects* (pp. 41–56). Oxford: Oxford University Press.

van Woerden, E. E., van Geijn, H. P., Caron, F. J. M., Mantel, R., Swartjes, J. M., & Arts, N. F. T. (1989). Automated assignment of fetal behavioural states near term. *Early Human Development, 19*, 137–146.

Visser, G. H. A. (1992). The second trimester. In J. G. Nijhuis (Ed.), *Fetal behaviour, developmental and perinatal aspects* (pp. 17–26). Oxford: Oxford University Press.

Visser, G. H. A., Dawes, G. S., & Redman, C. W. G. (1981). Numerical analysis of the normal human antenatal fetal heart rate. *British Journal of Obstetrics and Gynaecology, 88*, 792–802.

Visser, G. H. A., Goodman, J. D. S., Levine, D. H., & Dawes, G. S. (1981). Micturition and the heart rate period cycle in the human fetus. *British Journal of Obstetrics and Gynaecology, 153*, 5, 803–805.

Visser, G. H. A., Poelman-Weesjes, G., & Cohen, T. M. N. (1987). Fetal behaviour at 30 to 32 weeks of gestation. *Pediatrics Research, 22*, 655–658.

6

Fetal Behavioral States and Behavioral Transitions in Normal and Compromised Fetuses

Domenico Arduini
University of Ancona, Ospedale Fatebene Fratelli "S. Giovanni Calabita," Rome, Italy

Giuseppe Rizzo
Carlo Romanini
University of Rome "Tor Vergata," Rome, Italy

Behavioral states are defined as combinations of physiological and behavioral variables, stable over time and repeatedly recurring, not only in the same subject, but also in similar forms in all studied subjects (Nijhuis, 1992).

From the first description made by Dawes and associates two decades ago of behavioral states in the fetus using a sheep model (Dawes, Fox, Leduc, Liggins, & Richards, 1970), there has been an increasing interest in this subject. In particular, the refinement of ultrasound methods and their application to the human fetus have allowed a noninvasive assessment of human fetal movements (Birnholz, Stephens, & Faria, 1978; Bots, Nijhuis, Martin, & Prechtl, 1981) and heart rate patterns (Evertson, Gauthier, Schifrin, & Paul, 1979). This technical advance opened up a new field of behavioral studies, confirming the results obtained from animal models. Indeed, Timor-Tritsch, Dierker, Hertz, Deagan, and Rosen (1978) showed that in the human fetus near term heart rate and body movements are clustered in episodes resembling quiet and active phases of animal behavior. Nijhuis, Prechtl, Martin, and Bots (1982) found evidence of stable and

83

recurring associations between heart rate, body movements, and fetal eye movements, similar to those used by Prechtl (1974) to identify behavioral states in the newborn. These associations develop from the second trimester of pregnancy and become particularly evident from 36 weeks of gestation onward.

From these studies it has become evident that the fetal intrauterine condition is not a "stable state" but a continuous alternation of states characterized by significant changes not only in fetal motility and heart rate but also in fetal hemodynamics, response to stimulation, and metabolism. As a consequence, every researcher studying fetal pathophysiology and every clinician evaluating fetal health must be aware of behavioral states. Not taking them into account may lead to inconsistencies in the results obtained and to errors in patients management.

Recently, we have developed methods for the automated recognition of fetal behavioral states, and have used these methods to study state development in compromised fetuses. This chapter first describes the techniques for recording and analyzing fetal behavioral states. We then discuss the application of these techniques to the study of fetuses of normal pregnancies and the impact of states on different physiological parameters. Finally, we present some potential clinical applications of these methods; in particular, the characterization of abnormal patterns of state transitions in pathological pregnancies is reviewed.

STUDYING FETAL BEHAVIOR

Recording Technique

Fetal behavioral states are defined on the basis of fetal heart rate patterns (FHRP), fetal gross body movements (FM), and fetal eye movements (FEM). Therefore, it is necessary to record simultaneously fetal heart rate with a cardiotocograph and FM and FEM with two real-time ultrasound transducers. The probes of these two latter forms of equipment are positioned on the maternal abdomen in order to obtain respectively a parasagittal section through the fetal face and a transverse section at the level of the upper part of the fetal abdomen. With the first probe it is possible to obtain evidence of FEM as well as other head and facial movements (including mouth movements) and frequently forearm and hand movements. With the second, FM and breathing movements can be detected. Synchronization among these three behavioral variables is particularly important and may be performed automatically with computer programs (Rizzo, Arduini, Romanini, & Mancuso, 1988). To achieve this we developed a system controlled by a 386 personal computer that acquires fetal heart rate data from the cardiotocograph via its RS232 port (Arduini et al., 1993). Simultaneously the two observers, using the ultrasound probes, enter individual movements into the computerized system using two remote switching devices and codified keyboards to signal the onset and the end of each movement. They also enter the periods in which a reliable view of the fetus is not obtained. In order to minimize the influences of diurnal variation and maternal food intake, all the recordings should be performed around the same time of the day. In our laboratory all recordings are performed in the afternoon 2 hr after a standardized 1,000-kcal lunch.

Finally in order to record the complete cycle of fetal behavior the recording time should be at least 2 hr, and a moving window of 3 min shifted every minute is used to score epochs.

Analysis of Fetal Behavioral States

Behavioral states are defined as stable coincidences (at least 3 min) of FHRP, FEM, and FM according to one of the specific combinations listed in Table 6.1. In addition, in order for a specific combination of variables to be considered as a state, there must be rapid (less than or equal to 3 min) and simultaneous transitions in these values to new levels that are characteristic of another behavioral state.

Recognition of the presence or absence of FEM and FM is relatively easy and reproducible for expert investigators. However, classification of FHRP into the four classes A to D (Fig. 6.1) is more difficult and there are instances of poor agreement among experts (Arduini et al., 1993). The use of a computerized system capable of automatically classifying FHRP greatly improves the reproducibility of the heart rate analysis (Arduini et al., 1993). Furthermore, this system allows an automatic computation of the periods of coincidence, thus greatly shortening the analysis time.

TABLE 6.1
Criteria for Definition of Behavioral States

	*FHRP**	*FEM*	*FM*
1F (Quiet sleep)	A	Absent	Absent
2F (Active sleep)	B	Present	Present
3F (Quiet awake)	C	Present	Absent
4F (Active awake)	D	Present	Present

Note. FHRP, fetal heart rate patterns; FEM, fetal eye movements; FM, fetal gross body movements.

*A, Heart rate variability <10 bpm, absence of accelerations or isolated ones. B, Variability >10 bpm, frequent acceleration. C, Variability >10 bpm, absence of accelerations. D, Heart rate unstable with large and long-lasting accelerations.

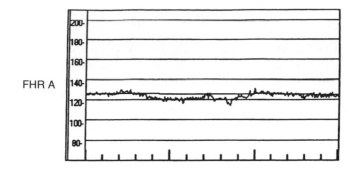

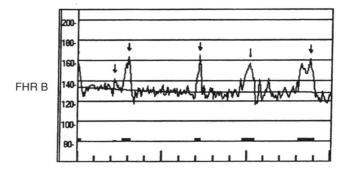

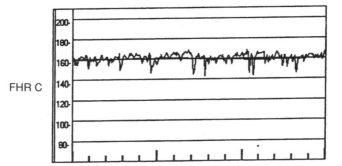

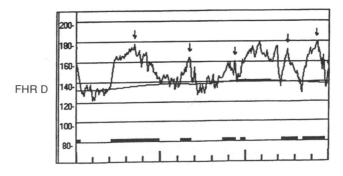

FIG. 6.1. Examples of the four fetal heart rate patterns (FHRP) A, B, C, and D that occur during behavioral states 1F, 2F, 3F, and 4F, respectively. Arrows indicate FHR accelerations, and thick bars mark minutes.

DEVELOPMENT OF FETAL BEHAVIORAL STATES

"True" behavioral states are clearly established by 36 weeks of gestation (Arduini et al., 1985; Nijhuis et al., 1982). Before this gestational age it is possible to recognize periods of stable (>3 min) and recurrent associations (coincidence) between the behavioral and physiological variables that are similar to those present during behavioral states 1F to 4F, but that do not have the short, synchronized transitions. Although these periods of associations, which are called *coincidences*, do not meet generally accepted criteria for state classification, their characterization is of great interest because many of the complications of pregnancy result in a delivery of the fetus prior to development of true states at 36 weeks.

As already stated, behavioral and physiological variables such as FHR, FM, and FEM show evident periodicities from 26 to 28 weeks of gestation onward (Arduini et al., 1986a). As fetuses grow older, fluctuations in these variables become more related temporally and form stable clusters, which we believe are the forerunners of behavioral states. In developmental studies we have used the percent of time during which there are none of these coincidences (percent no coincidence) as an index of the development of fetal behavioral states (Arduini et al., 1991). Since the percent of noncoincidence changes with gestation, it is possible to compare the developmental trend of this parameters in healthy fetuses with that of compromised fetuses, even earlier than 36 weeks of gestation when true states are not evident.

CIRCADIAN RHYTHMS

Although behavioral recordings are usually performed at the same time of the day in routine work, the assessment of fetal variables may be performed in different diurnal periods according to the clinical exigencies.

Diurnal variations of fetal activities (breathing movements, FM, FHR) are probably present before the appearance of behavioral states and have been described in the human fetus as early as 20–22 weeks of gestation (De Vries, Visser, Mulder, & Prechtl, 1987). These variations are characterized by an increased fetal activity during the evening associated with a reduced activity during the first hours of the day (Patrick, Campbell, Carmichael, & Richardson, 1982). Knowledge of these factors may be clinically useful to interpret the results obtained.

The underlying mechanism of this biological clock in the fetus is poorly understood, and caution is needed in determining causal links. Moreover, it is noteworthy that there is a negative correlation between maternal plasma cortisol concentrations and fetal activity, which suggests either a causal or a temporal relationship between fetal behavior and maternal cortisol levels (Arduini et al, 1987c). This hypothesis is supported by studies showing the absence of circadian rhythms in fetal behavior in patients with suppression of the adrenal glands of various origin (Arduini et al., 1986b; Arduini et al., 1986c; Patrick et al., 1981). The mechanism of action of maternal steroids on fetal behavior is still unclear, but cortisol may modulate the fetal production of pro-opiomelanocortin, and therefore of ß-endorphin, because it has been shown that naloxone causes rapid modifications of fetal behavior (Arduini et al., 1987b).

EFFECTS OF FETAL BEHAVIOR
ON CLINICAL TESTS

Doppler Velocimetry

Doppler flow velocity measurements are increasingly used in obstetrics for early detection of obstetrical complications such as hypertension and intrauterine growth retardation (IUGR) and for their continued monitoring ("Doppler Ultrasound," 1992). Indeed, some authors have suggested the use of Doppler velocimetry in making the decisions about the proper time of delivery in IUGR fetuses (Almstrom et al., 1992). Moreover, there are substantial changes in fetal hemodynamics associated with behavioral states that must be taken into account in the clinical evaluation of the results obtained, as values normal for a behavioral state may seem abnormal for a different state.

During state 2F healthy fetuses show a significant decrease of the pulsatility index (PI), an index believed to be expression of impedance to flow, at the level of fetal internal carotid artery and descending thoracic aorta (van Eyck et al., 1985; van Eyck, Wladimiroff, Wijngaard, Noordam, & Prechtl, 1987). Other hemodynamic changes are present at intracardiac level, including an increased right to left shunt at the level of foramen ovale (van Eyck & Stewart, 1990), an increase of left cardiac output (Rizzo, Arduini, Valensise, & Romanini, 1990), and a reduced flow through the ductus arteriosus (Mooren, van Eyck, & Wladimiroff, 1989). All these modifications are consistent with a behavioral state involving redistribution of fetal blood flow leading during state 2F to a preferential streaming of well-oxygenated blood to the left heart and consequently to the brain.

As was the case for circadian effects, these state-related variations in biological activities must be considered in the clinical interpretation of a result. For example, a low PI value in the internal carotid artery may be suggestive of either a brain-sparing phenomenon or a normal behavioral hemodynamic adaptive response to a period of fetal behavioral activity.

Nonstress Test

The recording of FHR in the absence of stimulation (nonstress test [NST]) is one of the standard tests of fetal surveillance, although several studies have recently questioned its significance. The main feature of normality in the interpretation of NST is the presence of FHR accelerations, that is, reactive tracing. The suggested optimum number of accelerations varies in the literature from one to five over a period of 20 or 30 min (Spencer, 1990). On the other hand, the absence of accelerations (nonreactive tracing) is considered suspicious. Fetal behavioral states greatly influence the results of NST, as the presence of a FHR pattern A appears similar to a nonreactive tracing. As a consequence, the interpretation of the NST should take into account the existence and the duration of the different behavioral states. In Fig. 6.2 are shown the median and maximum duration of FHR pattern A in healthy third-trimester fetuses. These values validate the data obtained by others (30) and demonstrate that healthy fetuses may show at term non reactive tracings lasting as long as 50 min. Thus, the management of a nonreactive NST requires as first step the extension of the recording time

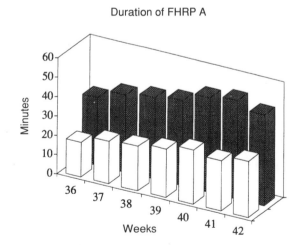

FIG. 6.2.   Duration (minutes) of fetal heart pattern (FHRP) A from 36 to 42 weeks of gestation calculated from routine fetal heart monitoring in 14,287 uncomplicated pregnancies. Data are expressed as median duration (white columns) and maximum duration (dashed columns).

to 50 min. Clinical evaluations performed on shorter time intervals may be misleading.

Vibroacoustic Stimulation

Fetal response to vibroacoustic stimulation, characterized by a transient tachycardia that may last several minutes and by an increase in fetal movements, is considered an indicator of fetal health (Serafini et al., 1984) and is part of the current clinical practice in different centers. However, the ability of the fetus to react to sound stimuli seems to vary with different behavioral states (Devoe, Murray, Faircloth, & Ramos, 1990). The response is more evident when the stimulus is applied during state 1F than during state 2F. Again, clinical interpretation of the test needs to take behavioral state into account.

Biochemical Indices

The possibility of collecting fetal blood samples by cordocentesis allowed physicians to obtain in selected cases direct data on fetal acid–base balance, metabolism, and endocrine conditions. It seems clear that this information will be used in the future for the management of sick fetuses. Although the invasive nature of cordocentesis has limited the possibilities of obtaining serial blood samplings in the human fetus, it is logical to predict that these biochemical indices will change in association with behavioral states as demonstrated on animal models (Reid, Jensen, Phernetton, & Rankin, 1990). This implies that the interpretation of biochemical results will require knowledge of the behavioral state during which the blood sampling was obtained.

BEHAVIORAL STATE TRANSITIONS

The long observation period usually required for behavioral state analysis (i.e., 2 hr) and the time-consuming off-line analysis of state variables have to date limited their clinical application. We recently restricted our studies to the analysis of behavioral transitions (Arduini et al., 1989). A *transition* is defined as the time elapsing between two different and consecutive behavioral states. The onset of transition is calculated from the beginning of the loss of coincidence between behavioral variables, and the end is the time of synchronization of the three behavioral variables in a different state. The computerized system previously described allows automatic recognition of FHRP (Fig. 6.3) and of the other behavioral variables. In this way

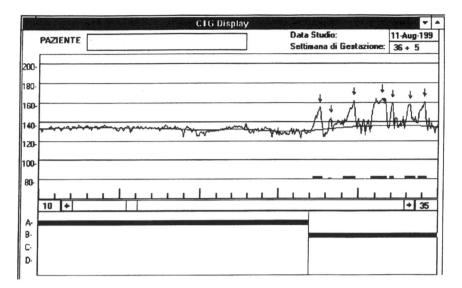

FIG. 6.3.   Example of a transition from fetal heart pattern A to fetal heart pattern B. The two fetal heart rate patterns are automatically recognized by the computer and traced as vectors (bottom panel). Each minor thick mark indicates a 1-min interval.

transitions may be analyzed in terms of either their duration or the sequence of change of behavioral variables.

In healthy fetuses there is a progressive reduction in the duration of transitions from 28 weeks of gestation onward and nomograms for gestational age have been constructed (Arduini et al., 1991) and are reported in Fig. 6.4. Of interest is that prior to 32 weeks of gestation there are virtually no transitions shorter than 3 min.

Concerning the sequence of change of behavioral variables, at first there is no prominent, leading variable whose appearance or disappearance heralds transitions. As gestational age increases (more than 34 weeks), FM is the most likely variable to change during transitions from coincidence 1F to 2F, followed by changes in FEM and FHRP. On the other hand, during transitions from 2F to 1F, FHRP most often changes first, followed by FM and FEM (Arduini et al., 1991). A graphic representation of the sequence of change of behavioral variables is given in Fig. 6.5.

It must be pointed out that the study of transitions allows a significant shortening of the observation time. In our experience a transition is usually evidenced after 45 min of recordings (range 15–87 min), a time interval compatible with clinical practice. Furthermore, the intraindividual variation in the duration of transition is reduced, thus allowing consideration of a single value as representative of the behavioral development of such subject (Arduini et al., 1989).

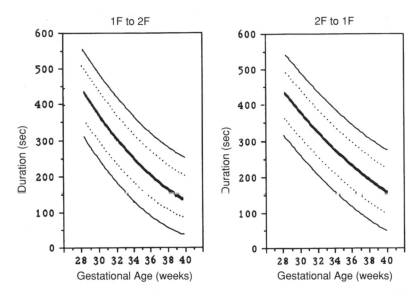

FIG. 6.4. Calculated curves of the duration of behavioral transitions from 1F to 2F (left) and from 2F to 1F (right). The bold lines indicate the 50th centile, the dotted lines the 10th and 90th centiles, and the plain lines the 5th and 95th centiles. From Arduini et al. (1991). Reprinted by permission.

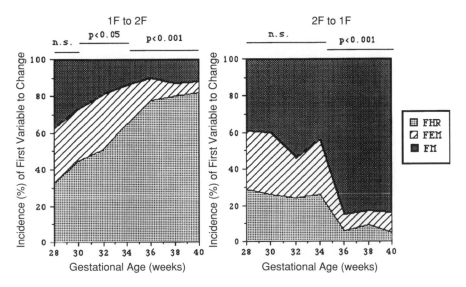

FIG. 6.5. Distribution of behavioral variables as first variable to change during transitions from 1F to 2F (left) and from 2F to 1F (right). From Arduini et al. (1991). Reprinted by permission

92

FETAL BEHAVIORAL STATES AND BEHAVIORAL TRANSITIONS IN PATHOLOGICAL CONDITIONS

An underlying assumption in the study of behavioral states is that they may reflect fetal brain development. Different factors may impair brain development, leading to abnormalities in the clustering between fetal behavioral variables (FHR, FEM, and FM) and thus resulting in anomalies in the incidence and occurrence of behavioral states.

IUGR Fetuses

The pathophysiology of IUGR is a reduced supply of nutrients and oxygen from the mother to the fetus through the placenta (so-called *uteroplacental insufficiency*). Under this condition of fetal starvation several behavioral state abnormalities have been reported (Van Vliet, Martin, Nijhuis, & Prechtl, 1985; Rizzo, Arduini, Pennestrì, Romanini, & Mancuso, 1987). These changes include an higher incidence of periods of no coincidence when compared to reference limits for gestation. In IUGR fetuses identified early in gestation by Doppler ultrasonography we found that the development of behavioral states is impaired, and this modification precedes by weeks the occurrence of abnormal heart rate tracings requiring prompt delivery (Fig. 6.6). However, there is high interfetal variability in the time interval elapsing between abnormalities of behavioral state and the occurrence of abnormal heart rate tracings.

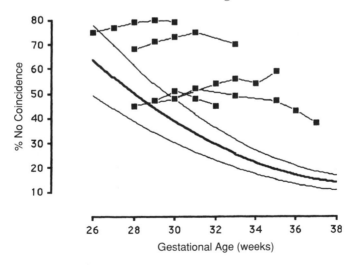

FIG. 6.6.   Individual values of percentage of no coincidence found in five IUGR fetuses diagnosed in early pregnancy by Doppler ultrasonography and that later developed abnormal (late decelerations) heart rate tracings. Reference limits are shown as mean ± 2SD.

The already reported difficulties in using clinically the analysis of behavioral states have turned our attention to the study of transitions. In IUGR fetuses transitions were longer and the sequence of change of variables remained disorganized at comparable gestational age (Fig. 6.7) (Arduini et al., 1989). Furthermore, when transitions were evaluated longitudinally, in IUGR fetuses a progressive abnormal duration of transitions was evidenced, suggesting a potential role for their analysis in the monitoring of fetal condition (Fig. 6.8).

It is not clear whether hypoxia is the major cause affecting central nervous system (CNS) function or whether the deprivation of other nutrients such as glucose and amino acids may play a role. Experiments on instrumented lamb fetuses have shown that chronic hypoxemia induces changes in fetal behavior similar to those described in human IUGR

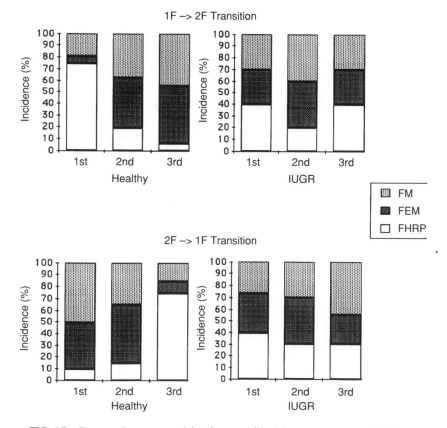

FIG. 6.7.   Temporal sequence of the changes of fetal heart rate patterns (FHRP), eye movements (FEM), and body movements (FM) during transitions from 1F to 2F and 2F to 1F in healthy and IUGR fetuses. Redrawn from Arduini et al. (1989). Adapted by permission.

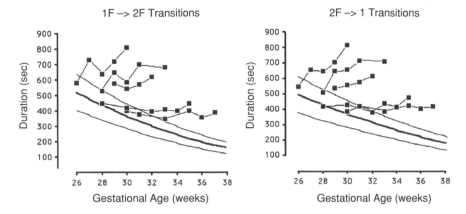

FIG. 6.8.   Duration of transitions in five IUGR fetuses diagnosed in early pregnancy by Doppler ultrasonography and that later developed abnormal (late decelerations) heart rate tracings. Reference limits are shown as mean ± 2SD.

fetuses (Bocking, Gagnon, Milne, & White, 1988). On the other hand, serial studies in deteriorating IUGR fetuses have evidenced behavioral abnormalities at a clinical stage preceding that of hypoxemia, thus suggesting that malnutrition itself may induce a cortical dysfunction (Visser, Bekedam, & Ribbert, 1990).

Fetuses of Diabetic Mothers

The development of behavioral states is also disturbed in fetuses of insulin-dependent diabetic mothers. As early as the first trimester there is a 1- to 2-week delay in the appearance of fetal movements (Mulder & Visser, 1991). Moreover, the emergence of behavioral states is impaired, and these fetuses are characterized by a low incidence of state 1F whereas the incidence of state 2F is similar to normal fetuses (Mulder, Visser, Bekedam, & Prechtl, 1987). Modifications occurring in transitions are still under evaluation.

The behavioral abnormality differs from that present in IUGR and other pathological conditions. The reason for this difference is unknown, but it may suggest that either a different timing of exposure of the central nervous system to a nonoptimal metabolic environment or that differences in the action of the causative factors may play a role.

Tight glycemic control does not prevent these abnormalities. It is of interest, however, that macrosomic fetuses show a more severe compromise of behavioral indices (Mulder, Visser, Bekedam, & Prechtl, 1987) . This suggests that adequate glycemic control does not prevent other metabolic disturbances (lipids, amino acids) that may influence fetal growth and cortical function. On this basis the need for a different metabolic control of diabetic pregnancies may be suggested.

Fetuses with Central Nervous System Anomalies

Hydrocephalic fetuses show grossly abnormal behavioral states. Of interest is the fact that the incidence of FHRP A and B may be normal in such fetuses whereas the clustering with FM and FEM is extremely low, thus resulting in a high percentage of no coincidence (Arduini et al., 1987a).

In this study there were also significant differences in behavioral states between hydrocephalic fetuses with a good prognosis after birth and those with a poor outcome (i.e., death or severe neurological impairment). This finding demonstrates a potential clinical usefulness of this technique in the management of such fetuses. Furthermore, serial recordings could improve choosing the optimum time of delivery for these fetuses.

Abnormalities of fetal behavioral states have also been found in lethal congenital anomalies (Pillai, Garrett, & James, 1991), despite normal NST and biophysical profile.

Medication and Drug Assumption

Few data are available on the neuroteratology of drugs used during human pregnancies, but animal data indicate that short- and long-term sequaele may result from their use (Mirmiran & Swaab, 1992). Moreover, abnormal fetal behavior has been evidenced in fetuses of mothers treated with antiepileptics (Van Geijn et al., 1986). Similarly abnormalities were found in fetuses of cocaine-addicted mothers (Hume, O'Donnell, Stanger, Killam, & Gingras, 1989). No systematic data are available on other medications used during pregnancy or other drug of abuse.

CONCLUSIONS

Fetal behavioral states can be easily recognized in utero by using computerized techniques of analysis. Their influence on the routine tests of assessment of fetal well-being is evident. Ignoring their presence in the interpretation of these tests can lead to erroneous results.

As indices of fetal CNS function, behavioral states may be used in selected cases to assess the integrity of central nervous system. Their use has been so far limited mainly because of the complexity of analysis and the long periods of observation required. The use of the computerized approach and the limitation of the analysis more to transitional periods may make this analysis compatible with clinical practice.

ACKNOWLEDGMENT

These studies were supported by a grant of the Italian National Council of Research (CNR Grant No. 94.0001; PF41).

REFERENCES

Almstrom, H., Axelsson, O., Cnattingius, S., Ekman, G., Maesel, A., Ulmsten, U., Arstrom, K., & Marsal, K. (1992). Comparison of umbilical artery velocimetry and cardiotocography for surveillance of small for gestational age fetuses. *Lancet, 340,* 936–940.

Arduini, D., Rizzo, G., Caforio, L., Boccolini, M. R., Romanini, C., & Mancuso, S. (1989). Behavioural state transitions in healthy and growth retarded fetuses. *Early Human Development, 19,* 155–162.

Arduini, D., Rizzo, G., Caforio, L., Romanini, C., & Mancuso, S. (1987a). The development of behavioural states in hydrocephalic fetuses. *Fetal Therapy, 2,* 135–143.

Arduini, D., Rizzo, G., Dell'Acqua, S., Mancuso, S., & Romanini, C. (1987b). Effects of naloxone on fetal behaviour near term. *American Journal of Obstetrics and Gynecology, 156,* 474–478.

Arduini, D., Rizzo, G., Giorlandino, C., Dell'Acqua, S., Valensise, H., & Romanini, C., (1986a). The development of fetal behavioural states: A longitudinal study. *Prenatal Diagnosis, 6,* 117–124.

Arduini, D., Rizzo, G., Giorlandino, C., Nava, S., Dell'Acqua, S., Valensise, H., & Romanini, C. (1985). The fetal behavioural states: An ultrasonic study. *Prenatal Diagnosis, 5,* 269–276.

Arduini, D., Rizzo, G., Massacesi, M., Boccolini, M. R., Romanini, C., & Mancuso, S. (1991). Longitudinal assessment of behavioural transitions in healthy human fetuses during the last trimester of pregnancy. *Journal of Perinatal Medicine, 1,* 67–72.

Arduini, D., Rizzo, G., Parlati, E., Dell'Acqua, S., Mancuso, S., & Romanini, C. (1987c). Are the fetal heart rate patterns related to fetal maternal endocrine rhythms at term of pregnancy? *Journal of Fetal Medicine, 6,* 53–57.

Arduini, D., Rizzo, G., Parlati, E., Giorlandino, C., Valensise, H., Dell'Acqua, S., & Romanini, C., (1986b). Modifications of ultradian and circadian rhythms of fetal heart rate after fetal-maternal adrenal gland suppression: A double blind study. *Prenatal Diagnosis, 6,* 409–417.

Arduini, D., Rizzo, G., Parlati, E., Valensise, H., Dell'Acqua, S., & Romanini, C. (1986c). Loss of circadian rhythms of fetal behaviour in a total adrenalectomized pregnant woman. *Gynecological and Obstetrical Investigation, 23,* 226–229.

Arduini, D., Rizzo, G., Piana, G., Bonalumi, R., Brambilla, P., & Romanini, C. (1993). Computerized analysis of fetal heart rate: I. Description of the system (2CTG). *Journal of Maternal and Fetal Investigation, 3,* 159–164.

Birnholz, J. C., Stephens, J. C., & Faria, M. (1978). Fetal movements patterns: A possible means of defining neurological milestones in utero. *American Journal of Roentgenology, 130,* 537–540.

Bocking, A. D., Gagnon, R., Milne, K. M., & White, S. E. (1988). Behavioural activity during prolonged hypoxemia in fetal sheep. *Journal Applied Physiology, 65,* 2420–2426.

Bots, R. S. G. M., Nijhuis, J. G., Martin, C. B., Jr., & Prechtl, H. F. R. (1981). Human fetal eye movements: Detection in utero by means of ultrasonography. *Early Human Development, 5,* 87–94.

Dawes, G. S., Fox, H. E., Leduc, B. M., Liggins, G. C., & Richards, R. T. (1970). Respiratory movements and paradoxical sleep in foetal lambs. *Journal of Physiology, 210,* 47–48.

De Vries, J. I. P., Visser, G. H. A., Mulder, E. J. H., & Prechtl, H. F. R. (1987). Diurnal and other variations in fetal movements and other heart rate patterns. *Early Human Development, 15,* 99–114.

Devoe, L. D., Murray, C., Faircloth, D., & Ramos, F. (1990). Vibroacoustic stimulation and fetal behavioural state in normal term human pregnancy. *American Journal of Obstetrics and Gynecology, 163,* 1156–1161.

Doppler ultrasound in obstetrics [Editorial]. (1992). *Lancet, 339,* 1083–1084.

Evertson, L. R., Gauthier, R. S., Schrifin, B. S., & Paul, R. H. (1979). Antepartum fetal heart testing. I. Evolution of the non stress test. *American Journal of Obstetrics and Gynecology, 133,* 29–33.

Hume, R. F., Jr., O'Donnell, K. J., Stanger, C. L., Killam, A. P., & Gingras, A. L. (1989). In utero cocaine exposure. Observations of behavioural states may predict neonatal outcome. *American Journal of Obstetrics and Gynecology, 161,* 685–690.

Mirmiran, M., & Swaab, D. F. (1992). Effects of perinatal medications on the developing brain. In J. G. Nijhuis (Ed.), *Fetal behaviour. Developmental and perinatal aspects* (pp. 112–128). Oxford: Oxford University Press.

Mooren, K., van Eyck, J., & Wladimiroff, J. W. (1989). Human fetal ductal flow velocity waveforms relative to behavioural states in normal term pregnancy. *American Journal of Obstetrics and Gynecology, 160,* 371–374.

Mulder, E. J. H., & Visser, G. H. A. (1991). Growth and motor development in fetuses of women with type 1 diabetes. II. Emergence of specific movement pattern. *Early Human Development, 25,* 107–115.

Mulder, E. J. H., Visser, G. H. A., Bekedam, D. J., & Prechtl, H. F. R. (1987). Emergence of behavioural states in fetuses of type I diabetic mothers. *Early Human Development, 15,* 231–252.

Nijhuis, J. G. (1992). The third trimester. In J. G. Nijhuis (Ed.), *Fetal behaviour. Developmental and perinatal aspects* (pp. 26–40). Oxford: Oxford University Press.

Nijhuis, J. G., Prechtl, H. F. R., Martin, C. B., Jr., & Bots, R. S. G. M. (1982). Are there behavioural states in the human fetus? *Early Human Development, 6,* 177–195.

Patrick, J., Campbell, K., Carmichael, L., & Richardson, B. (1982). Patterns of fetal gross body movement over 24 hours observation intervals during the last 10 weeks of pregnancy. *American Journal of Obstetrics and Gynecology, 146,* 363–371.

Patrick, J., Challis, J., Campbell, K., Carmichael, L., Richardson, B., & Tevaarwerk, G. (1981). Effects of synthetic glucocorticoid on the human fetal breathing movements at 34–35 weeks gestation. *American Journal of Obstetrics and Gynecology, 139,* 324–328.

Pillai, M., Garrett, C., & James, D. (1991). Bizarre fetal behaviour associated with lethal congenital anomalies: A case report. *European Journal of Obstetrics, Gynecology and Reproductive Biology, 39,* 215–218.

Prechtl, H. F. R. (1974). The behavioural states of newborn infant (a review). *Brain Research, 76*, 185–212.

Reid, D. L., Jensen, A., Phernetton, T. M., & Rankin, J. H. G. (1990). Relationship between plasma catecholamine levels and electrocortical state in the mature fetal lamb. *Journal of Developmental Physiology, 13*, 75–79.

Rizzo, G., Arduini, D., Romanini, C., & Mancuso, S. (1988). Computer-assisted analysis of fetal behavioural states. *Prenatal Diagnosis, 8*, 479–484.

Rizzo, G., Arduini, D., Pennestrì, F., Romanini, C., & Mancuso, S. (1987). The fetal behaviour in growth retardation: Its relationship to fetal blood flow. *Prenatal Diagnosis, 7*, 229–238.

Rizzo, G., Arduini, D., Valensise, H., & Romanini, C. (1990). Effects of behavioral states on cardiac output in healthy human fetuses at 36–38 weeks of gestation. *Early Human Development, 23*, 109–115.

Serafini, P., Lindsay, M. B. J., Nagey, D. A., Pupkin, M. J., Tseng, P., & Crenshaw, C. J. (1984). Antepartum fetal heart response to sound stimulation: The acoustic stimulation test. *American Journal of Obstetrics and Gynecology, 48*, 41–45.

Spencer, J. A. D. (1990). Antepartum cardiotocography. In G. Chamberlain (Ed.), *Modern antenatal care of the fetus* (pp. 163–188). Oxford: Blackwell.

Tas, B. A. P. J., & Nijhuis, J. G. (1992). Consequence for fetal monitoring. In J. G. Nijhuis (Ed.), Fetal behaviour. Developmental and perinatal aspects (pp. 258–267). Oxford: Oxford University Press.

Timor-Tritsch, I. E., Dierker, L. J., Hertz, R. H., Deagan, N. C., & Rosen M. G. (1978). Studies of antepartum behavioural state in the human fetus at term. *American Journal of Obstetrics and Gynecology, 132*, 524–528.

van Eyck, J., Stewart, P. A., & Wladimiroff, J. W. (1990). Human fetal foramen ovale flow velocity waveforms relative to behavioural states in normal term pregnancy. *American Journal of Obstetrics and Gynecology, 163*, 1239–1242.

van Eyck, J., Wladimiroff, J. W., Noordam, M. J., Tonge, H. M., Prechtl, H. F. R. (1985). The blood flow velocity waveforms in the fetal descending aorta; Its relationship to behavioural states in normal pregnancy at 37–38 weeks of gestation. *Early Human Development, 14*, 99–107.

van Eyck, J., Wladimiroff, J. W., Wijngaard, J. A. G. W., Noordam, H. M., & Prechtl, H. F. R. (1987). The blood flow velocity waveforms in the fetal internal carotid and umbilical artery; Its relationship to behavioural states in normal pregnancy at 37–38 weeks of gestation. *British Journal of Obstetrics and Gynaecology, 94*, 736–741.

van Geijn, H. P., Swartjes, J. M., van Woerden, E. E., Caron, F. J. M., Brons, J. T. J., & Arts, N. T. F. (1986). Fetal behavioural states in epileptic pregnancies. *European Journal of Obstetrics, Gynecology and Reproductive Biology, 21*, 309–314.

van Vliet, M. A. T., Martin, C. B., Jr., Nijhuis, J. G., & Prechtl, H. F. R. (1985). Behavioural states in growth retarded fetuses. *Early Human Development, 12*, 183–197.

Visser, G. H. A., Bekedam, D. J., & Ribbert, L. S. M. (1990). Changes in antepartum heart rate patterns with progressive deterioration of the fetal condition. *International Journal of Biomedical Computing, 25*, 239–246.

7

Neurobehavioral Development in the Human Fetus

David James
Queen's Medical Center,
Nottingham, United Kingdom

Mary Pillai
John Smoleniec
St. Michael's Hospital, Bristol, United Kingdom

In the western world the majority of pregnancies result in the delivery of a normal healthy baby who subsequently develops normally through infancy and childhood into adolescence. Thus, the impact is great when this postnatal development is not normal and the child is recognized to have some neurodevelopmental disability in infancy (NDDI).

In the United States, mental retardation affects about 850,000 children and cerebral palsy affects 750,000. In the United Kingdom the incidence is similar with approximately 1 in 300 newborns developing some form of NDDI (Emond, Golding, & Peckham, 1981). It has been estimated that in the United States the financial costs of neurological and communicative disorders amounted to $14 billion in 1985. The preface to the U.S. Department of Health and Human Services report "Prenatal and Perinatal Factors Associated with Brain Disorders" concluded that an overview of pre- and perinatal causes of mental retardation, cerebral palsy and epilepsy revealed how little was known of the factors controlling, altering or modifying brain development or of what the causes of these disabling conditions were (Freeman, 1985).

It has been estimated that of the cases of neurodevelopmental disability identified during infancy and childhood approximately 30% are caused by factors operating after birth (e.g., infection, trauma, and tumors), 10% are caused by events during labor and delivery (principally hypoxia), and approximately 60% are caused by factors operating before labor and delivery (Lamb & Lang, 1992). Some of these factors are recognized and clearly documented, for example, chromosomal abnormalities and inborn errors of metabolism. However, the majority have not been identified.

The 1985 statement relating to the lack of knowledge of normal brain development and pathological influences still holds true today (Freeman, 1985).

REASONS FOR STUDYING HUMAN FETAL NEURODEVELOPMENTAL MILESTONES

The are three reasons for studying fetal neurobehavioral development. The first is to study the etiology and pathogenesis of abnormal development with the goal of devising and testing therapeutic and preventative measures. This is the most important reason. Second is to make possible early intervention in the form of assessment, treatment and support after birth for those babies with suspected abnormal fetal development, because there is evidence that the overall outcome in babies is improved the earlier such intervention can be implemented (Shonoff & Hauser-Grau, 1987). Third is to assess what proportion of NDDI is due to factors operating before labor and delivery.

One approach to the study of fetal neurobehavioral development uses the concept of establishing fetal neurobehavioral developmental milestones and is analogous to the milestones used in screening during childhood and infancy. Certainly, this approach should meet the three aims just set out. By identifying normal neurodevelopmental milestones and their variation in the human fetus, it should be possible to define "normal" development. If specific milestones are not achieved it may be possible to identify a point in pregnancy prior to which the "insult" must have occurred and thus have a starting point for studying possible insults and their mode of action. Such milestone testing may identify the newborn who will need detailed assessment and proven therapeutic intervention after birth. Finally, it may also identify the fetuses with neurodevelopmental compromise before labor and delivery. The use of real-time ultrasound has opened the door to neurological assessment of the intact human fetus. The possibility of establishing developmental milestones for the fetus was proposed over a decade ago (Birnholz, Stephens, & Faria, 1978).

WHICH MILESTONES?

The first step in undertaking this approach to fetal neurodevelopmental research is to decide which neurodevelopmental features to study. There are a number of possible candidates.

Movement

In early pregnancy the ontogeny of different movements has been studied by several groups (Birnholz et al., 1978; De Vries, Visser, & Prechtl, 1982, 1988; Iannoruberto & Tajani, 1981). Van Dongen and Goudie (1980) observed four patterns of behavior in fetuses between 10 and 12 weeks gestation, namely, periods of absence of movement, lasting not longer that 5 mins, periods of rolling, flexion, extension, and head rotating, involving all parts of the body, periods of isolated limb movements, and periods of strong pulsed movement of the thorax, akin to hiccups. Iannoruberto and Tajani (1981) noted that smooth vermicular movements of the early embryo ceased at 10 weeks, whereas jerky jumps or flexion/extension of the whole body were common up to 20 weeks. The most detailed analysis of early pregnancy has been performed by De Vries et al. (De Vries et al., 1982, 1988), who found that the first fetal movements consist of extensions and flexions of the fetal head and spine, which could be observed from 7 weeks gestation. This was followed by rapid onset of a wide variety of distinct types of movement over the next 6–8 weeks. All the movements observed in term fetuses were already present at the age of 15 weeks, provided a sufficiently long observation time was used to compensate for the low incidence of many movements, such as breathing in early pregnancy. The mean age of onset of specific movement patterns reported in the literature has a range of 2 weeks in the first half of pregnancy (De Vries et al., 1982, 1985, 1988; Iannoruberto & Tajani, 1981).

The fluency and variability of movements in normal fetuses in the first half of pregnancy have been noted to contrast sharply with the forceful, jerky and repetitive movements of anencephalic fetuses, in whom no distinct patterns can be recognized (Visser, Laurinin, De Vries, Bekedam, & Prechtl, 1985). Also, fetuses of diabetic women have been found to have a delay in onset of many types of movement (Visser, Bekedam, Mulder, & van Ballegooie, 1985; Visser, Mulder, Bekedam, van Ballegooie, & Prechtl, 1986). This is not specific but parallels the degree of early growth retardation also commonly present in fetuses of diabetics during the first trimester (Pedersen & Molsted-Pedersen, 1981; Pederson, Molsted-Pederson, & Mortensen, 1984).

The main limitation of establishing developmental milestones in the

TABLE 7.1
The Appearance of Fetal Movements in Early Pregnancy

Movement	Gestation of First Appearance
Any movement	7
Startle	8
Generalized movements	8
Hiccups	8
Isolated arm movements	9
Head retroflexion	9
Hand–face contact	10
Breathing	10
Jaw opening	10
Stretching	10
Head anteflexion	10
Yawn	11
Suck and swallow	12

Note. From De Vries et al. (1982). Adapted by permission

fetus is that in practice only relatively short intervals are commonly observed in a research setting. In the first half of pregnancy circadian rhythms (frequency of one per 24 hr) and ultradian rhythms (frequency of more than one per 24 hr) do not play a role, so that records of 60 min are representative. However, in the second half of pregnancy fluctuations in behavior are such that recordings need to last at least 90 min (Nijhuis, Prechtl, Martin, & Bots, 1982).

The range of movements described by De Vries and colleagues (1982) is summarized in Table 7.1. Indeed, most movements seen in a full-term human fetus have been identified by the end of the first trimester. The difference, however, is that although at the beginning of pregnancy these movements appear to be random and uncoordinated (or at least no pattern has yet been recognized), as pregnancy advances they become increasingly sophisticated and integrated.

The precise timing of onset of the diurnal pattern of behavior has yet to be established; however, such rhythms are not demonstrable at 13 weeks, but have been reported at 20–22 weeks (De Vries, Visser, Mulder, & Prechtl, 1987), at 24–28 weeks (Nasello-Paterson, Natale, & Connors, 1988), and during the last 10 weeks of pregnancy (Patrick, Campbell, Carmichael, Natale, & Richardson, 1982). All of these studies found peaks of fetal activity occurring in the late evening, in keeping with the reported pattern of maternally perceived movements. Administration of corticosteroids to the mother suppresses these rhythms (Arduini et al., 1986), and they are temporarily lost immediately following birth (Dawes, 1986; Mills, 1975).

Using real-time ultrasound recordings of fetal eye movements and motility with simultaneous continuous recording of the fetal heart rate (FHR), Martin (1981) and Nijhuis et al. (Nijhuis et al., 1982; Nijhuis, Martin, & Prechtl, 1984) analyzed the temporal association of different types of somatic movements, eye movements, and heart rate patterns of fetuses of multiparous women at term, and between 32 and 40 weeks gestation. After 36 weeks they found distinct, recurring combinations of these variables that they considered analogous to the first four of the five states in infants (S1–S4; Prechtl, 1974), and they therefore designated them states 1F–4F, each with a specific heart rate pattern, A–D respectively. We examined individual consistencies and variations in the behavior of healthy mature fetuses. This revealed only two minor discrepancies compared with the original description of fetal states. The first was that within individual fetuses transition times were not consistently and clearly completed within 3 min once behavioral state were observed. Second, we did not observe state 3F; however, it is noteworthy that this state only occurred very briefly in the original studies reporting its existence (Figs. 7.1 and 7.2).

The stability, close linkage, and simultaneous change of the conditions of the different behavioral state variables is present in healthy fetuses from around 36 weeks gestation (Nijhuis et al., 1982). Prior to this, linkage of the state variables is less consistent, and intervals where the state variables conform to the pattern observed during the behavioral states have been

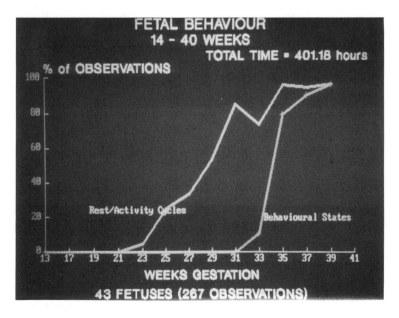

FIG. 7.1.   Definitions of behavioral states in the normal human fetus. From Pillai and James (1990a). Reprinted by permission.

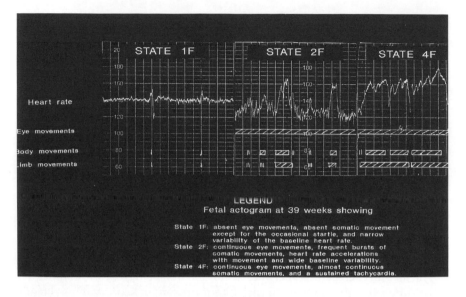

FIG. 7.2.   Characteristics of behavioral states in the normal human fetus. From Pillai
and James (1990a). Reprinted by permission.

called periods of coincidence. These periods of coincidence gradually
increase from 32 weeks gestation to term (Nijhuis et al., 1982, 1984) and
reflect advancing fetal neurological maturation. Before the appearance of
well-defined behavioral states or periods of coincidence, alternating cycles
of quiet and activity are evident. These have been called *active–quiet cycles*
(Dierker, Pillay, Sorokin, & Rosen, 1982a, 1982b), *rest–activity cycles*
(Nasello-Paterson et al., 1988) or *ultradian rhythms* (Campbell, 1980). We
have made longitudinal observations on a group of 45 low-risk singleton
pregnancies from 14 to 41 weeks gestation with the aim of describing the
development of these ultradian rhythms (Pillai & James, 1990c). With
advancing gestational age there was a significant increase in the longest
interval complete quiescence ($p \leq .001$; Fig. 7.3), revealing that fetal inactivity is gestational age dependent. Although evaluating complete inactivity
is not necessarily an appropriate way to discriminate intervals of rest and
activity, as it is established that cycles of state 1F (Nijhuis et al., 1982) in the
fetus and quiet sleep in the newborn (Prechtl, 1974) may be interrupted by
the occasional startle without a change of state occurring, it does provide a
simple means of distinguishing cyclical behavior without the use of complex mathematical formulas.

Prior to 24 weeks the majority of longest identifiable quiet intervals
were less than 5 min, whereas after 32 weeks most quiet intervals were
between 10 and 35 min and only one was longer than 40 min. Thus a

change in the distribution of behavior is evident between 24 and 32 weeks, with a relatively high base rate of fetal movements characteristic of the first half of pregnancy, becoming increasingly interrupted by periods of quiescence lasting 6 min or more in the second half of pregnancy. Using this arbitrary 6-min rule, rest–activity cycles were rarely observed prior to 24 weeks, but by 29 weeks they were present in over 80% of recordings (Fig. 7.4). Fixed and recurring associations of body movements, eye movements, and FHR pattern into well-defined fetal behavioral states, with simultaneous change (within 3 min) of all three variables at the times of state transition (Nijhuis et al., 1982), were first observed in one fetus at 33 weeks, and were present in over 80% of recordings after 36 weeks.

The high rate of activity at younger gestations supports the hypothesis that advancing fetal maturity is associated with the development of inhibitory neural pathways. It is of interest that anencephalic fetuses maintain this high level of activity throughout pregnancy, suggesting that such inhibitory neural pathways derive from the cerebral cortex.

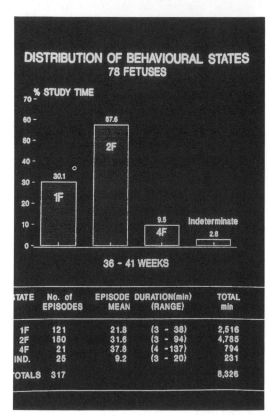

FIG. 7.3.   Duration of quiescence in the normal human fetus. From Pillai and James (1990c). Reprinted by permission.

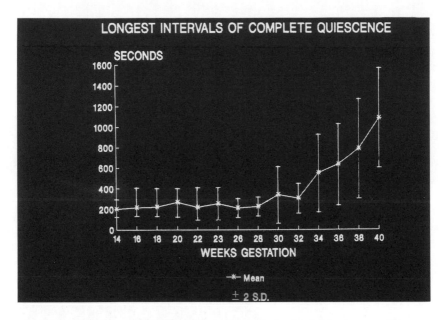

FIG. 7.4.   Development of rest–activity cycles and behavioral states in normal human pregnancy. From Pillai and James (1990c). Reprinted by permission.

The comparability of fetal states with those of the newborn has been studied (Pillai & James, 1990b). Comparisons were made between ultrasound behavioral recordings of 18 healthy term fetuses and recordings of the same variables of the same individuals at 3–5 days postnatally (Tables 7.2–7.4). Statistical comparison of the frequency of eye movements and limb and body movements revealed that the fetal states 1F and 2F were comparable to quiet sleep (S1), and rapid eye movement (REM) sleep (S2), respectively, in the newborn (Tables 7.2 and 7.3). Comparisons between the fetal states and wakefulness were less clear-cut. The heart rate in each of the three states in the fetus was about 20 beats per minute (bpm) higher than in the corresponding postnatal state, although the patterns were similar (Table 7.4). States 1F and 2F accounted for a higher percentage of fetal observations (86%) than states S1 and S2 in the neonatal observations (64%), but the ratio of the different types of sleep was similar in both recordings (approximately 30% quiet sleep to 70% REM sleep) (Table 7.2). State S3 (quiet awake) always and only occurred in the postnatal observations in association with feeding. No comparable behavior was observed during the prenatal observations (2,050 min in 18 fetuses). Prenatal observations of the fetus were conducted in a quiet room with the mother in a semirecumbent position. Numerically the movements observed in S5 (crying) were not significantly different from 2F; however, qualitatively there

TABLE 7.2
Comparison of Fetal and Neonatal Behavior: Total Relative State
Percentage in 18 Babies Before and After Birth

| | Fetal | | Neonatal | |
	State	%	State	%
"Sleep"	1F	28.5	S1	18.3
	2F	57.4	S2	45.5
	Total	85.9	Total	63.8
"Awake"			S3	7.2
	4F	11.0	S4	21.0
			S5	8.0
	Total	11.0	Total	36.2
Indeterminate	3.1			

Note. Paired observations were made in 18 fetuses/newborns before and after birth: 2050 min fetal and 2250 min neonatal observations. From Pillai and James (1990b). Reprinted by permission.

TABLE 7.3
Numbers (Mean + SD) of Eye, Limb and Body Movements per 10
Min in Stable State Epochs (Paired Observations in 18 Individuals)

State	Eye, Mean (SD)	Limb, Mean (SD)	Body, Mean (SD)
1F	2.8 (4.6)	6.6 (7.8)	3.2 (4.3)
2F	126.7 (50.4)	91.3 (41.2)	52.9 (25.7)
4F	226.6 (29.6)	143.0 (28.5)	95.4 (21.4)
S1	3.4 (2.7)	10.3 (10.7)	7.1 (8.3)
S2	123.5 (56.3)	115.0 (48.9)	58.4 (29.1)
S3	178.1 (67.6)	1.2 (3.8)	0.1 (0.3)
S4	229.6 (71.1)	191.3 (64.6)	120.1 (42.8)
S5	174.4 (107.3)	157.4 (83.9)	131.2 (98.8)

Note. From Pillai and James (1990b). Reprinted by permission

TABLE 7.4
Comparison of Fetal and Neonatal Heart Rates as Mean Values
(Standard Deviation), Paired Observations in 18 Individuals

Fetal State	Heart Rate (bpm)	Neonatal State	Heart Rate (bpm)	Change in Heart Rate
1F	135.8 (8.8)	S1	110.4 (8.6)	−25.4
2F	135.8 (8.7)	S2	113.4 (10.4)	−22.4
		S3	141.3 (16.9)	
4F	163.3 (8.0)	S4	143.8 (10.0)	−19.5
		S5	188.3 (14.1)	

Note. From Pillai and James (1990b). Reprinted by permission.

were marked differences, and S5 was characterized by a heart rate pattern quite unlike anything observed prenatally (often with a rate in excess of 200 bpm). We postulate that S3 and S5 are postnatal behavioral adaptations to extrauterine existence.

In conclusion, if movement were to be a useful milestone then the criteria that would seem reasonable to study would be prolonged quiescence. Before the 28th week of pregnancy less than 5% of normal fetuses are quiescent for 6 min or more (Fig. 7.3 and 7.4) (Pillai, 1992). This time "window" of acceptable quiescence would increase to 40 min at term (Pillai & James, 1990d).

Tone

There is a progressive increase in the tone of the fetus as pregnancy advances. This reflects maturation of both the central nervous system (especially the cerebellum) and the musculoskeletal system. It is diagrammatically summarized in Fig. 7.5.

This may be useful as a general neurological screening tool in the future.

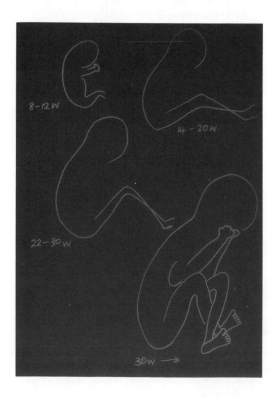

FIG. 7.5.   Diagrammatic representation of development of muscular tone in the human fetus.

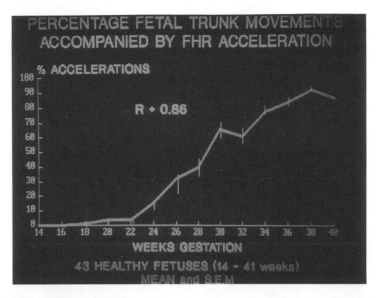

FIG. 7.6.   Proportion of fetal movements associated with FHR accelerations during normal human pregnancy.

If the features of this aspect of development could be quantified and documented, then it might play a role in the diagnosis and/or evaluation of fetal neuromuscular disorders in pregnancies of women with a family history of such conditions or in the general population for screening. Individual case reports of diagnosis of neuromuscular dysfunction using such criteria should prompt further study (Anthony, Mascarenhas, O'Brien, Battacharge, & Gould, 1993).

Heart Rate

The development of FHR characteristics during normal pregnancy represents a combination of the effects of both local and central factors (Pillai & James, 1990f).

During normal pregnancy the mean baseline FHR declines significantly as gestation advances, with the mean value being approximately 155 bpm at 16 weeks and falling by approximately 1 bpm per week to reach a mean value of 130 bpm at 40 weeks (Pillai & James, 1990f). Thus, the normal range for the FHR at the start of the third trimester is 120–160 bpm, whereas at term it is 110–150 bpm. Most of the other characteristics of the FHR trace are positively correlated with advancing gestation. Thus, as pregnancy progresses there are significant rises in the proportion of fetal movements associated with FHR accelerations (Fig. 7.6), the rate of rise of

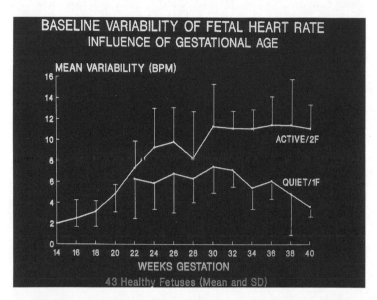

FIG. 7.7.   Baseline variability of FHR in normal human pregnancy.

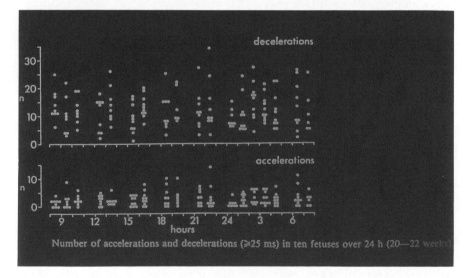

FIG. 7.8.   Relative frequency of accelerations and decelerations in the immature human fetus.

the accelerations, and the maximum height of the accelerations (Pillai & James, 1990f). There is also an initial increase in the variability of the baseline FHR over the first two trimesters. However, over the last trimester this continues to rise in periods of quiescence, but falls again in periods of activity (Fig. 7.7) (Pillai & James, 1990f). Certain features of the FHR trace have been shown to be markers of underlying neurological abnormality.

Although a "flat" unreactive FHR trace in the last trimester of pregnancy might merely reflect a fetus in 1F, if this were to last for longer than 40 min it should be regarded as pathological (Pillai & James, 1990d). Causes include anencephaly, brain death, and hypoxia (de Haan, van Bemmel, & Stolte, 1971; Nijhuis, Krayt, & Van Wijck, 1987; Visser, Laurenin, De Vries, Bekedam, & Prechtl, 1985b). It must be emphasized that these observations refer to the FHR pattern in the last trimester. Before that time an unreactive trace my be normal (Pillai & James, 1990f). Indeed, FHR decelerations, which in a pregnancy after 28 weeks might be regarded as pathological and especially suspicious of hypoxia, may be normal in the very immature fetus (Fig. 7.8) (Pillai & James, 1990f).

Mouthing

A sinusoidal FHR pattern may also reflect underlying pathology (especially fetal anemia or acute blood loss) (Rosenn, Ben Chetrit, Palti, & Hurwitz, 1990). However, it can also be a normal feature often found coexisting with fetal mouthing movements (Pillai & James, 1990g).

Yet the presence of fetal mouthing may be a useful discriminator of neurological integrity in the quiescent fetus with an unreactive FHR. In a study of 46 fetuses in quiescence, the ability of a variety of parameters to predict fetal compromise was compared.

Four of the fetuses were compromised as defined by acidosis. The results are illustrated in Table 7.5 and demonstrate that fetal mouthing in the quiescent fetus is possibly the best discriminator of fetal acidosis. Confirmation of these observations is necessary.

TABLE 7.5
Predictive Value of Biophysical Tests to Detect a Healthy Fetus (No Acidosis) During Quiescence

Test	Sensitivity	Specificity	Positive Predictive Value
Fetal breathing	100	53.8	11.8
Fetal movements	100	46.2	10.3
Nonstress test (FHR)	75	69.2	13.0
Biophysical Score	100	60.0	13.3
Rhythmical mouthing	100	93.0	50.0

Note. From Pillai and James (1990g). Reprinted by permission.

114   JAMES, PILLAI, SMOLENIEC

Respiratory Activity

The human fetus exhibits a number of different types of diaphragmatic movement; however, with the exception of fetal breathing, there are very few published data on these. Other types of diaphragmatic movement that have been described include sighs, hiccups and gasping. Of these, fetal hiccups are the most obvious, but in contrast to breathing they have received scant attention, and knowledge of the physiological mechanisms underlying their control and the role they play in fetal development is wanting.

Human fetal breathing movements have been recognized since 1888 (Ahlfeld, 1888). They have been defined as downward movement of the diaphragm with outward movement of abdominal contents and inward displacement of the thorax (Marsal, 1983). It is now well established that breathing is a normal feature of fetal life and is episodic in nature, with circadian and ultradian biological rhythms (Boddy & Dawes, 1975; Patrick, Campbell, Carmichael, Natale, & Richardson, 1980; Patrick, Natale, & Richardson, 1978; Roberts, Little, Cooper, & Campbell, 1979; van Vliet, Martin, Nijhuis, & Prechtl, 1985) and a tendency to be stimulated by glucose (Bocking et al., 1982; Harper, Meis, Rose, & Swain, 1987; Lewis, Trudinger, & Mangez, 1978; Natale, Patrick, & Richardson, 1978) and carbon dioxide (Connors et al., 1988; Ritchie & Lakhani, 1980) and inhibited by hypoxia (Bekedam & Visser, 1985; Boddy & Dawes, 1975; Manning & Platt, 1979). Much data has been accumulated on fetal breathing in chronically instrumented fetal animal preparations, especially the fetal lamb. With the development of noninvasive technology for fetal observation, interest in fetal breathing extended to its use as a parameter of well-being in the human fetus (Devoe, Reudrich, & Searle, 1989; Platt, Manning, Lemay, & Sipos, 1978). Suppression of fetal breathing has been suggested as an early predictor of fetal infection in patients with ruptured membranes, as a predictor of true preterm contractions (Agustsson & Patel, 1987), and as a predictor of the development of pulmonary hypoplasia in fetuses at high risk of this complication (Blott & Greenough, 1988; Blott et al., 1987).

All these predictive abilities were claimed with no account taken of the fact that fetal breathing in uncomplicated pregnancies showed a significant relationship with gestational age and a large degree of variability (Fox, Inglis, & Steinbrecher, 1979).

In a longitudinal study in low-risk fetuses, documenting developmental trends in fetal breathing and hiccups and their relationship to developing patterns of fetal behavior (Pillai & James, 1990e), all episodes of fetal breathing were considered significant if they contained a minimum of four consecutive breaths sustained over at least 5 sec. In accordance with the published criteria of others, all episodes where the breath-to-breath interval was 6 sec or more were excluded (Patrick et al., 1980). Isolated dia-phragmatic movements were not counted. Fetal hiccups were character-ized by more forceful and regular diaphragmatic contractions at a slower rate than breathing. Because there is no accepted definition for hiccups, this was arbitrarily defined as significant all episodes containing a mini-mum of five hiccups in 30 sec.

One hundred and five recordings were made prior to 26 weeks and were characterized by a low percentage of fetal breathing movements (median 1.4%, range 0–26%), with no breathing at all observed during 45 (43%) of the recordings. Between 26 and 30 weeks there was a marked increase in the percentage of breathing with a continuing upward trend until 36 weeks. The longest sustained intervals of fetal breathing showed a similar upward trend but peaked 2–4 weeks earlier. During normal preg-nancy fetal breathing is state dependent, being more common during active cycles. These features are illustrated in Fig. 7.9 (Pillai & James, 1990e).

Fetal hiccups showed a very different development course, being sig-nificantly more common prior to 24 weeks than subsequently ($p \leq .0001$), and this was solely due to a greater frequency of hiccup episodes prior to 24 weeks. Van Woerden et al. (1989) analyzed hiccups in a cross-sectional study of healthy fetuses at term and also found them to be present for less than 5% of the recording period.

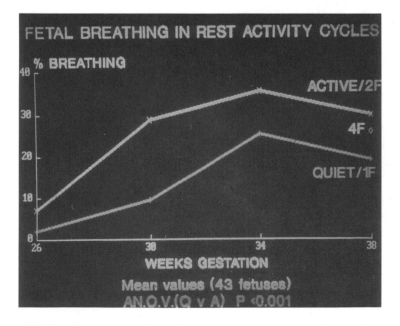

FIG. 7.9.   Development of breathing movements in the normal human fetus.

The onset of both hiccups and breathing has been described at 8–10 weeks gestation, respectively, corresponding to the time of development of the diaphragm (De Vries et al., 1982); however, their developmental trends thereafter are very different, with fetal hiccups being the predominant type of diaphragmatic movement up to 26 weeks gestation, and fetal breathing predominating thereafter. This suggests that the centers controlling fetal breathing are not only different but also are probably more complex than those that control hiccups. The early appearance of both types of activity suggests their ontogeny may only depend on relatively simple mechanisms; however, the subsequent developmental course of breathing and experimental destructive lesions in the fetal lamb show that development of higher centers has a profound influence on fetal breathing (Dawes, Gardner, Johnston, & Walker, 1983; Johnson, 1978).

Such data on the developmental trends and influence of higher centers on hiccups are lacking; however, the observation that they decline with advancing maturity suggests that if subsequent brain development does influence hiccups the effect may well be inhibitory. Evidence to support this is the finding that growth-retarded fetuses hiccup more often than normally growing fetuses (Bots, Broeders, Farman, Haverkorn, & Stolte, 1978), and also an increased incidence in fetuses of diabetic mothers and fetuses with congenital malformations (Wittman et al., 1983). Further anecdotal evidence is the observation of hiccups in compromised fetuses long after other types of normal behavior, including breathing, have ceased to be observed (unpublished data).

In conclusion, the periodic nature of fetal breathing makes it a poor candidate as a fetal neurodevelopmental milestone. However, hiccups warrant further investigation. As discussed already, it would appear that hiccups are a neurologically very immature or dysmature activity. For example, although at 14 weeks normal fetuses exhibit hiccups for over 10% of the time, this percentage is no more than 2% at 40 weeks. They are probably controlled and/or initiated at the level of the brainstem. It would seem a reasonable hypothesis that if fetal cortical activity were compromised, then one might expect the proportion of time a fetus exhibits hiccups to increase. This hypothesis needs to be tested prospectively.

Behavioral States

It is possible that the evidence of a fetus's exhibition of behavioral states itself may serve as a neurodevelopmental marker. For example, there are two cases reported where the fetus's failure to manifest behavioral states (i.e., an absence of the linkage of behavioral state variables of FHR somatic and eye movements) was associated with profound neurodevelopmental compromise (Pillai, Garrett, & James, 1991; Pillai & James, 1992).

In the first case this neurodevelopmental abnormality was observed in a

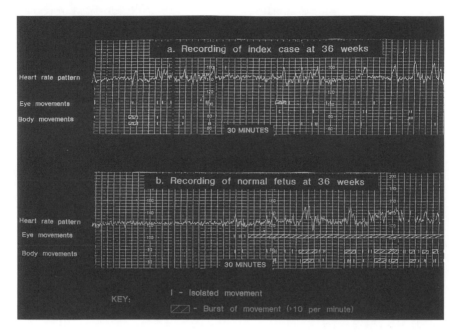

FIG. 7.10.   Fetal actograms from normal fetus and fetus with Smith-Lemli-Opitz syndrome type II. From Pillai, Garrett, and James (1991). Reprinted by permission.

fetus with the lethal Smith-Lemli-Opitz syndrome (Fig. 7.10). That fetus had characteristic abnormal anatomical features recognized on ultrasound and confirmed at birth. However, in the second case (Fig. 7.11) the newborn was passed as normal after birth and discharged home only to be readmitted on many occasions during infancy with poorly controlled seizures and recurrent upper airways obstruction. At the age of 18 months she had severe developmental delay, microcephaly, myoclonic epilepsy, and hearing impairment. The cause of this infant's disability was not identified.

Response to a Stimulus

All the potential fetal neurobehavioral developments discussed so far are based on observation. Testing that involves eliciting a response to a stimulus might be more useful. Benefits of direct testing might include a shorter period of time to sample behavior adequately. Furthermore, it represents a method that is used for neurodevelopmental evaluation in infancy and childhood.

The response to a stimulus can be evaluated as the presence/absence of a response, the latency/response time, or the time taken to habituate (cease to respond after repeated exposures to the stimulus).

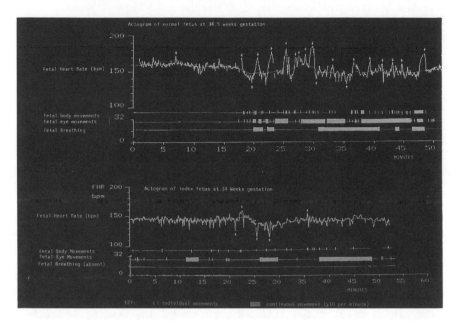

FIG. 7.11.   Fetal actograms from normal fetus and fetus that manifested neurodevelopmental compromise in infancy of unknown cause. From Pillai and James (1992). Reprinted by permission.

Habituation holds out the most hope as a potential neurodevelopmental milestone. Leader, Baillie, Martin, and Vermeulen (1982) demonstrated that fetuses with abnormal habituation patterns to a vibroacoustic stimulus before birth have significantly lower Griffiths Developmental Scores by 1 year of age (Leader et al., 1982). Hepper et al. demonstrated that fetuses with Down syndrome take longer to habituate to an auditory (single tone) stimulus (Hepper & Shahidullah, 1992). Furthermore, they suggested that different degrees (defined by the presence of cardiac defect) of Down syndrome (and, by implication, neurodevelopmental compromise) may be distinguished by different habituation patterns. These observations are discussed at greater length elsewhere in this volume.

In addition to the use of the response to a stimulus as a population screening method, this test could also be used in a selective way in women whose fetus may be at risk of, for example, congenital deafness.

WHAT ARE THE NEXT STEPS?

In summary, we believe the main assessment methods for possible human fetal neurodevelopmental evaluation are either observation of spontaneous behavior or response to a present stimulus. Observation lends itself to study of the duration of quiescence, the manifestation of linkage of fetal movements and FHR, and exhibition of behavioral states. Specific stimulus presentations are useful in studying the response to an auditory (or vibroacoustic) stimulus and analyzing the response, the latency of response, and the decrement of response with repeated stimulus (habituation).

However, all the results presented were obtained in a research setting and have not been immediately relevant or applicable to population screening. Before one can study fetal development as a population screening method there are two technological developments that are important. The first is a method of recording fetal variables (such as FHR and fetal movements) that is applicable as a screening method rather than as a research tool. The second is a computerized analysis of the fetal variables recorded in this way, made to make the analysis both faster and more objective.

Easier Recording of Variables

The methods currently used for study of both observed and stimulated fetal behavior are impractical for clinical use. For example, conventional behavioral state evaluation requires two ultrasound machines, an FHR machine, and a polygraphic recorder to integrate the signals (Pillai & James, 1990c) (Fig. 7.12). This method produces a comprehensive actogram (Fig. 7.13). However, the analysis of this actogram then has to be carried out retrospectively, which even with computer assistance is a time-consuming undertaking. Habituation research is also cumbersome and time-consuming.

In order to improve the ease of recording in a way that is more acceptable in clinical practice, one approach is to use Doppler ultrasound using a conventional FHR recording transducer. In its customary role as a recorder of the FHR signal, the transducer Doppler ultrasound signal identifies and records all movement in its path (fetal heart, breathing, limb and body movements, and maternal aorta and bowel activity). In its normal mode of operation as a FHR recorder this "raw" Doppler signal is filtered so that the FHR is selected out and displayed. It is possible to incorporate a separate broad-pass filter covering a frequency range below that for the FHR and to identify fetal movements. The resultant Doppler actogram (Fig. 7.14) only displays FHR and fetal movement (FM; James, Pillai, & Smoleniec, 1992), but these are arguably the most important variables that one would wish to study in both observed and stimulated fetal neurobehavioral research. This Doppler-generated actogram is currently being tested and its applicability for population study and screening is being characterized.

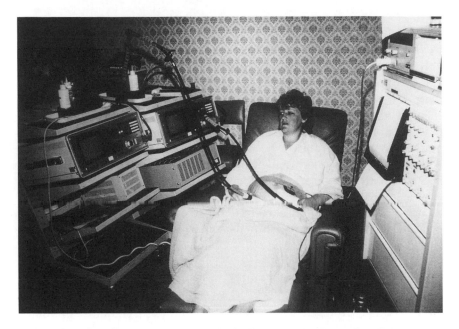

FIG. 7.12.   Set-up for recording the fetal actogram in a research setting.

Computerized Analysis of the Fetal Variables

Provided the evaluation of the Doppler generated actogram of FHR and FM is acceptable, then the filtered FHR and FM recordings can be analyzed using computer programs that extract both signals through an RS232 serial port. This computerized analysis of FHR and FM output could be adapted for both unstimulated/observed and stimulated studies.

We have undertaken and reported preliminary studies of this approach and are attempting to predict fetal behavioral state by computerized analysis of the FHR alone (Smoleniec, Parker, & James, 1990). In a study of 10 uncomplicated singleton pregnancies at full-term, we carried out simultaneous conventional fetal behavioral studies and FHR analysis using a commercially produced computer analysis program (System 8000; Davies, Visser, Goodman, & Redman, 1981). Each study was undertaken for 60 min. When the 600 min of observation were combined, the distribution of behavioral states was F1 43.5%, F2 55.8%, and F4 0.7%, as expected from previous work (Pillai & James, 1990a, 1990b). There was good correlation between the computer FHR analysis-identified "low FHR variation" and periods of F1 (r = .90) and the computer FHR analysis-identified "high FHR variation" and periods of F2/4 (r = .88). However, the prediction of behavioral state by FHR analysis (i.e., "low FHR variation" predicting F1 and "high FHR variation" predicting F2/4) was not good (see Table 7.6).

This work illustrates the principles of one approach to clinical applica-

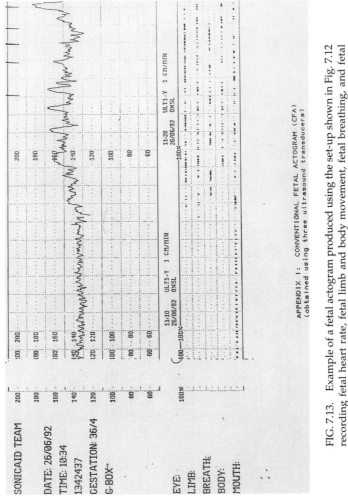

FIG. 7.13. Example of a fetal actogram produced using the set-up shown in Fig. 7.12 recording fetal heart rate, fetal limb and body movement, fetal breathing, and fetal mouthing.

121

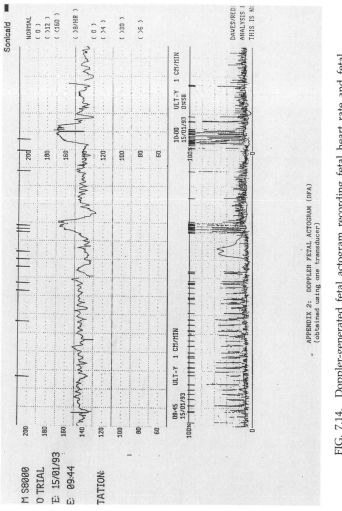

APPENDIX 2: DOPPLER FETAL ACTOGRAM (DFA)
(obtained using one transducer)

FIG. 7.14. Doppler-generated fetal actogram recording fetal heart rate and fetal movements.

TABLE 7.6
Prediction of Fetal Behavioral State Using Computerized FHR
Analysis (System 8000, Davies et al., 1981)

Positive Predictive Rates		
High FHR variation predicting	F2/4	84.1%
Low FHR variation predicting	F1	100%
Sensitivities		
High FHR variation predicting	F2/4	66.9%
Low FHR variation predicting	F1	40%
False Positive Prediction Rates		
High FHR variation during	F1	15.9%
Low FHR variation during	F2/4	0%
Accuracy (Combined Sensitivities)		55.6%

Note. From Smoleniec et al. (1990). Reprinted by permission.

tion of studies of fetal development. Yet it also highlights the limitations and pitfalls. Both by modifying the computer program of FHR analysis and by linking it with FM the aim is to improve the identification or prediction of fetal behavioral state.

CONCLUSIONS/SUMMARY

Screening for fetal neurodevelopmental compromise in practice is still in the future. The two immediate priorities are to develop more practical methods of recording FHR and FM and to generate more objective analysis of these recordings using computers.

Once these practical technical issues have been addressed, the three long-term goals are, in order, to make identifications from small population studies, both unstimulated and stimulated tests that will be most practical and feasible for use in population screening; to document the variation of these parameters in normal fetal development and the influence of nonpathological factors on them; and finally, to apply the best neurodevelopmental tests to a large population of fetuses who can be followed up to school age and beyond.

It will be this final stage that will start to address more closely the relationship between pathological prenatal influences on fetal neurobehavioral development and subsequent NDDI.

REFERENCES

Agustsson, P., & Patel, N. B. (1987). The predictive value of fetal breathing movements in the diagnosis of preterm labour. *British Journal of Obstetrics and Gynaecology, 94*, 860–863.

124   JAMES, PILLAI, SMOLENIEC

Ahlfeld, E. (1888). Uber bisher noch nicht beschriebene intrauterine Bewegungen des Kindes. [Concerning the hitherto undescribed intrauterine movement of the child]. *Verh. Dtsch. Ges. Gynakol., 2*, 203.

Anthony, J., Mascarenhas, L., O'Brien, J., Battacharge, A. K., & Gould, S. (1993). Lethal multiple pterygium syndrome. The importance of fetal posture in mid-trimester diagnosis by ultrasound: Discussion and case reports. *Ultrasound in Obstetrics and Gynaecology, 3*, 212–216.

Arduini, D., Rizzo, G., Parlati, E., Giorlandino, C., Volensise, H., Dell'acqua, S. & Romanini, C. (1986). Modifications of ultradian and circadian rhythms of fetal heart rate after fetal-maternal adrenal gland suppression: A double blind study. *Prenatal Diagnosis, 6*, 409–417.

Bekedam, B. J., & Visser, G. H. A. (1985). Effects of hypoxemic events on breathing, body movements, and heart rate variation: A study in growth-retarded human fetuses. *American Journal of Obstetrics and Gynecology, 153*, 52.

Birnholz, J. C., Stephens, J. C., & Faria, M. (1978). Fetal movement patterns: A possible means of defining neurologic development milestones in utero. *American Journal of Roentgenology, 130*, 537–540.

Blott, M., & Greenough, A. (1988). Oligohydramnios in the second trimester of pregnancy, fetal breathing and normal lung growth. *Early Human Development, 17*, 37–40.

Blott, M., Greenough, A., Nicolaides, K. H., Moscoso, G., Gibb, D., & Campbell, S. (1987). Fetal breathing movements as a predictor of favorable pregnancy outcome after oligohydramnios due to membrane rupture in second trimester. *Lancet, 2*, 129–131.

Bocking, A., Adamson, L., Cousin, A., Campbell, K., Carmichael, L., Natale, R., & Patrick, J. (1982). Effects of intravenous glucose injections on human fetal breathing movements at 38–40 weeks gestational age. *American Journal of Obstetrics and Gynecology, 142*, 606–611.

Boddy, K., & Dawes, G. S. (1975). Fetal breathing. *British Medical Bulletin, 31*, 1–7.

Bots, R. S. G. M., Broeders, G. H. B., Farman, D. J., Haverkorn, M. J., & Stolte, L. A. M. (1978). Fetal breathing movements in the normal and growth retarded fetus: A multiscan/M-mode echofetographic study. *European Journal of Obstetrics, Gynecology, and Reproductive Biology, 8*, 21–29.

Campbell, K. (1980). Ultradian rhythms in the human fetus during the last ten weeks of gestation. A review. *Seminars in Perinatology, 4*, 301–309.

Connors, G., Hunse, C., Carmichael, L., Natale, R., & Richardson, B. (1988). The role of carbon dioxide in the generation of human fetal breathing movements. *American Journal of Obstetrics and Gynecology, 158*, 322–327.

Davies, G. S., Visser, G. H. A., Goodman, J. O. S., & Redman, C. W. G. (1981). Numerical analysis of the human fetal heart rate: The quality of the ultrasound records. *American Journal of Obstetrics and Gynecology, 141*, 43–52.

Dawes, G. S. (1986). The central nervous control of fetal behavior. *European Journal of Obstetrics and Reproductive Biology, 21*, 341–346.

Dawes, G. S., Gardner, W. N., Johnston, B. M., & Walker, D. W. (1983). Breathing in fetal lambs: Effect of brain stem section. *Journal of Physiology, 335*, 535–553.

de Haan, J., van Bemmel, J. H., & Stolte, L. A. M. (1971). Quantitative evaluation of fetal heart rate patterns. II. The significance of the fixed heart rate during pregnancy and labour. *European Journal of Obstetrics, Gynecology, and Reproductive Biology, 3,* 103–110.

Devoe, L. D., Reudrich, D. A., & Searle, N. S. (1989). Value of observing fetal breathing activity in antenatal assessment of high-risk pregnancy. *American Journal of Obstetrics and Gynecology, 160,* 166–171.

De Vries, J. I. P., Visser, G. H. A., Mulder, E. J. H., & Prechtl, H. F. R. (1987). Diurnal and other variations in fetal movement and heart rate patterns at 20 to 22 weeks. *Early Human Development, 15,* 333–348.

De Vries, J. I. P., Visser, G. H. A., & Prechtl, H. F. R. (1982). The emergence of fetal behavior: I. Qualitative aspects. *Early Human Development, 7,* 301–322.

De Vries, J. I. P., Visser, G. H. A., & Prechtl, H. F. R. (1985). The emergence of fetal behavior: II. Quantitative aspects. *Early Human Development, 12,* 99–120.

De Vries, J. I. P., Visser, G. H. A., & Prechtl, H. F. R. (1988). The emergence of fetal behavior. III. Individual differences and consistencies. *Early Human Development, 16,* 85–104.

Dierker, L. J., Pillay, S. K., Sorokin, Y., & Rosen, M. G. (1982a). Active and quiet periods in the preterm and term fetus. *Obstetrics and Gynecology, 60,* 65–70.

Dierker, L. J., Pillay, S. K., Sorokin, Y., & Rosen, M. G. (1982b). The change in fetal activity periods in diabetic and nondiabetic pregnancies. *American Journal of Obstetrics and Gynecology, 143,* 181–185.

Emond, A., Golding, J., & Peckham, C. (1981). Cerebral palsy in two national cohort studies. *Archives of Disease of Childhood, 64,* 848–852.

Fox, H. E., Inglis, H., & Steinbrecher, M. (1979). Fetal breathing movements in uncomplicated pregnancies. I. Relationship to gestational age. *American Journal of Obstetrics and Gynecology, 134,* 544–546.

Freeman, J. M. (Ed.). (1985). *Prenatal and perinatal factors associated with brain disorders* (NIH publication No. 85-1149). National Institute of Child Health and Human Development, Baltimore, NIH.

Harper, M. A., Meis, P. J., Rose, J. C., & Swain, M. (1987). Human fetal breathing response to intravenous glucose is directly related to gestational age. *American Journal of Obstetrics and Gynecology, 157,* 1403–1405.

Hepper, P., & Shahidullah, S. (1992). Abnormal fetal behaviour in Down's syndrome fetuses. *Quarterly Journal of Clinical Psychology, 44,* 305–137.

Iannoruberto, A., & Tajani, E. (1981). Ultrasonographic study of fetal movements. *Seminars in Perinatology, 5,* 175–181.

James, D., Pillai, M., & Smoleniec, J. (1992, June). Fetal neurodevelopmental milestones—How near in practice? *Proceedings of the 26th British Congress of Obstetrics and Gynecology* (p. 100). Manchester, UK.

Johnson, P. (1978). In lambs fetal breathing in slow wave sleep becomes inhibited. In C. von Euler & H. Lagercrantz (Eds.), *Central nervous control mechanisms in breathing* (pp. 337–351). Oxford: Pergamon Press.

Lamb, B., & Lang, R. (1992). Aetiology of cerebral palsy. *British Journal of Obstetrics and Gynecology, 99,* 176–178.

Leader, L. R., Baillie, P., Martin, B., & Vermeulen, E. (1982). The assessment and significance of habituation to a repeated stimulus by the human fetus. *Early Human Development, 7,* 211–219.

Lewis, P. J., Trudinger, B. J., & Mangez, J. (1978). Effect on maternal glucose ingestion on fetal breathing and body movement in late pregnancy. *British Journal of Obstetrics and Gynecology, 85,* 86–89.

Manning, F. A., & Platt, L. D. (1979). Human fetal breathing movements and maternal hypoxemia. *Obstetrics and Gynecology, 53,* 758.

Marsal, K. (1983). Ultrasonic assessment of fetal activity. *Clinical Obstetrics and Gynecology, 10,* 541–563.

Martin, C. B., Jr., (1981). Behavioural states in human fetus. *Journal of Reproductive Medicine, 26,* 425–432.

Mills, J. N. (1975). Development of circadian rhythms in infancy. *Chronobiologica, 2,* 363–371.

Nasello-Paterson, C., Natale, R., & Connors, G. (1988). Ultrasonic evaluation of fetal body movements over twenty-four hours in the human fetus at twenty-four to twenty-eight weeks gestation. *American Journal of Obstetrics and Gynecology, 158,* 312–316.

Natale, R., Patrick, J., & Richardson, B. (1978). Effects of human maternal venous plasma glucose concentrations on fetal breathing movements. *American Journal of Obstetrics and Gynecology, 132,* 36–41.

Nijhuis, J. G., Kruyt, N., & Van Wijck, J. A. M. (1987). Fetal brain death: Two case reports. *British Journal of Obstetrics and Gynaecology, 95,* 197–200.

Nijhuis, J. G., Martin, C. B., Jr., & Prechtl, H. F. R. (1984). Behavioural states of the human fetus. In H. F. R. Prechtl (Ed.), *Continuity of neural functions from prenatal to postnatal life. Clinics in developmental medicine* (Vol. 94, pp. 65–79). Oxford: Blackwell.

Nijhuis, J., Prechtl, H. F. R., Martin, C. B., & Bots, R. S. G. M. (1982). Are there behavioural states in the human fetus? *Early Human Development, 6,* 177–195.

Patrick, J., Campbell, K., Carmichael, L., Natale, R., & Richardson, B. (1980). A definition of human fetal apnea and the distribution of fetal apneic intervals during the last ten weeks of pregnancy. *American Journal of Obstetrics and Gynecology, 136,* 471–477.

Patrick, J., Campbell, K., Carmichael, L., Natale, R., & Richardson, B. (1982). Patterns of gross fetal body movements over 24 hours observation interval in the last 10 weeks of pregnancy. *American Journal of Obstetrics and Gynecology, 136,* 471–477.

Patrick, J., Natale, R., & Richardson, B. (1978). Patterns of human fetal breathing activity at 34 to 35 weeks gestational age. *American Journal of Obstetrics and Gynecology, 132,* 507–513.

Pedersen, J. F., & Molsted-Pedersen, L. (1981). Early fetal growth delay detected by ultrasound marks increased risk of congenital malformation in diabetic pregnancy. *British Medical Journal, 283,* 269–271.

Pedersen, J. F., Molsted-Pedersen, L., & Mortensen, H. B. (1984). Fetal growth delay and maternal hemoglobin Alc in early diabetic pregnancy. *Obstetrics and Gynaecology, 64,* 351–352.

Pillai, M. (1992). *Development of behavioural states in the human fetus.* Unpublished doctoral dissertation, University of Bristol, UK.

Pillai, M., & James, D. K. (1990a). Behavioral states in normal mature human fetuses. *Archives of Disease of Childhood, 65,* 39–43.

Pillai, M., Garrett, C., & James, D. (1991). Bizarre fetal behaviour associated with lethal congenital abnormalities: A case report. *European Journal of Obstetrics, Gynecology, and Reproductive Biology, 39,* 215–218.

Pillai, M., & James, D. (1990b). Are the behavioural states of the newborn comparable to those of the fetus? *Early Human Development, 22,* 39–39.

Pillai, M., & James, D. (1990c). Development of human fetal behaviour, A review. *Fetal Diagnosis of Therapy, 5,* 15–32.

Pillai, M., & James, D. (1990d). The importance of the behavioural state in biophysical assessment of the term human fetus. *British Journal of Obstetrics and Gynecology, 97,* 1130–1134.

Pillai, M., & James, D. K. (1990e). Hiccups and breathing in the human fetus. *Archives of Disease of Childhood, 65,* 1072–1075.

Pillai, M., & James, D. K. (1990f). The development of fetal heart rate patterns during normal pregnancy. *Obstetrics and Gynecology, 76,* 812–816.

Pillai, M., & James, D. K. (1990g). Sinusoidal fetal heart rate associated with fetal mouthing. *European Journal of Obstetrics, Gynecology, and Reproductive Biology, 38,* 151–156.

Pillai, M., & James, D. (1992). Absence of fetal breathing and abnormal fetal behaviour in prolonged preterm ruptured membranes; case report. *Ultrasound in Obstetrics and Gynecology, 2,* 44–47.

Platt, L. D., Manning F. A., Lemay, M., & Sipos, L. (1978). Human fetal breathing: Relationship to fetal condition. *American Journal of Obstetrics and Gynecology, 132,* 514–518.

Prechtl, H. F. R. (1974). The behavioural states of the newborn infant (A review). *Brain Research, 76,* 185–212.

Ritchie, J. W. K., & Lakhani, K. (1980). Fetal breathing movements in response to maternal inhalation of 5% carbon dioxide. *American Journal of Obstetrics and Gynecology, 136,* 386–388.

Roberts, A. B., Little, D., Cooper, D., & Campbell, S. (1979). Normal patterns of fetal activity in the third trimester. *British Journal of Obstetrics and Gynecology, 86,* 4–9.

Rosenn, B., Ben Chetrit, A., Palti, Z., & Hurwitz, A. (1990). Sinusoidal fetal heart rate pattern due to massive feto-maternal transfusion. *International Journal of Gynecology & Obstetrics, 31,* 271–273.

Shonoff, J. P., & Hauser-Grau, P. (1987). Early intervention for disabled children and their families. *Paediatrics, 80,* 650–658.

Smoleniec, J., Parker, M., & James, D. (1990, September). Computer evaluation of the fetal heart rate pattern at term predicts behavioural state. In: *Proceedings of the First International Scientific Meeting of the Royal College of Obstetricians and Gynecologists* (p. 99) London: RCQG.

Van Dongen, L. G. R., & Goudie, E. G. (1980). Fetal movement patterns in the first trimester of pregnancy. *British Journal of Obstetrics and Gynecology, 87,* 191–193.

van Vliet, M. A. T., Martin, C. B., Jr., Nijhuis, J. G., & Prechtl, H. F. R. (1985). The relationship between fetal activity and behavioural states and fetal breathing movements in normal and growth-retarded fetuses. *American Journal of Obstetrics and Gynecology, 153,* 582–588.

van Woerden, E. E., van Geijn, H. P., Caron, F. J. M., Mantel, R., Swartjes, J. M., & Arts, N. F. T. (1989). Fetal hiccups; Characteristics and relation to fetal heart rate. *European Journal of Obstetrics, Gynecology, and Reproductive Biology, 30,* 209–216.

Visser, G. H. A., Bekedam, D. J., Mulder, E. J. H., & van Ballegooie, E. (1985). Delayed emergence of fetal behavior in type-1 diabetic women. *Early Human Development, 12*, 167–172.

Visser, G. H. A., Laurinin, R. N., De Vries, J. I. P., Bekedam, D. J., & Prechtl, J. F. R. (1985). Abnormal motor behavior in anencephalic fetuses. *Early Human Development, 12*, 173–182.

Visser, G. H. A., Mulder, E. J. H., Bekedam, D. J., van Ballegooie, E., & Prechtl, H. F. (1986). Fetal behavior in type-1 diabetic women. *European Journal of Obstetrics, Gynecology, and Reproductive Biology, 21*, 315–320.

Wittman, B. K., Brown, S., Davison, B., Rurak, D. W., & Gruber, N. (1983, June). Observation on hiccoughs in normal and abnormal pregnancy. *Abstracts Xth Conference on Fetal Breathing and Other Fetal Movements*, Malmo.

8

Developmental Aspects of Alterations in Fetal Behavioral States

Robert Gagnon
St. Joseph's Health Centre, London, Ontario, Canada

Initially described in the chronically instrumented fetal lamb (Dawes, Fox, Leduc, & Richards, 1972), the organization of different fetal biophysical variables such as electrocortical activity, fetal breathing activity, and fetal eye movements into well-defined patterns corresponding to different fetal behavioral states has provided the physiological basis for assessing fetal health (Patrick, 1989). More recently, it has been observed that transabdominal vibroacoustic stimulation (VAS) can reproducibly alter fetal behavioral activity (Gagnon, Hunse, Carmichael, Fellows, & Patrick, 1987a, 1987b). As a result, fetal behavioral responses to VAS have been suggested as a new and effective tool to discriminate between the healthy and compromised fetus (Smith, Phelan, Platt, Broussard, & Paul, 1986). Unfortunately, the introduction of VAS in clinical practice has rapidly disseminated prior to the establishment of adequate knowledge of its underlying physiological mechanism and its effectiveness as a clinical tool. Therefore, this review concentrates on the developmental aspects of fetal behavioral responsiveness to sound and vibration under normal and pathological conditions. The clinical significance of the fetal behavioral responses to a changing maternal environment is also described.

BIOLOGICAL SIGNIFICANCE OF FETAL
BEHAVIORAL STATES

Fetal Cerebral Metabolism

Fetal cerebral metabolism has been extensively studied in the fetal sheep. Cerebral oxidative metabolism is increased approximately 20% during the low-voltage electrocortical state (equivalent to rapid eye movement [REM] sleep state) when compared to non-rapid eye movement [NREM] sleep (Richardson, Patrick, & Abduljabbar, 1985). A similar synchronous increase in cerebral metabolic rate during REM sleep has been described using the 2-deoxyglucose technique (Abrams, Hutchison, Jay, Sokoloff, & Kennedy, 1988). In addition, the incidence of REM sleep state decreases with advancing biological age (Roffward, Muzio, & Demerk, 1966). This close relationship between cerebral metabolic activity and fetal behavioral states suggests a major role of the presence of REM sleep state in the brain's growth and development (Drucker-Colin, 1979).

Consistent with the tight blood flow and metabolism coupling present in the brain tissue, there is an increase in cerebral blood flow during REM sleep state compared to NREM sleep state (Rankin, Landauer, Tian, & Phernetton, 1987; Richardson et al., 1985). In the human fetus, using Doppler flow velocity waveforms measured in the cerebral vessels as an indirect index of downstream vascular resistance, there is evidence of a decrease in cerebral vascular resistance during fetal behavioral state 2F (similar to REM sleep; see chapter 5 by Nijhuis, this volume) compared to behavioral state 1F (NREM sleep), indicating that the increase in cerebral blood flow during REM sleep is largely the result of a decrease in cerebral vascular resistance (van Eyck, Wladimiroff, van den Wyngaard, Noordam, & Prechtl, 1987). It remains to be determined whether or not changes in the maternal environment that alter fetal behavioral states could eventually have a significant impact on subsequent brain growth and development.

Fetal Heart Rate Patterns in Normal and Growth-Restricted Fetuses

Since antepartum fetal heart rate (FHR) testing was introduced into clinical practice in the late 1970s, only the recent introduction of computerized FHR analysis has allowed the feasible characterization of FHR patterns throughout gestation (Dawes, Redman, & Smith, 1985; Gagnon, Campbell, Hunse, & Patrick, 1987c). With advancing gestational age, there is a decrease in baseline FHR, an increase in the mean amplitude of FHR accelerations, an increase in FHR variability, and the establishment of an inverse relationship between baseline FHR and the amplitude of FHR accelerations (Gagnon, Campbell, Hunse, & Patrick, 1987c). The distribution of

FHR accelerations' amplitude is characterized by a higher proportion of small-amplitude FHR accelerations (<10 beats/min) prior to 30 weeks. After 30 weeks, large-amplitude FHR accelerations (>10 beats/min) become predominant (Gagnon, Campbell, Hunse, & Patrick, 1987c). These developmental changes in FHR patterns occur during a narrow period between 28 and 30 weeks gestation and are reflecting the autonomic maturation of the control of the fetal heart. After 36 weeks, FHR patterns are well defined and alternate between episodes of low and high FHR variation characteristic of state 1F and state 2F, respectively, interrupted by brief episodes of large FHR accelerations often fused into sustained tachycardia (state 4F or analogous to the state of wakefulness described in the newborn; Prechtl, 1974). More than 90% of FHR accelerations are associated with fetal movements (Patrick, Carmichael, Chess, & Staples, 1984; Timor-Tritsch, Dierkar, Zador, Hertz, & Rosen, 1978) and occur during episodes of high FHR variation and rapid eye movements (see Nijhuis, chapter 5, this volume), reflecting the organization of different biophysical variables into well-defined behavioral states.

In fetuses with intrauterine growth restriction (IUGR), FHR patterns are markedly altered after 30 weeks. Although the baseline FHR is unaffected, FHR variability is decreased by 25% (Gagnon, Hunse, Fellows, & Patrick, 1988; Gagnon, Hunse, Carmichael, & Patrick, 1989), the number of FHR accelerations is decreased by 40 to 50%, and FHR accelerations are characterized by a high proportion of low-amplitude accelerations (Gagnon, Hunse, & Bocking, 1989) similar to those seen in healthy human fetuses prior to 28 weeks. The relationship between baseline FHR and the mean amplitude of FHR accelerations is also lost (Gagnon, Hunse, & Bocking, 1989), indicating that the autonomic control of the fetal heart is significantly altered in IUGR fetuses. There is also evidence that fetal behavioral state organization is significantly delayed as indicated by a larger amount of periods of no coincidence at term when compared with low-risk fetuses (van Vliet, Martin, Nijhuis, & Prechtl, 1985). These observations along with the differences observed in the detailed analysis of FHR patterns in IUGR fetuses suggest abnormalities in the functional development of the central nervous system early during gestation in the fetus exposed to chronic nutritional deprivation compared to the healthy fetus.

Fetal Responsiveness to External Vibroacoustic Stimulation

Sound Intensity During Vibroacoustic Stimulation

In contrast to the neonate, the human fetus is surrounded by the amniotic cavity and fluid. Until recently, it was not technically feasible and safe to measure the fetal sound environment during the application of vibroacoustic stimulation (VAS) on the surface of the maternal abdomen. Benzaquen, Gagnon, Hunse, and Foreman (1990), using a miniaturized hydrophone inserted under ultrasound guidance, recorded the background fetal sound environment in 10 pregnant women in active labor. The intrauterine sound consisted predominantly of low-frequency (<100 Hz) noise with maximum intensity of 85 dB at 12.5 Hz, which is below the audible range of frequency, but similar to the resonance frequency of the human body (Wasserman, 1990). This quiet background noise was interrupted only by maternal voice and bowel sounds. Maternal cardiovascular sounds were usually not a major feature of the intrauterine background noise (Benzaquen et al., 1990).

Although a wide variety of intensity and frequency of acoustic and vibroacoustic stimuli has been suggested to increase FHR reactivity (Davey, Dommisse, Macnab, & Dacre, 1984; Grimwade, Walker, Bartlett, Gordon, & Wood, 1971; Jensen, 1984; Luz, Lima, Luz, & Feldons, 1980; Querleu, Boutteville, & Renard, 1984; Read & Miller, 1977), only vibroacoustic stimulation (VAS) can reproducibly alter FHR patterns (Gagnon et al., 1987a; Gagnon, Hunse, Carmichael, Fellows, & Patrick, 1988; Smith, Nguyen, Phelan, & Richard, 1986; Smith, Phelan, Platt, Broussard, & Paul, 1986). Although other devices such as an electric toothbrush (Davey et al., 1984; Leader et al., 1982) have been used as a vibroacoustic stimulus, the most widely used stimulus in North America as a complement to antepartum FHR testing is an electronic artificial larynx (EAL). The device produces a broadband noise at a fundamental frequency of 87 Hz with multiple harmonics up to 20,000 Hz (Gagnon, Patrick, Foreman, & West, 1986; Gagnon, 1989). The surface of the instrument also vibrates at all frequencies between 10 Hz and 15,000 Hz (Gagnon, Foreman, Hunse, & Patrick, 1989). Estimations of intrauterine sound pressure levels during VAS have varied from 95 dB (Birnholz & Benacerraf, 1983), to 139 dB (Gerhardt, Abrams, & Kovaz, 1988). We measured an average intrauterine sound pressure level (SPL) reached during VAS applied during active labor of 95 dB, which can be as high as 125 dB (Gagnon, Benzaquen, & Hunse, 1992). It is therefore not clinically relevant that SPL measured in air at 1 meter from the surface of the EAL is approximately 82 dB (Smith, Nguyen, Phelan, & Richard, 1986). There is still no case report of cochlear damage in human fetuses exposed in utero to VAS.

Figure 8.1 illustrates the effect of decreasing the distance between the EAL and the surface of the maternal abdomen on intrauterine sound pressure levels reached during stimulation with the EAL as measured in nine pregnant women in active labor (Gagnon et al., 1992). Intrauterine sound pressure levels remained little altered when the EAL was moved from 10 cm to 5 cm (10–5 cm) and 1 cm (10–1 cm) from the surface of the

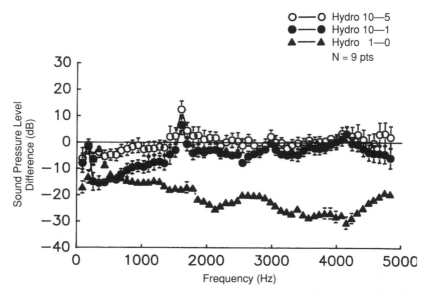

FIG. 8.1.   Mean (± SEM) intrauterine sound pressure level differences (dB at 20 μPa) during vibratory acoustic stimulation were plotted for frequencies between 87 and 5000 Hz. Hydro 10-5 (open circles), hydro 10-1 (closed circles), and hydro 1-0 (closed triangles) indicated the differences in sound pressure levels between the electronic artificial larynx held at 10 and 5 cm, 10 and 1 cm, and 1 and 0 cm from the surface of the maternal abdominal wall.

maternal abdomen. However, when touching the surface of the maternal abdomen (1–0 cm) the coupling between the vibrating surface of the device and maternal soft tissues greatly enhanced (up to 30 dB) the transmission of high-frequency sounds (>1000 Hz) across the maternal abdominal wall (Fig. 8.1). Because of this enhancement in sound transmission when touching the surface of the maternal abdomen, intrauterine sound pressure levels reached during VAS as currently used in clinical practice should be expected to be at least 30 dB higher than measured in air.

Fetal Heart Rate and Fetal Movement Responses

It is well recognized by clinicians that the presence of fetal heart rate (FHR) accelerations with fetal body movements and episodes of high FHR variability (state 2F) is a reliable indicator of fetal health (Brown & Patrick, 1981). However, due to the inherent pattern of alternation between episodes of rest and activity, several types of external stimulation have been suggested to increase FHR variability and fetal body movements. Fetal behavioral activity remains unchanged during stimulation using an external source of light (Polishuk, Laufer, & Sadovsky, 1975), external manipulation of the fetus (Druzin, Gratacos, & Paul, 1985; Richardson, Campbell, Carmichael, & Patrick, 1981), and maternal ingestion of glucose (Bocking et al., 1982). In contrast, significant alterations in fetal behavior have been reported following external auditory and vibratory external stimulation (Gagnon et al., 1987b). Fetal heart rate response to vibroacoustic stimulation, being relatively easy to measure accurately, has been the most widely studied.

The characteristics of the first FHR acceleration following VAS have been previously described in detail (Gagnon, Hunse, & Patrick, 1988) and are similar to spontaneous FHR accelerations (see earlier discussion). There is a developmental maturation in the immediate FHR response to VAS that appears between 28 and 30 weeks gestation, and that consists of an increase in the amplitude of the first acceleration following stimulus and the appearance of an inverse relationship between the prestimulus baseline FHR and the amplitude of the first acceleration (Gagnon, Campbell, Hunse, & Patrick, 1987). These developmental changes in the FHR response to VAS occurring between 28 and 30 weeks indicate that the immediate FHR response to VAS is the result of direct stimulation of the autonomic nervous system, which is functionally mature by 30 weeks gestation (Gagnon, Campbell, Hunse, & Patrick, 1987). Recent observations using cordocentesis to measure fetal plasma catecholamine concentrations indicated that there is no change in circulating catecholamines during VAS (Fisk et al., 1991). These observations and the rapidity of FHR response to VAS (≤ 10 sec) (Gagnon et al., 1986) support the concept of a direct fetal central nervous system stimulation rather than an FHR response mediated through catecholamine release by the adrenal medulla.

Following the immediate FHR response, there is a delayed FHR response that is gestational-age dependent, being present only after 33 weeks gestation (Gagnon et al., 1987a, 1987b). This delayed FHR response to VAS consists of an increase in the number of FHR accelerations between 10 and 20 min following a 5-sec stimulus. In approximately 15% of term fetuses, there is a profound fetal tachycardia lasting up to 90 min following a 5-sec stimulus (Gagnon et al., 1987a, 1987b; Visser, Mulder, Wit, Mulder, & Prechtl, 1989), which does not correspond to any typical FHR pattern observed under resting conditions. These observations of profound changes in FHR patterns following a relatively short stimulus of only a few seconds have led to questioning the validity and safety of introducing VAS into clinical practice (Gagnon, 1989; Visser et al., 1989).

In addition to the changes in FHR, fetal body and breathing patterns are significantly altered during VAS after 33 weeks. There is a delayed increase in the number and incidence of gross fetal body movements between 10 and 20 min following VAS that could persist up to 1 hr in some fetuses. Term fetuses (36–40 weeks) are breathing less and more irregularly following stimulus (Gagnon et al., 1987b; Gagnon, Hunse, & Foreman, 1989). Fetal breathing movements are not altered in fetuses of 26 - 35 weeks gestational age. These complex changes in fetal biophysical variables following VAS are all indicative of alterations in fetal behavioral states.

Fetal Behavioral States and Acoustic Stimulation

Concerns regarding possible adverse effects of loud noise on human fetal brain development have led investigators (Gagnon, Foreman, Hunse, & Patrick, 1989; Visser et al., 1989) to study the effects of low-frequency vibration (100 Hz, square wave) as a stimulus applied on the surface of the maternal abdomen in late gestation during state 1F (Gagnon, Foreman, Hunse, & Patrick, 1989; Gagnon, Hunse, & Foreman, 1989). The transition time from the stimulus to the onset of state 2F was 3 min in stimulated fetuses compared to 23 min following a sham stimulus (Gagnon, Hunse, & Foreman, 1989; Parkes, Morre, Moore, Fish, & Hanson, 1991). These changes in fetal behavioral states persisted for 20 min and were associated with a sustained increase in long-term FHR variability, the number of FHR accelerations, and fetal body movements (Gagnon, Foreman, Hunse, & Patrick, 1989; Gagnon, Hunse, & Foreman, 1989).

   Visser et al. (1989) reported on a small number of healthy pregnant women at term; following stimulation with the EAL, there was either a switch from fetal state 1F to 2F or 4F. On one occasion, the healthy term fetus had a switch from state 1F to an indeterminate state characterized by a sustained fetal tachycardia that lasted 1.5 hr, suggesting disorganization of fetal behavioral states following VAS. It is important to note that under normal conditions, the human fetus experiences spontaneous transitions from state 1F to state 2F, and then to state 4F (see Nijhuis, chapter 5, this volume). This is in contrast to the direct transition from state 1F to state 4F that can occur following stimulation with the EAL (Gagnon et al., 1987a, 1987b), which appears to be nonphysiological in nature. Due to the close relationship between cerebral metabolic rate and behavioral states, it is reasonable to believe that these changes in behavioral states of the human fetus would be accompanied by alterations in fetal cerebral glucose and perhaps oxidative metabolism. However, the latter remains to be confirmed in controlled animal experiments.

   Although profound changes in FHR and fetal body and breathing movements of long duration may occur following VAS, Devoe, Murray, Faircloth and Ramos (1990), using a 2-sec VAS, observed prolonged disruption of fetal behavioral states in only 10-15% of fetuses studied. Spencer, Deans, Nicolaides, and Arulkumaran (1991), in contrast to others, did not observe prolonged changes in fetal behavioral activity following VAS, suggesting that the intensity, and duration of the fetal responses to VAS are probably related to the type, intensity, and duration of the stimulus used and to the degree of perception of the stimulus by the fetus. Other unusual changes in fetal behavioral activity in healthy term fetuses have been reported following VAS, including evoked fetal micturition (Zimmer, Chao, Guy, Marks, & Fifer, 1993), fetal panting (Sherer, Abramowicz, D'Amico, Allen, & Woods, 1991), increased fetal swallowing (Petrikovsky, Schifrin, & Diana, 1993), and fetal bradycardia presumably as a result of umbilical cord compression (Sherer, Menashe, & Sadovsky, 1988). In regards to fetal habituation response to VAS, see chapter 21 by Leader and chapter 14 by Kisilevsky, this volume.

Intrauterine Growth Restriction and Acoustic Stimulation

Using the rationale that fetuses with severe intrauterine growth restriction (birthweight less than third percentile) might have altered FHR response to VAS, FHR and movement responses have been described in IUGR fetuses between 28 and 40 weeks gestation (Gagnon, Hunse, Carmichael, & Patrick, 1989; Gagnon, Hunse, Fellows, & Patrick, 1988).

Two distinct groups were identified; the first consisted of fetuses with early-onset IUGR (< 32 weeks) that delivered at a mean gestational age of 32.8 weeks (Gagnon, Hunse, Carmichael, & Patrick, 1989). Before stimulation, the fetuses exhibited diminished FHR variability, FHR accelerations, and fetal movements. In contrast to the increase in FHR observed in normally grown fetuses, there was no significant effect of VAS on either FHR or fetal movement patterns. In addition, all but one fetus had a normal umbilical artery pH at birth. These observations indicated that the absence of a FHR response to VAS in fetuses with early-onset IUGR does not reflect a deteriorating fetal metabolic status but most likely an abnormal function of sensory pathways.

The second group consisted of 17 IUGR fetuses detected after 32 weeks (late onset) (Gagnon, Hunse, Fellows, & Patrick, 1988). Although these fetuses had a slightly lower umbilical artery pO_2 (3 mm Hg less) than normally grown fetuses, there was no difference in pH. Prior to VAS, the IUGR fetuses demonstrated a 40% decrease in the incidence of gross fetal body movements, and a 25% decrease in long-term FHR variability compared to normally grown fetuses. Following VAS, FHR response in IUGR fetuses was similar to normally grown fetuses, but was of shorter duration and amplitude (Gagnon, Hunse, Fellows, & Patrick, 1988). The increase in the incidence of gross fetal body movements following stimulus was similar in IUGR and normally grown fetuses. These data suggested that fetal responses to VAS, although significantly different between IUGR and normally grown fetuses, could not be used to differentiate late-onset IUGR from normally grown fetuses because of large overlap. For more discussion of fetal habituation patterns to VAS in IUGR fetuses and their poten-

TABLE 8.1
Summary of Factors Influencing Fetal Heart Rate Acceleration
Response to Vibroacoustic Stimulation.

Factors	Effect on FHR Response
Early gestational age	Decrease amplitude
	Decrease duration
	Decrease number
< 30 weeks	No response 35% of the time
Intrauterine growth restriction	
Early onset (<32 weeks)	Usually no FHR response
Late onset (>32 weeks)	Decrease amplitude
	Decrease duration
Prestimulus baseline	Inversely related to amplitude
Prestimulous behavioral state	More consistent responses in state 1F
Labor	Decrease with advancing labor
Rupture of membranes	Decrease amplitude
Intensity of external sound stimulus	Positively related
Intrauterine sound pressure level reached	Positively related
Duration of stimulus	Positively related
Position of stimulus	No effect
Meperidine	Decrease amplitude

tial role in predicting IUGR (Leader et al., 1984), see chapter 21 by Leader, this volume. There is no longitudinal study yet to assess the onset of FHR and fetal movement response to VAS in growth-restricted fetuses.

A variety of biological factors beside deteriorating fetal metabolic status may influence the antenatal fetal heart rate responsitivity to vibroacoustic stimulation as indicated in Table 8.1. Therefore if VAS is to be used in conjunction with antepartum fetal heart rate testing, these limitations should be taken into account when interpreting test results.

Animal Studies of Fetal Auditory Responsitivity

Newborns exposed to sound stimuli have auditory evoked brainstem potentials (AEBPs), which are neuroelectric signals recorded from electroencephalograph (EEG) electrodes placed on the scalp (Allen & Capute, 1986). The AEBPs are considered to be of value in the assessment of newborn neurological and hearing functions. It has been shown that wave I originates from the auditory nerve, wave II from the cochlear nuclei, wave III from the superior olivary nucleus, wave IV from the lateral lemniscus, and wave V from the inferior colliculus. A fetal AEBP has been well characterized in the fetal lamb by Woods, Plessinger, and Mack, (1984). The fetal AEBP first appears at 117 - 125 days (term = 147 days) and by day 126 is comparable to the 1-day-old newborn lamb. In addition, latencies to each wave decrease with advancing gestational age (Plessinger

& Woods, 1987). The configurations of the AEBPs are similar with both extrauterine and intrauterine stimulation (Plessinger & Woods, 1986). However, the AEBP generated by an extrauterine acoustic stimulation is delayed in latency when compared to intrauterine acoustic stimulation (Woods & Plessinger, 1989), presumably as a result of the differences in distance from the fetal ear between extrauterine and intrauterine stimulation. In addition, there is evidence that an acoustic stimulation of at least 100 dB is necessary to obtain a reliable fetal AEBP (Plessinger & Woods, 1986), which is similar to the previously suggested threshold of 94 dB intrauterine sound pressure level necessary to obtain a reliable FHR response to VAS (Gagnon et al., 1992). Although AEBPs may provide a model for assessing development of the auditory system in utero (Woods et al., 1984), there is no evidence that AEBPs are altered during acute fetal hypoxia. It is not known whether AEBPs will be altered following recovery of an intrauterine asphyxial insult resulting in permanent brain damage.

In both the fetal lamb (Abrams, Hutchison, Gerhardt, Evans, & Pendergast, 1987) and the guinea pig fetus (Horner, Seriere, & Granier-Deferre, 1987), an increase in cerebral metabolic activity has been demonstrated following exposure to intense sound stimulation. By using a function generator providing a square-wave output and a mechanical oscillator similar to the one previously described by Gagnon et al. (Gagnon, Foreman, Hunse, & Patrick, 1989; Gagnon, Hunse, & Foreman, 1989) in humans, Parkes et al. (1991) developed a fetal sheep model that was effective in reducing the high-voltage fetal electrocorticogram (ECoG) characteristic of NREM sleep to a low-voltage electrocortical state analogous to REM sleep. However, the low-voltage ECoG remained usually unaltered after VAS, suggesting a state dependency of the fetal responses to sound and vibration. Interestingly, no consistent change in fetal heart rate was observed and the fetal electrocortical response to VAS was abolished by cochlear ablation. These observations in the fetal lamb indicated that a good functioning auditory pathway is essential to obtain fetal response to VAS.

FETAL BEHAVIORAL ACTIVITY AND HYPOXIA

An underlying assumption in the measurement of fetal behavioral state variables such as fetal breathing activity, fetal body movements, fetal heart rate patterns, and more recently FHR variability (Dawes et al., 1992) is that they may reflect the integrity of fetal cortical function. In the human fetus, clustering of these variables into fetal behavioral states similar to those described in the full-term neonate (Prechtl, 1974) has been shown to develop after 36 weeks gestation (see Nijhuis, chapter 5, this volume). Using the chronically instrumented fetal sheep, it has been demonstrated that fetal breathing movements (Boddy, Dawes, Fisher, Pinter, & Robinson, 1974) and fetal forelimb activity (Natale, Clewlow, & Dawes, 1981) are abolished during acute hypoxia. These observations have lead to the assumption that fetal cortical function might be an important marker of fetal hypoxia and therefore useful in the assessment of fetal health and neurological function. It is not clear yet if this assumption is valid.

For instance, despite the development of new methods of assessment of fetal health, the prevalence of cerebral palsy has remained relatively unchanged for the past 50 years at 2-3 per thousand live births (Jarvis & Hay, 1984; Nelson & Ellenberg, 1986). Recent data have demonstrated that certain hypoxic conditions that result in diminished breathing and rapid eye movement activity in the fetal lamb have different time courses of effect on these measurements. Bocking, Gagnon, Milne, and White (1988) induced fetal hypoxemia in sheep by reducing uteroplacental blood flow over a period of 24 hrs. Under these experimental conditions, fetal rapid eye movement returned to control levels hours before the return of fetal breathing movements, despite continuing fetal hypoxemia. Electrocortical activity was not altered throughout the time fetal hypoxemia was maintained. More recently, in the fetal sheep, there has been suggestion that following recovery of an episode of severe and prolonged intrauterine hypoxia with progressive metabolic acidosis, fetal behavioral activity returned to normal level despite evidence of grey- and white-matter necrosis on neuropathology (Matsuda, Carmichael, Patrick, & Richardson, 1992; Penning, Grafe, Matsuda, Hammond, & Richardson, 1992). Therefore, under normal conditions, the clustering of variables such as rapid eye movements, fetal breathing activity, body movements, and FHR changes might be used as reasonable indicators of fetal electrocortical activity and/or maturity of the fetal central nervous system. However, under conditions of different gestational ages, hypoxia, and other stimuli such as sound and vibration, these variables are dissociated from each other in time. In addition, observations of normal fetal biophysical activity are unlikely to be a useful marker of the integrity of the fetal cortex. It is against this background that the clinical significance of changes in human behavioral activity following external vibroacoustic stimulation must be considered.

CLINICAL IMPLICATIONS FOR FETAL MONITORING

Antepartum Monitoring

Although originally used to detect deafness antenatally (Dwornicka, Jasienska, Smolarz, & Wawryk, 1964; Johansson, Wedenberg, & Westin, 1964), fetal acoustic stimulation was shown to be associated with an increase in fetal heart rate. These original attempts to identify deafness were unsuccessful and therefore abandoned. With the introduction of antepartum FHR testing, several investigators using a variety of acoustic stimuli (Davey et al., 1984; Grimwade et al., 1971; Jensen, 1984; Luz et al., 1980; Querleu et al., 1984; Read & Miller, 1977) have suggested use of FHR response to external acoustic stimulation as an indicator of fetal health and metabolic status. Due to lack of standardization and technical difficulties in producing an optimal sound stimulus to elicit a reproducible response, fetal acoustic stimulation was not used clinically until the introduction of vibroacoustic stimulation with an electronic artificial larynx (Smith, Phelan, Platt, Broussard, & Paul, 1986). This stimulus, as described earlier, can reproducibly alter fetal heart rate and behavioral activity (Gagnon et al., 1987a, 1987b). Using the rationale that an FHR response to VAS may exclude fetal hypoxia and/or acidosis, this method of antepartum surveillance has disseminated rapidly into clinical practice as a complement to unstressed antepartum FHR testing.

Read and Miller (1977), in a small study, used fetal acoustic stimulation (FAS) in patients who were having contraction stress tests. They observed that patients without FHR response to stimulation tended to have a higher prevalence of abnormal contraction status tests. Typically, the sensitivity of FAS or VAS used antenatally to predict intrapartum fetal distress or low 5-min Apgar score has been less than 60% and the positive predictive value less than 20%. These results are not surprising. Many acute events occurring during labor, such as umbilical cord compression, placental abruptio, shoulder dystocia, administration of narcotic, or premature labor and delivery, are not present at the time of antepartum FHR testing and may lead to fetal distress or low Apgar score. Recent observations by Schwartz et al. (1991) reported 38 patients with both a nonreactive NST and reactive VAS. Following assessment included an oxytocin challenge test or biophysical profile, which was nonreassuring in five cases (13.5%) and in four out of these five cases there was evidence of fetal compromise. These observations suggested that VAS may have evoked reactivity in fetuses with early compromise and raised concerns about using VAS to discriminate between the healthy and unhealthy fetuses.

In the only randomized controlled trial of VAS for antepartum monitoring (Smith, Phelan, Platt, Broussard, & Paul, 1986), there was no difference in outcomes when the VAS was used compared with a control group followed with standard antepartum FHR monitoring. Monitoring time was 4 min shorter in the VAS group than controls. However, because the total monitoring time required for further monitoring following a nonreactive VAS was not included, it is difficult to make any firm conclusions as to the cost-effectiveness of using VAS for antepartum fetal monitoring. Smith, Phelan, Nguyen, Jacobs, and Paul (1988) described their continuing experience using VAS in a total of 3,100 women undergoing

8,258 tests and reported a fetal death rate within a week of 1.9 per 1,000, which was not different from 1.6 per 1,000 using standard nonstress testing. In another uncontrolled clinical trial, Clark, Sobey, and Jolley (1989) reported their experience in 2,628 women with singleton high-risk pregnancies with gestational age that ranged from 28 to 44 weeks. The FHR response to VAS was combined with amniotic fluid volume assessment. In 9 out of 2628 (0.45%) patients, delivery was done because of variable FHR decelerations following VAS. There was no antepartum death when an FHR acceleration occurred following VAS. Clarke et al. noted that during the same period, in their low-risk population, fetal death rate was 2 to 3 per 1,000, and they suggested that VAS in conjunction with amniotic fluid volume assessment was beneficial in reducing fetal death rate in their high-risk group. Despite these promising results, this sample size was still too small to demonstrate any significant benefit, and the absence of fetal deaths in the VAS group may have been due to chance alone. From these two studies, currently available data suggest that the risk of intrauterine fetal death in the presence of an FHR response to fetal vibroacoustic stimulation is probably not higher than following a spontaneously reactive nonstress test (1.6 per 1,000).

If clinicians wish to use antepartum VAS to assess fetal health and save testing time, criteria for reactivity such as one FHR acceleration of ≥10 bpm for ≥15 sec and/or an increase in FHR baseline of ≥10 bpm for ≥2 minutes following a 3-sec stimulus would be adequate criteria after 30 weeks gestation based on data obtained in healthy fetuses (Gagnon et al., 1987a, 1987b; Gagnon, Hunse, & Patrick, 1988; Davey et al., 1984; Jensen, 1984; Johansson et al., 1964). Occasionally, more than one stimulus may be required (Smith, Phelan, Platt, Broussard, & Paul, et al. 1986; Smith et al., 1988; Clark et al., 1989). If no FHR response is observed, the interpretation of test results should take into account other factors that could influence FHR response to VAS (Table 8.1). It would be advisable to continue FHR recording if no FHR response following VAS occurred, to differentiate the healthy fetus in quiet sleep state (see Nijhuis, chapter 5, this volume) from the metabolically compromised fetus with a flat FHR tracing requiring immediate delivery (Brown & Patrick, 1981). It should also be recognized that occasionally emergency intervention may be required if profound and persistent bradycardia occurs following VAS (Sherer et al., 1988).

Intrapartum Monitoring

There is evidence that the premature introduction into clinical practice of continuous FHR monitoring during labor has had deleterious effects. In recent randomized clinical trials comparing intermittent FHR auscultation and continuous FHR monitoring, it has been shown that continuous FHR monitoring during labor increases the rate of operative deliveries and is not superior to intermittent auscultation in low-risk pregnant women to detect fetal compromise (MacDonald, Grant, Sheridan-Periera, Boylan, & Chalmers, 1985; Leveno et al., 1986). In addition, persistently abnormal FHR patterns in laboring women have a false positive rate of 50% to predict adverse outcome. Fetal scalp blood sampling is currently the diagnostic test of choice to confirm progressive metabolic acidosis and fetal distress. However, it is not always feasible, and visual assessment of FHR tracings during labor might not be a good screening test due to its low sensitivity to decide which fetus needs to be sampled. For these reasons, FHR response to vibroacoustic stimulation has been suggested as a good screening test to detect the fetus potentially compromised and acidotic during labor (Smith, Nguyen, Phelan, & Richard, 1986).

The effectiveness of VAS to detect fetal acidosis during labor depends on the threshold used to define significant metabolic acidosis. Using a pH of <7.20, approximately 1.3% of acidotic fetuses have a normal FHR response to VAS (Edersheim, Hutson, Druzin, & Kogut, 1987; Ingemarsson, & Arulkumaran, 1989; Smith, Nguyen, Phelan, & Richard, 1986; Polzin, Blakemore, Petrie, & Amon, 1988), suggesting that normal FHR responsiveness to VAS might be falsely reassuring. This false negative rate also indicates that VAS may occasionally be a stimulus too strong to differentiate the healthy fetus from the acidotic fetus. The low positive predictive value (usually 8 to 9%) to detect fetal acidosis clearly demonstrates the necessity of performing fetal scalp sampling if an FHR response is absent. In our experience on a small number (n = 9) of term fetuses who all had normal umbilical artery cord gases at birth (Gagnon et al., 1992), two fetuses did not have an FHR response to VAS during labor. Our data suggested that the non-reactivity of FHR was due only to inadequate intrauterine sound pressure levels reached during VAS. It is therefore prudent to take into consideration factors (Table 8.1) that could influence FHR response to VAS during labor for accurate test interpretation and subsequent management.

SUMMARY AND FUTURE DIRECTIONS

There is a clear developmental aspect in fetal heart rate patterns in healthy human fetuses that can be altered with chronic fetal nutritional deprivation and perhaps fetal hypoxemia. Similarly, development of fetal behavioral activity patterns is strongly influenced by gestational age and the functional maturation of the central nervous system. External vibroacoustic stimulation can reproducibly alter fetal behavioral variables, with the most affected being fetal heart rate as early as 26 weeks, followed by a disturbance in fetal body movements after 32 weeks, and fetal breathing movements after 36 weeks' gestation. More important is that profound nonphysiological changes in fetal behavioral activity may persist for up to 1.5 hr following a 5-sec stimulus, suggesting that vibroacoustic stimulus might be too strong to differentiate the healthy from the compromised fetuses. Although the fetus at risk might respond differently than the healthy fetus, considerable overlap still exists between a normal and abnormal response. Future research should focus to understand better the mechanisms underlying disturbances in fetal behavioral activity such as seen with sound and vibration stimuli. There is also a need to develop new diagnostic tests to assess in utero the neurological maturation and function of the developing fetus in relation to subsequent neurological outcome and ultimately, to establish strategies to prevent antenatal brain damage.

REFERENCES

Abrams, R. M., Hutchison, A. A., Gerhardt, K. J., Evans, S. L., & Pendergast, J. (1987). Local cerebral glucose utilization in fetal sheep exposed to noise. *American Journal of Obstetrics and Gynecology, 157,* 456–460.

Abrams, R. M., Hutchison, A. A., Jay, T. M., Sokoloff, L., & Kennedy, C. (1988). Local cerebral glucose utilization nonselectively elevated in rapid eye movement sheep of the fetus. *Developmental Brain Research, 40,* 65–70.

Allen, M. C., & Capute, A. J. (1986). Assessment of early auditory and visual abilities of extremely premature infants. *Developmental Medicine and Child Neurology, 28,* 458–466.

Benzaquen, S., Gagnon, R., Hunse, C., & Foreman, J. (1990). The intrauterine sound environment of the human fetus during labour. *American Journal of Obstetrics and Gynecology, 163,* 484–490.

Birnholz, J. C., Benacerraf, B. R. (1983) The development of human fetal hearing. *Science, 222,* 516–518.

Bocking, A. D., Adamson, L., Cousin, A., Campbell, K., Carmichael, L., Natale, R., & Patrick, J. (1982). Effect of intravenous glucose injection on fetal breathing movements and gross fetal body movements at 38–40 weeks gestational age. *American Journal of Obstetrics and Gynecology, 142,* 606–611.

Bocking, A. D., Gagnon, R., Milne, K. M., & White, S. (1988). Behavioural activity during prolonged hypoxemia in fetal sheep. *Journal of Applied Physiology, 65,* 2420–2426.

Boddy, K., Dawes, G. S., Fisher, R., Pinter, S., & Robinson, J. S. (1974). Foetal respiratory movements, electrocortical and cardiovascular responses to hypoxemia and hypercarbia in sleep. *Journal of Physiology, 243,* 599–618.

Brown, R., & Patrick, J. (1981). The nonstress test, How long is long enough? *American Journal of Obstetrics and Gynecology, 141,* 646–651.

Clark, S. L., Sobey, P., & Jolley, K. (1989). Nonstress testing with acoustic stimulation and amniotic fluid volume measurement, 5973 tests without unexpected fetal death. *American Journal of Obstetrics and Gynecology, 160,* 694–697.

Davey, D. A., Dommisse, J., Macnab, M., & Dacre, D. (1984). The value of an auditory stimulatory test in antenatal fetal cardiotocograph. *European Journal of Obstetrics, Gynecology and Reproductive Biology, 18*, 273–277.

Dawes, G. S., Fox, H. E., Leduc, B. M., & Richards, R .T. (1972). Respiratory movements and rapid eye movement sleep in the foetal lamb. *Journal of Physiology, (London), 220*, 119–143.

Dawes, G. S., Moulden, M., & Redman, C. W. G. (1992). Short-term fetal heart rate variation, decelerations & umbilical flow velocity waveforms before labour. *Obstetrics and Gynecology, 80*, 673–678.

Dawes, G. S., Redman, C. W. G., & Smith, J. H. (1985). Improvements in the registration and analysis of fetal heart rate records at the bedside. *British Journal of Obstetrics and Gynaecology, 92*, 317–325.

Devoe, L. D., Murray, C., Faircloth, D., & Ramos, E. (1990). Vibroacoustic stimulation and fetal behavioural state in normal term human pregnancy. *American Journal of Obstetrics and Gynecology, 163*, 1156–1161.

Drucker-Colin, R. (1979). Protein molecules and the regulation of REM sleep. Possible implications for function. In, R., Drucker-Colin, M., Sckurovich, & M. B. Sterman, (Eds.), The function of sleep (pp. 99-111). New York. Academic Press.

Druzin, M., Gratacos, J., & Paul, R. H.(1985). Antepartum fetal heart rate testing XII. The effect of manual manipulation of the fetus on the nonstress test. *American Journal of Obstetrics and Gynecology, 151*, 61–65.

Dwornicka, B., Jasienska, A., Smolarz, W., & Wawryk, R. (1964). Attempt of determining the fetal reaction to acoustic stimulation. *Acta Otolaryngologica, 57*, 571–574.

Edersheim, T. G., Hutson, J. M., Druzin, M. L., & Kogut, E. A.(1987). Fetal heart rate response to vibratory acoustic stimulation predicts fetal pH in labor. *American Journal of Obstetrics and Gynecology, 157*, 1557–1560.

Fisk, N. M., Nicolaides, P. K., Arulkumaran, S., Weg, M .W., Tannirandorn, Y., Nicolini, U., Parkes, M. J., & Rodeck, C. H. (1991). Vibroacoustic stimulation is not associated with sudden fetal catecholamine release. *Early Human Development, 25*, 11–17.

Gagnon, R. (1989). Stimulation of human fetuses with sound and vibration. *Seminars in Perinatology, 13*, 393–402.

Gagnon, R., Benzaquen, S., & Hunse, C. (1992). The fetal sound environment during vibroacoustic stimulation in labour, Effect on fetal heart rate response. *Obstetrics and Gynecology, 79*, 905–955.

Gagnon, R., Campbell, K., Hunse, C., & Patrick, J. (1987). Patterns of human fetal heart rate accelerations from 26 weeks to term. *American Journal of Obstetrics and Gynecology, 157*, 743–749.

Gagnon, R., Foreman, J., Hunse, C., & Patrick, J. (1989). Effects of low-frequency vibration on human term fetus. *American Journal of Obstetrics and Gynecology, 161*, 1479–1476.

Gagnon, R., Hunse, C., & Bocking, A. D. (1989b). Fetal heart rate patterns in the small-for-gestational-age human fetus. *American Journal of Obstetrics and Gynecology, 161*, 779–784.

Gagnon, R., Hunse, C., Carmichael, L., Fellows, F., & Patrick, J. (1987). External vibratory acoustic stimulation near term, Fetal heart rate and heart rate variability responses. *American Journal of Obstetrics and Gynecology, 156*, 323–327.

Gagnon, R., Hunse, C., Carmichael, L., Fellows, F., & Patrick, J. (1987). Human fetal response to vibratory acoustic stimulation from twenty-six weeks to term. *American Journal of Obstetrics and Gynecology, 157*, 1375–1381.

Gagnon, R., Hunse, C., Carmichael, L., Fellows, F., & Patrick, J. (1988). Fetal heart rate and fetal activity patterns after vibratory acoustic stimulation at thirty to thirty-two weeks' gestational age. *American Journal of Obstetrics and Gynecology, 158*, 75–79.

Gagnon, R., Hunse, C., Carmichael, L., & Patrick, J. (1989). Vibratory acoustic stimulation in 26- to 32-week, small-for-gestational-age fetus. *American Journal of Obstetrics and Gynecology, 160*, 160–165.

Gagnon, R., Hunse, C., Fellows, F., & Patrick, J. (1988). Fetal heart rate and activity patterns in growth retarded fetuses, Changes following vibratory acoustic stimulation. *American Journal of Obstetrics and Gynecology, 158*, 265–271.

Gagnon, R., Hunse, C., & Foreman, J. (1989). Human fetal behavioural states after vibroacoustic stimulation. *American Journal of Obstetrics and Gynecology, 161*, 1470–1476.

Gagnon, R., Patrick, J., Foreman, J., & West, R. (1986). Stimulation of human fetuses with sound and vibration. *American Journal of Obstetrics and Gynecology, 155*, 848–851.

Gagnon, R., Hunse, C., & Patrick, J. (1988c). Fetal responses to vibratory acoustic stimulation, Influence of basal heart rate. *American Journal of Obstetrics and Gynecology, 159*, 835–839.

Gerhardt, K. J., Abrams, R. M., & Kovaz, B. M., (1988). Intrauterine noise levels in pregnant ewes produced by sound applied to the abdomen *American Journal of Obstetrics and Gynecology, 159*, 228–232,

Grimwade, J. C., Walker, D. W., Bartlett, M., Gordon, S., & Wood, C. (1971). Human fetal heart rate change and movement in response to sound and vibration. *American Journal of Obstetrics and Gynecology, 109*, 86–90.

Horner, K. C., Seriere, J., & Granier-Deferre, C. (1987). Deoxyglucose demonstration of an in utero hearing in the guinea-pig foetus. *Hearing Research, 26*, 327–333.

Ingemarsson, I., & Arulkumaran, S. (1989). Reactive fetal heart rate response to vibroacoustic stimulation in fetuses with low scalp blood pH. *British Journal of Obstetrics and Gynaecology, 96*, 562.

Jarvis, S., & Hay, E. (1984). Measuring disability and handicap due to cerebral palsy. In F., Stanley, E., Alberman, (Eds.), *The epidemiology, of the cerebral palsies* (pp. 35–45). Clinics in Developmental Medicine (No. 87). Suffolk, Lavenhorn.

Jensen, O. H. (1984). Fetal heart rate response to controlled sound stimuli during the third trimester of normal pregnancy. *Acta Obstetrics et Gynecologica Scandinavica, 63*, 193–197.

Johansson, B., Wedenberg, E., & Westin, B. (1964). Measurement of tone response by the human fetus. A preliminary report. *Acta Otolaryngologica, 57*, 188–192.

Leader, L. R., Baillie, P., Martin, B., & Vermeulen, E. (1982). The assessment and significance of habituation to a repeated stimulus by the human fetus. *Early Human Development, 7*, 211–219.

Leader, L. R., Baillie, P., Martin, B., Molteno, C., & Wynchank, S. (1984). Fetal responses to vibrotactile stimulation, a possible predictor of fetal and neonatal outcome. *Australian & New Zealand Journal of Obstetrics and Gynecology, 24*, 251–256.

Leveno, R. J., Cunningham, F. G., Nelson, S., Roark, M., Williams, M. L., Guzick, D., Dowling, S., Rosenfeld, C. R., & Buckley, A. (1986). A prospective comparison of selective and universal electronic fetal monitoring in 34995 pregnancies. *New England Journal of Medicine, 315*, 615–619.

Luz, N. P., Lima, C. P., Luz, S. H., & Feldons, V. L. (1980). Auditory evoked responses of the human fetus. I. Behaviour during progress of labor. *Acta Obstetrica et Gynecologica Scandinavia, 59*, 395–404.

MacDonald, D., Grant, A., Sheridan-Pereira, M., Boylan, P. & Chalmers, I. (1985). The Dublin randomized controlled trial of intrapartum fetal heart rate monitoring. *American Journal of Obstetrics and Gynecology, 152*, 524–539.

Matsuda, Y., Carmichael, L., Patrick, J., & Richardson, B. (1992, August). Recovery of the ovine fetus from sustained hypoxia, Effects on biophysical activity. *Proceedings of the 19th Annual Meeting of the Society for the Study of Fetal Physiology*, Niagara-on-the-Lake, Ontario.

Natale, R., Clewlow, F., & Dawes, G. S. (1981). Measurement of fetal forelimb movements in the fetal lamb in utero. *American Journal of Obstetrics and Gynecology, 140*, 545–551.

Nelson, R. B., & Ellenberg, J. H. (1986). Antecedents of cerebral palsy. Multivariate analysis of risk. *New England Journal of Medicine, 315*, 81–86.

Parkes, T. J., Morre, P. J., Moore, D. R., Fish, N. M., & Hanson, M. A. (1991). Behavioural changes in fetal sheep caused by vibroacoustic stimulation: The effects of cochlear ablation. *American Journal of Obstetrics and Gynecology, 164*, 1336–1343.

Patrick, J. (1989). The physiological basis for fetal assessment. *Seminars in Perinatology, 13*, 403–408.

Patrick, J., Carmichael, L., Chess, L., & Staples, C. (1984). Accelerations of the human fetal heart rate at 38 to 40 weeks' gestational age. *American Journal of Obstetrics and Gynecology, 148*, 35–41.

Penning, D. H., Grafe, M. R., Matsuda, Y., Hammond, R., & Richardson, B. (1992, September). The histopathological response of the fetal sheep brain to mid-gestational hypoxia. *Proceedings of the Annual Meeting for the Society for Neurosciences*, Anaheim, CA.

Petrikovsky, B. M., Schifrin, B., & Diana L. (1993). The effect of fetal acoustic stimulation on fetal swallowing and amniotic fluid index. *Obstetrics and Gynecology, 81*, 548–550.

Plessinger, M. A., & Woods, J. R., Jr. (1986). Fetal auditory brainstem response: External and intrauterine auditory stimulation. *American Journal of Physiology, 250*, R137–R141.

Plessinger, M. A. & Woods, J. R. (1987). Fetal auditory brainstem response, effect of increasing stimulus date during functional auditory development. *American Journal of Obstetrics and Gynecology, 157*, 1382–1387.

Polishuk, W. J., Laufer, N., & Sadovsky, E. (1975). Fetal responses to external light stimulus. *Harefuah, 89*, 395–397.

Polzin, G. B., Blakemore, D. J., Petrie, R. G., & Amon, E. (1988). Fetal vibroacoustic stimulation: Magnitude and duration of fetal heart rate accelerations as a marker of fetal health. *Obstetrics and Gynecology, 72,* 621–626.

Prechtl, H. F. R. (1974). The behavioural states of the newborn infant (A review). *Brain Research, 76,* 185–212.

Querleu, D., Boutteville, C., & Renard, X. (1984). Evaluation diagnostique de la souffrance foetale pendant la grossesse au moyen d'un test de stimulation sonore. *European Journal of Gynecology, Obstetrics, and Biological Reproduction, 13,* 789–796.

Rankin, J. H. G., Landauer, M., Tian, Q., & Phernetton, T. M. (1987). Ovine fetal electrocortical activity and regional cerebral blood flow. *Journal of Developmental Physiology, 9,* 537–542.

Read, J. A., & Miller, F. C. (1977). Fetal heart rate acceleration in response to acoustic stimulation as a measure of fetal well-being. *American Journal of Obstetrics and Gynecology, 129,* 512–517.

Richardson, B., Campbell, K., Carmichael, L., & Patrick, J. (1981). Effects of external physical stimulation on fetuses near term. *American Journal of Obstetrics and Gynecology, 39,* 344–352.

Richardson, B. S., Patrick, J. E., & Abduljabbar, H. (1985). Cerebral oxidative metabolism in the fetal lamb, Relationship to electrocortical state. *American Journal of Obstetrics and Gynecology, 153,* 426–431.

Roffward, H. P., Muzio, J. N., & Demert, W. C. (1966). Ontogenetic development of the human sleep-dream cycle. *Science, 152,* 604–619.

Schwartz, D. B., Sherman, S. J., Gayert G. L., Fields, P., Simkins, S., & Daoud, Y. (1991). An evaluation of antenatal fetal acoustic stimulation. *European Journal of Obstetrics, Gynecology and Reproductive Biology, 40,* 97–103.

Sherer, D. M., Abramowicz, J. S., D'Amico, M. L., Allen, T., & Woods, J. R. (1991). Fetal panting, yet another response to the external vibratory acoustic stimulation test. *American Journal of Obstetrics and Gynecology, 164,* 591–592.

Sherer, D. M., Menashe, M., & Sadovsky, E. (1988). Severe fetal bradycardia caused by external vibratory acoustic stimulation. *American Journal of Obstetrics and Gynecology, 159,* 334–335.

Smith, C. V., Phelan, J. P., Platt, L. D., Broussard, P., & Paul, R. H. (1986). Fetal acoustic stimulation testing: II. A randomized clinical comparison with the nonstress test. *American Journal of Obstetrics and Gynecology, 155,* 131–134.

Smith, C. V., Nguyen, H. N., Phelan, J. P., & Richard, H. D. (1986). Intrapartum assessment of fetal well-being, A comparison of fetal acoustic stimulation with acid-base determinations. *American Journal of Obstetrics and Gynecology, 155,* 726–728.

Smith, C. V., Phelan, J. P, Nguyen, H. N., Jacobs, N., & Paul, R. H. (1988). Continuing experience with the fetal acoustic stimulation test. *Journal of Reproductive Medicine, 33,* 365–368.

Spencer, J. A. D., Deans, A., Nicolaides, P., & Arulkumaran, S. (1991). Fetal heart rate response to vibroacoustic stimulation during low and high heart rate variability episodes in late pregnancy. *American Journal of Obstetrics and Gynecology, 165,* 86–96.

Timor-Tritsch, I. E., Dierkar, L. T., Zador, I., Hertz, R. H., & Rosen, M. G. (1978). Fetal movements associated with fetal heart rate accelerations and decelerations. *American Journal of Obstetrics and Gynecology, 131*, 276–280.

van Eyck, J., Wladimiroff, J. W., van den Wyngaard, J. A. G., Noordam, M. J., & Prechtl, H. E. (1987). The blood flow velocity waveform in the fetal internal carotid and umbilical artery; its relation to fetal behavioural states in normal pregnancy at 37–38 weeks. *British Journal of Obstetrics and Gynaecology, 94*, 736–741.

van Vliet, M. A. T., Martin, C. B., Nijhuis, J. G., & Prechtl, A. F. (1985). Behavioural states in growth-retarded human fetuses. *Early Human Development, 12*, 183–197.

Visser, G. H. A., Mulder, H. H., Wit, H. P., Mulder, E. J., & Prechtl, H. F. (1989). Vibro-acoustic stimulation of the human fetus: Effects on behavioural state organization. *Early Human Development, 19*, 285–296.

Wasserman, D. E. (1990). Vibration, Principles, measurements & health standards. *Seminars in Perinatology, 14*, 311–321.

Woods, J. R., Plessinger, M. A., & Mack, C. E. (1984). Fetal auditory brainstem evoked response (ABR). *Pediatric Research, 18*, 83–85.

Woods, J. R., Jr., & Plessinger, M. A. (1989). Fetal sensory sequencing: Applications of evoked potentials in perinatal physiology. *Seminars in Perinatology, 13*, 380–392.

Zimmer, E. Z., Chao, C. R., Guy, G. P., Marks, F., & Fifer, W. P. (1993). Vibroacoustic stimulation evokes human fetal micturition. *Obstetrics and Gynecology, 81*, 178–180

9

Nutrition and Behavioral States in the Developing Human Infant

Karl F. Schulze
Sudha Kashyap
Rakesh Sahni
William P. Fifer
Michael M. Myers
Columbia University College of Physicians and Surgeons, Babies and Children's Hospital of New York (Presbyterian Hospital) and New York's State Psychiatric Institute

For many years it has been assumed that developing human infants are able to regulate their food intake using the same complex systems that control hunger and satiety of older children and adults. Given this assumption, it was considered safe to offer a wide range of nutrient intakes and rely on the infant's appetite and feeding pattern to maintain a balanced intake of nutrients. This approach to nutritional management of infants was reinforced by the belief that, apart from the sequelae of inborn errors of metabolism, few adult health problems were related to nutritional disturbances experienced during early development. The fact that infants can grow well and remain healthy on many different diets has been justification to avoid micromanagement of their feeding activity.

However, there are at least two circumstances where innate regulatory mechanisms are bypassed, effectively uncoupling nutrient intake from metabolic requirements: the fetus who is fed intravenously across the placenta, and the immature low-birth-weight (LBW) infant who is tube-fed by caretakers. In neither of these situations is the nutrient intake of the developing organism necessarily linked directly to its metabolic needs. The consequences of this dissociation of nutrient intake from regulatory control systems have not been well studied; however, recent evidence from several sources suggests that the nutritional experience of fetuses and tube-fed infants may impact significantly on subsequent health. For example, the fetus who suffers from intrauterine growth retardation is now known to be at increased risk for cardiovascular disease, diabetes, and other health problems during adult life (Barker, Osmund, Golding, Kuh, & Wadsworth, 1989). Also, low-birth-weight infants fed unusually high intakes of protein do not perform as well on intelligence testing at school age compared to those fed less protein (Goldman, Goldman, Kaufman, & Liebman, 1974). These two observations, and other recent data, suggest the general hypothesis that relatively small differences in nutrient availability during early life may have serious consequences, and that perinatal nutritional status may be an important determinant of adult health and behavior.

This hypothesis acquired additional support with the publication of the now classic studies by Fernstrom and Wurtman (1971, 1972), which showed that the brain content of serotonin, an important neurotransmitter with effects on gastrointestinal, cardiorespiratory, behavioral, and other variables, is dependent on the plasma concentration of tryptophan and other large neutral amino acids. Plasma amino acid levels, in turn, are directly dependent on protein and energy intake. This observation suggests a direct effect of diet on brain function. In addition, other investigators have reported that functional tests of visual development are influenced by the amount and quality of fat in the diet (Uauy, Birch, Birch, Tyson, & Hoffman, 1990). These and other findings suggest a theoretical mechanism for the effects of nutrition on brain development and indicate pathways through which nutrition, physiology and behavior can interact. Needless to say, the idea that brain growth and brain function may be sensitive to rather small variations in nutrient intake is somewhat disquieting to those who have assumed that the internal milieu of the infant is well defended against such apparently innocuous perturbations as a high protein diet.

Coincident with the recognition that nutrient intake can influence brain growth and brain function, several interesting hypotheses have been formulated that bear directly or indirectly on this interaction. First, it is now clear that nutrient intake is accompanied by activation of the sympathetic nervous system. Sympathetic activity, whether assayed by plasma catecholamines (Astrup, Buemann, Christensen, Madsen, 1992), urinary excretion of catecholamines (Young, Rosa, & Landsberg, 1984), norepinephrine turnover (Young & Landsberg, 1977), or sympathetic neurograms (Sakaguchi, Arase, Fisler, & Bray, 1988), is known to increase with nutrient intake, particularly carbohydrate intake. Second, it has been suggested that stimulation of catecholamine metabolism within the central nervous system is dependent on the availability of the precursor amino acid, tyrosine. Although some changes in cerebral catecholamine metabolism appear to be driven by changes in plasma tyrosine concentration (Gibson & Wurtman, 1978), the data are less convincing than those supporting the relationship between serotonin and tryptophan. Taken together, however, the available evidence indicates an unequivocal effect of diet on sympathetic tone.

There is also evidence that nutritional intake influences behavior, perhaps through mechanisms involved in the metabolism of protein. Dietary intake of protein is known to stimulate protein synthesis and protein storage (Catzeflis et al., 1988), and protein synthesis is thought to occur primarily during active sleep (Drucker-Colin, 1979; Oswald, 1969). This association suggests the hypothesis that protein intake stimulates active sleep, a behavioral state that is known to be associated with increased sympathetic activity (Somers, Dyken, Mark, & Abboud, 1993). Thus, a case can be made that both behavior (i.e., active sleep) and the activity of the sympathetic nervous system may be linked to each other by a common dependence on nutritional intake.

Finally, it has also been reported that time spent in active sleep and other parameters of the sleep cycle are sensitive to plasma concentrations of tryptophan and the large neutral amino acids (MacFadyen, Oswald, & Lewis, 1973; Bakalian & Fernstrom, 1990) presumably through the stimulating effects of tryptophan on brain serotonin content. Serotonin is also thought to regulate the balance between active and quiet sleep (Jouvet, 1984). Because plasma amino acids concentrations vary with the amount of protein ingested, the flux of tryptophan into the brain is almost certainly diet dependent.

In summary, direct nutritional effects on both noradrenergic and serotonergic neurotransmitter metabolism have been demonstrated. We hypothesize that these effects serve as fundamental mechanisms linking nutrition and sleep. Although the evidence in favor of these hypotheses is quite strong for experimental animals and adult humans, little is known about these relationships in immature humans. We postulate that diet-induced alterations in the neurotransmitter systems of developing human beings, sustained over weeks or months of early life and spanning a time of rapid brain development, might ultimately lead to neurobehavioral and other physiological differences in later life. As a first step to testing this general hypothesis we studied the relationships among nutrient intake, cardiorespiratory activity, and behavior in a cohort of LBW infants fed various diets. The specific objective of this chapter is to review the effects of differences in the absolute amount and relative proportions of dietary protein and energy on the weight gain, energy expenditure, heart rate, respiratory frequency, protein metabolism, and the distribution of states of sleep of low-birth-weight infants. Although the fetus is not discussed directly, it is very likely that similar, if not identical, processes would contribute to in utero growth and neurobehavioral development. To understand the nature of the experimental differences in these infants it is first necessary to review briefly the study population and the experimental protocol and to describe the techniques and timing of the measurement of dependent variables.

MATERIALS AND METHODS

Study Population

The total study population consisted of 142 healthy growing LBW infants, all of whom were participants in studies of the effects of variations in protein and energy intake on the rate and composition of weight gain (Kashyap et al., 1986, 1988, 1990; Kashyap, Schulze, Ramakrishnan, Dell, & Heird, 1994). To study the relationships between diet and the cardiorespiratory variables, 6-hr FM tape recordings of electrocardiograms and impedance pneumograms were obtained in a subset of 66 infants. All studies were approved by the Institutional Review Board at Columbia Presbyterian Medical Center, and written informed consent was obtained from the parents of all participants. The characteristics of the infants, grouped by diet, are shown in Table 9.1.

Feeding Protocols

Both formula-fed and human milk-fed infants were studied. Formula-fed infants were assigned randomly to experimental formulas. The ranges of protein and energy intakes of the formula fed infants were targeted at 2.25–4.5 g/kg·day and 100 to 150 kcal/kg·day, respectively. Nonprotein energy in all formulas was 50% carbohydrate and 50% fat. Human milk-fed infants were randomly assigned to be fed their mother's milk or mother's milk with a supplement of protein, calcium, phosphorus, and sodium. If mothers were unable to provide adequate amounts of milk their infants were fed pooled banked human donor milk with the supplement. In all, 13 different diets were utilized.

After consent for participation in the study was obtained, the infants were begun on their assigned formula or human milk. Feedings were then advanced as tolerated until the desired intake, 180 ml/kg·day, was reached and the formal study period commenced. The composition of the diet was not changed during the study period, but the volume of intake was

TABLE 9.1
Characteristics of the Study Population

Group	Diet [protein(g/kg · day)/ energy(kcal/kg · day)]	n	Birth Weight (g)	Study Weight (g)	Gestational Age (weeks)	Post Conceptional Age (weeks)	Postnatal Age (days)
1	2.25/118	7	1495±205	1770±256	31.4±1.8	35.7±1.9	28.7±11.6
2	3.62/117	3	1435±215	1772±177	31.2±2.5	35.2±1.7	26.6±3.3
3	3.51/155	6	1501±200	1772±155	31.7±3.0	34.7±2.2	21.3±7.9
4	3.75/120	10	1497±201	1890±297	31.8±1.5	35.4±1.9	25.0±6.0
5	3.79/118	12	1410±199	1744±214	32.1±1.2	35.9±1.8	27.5±10.7
6	3.87/141	11	1477±193	2025±225	31.7±1.4	35.5±1.3	26.3±4.0
7	4.09/142	15	1320±222	1932±223	31.5±2.2	35.5±2.2	28.7±9.4
8	3.26/98	14	1308±267	1843±180	30.8±1.8	35.6±1.7	33.7±8.8
9	4.20/118	15	1326±252	1854±149	30.8±1.9	34.5±1.3	27.7±10.7
10*	2.49/130	10	1350±283	1662±268	30.6±1.6	34.8±2.0	30.6±10.5
11*	3.08/132	6	1356±205	1740±223	29.8±1.9	33.9±1.3	28.9±9.1
12*	2.85/122	12	1352±243	1791±272	31.1±1.1	35.8±1.5	32.1±5.8
13	3.39/125	21	1230±156	1759±193	29.7±1.7	34.4±1.1	33.7±6.9
Study means (n= 142)			1364±224	1819±230	31.0±1.9	35.1±1.7	29.4±8.9

*Human milk group.

153

adjusted daily for increases in weight until the infants completed the study at 2,200 g. The infants were cared for in the pediatric General Clinical Research Center as soon as permitted by their medical condition.

Measurement of Nutritional Variables

Each of the experimental formulas was from a special lot prepared and supplied by Ross Laboratories. Analysis of each nutrient was performed for each formula at the beginning, middle, and end of the study. Human milk samples were analyzed each week using a pool of daily samples.

Nitrogen balance and protein stored were measured weekly as previously described (Kashyap et al., 1986). In addition, every 2 weeks energy balance was determined from measurements of gross energy intake, energy excreted, and energy expenditure (Schulze et al., 1987). Energy expenditure was estimated from 6-hr measurements of oxygen consumption, carbon dioxide production, and daily urinary nitrogen excretion as previously described (Schulze et al., 1987; Schulze, Kashyap, & Ramakrishnan, 1993). During the 6-hr measurements of energy expenditure, cardiorespiratory variables and sleep states were measured.

Plasma samples for amino acid determination were obtained each week from all patients. The samples were drawn 2 hr after feeding, placed on ice, and taken immediately to the laboratory where they were analyzed as reported earlier (Schulze, Kashyap, Sahni, Fifer, & Myers, in press). The ratio of tryptophan to the other large neutral amino acids (Trp ratio) was computed by dividing the concentration of tryptophan by the sum of the concentrations of valine, leucine, isoleucine, tyrosine, and phenylalanine.

Measurement of Cardiorespiratory Variables

The electrocardiogram (ECG), impedance pneumogram, and a time code signal (Datum, Inc., Anaheim, CA) were recorded continuously on FM analog tape throughout the study. Analog signals were digitized and processed using an AST 286 microcomputer and special-purpose software (VitalTrends Technologies, Inc., New York, NY). The ECG was preprocessed and filtered by an HP3680 fetal monitor and fed to a custom-built microcomputer-based ECG preprocessor, which computed respiratory rate RR intervals with resolution of less than 0.1 msec. The RR intervals were then processed by additional special-purpose software to remove artifacts and to compute heart rate (HR) for each minute of the study. The impedance and time code tracings were digitized at 25 Hz. The impedance signal was filtered to reduce cardiac artifact, using a 25-point moving average of the first derivative of the digitized data. The mean time of each respiratory cycle (Ttot) was determined by marking troughs in the impedance tracing using pattern-recognition software specific for respiratory wave forms (Korten & and Haddad, 1989). The behaviorally coded state of sleep of the infant was added to each minute's record during data analysis, making it possible to separate minutes of cardiorespiratory data for active (AS) and quiet sleep (QS).

Assessment of States of Sleep

Every other week, as part of the protocol for measurement of energy expenditure, heart rate, respiratory rate, and states of sleep and wakefulness were coded each minute for approximately 6 hr. Coding began after the 8 a.m. feeding, continued until the 11 a.m. feeding, resumed after the 11 a.m. feeding, and terminated prior to the 2 p.m. feeding. During the postprandial period the infant was left undisturbed, warmed by a radiantly heated respiratory chamber and monitored as if in the intensive care unit (ICU). Behavioral codes were assigned each minute according to a coding system developed and validated in our laboratory (Stefanski et al., 1984). Briefly, active sleep was coded whenever at least one rapid eye movement was observed during the minute, and quiet sleep was coded when the infant was asleep without rapid eye movements. During quiet sleep the infant typically appeared "rag-doll" floppy with few or no movements apart from brief generalized startles. Although quiet sleep is known to be associated with increased activity in the electromyogram, the infant typically appears relaxed and hypotonic. Codes were also assigned for wakefulness, crying, and feeding. Percent active sleep (AS%) was computed as minutes of active sleep divided by minutes of active plus quiet sleep times 100. In 36 infants the electroencephalogram (EEG) was also recorded on a polygraph (Grass, model 6). In this subset of infants, the concordance between behavioral versus EEG coding of sleep states was 92% for EEG coded active sleep and 85% for quiet sleep (Sahni, Schulze, Stefanski, Fifer, & Myers, in press).

Data Analysis

Multiple measurements were made of most variables. For example, nitrogen and energy intakes were measured daily, amino acid concentrations were measured weekly, and states of sleep were assessed every other week. When age or weight trends were present, as was the case for heart rate, for example, the data were adjusted to a common, representative, postnatal age (28 days) or weight (2,200 g) using the data obtained from infants studied at two or more ages or weights (see Results section). When age and weight trends were not present, multiple nutritional and sleep state measurements of individual subjects were averaged and logged as subject means. The ages at study, weights at study, and postnatal ages at study were also averaged. Thus, measurements of AS% made at 32 and 34 weeks were averaged and taken to represent the AS% at 33 weeks and so forth. As a result of this averaging, all study infants were represented equally in the final data, although the number of observations made in individual infants may have differed. All regression analyses and tests of significance were run using the Multiple General Linear Hypotheses (MGLH) module of the Systat statistical analysis package (Systat, Evanston, IL).

RESULTS

Nutrition and Cardiorespiratory Activity

Because our goal was to focus on the effects of diet, we wanted to first remove differences that might have been related to age. Thus, the first phase of the analysis focused on the known trends in heart rate and respiratory frequency with time (Harper, Hoppenbrouwers, Sterman, McGinty, & Hodgeman, 1976.). The slopes of heart rate and respiratory frequency versus postnatal age were computed using the infants with cardiorespiratory data who were studied more than once. The group means of the slopes in active and quiet sleep and their standard deviations were:

$$\text{HR (AS) vs. postnatal age} = 0.43 \pm 0.46 \text{ beats/day} \qquad (1)$$

$$\text{HR (QS) vs. postnatal age} = 0.41 \pm 0.55 \text{ beats/day} \qquad (2)$$

Both slopes were significantly different from zero, $p<.0001$. The patient means were then adjusted to age 28 days using the mean slope for the group. Over the ranges tested there was no effect of either age or weight on respiratory frequency. All effects of diet on cardiorespiratory variables were similar for active and quiet sleep; therefore, only values for active sleep, the more common state (72% of sleep time), are reported. The results of simple linear regression of dietary nitrogen-energy ratio (mg/kcal; N/E), weight gain (g/kg·day; WG) and energy expenditure (kcal/kg·day; EE) against age-adjusted heart rate during active sleep (HR_{adj}) are listed here and shown in Fig. 9.1.

$$\text{AS HR}_{adj} = (0.97 \pm 0.29)(WG) + 144 \qquad r^2 = .15 \qquad p<0.01 \qquad (3)$$

$$\text{AS HR}_{adj} = (5.9 \pm 1.4)(N/E) + 139 \qquad r^2 = .22 \qquad p<0.01 \qquad (4)$$

$$\text{AS HR}_{adj} = (0.53 \pm 0.17)(EE) + 129 \qquad r^2 = .13 \qquad p<0.01 \qquad (5)$$

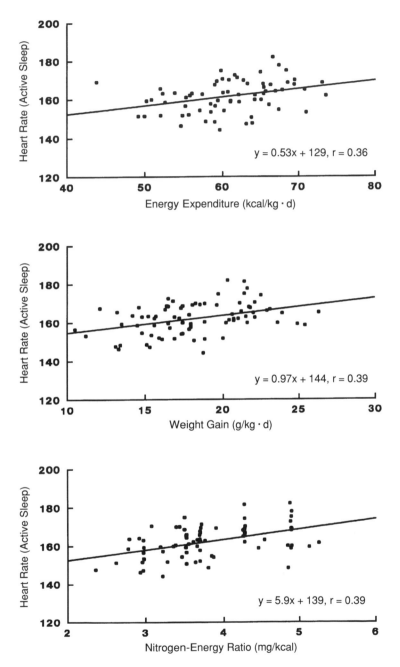

FIG. 9.1. Simple linear regression of dietary nitrogen–energy ratio (bottom panel), weight gain (middle panel), and energy expenditure (top panel) versus heart rate during active sleep. Heart rate has been adjusted to a postnatal age of 28 days.

157

Multiple regression of AS HR_{adj} against nitrogen intake (mg/kg·day), calorie intake (kcal/kg·day), nitrogen-energy product [mg kcal/(kg·day)^2], nitrogen-energy ratio (mg/kcal), weight gain (g/kg·day), energy expenditure (kcal/kg·day), hematocrit, study weight (g), postconceptional age (weeks), gestational age (weeks), and birth weight (g) yielded an equation with three variables:

$$AS\ HR_{adj} = (0.59\pm0.28)(WG) + (3.80\pm1.5)(N/E) \qquad (6)$$
$$+ (0.33\pm0.16)(EE) + 116$$

$$r^2 = .31 \qquad p \text{ value for each coefficient} <.05$$

Thus, after age adjustment, approximately 30% of the variability in mean heart rate during active sleep could be accounted for by variations in rate of weight gain, relative "leanness" of the diet, and the prevailing metabolic rate. Each variable in this model was independently significant and enhanced predictive accuracy when added to the model.

In other analyses, respiratory frequency during active sleep was found to be significantly related to weight gain. Nitrogen intake and hematocrit were also significant predictors of respiratory rate but substantially less powerful than weight gain. Combining variables did not lead to an improvement in r^2.

$$\text{Respiratory frequency (AS)} = (0.18\pm0.11)(WG) + 48 \qquad (7)$$

$$r^2 = .17 \qquad p <.001$$

Nutrition and Sleep

To investigate the relationship between macronutrient intake and sleep, AS% was regressed against the following independent variables: nitrogen intake (mg/kg·day; NI), energy intake (kcal/kg·day; EI), birth weight (g; BW), gestational age (weeks; GA), study weight (kg; SW), postconceptional age at study (weeks; PCA), and postnatal age at the time of study (days; PNA). The results of this regression are:

$$AS\% = (15.6\pm6.1)(NI) - (5.6\pm2.5)(SW) + (78.6\pm4.8) \qquad (8)$$

$$r^2 = .06 \qquad p=.014$$

In this two-variable model, both predictor variables were significantly related to AS% (NI, $p = .012$; SW, $p = .028$).

It is likely that study weight is a variable that parallels the known developmental decrease in the percent of time spent in active sleep (Roffwarg, Muzio, & Dement, 1966). Larger and more mature infants have less active sleep. Study weight was therefore included in all subsequent regression analyses.

Active Sleep, Protein Storage, and Weight Gain

The hypothesis that AS% is related not only to dietary nitrogen intake but also to its correlates—protein stored (g·kg·day; PS) and weight gain (g/kg·day; WG)—was tested by substituting these variables for nitrogen intake in the model. Both were significant predictors. Weight gain exhibited the stronger effect and, interestingly, was also stronger than nitrogen intake. The fact that weight gain explained more variation in AS% than nitrogen intake and protein stored suggests other growth-related variables may influence time spent in active sleep. The regression relationship with weight gain and study weight as independent variables is shown in Equation 9 and also plotted in Fig. 9.2.

$$AS\% = (0.51\pm0.18)(WG) - (5.6\pm2.5)(SW) + (74.4\pm4.9) \qquad (9)$$

$$r^2 = .11 \qquad p = .001$$

Again, in this two-variable model, each predictor variable was, in the presence of the other variable, significantly related to AS% (WG, $p = .006$; SW, $p = .028$).

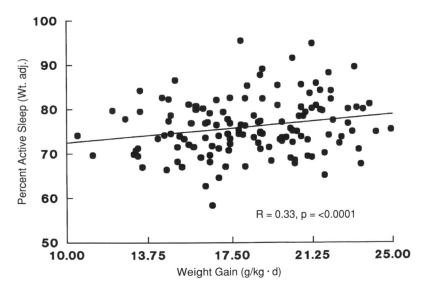

FIG. 9.2.   Percent active sleep is plotted against weight gain. Percent active sleep was adjusted for the effect of study weight using the relationship given in Equation 3: $AS\%_{adjusted} = AS\% + 5.6*$ (infant weight at study – population mean weight at study).

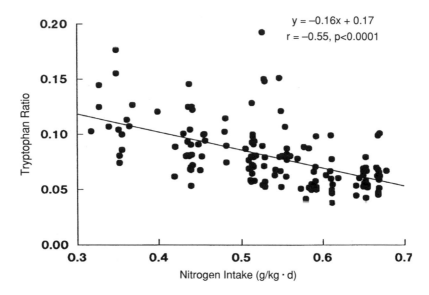

FIG. 9.3.   Trp ratio is plotted against nitrogen intake. The change in Trp ratio with increasing nitrogen intake is due to the fact that the plasma concentration of tryptophan, unlike the other LNAA, did not increase with nitrogen intake.

Nitrogen Intake and Trp ratio

In general, increases in nitrogen intake were associated with increases in plasma concentration of amino acids. However, the plasma concentrations of certain amino acids, such as tryptophan, were not correlated with nitrogen intake. The individual correlations of nitrogen intake and plasma amino acid concentrations of the large neutral amino acids (LNAA) were: tyrosine, r = .56; phenylalanine, r = 0.44; leucine, r = .58, valine, r = .75; isoleucine, r = 0.69; and tryptophan, r = –.04. Because plasma concentrations of LNAA increased with nitrogen intake and concentration of tryptophan did not, Trp ratio (TR) was negatively correlated with nitrogen intake as shown in Equation 10 and in Fig. 9.3.

$$TR = (-0.16 \pm 0.02)(NI) + (0.17 \pm 0.01) \qquad (10)$$
$$r^2 = 0.30 \qquad p < .0001$$

Active Sleep and Trp Ratio

The hypothesis that tryptophan may be involved in regulating AS% through the Trp ratio was then tested by substituting Trp ratio for weight gain.

$$AS\% = (-44.7 \pm 20.3)(TR) - (5.0 \pm 2.5)(SW) + (89 \pm 5.2) \qquad (11)$$
$$r^2 = .05 \qquad p = .019$$

Once more, in the two-variable model, each predictor variable was significantly related to AS% (TR, $p = .03$; SW, $p = .047$).

The relationships summarized by these regressions indicate that AS% is related to nitrogen intake, weight gain, protein storage, and/or Trp ratio. Thus, the hypotheses linking active sleep to both protein synthesis and the Trp ratio are supported by the data. To determine whether the effects of weight gain and Trp ratio are distinct or overlapping, both variables were included in the analysis. In the presence of weight gain the Trp ratio does not improve r^2.

These observations should be qualified in two ways. First, although these regressions are statistically significant, the r^2 values are small. The message is not that nutritional variables are good predictors of AS%, but rather that these variables should be considered among the many factors involved in the regulation of sleep. Second, the nutritional variables— nitrogen intake, protein stored, weight gain, and Trp ratio—are all strongly intercorrelated. It was not feasible to separate their effects in the study design. The significance of each individual regression relationship should be interpreted with this in mind.

DISCUSSION

The responses of these LBW infants to different nutritional intakes provide support for prevailing hypotheses relating diet and sleep. An infant who is growing rapidly, especially one who is fed a protein-rich diet, expends energy at a higher rate and has a higher resting heart rate and respiratory rate than a slow grower. The increases in heart rate, respiratory rate, and energy expenditure that accompany increases in weight gain in our infants would be expected to be associated with increased sympathetic tone. Unfortunately, we have no specific measures of sympathetic activity to support directly the hypothesis that sympathetic activity was altered by the experimental diets. Support for the relationship between feeding and activation of the noradrenergic system is therefore entirely indirect.

The outcomes we observed in LBW infants are compatible with current hypotheses relating protein metabolism to active sleep. Experimental evidence linking active sleep to protein synthesis has been derived primarily from studies of animals. Positive correlations between the amount of active sleep and the rate of protein synthesis have been reported in animals when protein synthesis is spontaneously activated (Drucker-Colin, Spanis, Cotman, & McGaugh, 1977), stimulated by parenteral amino acids (Danguir & Nicholaidis, 1980) or inhibited by chloramphenicol (Pegram, Hammond, & Bridgers, 1973). Limited data from human studies also support a relationship between sleep and protein metabolism. In adult humans, decreases in active sleep are observed when protein synthesis is inhibited by drugs (Oswald, 1969) or starvation (MacFadyen et al., 1973). The fact that rapidly growing, human infants have disproportionately high AS% has been cited as further evidence for a link between sleep and protein metabolism (Oswald, 1969).

As protein intake and protein storage increase, the plasma concentration of tryptophan relative to other large neutral amino acids (Trp ratio) decreases and the infants spend proportionately more time in active sleep. Our data are therefore compatible with the hypothesis that enhanced influx of tryptophan into the brain increases brain serotonin content and reduces active sleep, a situation that is similar to that reported in rats (Bakalian & Fernstrom, 1990). The results of this investigation are thus consistent with the relationship between brain serotonin and dietary tryptophan hypothesis first described by Fernstorm and Wurtman (1971, 1972). In this model, plasma tryptophan competes with other LNAA for a common transport carrier into the central nervous system, rendering the flux of tryptophan into the brain proportional to the ratio of tryptophan to LNAA. Upon entry to the brain, tryptophan promotes serotonin synthesis in direct relationship to its tissue concentration. Serotonin, in turn, has an acute hypnotic effect on both animals and humans (Jouvet, 1984) and appears to reduce active sleep preferentially. Changes in sleep latencies of term infants have been reported to follow feedings designed to perturb this ratio (Yogman & Zeisel, 1982).

The relationship between dietary tryptophan, competing LNAA, and the synthesis of brain serotonin in chronic experiments is less clear than the outcomes of acute studies (Fernstrom, Fernstrom, Grubb, & Volk, 1985). When nitrogen intake is increased for long periods of time, induction of pathways for tryptophan catabolism causes a down-regulation of tryptophan plasma concentration. No such change occurs in the pathways for metabolism of the LNAA; hence, concentrations of LNAA increase directly with protein intake (Harper, Benevenga, & Wohlhueter, 1970; Peters & Harper, 1981). The Trp ratio of the LBW infants decreased with increased nitrogen intake, the decrease being due to large increases in LNAA with little or no change in tryptophan. Whether human brain tryptophan and serotonin metabolism change in parallel with chronic changes in the plasma Trp ratio requires further study. Although AS% is inversely related to the Trp ratio, the effects of the tryptophan cannot be separated from the effects of correlated variables such as nitrogen intake and protein storage or other unmeasured variables.

The data obtained in these studies of LBW infants fed different, but not unusual, amounts of protein and energy support the general hypothesis that nutrition and behavior are interactive. Whether the noradrenergic system is activated and/or whether the serotonergic system is suppressed by nutrient intake will take additional studies and additional measurements, including direct measurements of neurotransmitter activity, and whether any changes in these systems will prove to be of general importance also remains to be determined.

The optimal feeding strategy for the LBW infant remains controversial. Using today's feeding regimens it is possible to achieve a wide range of differences in the rate and composition of weight gain (Kashyap et al., 1994). Rapid growth requires relatively high protein intakes, and there is suggestive evidence that protein-rich formulas lead to superior neurobehavioral outcomes at 18 months (Lucas et al., 1990). But the same observers have reported that human milk feeding (with unspecified but probably lower protein content) is associated with higher 7–8 year IQ (Lucas, Morley, Cole, Lister, & Leeson-Payne, 1992). The value of protein supplementation has not yet been defined. However, at this time it seems clear that alterations in the protein intake of healthy growing LBW infants are associated with subtle but pervasive effects on neonatal physiology and behavior. The fact that differences in biochemistry and behavior occur during a time of active brain development suggests the stakes may be high.

What parallels might exist between postnatal, enteral feeding of the low-birth-weight infant and transplacental feeding of the fetus in utero? First, it is known that the transfer of nutrients across the placenta involves at least some of the same mechanisms as the transfer of nutrients across the blood–brain barrier. Second, as described elsewhere in this volume, there is emerging evidence that differences in fetal nutrition and growth are associated with alterations in the distribution of fetal behavioral states. Nutritional therapies for the undergrown fetus, which are now under study in experimental animals, may prove to be effective in human gestations. If this occurs, monitoring of behavioral variables should prove useful in tracking the fetal response to treatment. Fetal diagnosis is progressing at an extraordinarily rapid rate. As techniques for assessment of fetal growth and behavior improve, it is likely that a better understanding of the interactions of nutrition and behavior will be needed.

SUMMARY AND SPECULATION

A number of biochemical and physiological variables of the developing human appear to be influenced by relatively subtle differences in quality or quantity of nutritional intake. Although diet effects are small, they involve basic physiological and behavioral variables and they occur for substantial periods of time while the brain of infant is growing and differentiating. Today, despite careful attention from obstetricians and pediatricians, fetal and neonatal growth often fails to meet expected standards, and when growth failure occurs, long-term morbidity increases. Whether small differences in blood biochemistry and behavior due to variations in food intake, such as those described in this chapter, are associated with meaningful differences in subsequent health is not known. However, the fact that differences in weight at birth are associated with differences in such basic indices of adult health as arterial blood pressure, body weight, and cardiovascular morbidity suggests that nutritional experience during early life may be an important variable in determining adult health and behavior. Preliminary studies suggest that therapy for intrauterine growth failure may someday be practical. Perhaps fetal behavior will provide the diagnostic information required to evaluate fetal growth and the response of the fetus to nutritional interventions. Clearly, from both a theoretical and an experimental perspective there is much important work to be done in the interaction of perinatal nutrition and behavior.

ACKNOWLEDGMENT

This work was supported by U.S. Public Health Service grants HD 13020, HD 27564, RR00645, and HD 13063.

REFERENCES

Astrup, A., Buemann, B., Christensen, N., & Madsen, J. (1992). 24-hour energy expenditure in postobese women consuming a high-carbohydrate diet. *American Journal of Physiology, 262*, E282–E288.

Bakalian, M. J., & Fernstrom, J. D. (1990). Effects of 1-tryptophan and other amino acids on electroencephalographic sleep in the rat. *Brain Research, 528*, 300–307.

Barker, D. J. P., Osmund, C., Golding, J., Kuh, D., & Wadsworth, M. E. J. (1989). Growth in utero, blood pressure in childhood and adult life and mortality from cardiovascular disease. *British Medical Journal, 298*, 564–567.

Catzeflis, C., Schutz, Y., Micheki, J. L., Welsch, C., Arnaud, M. J., & Jequier, E. (1988). Whole body protein synthesis and energy expenditure in very low birth weight infants. *Pediatric Research, 19*, 679–687.

Danguir, J., & Nicholaidis, S. (1980). Intravenous infusions of nutrients and sleep in the rat: An ischymetric sleep regulation hypothesis. *American Physiology, 238*, E307–E312.7.

Drucker-Colin, R. (1979). Protein molecules and the regulation of REM sleep: Possible implications for function. *The functions of sleep* (pp. 99–111). New York: Academic Press.

Drucker-Colin, R., Spanis, C. W., Cotman, C. W., & McGaugh, J. L. (1977). Changes in protein levels in perfusates of freely moving cats: Relation to behavioral state. *Science, 187*, 963–965.

Fernstrom, J. D., Fernstrom, M. H., Grubb, P. E., Volk, E. A. (1985). Absence of chronic effects of dietary protein content on brain tryptophan concentrations in rats. *Journal of Nutrition, 115,* 1337–1344.

Fernstrom, J. D., & Wurtman, R. J. (1971). Brain serotonin content: Physiological dependence on plasma tryptophan levels. *Science, 173,* 149–152.

Fernstrom, J. D., & Wurtman, R. J. (1972). Brain serotonin content: Physiological regulation by plasma neutral amino acids. *Science, 178,* 414–416.

Gibson, C. J., Wurtman, R. J. (1978). Physiological control of brain norepinephrine synthesis by brain tyrosine concentration. *Life Sciences, 22,* 1399–1406.

Goldman, H. I., Goldman, J. S., Kaufman, I., & Liebman, O. B. (1974). Late effects of early protein intake on low birthweight infants. *Journal of Pediatrics, 85,* 764–769.

Harper, A. E., Benevenga, N. J., Wohlhueter, R. M. (1970). Effects of ingestion of disproportionate amounts of amino acids. *Physiological Reviews, 50,* 428–558.

Harper, R. M., Hoppenbrouwers, T., Sterman, M. B., McGinty, D. J., & Hodgeman, J. (1976). Polygraphic studies of normal infants during the first six months of life. I. Heart rate and variability as a function of state. *Pediatric Research, 10,* 945–951.

Jouvet, M. (1984). Indolamines and sleep-inducing factors. *Experimental Brain Research, Suppl. 8,* 81–94.

Kashyap, S., Forsyth, M., Zucker, C., Ramakrishnan, R., Dell, R. B., & Heird, W. C. (1986). Effects of varying protein and energy intakes on growth and metabolic response in low birth weight infants. *Journal of Pediatrics, 108,* 955–963.

Kashyap, S., Schulze, K., Forsyth, M., Zucker, C., Dell, R., Ramakrishnan, R., & Heird, W. C. (1988). Growth, nutrient retention, and metabolic response in low birth weight infants fed varying intakes of protein and energy. *Journal of Pediatrics, 113,* 713–721.

Kashyap, S., Schulze, K., Forsyth, M., Zucker, C., Dell, R., Ramakrishnan, R., & Heird, W. C. (1990). Growth, nutrient retention, and metabolic response of low birth weight infants fed supplemented and unsupplemented human milk. *American Journal of Nutrition, 52,* 254–262.

Kashyap, S., Schulze, K. F., Ramakrishnan, R., Dell, R. B., & Heird, W. C. (1994). Evaluation of a mathematical model for predicting the relationship between protein and energy intakes of low birth weight infants and the rate and composition of weight gain. *Pediatric Research, 35,* 704–712.

Korten, J. B., & Haddad, G. (1989). Respiratory waveform pattern recognition using digital techniques. *Computers in Biology and Medicine, 19,* 207–217.

Lucas, A., Morley, R., Cole, T. J., Gore, S. M., Lucas, P. J., Crowley, P., Pearse, R., Boon, A. J., & Powell, R. (1990). Early diet in preterm babies and developmental outcome status at 18 months. *Lancet, 335,* 1477–1481.

Lucas, A., Morley, R., Cole, T. J., Lister, G., & Leeson-Payne, C. (1992). Breast milk and subsequent intelligence quotient in children born preterm. *Lancet, 339,* 261–264.

MacFadyen, U. M., Oswald, I., & Lewis, S. A. (1973). Starvation and human slow-wave sleep. *Journal of Applied Physiology, 35* (3), 391–394.

Oswald, I. (1969). Human brain protein, drugs and dreams. *Nature, 223,* 893–897.

Pegram, V., Hammond, D., & Bridgers, W. (1973). The effects of protein synthesis inhibition on sleep in mice. *Behavioral Biology, 9,* 377–382.

Peters, J. C., & Harper, A. E. (1981). Protein and energy consumption, plasma amino acid ratio, and brain neurotransmitter concentrations. *Physiology & Behavior, 27,* 287–298.

Roffwarg, H. P., Muzio, J. N., & Dement, W. C. (1966). Ontogenetic development of the human sleep-dream cycle. *Science, 152,* 604–619.

Sahni, R., Schulze, K., Stefanski, M., Fifer, W., & Myers, M. (in press). Methodological issues in coding sleep states in immature infants *Developmental Psychobiology.*

Sakaguchi, T., Arase, K., Fisler, J. S., & Bray, G. (1988). Effect of starvation and food intake on sympathetic activity. *American Journal of Physiology, 255,* R284–R288.

Schulze, K., Kashyap, S., & Ramakrishnan, R. (1993). The cardiorespiratory costs of growth. *Journal Developmental Physiology. 19,* 85–93.

Schulze, K., Kashyap, S., Sahni, R., Fifer, W., & Myers, M. (in press). Diet, sleep and the developing autonomic nervous system. *Journal of Developmental Physiology.*

Schulze, K. F., Stefanski, M., Masterson, J., Spinnazola, R., Ramakrishnan R., Dell, R. B., & Heird, W. C. (1987). Energy expenditure, energy balance, and composition of weight gain in low birth weight infants fed diets of different protein and energy content. *Journal of Pediatrics, 110,* 753–759.

Somers, V. K., Dyken, M. E., Mark, A. L., & Abboud, F. M. (1993). Sympathetic nerve activity during sleep in normal subjects. *New England Journal of Medicine, 328,* 303–307.

Stefanski, M., Schulze, K. F., Bateman, D., Kairam, R., Pedley, T., Masterson, J., & James, L. S. (1984). A scoring system for states of sleep and wakefulness in term and preterm infants. *Pediatric Research, 18,* 58–63.

Uauy, R. D., Birch, D. G., Birth, E. E., Tyson, J. E., & Hoffman, D. R. (1990). Effect of dietary omega-3 fatty acids on retinal function of very low birth weight neonates. *Pediatric Research, 28,* 485–492.

Yogman, M. W., & Zeisel, S. H. (1982). Diet and sleep patterns in newborn infants. *New England Journal of Medicine, 309*(19), 1147–1149.

Young, J. B., Rosa, R. M., & Landsberg, L. (1984). Dissociation of sympathetic nervous system and adrenal medullary responses. *American Journal of Physiology, 247,* E35–E40.

Young, J. B., & Landsberg, L. (1977). Stimulation of sympathetic nervous system during sucrose feeding. *Nature, 269,* 615–617.

Part IV

MOTOR AND SENSORY DEVELOPMENT OF THE FETUS

10

Oscillation and Chaos in Fetal Motor Activity

Steven S. Robertson
Leigh Foster Bacher
Cornell University

In the human fetus and neonate, there is now substantial evidence for the existence of cyclic fluctuations in spontaneous motor activity (CM, Fig. 10.1), comprised of general movements of the limbs, trunk, and head, on a time scale of minutes (Robertson, 1990). The cyclic fluctuations emerge before midgestation, perhaps as early as the 12th postmenstrual week (de Vries, Visser, & Prechtl, 1982). The quantitative properties of CM are remarkably stable during the second half of gestation, and the physiologic changes at birth do not appear to induce changes in CM (Robertson, 1985, 1987). However, fetal CM is influenced by maternal diabetes (Robertson & Dierker, 1986; Robertson, Klugewicz, & Lalley, 1992), yet returns to normal by the end of gestation and remains normal after birth, even in those infants with clinical evidence of having been exposed to an abnormal metabolic environment in utero (Robertson, 1988). CM persists for at least the first 4 postnatal months; during active sleep it remains nearly identical to fetal CM. However, awake CM becomes somewhat weaker and less predictable, as more complex fluctuations emerge at higher frequencies (Robertson, 1993b).

Quantitatively similar oscillations in spontaneous motor activity exist in the fetal rat (Smotherman, Robinson, & Robertson, 1988). Experiments with the fetal rat indicate that there is more than one source of CM in the motor system, and that the multiple sources have different preferred frequencies (Robertson & Smotherman, 1990a). Data from the human neonate are at least consistent with this multisource hypothesis (Robertson, 1993a). There is also preliminary evidence from the human infant and fetal rat that the mechanism underlying CM is governed by chaotic dynamics

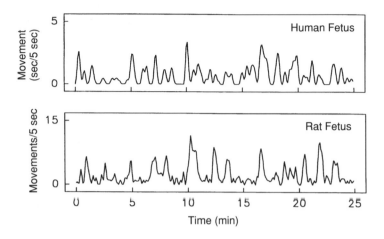

FIG. 10.1.   Cyclic fetal motor activity (CM). Top: The total duration of spontaneous fetal movement in successive 5-sec intervals in a human fetus at 240 postmenstrual days of gestation. Fetal movement was detected by two strain gauges on the mother's abdomen. The pregnancy was complicated by maternal diabetes (class C). The fetus was subsequently born without complications at 270 days of gestation but was large for gestational age with a birth weight of 4.41 kg. Bottom: The number of movements observed in successive 5-sec intervals in a rat fetus on day 20 of gestation. The fetus was observed undisturbed in a warm saline bath following delivery from the uterus and amniotic sac, with fetal-placental-uterine connections intact (Smotherman et al., 1988). Both time series were smoothed with a 15-sec moving average.

(Robertson, Cohen, & Mayer-Kress, 1993; Robertson & Smotherman, 1990b).

The functional significance of CM has only begun to be studied. However, new evidence in human infants suggests that CM may regulate perceptual exploration of the postnatal environment. When 2- to 3-month old infants look at interesting pictures, there is an inverse relationship between the rates of change of movement and visual fixation; infants can move and look at the same time, but changes in one entail opposite adjustments in the other (Robertson & Bacher, 1992). Intrinsic fluctuations in motor activity may both permit attention to visual information in the environment and trigger shifts in the infant's focus of attention. Additional evidence indicates that the spectral properties of CM change in response to social stimulation in ways that might facilitate interaction with a caregiver (Lalley, 1993).

WHY STUDY CM?

Since CM was first described in the human fetus and neonate (Robertson, 1982; Robertson, Dierker, Sorokin, & Rosen, 1982), it has been found to be a robust property of early neurobehavioral organization. Similar temporal patterns have been found in other vertebrate species as well (Corner, 1977; Hamburger, Wenger, & Oppenheim, 1966; Smotherman et al., 1988). Any explanation of spontaneous activity must be able to account for these intrinsic temporal patterns.

There are, in addition, several quite specific reasons to study CM. First, to the extent that CM is a robust property of early behavioral organization, it is likely to be an important factor in adaptive interactions with the environment. It is therefore essential that we begin to understand precisely how CM constrains or regulates such interactions. Understanding the functional significance of CM may also provide insights into the costs or benefits of spontaneous fluctuations in other biological systems. In addition, the underlying mechanism in CM may be a very common one, so that understanding it would have broader significance.

Finally, the potential theoretical consequences of building a successful dynamical model of CM are also significant. The field of dynamics, which includes the study of natural phenomena and their time dependence, the theory of change based on differential equations and geometry, and the experimental modeling of dynamical systems, is concerned with phenomena precisely like CM. The field is not new (Abraham & Shaw, 1982), but it has recently been applied to the organization and development of behavior (Kelso, Mandell, & Shlesinger, 1988; Smith & Thelen, 1993). The promise of dynamical systems theory lies in the way its powerful concepts are integrated in a coherent theory of change and stability, which may lead to a deeper understanding of behavior and development. The test of this theoretical perspective must go beyond metaphorical arguments, however, and deal with real data. The study of CM provides an excellent opportunity to test hypotheses that are central to the success of dynamical systems theory.

Dynamical systems theory may also help explain the core characteristics of the fluctuations in spontaneous motor activity that constitute CM: their persistence and their irregularity. Both may be equally fundamental properties of the same mechanism. That is, it may not be necessary to postulate stochastic events or noisy environments as sources of the irregularity distinct from the regularity. The study of CM dynamics may also lead to new insights into its possible functional significance: What might be the costs or benefits of bounded unpredictability built into the mechanism controlling spontaneous motor activity?

In this chapter we describe some of the basic spectral properties of CM in the fetal sheep and the influence that spontaneous uterine activity appears to have on CM. We also present some preliminary evidence that in the fetal sheep, as in the human and rat, CM is governed by chaotic dynamics. The results are some of the initial findings from a program project examining neurobehavioral development in the fetal sheep, being done in collaboration with Peter Nathanielsz (this volume), and with William Smotherman and Scott Robinson (this volume).

WHY STUDY CM IN THE FETAL SHEEP?

There are some important reasons to study CM in the fetal sheep.

1. The fetal sheep is a standard animal model of human fetal and perinatal physiology, and important information relevant to understanding CM may already be known.
2. It is possible to manipulate the fetal environment experimentally.
3. It is also possible to directly measure a large number of maternal and fetal variables, including electromyographic (EMG) activity in multiple limb muscles.
4. Finally, continuous data acquisition is possible over substantial periods during gestation.

The fourth point is especially important. One of the biggest practical barriers to the quantitative application of dynamical systems theory to behavior is the requirement for large amounts of low-noise, high-resolution data (Robertson et al., 1993). The chronic instrumentation of the fetal sheep provides continuous measurement of motor activity, which in turn yields time series of a length sufficient to analyze important dynamic properties of the mechanism generating CM.

METHODOLOGICAL OVERVIEW

The primary data in the study of CM are time series of motor activity. In the human fetus, motor activity has been measured using the differential output of two strain gauges on the mother's abdomen, above the upper and lower portions of the fetal body. In the human infant, motor activity is measured directly by movement sensors. In the fetal rat, motor activity has been measured by the direct observation of behavior using techniques perfected by Smotherman and Robinson (Smotherman, Richards, & Robinson, 1984).

In the sheep fetus, motor activity is measured by recording EMG from flexor (brachialis) and extensor (triceps) muscles in the forelimbs, and flexor (tibialis anterior) and extensor (gastrocnemius) muscles in the hindlimbs. The rectified EMG signals are averaged over 1-sec intervals and digitized on-line (Fig. 10.2). Depending on the specific hypothesis being tested, analysis focuses on EMG activity recorded from individual muscles,

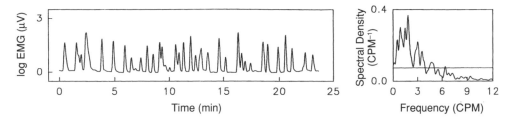

FIG. 10.2. Pooled limb EMG time series and corresponding spectrum from a fetal sheep studied at 130 days of gestation. The time series in this illustration has been smoothed with a 15 sec moving average; unsmoothed data were used to compute the spectrum. The horizontal line in the spectrum is the upper 99% confidence limit of the spectral estimates for a white noise process. The dominant frequency of oscillation in this sample of pooled EMG activity, estimated by the location of the dominant peak in the spectrum, is 1.86 cycles/min.

or EMG activity pooled from different muscles. EMG activity from individual muscles is pooled by computing the unweighted average of the signals on a second-by-second basis.

As in previous work on CM (e.g., Robertson, 1985), each time series of motor activity is spectral analyzed (after removing linear and very slow curvilinear trends) to identify specific cyclic patterns and quantify their basic properties. In addition to spectral analysis, new methods are being employed that use the information in the movement time series to estimate the dynamic properties of the system responsible for CM (Robertson et al., 1993). These techniques are described in subsequent sections.

EXISTENCE OF CM IN THE FETAL SHEEP

Clearly the first question that must be addressed in the fetal sheep is whether there is any evidence for the existence of cyclic organization in spontaneous motor activity. Pooled EMG activity from flexor and extensor muscles in the forelimbs and hindlimbs was examined first because the pooled data are closest to the behavioral level at which CM has previously been studied. Spectral analysis (Fig. 10.2) of 10–24 min of EMG data from six fetuses studied between 119 and 136 days of gestation revealed strong cyclic organization in every EMG time series. The rate of oscillation in pooled EMG activity, measured by the frequency of the dominant peak in the spectrum, appears to be somewhat faster in the fetal sheep (1.15 ± 0.33 cycles/min, mean $\pm$ SEM) than in the fetal rat (0.61 ± 0.09 cycles/min; Smotherman et al., 1988), $t(21) = 1.92$, $p = .07$, and the fetal human (0.42 ± 0.04 cycles/min; Robertson, 1987), $t(37) = 4.53$, $p<.01$. However, the small number of sheep fetuses for which data are currently available makes inferences about species differences risky. In any case, the data provide strong evidence for the existence of cyclic organization in pooled limb EMG activity in the fetal sheep that is qualitatively similar to results obtained from direct observation of fetal rat behavior and indirect recording of human fetal movement.

EFFECTS OF NONLABOR UTERINE CONTRACTIONS

The intrauterine environment is rich with varied forms of stimulation, and their effects on fetal behavior and development are of both scientific and clinical interest. A major source of mechanical stimulation of the fetus is the repeated contractions of uterine muscle, which occur long before labor begins in sheep (Harding, et al., 1982) as they do in humans (Braxton Hicks, 1872; Mulder & Visser, 1987). Various mechanical, physiologic, and neuroelectric changes associated with nonlabor contractions [also called contractures (Nathanielsz, et al., 1977) and type A contractions (Lye, Wlodek, & Challis, 1984)] have been documented in the fetal sheep. They include decreases in arterial oxygen tension and saturation, deformation of the chest wall, and the transition from low-voltage to high-voltage electrocortical activity (e.g., Harding & Poore, 1984; Jansen et al., 1979; Llanos, Court, Block, Germain, & Parer, 1986; Nathanielsz, Bailey, Poore, Thorburn, & Harding, 1980). Induced contractures also seem to accelerate the development of fetal electrocortical activity (Martel, Poore, Sadowsky, Cabalum, & Nathanielsz, 1990). Examining how CM responds to nonlabor contractions may lead to a better understanding of this robust feature of fetal behavioral organization and extend our knowledge of how the fetal central nervous system responds to the dynamic aspects of the intrauterine environment.

Our preliminary data have revealed systematic effects of spontaneous nonlabor contractions on fetal CM. Uterine EMG was sampled at 32 Hz, rectified, and averaged over 1-sec intervals. Contractures were defined as the sustained elevation (above baseline for 3 min or more) of the 15-sec moving average of this signal. In four fetuses studied between 119 and 131 days of gestation, extended periods of fetal motor activity were identified during which there was a spontaneous uterine contracture. The contractures lasted 6–9 min, and were preceded by 8–15 min and followed by 7–12 min of fetal activity without uterine contractures. The pooled limb EMG time series were divided into three sections corresponding to before, during, and after the contracture and spectral analyzed (Fig. 10.3). The results revealed an increase in the dominant frequency of oscillation during the contracture in all four fetuses; the change in frequency ranged from 0.40 to 1.97 cycles/min. In each fetus, the dominant frequency of oscilla-

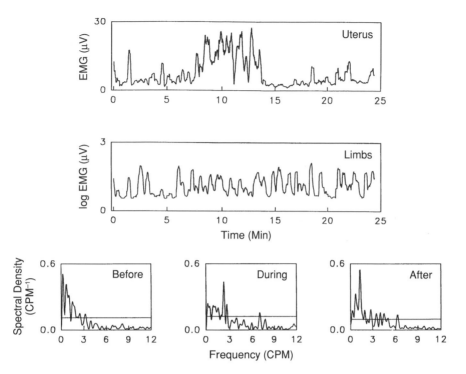

FIG. 10.3. Spontaneous uterine contracture and fetal CM at 119 days of gestation. Top: EMG activity from the body of the uterus. Center: Pooled limb EMG activity. In this illustration, the uterine and pooled limb EMG time series have been smoothed with a 15-sec moving average. Bottom: Pooled limb EMG spectra corresponding to before, during, and after the uterine contracture. The dominant peak in the spectrum shifts to a higher frequency during the contracture (from 0.26 to 2.23 cycles/min), and remains somewhat elevated (1.29 cycles/min) after the contracture. The spectra were computed from the unsmoothed EMG time series.

tion in pooled limb EMG activity after the contracture remained above the rate measured before the contracture (by 0.16 to 1.8 cycles/min). No systematic effects of contractures on the strength (measured by the height of the dominant peak in the spectrum) or irregularity (measured by the width of the dominant peak at half-maximum) of CM were found.

The mechanism by which nonlabor contractions influence the rate of oscillation in CM and the possible role of other documented neural and physiologic changes in the fetus during contractures remain to be investigated. However, the finding that only the rate of CM changed is consistent with the results of experiments designed to perturb CM in the fetal rat and human neonate. In the rat, spinal cord transection revealed that there is more than one source of CM, and that caudal sources have a higher preferred frequency than rostral sources (Robertson & Smotherman, 1990a).

The results of a perturbation experiment in human neonates (Robertson, 1993a) are consistent with this interpretation of the fetal rat data. If there are also multiple sources of CM in the fetal sheep, uterine contractures may accelerate most of them, selectively enhance (or attenuate) the influence of fast (or slow) sources, or alter the coupling between them. There was no evidence in these four fetuses that bursts of fetal motor activity were being directly triggered or otherwise entrained by fluctuations in uterine activity during the contractures.

Experimental induction of nonlabor uterine contractions will permit a more detailed analysis of the time constant in the transient acceleration of CM. Manipulation of the number or strength of nonlabor contractions may also provide some insight into any long-term consequences of spontaneous contractures on the prenatal development of CM, including its characteristic irregularity.

LOCAL VERSUS GLOBAL

In all of the previous research on the quantitative properties of CM, cyclicity has been studied in the pooled output of the motor system. In the human fetus (Robertson, 1982, 1985), motor activity has been detected by conformational changes in the mother's abdomen, which effectively integrates movements of the fetal head, trunk, and limbs. The human infant has been studied using movement sensors that also pool the activity of different parts of the body (Robertson, 1987, 1993b). Similarly, CM in the fetal rat has been studied by analyzing time series of total motor activity obtained by direct observation of the fetus (Smotherman et al., 1988). In the analyses reported earlier, EMG activity from individual limb muscles was combined as a way to estimate total motor activity in the fetal sheep.

A basic unanswered question about CM is whether the cyclicity is a property that emerges only at a global level that pools activity from many parts of the motor system, or whether it characterizes fluctuations in activity at a more local level as well. That is, the existence of global CM does not necessarily imply the existence of local CM, in either a mathematical or neurobehavioral sense. Analysis of the temporal organization of EMG activity from individual muscles in the forelimbs and hindlimbs of the fetal sheep is a straightforward first step in addressing the local–global question in the intact mammal.

Pooled limb EMG activity from the six sheep fetuses studied between 119 and 136 days of gestation was decomposed into the EMG activity of the brachialis, triceps, gastrocnemius, and tibialis muscles. Gastrocnemius and tibialis EMG recordings were not available in two of the fetuses.

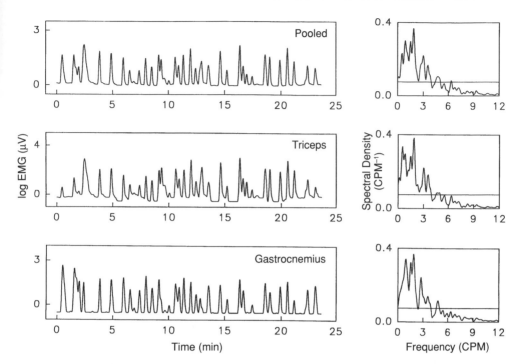

FIG. 10.4.   Limb EMG activity and corresponding spectra in a fetal sheep at 130 days of gestation. Top: Unweighted average of EMG activity recorded from the left brachialis, triceps, gastrocnemius, and tibialis, and the corresponding spectrum. Center: Triceps EMG activity and corresponding spectrum. Bottom: Gastrocnemius EMG activity and corresponding spectrum. The time series in this illustration were smoothed with a 15-sec moving average; all spectra were computed from the unsmoothed data.

Spectral analysis of the separate time series revealed cyclic organization in the EMG activity of the individual muscles (Fig. 10.4). The dominant frequency of oscillation was 1.40 ± 0.44 cycles/min (range 0.34–3.00) in brachialis EMG, 1.14 ± 0.33 (0.31–2.23) in triceps, 1.00 ± 0.38 (.37–1.87) in gastrocnemius, and 0.82 ± 0.24 (0.40–1.52) in tibialis. There was no evidence for systematic differences in the dominant frequency of oscillation between forelimbs and hindlimbs, nor between flexor and extensor muscles acting on the same joint.

These results demonstrate that CM in the fetal sheep does not emerge only at a global level that pools activity from many parts of the motor system, but exists at a more local level as well. This analysis does not address the short-term timing relations between individual contractions of different muscles. Rather, it is designed to reveal longer term temporal organization in the waves of activity over many minutes. However, the existence of such cyclic organization in the activity of individual muscles raises many questions that cannot be answered by the present data:

1. Does local CM reflect the distributed effects of a single oscillatory network? Data from the fetal rat (Robertson & Smotherman, 1990a) and chick embryo (Hamburger et al., 1966; Oppenheim, 1975; Provine & Rogers, 1977) are not consistent with a single localized source.
2. If oscillations arise at many locations in the fetal sheep motor system, how are they generated and do they influence each other? If they do interact, what is the mechanism by which they are coupled?
3. At what level is cyclic organization no longer apparent? For example, does cyclic organization characterize the firing pattern of the many separate motor units underlying the EMG activity recorded from individual muscles?

DYNAMIC PROPERTIES OF CM

Based on the results from numerous studies, including the results summarized earlier, the core properties of CM are clear. First, the fluctuations in spontaneous motor activity are sustained. Cyclic organization has been found at the level of individual muscle EMG and global behavior, in a number of species, during different developmental stages, and under at least some pathological conditions. The oscillations that define CM appear to be intrinsic to the developing motor system. Second, the oscillations are irregular, as can be easily seen in any time series of motor activity based on behavioral or EMG measurements.

The irregularity of CM poses a significant challenge in trying to understand the mechanism responsible for these ubiquitous fluctuations: Is the irregularity signal or noise? If it is signal, can we account for it with the same mechanism that may be generating the cyclicity itself? From work in other fields we now know that some relatively simple dynamical systems can produce highly irregular fluctuations, that is, chaos (Thompson & Stewart, 1986). Is there evidence for chaotic dynamics in CM? Is there evidence for structure in the fluctuations of spontaneous motor activity, and does the structure exhibit the characteristic features of chaos (Fraser & Swinney, 1986)?

The first step in answering these questions is to reconceptualize the goals of the data analysis. Rather than viewing the time series of motor activity as the object of study, we acknowledge that it is, in fact, a single-variable read-out from a system with potentially many degrees of free-

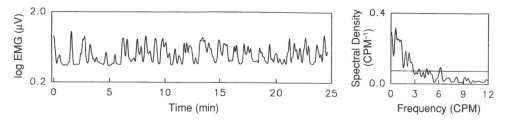

FIG. 10.5.   Gastrocnemius EMG activity and corresponding spectrum from a fetal sheep studied at 119 days of gestation. The time series was smoothed with a 15-sec moving average; the spectrum was computed from the unsmoothed data.

dom. If we knew (and could measure) the collection of variables that fully specify the state of the mechanism responsible for CM at any instant in time, we could examine the time-dependent relations among the changes in those variables directly. That is, we could study the dynamics of CM. For example, we could construct a state space in which the collection of variables are the coordinate axes. The temporal evolution of these state variables, represented as trajectories in the state space, could then be examined for evidence of structure. In particular, do the trajectories tend to flow through some regions but not others (are certain sequences of states observed, but not others)? If a perturbation deflects the trajectory, does it return to its previous course? That is, is there evidence for an attractor governing the dynamics of CM? If so, how complex is it? Is there evidence that the dynamics are chaotic? That is, do nearby trajectories diverge at an exponential rate, giving rise to the sensitive dependence on initial conditions that is the signature of chaotic dynamics? Evidence for chaotic dynamics underlying the fluctuations in spontaneous motor activity would mean that both the sustained oscillations and their irregularity might be equally fundamental properties of the mechanism responsible for CM.

But we do not know the state variables for CM. Therefore, it is necessary to use techniques developed in other fields for reconstructing a phase portrait (the trajectories followed by a system in its state space) from a single-variable readout of the system, such as motor activity (Packard, Crutchfield, Farmer, & Shaw, 1980; Takens, 1981). The techniques are based on the fact that the readout, under certain conditions, will contain useful information about the underlying dynamics. Detailed discussion of these methods and their application to human CM can be found in Robertson et al. (1993). In the following sections, these methods are used to analyze gastrocnemius EMG activity from a sheep fetus studied at 119 days of gestation (Fig. 10.5) for evidence of chaotic dynamics. Programs written by Schaffer and his colleagues (Schaffer, Truty, & Fulmer, 1990) were used to perform the calculations reported in the following sections.

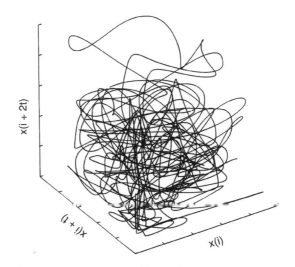

FIG. 10.6.   Phase portrait reconstructed in three dimensions from the time series in Fig. 10.5 using Takens' (1981) method with a time delay of t = 15 sec. For this illustration, successive points along the trajectory have been connected using a cubic spline method. The $x(i+2t)$ axis is tilted 30 degrees up from the plane of the paper.

The phase portrait in Fig. 10.6 was reconstructed from the time series in Fig. 10.5 using Takens' (1981) method of delays. In this method, the time series is plotted against multiple, lagged versions of itself. More formally, vectors $\mathbf{y}(i)$ are constructed whose components are the successive values of the time series $x(i)$ separated by a time delay, t, so that $\mathbf{y}(i) = [x(i), x(i+t), x(i+2t), \ldots, x(i+2mt)]$, where m is the dimension of the manifold within which the unknown attractor exists. Thus, the vectors $\mathbf{y}(i)$ define points in a $(2m+1)$-dimensional embedding space where the axes are measurements of the time series separated by integer multiples of the delay t. Points in the reconstructed phase portrait therefore represent the recent history of values in the time series of motor activity. The sequence of points in the reconstructed phase portrait, $\mathbf{y}(i)$, $\mathbf{y}(i+1)$, $\ldots$, defines a trajectory. Takens proved that some important properties of the real attractor are preserved in the reconstructed phase portrait if (among other things) the reconstruction is done in enough dimensions, that is, if enough lagged versions of the time series are used. For the illustration in Fig. 10.6, the reconstruction was done in only three dimensions: Each point in the time series was plotted against the two subsequent points in the series separated by a delay of t = 15 sec. The complexity of the phase portrait in this illustration is due, in part, to the fact that the dimension of the embedding space is too low (see later discussion). In a sense, we are looking at a shadow of the attractor in which higher dimensions are collapsed and overlapping.

ATTRACTOR DIMENSION

One important property of an attractor, and a measure of its geometric complexity, is its dimension. For example, a closed loop representing perfectly periodic behavior (limit cycle) has a dimension of 1, and a torus representing doubly periodic behavior has a dimension of 2. Chaotic attractors often, but not always (Grebogi, Ott, Pelikan, & Yorke, 1984), have a noninteger dimension. The dimension of an unknown attractor can be estimated by analyzing the reconstructed phase portrait.

Because the dimension of the unknown attractor is not known when the analysis begins, the phase portrait is reconstructed in successively higher dimensional embedding spaces and an estimate of the attractor's dimension is computed at each step. A common method of computing the estimate, used here, was developed by Grassberger and Procaccia (1983). This procedure is continued until the estimates stabilize or there are insufficient data to perform the calculations. That is, if the attractor has a finite and relatively small dimension, the estimates will increase until the attractor has been disentangled, and then level off. In this example, the estimated dimension of the attractor levels off at about 3.2 (the plateau formed by the last four estimates in Fig. 10.7). If the time series was just

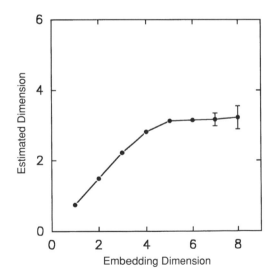

FIG. 10.7.   Estimated dimension of CM attractor based on the data in Fig. 10.5. The time series was filtered to remove high frequency fluctuations (above 12 cycles/min) and embedded in 1–8 dimensions using Takens' (1981) method with a delay of 15 sec. At each step, Grassberger and Procaccia's (1983) method was used to estimate the dimension of the reconstructed phase portrait. The error bars are 95% confidence limits.

noise, the estimated dimension of the reconstructed phase portrait would continue to climb.

The convergence of the dimension estimates to a stable value is evidence for dynamic structure underlying the irregularity in CM. A finite dimension for the reconstructed phase portrait is evidence that the fluctuations in spontaneous activity are not simply due to noise. Furthermore, the estimated dimension of the CM attractor puts a lower bound on the number of state variables that will be needed to model the dynamics on the attractor (Farmer, Ott, & Yorke, 1983). Finally, the relatively low dimension suggests that the complex and irregular fluctuations in spontaneous motor activity in the fetal sheep, as in the fetal rat and human infant, are generated by a mechanism with relatively few effective degrees of freedom in a motor system with potentially very many degrees of freedom.

SENSITIVITY TO INITIAL CONDITIONS

A defining property of chaotic attractors is the exponential divergence of nearby trajectories, which accounts for the sensitivity to initial conditions and the long-term unpredictability of chaotic systems (Guckenheimer, 1982; Wolf, Swift, Swinney, & Vastano, 1985). The divergence (and convergence) of nearby trajectories is quantified by Lyapunov exponents, for which there are a number of equivalent definitions. One of the more intuitive (Wolf et al., 1985) defines the largest Lyapunov exponent, λ_1, as the rate at which an infinitesimal volume of states expands in the direction of greatest divergence. It is common to take $\lambda_1 > 0$ as the definition of chaos (Farmer et al., 1983).

Wolf's algorithm (Wolf et al., 1985) was used to estimate λ_1 from the data in Fig. 10.5. The algorithm takes the nearest neighbor to the initial point in the reconstructed state space and calculates the increase in separation between them during a fixed evolution time. This process is repeated until the end of the data set, and the time average of the values of $\log_2 D'/D$ where D and D' are the initial and final separations of the neighboring points in each step, is used to estimate λ_1. Because short evolution times overestimate λ_1 and long times underestimate λ_1, the calculation is repeated for a range of evolution times spanning the average recurrence time (estimated by the dominant peak in the spectrum), and evidence of a plateau is sought.

Figure 10.8 shows the exponential rate of divergence of nearby trajectories in the phase portrait reconstructed from the data in Fig. 10.5. The phase portrait was reconstructed in a 5-dimensional embedding space, which corresponds to the beginning of the plateau in Fig. 10.7. For evolution times around 100 sec, which is the average cycle time of EMG activity in

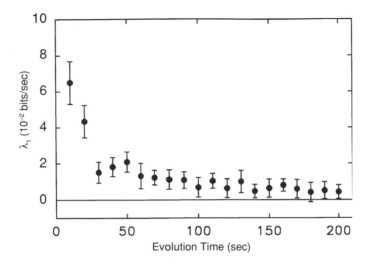

FIG. 10.8.   Estimated rate of divergence of nearby trajectories (largest Lyapunov exponent, λ_1) in a phase portrait reconstructed from the data in Fig. 10.5 using Takens' (1981) method with an embedding dimension of 5 and a time delay of 15 sec. Estimates of λ_1 were computed using Wolf's method (Wolf et al., 1985) for evolution times of 10–200 sec. The error bars are 95% confidence limits.

this fetus (see spectrum in Fig. 10.5), the estimated rate of divergence is relatively stable and positive, a sign that chaotic dynamics govern the fluctuations in CM.

IMPLICATIONS OF CHAOS

If confirmed by analyses of other suitable data sets in the fetal sheep, these results would provide some justification for considering the cyclic organization in fetal EMG activity and its irregularity as properties of the same mechanism. Thus it may not be necessary (or wise) to search for a mechanism capable of generating sustained oscillations on a time scale characteristic of CM and separate sources of noise or instability to account for the irregularity of CM.

These results also raise some interesting questions about the possible functional significance of CM. Are there any special consequences, beneficial or adverse, of built-in irregularity in the system controlling spontaneous fetal motor activity? In postnatal animals, the literature on foraging and search behavior has identified some advantages to elements of randomness (Bell, 1991; Hoffman, 1983). A system controlled by chaotic dynamics exhibits output that shares some of the irregularity, unpredictability, and nonrepeating characteristics of a random process.

Some have therefore speculated about the benefits of chaotic dynamics in search behavior (Auslander, Guckenheimer, & Oster, 1978; Conrad, 1986; Robertson, 1993b).

However, it is unclear whether these speculations have any relevance to the functional significance (if any) of chaotic dynamics in fetal CM. If fetal CM has important consequences, it may be on neuromuscular development where the intrinsic fluctuations could balance the benefits of activity and inactivity (Robertson, 1989). The nonrepeating characteristic of chaotic fluctuations might have additional consequences that are beneficial. Of course, there may be no important prenatal consequences of fetal CM. For that matter, the irregular oscillations in spontaneous fetal activity might actually have negative consequences: CM might, for example, interfere with fetal learning (Smotherman & Fifer, this volume). The possible consequences of irregular fluctuations in spontaneous fetal activity, whether they are beneficial, neutral, or adverse, are empirical questions of great theoretical interest that must be addressed by future research on CM.

SUMMARY

The results to date have confirmed the existence of CM in the fetal sheep, with spectral properties similar to CM found in the human and rat fetus. The similarity is found in spite of the different operational definitions of motor activity that have been used in studies of the three species. In addition, preliminary evidence indicates that nonlabor contractions in the sheep are associated with a transient acceleration in fetal CM. Thus the fetal sheep, a standard model of human prenatal physiology, may also be a useful animal model in which to study the intrinsic temporal organization of spontaneous behavior and how it responds to the dynamic aspects of the intrauterine environment.

Analysis of EMG activity from individual limb muscles in the fetal sheep has already yielded two important findings. First, the oscillations in spontaneous activity do not emerge only at the global level of pooled behavior. The characteristic cyclicity appears to be a local property in the developing motor system. This puts speculation about the distributed nature of CM in the human and rat fetus on a more substantial empirical foundation.

EMG time series from the fetal sheep have also provided an excellent opportunity to take the behavioral application of dynamical systems theory beyond metaphorical discussion. The calculations carried out to date have yielded evidence for chaotic dynamics underlying the fluctuations in spontaneous activity. This, in turn, raises the possibility of a unified explanation for both the cyclicity and its irregularity. It also raises new questions about the functional consequences of built-in unpredictability in the system controlling general activity.

FUTURE DIRECTIONS

We believe there are four classes of questions (Tinbergen, 1963) that should be addressed in trying to understand why spontaneous motor activity in the fetus and infant exhibits irregular cyclic organization. These are questions that have motivated and guided the research program to date (including studies of human, rat, and sheep), and will continue to do so in the future.

Mechanism.   What causes CM, and what intrinsic and extrinsic factors influence its expression? One approach is to search for the neural substrate of CM in animal models. Another approach is to examine pathological conditions in humans, such as pregnancy complicated by maternal diabetes. Yet another approach is to attempt to build more formal, perhaps mathematical, models of CM. This approach may benefit the most from the application of dynamical systems theory. It is the hope that these various approaches to uncovering the mechanism of CM will converge on the same explanation.

Function.   What are the consequences, if any, of irregular cyclic organization in spontaneous motor activity? Are the consequences limited to prenatal neuromuscular development, or do they extend to postnatal life by regulating interactions with the physical and social environment? Are the consequences beneficial, neutral, or adverse? How does this robust aspect of intrinsic behavioral organization influence behavioral and psychological development, and do disruptions in CM constitute a developmental risk? Because it appears that the organization of behavior may be a more sensitive measure of fetal status than its amount (Prechtl, 1990), perhaps CM could provide additional useful information in assessing the condition of the fetal central nervous system.

Development.   What is the ontogenetic history and subsequent fate of CM in humans and other animals? Does it characterize the earliest activity of the embryo, or is it the result of emerging communication and coupling between active elements in the developing motor system? Does CM persist beyond early infancy as more coordinated and intentional behavior comes to dominate spontaneous activity? Does the mechanism responsible for CM continue to influence activity in other systems (e.g., perceptual and cognitive), even if behavioral expression of cyclicity is limited?

Evolution. Most of us never really address the question of the evolutionary origins of the behavioral organization that we study. The study of CM is likely to be no exception. However, there is mounting evidence that CM exists in a number of mammalian species, so that comparative (if not evolutionary) analyses will be possible. In any case, it will be important to heed the warnings of Gould and Lewontin (1979) and not take the widespread existence of CM as evidence of its adaptive value; the possible adaptive value of CM is an empirical question. Furthermore, if CM turns out to have important consequences, it must not be assumed that those consequences played a role in the evolution of CM; that, too, is an empirical question.

REFERENCES

Abraham, R. H., & Shaw, C. D. (1982). *Dynamics—The geometry of behavior. Part one: Periodic behavior.* Santa Cruz, CA: Aerial Press.

Auslander, D., Guckenheimer, J., & Oster, G. (1978). Random evolutionarily stable strategies. *Journal of Theoretical Population Biology, 13,* 276–293.

Bell, W. J. (1991). *Searching behaviour: The behavioural ecology of finding resources.* London: Chapman and Hall.

Braxton Hicks, J. (1872). On the contractions of the uterus throughout pregnancy: Their physiological effects and their value in the diagnosis of pregnancy. *Transactions of the Obstetrical Society of London, 13,* 216–231.

Conrad, M. (1986). What is the use of chaos? In A. V. Holden (Ed.), *Chaos* (pp. 3–14). Princeton, NJ: Princeton University Press.

Corner, M. A. (1977). Sleep and the beginnings of behavior in the animal kingdom—Studies of ultradian motility cycles in early life. *Progress in Neurobiology, 8,* 279–295.

de Vries, J. I. P., Visser, G. H. A., & Prechtl, H. F. R. (1982). The emergence of fetal behaviour. I. Qualitative aspects. *Early Human Development, 7,* 301–322.

Farmer, J. D., Ott, E., & Yorke, J. A. (1983). The dimension of chaotic attractors. *Physica, 7D,* 153–180.

Fraser, A. M., & Swinney, H. L. (1986). Independent coordinates for strange attractors from mutual information. *Physical Review A, 33,* 1134–1140.

Gould, S. J., & Lewontin, R. C. (1979). The spandrels of San Marco and the Panglossian paradigm: A critique of the adaptationist programme. *Proceedings of the Royal Society of London, B205,* 581–598.

Grassberger, P., & Procaccia, I. (1983). Characterization of strange attractors. *Physical Review Letters, 50,* 346–349.

Grebogi, C., Ott, E., Pelikan, S., & Yorke, J. A. (1984). Strange attractors that are not chaotic. *Physica, 13D,* 261–268.

Guckenheimer, J. (1982). Noise in chaotic systems. *Nature, 298,* 358–361.

Hamburger, V., Wenger, E., & Oppenheim, R. (1966). Motility in the chick embryo in the absence of sensory input. *Journal of Experimental Zoology, 162,* 133–160.

Harding, R., & Poore, E. R. (1984). The effects of myometrial activity on fetal thoracic dimensions and uterine blood flow during late gestation in the sheep. *Biology of the Neonate, 45,* 244–251.

Harding, R., Poore, E. R., Bailey, A., Thorburn, G. D., Jansen, C. A. M., & Nathanielsz, P. W. (1982). Electromyographic activity of the nonpregnant and pregnant sheep uterus. *American Journal of Obstetrics and Gynecology, 142,* 448–457.

Hoffmann, G. (1983). The random elements in the systematic search behavior of the desert isopod *Hemilepistus reaumuri. Behavioral Ecology and Sociobiology, 13,* 81–92.

Jansen, C. A. M, Krane, E. J., Thomas, A. L., Beck, N. F. G., Lowe, K. C., Joyce, P., Parr, M., & Nathanielsz, P. W. (1979). Continuous variability of fetal PO_2 in the chronically catheterized fetal sheep. *American Journal of Obstetrics and Gynecology, 134,* 776–783.

Kelso, J. A. S., Mandell, A. J., & Shlesinger, M. F. (Eds.). (1988). *Dynamic patterns in complex systems.* Singapore: World Scientific.

Lalley, N. M. (1993, March). *Capturing cyclic motility with rhythmic stimulation.* Paper presented at the Society for Research in Child Development, New Orleans, LA.

Llanos, A. J., Court, D. J., Block, B. S., Germain, A. M., & Parer, J. T. (1986). Fetal cardiorespiratory changes during spontaneous prelabor uterine contractions in sheep. *American Journal of Obstetrics and Gynecology, 155,* 893–897.

Lye, S. J., Wlodek, M. E., & Challis, J. R. G. (1984). Relation between fetal arterial PO_2 and oxytocin-induced uterine contractions in pregnant sheep. *Canadian Journal of Physiology and Pharmacology, 62,* 1337–1340.

Martel, J., Poore, G., Sadowsky, D. W., Cabalum, T., & Nathanielsz, P. W. (1990). *Pulsatile oxytocin (OT) administered to ewes at 120 to 135 days gestational age (dGA) increases rate of synchronization and maturation of fetal biparietal electrocorticogram (FECoG) into distinct high voltage (HV) and low voltages (LV) epochs* (Abstract, p. 154). Society for Gynecologic Investigation, St. Louis, MO. March.

Mulder, E. J. H., & Visser, G. H. A. (1987). Braxton Hicks' contractions and motor behavior in the near-term human fetus. *American Journal of Obstetrics and Gynecology, 156,* 543–549.

Nathanielsz, P. W., Bailey, A., Poore, E. R., Thorburn, G. D., & Harding, R. (1980). The relationship between myometrial activity and sleep state and breathing in fetal sheep throughout the last third of gestation. *American Journal of Obstetrics and Gynecology, 138,* 653–659.

Nathanielsz, P. W., Jack, P. M. B., Krane, E. J., Thomas, A. L., Ratter, S., & Rees, L. H. (1977). The role and regulation of corticotropin in the fetal sheep. In J. Knight (Ed.), *The fetus and birth* (pp. 73–89), Amsterdam: Elsevier.

Oppenheim, R. W. (1975). The role of supraspinal input in embryonic motility: A reexamination in the chick. *Journal of Comparative Neurology, 160,* 37–50.

Packard, N. H., Crutchfield, J. P., Farmer, J. D., & Shaw, R. S. (1980). Geometry from a time series. *Physical Review Letters, 45,* 712–716.

Prechtl, H. F. R. (1990). Qualitative changes of spontaneous movements in fetus and preterm infant are a marker of neurological dysfunction. *Early Human Development, 23,* 151–158.

Provine, R. R., & Rogers, L. (1977). Development of spinal cord bioelectric activity in spinal chick embryos and its behavioral implications. *Journal of Neurobiology, 8,* 217–228.

Robertson, S. S. (1982). Intrinsic temporal patterning in the spontaneous movement of awake neonates. *Child Development, 53,* 1016–1021.

Robertson, S. S. (1985). Cyclic motor activity in the human fetus after midgestation. *Developmental Psychobiology, 18,* 411–419.

Robertson, S. S. (1987). Human cyclic motility: Fetal-newborn continuities and newborn state differences. *Developmental Psychobiology, 20,* 425–442.

Robertson, S. S. (1988). Infants of diabetic mothers: Late normalization of fetal cyclic motility persists after birth. *Developmental Psychobiology, 21,* 477–490.

Robertson, S. S. (1989). Mechanism and function of cyclicity in spontaneous movement. In W. P. Smotherman & S. R. Robinson (Eds.), *Behavior of the fetus* (pp. 77–94). Caldwell, NJ: Telford Press.

Robertson, S. S. (1990). Temporal organization in fetal and newborn movement. In H. Bloch & B. I. Bertenthal (Eds.), *Sensory-motor organizations and development in infancy and early childhood* (pp. 105–122). Dordrecht, The Netherlands: Kluwer Academic Publishers.

Robertson, S. S. (1993a). Probing the mechanism of oscillations in newborn motor activity. *Developmental Psychology, 29,* 677–685.

Robertson, S. S. (1993b). Oscillation and complexity in early infant behavior. *Child Development, 64,* 1022–1035.

Robertson, S. S., & Bacher, L. F. (1992, May). *Coupling of spontaneous movement and visual attention in infants.* Paper presented at the International Conference on Infant Studies, Miami, FL.

Robertson, S. S., Cohen, A. H., & Mayer-Kress, G. (1993). Behavioral chaos: Beyond the metaphor. In L. Smith & E. Thelen (Eds.), *A dynamic systems approach to development: Applications* (pp.   ). Cambridge, MA: MIT Press.

Robertson, S. S., & Dierker, L. J. (1986). The development of cyclic motility in fetuses of diabetic mothers. *Developmental Psychobiology, 19,* 223–234.

Robertson, S. S., Dierker, L J., Sorokin, Y., & Rosen, M. G. (1982). Human fetal movement: Spontaneous oscillations near one cycle per minute. *Science, 218,* 1327–1330.

Robertson, S. S., Klugewicz, D. A., & Lalley, N. M. (1992, May). *Fetal cyclic motor activity: Sensitivity to maternal glucose metabolism.* Paper presented at the International Conference on Infant Studies, Miami, FL.

Robertson, S. S., & Smotherman, W. P. (1990a). The neural control of cyclic motor activity in the fetal rat. *Physiology and Behavior, 47,* 121–126.

Robertson, S. S., & Smotherman, W. P. (1990b, April). *Behavioral chaos?* Paper presented at the International Conference on Infant Studies, Montreal, Quebec.

Schaffer, W. M., Truty, G. L., & Fulmer, S. L. (1990). *Dynamical software,* versions I.4.I and II.2.I. Tucson, AZ: Dynamical Systems, Inc.

Smith, L., & Thelen E. (Eds.). (1993). *A dynamic systems approach to development: Applications.* Cambridge, MA: MIT Press.

Smotherman, W. P., Richards, L. S., & Robinson, S. R. (1984). Techniques for observing fetal behavior in utero: A comparison of chemomyelotomy and spinal transection. *Developmental Psychobiology, 17,* 661–674.

Smotherman, W. P., Robinson, S. R., & Robertson, S. S. (1988). Cyclic motor activity in the rat fetus. *Journal of Comparative Psychology, 102,* 78–82.

Takens, F. (1981). Detecting strange attractors in turbulence. In D. A. Rand & L. S. Young (Eds.), *Dynamical systems and turbulence* (pp. 366–381). New York: Springer-Verlag.

Thompson, J. M. T., & Stewart, H. B. (1986). *Nonlinear dynamics and chaos.* New York: Wiley.

Tinbergen, N. (1963). On aims and methods of ethology. *Zeitschrift fuer Tierpsychologie, 20,* 410–433.

Wolf, A., Swift, J. B., Swinney, H. L., & Vastano, J. A. (1985). Determining Lyapunov exponents from a time series. *Physica, 16D,* 285–317.

11

Development of Motor Behavior in Chick Embryos

Anne Bekoff
University of Colorado

Our understanding of the mechanisms involved in the development of fetal behavior has greatly benefited from the use of animal models. One of these, the chick embryo, provides an opportunity for extensive observation and experimental manipulation of the developing embryo without the technical complications introduced when dealing with the mother. Ultimately, of course, the interactions between fetus and mother must also be addressed, but the advantages of studying fetal behavior in isolation should not be overlooked. For this purpose, chick embryos are ideal because fertile eggs are available throughout the year and the embryos develop readily in an incubator with little care other than maintenance of temperature and humidity. In addition, each embryo is encased in a hard, protective shell, which provides a secure environment for the developing chick. Access to the embryo can be obtained by simply making a hole or "window" in the shell, through which the embryo can be observed or manipulated (Hamburger & Oppenheim, 1967) . As long as sterile conditions are maintained, the window in the egg can be covered with tape or a glass coverslip sealed with paraffin and the egg returned to the incubator so that development can continue (e.g., Hamburger, Wenger, & Oppenheim, 1966).

The accessibility of the chick embryo allows the application of two powerful techniques, kinematic and electromyographic (EMG) recordings, throughout the entire embryonic period. This means that detailed analysis of the actual embryonic movements (kinematic analysis; see Fig. 11.1) can be combined with quantified recordings of the underlying patterns of muscle contraction (EMG analysis; see Fig. 11.2) to provide information about both the output of the nervous system and the resulting behavior. This has been particularly useful in studies of fetal behavior for several reasons. One is that in developmental studies, a significant problem derives from the fact that the organism differs in appearance, and in the environment in which it is found, at different stages. This complicates the comparison of behaviors performed at different times during development (Bekoff, 1992). For example, a chick embryo at early stages of incubation differs dramatically in size, morphometry, and postural configuration from an embryo at later stages. Furthermore, embryos differ from the newly hatched chicks that emerge on day 21 of incubation in these factors as well as in the environment. From the time that movement begins at 3.5 days of incubation, until about 13 days, the embryo is freely floating on its left side in the amniotic fluid. Its movements do not appear to be markedly constrained by the amnion or the eggshell. As it increases in size after 13 days, the embryo becomes increasingly constrained within the egg. In addition, near the time of hatching, the chick becomes firmly confined within the shell in a particular postural configuration called the hatching position (discussed later). After hatching, the chick is neither floating in a fluid environment nor are its movements and posture confined by the eggshell. However, it must then contend with supporting its body on its legs against the forces of gravity.

Given these changes, how can we assess whether it is these factors or changes in the underlying motor patterns that are responsible when behavioral changes are seen? That is, the appearance of the behavior could be altered even if the chick were producing the same sequence of muscle contractions. Alternatively, the motor patterns could be changed due to developmental maturation of the nervous system independent of changes in the body or environment. A third possibility is that the behavioral changes that are seen occur in response to alterations in sensory input that result from such factors as postural or environmental changes (e.g., Chambers & Bradley, 1992; Robinson & Smotherman, 1992; Smotherman & Robinson, 1990). One of the advantages of both EMG and kinematic recording techniques is that muscle activation patterns and joint angles can easily be compared among subjects at different stages of ontogeny and in different environments.

Another issue is that the appearance and organization of early fetal movements differ from those of adults. For example, early fetal behavior has often been described as uncoordinated and disorganized (Hamburger, 1963, 1975). Difficulties in describing such behavior have led to qualitative characterizations of fetal movements as "local" when one body part such as the head or a leg moves alone, or "total" when many parts move together (e.g., Narayanan, Fox, Hamburger, 1971; Windle, 1944), or to simply quantifying the fetal behavior in terms of numbers of movements per unit time (e.g., Oppenheim, 1972). Significant progress has been made by Smotherman and Robinson (1986) in recognizing categories of fetal movements in rats, such as mouth, foreleg, dorsal trunk stretch, thoracic twitch, etc. (see also Ronca & Alberts, chapter 18, this volume). Prechtl and his colleagues have used this type of classification system for preterm infants (Cioni & Prechtl, 1989; Prechtl, Fargel, Weimann, & Bakker, 1979). Nevertheless, these types of descriptions tend to emphasize the differences in appearance between early fetal behaviors and more organized and goal-directed behaviors appearing in late fetal or postnatal life, such as hatching or walking in chicks or face wiping (Smotherman & Robinson, 1988) and swimming-like leg movements (Bekoff & Lau, 1980) in rats.

Thus the behavioral studies have pointed to major discontinuities in behavior near the time of hatching or birth. However, as useful as these approaches have been for behavioral studies, they have not resulted in descriptions of fetal behavior that facilitate attempts to correlate the behavior with underlying neural activity. And, as discussed later, there is evidence for continuity at the level of neural circuitry.

In the following sections, the results of several studies of chick embryos using EMG and kinematic techniques are presented. The first studies address the issue of why fetal behavior is so unique in appearance. Next the question of what relationship fetal behavior has to postnatal behavior is examined. In this section the concept of multifunctional pattern generating circuitry is introduced and its relevance to developmental studies is discussed. Finally, the role of sensory information in the initiation of one particular chick behavior, hatching, is explored.

UNCOORDINATED APPEARANCE
OF FETAL BEHAVIOR

In chick embryos, as in mammalian fetuses, the majority of movements are organized into regular episodes of activity and inactivity and yet the movements appear jerky, "random," and uncoordinated (Hamburger & Oppenheim, 1967). To determine whether there were any elements of coordination that remained undetected by standard behavioral analyses, a kinematic study of embryonic chick leg movements was undertaken to examine the fetal movements in more detail (Watson & Bekoff, 1990). The movements of the right leg were chosen because the leg is relatively large and the chick lies on its left side as it floats in the amniotic fluid, so that the right leg is easily visible. A window was made in the eggshell of 9- and 10-day-old embryos and small dots were placed on the skin overlying the hip, knee, and ankle joints and along the back. The eggs were then placed in a chamber that maintained normal temperature and humidity conditions

and the embryos were videotaped as they performed their normal, spontaneous repertoire of movements. Using a computer program, the dots were
digitized from the videorecords and hip, knee and ankle joint angles were
calculated and then plotted (Fig. 11.1).

Using these data it was possible to show that the jerky appearance of the
fetal movements is due to the fact that very short duration movements
(Fig. 11.1a, d), which appear as abrupt jerks of the leg, are interspersed
among longer, smoother movements (Fig. 11.1c, f). The jerks thereby
interfere with our ability to perceive the elements of coordination that are
present (Watson & Bekoff, 1990). In fact, the kinematic analysis allowed us
to determine that in almost all of the movements that were analyzed, all of
the joints that participated moved together in a coordinated fashion, beginning and ending the movement at the same time and flexing and
extending together (for two of the relatively rare exceptions, see Fig. 11.1b,
e). Thus, the leg movements consist of alternating extension and flexion of
all of the joints of the limb simultaneously. This is true of both the short
jerks and the longer, smoother movements and thus represents a basic
pattern of coordinated leg movement that is not dependent on movement
duration. In fetal mammals, the short jerks occur at a lower frequency so
that overall the behavior appears smoother and more coordinated (Hamburger, 1975). However, movements that appear to be "random" and
uncoordinated are commonly seen in rat fetuses (Bekoff & Lau, 1980;
Narayanan et al., 1971; Smotherman & Robinson, 1986) as well as in
human fetuses and premature newborns (Cioni & Prechtl, 1989; de Vries,
Visser, & Prechtl, 1982). Kinematic analyses of the type just described in
chick embryos have not yet been applied to mammalian fetuses, so it is not
known whether they exhibit a basic pattern of interjoint coordination
similar to chicks.

Embryonic leg movements in chicks were also found to be more variable than adult behaviors in other ways. For example, the kinematic
analysis showed that not all joints participated in all movements (Watson
& Bekoff, 1990). For example, the ankle might flex and extend alone (Fig.
11.1f), or the knee and ankle might move without the hip (Fig. 11.1d, e).
Nevertheless, with few exceptions, when more than one joint participated
in a movement, all active joints moved at the same time and in the same
direction.

As with coordination within a limb, coordination between the legs is not
evident throughout most of embryonic development. For example, kinematic analyses show that coordination between the two legs in 9- and 10-
day-old chick embryos is highly variable, including alternation of the two
legs (47%), synchrony (18%), and unilateral leg movements (35%) (Watson
& Bekoff, 1990). Coordination between wing and leg movements is also
variable (Chambers & Bradley, 1991). This again is likely to contribute to

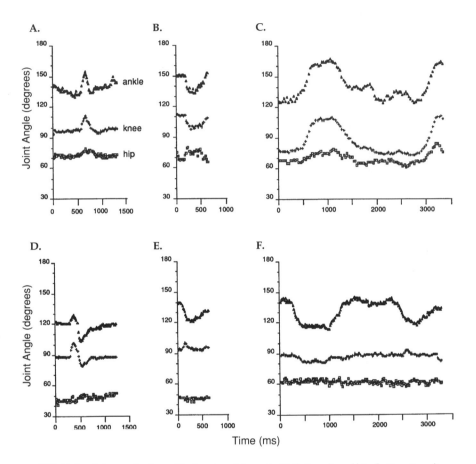

FIG. 11.1. Joint angles for ankle (top trace), knee (middle trace), and hip (bottom trace) are plotted against time for six different examples of leg movement patterns in 9- and 10-day old chick embryos. (A) An individual extension–flexion movement occurs synchronously at all three joints. (B) An individual flexion–extension movement of ankle and knee occurs synchronously with extension–flexion of the hip. (C) A sequence of rhythmic cycles is seen in which all three joints move synchronously and in the same direction. (D) A sequence consisting of a single cycle of synchronous movements at ankle and knee is seen while the hip remains in the rest position. (E) An individual flexion–extension at the ankle occurs synchronously with an extension–flexion at the knee. The hip does not participate in this movement. (F) Only the ankle moves in this sequence of two rhythmic cycles. From Watson and Bekoff (1990). Reprinted by permission.

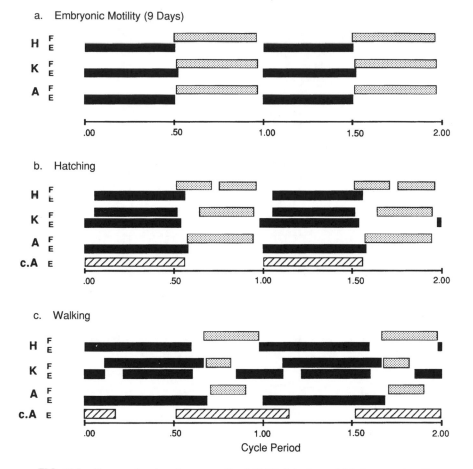

FIG. 11.2.   Bar graphs showing normalized EMG data from chick leg muscles. For muscles of the right leg, hip (H), knee (K), and ankle (A), extensor bursts are indicated by solid black bars and flexor bursts by gray bars. The activity of the left (contralateral) ankle extensor (c. AE) is indicated by the striped bars in (B) and (C). Two cycle periods, beginning with the onset of activity in the ankle extensor, are shown for each behavior. From Bekoff (1992). Reprinted by permission.

the apparent lack of coordination that is evident at the level of behavioral observations. Lack of coordination between limbs is also a characteristic of mammalian fetal movements (Hamburger, 1975).

There is an increase in concurrent movements of various body parts over the course of development in both chick embryos (Provine, 1980) and rat fetuses (Robinson & Smotherman, 1987). As yet, however, no studies have addressed the issue of whether the concurrent movements are organized into specific patterns of interlimb coordination (Bekoff, 1992). For example, each leg could perform the same sequence of movements, which could be organized in an alternating pattern, as in walking, or a synchronous pattern, as in hatching or hopping. On the other hand, the two legs could move at the same time, but each leg could perform a different sequence of movements.

At the end of the gestation period, just prior to birth or hatching, there is a relatively abrupt change in the appearance of embryonic behavior. Even without the help of EMG or kinematic techniques, the leg movements are seen to be coordinated (Bakhuis, 1974; Hamburger & Oppenheim, 1967; Oppenheim, 1973). For example, at the end of the incubation period, the chick embryo performs the hatching behavior. Both kinematic and EMG studies confirm that these leg movements are coordinated both within and between legs as the chick thrusts its legs against the shell in synchrony (Fig. 11.2b; Bekoff & Kauer, 1982, 1984). Likewise, analysis of videotaped records of 20-day-old rat fetuses shows that alternation of forelimbs, as in stepping, is present (Bekoff & Lau, 1980). Thus, at the beginning of the perinatal period, there is a clear transition from behavior that is strikingly different in appearance from typical postnatal behaviors to behavior that becomes increasingly similar to smoothly coordinated, goal-directed postnatal behaviors.

Kinematic analyses have been particularly useful in allowing us to see that fetal movements are more coordinated than behavioral observations had suggested. Because of differences in size, postural configuration, and smoothness of fetal versus postnatal behaviors, visual observations had indicated that there was a striking discontinuity in the overall appearance of the behaviors at these different stages. In contrast, the results of the kinematic analysis suggested that further examination of the relationship of the apparently uncoordinated fetal movements to the clearly coordinated perinatal and postnatal behaviors would be fruitful.

BASIC PATTERN OF EMBRYONIC LEG MOVEMENTS AND ITS RELATIONSHIP TO POSTNATAL BEHAVIORS: EVIDENCE FOR MULTIFUNCTIONAL CIRCUITS

Analysis of the EMG recordings made from leg muscles of 9-day-old chick embryos has shown that there are basic similarities among the leg motor patterns of embryonic motility, hatching and walking in chicks (Fig. 11.2; Bekoff, 1988, 1992). The EMG data are obtained under conditions similar to those used for the kinematic recordings (Bekoff, 1976). A window is first opened in the shell and fine, flexible electrodes are placed on two to six muscles of the right leg. The egg is maintained in a temperature- and humidity-controlled chamber, and recordings are made during normal, spontaneous leg movements. These recordings are analyzed using a computer program that enables quantitative measurements to be made of the relative timing of the onset and offset of activity in each muscle (Bradley & Bekoff, 1990). The results show that a rather simple pattern of muscle activity is present: Extensor muscles are coactive, flexor muscles are coactive, and extensors and flexor alternate (Fig. 11.2a; Bekoff, 1976; Bradley & Bekoff, 1990). We have called this the *basic pattern* because it is simple and occurs early in development.

Elements of the embryonic basic pattern can be recognized in the more complex patterns seen in postnatal behaviors (Fig. 11.2; Bekoff, 1988, 1992). For example, muscles that are activated together in the embryo are also coactivated in adult behaviors, whereas muscles that are activated in alternation in the embryo also tend to alternate in adult behaviors. This is true despite the fact that many other features of the muscle activity patterns show large differences. Such aspects as burst durations, cycle periods, and latencies can vary over a wide range, and specific values are characteristic of each behavior. For instance, cycle period, which is measured as the time from the beginning of a movement in one leg to the beginning of the next movement in the same leg, can vary from a mean in the range of several seconds in embryonic motility in 9-day-old embryos (Bradley & Bekoff, 1990), to around 350 ms in walking in 1-day-old chicks (Johnston & Bekoff, 1992), to under 100 ms during unilateral footshaking (Woolley, Bradley, & Bekoff, 1990).

Furthermore, removal of sensory input in posthatching chicks results in the reappearance of elements of the basic pattern (Bekoff, Nusbaum, Sabichi, & Clifford, 1987). This was shown in a study in which the legs of 1- to 4-day old chicks were deafferented by cutting the dorsal roots in the lumbosacral region of the spinal cord. These chicks were able to perform stepping-like leg movements. However, detailed analysis of the EMG recordings showed that the muscle activity patterns had lost some of the complexity normally associated with walking. The patterns became simpler and more symmetrical—similar to the basic pattern typical of embryos. These results suggest that the neural circuitry used for producing the leg movements of embryonic motility is conserved through development. It is not lost at the time of hatching and replaced by new circuitry appropriate for postnatal behaviors, but instead this circuitry is normally modulated by sensory input to produce the more complex patterns characteristic of later behaviors.

The results obtained from developing chicks are consistent with recent advances in understanding the function and organization of multifunctional circuits in invertebrates (Marder, 1984). In invertebrate organisms such as crabs and lobsters, it has been possible to record from every neuron involved in the production of a particular behavior. The surprising out-come of such studies has been the discovery that, rather than having separate and unique neural circuits for different behaviors, multifunc-tional neural circuits are used to produce many behaviors. This is possible because the multifunctional circuits are very flexible and can produce different outputs in response to different modulatory inputs (Harris-Warrick & Johnson, 1989; Marder & Nusbaum, 1989).

These results have important implications for our understanding of behavioral ontogeny. They imply that developmental changes in behavior could come about as a result of changes in modulation of a multifunctional circuit rather than the development of new circuitry. Instead, multifunc-tional neural circuitry may be assembled early in development and may remain present throughout life. These multifunctional circuits may be used to produce different behaviors as a results of modulation. Such changes in modulation could occur in a variety of ways, including the development of new transmitter systems, altered sensory input due to changes in postural configuration, new sources of sensory input such as that due to weight support, and the development of new descending inputs impinging on the circuitry. An example of a case in which a change in sensory input appears to switch on a new behavior is presented in the next section.

ROLE OF SENSORY SIGNALS IN THE INITIATION OF HATCHING IN CHICKS

Numerous examples of behaviors that suddenly appear, disappear, or reappear in an animal's repertoire are known (see Smotherman & Robinson, chapter 2, this volume). One behavior that suddenly appears in the chick's repertoire is hatching. Hatching is a unique and easily recognizable behav-ior that is normally initiated at the end of the 21-day incubation period (Bakhuis, 1974; Bekoff & Kauer, 1982, 1984; Hamburger & Oppenheim, 1967; Oppenheim, 1973). As mentioned earlier, it is smooth and coordi-nated in appearance. The behavior is initiated rather abruptly about 45 min to 1½ hr prior to emergence from the egg. The chick uses its legs to thrust against the shell while the upper body rotates and the head thrusts back-ward so that the beak hits against the shell and cracks it. The legs provide the force that causes the chick to rotate (Oppenheim & Narayanan, 1968). This ensures that the beak does not hit over and over in the same place, but progressively advances around the circumference of the shell so that eventually a cap lifts off and the chick can emerge. Hatching behavior is organized into episodes of movements that occur at 20- to 30-sec intervals.

Typically the legs thrust once or twice per episode, and each episode lasts 1–3 sec. Between episodes, the chick is inactive.

Hatching behavior is strikingly different from earlier embryonic motility. However, it does have some similarities to the prehatching behaviors that occur between days 17 and 21 (Hamburger & Oppenheim, 1967). For example, tucking is the prehatching behavior that begins on day 17. Like hatching, it appears smooth and coordinated and has a distinct goal. Nevertheless, it involves head and neck movements that are distinctly different in orientation and function from hatching head and neck movements. For example, tucking behavior is designed to place the head under the right wing in the hatching position. The head and neck movements of tucking are therefore initially directed downward and then laterally as the right wing is lifted (Bekoff & Li, unpublished results). During hatching, the head is thrust sharply backward so that the upper surface of the tip of the beak can break the shell. In addition, tucking does not appear to involve leg movements while leg thrusts are an essential component of hatching (Bekoff, 1976).

The other major prehatching behavior is pipping, the behavior by which the chick first breaks a hole in the shell (Hamburger & Oppenheim, 1967). Pipping typically first appears on day 19. Less is known about pipping, but the head and neck movements of pipping are likely to be similar to those of hatching because they are used to break the shell. However, there is not yet any evidence that this behavior involves leg movements (Bekoff, 1976). Thus, hatching may incorporate some components of earlier behaviors (e.g., the head and neck movements of pipping), but also includes smooth and coordinated leg movements unlike any that have been seen previously.

The question of how the initiation of hatching behavior is controlled has been extensively investigated (Bekoff & Kauer, 1982; Bekoff & Sabichi, 1987; Corner & Bakhuis, 1969; Corner, Bakhuis, & van Wingerden, 1973; Oppenheim, 1973). It is now clear that sensory signals play a major role in turning this behavior on and off. For example, unbending the neck while the chick is engaged in the hatching behavior will terminate hatching (Bekoff, 1992), and taping the shell so that the chick cannot open the top and unbend its neck causes hatching to continue much longer than normal (Provine, 1972). In addition, we have shown that bending the neck into the hatching position, where it is placed underneath the right wing and the beak is oriented toward the top of the shell, is a specific signal for the initiation of hatching (Bekoff & Kauer, 1982). Just bending the neck to one side, even in a chick that is not inside an egg, is sufficient to switch the pattern of leg coordination from alternation, which is characteristic of walking, to synchrony, which is typical of hatching (Fig. 11.3). Further-

A. Head Free

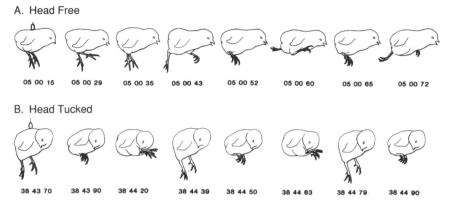

| 05 00 15 | 05 00 29 | 05 00 35 | 05 00 43 | 05 00 52 | 05 00 60 | 05 00 65 | 05 00 72 |

B. Head Tucked

| 38 43 70 | 38 43 90 | 38 44 20 | 38 44 39 | 38 44 50 | 38 44 63 | 38 44 79 | 38 44 90 |

FIG. 11.3.   Drawings made from single frames of videotape records. Numbers represent real time in minutes, seconds, and hundredths of seconds, read from a digital stopwatch in the field of view. (a) Chick suspended by a small ring glued to the middle of its back with head and neck free. (b) Chick suspended with head bent to the right and taped in place (tape not shown). From Bekoff and Kauer (1982). Reprinted by permission.

more, by placing postnatal chicks in an artificial glass eggshell with the neck bent into the hatching position, we have shown that the neck signal from the neck is still effective up to 61 days after hatching (Bekoff & Kauer, 1984).

It seems likely that a proprioceptive signal from receptors that are stimulated asymmetrically on the two sides of the neck serves as the specific initiation signal for hatching. For example, only bending the neck to the side is effective in turning on hatching (Bekoff & Kauer, 1982). Bending the neck up or down or immobilizing it in a straightened position will not initiate the behavior. Furthermore if the local anesthetic lidocaine is injected into the neck, hatching is delayed until the anesthetic wears off (Bekoff & Sabichi, 1987).

These results are consistent with the concept of a multifunctional circuit whose output is altered by various kinds of modulatory inputs as well as with ideas about development coming from dynamical systems analysis (e.g., Thelen, 1988). For example, as a dynamical system, a multifunctional circuit might be expected to produce a stable, rhythmic pattern under one set of conditions. However, if one particular variable is altered (e.g., a modulatory input is added), this could act as a control parameter to shift the circuit to a completely different, but equally stable, output pattern. Thus, proprioceptive input from the bent neck appears to act as a control parameter, turning on hatching and switching interlimb coordination from an alternating to a synchronous pattern. As discussed earlier, the available evidence suggests that a multifunctional circuit is used for producing leg movements throughout development, and the specific behavior produced is dependent on the sensory context.

SUMMARY AND FUTURE DIRECTIONS

In summary, although embryonic motility initially appears to be quite different and unrelated to later behaviors, there is considerable evidence for continuity of pattern generating circuitry throughout development in a variety of organisms. This suggests that such circuits are, in fact, multifunctional networks. By modulating these networks, sensory inputs may serve as control parameters, shifting motor patterns from one stable pattern to another and resulting in the "sudden appearance" of new behaviors at the appropriate times during ontogeny. Future research on the nature of those sensory signals and the mechanisms by which they modulate network output will undoubtedly be fruitful.

ACKNOWLEDGMENT

This work has been generously supported by National Institutes of Health grants NS20310 and HD28247.

REFERENCES

Bakhuis, W. L. (1974). Observations on hatching movements in the chick (*Gallus domesticus*). *Journal of Comparative and Physiological Psychology, 87,* 997–1003.

Bekoff, A. (1976). Ontogeny of leg motor output in the chick embryo: A neural analysis. *Brain Research, 106,* 271–291.

Bekoff, A. (1986). Is the basic output of the locomotor CPG to flexor and extensor muscles symmetrical? Evidence from walking, swimming and embryonic motility in chicks. Society for Neuroscience Abstracts, 12, 880.

Bekoff, A. (1988). Embryonic motor output and movement patterns: Relationship to postnatal behavior. In W. P. Smotherman & S. R. Robinson (Eds.), *Behavior of the fetus* (pp. 191–206). Caldwell, NJ: Telford.

Bekoff, A. (1992). Neuroethological approaches to the study of motor development in chicks: Achievements and challenges. *Journal of Neurobiology, 23,* 1486–1505.

Bekoff, A., & Kauer, J. A. (1982). Neural control of hatching: Role of neck position in turning on hatching leg movements in post-hatching chicks. *Journal of Comparative Physiology, 145,* 497–504.

Bekoff, A., & Kauer, J. A. (1984). Neural control of hatching: Fate of the pattern generator for the leg movements of hatching in posthatching chicks. *Journal of Neuroscience, 4,* 2659–2666.

Bekoff, A., & Lau, B. (1980). Interlimb coordination in 20-day-old rat fetuses. *Journal of Experimental Biology, 173–175.*

Bekoff, A., & Li, T. (1994). [Video analysis of tucking behavior in 17-day chick embryos.] Unpublished raw data.

Bekoff, A., Nusbaum, M. P., Sabichi, A. L., & Clifford, M. (1987). Neural control of limb coordination: I. Comparison of hatching and walking leg motor output patterns in normal and deafferented chicks. *Journal of Neuroscience, 7,* 2320–2330.

Bekoff, A., & Sabichi, A. L. (1987). Sensory control of the initiation of hatching in chicks: Effects of a local anesthetic injected into the neck. *Developmental Psychobiology, 20,* 489–495.

Bradley, N. S., & Bekoff, A. (1990). Development of coordinated movement in chicks. I. Temporal analysis of hindlimb synergies at embryonic days 9 and 10. *Developmental Psychobiology, 23,* 763–782.

Chambers, S. H., & Bradley, N. S. (1991) Intralimb and interlimb coordination during motility in chick embryos. *Society for Neuroscience Abstracts, 17,* 937.

Chambers, S. H., & Bradley, N. S. (1992). Does buoyancy mask the potential for coordinated motility *in ovo*? *Society for Neuroscience Abstracts, 18,* 962.

Cioni, G., & Prechtl, H. F. R. (1989). Development of posture and motility in preterm infants. In C. von Euler, H. Forssberg, & H. Lagerkrantz (Eds.), *Neurobiology of early infant behaviour* (pp. 69–76). Hampshire, England: Macmillan.

Corner, M. A., & Bakhuis, W. L. (1969). Developmental patterns in the central nervous system of birds: V. Cerebral electrical activity, forebrain functions and behavior in the chick at the time of hatching. *Brain Research, 13,* 541–555.

Corner, M. A., Bakhuis, W. L., & van Wingerden, C. (1973). Sleep and wakefulness during early life in the domestic chicken, and their relationship to hatching and embryonic motility. In G. Gottlieb (Ed.), *Behavioral embryology* (pp. 245– 279). New York: Academic Press.

de Vries, J. I. P., Visser, G. H. A., & Prechtl, H. F. R. (1982). The emergence of fetal behavior. I. Qualitative aspects. *Early Human Development, 7,* 301–322.

Hamburger, V. (1963). Some aspects of the embryology of behavior. *Quarterly Review of Biology, 38,* 342–365.

Hamburger, V. (1975). Fetal behavior. In E.S.E. Hafez (Ed.), *The mammalian fetus* (pp. 68–81). Springfield, IL: Charles C. Thomas.

Hamburger, V., & Oppenheim, R. W. (1967). Prehatching motility and hatching behavior in the chick. *Journal of Experimental Zoology, 166,* 171–204.

Hamburger, V., Wenger, E., & Oppenheim, R. (1966). Motility in the chick embryo in the absence of sensory input. *Journal of Experimental Zoology, 162,* 133–160.

Harris-Warrick, R. M., & Johnson, B. R. (1989). Motor pattern networks: Flexible foundations for rhythmic pattern production. In T. J. Carew & D. B. Kelley, (Eds.), *Perspectives in neural systems and behavior* (pp. 51–71). New York: Alan R. Liss.

Johnston, R. M., & Bekoff, A. (1992). Constrained and flexible features of rhythmical hindlimb movements in chicks: Kinematic profiles of walking, swimming and airstepping. *Journal of Experimental Biology, 171,* 43–66.

Marder, E. (1984). Mechanisms underlying neurotransmitter modulation of a neuronal circuit. *Trends in Neuroscience, 7,* 48–53.

Marder, E., & Nusbaum, M. P. (1989). Peptidergic modulation of the motor pattern generator in the stomatogastric ganglion. In T. J. Carew & D. B. Kelley, *Perspectives in neural systems and behavior* (pp. 73–91). New York: Alan R. Liss.

Narayanan, C. H., Fox, M. W., & Hamburger, V. (1971). Prenatal development of spontaneous and evoked activity in the rat (*Rattus norvegicus albinus*). *Behaviour, 40,* 100–134.

Oppenheim, R. W. (1972). An experimental investigation of the possible role of tactile and proprioceptive stimulation in certain aspects of embryonic behavior in chicks. *Developmental Psychobiology, 5,* 71–91.

Oppenheim, R. W. (1973). Prehatching and hatching behavior: A comparative and physiological consideration. In C. Gottlieb (Ed.), *Behavioral embryology* (pp. 163–244). New York: Academic Press.

Oppenheim, R. W., & Narayanan, C. H. (1968). Experimental studies on hatching behavior in the chick. I. Thoracic spinal gaps. *Journal of Experimental Zoology, 168,* 387–394.

Prechtl, H. F. R., Fargel, J. W., Weimann, H. M., & Bakker, H. H. (1979) Postures, motility and respiration of low risk preterm infants. *Developmental Medicine and Child Neurology, 21,* 3–27.

Provine, R. R. (1972). Hatching behavior of the chick (*Gallus domesticus*): Plasticity of the rotatory component. *Psychonomic Science, 2,* 27–28.

Provine, R. R. (1980). Development of between-limb movement synchronization in the chick embryo. *Developmental Psychobiology, 13,* 151–163.

Robinson, S. R., & Smotherman, W. P. (1987). Environmental determinants of behavior in the rat fetus. II. Emergence of synchronous movement. *Animal Behavior, 35,* 1652–1662.

Robinson, S. R., & Smotherman, W. P. (1992). Fundamental motor patterns of the mammalian fetus. *Journal of Neurobiology, 23,* 1574–1600.

Smotherman, S. R., & Robinson, W. P. (1986). Environmental determinants of behavior in the rat fetus. *Animal Behavior, 34,* 1859–1873.

Smotherman, S. R., & Robinson, W. P. (1988). Dimensions of fetal investigation. In W. P. Smotherman & S. R. Robinson (Eds.), *Behavior of the fetus* (pp. 19–34). Caldwell, NJ: Telford.

Smotherman, S. R., & Robinson, W. P. (1990). The prenatal origins of behavioral organization. *Psychological Science, 1,* 97–106.

Thelen, E. (1988). On the nature of developing motor systems and the transition from prenatal to postnatal life. In W. P. Smotherman & S. R. Robinson (Eds.), *Behavior of the fetus* (pp. 207–224). Caldwell, NJ: Telford.

Watson, S. J., & Bekoff, A. (1990). A kinematic analysis of hindlimb motility in 9- and 10-day old chick embryos. *Journal of Neurobiology, 21,* 651–660.

Windle, W. F. (1944). Genesis of somatic motor function in mammalian embryos: A synthesizing article. *Physiological Zoology, 17,* 247–260.

Woolley, S. M. , Bradley, N. S., & Bekoff, A. (1990). An EMG study comparing footshaking and walking in chicks. *Society for Neuroscience Abstracts, 16,* 118.

12

Odor Sensing in the Human Fetus: Anatomical, Functional, and Chemoecological Bases

Benoist Schaal
CNRS, Paris, France and CNRS-INRA, Nouzilly, France

Pierre Orgeur
INRA-CNRS, Nouzilly, France

Christian Rognon
Université Claude Bernard, Villeurbanne, France

Among vertebrate embryos, sensory structures develop according to an invariant orderly sequence (Bradley & Mistretta, 1975; Gottlieb, 1971). In that developmental succession, the morphogenesis of the chemosensory modalities (oral and nasal chemoreception) closely follows that of the early somesthesic and vestibular modalities, but precedes the auditory and visual modalities. Despite the fact that this precocity of chemosensory structures has been well established, the possibility of a prenatal onset of olfactory functions was never seriously considered. To support this presumed sensory hindrance, some influential scholars argued for either the necessity for chemicals to be airborne in order to trigger an olfactory sensation (Carmichael, 1970; Gueubelle, 1984; Preyer, 1881), the absence of fluid currents flowing through the nose (Humphrey, 1978), or the total lack of odorous compounds in the prenatal environment (Feldman, 1920; Ferril, 1987).

The present state of knowledge benefits, however, from considerable advances in our understanding of neonatal olfactory structures and functions, both in human and animal newborns, and from direct assessments of antenatal chemoreception in animals. These findings indicate that nasal chemoreception might occur in the human fetus and have, as a result, awakened interest in the earliest phases of its functional development.

In the present chapter, we bring together behavioral, anatomical, physiological, and chemoecological arguments that support the possibility of prenatal functioning of nasal chemoreceptors in the human fetus. First we describe empirical findings on odor preferences displayed by humans immediately after birth and argue that these results suggest the persistence of a chemosensory memory of prenatal origin. Next we outline the ontogeny of nasal chemosensory structures in the human embryo and fetus to provide structural bases for these functions. In the third section, we review evidence from a variety of sources that suggest prenatal chemosensory function. Finally, we describe the fetal compartment and show how this "liquid atmosphere" (Barcroft & Mason, 1938) may carry many potential chemostimulants, and how it is available to external (i.e., maternal) influences.

POSTNATAL EVIDENCE OF PRENATAL ODOR ENCODING?

Mammalian neonates have been observed to exhibit interest and attraction to particular odors normally present at birth. These attractive volatile compounds are found in the amniotic fluid. Teicher and Blass (1977) provided the initial evidence that newborn rats are attracted to amniotic fluid and that the olfactory cues contained in it guide the initial suckling episode. Although the importance of amniotic fluid odor was demonstrated with samples of fluid taken from any parturient female, a more specific preference could also be shown for the amniotic fluid of a rat pup's own mother (Hepper, 1987). Similar attraction to the odor of amniotic fluid was later reported in mice (Kodama, 1990), piglets (Parfet & Gonyou, 1991) and lambs (Schaal, Orgeur, & Arnould, submitted).

Newborns are also highly responsive to biological substrates to which they have apparently never been exposed prior to the postnatal preference tests. These include the dam's saliva in rats, (Teicher & Blass, 1977), an odor cue excreted in the milk or on the dam's abdomen around the nipples in rabbits (Hudson & Distel, 1983; Keil, von Stralendorff, & Hudson, 1990), the ewe's inguinal gland secretion in lambs (Vince & Ward, 1984), and maternal feces in piglets (Morrow-Tesch & McGlone, 1990). But it is probable that the sensory features of some compounds in these various postnatal substrates relate to the prenatal environment, and that the newborns detect the chemosensory continuity of the two environments.

Although the evidence is not as substantial for humans, similar early olfactory influences may also be present. A first hint of human newborns' preference for certain odors was provided by Steiner (1977, 1979) in his search for selective neonatal responsiveness to hedonically contrasted odorants. The presentation to neonates of artificial odors "evaluated as pleasant by adults" (fruity, milky odors) triggered facial responses decoded by blind raters as neutral or positively valenced. Conversely, rejecting or "negative" faces were elicited in neonates by the presentation of unpleasant odors (fishy or rotten odors). The precocity of this differential response (tests made before postnatal hr 12), its independence from postnatal experience (tests made before the first feed), and the fact that it was observed in an anencephalic baby led Steiner to conclude the existence of an "innate, possibly inherited" (1979, p. 278) selective responsiveness to odors or odor categories.

More recent experiments by Porter and his co-workers have revealed biased responses to odors in human infants, that cannot be easily explained by postnatal experience. When simultaneously presented with two gauze pads, one bearing the odor of an unfamiliar lactating mother's breast and the other bearing either the odor of the same mother's axilla or the breast odor of a nonparturient woman, 2-week-old bottle-fed neonates oriented more to the former pad (Makin & Porter, 1989). As these babies had never been breast-fed nor had direct exposure to human milk, postnatal associative learning or familiarization could not have played a key role. The same pattern of preference for the odor of the lactating breast was further shown in subsequent tests with breast-fed babies (Porter, Makin, Davis, & Christensen, 1992), indicating the general attracting power of that odor for infants. In an additional choice test with bottle-fed infants, the odor of an unfamiliar lactating mother's breast and that of the infant's own familiar formula were presented concurrently (Porter, Makin, Davis, & Christensen, 1991). The former odor elicited longer head orientation time as compared to the latter, suggesting that these infants preferred an odor to which they had virtually no postnatal exposure more than an odor they were exposed to at each feeding since birth (the infants were aged 2 weeks when tested).

As already indicated, early olfactory preferences are likely to reflect prenatal and postnatal experience. First, the acquisition (or stabilization) of neonatal odor preferences can be effective within a very short time window postnatally (cf., e.g., Caza & Spear, 1984; Kindermann, Hudson, & Distel, 1994; Sullivan & Wilson, 1991), facilitated by the strongly reinforcing power of the initial interactions with the mother. Second, the fetal chemoreceptor system may be genetically predisposed to detect particular odor cues that are critical for neonatal survival. Third, the chemical composition of the amniotic environment at a given moment of fetal development may induce a specific pattern of receptor expression in the olfactory neuroreceptors, and determine their odorant specificity and sensitivity (cf., e.g., Wang, Wysocki, & Gold, 1993). Finally, prenatal experience with chemicals present in the womb may fully determine (e.g., Smotherman, 1982b) or facilitate (Pedersen & Blass, 1982) postnatal preference acquisition for similar substances present in the neonatal environment. Although all these mechanisms may combine to a certain degree, the latter alternative may be priviledged by the fact that there is a degree of transnatal continuity in the volatiles present in the fetal and neonatal compartments. Prenatal experience with odorants in the amniotic fluid might thus prepare the chemosensory systems to detect and/or bias the motivational mechanisms of the neonate organism to search certain odors or classes of odors. In other words, prenatal odor experience may contribute to the formation of a chemical "search image" (Tinbergen, 1960) of the mother or of a significant area of her body.

To date, the possibility of fetal responsiveness to odors present in the prenatal environment has been successfully assessed in the fetus of only one placental group, the rodents, with a pronounced emphasis on the laboratory rat. Several experimental paradigms have demonstrated that infant rats can associate chemosensory stimulation experienced in utero contingently with aversive or appetitive reinforcements, or that they can recognize chemosensory stimuli following prenatal mere exposure (Chotro & Molina, 1990; Pedersen & Blass, 1981, 1982; Smotherman, 1982a; Smotherman & Robinson, 1987; Stickrod, Kimble, & Smotherman, 1982). Furthermore, such abilities to retain odor inputs could be demonstrated between two embryonic stages (Smotherman & Robinson, 1987). The sensory system supporting these prenatal responses to odors was initially thought to be the vomeronasal organ (Pedersen, Steward, Greer, & Sheperd, 1983), which is a distinct field of chemoreceptors known to be active in most terrestrial mammals, such as rodents (see later discussion). This means that species lacking a functional vomeronasal organ in utero might not be sensitive to some odors in their prenatal milieu.

Two recent findings, however, have challenged this view. First, although the vomeronasal organ was believed until recently to degenerate in the human fetus, anatomical evidence has now demonstrated its presence in older fetuses, newborns, and even in a considerable proportion of adults (discussed later). Thus it is not unlikely that the vomeronasal system plays a sensory role in the human species as well. Second, the exclusive affinity of amniotic odorants for vomeronasal receptors has been questioned. In the mouse, the vomeronasal organ, although mature, does not appear to be able to function prenatally (Coppola & O'Connell, 1989), or even prepubertally (Coppola, Budde, & Milar, 1993), although the fetus has been shown to be sensitive to odorants injected into the amniotic sac (Kodama, 1987). Different combination of chemosensory subsystems may thus be activated by the same stimuli in closely related species, and, accordingly, constituents from the prenatal environment may activate the whole range, or part of the chemoreceptors present in the mammalian fetus's nose.

DEVELOPMENT OF NASAL CHEMOSENSORY STRUCTURES

In mammals, the nasal chemosensory system is a complex arrangement of anatomically distinct subsystems variably distributed within the nasal cavities and believed to work under different operational conditions (Graziadei, 1977; Shepherd, Pedersen, & Greer, 1987; Tücker, 1971). In humans, this nasal chemoreceptive system is composed of four subsystems: the main olfactory, the trigeminal, the vomeronasal, and the terminal. The main olfactory system is composed of the main olfactory epithelium (MOE) situated at the apical part of each nasal cavity, linked by the olfactory nerve to the primary olfactory center, the main olfactory bulbs (MOB), and then to higher diencephalic and telencephalic centers. Originating from the Vth cranial nerve, the trigeminal system comprises a network of free nerve endings diffusely distributed in the respiratory and olfactory mucosae lining the nasal cavities. The vomeronasal system (VNO) is formed by symmetrical invaginations on each side of the lower nasal septum, lined with bipolar sensory cells sending their axons to the accessory olfactory bulb (AOB). Finally, the Nervus terminalis system comprises free nerve endings in the anterior part of the nasal septum and in the MOE.

All of these sensory structures differentiate very early during embryonic and fetal life (for reviews, cf. Farbman, 1991; Meisami, 1987; Schaal, 1988a). We outline the prenatal development of these subsystems, with a special emphasis on the period when they reach presumable functional onset, as inferred from morphological evidence.

Formation of the Nasal Structures

The nasal tissue supporting and enclosing the human chemoreceptors takes the form of a "miniature" nose between 6 and 8 gestational weeks (G weeks). Mesenchymal tissue proliferates medially and laterally from the nasal pit to form the septum and the alae nasi, respectively. By the seventh to eighth week, these elevations blend to form two partitioned nasal cavities separated from the oral cavity (Gasser, 1977). They open anteriorly by the nostrils and posteriorly by the primitive choanas. The fetal nose is reliably detected by ultrasonography from 11 to 15 G weeks (Christ & Meiniger, 1983). Amniotic fluid is then supposed to circulate in these respiratory channels, at least after the resorption of nasal plugs (which original description by Schaffer, 1910, has never since been repeated to our knowledge) between 2–4 and 6 G months.

Main Olfactory Subsystem

The main olfactory subsystem organizes most intensively during the first trimester of gestation. The appearance of placodes on both sides of the anterior cephalic surface of the embryo is the first sign of an olfactory region, which becomes visible at 4–5 G weeks (Humphrey, 1940). The olfactory neuroreceptors derive from neuroblasts located in the olfactory placode. Between 7 and 11 G weeks, the bipolar neuroreceptors first grow out a dendritic process ending in surface knobs. The olfactory cilia burgeon from these knobs to attain adult-like morphology and number toward G week 11 (Chuah & Zheng, 1987; Pyatkina, 1982). Closely following dendritic growth, during G week 8, the cell bodies of the MOE neurons begin to form axons that extend toward the forebrain, inducing there the evagination of the primordial olfactory bulb. Several aggregations of such axons (fila olfactoria) then form the lateral and medial bundles of the olfactory nerve, which enter their respective zones of the bulb (Pearson, 1941). It should be emphasized that the topography of the fetal MOE is wider than that observed in adults: Its extension ranges from the middle of the nasal septum to the superior turbinate without any of the discontinuities often seen in adults (Nakashima, Kimmelman, & Snow, 1984).

The neuron classes typical of the MOB (i.e., mitral, tufted, granular) differentiate rapidly, with their characteristic stratification being visible from week 10 onward. The main secondary relay (mitral) cells are disposed in a clear layer by G weeks 10–18 (Humphrey, 1940), and, from that period (Bossy, 1980), they grow dendrites to the glomeruli (i.e., increased synaptogenesis between the first and second order neurons). The ontogeny of higher level connections of the MOB with the limbic forebrain, the olfactory paleocortex, and the frontal neocortex is imperfectly known. The secondary (e.g., anterior olfactory nucleus, prepiriform cortex, medial septal nucleus) and tertiary (e.g., entorhinal cortex, amygdaloid complex, hippocampus) olfactory structures have been studied anatomically by Macchi (1951) and Humphrey (1963, 1967, 1968). From the fourth gestational month, these structures reorganize developmentally (i.e., reductions or extensions) in relative size.

Thus, from the end of the first trimester, the olfactory subsystem presents as a sheet of receptors "mature enough to be capable of sensory performance" (Pyatkina, 1982, p. 371) and shows a pattern compatible with functional ability at the primary and higher centers of integration during the last G trimester. Neurochemical evidence discussed later further suggests that olfactory function may begin during that period.

Trigeminal Subsystem

The trigeminal subsystem is one of the earliest developing sensory structures in the embryo and, as it does not require specialized sensory receptors (free nerve endings), it may also be the earliest functioning chemosensor. It innervates the nasal cavity through its maxillary and ophthalmic divisions (Cauna, Hinderer, & Wentges, 1969). The maxillary division (superior nasal and naso-palatine branches) innervates the perinasal epidermis (alae nasi, bridge of the nose) as well as the lower interior mucosa. The ophthalmic division (interior nasal branch) innervates the mucosa lining the upper interior mucosa, including the MOE. Free trigeminal endings are evident in the respiratory mucosa in embryos 4 G weeks old (Hogg, 1941). They grow close to the epidermal or mucosal surface between 5.5 and 14 G weeks (Hogg, 1941; Humphrey, 1966). By G week 18, they reach the lamina propria, immediately below the MOE (Chuah & Zheng, 1987). The cell bodies of these sensory trigeminal neurons are located in the Gasserian ganglion, whose prenatal maturation is heterochronous, as evidenced by the sequential development of the tactosensitive cutaneous fields of the face (Brown, 1974).

The sensitive fascicles of the maxillary divisions of the trigeminal nerve respond to touch in the 5.5–7.5 G week embryo (Humphrey, 1978). Reflexes induced by touching receptive fields of the ophthalmic branch were recorded slightly later, that is, from 8 to 10 G weeks (Humphrey, 1978). Responses to tactile stimulations applied inside the nose were reported at 22 G weeks (Golubeva, Shulejkina, & Vainstein, 1959). From these early ages, adequate sensory receptors for somesthetic reflexes are thus present in the fetus. Since these thermotactile receptors also mediate the "common chemical sense," they are likely to be reactive to chemicals from the prenatal environment.

Vomeronasal Subsystem

The vomeronasal subsystem is well developed in the trimester-old human fetus (Humphrey, 1940; Kreutzer & Jafek, 1980; Nakashima et al., 1984). At the periphery, the vomeronasal groove is first evident in the fetus 5 G weeks old (Bossy, 1980). During the next 3 weeks, the vomeronasal fibers course parallel to the terminal and olfactory axons to end in the accessory olfactory bulb, located dorso-laterally to the MOB. The fetal VNO attains a maximum length of 4–8 mm, that is, a dimension bigger than the adult VNO (Johnson, Josephson, & Hawke, 1985; Moran, Jafek, & Rowley, 1991). The appearance of sensory-like neurons is reported between 5 and 13 G weeks (Bossy, 1980; Ortmann, 1989). The central structure directly linked with the VNO can be clearly localized between 8.5 and 18.5 weeks

(Humphrey, 1940). At 18.5 weeks, its degree of differentiation (e.g., characteristic lamination) is morphologically comparable to that of other adult mammals (Humphrey, 1940). During this time, regressive changes have been reported in the accessory olfactory bulb, resulting in a "rudimentary structure" in the older fetus and the newborn. The degree of this involutive trend appears, however, to be individually variable, and it is of interest to note that the left AOB remained better developed in the fetuses examined by Humphrey (1940). Whether these changes are regressive or represent reorganization remains to be ascertained, however. Humphrey suggested that "in at least certain cases in which regression occurs in the accessory olfactory formation, some of its mitral cells appear to become a part of the anterior olfactory nucleus" (1940, p. 460). The recent evidence of vomeronasal function in the human is further discussed later.

Terminal Subsystem

The terminalis subsystem is the least explored (supposed) chemosensor, although its presence was reported early in this century (in the embryo, McCotter, 1915; in the infant, Brookover, 1917). At the peripheral level, it is composed of plexiform clusters of ganglion cells spread in the mucosa of the nasal septum (Brookover, 1914; Brown, 1987; Johnston, 1914; Oelschläger, Bühl, & Dann, 1987). There, terminal fiber free endings are apposed either along blood vessels and Bowman glands or terminate in the olfactory mucosa, suggesting both effector and sensory functions (Larsell, 1950; Oelschläger et al., 1987). On the central side, the terminal afferents lie with olfactory and vomeronasal nerves to enter, in close proximity with them, the ventromedial surface of the forebrain where they have a complex pattern of connections with the olfactory tubercle, the ventral septal nuclei, and the posterior part of the anterior commissure (Larsell, 1950; Pearson, 1942). The embryonic appearance of the terminal elements is situated at circa G week 6 (Bossy, 1980; Pearson, 1942). By the seventh week, the terminal nerve can be traced from the nasal roof to the brain. The terminal ganglion decreases in size around the eighth week (Bossy, 1980), but it remains well developed in 5-, 7-, and 9-month-old fetuses and in newborns (Johnston, 1914; Brookover, 1917; Oelschläger et al., 1987). From the fact that terminal fibers contain luteinizing hormone-releasing hormone since the fetal period, the possibility of their involvement in the development of neuroendocrine responses to odors has been proposed (Demski & Schwanzel-Fukuda, 1987), but has not yet been experimentally verified (e.g., Schwanzel-Fukuda & Pfaff, 1987).

Based on anatomical evidence, all nasal chemosensors appear to be able to process sensory stimuli before birth. The ratio of contribution of each of these composite sources of inputs to what we loosely call the "olfactory sensation" is unclear, even in adults. There is conventional agreement that the olfactory system (mediating olfaction *sensu stricto*) is most finely tuned to analyze low concentrations of volatile molecules in gaseous phase, whereas the trigeminal system (mediating irritation) is sensitive chiefly to the tactile side effects of chemical stimulations delivered at higher concentrations. The vomeronasal organ (mediating vomerolfaction; Cooper & Burghard, 1990) is considered (from comparative inference) as an organ devised to detect nonvolatile compounds carried in an aqueous medium. The sensory functions and properties of the terminal system are not known. The operating characteristics of these different subsystems are thus segregated on the basis of the physicochemical features of the stimulus (mainly vapor pressure, hydrophilicity, and concentration). The functional role distribution in nasal chemoreception appears, however, not to be so exclusively defined for each subsystem (cf. next section).

POTENTIAL ABILITY TO SENSE ODORANTS IN UTERO

Thus far, there is no direct, in utero demonstration for nasal chemosensation in the human fetus. However, indirect evidence for nasal chemosensation may be derived from several converging lines of study. First, the chemosensory areas of the nose do not develop in isolation from their environment: Potential stimulation may reach these areas through different pathways, some of them being probably favored by the behavior of the fetus itself. Second, instead of being inhibited by the aquatic conditions of stimulation, the preneural events leading to chemosensory transduction may be facilitated in the fetus. Third, the investigation of premature infants' chemosensory responses may allow inferences about the functional status of chemoreception in the fetus of the same G age: In this regard, the sensory performance of developing nasal chemosensory subsystems is examined in the light of recent findings in adults. Finally, preliminary evidence of chemoreception is provided from in utero investigation in sheep, an animal model that shares fundamental ontogenetic commonalities with human fetuses.

Transport of Chemostimuli to Fetal Receptor Areas

The most obvious way to stimulate the nasal receptors is through compounds external to the fetus, that is, borne by the amniotic fluid flowing through the narinal-choanal pathways, after the dissolution of the narinal plugs presumed to obstruct the passage. But even before the resorption of the nasal plugs, the olfactory epithelia could be approached by odorants from the retronasal route. Because human amniotic fluid has an aqueous consistency throughout gestation, it may be an efficient odor carrier until term. The continual turnover of the amniotic fluid bathing the chemoreceptors may be facilitated by the bursts of swallowing and breathing behavior of the fetus (Pritchard, 1966). In fact, the fetus inhales more than twice the volume of fluid it swallows (Duenholter & Pritchard, 1976), suggesting an intense movement of fluid through the nose. This was confirmed by real-time ultrasonography (Logvinenko, 1990). The short-period respiratory movements of the fetus induce pulsatile displacements of fluid in the nasal fossae and as a result may be hypothesized to be a kind of reflexive "amniotic sniffing." This intermittent renewal of the fluid bathing receptors may offset any presumed adaptation phenomena (discussed later).

Another, more passive, putative access of odorants to the nasal chemoreceptors might be through the fetal blood itself, that is, through the hematogenic pathway (Bradley & Mistretta, 1975). This mechanism of stimulation is presumed to work by diffusion of blood-borne odorants from the capillary vessels running close to the olfactory mucosa. To date, this odorant access route has not been tested in the fetus, but empirical data exist for hematogenic smell (and taste) in adult animals and humans (Bradley & Mistretta, 1971; Kasama & Zusho, 1981; Maruniak, Silver, & Moulton, 1983; Teatini & Pincini, 1961). Indeed, the intravenous infusion of an odorant is followed after several seconds by an electrical response recorded in the olfactory nerve in rats (Maruniak et al., 1983). The odor access to chemoreceptors through blood may be facilitated in the fetus because of a considerably more intensive vascularization of the MOE as compared to the adult. In fact, in the 12–24 G week fetus, numerous capillaries are located close to the basal lamina below the MOE, and some were observed within the MOE itself, in actual contact with neuroreceptors (L. Astic, personal communication, 1993; Chuah & Zheng, 1987; Naessen, 1971). This more intimate association between intra-epithelial capillaries and the MOE, coupled with a greater extension of the fetal MOE, makes plausible the hypothesis of hematogenic chemoreception in the fetus.

Hematogenic chemoreception may be the most direct route for chemostimulants to the various receptor areas, because no metabolism occurs between the placenta and the fetal nasochemoreceptors. As much as 50% of umbilical vein blood flow is shunted through the ductus venosus to the brain without metabolic degradation, with the remaining blood fraction flowing to the liver (Edelstone, Merick, Caritis, & Müller-Heubach, 1980). In contrast, in order to be excreted via micturition into the amniotic pool, odorants have to cross multiple fetal sites of metabolic activities (e.g., brain, liver, kidneys), potentially weakening or altering their olfactory power. Nonetheless, there are other transfer routes that can bypass one or several of these potential degradation sites (e.g., excretion via the fetal pulmonary fluids [Riggs et al., 1987] and saliva [Harding, Bocking, & Sigger, 1984]), but these are minor exchange routes between the fetus and amniotic fluid (Lotgering & Wallenburg, 1986).

Physicochemical Interactions Between Odorants and Receptors

Once the odorigenic solutes have moved close to the receptor areas by the amniotic route, they are still influenced by different processes that modulate the final binding to the receptor sites. Specifically, one may wonder if and how an odor sensation is possible with water-borne stimuli. Le Magnen (1969) argued that there is no reason to make a radical distinction in the process of olfactory detection based on whether it takes place in aerial or in aquatic conditions. Odorivector molecules must in every case solubilize and diffuse in the aqueous mucus film spread over all mucous (including olfactory, vomeronasal, and respiratory) areas to reach the receptor sites. Thus, they necessarily act in a liquid medium (~95% water: Getchell & Getchell, 1990). In air, besides its obvious protective function, this mucus film acts as a supplier of ions and proteins involved in normal neuroreceptor function. One may then wonder whether the fetal MOE is covered with a mucus layer, and whether the presence of the mucus layer is necessary for olfactory response to occur in a water environment.

The glandular elements (i.e., Bowman's glands) that secrete the serous fluid constituting the aqueous mucus layer are located beneath the MOE. First seen in the 10–11 G week fetus (Pyatkina, 1982), with their number increasing after 15–16 G weeks (Tos & Poulsen, 1975; Chuah & Zheng, 1987), these glands seem to develop massively later in fetal life (5, 6, and 7 G months fetuses show sparse Bowman's glands; Nakashima et al., 1984). Some authors (Breipohl, 1972) presume that the contact with air is the stimulus that initiates mucus secretion, although others (Bang, 1964) report the presence of mucus several months prior to birth. It is still not known when the olfactory mucus layer appears, and what its structure and topography are in the human fetus.

Experimental arguments suggest that chemosensory responses precede the formation of the mucus film. In the rat fetus, the development of Bowman's glands begins around G day 18 (Farbman, 1986), whereas fetuses respond to water-diluted odorants in utero by G day 17 (Smotherman & Robinson, 1987). Moreover, rat fetuses were shown to react behaviorally (by G day 17) to air-diluted odorants injected into their mouth (Smotherman & Robinson, 1990), and even isolated olfactory neuroreceptors responded to odorants delivered in air by G day 16 (Gesteland, Yancy, & Farbman, 1982). Hence, the mucus film does not appear to be necessary for adequate stimulation to occur in an aqueous environment (at least in the short term of an experiment).

The question arises then of whether the chemosensory response is different when it takes place in either aquatic or aerial conditions of stimulation. The air/mucus layer interface appears to be the final limiting constraint to the odorant adsorption (Holley & MacLeod, 1977), and it should thus constitute a "formidable barrier" (Getchell & Getchell, 1990, p. 224) for the highly diluted, often hydrophobic, odorivector molecules. Although facilitating mechanisms (i.e., olfactory binding proteins) exist within the mucus and the MOE for the uptake of airborne odorants (Hornung, Yougentob, & Mozell, 1987), these may not be required in aquatic conditions (Carr, Gleeson, & Trapido-Rosenthal, 1990). The discontinuity between the aqueous mucus and the amniotic fluid is probably not as marked during the fetal period, with both media presumably sharing similar diffusion rates. Therefore it is possible that chemosensory stimulation may be equal, if not facilitated, in aquatic conditions. The temperature of the amniotic environment may be an additional facilitating factor of fetal nasal (and oral) chemoreception. Partial support for this idea comes from the positive relationship between the amplitude of the electrical response of the MOE and the temperature of the odorant (Ottoson, 1956).

In a behavioral study, rat fetuses stimulated with water solutions of cyclohexanone or lemon extract reacted more intensely than those exposed to the same odorants in air (Smotherman & Robinson, 1990). In addition, in amphibious animals (the frog), the electro-olfactogram is similar to water solutions of compounds that are odorous or even nonodorous in air (Getchell, 1969); this suggests that the same receptors can be functional in both environments, and that the spectrum of odorigenic compounds is broader in water than in air. This latter point is supported by early experiments administering odor solutions to adult humans (Aronsohn, 1884; Veress, 1903). Some low-vapor-pressure compounds lacking odor properties in air could be shown to evoke chemosensory sensation when dissolved and directly infused into the nasal passages. In summary, it may be expected that chemosensory stimulations are detectable at equal or lower threshold, and that the range of detectable chemicals is wider, in water as compared to air conditions.

Empirical Data on Early Functional Capacities of the Different Chemosensory Subsystems

It is now well established that human newborns display good sensivity to chemosensory stimuli administered nasally (for recent reviews, cf. Crook, 1987; Doty, 1992; Engen, 1986; Porter, Balogh, & Makin, 1988; Porter & Schaal, 1994; Schaal, 1988a, 1988b, 1991; Schmidt & Beauchamp, 1992;). Odor tests given to newborns shortly after birth (first hour, Peterson & Rayney, 1911; first day, Steiner, 1979) are indicative of a very precocial

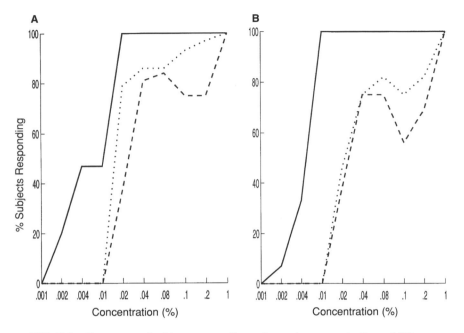

FIG. 12.1. Percentage of subjects responding to increasing concentrations of (A) asa fetida (A) and (B) a floral odor (unspecified) in adults (bold line), term newborns (dotted lines), and preterm newborns (dashed lines). After data from Kulakowskaia (1929).

onset of this ability, although it later improves (e.g., Lipsitt, Engen, & Kaye, 1963).

Odor reactivity tests have rarely been performed on prematures. They do, however, suggest the possibility of a comparable functional ability in the fetuses of equivalent G age. Initial studies of olfaction (Kulakowskaia, 1929; Peterson & Rayney, 1911; Stirnimann, 1936) indicated that premature infants responded to odorants (as attested by concurrent changes in the oral, facial, segmental, and general motor activity). Kulakowskaia (1929) compared the responsiveness to increasing concentrations of two odorants (oil of asa fetida and an unspecified floral odor) in preterm infants, term infants, and a sample of adults. Although the direct comparability of behavioral measures may be questioned between adults and newborns, it appears to be valid between term and preterm infants. The term newborns ($n = 29$) were tested between 1 hr and 5 days of age, whereas the preterms ($n = 16$) were tested within the 20 hr to 5 days range.[1] Figure 12.1 depicts the frequency of response in subjects in the three age groups. All premature infants reacted to both odorants. At lower concentrations they showed a detection deficit compared to the term infants, but both groups re-

---

[1]The G age of the preterm infants is not précised, but their birth weights ranged from 800 to 2,500 g, and their crown–heel length ranged from 36 to 45 cm.

sponded very similarly to the higher concentrations of both odorants. This finding suggests functional chemosensation in prematures, but at a lower level of performance than in term babies (see also Shimada, Takahashi, Imura, & Baba, 1987). Unfortunately, the prematures were not segregated for G age or postnatal age at testing, limiting the import of Kulakowskaia's findings. A more recent study with prematures of known G age showed that the proportion of newborns detecting mint odor at birth is related to G age (Fig. 12.2A; Sarnat, 1978). The majority of subjects responded to the stimulus between G weeks 28 and 32.

The increasingly consistent responsiveness to mint odor in premature infants can be compared with what is known about the neurochemical maturation of the olfactory tract (Fig. 12.2). In rats, olfactory neurons are thought to express specific olfactory marker protein (OMP) when they reach functional maturity, that is, when they synapse with mitral cells in the MOB and show selective responsiveness (Gesteland et al., 1982). Whether the same neurochemical functional correlation applies to humans is not ascertained, but the following data lean in that direction. In the human fetus, OMP is not detected before G week 28 (Chuah & Zheng, 1987; Nakashima, Kimmelman, & Snow, 1985); from that time onward, at a period when behavioral responses to odors are still weak and unreliable, OMP appears only at the periphery, in cell bodies and dendrites of the receptor cells, but not in axons (Chuah & Zheng, 1987). The appearance of OMP in the olfactory nerve was clear at 32 weeks, and from 35 weeks it was detected in the glomerular layer of the olfactory bulb as well. By that time, premature infants' behavioral responsiveness to odors is stable and comparable to that of term infants.

Some investigations report erratic chemosensory responses earlier than 28 week G age (Stirnimann, 1936). The stimulus used in these studies (anise oil) may have activated trigeminal responses, as may have the mint stimulus used in Sarnat's (1978) report. Indeed, the trigeminal subsystem is responsive to somesthesis as early as the first G trimester. Functional trigeminal input is further indicated by autonomic effects elicited by intranasal injections of pure air in prematures 26–45 G weeks old (Ramet, Praud, D'allest, Dehan, & Gaultier, 1990). By that age, it is likely that the trigeminus should also detect irritating properties of chemosensory stimuli.

Finally, recent (but still controversial) evidence of vomeronasal function in human adults again raises the question of its functional status during fetal life, that is, the time of maximal development (Humphrey, 1940). Monti-Bloch and Grosser (1991) reported that the elective chemical stimulation of the adult VNO produces receptor potential responses that cannot be assigned to olfactory or trigeminal terminals. The electrical responses are easily triggered by a class of undefined compounds referred to as *putative pheromones*, but not by olfactory stimuli such as clove, suggesting a

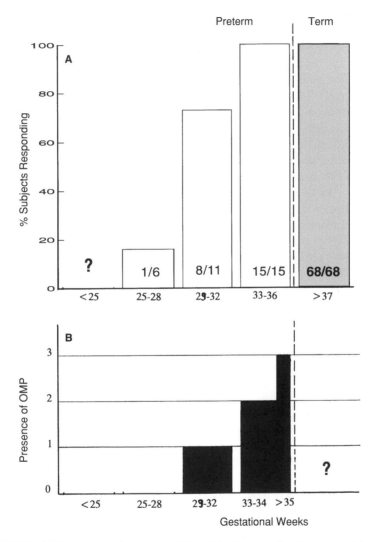

FIG. 12.2.   (A) Percentage of preterm and term infants responding to peppermint odor according to gestational age (the question mark indicates that no subjects were tested below 25 weeks; the number of subjects tested is indicated for each age group). After data from Sarnat (1978). (B) Detection of olfactory marker protein (OMP) at different levels of the olfactory subsystem according to gestational age (level 1, cell bodies and dendrites of the olfactory neuroreceptors; level 2, axons of the neuroreceptors, nerve layer of the olfactory bulb; level 3, glomerular layer of the olfactory bulb). The question mark indicates that no data were available for term newborns. After data from Nakashima et al. (1985) and Chuah and Zheng (1987).

specialized detector function of the VNO. A similar suggestion has been made for the functioning conditions of the VNO in other animals (Halpern, 1987; Wysocki, 1979). The vomeronasal system may thus have evolved as a *Wassergeruchsorgan* (Broman, 1920), an organ devised to smell water-dissolved compounds, and may thus play a significant role in the fetus. As yet, this hypothesis has been confirmed in rat fetuses only (Pedersen et al., 1983).

Because many chemical stimuli can stimulate the nasal chemoreceptors, these subsystems may well interact in the fetus. Functional overlap, synergy, or adaptive inhibition have indeed been reported in mature chemosensors. Mutual central inhibitory interactions have been described between olfactory *stricto sensu* and trigeminal sensations (Cain, 1976, Cain & Murphy, 1980). Nasal and oral chemoreceptive convergence has also been documented both structurally and functionally (e.g., Faurion, 1987). Further, if transfer of information exists between different sensory modalities (e.g., between visual, auditory, or tactile inputs; cf. Lewkowicz & Lickliter, 1994), then information transfer should also be possible in synergistic modalities (e.g., between olfactory and trigeminal, or olfactory and vomeronasal inputs). The different chemoreceptors can substitute for each other in transmitting chemosensory cues to the brain. For example, subjects totally lacking olfaction *sensu stricta* can detect and discriminate odorants with their trigeminal inputs (Doty et al., 1978). In the rat, the removal of the vomeronasal organ is compensated for by the main olfactory subsystem (Ichikawa, 1989). In total, the chemosensory equipment of the fetus should be considered as a range of sensors potentially capable of integrating qualitatively and quantitatively rich informations about its chemical environment.

Evidence of In Utero Chemosensory Function in the Sheep Model

We have strengthened the preceding arguments from humans by a direct test of odor responsiveness in sheep. Because it is often used to model physiological processes in the human fetus (e.g., Nathanielsz, 1984), and because of the ease of its experimental usage, the ovine fetus was chosen. More fundamental reasons make the fetal lamb a good model for human fetal development and function. In both species: (a) the chemosensory structures and processes investigated are homologous, (b) the maturation of the chemosensory system is nearly complete during the last months of gestation, implying that they developed within the prenatal chemosphere, and (c) the long gestation span results in sensorily precocial neonates.

Initial data on the functional status of the fetal lamb olfactory processing have been obtained recently (Schaal et al., 1991). Two near-term fetuses (G day 144) were externalized from the uterus and amnion, and were implanted with intranasal catheters and electrodes. Three catheters were sutured to the *alae nasi*, two in the left nare, and one in the opposite nare. The proximal end of the catheters was positioned in the postero-apical part of the nasal fossae, in the immediate vicinity of the MOE. The distal end of the catheters was connected to a hand-operated syringe in order to inject contrasted odorant solutions. The odorants consisted of citral and 2-methyl-2-thiazoline solutions in isotonic saline, which also served as the control stimulus. The rationale for choosing these substances was that citral (a lemon odor) was effective in fetal rats and 2-methyl-2-thiazoline (a foul odor) was shown to be strongly aversive in adult ewes. The injections of stimuli were at fetal temperature with low, regular pressure. Both odorants were infused into the left nare, with the right nare receiving the control infusions. Fetal heart rate was recorded through three silver electrodes implanted subcutaneously.

The intranasal infusions of distinct odor qualities to sheep fetuses induced differential heart rate responses. The most dramatic effects were triggered by 2-methyl-2-thiazoline infusions, which induced reliable bradycardias in both fetuses. Infusions of citral induced a weak accelerative effect in one fetus, but not in the other. Finally, no significant fetal heart rate variations were obtained in either fetus in response to control isotonic saline injections. Because control injections did not elicit significant heart rate changes, the potential confounding effects of somesthesis associated with the injection of fluids can be ruled out. In addition, the fact that the injections were of small quantities and made into the nasal passages rules out potential fetal heart rate changes triggered by the laryngeal chemoreflex.

The differential effectiveness of both stimuli might be related to contrasts in physicochemical (intensity, hydrophilicity) and/or hedonic properties in both stimuli. The weak effect of intranasal citral injections in the present experimental conditions was surprising compared to the clear results obtained in fetal rats (Pedersen & Blass, 1982; Smotherman & Robinson, 1987). These initial data indicate, however, that the ovine chemoreceptors can detect the presence of experimental odorants infused into the nose. Additional studies are needed to explore the stimulus–response relationships along both psychophysical and hedonic dimensions.

Permanent Chemosensory Adaptation In Utero?

How can nasal chemoreception take place in utero without being swamped by sensory adaptation due to chronic stimulation? Several mechanisms that disrupt presumed receptor fatigue can be proposed (e.g., Schaal &

Orgeur, 1992). Some of them may relate to general state alterations or specific behaviors expressed by the fetus; others may relate to short-term changes in the chemical qualities of the internal or external environment. First, the behavioral states of the fetus are extremely labile and produce differential occurrences of behaviors that may be involved in the swift renewal of the fluid directly bathing the sensory areas. Variations in fetal respiratory movements have been related to mother's metabolic state: The manipulation of maternal glycosemia by ingestion or intravenous injection of glucose have been reported to increase the frequency and amplitude of fetal inhalation–exhalation of amniotic fluid (e.g., Luther, Gray, Stinson, & Allen, 1984). State-related changes in oral activities (swallowing or sucking) may further result in the pulsatile displacement of the fluid contacting the chemoreceptive areas, and reset their detection abilities. Second, several sources of short-term changes of the chemical composition of the fetal milieu intérieur are periodically activated. One case is after the mother ingests foods or drinks, when both metabolites and aromas concurrently reach the level of the chemoreceptors through the hematogenic route. Another case of acute change in amniotic chemical composition involves alterations in maternal–fetal transfer. For instance, maternal stress or smoking induces transitory drops in the placental blood flow, slowing down the fetal supply of oxygen and metabolites and the backflow of wastes. That the fetus can detect such chemical transient hypoxia has been recently shown with experimental compression of the umbilical cord. Fetal rats were exposed to a single hypoxic episode and an injection of orange into the amniotic fluid. When tested in two-choice tests between orange and water, the 12-day-old pups exposed to orange followed by hypoxia avoided orange, whereas those exposed to orange during the recovery from hypoxia preferred orange. Short-term physiological changes can thus be detected and promote the integration of contiguous chemical stimuli (Hepper, 1991). Finally, the fetus itself may initiate short-term chemosensory changes of its amniotic fluid through the release of urine. Apart from the normal urine emission, the human fetus has indeed been shown to respond to external stressful stimulations (e.g., an intense vibroacoustic stimulation) by phasic bladder emptying (Zimmer, Chao, Guy, Marks, & Fifer, 1993).

TOWARD A CHEMICAL ECOLOGY OF THE FETUS

The prenatal environment has been extensively investigated to extract diagnostic chemical markers or to assess the fate of medication applied to the mother or the fetus itself. In contrast, which normal properties of the chemical environment might imprint on fetal psychobiological development has received little attention. It is clear that the fine organization of the chemoreceptors is heavily dependent on environmental stimulation (Brunjes & Frazier, 1986), and that it is completed during the last months of fetal life (discussed earlier). This means that the intraamniotic chemosensory ecology may promote epigenetic specifications of the nasal chemoreceptive structures and functions. By fetal chemical ecology, we mean the chemostimulative potential of the internal (blood) and external (amniotic fluid) milieux that may affect the fetus's sensory, perceptual, and behavioral organization. Accordingly, some general issues are addressed next: Are odorivector compounds present in utero? Which influences affect the odor qualities of the fetal chemical niche?

In Utero Presence of Odorivector Compounds

Human and ovine amniotic fluids contain a wide range of chemical compounds. Some recent gas chromatographic-mass spectrometric analyses could detect as much as 390 distinct compounds in a pool of amniotic fluid samples collected from 10 different women as early as 18 G weeks; at that same age, an average of 120 compounds was detected in individual amniotic fluid samples (Antoshechkin, Golovkin, Maximova, & Bakharev, 1989). Using high-resolution gas-phase analytical techniques, we observed a similar chemical variety in both human and ovine amniotic fluids collected at term (Rognon, Schaal, Orgeur, & Chastrette, in preparation). The way putative odorigenic compounds were extracted from amniotic fluid samples provided different major constituents, however. Dynamic headspace analyses of ovine amniotic fluid provided a chromatographic profile dominated by volatile esters and aromatic ketones and acids. Extraction of both human and ovine amniotic fluid samples by an organic solvent resulted in chromatographic profiles in which organic acids predominated. Both methods of amniotic fluid extraction provided strongly odorous extracts (with a tenacious, distinctive animal note) after the removal of the solvent. Some of the compounds of these mixtures could be identified and described as having odor properties in aerial conditions (Rognon et al., in preparation). Previous analyses have also reported the presence of a variety of potentially odorous compounds in the human amniotic fluid, including among others, several derivates of short-chain fatty acids with very pungent rancid or goaty odors (propionic, two derivates; butyric, six; valeric, six; caproic acids, four), of long-chain fatty acids with faint waxy odors (lauric, oleic, maleic, linoleic, stearic acids), of indole derivates (two) having a strong fecal note, and of polyenes (e.g., squalene, which has a mild oily odor; Coude, Chadefaux, Rabier, & Kamoun, 1990; Hoffmann, Aramaki, Blum-Hoffman, Nyhan, & Sweetman, 1989; Ng et al., 1982; Nichols, Hähnel, & Wilkinson, 1978). The amniotic

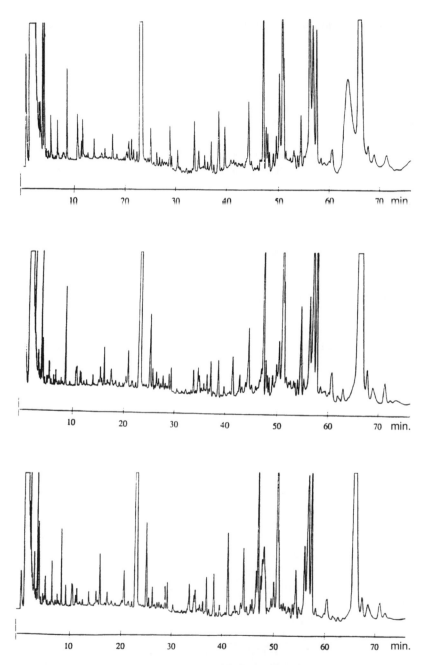

FIG. 12.3. Chromatograms obtained from three samples of human amniotic fluid (collected at term delivery; extracted with dichloromethane). Ordinate indicates the intensity of detected substances; the same elution program was used for all analyses, thereby permitting comparison of the different profiles. From Rognon, Schaal, Orgeur, and Chastrette (in preparation).

pool is thus rich in diverse putative odorants. Whether these compounds are present in concentrations sufficient to elicit chemosensation remains to be ascertained by both quantitative microanalysis and sensory evaluation with newborns. Rather low levels of concentrations are reported for organic acids (within the 1–15 ppm range; Hoffmann et al., 1989).

We are continuing our analyses to provide a descriptive picture of the main odoriferous compounds that the human fetus is exposed to near term. The capillary gas chromatograms in Fig. 12.3 are representative of the substance profiles obtained from amniotic fluid samples of three different parturient women who belong to the same culture. Visual examination of these profiles indicates a very similar pattern of peaks. There are observable differences that reflect quantitative rather than to qualitative variations, although these are not to be excluded (especially in the case of females living on different diets).

Sources of Odorivector Compounds

Long- and short-term alterations of the amniotic chemical ecology are under the control of both fetus and mother. During the second half of pregnancy, the amniotic chemical composition deviates increasingly from that of the surrounding compartments, due predominantly to the release of fetal urine. The volume of fetal micturition augments with advancing gestation, attaining a rate of 51 ml/hr near term (Rabinowitz, Peters, Vyas, Campbell, & Nicolaïdes, 1989). This is correlated with a huge increase in, among other compounds, urea during the second half of pregnancy with concentrations in amniotic fluid exceeding these of maternal serum (<20 weeks, 18 mg/100 ml; >38th week, 32 mg/100 ml; Lind, 1973; Räihä & Kekomäki, 1978). Such a change may be important for chemoreception because urea develops an ammonia-like odor (Budavari, 1989).

The profiles of constituents present in both fetal blood and amniotic fluid are dependent on maternal diet. For example, protocatechuic acid, which is present in only minute amounts in wheat grain, is easily detectable in ovine amniotic fluid (Rognon, Schaal, Orgeur, & Chastrette, in preparation). In humans also, the dominant odor quality of amniotic fluid can be influenced by what the mother has ingested. The infants and amniotic fluid of mothers that had eaten food strongly flavored with either cumin, fenugreek, or curry just prior to parturition were sufficiently tainted with these respective odors that they were detected by the obstetricians (Baum, 1981; Hauser, Chitayat, Berns, Braver, & Muhlhauser, 1985). In a controlled experiment, pregnant women (32–36 G weeks) were asked to ingest two cups of either regular or decaffeinated coffee during on-line registration of fetal breathing and heart rate (Salvador & Koos, 1989). The consumption of coffee had the same accelerative effect on fetal breathing rate, whether the coffee was decaffeinated or regular. This suggests that either psychoactive compounds other than caffeine are present in coffee, or that some of the various chemosensory compounds of coffee (e.g., Arnaud, 1988) are detected by the fetus.

To further investigate if and how maternal diet affects the olfactory qualities of the fetal environment, ewes were fed cumin seeds daily during the last two weeks of gestation (Schaal, Orgeur, Desage, & Brazier, 1994). At term, a number of fluids were sampled via cesarean section: These included maternal venous blood, fetal blood from both the umbilical and jugular veins, and amniotic and allantoic fluids. Compared with control ewes, which had ingested regular fodder, cumin-treated ewes had detectable plasma levels of the cumin aroma transfer markers. These compounds could also be detected in the umbilical venous plasma upstream from the fetal brain, in the fetal jugular venous plasma downstream from the fetal brain, but not in the amniotic fluid. Whether the absence of the cumin markers in the fluid pool external to the fetus is a consequence of fetal metabolization of these compounds, of their reexportation toward the maternal compartment, or of the inadequacy of our method to extract them from amniotic fluid remains to be determined. It is clear, however, that odorous constituents of the mother's diet are transferred into the fetal milieu intérieur at levels detectable by gas chromatography.

It should be noted, however, that in the previous experiment, the ratio of the ewe to fetus venous plasmatic levels of the cumin aroma markers was very high, suggesting a low rate of transplacental transfer of these compounds. This may be a consequence of the weak permeability of the ovine epithelochorial placenta (Boyd, Haworth, Stacey, & Ward, 1976). The situation may be different in the human haemomonochorial placenta where only two tissue layers separate maternal from fetal blood. Near term, this type of placenta is permeable to high-molecular weight solutes, up to 5,200 D (Thornburg, Burry, Adams, Kirk, & Faber, 1988; Willis, O'Grady, Faber, & Thornburg, 1986). Because of structural (increased exchange surface and reduced thickness of the placenta) and functional (increased utero-placental blood flow) modification in late gestation, the placental permeability is enhanced, thus reinforcing the influence of maternal dietary selection on the fetal environment. As Dancis noted, "given a sufficiently extended time scale and sufficiently sensitive detection methods, it is probably possible to demonstrate some transfer of all circulating material" (1978, p. 25).

To our knowledge, no serious verification of the transfer rate of maternal dietary flavors to the fetal compartment has been reported in the human literature, but experiments using pharmacologically active compounds are numerous (for reviews, cf. Mirkin & Singh, 1976; Seeds, 1980; Szeto, 1982). According to these studies, the placental crossing of individual compounds depends on their physicochemical properties. The permeability to hydrophilic constituents, for example, is proportional to the coefficient of free diffusion in water. Highly lipophilic substances (as the food flavors often are) are rapidly transferred to the fetal blood pool, but enter slowly into the amniotic pool (Seeds, 1980).

The variation range of fetal chemical ecology is thus first set by the chemical inputs provided by the mother's idiosyncratic diet, second by their selective passage through the placental barrier, and finally by their metabolic processing by the fetus. Whether fetuses are able to discriminate among odorants derived from amniotic fluid or from blood remains unanswered. This could be hypothesized if different populations of chemosensory receptors were differentially exposed to amniotic fluid or hematogenic stimuli. If such discrimination is possible, then fetuses may be able to distinguish odorants of maternal origin from odors resulting from fetal metabolism.

CONCLUSIONS AND FUTURE PERSPECTIVES

The present chapter has brought together data to support the idea that human olfactory function (detection abilities and preferences) may have an ontogenetic precedent in the chemoperceptions of the fetus. This is supported by a polymodal receptor equipment that develops very early during gestation. Among the four subsystems considered, two (olfactory and trigeminal) appear clearly functional during the last trimester, one (vomeronasal) is functional in human adults and in animal fetuses, and one (terminal) has as yet not been ascribed a sensory role. Whether these structures are operative in utero is not yet verified in the human fetus, but evidence from ex utero fetuses (prematures) indicates reactivity to air-diluted odor stimuli administered nasally. Animal studies demonstrate that these chemoreceptors are also responsive to water-diluted odorants in utero.

Chemical analysis presents the environment of the fetus as replete with varied potential odor stimuli. Two main media appear to convey these putative stimuli into contact with the fetal chemosensory areas. The amniotic flow through the nose channels putative odorants of mainly fetal origin, while the blood flow of the nasal mucosal capillaries may carry stimuli of mainly maternal origin. Although the chemical mixtures present in both media overlap because of the relative openness of the different compartments, the possibility exists that they are different, at least on quantitative grounds. This hypothesized dual possibility of stimulations provides an abundant and diverse source of chemosensory input to the fetus. Whether these chemosensory variations are eventually perceived by the fetus through both amniotic and hematogenic chemoreception remains central to our understanding of mammalian development of perception and motivation.

It may be objected that the fetal chemoreceptors do not detect odorants in the same way as a chromatograph does. The issue to be settled is: whether how, when, and what the human fetus perceives, and whether it retains postnatally chemosensory information from its amniotic ecology. The ultimate verification of olfactory perception in the human fetus would be to register psychophysiological or behavioral responses concurrent with odor infusion in utero. A direct approach on the human fetus is clearly not feasible on ethical grounds, and the use of animal models can satisfactorily help to test the biological validity of hypotheses formulated in humans. Increasingly sophisticated ultrasonographic visualization of fetal behavioral and autonomic responses could, however, be used to scrutinize potential responses to dietary compounds of known kinetics or to fetal release of urine in response to external stimulation. Alternatively, indirect strategies may be developed in parallel. A systematic screening of odor responsiveness in a sample of premature infants born at different G ages can provide interesting findings on the G age when chemosensation is beginning. Another approach may be to analyze the behavioral or autonomic responses of human newborns to odors extracted from the amniotic environment, which they were in contact with several hours or days before delivery.

ACKNOWLEDGMENTS

This research was supported by Ministère de la Recherche et de la Technologie (grant 89GO388 to B. Schaal) and by INRA (AIP Comportement et Adaptation des Animaux Domestiques). The authors are grateful to R. H. Porter, D. J. Lewkowicz, and J. P. Lecanuet for continuing discussions, to E. M. Blass, C. E. Evans, A. Faurion, and two anonymous referees for comments on earlier drafts, to Mrs. H. Bosc and M. Schmitz for the translation of Russian articles, and to C. Kervella, A.-Y. Jacquet, and E. Hertling for their generous help.

REFERENCES

Antoshechkin, A. G., Golovkin, A. B., Maximova, L. A., & Bakharev, V. A. (1989). Screening of amniotic fluid metabolites by gas chromatography-mass spectrometry. *Journal of Chromatography, 489*, 353–358.

Arnaud M. J. (1988). The metabolism of coffee constituents. In R. J. Clarke & R. Macrae (Eds.), *Coffee: Vol. 3. Physiology* (pp. 33–55). London: Elsevier.

Aronsohn, E. (1884). Beiträge zur Physiologie des Geruchs [Contributions to the physiology of olfaction]. *Archiven für Anatomie und Physiologie*, 163–167.

Bang, B. G. (1964). The mucous glands of the developing human nose. *Acta Anatomica, 59*, 297–314.

Barcroft, J., & Mason, M. F. (1938). The atmosphere in which the foetus lives. *Journal of Physiology (London), 93*, P22.

Baum, J. D. (1981). Parent-offspring relations in man. *Journal of Reproduction and Fertility, 62*, 651–656.

Bossy J. (1980). Development of olfactory and related structures in staged human embryos. *Anatomy and Embryology, 161*, 225–236.

Boyd, R. D., Haworth, C., Stacey, T. E., & Ward, R. H. T. (1976). Permeability of the sheep placenta to unmetabolized polar nonelectrolytes. *Journal of Physiology (London), 256*, 617–634.

Bradley R. M., & Mistretta C. M. (1971). Intravascular taste in rats as demonstrated by conditioned aversion to sodium saccharin. *Journal of Comparative and Physiological Psychology, 75*, 186–189.

Bradley, R. M., & Mistretta, C. M. (1975). Fetal sensory receptors. *Physiological Reviews, 55*, 352–382

Breipohl, W. (1972). Licht- und elektronmikroskopische Befunde zur Struktur der Bowmanschen Drüsen in Riechepithel der weissen Maus [Light- and electron-microscopic findings on the structure of Bowman's glands in the olfactory epithelium of the white mouse]. *Zeitschrift für Zellforschung, 131*, 329–346.

Broman, I. (1920). Das Organon Vomeronasale Jacobsoni—ein Wassergeruchsorgan. *Anatomische Hefte, 58*, 143–191.

Brookover, C. (1914). The peripheral distribution of the nervus terminalis in an infant. *Journal of Comparative Neurology, 28*, 349–360.

Brown, J. W. (1974). Prenatal development of the human chief sensory trigeminal nucleus. *Journal of Comparative Neurology, 156*, 307–336.

Brown, J. W. (1987). The nervus terminalis in insectivorous bats and notes on its presence during human ontogeny. *Annals of the New York Academy of Sciences, 519*, 184–200.

Brunjes P. C., & Frazier, L. L. (1986). Maturation and plasticity in the olfactory system of vertebrates. *Brain Research Reviews, 11*, 1–45.

Budavari, S. (Ed.). (1989). *The Merck Index*. Rahway, NJ: Merck.

Cain, W. S. (1976). Olfaction and the common chemical sense: Some psychophysical contrasts. *Sensory Processes, 1*, 57–67.

Cain, W. S., & Murphy, C. L. (1980). Interaction between chemoreceptive modalities of odour and irritation. *Nature, 284*, 255–258.

Carmichael, L. (1970). Onset and early development of behavior. In P. H. Mussen (Ed.), *Manual of child psychology* (Vol. 1., pp. 447–563). New York: Wiley.

Carr, W. E. S., Gleeson, R. A., & Trapido-Rosenthal, H. G. (1990). The role of peri–receptor events in chemosensory processes. *Trends in Neuroscience, 13*, 212–215.

Cauna, N., Hinderer, K. & Wentges, R. T. (1969). Sensory receptor organs of the human respiratory mucosa. *American Journal of Anatomy, 124*, 607–612.

Caza, P.A., & Spear, N. E. (1984). Short-term exposure to an odor increases its subsequent preference in preweanling rats: A descriptive profile of the phenomenon. *Developmental Psychobiology, 17,* 407–422.

Chotro, M. G., & Molina, J. C. (1990). Acute ethanol contamination of the amniotic fluid during gestational day 21: Postnatal changes in alcohol responsiveness in rats. *Developmental Psychobiology, 23,* 535–547.

Christ, J. E., & Meiniger, M. G. (1983). Ultrasound study of the nose and upper lip before birth. *Annals of Plastic Surgery, 11,* 308–312.

Chuah, M. I., & Zheng, D. R. (1987). Olfactory marker protein is present in olfactory receptor cells of human fetuses. *Neuroscience, 23,* 363–370.

Cooper, W. E., & Burghard, G. M. (1990). Vomerolfaction and vomodor. *Journal of Chemical Ecology, 16,* 103–105.

Coppola, D. M., & O'Connell, R. J. (1989). Stimulus access to olfactory and vomeronasal receptors in utero. *Neuroscience Letters, 106,* 241–248.

Coppola, D. M., Budde, J., & Millar, L. (1993). The vomeronasal duct has a protracted postnatal development in mouse. *Journal of Morphology, 218,* 59–64.

Coude M., Chadefaux, B., Rabier, D., & Kamoun, P. (1990). Early amniocentesis and amniotic fluid organic acid levels in the prenatal diagnosis of organic acidemias. *Clinica Chimica Acta, 187,* 329–332.

Crook, C. (1987). Taste and olfaction. In P. Salapatek & L. Cohen, L. (Eds.), *Handbook of infant perception: Vol. 1. From sensation to perception* (pp. 237–264). Orlando, FL: Academic Press.

Dancis, J. (1978). The placenta: An overview. In U. Stawe (Ed.), *Perinatal physiology* (pp. 19–26). New York: Plenum.

Demski, L. S., & Schwanzel-Fukuda, M. (Eds.). (1987). The terminal nerve (nervus terminalis): Structure, function and evolution. *Annals of the New York Academy of Sciences, 519,* 1–465.

Doty, R. L. (1992). Olfactory function in neonates. In D. G. Laing, R. L. Doty, & W. Breipohl (Eds.), *The human sense of smell* (pp. 155–165). Berlin: Springer Verlag.

Doty, R. L., Brugger, W. E., Lurs, P. C., Orndorff, M. A., Snyder, P. F., & Lowry, L. D. (1978). Intranasal trigeminal stimulation from odorous volatiles: Psychometric responses from anosmic and normal humans. *Physiology & Behavior, 20,* 175–187.

Duenholter, J. H., & Pritchard, J. A. (1976). Fetal respiration: Quantitative measurements of amniotic fluid inspired near term by human and rhesus fetuses. *American Journal of Obstetrics and Gynecology, 125,* 306–309.

Edelstone, D. I., Merick, R. E., Caritis, S. N., & Müller-Heubach, E. (1980). Umbilical venous blood flow and its distribution before and during autonomic blocade in fetal lambs. *American Journal of Obstetrics and Gynecology, 138,* 703–707.

Engen, T. (1986). Children's sense of smell. In H. L. Meiselman & R. S. Rivlin (Eds.), *Clinical measurement of taste and smell* (pp. 316–325). New York: Macmillan.

Farbman, A. I. (1986). Prenatal development of mammalian olfactory receptor cells. *Chemical Senses, 11,* 3–18.

Farbman, A. I. (1991). Developmental neurobiology of the olfactory system. In T. V. Getchell, R. L. Doty, L. M. Bartoshuk, & J. B. Snow (Eds.), *Smell and taste in health and disease* (pp. 19–33). New York: Raven Press.

Faurion, A. (1987). Physiology of the sweet taste. *Progress in Sensory Physiology, 8*, 129–201.

Feldman, W. M. (1920). *Principles of ante-natal and post-natal child physiology.* New York: Longmans-Green.

Ferrill, A. L. (1987). *The child before birth.* Ithaca, NY: Cornell University Press.

Gasser, R. F. (1977). *Atlas of human embryos.* New York: Harper & Row.

Gesteland, R. C., Yancey, R. A., & Farbman, A. I. (1982). Development of olfactory receptor neuron selectivity in the rat fetus. *Neurosciences, 7*, 3127–3136.

Getchell, T. V. (1969). The interaction of the peripheral olfactory system with non-odorous stimuli. In C. Pfaffman (Ed.), *Olfaction and taste III* (pp. 112–128). New York: Rockfeller University Press.

Getchell, T. V., & Getchell, M. L. (1990). Regulatory factors in the vertebrate olfactory mucosa. *Chemical Senses, 15*, 223–231.

Golubeva, E. L., Shulejkina, K. V., & Vainstein, I. I. (1959). The development of reflex and spontaneous activity of the human fetus during embryogenesis. *Obstetrics and Gynecology (USSR), 3*, 59–62.

Gottlieb, G. (1971). Ontogenesis of sensory function in birds and mammals. In E. Tobach, L. R. Aronson, & E. Shaw (Eds.), *Biopsychology of development*, (pp. 67–128). New York: Academic Press.

Graziadei, P. P. C. (1977). Functional anatomy of the mammalian chemoreceptor system. In D. Müller-Schwarze & M. M. Mozell (Eds.), *Chemical signals in vertebrates* (pp. 435–454). New York: Plenum.

Gueubelle, F. (1984). Perception of environmental conditions by fetus in utero. *Progress in Reproductive Biology and Medicine, 11*, 110–119.

Halpern, M. (1987). The organization and function of the vomeronasal system. *Annual Review of Neuroscience, 10*, 325–362.

Harding, R., Bocking, A. D., & Sigger, J. N. (1984). Composition and volume of fluid swallowed by fetal sheep. *Quarterly Journal of Experimental Physiology, 69*, 487–495.

Hauser, G. J., Chitayat, D., Berns, L., Braver, D., & Muhlhauser, B. (1985). Peculiar odours in newborns and maternal prenatal ingestion of spicy foods. *European Journal of Pediatrics, 144*, 403.

Hepper, P. G. (1987). The amniotic fluid: An important priming role in kin recognition. *Animal Behavior, 35*, 1343–1346.

Hepper, P. G. (1991). Transient hypoxic episodes: A mechanism to support associative fetal learning. *Animal Behavior, 41*, 477–480.

Hoffmann, G., Aramaki, S., Blum-Hoffmann, E., Nyhan, W., & Sweetman, L. (1989). Quantitative analysis for organic acids in biological samples: Batch isolation followed by gas chromatographic-mass spectrometric analysis. *Clinical Chemistry, 35*, 587–595.

Hogg, I. D. (1941). Sensory nerves and associated structures in the skin of human fetuses of 8 to 14 weeks of menstrual age correlated with functional capacity. *Journal of Comparative Neurology, 75*, 371–410.

Holley, A., & Macleod, P. (1977). Transduction et codage des informations olfactives chez les vertébrés [Transduction and coding of olfactory information in vertebrates]. *Journal de Physiologie (Paris), 73*, 725–828.

Hornung, D. E., Yougentob, S. L., & Mozell, M. M. (1987). Olfactory mucosa/air partitioning of odorants. *Brain Research, 413,* 147–154.

Hudson, R., & Distel, H. (1983). Nipple location by newborn rabbits: Evidence for pheromonal guidance. *Behaviour, 81,* 260–275.

Humphrey, T. (1940). The development of the olfactory and the accessory olfactory formations in human embryos and fetuses. *Journal of Comparative Neurology, 73,* 431–468.

Humphrey, T. (1963). The development of the anterior olfactory nucleus of human fetuses. *Progress in Brain Research, 3,* 170–190.

Humphrey, T. (1966). The development of trigeminal nerve fibers to the oral mucosa, compared with their development to cutaneous surfaces. *Journal of Comparative Neurology, 126,* 91–108.

Humphrey, T. (1967). The development of the human tuberculum olfactorium during the first three month of embryonic life. *Journal für Hirnforschung, 9,* 437.

Humphrey, T. (1968). The development of the human amygdala during early embryonic life. *Journal of Comparative Neurology, 132,* 135.

Humphrey, T. (1978). Functions of the nervous system during prenatal life. In U. Stave (Ed.), *Perinatal physiology* (pp. 651–683). New York: Plenum.

Ichikawa, M. (1989). Recovery of olfactory behavior following removal of accessory olfactory bulb. *Brain Research, 498,* 45–48.

Johnson, A., Josephson, R., & Hawke, M. (1985). Clinical and histological evidence for the presence of the vomeronasal (Jacobson's) organ in adult human. *Journal of Otolaryngology, 14,* 71–79.

Johnston, J. B. (1914). The nervus terminalis in man and mammals. *Journal of Comparative Neurology, 8,* 185–198.

Kasama, R., & Zusho, H. (1981). A study on concentrations of odorous substance in intravenous olfaction test. *Japanese Journal of Otology (Tokyo), 84,* 400–407.

Keil, W., von Stralendorff, F., & Hudson, R. (1990). A behavioral bioassay for analysis of rabbit nipple-seach pheromone. *Physiology and Behavior, 47,* 525–529.

Kindermann, U., Hudson, R., & Distel, H. (1994). Learning of suckling odors by newborn rabbits declines with age and suckling experience. *Developmental Psychobiology, 27,* 199–210.

Kodama, N. (1987, July). *Fetal memory in utero of mice.* Ninth Biennal Meeting of the International Society for the Study of Behavioral Development, Tokyo.

Kodama, N. (1990, July). *Preference for amniotic fluid in newborn mice.* Annual Meeting of the International Society of Developmental Psychobiology, Cambridge, UK.

Kreutzer, E. W., & Jafek, B. W. (1980). The vomeronasal organ of Jacobson in the human embryo and fetus. *Otolaryngology, Head and Neck Surgery, 88,* 119–123.

Kulakowskaia, E. C., (1929). Nablioudenia nad Tchouvstom vkusa i obanianiia novoro zhdennbikh [Observations on the sense of taste and smell in newborns], *Zhurnal Izucheniya Rannego Detskogo Vospr Vorasta (Moscow), 9,* 15–20.

Larsell, O. (1950). The nervus terminalis. *Annals of Otology, Rhinology and Laryngology, 59,* 414–438.

Le Magnen, J. (1969). Olfaction. In C. Kayser (Ed.), *Traité de physiologie* (pp. 749–801). Paris: Flammarion.

Lewkowicz, D. J., & Lickliter, R. E. (Eds.). (1994). *Development of intersensory perception: Comparative perspectives.* Hillsdale, NJ: Lawrence Erlbaum Associates.

Lind, T. (1973). The biochemistry of amniotic fluid. In D. V. Fairweather & T. Eskes (Eds.), *Amniotic fluid: Research and clinical applications* (pp. 60–81). Amsterdam: Excerpta Medica.

Lipsitt, L. P., Engen, T., & Kaye, H. (1963). Developmental changes in the olfactory threshold of the neonate. *Child Development, 34,* 371–376.

Logvinenko, A. V. (1990). Recording of fetal respiratory movements based on studying the shifting of the amniotic fluid in the trachea by the Doppler effect. *Akush Ginekologia (Moskow), 7,* 38–41.

Lotgering, F. K., & Wallenburg, H. C. S. (1986). Mechanisms of production and clearance of amniotic fluid. *Seminars in Perinatology, 10,* 94–102.

Luther, E. R., Gray, J. H., Stinson, D., & Allen, A. (1984). Characteristics of glusoce-stimulated breathing movements in fetus with intra-uterine growth retardation. *American Journal of Obstetrics and Gynecology, 148,* 640–644.

Macchi, G. (1951). The ontogenetic development of the olfactory telencephalon in man. *Journal of Comparative Neurology, 95,* 245–305.

McCotter, R. E. (1915). A note on the course and distribution of the nervus terminalis in man. *Anatomical Record, 9,* 243–246.

Macfarlane, A. J. (1975). Olfaction in the development of social preferences in the human neonate. *Ciba Foundation Symposia, 33,* 103–117.

Makin, J. W., & Porter, R. H. (1989). Attractiveness of lactating females' breast odors to neonates. *Child Development, 60,* 803–810.

Maruniak, J. A., Silver, W. L., & Moulton D. G. (1983). Olfactory receptors respond to blood-borne odorants. *Brain Research, 265,* 312–316.

Meisami, E. (1987). Olfactory development in the human. In E. Meisami & P. S. Timiras (Eds.), *Handbook of human growth and developmental biology: Vol. I. Neural, sensory and integrative development* (pp. 33–61). Boca Raton, FL: CRC.

Mirkin, B. L., & Singh, S. (1976). Placental transfer of pharmacologically active molecules. In B. L. Mirkin (Ed.), *Perinatal pharmacology and therapeutics* (pp. 1–10). New York: Academic Press.

Monti-Bloch, L., & Grosser B. I. (1991). Effect of putative pheromones on the electrical activity of the human vomeronasal organ and olfactory epithelium. *Journal of Steroid Biochemistry and Molecular Biology, 39,* 573–582.

Moran, D. T., Jafek, B. W., & Rowley, J. C. (1991). The vomeronasal (Jacobson's) organ in man: Ultrastructure and frequency of occurrence. *Journal of Steroid Biochemistry and Molecular Biology, 39,* 545–552.

Morrow-Tesch, J., & McGlone J. J. (1990). Sources of maternal odors and the development of odor preferences in baby pigs. *Journal of Animal Science, 68,* 3563–3571.

Naessen, R. (1971). An enquiry on the morphological characteristics and possible changes with age in the olfactory region of man. *Acta Otolaryngologica, 71,* 49–62.

Nakashima, T., Kimmelman, C. P., & Snow, J. B (1984). Structure of human fetal and adult olfactory neuro-epithelium. *Archives of Otolaryngology, 110,* 641–646.

Nakashima, T., Kimmelman, C. P., & Snow, J. B. (1985). Immunohistopathology of human olfactory epithelium, nerve and bulb. *Laryngoscope, 95,* 391–396.

Nathanielsz, P. W. (Ed.). (1984). *Animal models in fetal medicine.* New York: Perinatology Press.

Ng, K. J., Andresen, B. D., Bianchine, J. R., Iams, J. D., O'Shaugnessy, R. W., Stempel,

L. E, & Zuspan, F. (1982). Capillary gas chromatographis-mass spectrometric profiles of trimethylsilyl derivatives of organic acids from amniotic fluis of different gestational age. *Journal of Chromatography, 228,* 43–50.

Nicholls, T. M., Hähnel, R., & Wilkinson, S. P. (1978). Organic acids in amniotic fluid. *Clinica Chimica Acta, 84,* 11–17.

Oelschläger, H. A., Buhl, E. A., & Dann, J. F. (1987). Development of the nervus terminalis in mammals including toothed whales and humans. In L. S. Demski & M. Schwanzel-Fukuda (Eds.), The terminal nerve (nervus terminalis). Structure, Function, evolution. *Annals of the New York Academy of Sciences, 519,* 447–464.

Ortmann, R. (1989). Über Sinneszellen am fetalen vomeronasalen Organ des Menschen [On the sensory cells in the fetal vomeronasal organ in humans]. *Hals, Nase, Ohren, 37,* 191–197.

Ottoson, D. (1956). Analysis of the electrical activity of the olfactory epithelium. *Acta Physiologica Scandinavica, 35* (Suppl. 122), 1–83.

Parfet, K. A. R., & Gonyou, H. W. (1991). Attraction of newborn piglets to auditory, visual, olfactory and tactile stimuli. *Journal of Animal Science, 69,* 125–133.

Pearson, A. A. (1941). The development of the olfactory nerve in man. *Journal of Comparative Neurology, 75,* 199–217.

Pearson, A. A. (1942). The development of the olfactory nerve, nervus terminalis and the vomeronasal nerve in man. *Annals of Otology, Rhinology, Laryngology, 51,* 317–333.

Pedersen, P. A., & Blass, E. M. (1981). Olfactory control over suckling in albino rat. In R. N. Aslin, J. R. Alberts, & M. R. Petersen (Eds.), *The development of perception: Psycho-biological processes* (pp. 359–381). Hillsdale, NJ: Lawrence Erlbaum Associates.

Pedersen, P. A., & Blass, E. M. (1982). Prenatal and postnatal determinants of the 1st suckling episode in albino rats. *Developmental Psychobiology, 15,* 349–355.

Pedersen, P. A., Steward, W. B., Greer, C. A., & Sheperd G. M. (1983). Evidence for olfactory function in utero. *Science, 221,* 478–480.

Peterson, F., & Rayney, L. H. (1911). The beginnings of mind in the newborn. *Bulletin of the Lying-in Hospital of New York City, 7,* 99–122.

Porter, R. H., & Schaal, B. (1995). Olfaction and development of social preferences in neonatal organisms. In R. L. Doty (Ed.), *Handbook of clinical olfaction and gestation* (pp. 299–321). New York: Marcel Dekker.

Porter, R. H., Balogh, R. D., & Makin, J. W. (1988). Olfactory influences on mother-infant interactions. In C. Rovee-Collier & L. P. Lipsitt (Eds.), *Advances in infancy research* (Vol. 5, pp. 39–68). Norwood, NJ: Ablex.

Porter, R. H., Makin, J. W., Davis, L. B., & Christensen, K. M. (1991). An assessment of the salient olfactory environment of formula-fed infants. *Physiology and Behavior, 50,* 907–911.

Porter, R. H., Makin, J. W., Davis, L. B., & Christensen, K. M. (1992). Responsiveness of infants to olfactory cues from lactating females. *Infant Behavior and Development, 15,* 85–93.

Preyer, W. (1881). *Die Seele des Kindes* [the mind of the infant]. (French translation). Paris: Alcan.

Pritchard, J. A. (1966). Deglutition by normal and anencephalic fetuses. *Obstetrics and Gynecology, 25,* 289–299.

Pyatkina, G. A. (1982). Development of the olfactory epithelium in man. *Zeitschrift für Mikroskopie und Anatomische Forschung, 96*, 361–372.

Rabinowitz, R., Peters, M. T., Vyas, S., Campbell, S., & Nicolaides, K. (1989). Measurement of fetal urine production in normal pregnancy by real-time ultrasonography. *American Journal of Obstetrics and Gynecology, 161*, 1264–1266.

Räihä, N. C., & Kekomäki, M. (1978). Development of the ornithine-urea cycle. In U. Stawe (Ed.), *Perinatal physiology* (pp.   ). New York: Plenum.

Ramet, J., Praud, J. P., D'Allest, A. M., Dehan, M., & Gaultier, C. (1990). Trigeminal airstream stimulation: maturation-related cardiac and respiratory responses during REM sleep in human infants. *Chest, 98*, 92–96.

Riggs, K. W., Rurak, D. W., Yoo, S. D., McErlane, B. A., McMorland, G. H., & Axelson, J. E. (1987). Drug accumulation in lung fluids of the fetal lamb after maternal or fetal administration. *American Journal of Gynecology and Obstetrics, 157*, 1286–1291.

Rognon, C., Schaal, B., Orgeur, P., & Chastrette, M. (in preparation). The odorous compounds of amniotic fluid: First data on ovine and human samples.

Salvador H. S. & Koos B. J. (1989). Effects of regular and decaffeinated coffee on fetal breathing and heart rate. *American Journal of Obstetrics and Gynecology, 160*, 1043-1047.

Sarnat, H. B. (1978). Olfactory reflexes in the newborn infant. *Journal of Pediatrics, 92*, 624–626.

Schaal, B. (1988a). Olfaction in infants and children: Developmental and functional perspectives. *Chemical Senses, 13*, 145–190.

Schaal, B. (1988b). Discontinuité natale et continuité chimio-sensorielle. Modèles animaux et hypothèses pour l'homme [Natal discontinuity and chemosensory continuity. Animal models and hypotheses for the human case]. *l'Année Biologique, 27*, 1–41.

Schaal, B. (1991). L'organisation de la perception olfactive au cours de la période périnatale [The organization of olfactory perception during the perinatal period]. In F. Jouen & A. Hénocq (Eds.), *Du nouveau-né au nourrisson* (pp. 63–91). Paris: PUF.

Schaal, B., & Orgeur, P. (1992). Olfaction *in utero*: Can the rodent model be generalized? *Quarterly Journal of Experimental Psychology, 44B*, 245–278.

Schaal, B., Orgeur, P., Desage, M., & Brazier, J. L. (1994). *Transfer of the aromas of the pregnant and lactating mother's diet to the fetal and neonatal environments in the sheep.* Presented at the XIth Congress of the European Chemoreception Research Organization, Blois, France, July 1994.

Schaal, B., Orgeur, P., Lecanuet, J. P., Locatelli, A., Granier-Deferre, C., & Poindron, P. (1991). Chémoreception nasale in utero: Expériences préliminaires chez le foetus ovin [Nasal chemoreception in utero: Preliminary experiments in the fetal sheep]. *Comptes Rendus de l'Académie des Sciences (Paris), Série III, 113*, 319–325.

Schaal, B., Orgeur, P., & Arnould, C. (submitted). Olfactory preferences in newborn lambs: Possible influence of prenatal experience.

Schaffer, J. P. (1910). The lateral wall of the cavum nasi in man with special reference to the various developmental stages. *Journal of Morphology, 21*, 613–707.

Schmidt, H .J., & Beauchamp, G. K. (1992). Human olfaction in infancy and early childhood. In M. J. Serby & K. L. Chobor (Eds.), *Science of olfaction* (pp. 378–395). New York: Springer Verlag.

Schwanzel-Fukuda, M., & Pfaff, D. W. (1987). Passive immunization of fetal rats with antiserum to LHRH or transection of the central roots of the nervus terminalis does not affect rat pups' preference for home nest. *Physiology and behavior, 41*, 613–619.

Seeds, A. E. (1980). Current concepts of amniotic fluid dynamics. *American Journal of Gynecology and Obstetrics, 138*, 575–586.

Sheperd, G. M., Pedersen, P. A., & Greer, C. A. (1987). Development of olfactory specificity in the albino rat: a model system. In N. A. Krasnegor, E. M. Blass, M. A. Hofer, & W. P. Smotherman (Eds.), *Perinatal development, a psychobiological perspective* (pp. 127–144). Orlando, FL: Academic Press.

Shimada, M., Takahashi, S., Imura, S., & Baba, K. (1987). Olfaction in neonates. *Chemical Senses, 12*, 518.

Smotherman, W. P. (1982a). Odor aversion learning by the rat fetus. *Physiology and Behavior, 29*, 769–771.

Smotherman, W. P. (1982b). In utero chemosensory experience alters taste preferences and corticosterone responsiveness. *Behavioral and Neural Biology, 36*, 61–68.

Smotherman, W. P., & Robinson, S. R. (1987). Psychobiology of fetal experience in the rat. In N. A. Krasnegor, E. M. Blass, M. A. Hofer, & W. P. Smotherman (Eds.), *Perinatal development* (pp. 39–60). Orlando, FL: Academic Press.

Smotherman, W. P., & Robinson, S. R. (1988). Behavior of rat fetuses following chemical or tactile stimulation. *Behavioral Neuroscience, 102*, 24–34.

Smotherman, W. P., & Robinson, S. R. (1990). Rat fetuses respond to chemical stimuli in gas phase. *Physiology and Behavior, 47*, 863–868.

Steiner, J. E. (1977). Facial expressions of the neonate infant indicating the hedonics of food-related stimuli. In J. M. Weiffenbach (Ed.), *Taste and development, the genesis of sweet preference* (pp. 173–188). Bethesda, MD: National Institutes of Health, Department of Health, Education and Welfare.

Steiner, J. E. (1979). Human facial expressions in response to taste and smell stimulations. In L. P. Lipsitt, & H. W. Reese (Eds.), *Advances in child development* (Vol. 13, pp. 257–295). New York: Academic Press.

Stickrod, G., Kimble, D. P., & Smotherman, W. P. (1982). In utero taste odor aversion conditioning of the rat. *Physiology and Behavior, 28*, 5–7.

Stirnimann, F. (1936). Versuche über Geschmack und Geruch am ersten Lebenstag [Experiments on taste and smell during the first day after birth]. *Jahrbuch für Kinderheilkunde, 146*, 211–227.

Sullivan, R. M., & Wilson, D. A. (1991). Neural correlates of conditioned odor avoidance in infant rats. *Behavioral Neuroscience, 105*, 85–90.

Szeto, H. H. (1982). Pharmacokinetics in the ovine maternal-fetal unit. *Annual Review of Pharmacology and Toxicology, 22*, 221–243.

Teatini, G. P., & Pincini, G. (1961). Estimulacion olfatoria por via hematica [Olfactory stimulation through blood]. *Acta Oto-Rino-Laringologica Ibero-Americana, 12*, 377–400.

Teicher, M. H., & Blass, E. M. (1977). First suckling response in the newborn albino rat: the roles of olfaction and amniotic fluid. *Science, 198*, 635–636.

Thornburg, K. L., Burry, K. J., Adams, A. K., Kirk, E. P., & Faber, J. J. (1988). Permeability of placenta to inulin. *American Journal of Obstetrics and Gynecology, 158*, 1165–1169.

Tinbergen, N. (1960). The natural control of insects in pinewoods: 1. Factors influencing the intensity of predation by songbirds. *Archives Néerlandaises de Zoologie, 13*, 265–336.

Tos, M., & Poulsen, J. (1975). Mucous glands in the developing human nose. *Archives of Otolaryngology, 101*, 367–372.

Tücker, D. (1971). Nonolfactory responses from the nasal cavity: Jacobson's organ and the trigeminal system. In Beidler, L. M. (Ed.), *Handbook of Sensory Physiology: Vol. 4. Chemical Senses, Part 1, Olfaction* (pp. 151–181). Berlin: Springer Verlag.

Veress, E. (1903). Über die Reizung des Riechorgans durch direkte Einwirkung riechender Flüssigkeiten [On the stimulation of the olfactory organ through direct application of odorous solutions]. *Pflüger's Archivs für gesamte Physiologie, 95*, 368-408.

Vince, M. A., & Ward, T. M. (1984). The responsiveness of newly born clun-forest lambs to odour sources in the ewe. *Behaviour, 89*, 117–127.

Wang, H. W., Wysocki, C. J., & Gold, G. H. (1993). Induction of olfactory receptor sensitivity. *Science, 260*, 998–1000.

Willis, D. M., O'Grady, J. P., Faber, J. J., & Thornburg, K. L. (1986). Diffusion permeability of cyanocobalamin in human placenta. *American Journal of Physiology, 250*, R459–R464.

Wysocki, C. K. (1979). Neurobehavioral evidence for the involvement of the vomeronasal system in mammalian reproduction. *Neuroscience and Biobehavioral Reviews, 3*, 301–341.

Zimmer, E. Z., Chao, C. R., Guy, G. P., Marks, F., & Fifer, W. P. (1993). Vibroacoustic stimulation evokes human fetal micturition. *Obstetrics and Gynecology, 81*, 178–180.

13

Human Fetal Auditory Perception

Jean-Pierre Lecanuet
Carolyn Granier-Deferre
Centre National de la Recherche Scientifique
Ecole Pratique des Hautes Etudes

Marie-Claire Busnel
Centre National de la Recherche Scientifique, Paris

As recently as the 1920s and the 1930s, obstetricians began to consider the possibility of fetal audition and started to investigate fetal responsiveness to loud external sounds (Forbes & Forbes, 1927; Peiper, 1925; Ray, 1932; Sontag & Wallace, 1934, 1935, 1936). Two factors influenced the design of these studies and the majority of the ones that followed. First, due to the idea that the fetus was sensorially isolated and the observation of many pregnant women that their babies moved when a very loud noise occurred, it was believed that last trimester fetuses probably perceived only sudden, very loud sounds. Second, the major clinical concerns, which were antenatal detection of deafness and diagnosis of fetal well-being, required the use of acoustic stimuli that were easy to deliver and were known to elicit startle responses (sudden, strong motor responses), easily interpretable in daily medical practice. Thus, from the initial work of Peiper (1925), many studies have been conducted with stimuli of sound pressure levels (SPL) at or over 100 dB SPL (reference: 20 μPa in this chapter if not otherwise stated) applied directly to the mother's abdomen so as to reduce sound pressure loss. In the 1980s, vibroacoustic devices, such as the electroacoustic larynx, delivering broad-band noises with highest pressure levels in the low frequencies (>135 dB SPL in utero in the sheep), were adopted (Gagnon, Benzaquen, & Hunse, 1992; Gerhardt, 1989). The devices are designed to propagate sound pressure more efficiently through tissues and fluids than through air. The problem of impedance mismatch is therefore avoided. However, a problem with vibroacoustic devices for research on audition is that they introduce nonauditory stimulation. They might activate fetal cutaneous receptors, which mature very early in development (Hooker, 1952), and also possibly the sacculus. The latter, which is part of the vestibular system, matures 2 weeks earlier than the auditory apparatus (Pujol & Sans, 1986) and is known to be activated by loud low frequencies in different species including the human (Cazals, Aran, & Erre, 1983; Ribaric, Bleeker, & Witt, 1992). The possibility of such activation makes it difficult not only to rely on the data obtained to determine, for instance, the onset of auditory function, but also to draw any precise conclusions regarding fetal audition.

Because our main interest is fetal auditory abilities, a historical survey of the studies in which the experimental design minimized the possibility of multimodal fetal stimulation is presented. Studies that have used broadspectrum vibrators applied to the maternal abdomen are reported in several other chapters in this book (see Gagnon, chapter 8, Kisilevsky, chapter 14, and Leader, chapter 21, in this volume).

All recent studies have shown that the acoustic structure of the intrauterine environment includes many components of external sounds emitted at or over 60 dB in the close vicinity of a pregnant woman, including her own vocalizations (Abrams, Gehrardt, & Peters, chapter 17, this volume; Benzaquen, Gagnon, Hunse, & Foreman, 1990; Querleu, Renard, Boutteville, & Crépin, 1989). This means that the fetal cochlea is stimulated by many complex sounds during the last trimester of gestation and that the fetus may be capable of discriminating some of their acoustical features, such as intensity and frequency. Our attention is therefore focused on the effect of these parameters on fetal responsiveness to (a) startling auditory stimuli and (b) nonstartling complex noises. The results reported in this chapter are only from experiments carried out prior to labor on healthy nonrisk samples of subjects.

STARTLING AUDITORY STIMULATION

In the earliest studies, investigators used airborne stimuli that could be characterized as rough, intense, and "ecological"; examples of such stimuli are warning horns (Fleischer, 1955; Peiper, 1925) and wood claps (Forbes & Forbes, 1927; Ray, 1932; Spelt, 1948). In the 1950s experimenters utilized more carefully defined acoustic stimulation like pure tones and band noises. The airborne mode of stimulation was abandoned in favor of stimulation applied directly on the mother, near the fetal head, so as to avoid or minimize sound pressure loss (see Tables 13.1 and 13.2). Two procedures were used:

1. Stimulation was air-coupled, and in most cases the loudspeaker was isolated from the mother's abdomen with a rubber or foam ring (Table 13.1).

2. Stimulation was directly transmitted to the maternal abdomen by the oscillatory source, generally a bone vibrator or a tuning fork, placed near the fetal head (Table 13.2). Similar to the electroacoustic larynx, with this direct coupling method there is little or no impedance mismatch and, in contrast to the airborne condition, most of the acoustic pressure is transmitted to the amniotic fluid. This mode of stimulation may also activate cutaneous receptors, and this may mimic the body transmission (via bones and tissues) of the maternal voice. Compared to the air-coupled procedure, with an identical pressure level of emission, cochlear activation is probably stronger with direct vibratory stimulation; the precise amount of sound pressure transmitted to the maternal tissue by a vibrating device is unknown, but in any case is louder than the pressure levels measured in the adjacent air. The problem is, however, even more complex. The air-coupled procedure is likely to result in important alteration of stimulus if the loudspeaker is applied directly to the mother's abdomen. The loudspeaker membrane is partially blocked, which produces frequency distortions and high-frequency amplification. In contrast, when the loudspeaker is coupled with a rubber or a foam ring, it is the low frequencies that are more likely to be amplified. Therefore, the conditions produced by the two procedures just described are very different from the conditions of fetal auditory activation by external everyday sounds.

In addition to procedural differences, studies varied on a number of stimulus characteristics such as the spectral composition of a sound and its frequency, bandwidth, duration, or acoustic pressure level (measured or inferred). Studies also differed in the type of fetal responses recorded, response detection methods and criteria, and other experimental design characteristics, such as whether or not the mother could hear the acoustic stimulus. Thus, in the next subsection, it is shown that comparison of the results from these studies is not always possible and that it is difficult to derive general trends. Nonetheless, it is notable that several major findings concerning fetal hearing were obtained quite early in the development of this field of research, long before the use of ultrasound scanning systems increased the number of experimental studies.

TABLE 13.1

Cardiac and Motor Response to Auditory Stimulations in the Human Fetus: Air-Coupled Stimulations (Various Types of Loudspeakers Placed Directly or Via a Rubber or Foam Ring on the Mother's Abdomen)

Reference	n	Age Range	Stimulus	SPL	Duration	Motor Response	Acceleration	Comments
Bernard & Sontag (1947)	4	7.5–9 months	Pure tones: 0.02 to 6 KHz	—	5 sec	Present	0.02–2 kHz: 5–6 bpm 4–5 kHz: 2 bpm	One case of deceleration
Murphy & Smyth (1962)	290	Some subjects between 30 and 34 weeks	Pure tones: 0.5 kHz, 4 kHz	100 dB	15 sec	Not studied	0.5 Hz: 74%: 17 bpm 4 kHz: 21%: 11 bpm	—
Dwornicka et al. (1964)	32	9 months	Pure tones: 1 kHz, 2 kHz	100 dB	5 sec	—	91%; 1 kHz: 7 bpm 2 kHz: 11 bpm	Two cases of deceleration (5–10 bpm) / response decrement after repeated stimulus
Bench & Mittler (1967)	12	34–37 weeks	Pulsed pure tone: 0.5 kHz	105 dB	2.5, 5, 10, 15 sec	Present	—	Response decrement after repeated stimulus
Bench & Vass (1970)	40	—	Pure tones: 0.5 kHz, 4 kHz	100 dB	15 sec	—	0%	—
Grimwade et al. (1971)	14	38–42 weeks	Pure tones: 0.5 kHz, 1 kHz	80 dB in utero	20 sec	42% (83% of the cardiac responses)	47% 27 bpm	3% Deceleration (17 bpm) (6% of the cardiac responses)
Goodlin & Schmidt (1972)	50	35–42 weeks	Pure tone: 2 kHz	120 dB	5 sec	Present	56%	Cardiac & motor response in LV and HV / many decelerations / stimulus until response / response change after repeated stimulus
Goodlin & Lowe (1974)	60	36–41 weeks	Pure tone: 2 kHz	110 dB	5 sec	Present	92%	Response studied function of HR + fetal movement variation / response decrement after repeated stimulus / 8% deceleration

(Continued)

TABLE 13.1
(Continued)

Reference	n	Age Range	Stimulus	SPL	Duration	Motor Response	Acceleration	Comments
Goupil et al. (1975)	69	33–42 weeks	Low-frequency band noise	100 dB	10 sec	52%: Startles or sustained fetal movements	—	Response decrement after repeated stimulus
Gelman et al. (1982)	60	7–9 months	Pure tones: 0.5 kHz, 2 kHz	110 dB	60 sec	0% at 0.5 kHz, sustained fetal movements at 0.2 kHz for 30 min	—	Immediate response not studied
Shenhar et al. (1982)	35	>28 weeks	Pure tones: 0.5, 1, 3 kHz + white noise	>70 dB	—	100%	100%	5/19 Fetuses from additional deaf mothers did not respond and were found deaf after birth
Schmidt et al. (1985)	43	37–42 weeks	Pure tone: 2 kHz, Modulated tone: 0.5–2 kHz	120 dB	5 sec	1F, 0.04%; 2F, 34%; 3F, 75%; 4F, 78%; no difference between the two stimulus	Accelerations, decelerations, and/or movements are not different	No state change after any stimulus
Ishige, Numata, and Suzuki (1989)	19	—	Band noise + pure tone	—	—	Eye-blink, eye movement	—	—
Pereira-Luz (1991)	1286	—	Pulsed pure tone: 1.5 kHz	125 dB	2 sec × 5	57.2% Startles	Present	Retrospective study
Hepper & Shahidullah (1992)	10	34–36 weeks	Pure tone: 0.25 kHz	Subject's threshold 80–100 dB	2 sec	Head, trunk or arm movement in 5 subjects at 80–85 dB and in 5 subjects at 90–100 dB	—	Response decrement after repeated stimulus

Note. Only studies carried out prior to labor on healthy, non-risk, samples of subjects are reported. If more than one stimulation was presented in the experiment, response characteristics are given for the first stimulation only, except if not specified in the publication.

TABLE 13.2.

Cardiac and Motor Response to Auditory Stimulations in the Human Fetus: Pure Tone Vibroacoustic Stimulations (Bone Vibrator or Tuning Fork Placed on the Mother's Abdomen

Reference	n	Age Range	Stimulus	SPL	Duration	Motor Response	Cardiac Acceleration	Comments
Sontag & Wallace (1934)	4	End of gestation	Gong (0.12 kHz), tapping on a wooden block or tuning fork (0.384 kHz)	—	—	0.12 kHz: 80–97% within 15 sec 0.384 kHz: 0%	—	Response decrement after repeated stimulus; conditioning attempt
Sontag & Wallace (1935)	8	6–9 months	Gong (0.12 kHz), tapping on a wooden block	—	—	6–7 months: 20–54% 8–9 months: 81–86%	—	—
Sontag & Wallace (1936)	8	6–9 months	Gong (0.12 kHz), tapping on a wooden block	—	—	—	Present at 7 months, 8 bpm; 8–9 months, 13–14 bpm	Acceleration with motor response: 11 bpm Acceleration without motor response, 6 bpm
Ogawa (1955)	—	—	Tuning fork: 0.128 kHz, 4.024 kHz, 8.192 kHz	—	—	—	Present at 5–6 months	Response decrement after repeated stimulus
Fleischer (1955)	79	6–9 months	Tuning fork: 0.5 kHz, 1 kHz	100–110 phones	1 sec	Not reliable under 110 phones or at 0.5 kHz	—	—
Johansson et al. (1964)	10	35–40 weeks	Pure tone: 3 kHz	110 dB in utero	1 sec	Present	93%	Response decrement after repeated stimulus
Wedenberg (1965)	15	22–26 weeks	Bone vibrator: 0.5 kHz, 1 kHz, 2 kHz, 3 kHz	110 dB in utero	1 sec	—	26 weeks, first response;	Increased response with age
Tanaka & Arayama (1969)	134	6–10 months	Bone vibrator: 0.5 kHz, 1 kHz, 2 kHz	90 dB in rectum	5 sec	Motor response and/or acceleration 6 months, 0%; 7 months, 55%, >8 months, 96%; 48% of sustained motor response	0.5 kHz, 100%; 1 kHz, 97%; 2 kHz, 86%	Cases of deceleration

(Continued)

TABLE 13.2
(Continued)

Reference	n	Age Range	Stimulus	SPL	Duration	Motor Response	Cardiac Acceleration	Comments
Calvet, Coll, Laredo, and Camillieri (1972)	—	40–42 weeks	Pure tones: 1.5 kHz, 2 kHz	100 dB	2 sec	Present	Present	—
Vecchietti & Bouché (1976)	56	19–42 weeks	Pure tone: 3 kHz	120 dB	—	Startles or sustained motor response present at 27 weeks onward, 100% at term	Present at 27 weeks; 100% at term: 20 bpm	The sample ($n = 56$) included some pathology; deceleration and tachycardia; inhibition of ongoing movement; induced state changes
Bouché (1981)	38	31–41 weeks	Pure tone: 3 kHz	110–120 dB	—	Leg and/or arm movement, 87% arm latency shorter than leg latency	100%	89% inhibition of ongoing breathing, movement; 97% rotation toward the sound source
Jensen & Flottorp (1982)	35	36–40 weeks pregnancy	Bone vibrator in vagina: 2 kHz	65–80 dB in vagina	5 sec	Present	80 dB: 24 bpm 75 dB: 21bpm 70 dB: 17 bpm 65 dB: 16 bpm	The higher the prestimulus level, the smaller the acceleration amplitude/ response decrement after repeated stimulus
Jensen (1984b)	24	32–39 weeks pregnancy	Bone vibrator in vagina: 2 kHz	70–80 dB in vagina	5 sec	Present	80 dB: 15–18 bpm 75 dB: 10–15 bpm 70 dB: 10–12 bpm	Increasing response rate between 32 and 35 weeks; at 39 weeks same % for 70 and 80 dB; some biphasic response
Jensen (1984a)	20	38–42 weeks pregnancy	Bone vibrator in vagina: 2 kHz	80 dB in vagina	5 sec	Present	100%, 21 bpm	Only accelerations >10 bpm were considered
Jensen (1984c)	36	37–43 weeks pregnancy	Bone vibrator in vagina: 2 kHz	80 dB in vagina	5 sec	Present	100%, 19–20 bpm	—

Note. Only studies carried out prior to labor on healthy, non-risk, samples of subjects are reported. If more than one stimulation was presented in the experiment, response characteristics are given for the first stimulation only, except if not specified in the publication.

In the 1980s, some investigators began using airborne stimulation by placing loudspeakers at various distances from the maternal abdomen (10–100cm) (Granier-Deferre, Lecanuet, Cohen, & Busnel, 1983; Granier-Deferre, Lecanuet, Cohen, & Busnel, 1985; Kisilevsky & Muir, 1991; Kisilevsky, Muir, & Low, 1989; Lecanuet, Granier-Deferre, & Busnel, 1988; Lecanuet, Granier-Deferre, Cohen, Le Houezec, & Busnel, 1986; Querleu et al., 1989; Querleu, Renard, & Versyp, 1981). In this way it was possible to simulate as closely as possible the fetus's normal experience. These studies are reviewed in the subsequent subsection.

Air-Coupled and Vibroacoustic Studies

In addition to the earliest investigations already mentioned, 30 studies were conducted with these procedures in last trimester fetuses. Half of them used the air-coupled method; most stimulation used were pure tones (14/15 studies), and some were band noises (3/15), delivered from 70 to 125 dB SPL measured near the maternal abdomen (procedures and results are summarized in Table 13.1). The other half used *direct vibratory transducers* to deliver pure tones from 65 to 120 dB SPL measured at different sites (procedures and results are summarized in Table 13.2). Even though a wide range of SPLs was used, most motor and/or cardiac responses were studied with stimulation mostly at or above 100 dB SPL. The principal results of these studies are described next. Phasic and tonic changes were both reported, although most of the authors were interested in phasic, short latency effects (less than 5 sec after the onset of the stimulation). This is a radically different approach from the current clinical one, which generally uses the classical nonstress test criteria to define a significant fetal response (see Gagnon, chapter 8, this volume).

Motor Responses

In order to detect fetal motor responses, Peiper and other early investigators had to rely either on visual or tactile estimation of fetal movement or on mother's perception of movement. (It was more recently demonstrated that mother's perception of movement is only partially reliable [Kisilevsky, Killen, Muir, & Low, 1991]). Researchers attempted to objectively record modifications of the shape of the maternal abdominal wall due to fetal movement independently of those evoked by mother's breathing. Different systems with pressure transducers (Ray, 1932; Sontag & Wallace, 1934, 1936) or piezoelectric accelerometers (Goupil, Legrand, Breard, Le Houezec, & Sureau, 1975) were built to record the abdominal changes more precisely. Analysis of fetal motor responses entered a golden age with the development of real-time ultrasound scanning systems in the 1970s.

Since the earliest observations, motor responses have been classified either as isolated, strong, and sudden or as a sustained increase in fetal activity. As it is impossible to fully determine a startle response in the fetus, any short-latency motor response described by the authors as strong and sudden is referred to as a *startle response*. Inhibition of ongoing movements (Bouché, 1981; Fleischer, 1955; Tanaka & Arayama, 1969; Vecchietti & Bouché, 1976) and habituation to the stimulus (cessation or a decrement of responses after repetition of stimulation) were also described very early (Sontag & Wallace, 1934), and regularly observed in many subsequent studies (Bench & Mittler, 1967; Dwornicka, Jasienska, Smolarz, & Wawryk, 1964; Johansson, Wedenberg, & Westin, 1964; Ogawa, 1955) (Tables 13.1 and 13.2).

Cardiac Accelerative Changes

The early researchers computed heart rate (HR) changes with the help of a midwife stethoscope and a watch (Sontag & Wallace, 1934, 1935). Phonocardiography was used by many investigators (Bench & Mittler, 1967; Bench & Vass, 1970; Dwornicka et al., 1964; Johansson et al., 1964; Tanaka & Arayama, 1969), but most modern studies were performed with ultrasound cardiotocography. Mostly phasic HR accelerations, but also sustained HR modifications, such as tachycardia, or a change in HR variability, were described. Mean amplitudes of both large and small cardiac accelerations were reported (from 2 to 27 bpm, Tables 13.1 and 13.2). Some authors studied both motor and cardiac responses and showed that motor response rates were lower than cardiac acceleration rates (Grimwade, Walker, Bartlett, Gordon, & Wood, 1971; Tanaka & Arayama, 1969).

Ontogeny of Responses

In the very first vibroacoustic studies by Sontag and Wallace (1935, 1936), the increase in fetal activity after stimulation with a 120-Hz bell gong was reliably evoked at 6 months for a motor response and at 7 months for an accelerative change. Since then, vibroacoustic and air-coupled studies described the appearance of fetal responses to pure tones (between 500 and 4,000 Hz SPLs between 90 dB intraabdominal and 120 dB ex utero) at various ages from 24 to 30 weeks: Motor responses were first detected at 27–28 weeks (Shenhar, Da Silva, & Eliachor, 1982; Vecchietti & Bouché, 1976) or at around 7 months (Gelman, Wood, Spellacy, & Abrams, 1982; Tanaka & Arayama, 1969). Cardiac accelerative changes were described as early as 5–6 months (Ogawa, 1955), 26 weeks (Wedenberg, 1965), 27 weeks (Vecchietti & Bouché, 1976), 28 weeks (Shenhar et al., 1982), or 30 weeks (Tanaka & Arayama, 1969).

Because of the important experimental design differences, no precise conclusion can be made on the ontogeny of fetal responses to pure tones. However, a gradual increase in responsiveness was observed with gestational age for both motor responses (Sontag & Wallace, 1935; Tanaka & Arayama, 1969; Vechietti & Bouché, 1976) and cardiac accelerative changes (Jensen, 1984b; Tanaka & Arayama, 1969; Vecchietti & Bouché, 1976; Wedenberg, 1965). According to Sontag and Wallace (1936), cardiac accelerations display larger amplitudes as fetuses get older. By 8 months, motor response and accelerative change rates found in most studies are between 70% and 90% (Fleischer, 1955; Sontag & Wallace, 1935; Tanaka & Arayama, 1969; Vecchietti & Bouché, 1976; Wedenberg, 1965). These discrepancies may be explained by differences in response detection procedures and also because of stimulus characteristics. However, no systematic studies have been performed to analyze the effect of frequency, intensity, or duration of stimulation on the proportion and characteristics of early fetal responses. As discussed later, there are also very few studies in the near-term fetus.

Effects of Stimulus Characteristics

Frequency. Pure tones between 250 and 4,000 Hz were all efficient in inducing motor responses and/or accelerative changes: Response ratios between 50% and 100% were elicited at or over 90 dB SPL with 250 Hz (one study), 500 Hz (three studies), 1,000 Hz (six studies), 1,500 Hz (two studies), 2,000 Hz (six studies), and 3,000 Hz (eight studies). Some studies found 0% responses at 500 Hz (Fleischer, 1955; Gelman et al., 1982). Unfortunately, considering the differences in procedures and the fact that many early researchers did not publish precise data, it is impossible to compare these studies and determine whether response rates are a function of stimulus frequency. Some authors did study this issue but results are contradictory from one experiment to another. For example, for motor responses, Fleischer (1955) and Gelman et al. (1982) found more responses at 1,000 and 2,000 Hz than at 500 Hz, with approximately similar pressure levels, whereas Tanaka and Arayama (1969) described a slightly higher responsiveness at 500 Hz than at 2,000 Hz.

Intensity. Motor responses and cardiac accelerative change rates are highly variable across experiments for the same pressure level of stimulation and do not seem to vary as a function of intensity. Indeed, ranges of the evoked response rates are relatively similar for all tested SPLs; for example, at 100 dB ex utero (or 20–30 dB lower in utero), the response rates (between 42% and 100%) are similar to the ones observed at 120 dB ex utero (see Tables 13.1 and 13.2). Only Bench and Vass (1970) obtained no response at 100 dB. Only two studies measured the effect of various SPLs in comparable conditions. Fleischer (1955) noted that 110 phones induced more reliable responses than lower pressures, and Jensen (1984b), in the only systematic study performed with a pure tone delivered via a vibrator, demonstrated that the higher the intensity, the higher the accelerative change amplitude (Table 13.2). More recently, Hepper and Shahidullah (1992) attempted to determine subjects' thresholds to a 250-Hz pure tone and found cut-off values between 80 and 100 dB ex utero.

Duration.   In the majority (72%) of experiments reviewed (Table 13.1 and 13.2), stimuli were between 1 and 5 sec in duration. The remaining studies utilized between 10 and 60 sec duration. The longest duration was 60 sec of a 2,000-Hz bone vibrator (estimated level of 110 dB) by Gelman et al. (1982). It increased fetal motor activity during the following 30 min. However, it is not possible to determine whether magnitude of response is affected by the duration of the stimulus, since other studies also have found sustained motor responses with much shorter stimuli (Goupil et al., 1975, 10 sec; Tanaka & Arayama, 1969, 5 sec). The only systematic study comparing the effect of different short duration stimuli found no difference between them, neither on cardiac accelerations nor on motor responses (Bench & Mittler, 1967).

Behavioral State

Contradictory results in some of the data already mentioned can be explained by the many differences in stimulus characteristics and sources. Behavioral state is also likely to be an important factor, which, of course, was not controlled in most of these studies. In the early 1970s, Goodlin and his colleagues (Goodlin & Lowe, 1974; Goodlin & Schmidt, 1971) observed that when fetuses showed a "poorly reactive HR pattern" (i.e., low variability), it seemed that more stimulation was needed to elicit a response than when the HR pattern was "highly reactive" (i.e., high variability). However, the relationship between fetal HR variability and responsiveness was still not clear. This was the first known attempt at considering fetal arousal levels and responsiveness to external stimuli.

This issue was addressed again by Vecchietti and Bouché (1976), who observed induced state change with a vibratory transducer delivering a 3-kHz pure tone at 120 dB. It was thoroughly investigated by Schmidt, Bos, Gniers, Auer, and Schulze (1985) with air-coupled stimulation. These researchers did not observe any induced state change, even though their stimulus (0.5 and 2 kHz pure tones) was emitted at the same pressure level, but a clear connection was demonstrated between state and responsiveness: Fetuses in sleep states are less reactive than in a quiet alert state, and in active sleep are more reactive than in quiet sleep (see Table 13.1).

Airborne Studies

As mentioned earlier, only three groups of researchers have investigated the fetal response to well defined airborne stimuli: (a) Querleu et al. (1981, 1989); (b) Granier-Deferre et al. (1985) and Lecanuet et al. (1986, 1988); and (c) Kisilesky et al. (1989); Kisilevsky & Muir (1991).

Querleu et al. delivered 1,000, 1,500, and 2,000 Hz, as 5-sec band noises, between 100 and 110 dB SPL, and a nonfiltered white noise. These were presented via a loudspeaker placed 1 m away from the maternal abdomen of subjects between 23 and 40 weeks gestational age (GA). Reliable motor and cardiac responses were measured from 28 weeks onward. In the two other groups of studies, subjects were tested between 36 and 42 weeks GA.

In studies done in our laboratory, Lecanuet and his colleagues delivered: A high-pass filtered (at 800 Hz) pink noise (Granier-Deferre et al., 1985; Lecanuet et al., 1986), and three octave-band noises centered respectively at 500, 2,000, and 5,000 Hz (Lecanuet et al., 1988), which were all emitted at 100, 105, and 110 dB for 5 sec. The loudspeaker was placed 20 cm above the maternal abdomen at fetal head level. Mothers wore headphones emitting loud but not uncomfortable masking music during the test session. Masking of the experimental stimuli to the mother was improved by placing a thick blanket over the loudspeaker and around the mother's body extending down to the floor. A motor response was defined as flexing or extending of the fetal leg (tibia and fibula) before the end of the stimulation. An accelerative change was defined if the HR reached, before the end of the 5-sec period, an amplitude equal to or greater than a value one standard deviation above the mean HR of the 1-min prestimulus period.

Kisilevsky and her associates (1989, 1991) delivered 2.5-sec pulsed stimulus (divided in sound segments of 250 msec with 250 msec between segments): a white noise, high-pass filtered at 800 Hz and presented at 100, 105, or 110 dB SPL, and a 2,000-Hz pure tone delivered at 110 dB. Both types of stimuli were presented via a loudspeaker placed 10 cm above the maternal abdomen, pointing toward the fetal head. During the stimulation period mothers wore earphones and listened to continuous pink noise in one ear and to a musical selection of their choice in the other ear.

Pure Tone/Complex Noise

Consistent findings in all three studies were that broadband noise given at the same SPL, 110 dB, elicited much higher rates of accelerative changes and motor responses than pure tones or narrow-band noises. For example, with a 2,000-Hz pure tone at 110 dB, Querleu et al. (1981) observed that responsiveness was possible but inconsistent, whereas Kisilevsky and Muir (1991) found that responsiveness was no different from that obtained in control trials. This is in contrast to the air-coupled and direct vibratory conditions where high proportions of fetal responses were obtained with pure tones. A probable explanation is that the SPLs reaching the amniotic fluid are much greater in the latter condition. With narrow and broad band noises, reactiveness appears to be much greater than with pure tones. Lecanuet et al. (1988) found that 2,000-Hz and 5,000-Hz centered octave band noises presented at 110 dB induced high rates of cardiac accelerations (respectively 82% and 83%) and leg extension/flexion (58% and 73%, respectively) in a high-variability HR state.[1] These values are close to those obtained for accelerative changes to a broadband noise (pink noise) also presented at 110 dB in a high-variability HR state (96% accelerative changes and 71% motor responses).

Effect of Intensity, Frequency, and Behavioral State

Cardiac acceleration and motor response rates increase significantly as intensity increases from 100 to 110 dB SPL. This was clearly shown by both us (Granier-Deferre et al., 1985; Lecanuet et al., 1986) and Kisilevsky et al. (1989) with broadband noises. At 100 dB, Kisilevsky et al. (1989) found that accelerative change and movement response rates and accelerative change amplitudes were similar to those during silent control periods. According to the authors, the threshold intensity for a reliable HR acceleration is somewhere between 100–105 dB. Our results are a little different. A pilot study with 54 women indicated that, similar to Kisilevsky's results, a 100-dB pink noise also did not induce systematic HR accelerations or motor responses, but we believe this was due to the fact that behavioral states were not controlled in the pilot study. In a subsequent study (Lecanuet et al., 1988), data were analyzed as a function of the HR variability pattern at the time of stimulation.

When state was controlled, it was found that even at 100 dB relatively high percentages of HR accelerative responses were elicited with octave-band noises presented in a high variability HR state: 50% at 2,000 Hz and 55% at 5,000 Hz, with an average amplitude of 18 bpm for the two frequencies. Motor response rates were lower: 8% at 2,000 Hz, 30% at 5,000 Hz. These rates were significantly greater than in a low-variability HR

---

[1]Classification of the stimulation episodes in low- or high-variability states was performed by visual on-line and post hoc inspections of the hard copy of the heart rate. The high-variability pattern was defined after fetal heart rate pattern B, correlate of the 2F state in the Nijhuis, Prechtl, Martin and Bots (1982) classification, and the low-variability pattern after fetal heart rate pattern A, correlate of the 1F state in the same classification. After 36 weeks it is possible to correctly infer behavioral states from the visual identification of the heart rate patterns only. The proportion of misclassification should not exceed 5% according to Nijhuis (personal communication).

state: only 9% accelerative changes at 2,000 Hz and 29% at 5,000 Hz. This experiment demonstrated not only that behavioral states should be considered when studying fetal near-term reactiveness to external stimuli—a crucial influence that was also demonstrated by Schmidt et al. (1985) (see earlier discussion and Table 13.1)—but also that the effect of intensity was modulated by the frequency of the noise. Acoustic and behavioral parameters cannot be independently analyzed in fetal studies, and this was clearly apparent in the fetal response to the 500-Hz/100-dB noise. Movement response and accelerative change rates were lower in both states: In the high-variability state, 15% motor responses and 36% accelerative changes were detected, whereas these proportions dropped to 0% in the low variability state. In the next section, it is shown that, in fact, at lower intensities we cannot speak of a decrease in responsiveness but of a change in the nature of responsiveness.

In summary, accelerative changes and motor responses increased not only with sound pressure level but with the pitch of the noise, at least between 500 and 5,000 Hz. At an equivalent SPL, the higher the frequency, the higher the proportion of induced startle responses, the higher the cardiac acceleration amplitude and the shorter the motor response latencies. A motor response is never evoked independently of a cardiac acceleration. Due to a somatocardiac coupling, average amplitudes of cardiac responses are larger when accompanied by a startle than when there is no simultaneous movement or only a slight one. In the nine conditions studied (three frequencies × three SPLs), accelerative change rates were always higher than motor response rates, and reactiveness was higher in a high-variability state than in a low-variability state. However, when a high-SPL and/or high-frequency octave-band noise or a high-SPL broadband noise (pink noise) is given, there is no longer a significant difference between states, and the proportion of motor responses almost reaches the proportion of cardiac accelerations (for example, at 113 dB there are 100% HR accelerations and 91% motor startles with pink noise).

The importance of behavioral state for fetal responsiveness to stimuli at or below 110 dB SPL may partly explain the differences between our results and those of Kisilevsky et al. (1989), because Kisilevsky et al. did not analyze fetal responses as a function of HR variability patterns. Our data obtained with both the pink noise and medium-pitch octave-band noises (2,000 Hz and 5,000 Hz) show overall higher proportions of HR accelerations and motor responses in high variability state at 110 dB and in most conditions at 105 db SPL when compared to the Kisilevsky et al. results with white noise at 110 dB (57–58% of accelerations; 50–52% of motor responses). The difference is also clearly apparent for HR acceleration amplitude. For example, with our pink noise at 110 dB, median amplitudes were 23.2 bpm in a high-variability state, which is much larger than the average one found by Kisilevsky et al. (14 bpm) on the first trial. Response rates and cardiac acceleration mean amplitude found by Kisilevsky et al. are close to those found in our studies for the subjects showing no concomitant motor response in a low-variability state. It suggests that either the trunk movement observed by Kisilevsky et al. in response to their stimulus had a poor somatocardiac coupling, weaker than the one induced by the leg extension/flexion elicited by our stimulus, or there was a high proportion of subjects in a low variability HR state in their study. The fact that Kisilevsky et al. (1989) did not find any significant acceleration amplitude rise with an increase in SPL (from 105 to 110 dB) could also be masked by unknown differences in the proportions of high-variability and low-variability state subjects in each SPL group. Other experimental factors can explain the differences between our results and those of Querleu et al. and Kisilevsky et al.. First, the latter used a square-wave whereas the rise time of the stimuli used by Querleu et al. was 2 sec. This difference in rise time may have reduced the effect of the pure tones that Querleu employed. Second, the Kisilevsky et al. method for computing motor responses is based on three successive trials and the proportions on the first trial are not given.

NONSTARTLING AIRBORNE STIMULI

Unexpected and most interesting results were obtained in one of our experiments mentioned earlier (Lecanuet et al., 1988). High proportions of transient decelerative HR responses were found. These were of lower amplitude than the cardiac accelerative responses and were never accompanied by movements. Mean amplitudes were similar in both a low-variability and in a high-variability state (−10.4 vs. −10.2 bpm). In the low-variability state, cardiac decelerative changes represented the majority of HR responses for all frequencies at the lowest intensity tested (100 dB), and for all intensities at the lowest frequency tested (500 Hz) (50%–80% of all cardiac responses and 100% at 500 Hz/100 dB). Therefore, under certain stimulus and state conditions, near-term fetuses (36–41 weeks GA) may display only cardiac decelerative responses. In this experiment, the proportion of subjects responding with a decelerative change never exceeded 32%, even when it was the only type of response evoked by the stimulation. This type of response had been anecdotally mentioned by many authors (Bernard & Sontag, 1947; Dwornicka et al., 1964; Goodlin & Schmidt, 1972; Goodlin & Lowe, 1974; Grimwade et al., 1971; Tanaka & Arayama, 1969; Vecchietti & Bouché, 1976; see Tables 13.1 and 13.2). Only a few cases were reported in most of these studies, but decelerative changes constituted as much as 6% of the cardiac responses for Grimwade et al. (1971) and 8% for Goodlin and Lowe (1974). Most authors did not specify characteristics of the decelerative responses, but their amplitude was also described as lower than the amplitude of the observed cardiac accelerations: 5–10 bpm in Dwornicka et al. (1964), and 17 bpm in Grimwade et al. (1971). Some of the decelerative responses were described as part of biphasic cardiac responses. Possible explanations for these reports being only anecdotal are that most authors were looking for high-amplitude cardiac changes, and mostly high-SPL stimuli were delivered.

Based on such results we decided to investigate the cardiac impact of various types of low sound pressure levels (under 100 dB). It was found that, like newborns in quiet sleep (Eisenberg, Marmarou, & Giovachino, 1974), fetuses displaying HR pattern A, specific to the 1F state, may respond with a decelerative heart rate change to various brief, continuous or rhythmic, low- to medium-pitched sounds, including vocal or musical sequences, that are presented between 80 dB and 100 dB SPL ex utero. This responsiveness has a large interindividual variability, a phenomenon we have not yet studied.

Pilot studies also revealed that these decelerative changes quickly habituated when a brief stimulus was repeated at short intervals (e.g., a few seconds). This made it feasible to examine the possibility of discriminative auditory capacities at the end of the gestation period with the help of a habituation/dishabituation procedure derived from the one used by Clarkson and Berg (1983) to study speech discrimination in neonates. This type of experiment can only be performed in the 1F state, a period where few spontaneous movements are present and HR variability is low and remains stable long enough to run a habituation and a deshabituation phase.

In a first study (Lecanuet et al., 1987), it was demonstrated that 36–40 week GA fetuses exposed to the repeated presentation (every 3.5 sec) of a pair of French syllables ([ba] and [bi] or [bi] and [ba]), uttered by a female voice and emitted at the same acoustic pressure level (95 dB), showed a transient deceleration. A modification in the acoustic structure of the stimulus (reversing the order of the paired syllables) after 16 presentations also reliably induced the same type of response. This was observed in 15/ 19 fetuses in the BABI/BIBA condition and in 10/14 fetuses in the BIBA/ BABI condition. Response recovery suggested that fetuses discriminated between the two stimuli.

The classical group procedure for HR data analysis averages subjects HR over successive time intervals. This procedure does not give a proper estimation of the subject's response amplitude in experiments where there is a high interindividual variability in the slope of the HR response, and thus in the delay to reach peak amplitude. In the next study (Lecanuet, Granier-Deferre, Jacquet, & Busnel, 1992), a conservative data treatment procedure was developed to take into account interindividual variability to define for each subject: (a) whether the stimulus, and modification of its acoustic structure, induced a HR change, (b) whether the direction of the HR change was accelerative or decelerative, and (c) the amplitude of the HR change. The procedure considered the HR variability of the time period preceding the onset of the habituation stimulus and of the time period preceding the onset of the dishabituation stimulus.

Successive beat-to-beat intervals, collected with a Doppler cardiotocograph (HP 8030), were stored on a computer. Missing or erroneous beat-to-beat intervals were detected and corrected. A subject was rejected if one of his or her files included more than 25% of erroneous intervals or showed missing beats for more than two consecutive seconds (see Lecanuet et al., 1992, for details). The HR changes induced by a stimulus were defined by comparing HR variations within the first two successive 10-sec periods of presentation of a stimulus to the HR variation of the last 10 sec preceding this presentation.

The HR responses of 37–40 week GA fetuses exposed to a short sentence "Dick a du bon thé" [trans., "Dick has some good tea"] was studied. The sentence was uttered by a low-pitched male voice or a high-pitched female voice at the same hearing level (male voice level was adjusted to the female voice level delivered at a peak of 92 dB SPL). The sentence lasted 1.8 sec and was delivered every 3.5 sec. Presentation of the first voice (male or female) to the fetus started when the HR was stable with no more than ± 5 bpm variability on average. After return to a stable HR pattern—between 45 and 65 sec of presentation of the initial voice—this voice was either continued (in a control condition) or replaced by the other voice.

In the first 10 sec after onset of their initial presentation the two voices induced a high and similar proportion of decelerative changes (male voice 77%, female voice 66%). This was significantly more than in the silent control group (9% of decelerations/46% of accelerations). Average maximum amplitude of the decelerative changes was 4.8 bpm. Individual decelerative changes evoked by the voices varied widely in shape and duration. Most decelerative changes started within the first few seconds of voice presentation and peaked within the first 10 sec. Seventy percent of the male voice group and 59% of the female voice group still showed a decelerative change after 10 sec of presentation of the voice. Control subjects showed significantly fewer HR changes than stimulated ones; nevertheless, one may wonder why a relatively important amount of control subjects displayed an accelerative change. This is due to our testing procedure. The experimenter waited until the HR variability was extremely low for 10–20 sec before delivering the stimulation. Post hoc examination of 10-sec prestimulus HR showed that the mean second-by-second HR variability was less than 1 bpm. This is extremely low, compared to the mean HR variability during longer periods of low-variability (1F) states: 2.86 bpm (the average standard deviation computed on 1 min in 57 subjects between 37 and 40 week GA; unpublished data). It was therefore highly probable that a spontaneous change of several beats per minute occurred within the next 10–20 sec, as flat HR episodes rarely last long in healthy fetuses.

Within the first 10 sec following the voice change, 69% of the subjects exposed to the other voice displayed a decelerative change (average maximum amplitude –4.7 bpm), whereas 43% of the subjects still exposed to the initial voice displayed a significantly weaker amplitude acceleration (3.3 bpm)[2] (Lecanuet, Granier-Deferre, Jacquet, Capponi, & Ledru, 1993). In two-thirds of the experimental subjects the cardiac response lasted more than 10 sec. Thus, as in the habituation phase, decelerations were the dominant change in the experimental group and cardiac accelerations in the control group.

In the stimulated subjects, these significant novelty responses showed that near-term fetuses perceive differences between voice characteristics of two speakers, at least when the voices are highly contrasted for fundamental frequency and timbre. These results cannot be generalized for all female and male voices or to all utterances. It should be emphasized that HR deceleration occurred within the first seconds of exposure to the novel voice, suggesting that only a short speech sample is needed for the fetal auditory system to detect an acoustically relevant change in a human voice. Because the most obvious acoustic cues for this discrimination are fundamental frequency and timbre, near-term fetuses, like newborns, may be capable of pitch discrimination during the 1F state. Alho, Sainio, Sajaniemi, Reinkainen, and Näätänen (1990) found similar results in the newborn with event-related potentials during quiet sleep.

The fact that some subjects did not display any HR modification cannot be definitively explained. One possible explanation is that autonomic nervous system responsiveness may vary within a 1F episode; quiet sleep in the near-term fetus is similar to that of the newborn, and quiet sleep phases are not homogeneous in the latter. Despite the difficulty in understanding this intersubject variability and although this procedure can only be used during lengthy low-variability HR periods—therefore at and above 36 weeks GA—we feel that it is a very helpful technique for exploring auditory fetal abilities and has proven to be very fruitful thus far.

---

[2]The male/female group did not differ from the female/male group, and there was no difference between the two control groups; thus the experimental data were pooled and so were the control data for comparison.

CONCLUSIONS

Our historical survey on fetal responsiveness to startling and nonstartling auditory stimulation reveals that many important findings in this domain were made as early as the 1930s. When exposed to direct brief vibratory and air-coupled stimulation, near-term fetuses were found to be highly reactive to pure tones at or above 100 dB. Reliable cardiac accelerations and startle responses were observed as early as 7 months. These results are in agreement with those obtained in the airborne conditions with broadband or band noises that are 5–10 dB more intense.

Brief airborne auditory stimulation evokes mostly HR accelerations if the SPL is over 100 dB and HR deceleration, if the SPL is between 85 and 100 dB in the near-term fetus. This effect is especially displayed in the 1F state. The relation between SPLs and direction of HR responses is similar to the one described in neonates (Graham, Anthony, & Ziegler, 1983). The shift in the infant from decelerative responses to accelerative responses occurs at around 75–80 dB SPL, about 10 dB lower than in the fetus. This is in agreement with recent data demonstrating that in utero attenuation of external sounds does not exceed 10 dB, but with a large interindividual variability (Richards, Frenzen, Gerhardt, Abrams, & McCann, 1992; Abrams, Gerhardt, & Peters, chapter 17, in this volume). These results emphasize the transnatal continuity of neural and perceptive processes.

The discriminative abilities evidenced in our studies suggest that, in spite of the particular conditions of airborne sound transmission, third-trimester fetuses may benefit from prenatal exposure to a variety of sounds, including speech sounds. Many animal studies have demonstrated that auditory stimulation is necessary for the normal development of the auditory system (Gottlieb, 1978; see review in Granier-Deferre & Lecanuet, 1987, and in Moore, 1990). This early exposure may thus contribute to the maintenance, tuning, and specification of the auditory abilities necessary for the neonate to process sounds that will be relevant postnatally (Lecanuet et al., 1991; Ruben, 1992).

The finding of a variety of auditory perceptual capacities in the fetus provides further support and validation for the data demonstrating prenatal auditory learning obtained in studies of infants following birth. When presented with different categories of stimuli to which the fetuses had been systematically exposed during the last weeks of gestation, without any other postnatal exposure than during the postnatal testing, newborns (2–4 days old) display significant preferences (shown with nonnutritive sucking choice procedures) for previously experienced stimuli including: (a) specific musical sequences (Panneton, 1985; Satt, 1984, this volume); (b) specific speech sequences (DeCasper & Spence, 1986); and (c) a specific language, the mother's native tongue (Fifer & Moon, chapter 19, this volume; Mehler et al., 1988; Moon, Cooper, & Fifer, 1993). In the latter case, however, the neonates had some postnatal contact with this particular language prior to postnatal testing. These specific preferences imply underlying fetal discriminative auditory abilities. The results of our discrimination studies are direct evidence of the functionality of these abilities during the prenatal period.

A large amount of research should, of course, be performed to increase the knowledge on fetal auditory perceptions. These studies should include investigations on prenatal behavioral thresholds as a function of gestational age and of the frequency band of the stimulus. Electrophysiological studies conducted with preterm babies have shown that absolute auditory thresholds decrease from the 26th to the 35th week GA. At 35 weeks they are close to the adult level (the difference is not greater than 10–20 dB HL [hearing level]) (Krumholz, Felix, Goldstein, & McKenzie, 1985; Pasman, Näätanen, & Alho, 1991). Pitch and tempo discriminations should also be considered. They would help the understanding of the results of our discriminative studies based on complex vocal stimulations and would call for the development of other experiments using speech and nonspeech stimulation. The transnatal auditory continuity that has been demonstrated in many species is still restricted in the human being to experiments carried out with infants less than 1 week old. Concurrently, further experimental studies should also focus on the analysis of the long-term memorization of fetal learning during both the prenatal and the postnatal period.

ACKNOWLEDGMENT

The authors express their gratitude to David Lewkowicz for his editing of the manuscript.

REFERENCES

Alho, K., Sainio, K., Sajaniemi, N., Reinikainen, K., & Näätänen, R. (1990). Event-related brain potential of human newborns to pitch change of an acoustic stimulus. *Electroencephalography and Clinical Neurophysiology, 77,* 151–155.

Bench, R. J., & Mittler, P. J. (1967). Changes of heart rate in response to auditory stimulation in the human fetus. *Bulletin of the British Psychological Society, 20,* 14a.

Bench, J. R., & Vass, A. (1970). Fetal audiometry. *Lancet, 10,* 91–92.

Benzaquen, S., Gagnon, R., Hunse, C., & Foreman, J. (1990). The intrauterine sound environment of the human fetus during labor. *American Journal of Obstetrics and Gynecology, 163,* 484–490.

Bernard, J., & Sontag, L. W. (1947). Fetal reactivity to tonal stimulation: A preliminary report. *Journal of Genetic Psychology, 70,* 205–210.

Bouché, M. (1981). Echotomographic evaluation of fetal sound stimulation. *Ultrasons, 2,* 339–341.

Calvet, J., Coll, J., Laredo, C., & Camillieri, L. (1972). Les réactions auditives chez le nouveau-né et le foetus. *Folia Phoniatrica, 24,* 427–430.

Cazals, Y., Aran, J.-M., & Erre, J.-P. (1983). Intensity difference thresholds assessed with eighth nerve and auditory cortex potentials: Compared values from cochlear and saccular responses. *Hearing Research, 10,* 263–268.

Clarkson, M. G., & Berg, W. K. (1983). Cardiac orienting and vowel discrimination in newborns: Crucial stimulus parameters. *Child Development, 54,* 162–171.

DeCasper, A. J., & Spence, M. J. (1986). Prenatal maternal speech influences newborn's perception of speech sounds. *Infant Behavior and Development, 9,* 133–150.

Dwornicka, B., Jasienska, A., Smolarz, W., & Wawryk, R. (1964). Attempt of determining the fetal reaction to acoustic stimulation. *Acta Oto-Laryngologica (Stock.), 57,* 571–574.

Eisenberg, R. B., Marmarou, A., & Giovachino, P. (1974). Infant heart rate changes to a synthetic speech sound. *Journal of Audiological Research, 14,* 20–28.

Fifer, W. P., & Moon, C. (1989). Psychobiology of newborn auditory preferences. *Seminars in Perinatology, 13,* 430–433.

Fleischer, K. (1955). Untersuchungen zur Entwickllung der Innenohrfunktion (Intrauterine Kinderbewegungen nach Schallreizen) [Studies on the development of the inner ear (Fetal motor responses to acoustical stimuli]. *Zeitschrift für Laryngologie und Rhinologie, 3,* 733–740.

Forbes, H. S., & Forbes, H. B. (1927). Fetal sense reaction: Hearing, *Journal of Comparative & Physiological Psychology, 7,* 353–355.

Gagnon, R., Benzaquen, S., & Hunse, C. (1992). The fetal sound environment during vibroacoustic stimulation in labor: Effect on fetal heart rate response. *Obstetrics and Gynecology, 79,* 950–955.

Gelman, S. R., Wood, S., Spellacy, W. N., & Abrams, R. M. (1982). Fetal movements in response to sound stimulation. *American Journal of Obstetrics and Gynecology, 143,* 484–485.

Gerhardt, K. J. (1989). Characteristics of the fetal sheep sound environment. *Seminars in Perinatology, 13,* 362–370.

Goodlin, R. C., & Lowe, E. W. (1974). Multiphasic fetal monitoring: A preliminary evaluation. *American Journal of Obstetrics and Gynecology, 119,* 341–357.

Goodlin, R. C., & Schmidt, W. (1971). Human fetal arousal levels as indicated by heart rate recordings. *American Journal of Obstetrics and Gynecology, 114,* 613–621.

Gottlieb, G. (1978). Development of species identification in ducklings: IV. Changes in specific perception caused by auditory deprivation. *Journal of Comparative & Physiological Psychology, 92,* 375–387.

Goupil, F., Legrand, H., Breard, G., Le Houezec, R., & Sureau, C. (1975). *Sismographie et réactivité foetales. 5e Journées Nationales de Médecine Périnatale* [Sismography and fetal responsiveness, 5th National Meeting of Perinatal Medicine] (pp. 262–266).

Graham, F. K., Anthony, B. J., & Zeigler, B. L. (1983). The orienting response and developmental processes. In D. Siddle (Ed.), *Orienting and habituation: Perspectives in human research* (pp. 371–340). Sussex, England: John Wiley.

Granier-Deferre, C. & Lecanuet, J-P. (1987). Influence de stimulations auditives précoces sur la maturation anatomique et fonctionnelle du système auditif [Effects of early auditory stimulation on the anatomical and functional maturation of the auditory system]. *Progrès en Néonatologie, 7*, 145–155.

Granier-Deferre, C., Lecanuet, J.-P., Cohen, H., & Busnel, M.-C. (1985). Feasability of prenatal hearing test. *Acta Oto-Laryngologica (Stock.) Suppl., 421*, 93–101.

Granier-Deferre, C., Lecanuet, J.-P., Cohen, H., & Busnel, M.-C. (1983). Preliminary evidence on fetal auditory habituation. In G. Rossi (Ed.), *Noise as a public health problem* (pp. 561–572).

Grimwade, J. C., Walker, D. W., Bartlett, M., Gordon, S., & Wood, C. (1971). Human fetal heart rate change and movement in response to sound and vibration. *American Journal of Obstetrics and Gynecology, 109*, 86–90.

Hopper, P. C., & Shahidullah, S. (1992). Habituation in normal and Down's syndrome fetuses. *Quarterly Journal of Experimental Psychology, 44B*, 305–317.

Hooker, D. (1952). *The prenatal origin of behavior.* Lawrence: University of Kansas Press.

Ishige, T., Numata, T., & Suzuki, H. (1989). *Human fetal response to acoustic stimulation* (video meeting). Proceedings of the 14th world congress of otorhinolaryngology, head and neck surgery, Madrid, Kugler and Ghedini, Amsterdam.

Jensen, O. H. (1984a). Fetal heart rate response to a controlled sound stimulus as a measure of fetal well-being. *Acta Obstetrica et Gynecologica Scandinavica, 64*, 97–101.

Jensen, O. H. (1984b). Fetal heart rate response to controlled sound stimuli during the third trimester of normal pregnancy. *Acta Obstetrica et Gynecologica Scandinavica, 63*, 193-197.

Jensen, O. H. (1984c). Accelerations of the human fetal heart rate at 38 to 40 weeks' gestational age. *American Journal of Obstetrics and Gynecology, 149*, 918.

Jensen, O. H., & Flottorp, G. (1982). A method for controlled sound stimulation of the human fetus. *Scandinavian Audiology, 11*, 145–150.

Johansson, B., Wedenberg, E., & Westin, B. (1964). Measurement of tone response by the human fetus. A preliminary report. *Acta Oto-Laryngologica, 57*, 188–192.

Kisilevsky, B. S, Killen, H., Muir, D. W., & Low, J. A. (1991). Maternal and ultrasound measurements of elicited fetal movements: A methodologic consideration. *Obstetrics and Gynecology, 77*, 889–892.

Kisilevsky, B. S., & Muir, D. W. (1991). Human fetal and subsequent newborn responses to sound and vibration. *Infant Behaviour and Development, 14*, 1–26.

Kisilevsky, B. S., Muir, D. W., & Low, J. A. (1989). Human fetal response to sound as a function of stimulus intensity. *Obstetrics & Gynecology, 73*, 971–976.

Kisilevsky, B. S., Stack, D. A., & Muir, D. W. (1991). Fetal and infant response to tactile stimulation. In M. J. S. Weiss & P. R. Zelazo (Eds.), *Newborn attention: Biological constraints and the influence of experience* (pp. 63–98). Norwood, NJ: Ablex.

Krumholz, A., Felix, J. K., Goldstein, P. J., & McKenzie, E. (1985). Maturation of the brain-stem auditory evoked potential in premature infants. *Electroencephalography and Clinical Neurophysiology, 62*, 124–134.

Lecanuet, J.-P., Granier-Deferre, C., & Busnel, M.-C. (1988). Fetal cardiac and motor responses to octave-band noises as a function of central frequency, intensity and heart rate variability. *Early Human Development, 18,* 81–93.

Lecanuet, J.-P., Granier-Deferre, C., & Busnel, M.-C. (1991). Prenatal familiarization. In G. Piéraut-Le Bonniec & M. Dolitsky (Eds.), *From basic language to discourse bases* (pp. 31–44). Philadelphia: Benjamin.

Lecanuet, J.-P., Granier-Deferre, C., Cohen, H., Le Houezec, R., & Busnel, M.-C. (1986). Fetal responses to acoustic stimulation depend on heart rate variability pattern, stimulus intensity and repetition. *Early Human Development, 13,* 269–283.

Lecanuet, J.-P., Granier-Deferre, C., DeCasper, A. J., Maugeais, R., Andrieu, A.-J., & Busnel, M.-C. (1987). Perception et discrimination foetale de stimuli langagiers, mise en évidence à partir de la réactivité cardiaque. Résultats préliminaires. *Compte-Rendus de l'Academie des Sciences de Paris, 305,* 161–164.

Lecanuet, J.-P., Granier-Deferre, C., Jacquet, A. Y., & Busnel, M.-C. (1992). Decelerative cardiac response to acoustic stimulation in the near term foetus. *Quarterly Journal of Experimental Psychology, 44b,* 279–283.

Lecanuet, J.-P., Granier-Deferre, C., Jacquet, A. Y., Capponi, I., & Ledru, L. (1993). Prenatal discrimination of a male and a female voice uttering the same sentence. *Early Development and Parenting, 2,* 217–228.

Mehler, J., Jusczyk, P., Lamberz, G., Halstead, N., Bertoncini, J., & Amiel-Tison, C. (1988). A precursor of language acquisition in young infants. *Cognition, 29,* 143–178.

Moon, C., Cooper, R. P., & Fifer, W. P. (1993). Two-day-olds prefer their native language. *Infant Behavior and Development, 16,* 495–500.

Moore, D. R. (1990). Effects of early auditory experience on development of binaural pathways in the brain. *Seminars in Perinatology, 14,* 294–298.

Murphy, K. P., & Smyth, C. N. (1962). Response of fetus to auditory stimulation. *Lancet, 1,* 972–973.

Nijhuis, J. G., Prechtl, H. F. R., Martin, C. B., & Bots, R. S. G. M. (1982). Are there behavioural states in the human fetus? *Early Human Development, 6,* 177–195.

Ogawa, G. (1955). The audiovisual sensories of fetus. *Journal of Obstetrics & Gynecology, Hokkaido, 6,* 60–65.

Panneton, R. K. (1985). *Prenatal auditory experience with melodies: Effects on postnatal auditory preferences in human newborns.* Unpublished doctoral dissertation, University of North Carolina at Greensboro.

Pasman, R. L., Näätanen, R., & Alho, K. (1991) Auditory evoked responses in prematures. *Infant Behaviour and Development, 14,* 129–135.

Peiper, A. (1925). Sinnesempfindugen des Kinder vor Seiner Geburt. *Monatsschrift Kinderheilkunde, 29,* 236–241.

Pujol, R, & Sans, A. (1986). Synaptogenesis in the cochlear and vestibular receptors. In R. E. Aslin (Ed), *Advances in neural and behavioral development, Vol. 2, Auditory development* (pp. 1–18). Norwood, NJ: Ablex.

Querleu, D., Renard, X., & Versyp, F. (1981). Les perceptions auditives du foetus humain [Human fetal auditory perceptions]. *Médecine et Hygiène, 39,* 2101–2110.

Querleu, D., Renard, X., Boutteville, C., & Crepin, G. (1989). Hearing by the human fetus? *Seminars in Perinatology, 13,* 430–433.

Ray, W. S. (1932). A preliminary study of fetal conditioning. *Child Development, 3,* 173–177.

Ribaric, K., Bleeker, J. D., & Wit, H. P. (1991). Perception of audio-frequency vibrations by profoundly deaf subjects after fenestration of the vestibular system. *Acta Oto-Laryngologica (Stockh.), 112,* 45–49.

Richards, D. S., Frentzen, K. J., Gerhardt, K. J., Abrams, R. M., & McCann, M. E. (1992). Sound levels in the human uterus. *Obstetrics and Gynaecology, 80,* 186–190.

Ruben, R. J. (1992). The ontogeny of human hearing. *Acta Oto-Laryngologica (Stockh), 112,* 192-196.

Satt, B. J. (1984). *An investigation into the acoustical induction of intra-uterine learning.* PhD dissertation, California School of Professional Psychology, Los Angeles.

Schmidt, W., Boos, R., Gniers, J., Auer, L., & Schulze, S. (1985). Fetal behavioural states and controlled sound stimulation. *Early Human Development, 12,* 145–153.

Shenhar, B., Da Silva, N., & Eliachor, I. (1982, September). Fetal reactions to acoustic stimuli: A clinical trial. *XVIe International Congress of Audiology,* Helsinki.

Sontag, L. W., & Wallace, R. F. (1934). Study of fetal activity. Preliminary report of the Fels Fund. *American Journal of Diseases of Children, 48,* 1050–1057.

Sontag, L. W., & Wallace, R. F. (1935). The movement response of the human fetus to sound stimuli. *Child Development, 6,* 253–258.

Sontag, L. W., & Wallace, R. F. (1936). Changes in the rate of the human fetal heart in response to vibratory stimuli. *American Journal of Diseases of Children, 51,* 583–589.

Spelt, D. K. (1948). The conditioning of the human fetus in utero. *Journal of Experimental Psychology, 38,* 338–346.

Spence, M. J., & DeCasper, A. J. (1987). Prenatal experience with low frequency maternal voice sounds influences neonatal perception of maternal voice samples. *Infant Behavior and Development, 10,* 133–142.

Tanaka, Y., Arayama, T. (1969). Fetal responses to acoustic stimuli. *Practica Oto-Rhino-Laryngologica, 31,* 269–273.

Vecchietti, G., & Bouché, M. (1976). La stimulazione acustica fetale: indagni preliminari sul significato delle reazioni evocate [Fetal acoustical stimulation: Preliminary data on the meaning of the evoked response]. *Attualita di Ostetrica e Ginecologia, 22,* 367–378.

Wedenberg, E. (1965). Prenatal test of hearing. *Acta Oto-Laryngologica (Suppl.), 206,* 27–30.

14

The Influence of Stimulus and Subject Variables on Human Fetal Responses to Sound and Vibration

B. S. Kisilevsky
Queen's University, Kingston, Ontario, Canada

Since the 1980s, researchers have been systematically examining the influence of stimulus and subject variables on elicited fetal responses. In addition, questions related to methodologies employed in fetal and fetal-newborn studies have been addressed. This chapter begins by outlining several methodological issues that influence the conduct of human fetal research describing how these issues are dealt with in particular studies. The issues include identifying the proximal stimulus, measuring fetal movement, and determining fetal well-being. Next, several studies characterizing the effect of selected stimulus variables (i.e., intensity, modality, repeated presentations) are reviewed. Finally, several studies exploring the influence of subject variables (i.e., gestational age, risk status) are considered. Coverage of the topic is limited to those areas that have been studied in the author's laboratory.

METHODOLOGICAL ISSUES

A major methodological issue in the study of fetal perception is determination of the proximal stimulus. The intact human fetus is housed in a liquid environment within the maternal abdomen and is not accessible to direct stimulation. Typically, acoustic stimuli are delivered in air above the maternal abdomen, and vibroacoustic stimuli are delivered on the maternal abdomen. Alterations in stimulus characteristics reaching the fetus through air, the maternal abdomen, and amniotic fluid are beginning to be described (e.g., Benzaquen, Gagnon, Hunse, & Foreman, 1990; Richards, Frentzen, Gerhardt, McCann, & Abrams, 1992; Smith, Satt, Phelan, & Paul, 1990). Nevertheless, currently the proximal stimulus must be considered a "guesstimate." Therefore, in the studies discussed next, the characteristics of the distal stimuli are described and manipulated recognizing that these vary from the proximal stimulus (for a discussion of this issue, see Kisilevsky, Stack, & Muir, 1991).

A second methodological issue is selection of an appropriate fetal response. Typically, measurements of fetal heart rate (FHR) accelerations and body movements are used to examine fetal responding to sensory stimuli. The FHR is obtained using one of several commercially available FHR monitors. Movement, however, is obtained in several ways. Two common methods are ultrasound scan observation, which requires expensive equipment and technical skill, and maternal perception, which is readily available and inexpensive, requiring no equipment. Several reports suggested that maternal perceptions of movement were a reliable method of evaluating fetal response (e.g., Arulkumaran, Anandakumar, Wong, & Ratnam, 1989; Nymen & Westgren, 1989). To determine whether both techniques yielded the same results and could be used interchangeably, Kisilevsky, Killen, Muir, and Low (1991) compared maternal perceptions and ultrasound scan observations of vibroacoustically elicited fetal movements in groups of low-risk and high-risk fetuses. Using a handheld, battery-powered, commercial vibrator (Allied Traders), they demonstrated that maternal perceptions were poor compared to ultrasound scan observations. Figure 14.1 illustrates the percentages of movements observed by each method. Clearly, mothers perceived fewer movements regardless of gestational age (23–36 weeks) or risk status (high versus low). Furthermore, those movements that mothers perceived were not consistent with those observed using ultrasound scan until 29–31 weeks. In a subsequent study, it was demonstrated that the stimulus used also influences maternal perception (Kisilevsky, Kilpatrick, & Low, 1993). It was concluded that maternal perceptions of fetal movements cannot be substituted for ultrasound scan observations for accurate assessment of fetal movement. In the studies reported in this chapter, movement responses were observed using real-time ultrasound scan.

A third methodological issue is the well-being of the fetus at the time of testing. Normative data regarding fetal sensory development needs to be obtained from healthy fetuses. In the normative studies that follow, health status was determined at the time of testing and confirmed after birth. At

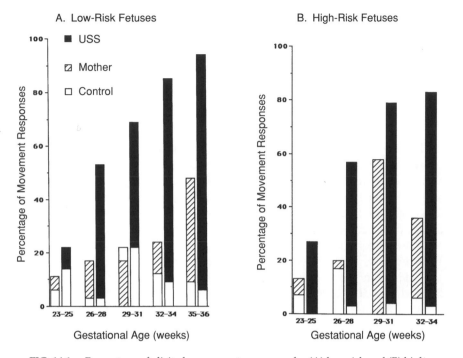

FIG. 14.1.   Percentage of elicited movement responses for (A) low-risk and (B) high-risk fetuses as a function of gestational age and scoring method (maternal perceptions and ultrasound scan observations) on vibroacoustic stimulus and no-stimulus control trials. Note: For high-risk fetuses at 23–25 (ultrasound) and 29–31 (maternal perceptions) weeks gestation there were 0% movement responses on control trials.

the time of testing, pregnancies were judged to be of low risk and uneventful by the attending obstetrician. At birth all infants included in data analyses were 37–42 weeks gestational age and had a birth weight greater than 2,500 g, an Apgar score of 6–10 at 5 min, a cord artery buffer base greater than 34 mMol/L (if obtained), and a diagnosis of healthy term infant on first-day physical examination.

STIMULUS VARIABLES

Identifying acoustic and vibroacoustic stimulus variables that might influence fetal behavior is relatively straightforward. Sounds that are heard and vibrations that are felt result from waves generated by a vibrating body. Waves may be described in terms of their intensity and frequency; they occur in gaseous (e.g., air), liquid (e.g., amniotic fluid), and solid (e.g., skin or bone) mediums. The intensity and frequency of airborne sound can be manipulated independently, and the results of such manipulations are presented next. In addition, the following subsections describe studies examining the influence of stimulus modality and stimulus repetition (i.e., habituation).

Airborne Sound Intensity

In the early 1980s when initial studies were undertaken, fetal response to sound was still a contentious issue. In particular, not all researchers were able to demonstrate a reliable FHR acceleration using a sound stimulus (e.g., Patrick, 1984). Hence, selection of a complex sound stimulus for the following study was based on the literature where it was apparent that those investigators reporting failure to elicit fetal responding had used pure tones (e.g., Bench & Vass, 1970; Gelman, Wood, Spellacy, & Abrams, 1982; Patrick, 1984). Even those reporting successes with pure tones observed responding on only 30%–50% of stimulus trials (Grimwade, Walker, Bartlett, Gordon, & Wood, 1971; Schmidt, Boos, Gnirs, Auer, & Schulze, 1985). In addition, there was evidence that neonates responded more often and more reliably to complex sounds than to pure tones (e.g., Levarie & Rudolph, 1978; Turkewitz, Birch, & Cooper, 1972) and that neonates responded to the rapid onset (rise time) of a stimulus (Kearsley, 1973). Surmising that term fetuses (i.e., 37–42 weeks gestational age) and newborn infants might behave in similar ways, a pulsed, complex airborne sound was used to study the impact of sound intensity on movement and FHR acceleration responses in a group of healthy term fetuses (Kisilevsky, Muir, & Low, 1989). The complex sound consisted of a computer-generated white noise with frequencies below 800 Hz and above 20,000 Hz removed. Eliminating the lower frequencies reduced the tactile component of the sound, permitting examination of the effects of sound alone rather than a combination of sound and vibration (Iggo, 1982). Eliminating the high frequencies above threshold produced a lower-pitched, softer sound (Pickles, 1982), which was less disturbing in the clinic where volunteers were tested. The sound was delivered in air, approximately 10 cm above the maternal abdomen, at 100, 105, and 110 dB(C). No-stimulus trials were interspersed randomly to control for spontaneous activity, which is common (Patrick, Campbell, Carmichael, Natale, & Richardson, 1982; Wheeler & Murrills, 1978), as well as to control for changes in state of arousal during testing. Table 14.1 demonstrates that the average FHR acceleration and movement responses varied as a function of stimulus intensity. Also, it can be seen that the threshold for a response was between 100 and 105 dB(C). These results are in keeping with other reports (e.g.,

TABLE 14.1
Changes in Fetal Responses with Increasing Sound Intensity

Intensity	Mean FHR Acceleration (bpm), Sound/No-Sound	Mean Movement Score, Sound/No-Sound
100 dB	5.3/5.4	0.6/0.2
105 dB	10.6/6.7	1.9/0.6
110 dB	10.7/4.4	3.0/0.4

Lecanuet, Granier-Deferre, Cohen, Le Houezec, & Busnel, 1986) in which spontaneous activity was not controlled. In addition, the study showed that small sample sizes can provide reliable behavioral data. In a group of 10 compared to a group of 93 fetuses, the percentages of subjects responding to the 110-dB airborne sound with an FHR acceleration >10 bpm (58% vs. 57%, respectively) and movement responses (52% vs. 50%, respectively) were essentially the same. Clearly, the intensity of an airborne sound stimulus determines whether a response will be elicited as well as the magnitude of the response. Also, success in using the neonatal literature to select a stimulus that elicited fetal responding suggested that there may exist a continuity in fetal-newborn sensitivity to auditory stimuli. This issue was examined in a subsequent study described later.

The influence of the frequency characteristics of airborne sound has been studied by others. For example, Lecanuet, Granier-Deferre, and Busnel (1988) demonstrated that increasing the central frequency of octave-band airborne noise increases fetal responsiveness. Their findings indicated that the effect of increasing frequency is independent of the effect of increasing intensity. A more detailed discussion of this work appears elsewhere in this volume.

Vibroacoustic Stimulus Intensity

After establishing a sensitivity function for an airborne sound stimulus, an attempt was made to do the same for a vibroacoustic stimulus. The task was formidable. To begin with, a vibroacoustic stimulus is delivered on the maternal abdomen as opposed to in air and includes both an airborne sound and a mechanical tactile vibration. The multimodal nature of the stimulus presents at least two problems. First, how does one determine intensity? Is it a measure of the airborne sound or the mechanical vibration or both? Second, how does one manipulate the stimulus components (i.e., sound and vibration) independently? Altering the airborne component also alters the amplitude and/or frequency components of the mechanical vibration and vice versa. Studies in this laboratory to determine the "inten-

TABLE 14.2
Fetal Responses Elicited by Four Different Stimuli

Stimulus	Mean FHR Acceleration (bpm), Stimulus/Control, First Trial	Mean Movement Score, Stimulus/Control, First Two-Trial Block,
Vibroacoustic	20.2/9.2	1.9/0.3
Complex noise	13.9/5.9	0.8/0.1
Ballottement[a]	12.6/3.5	1.1/0.1
Tone	7.3 / 6.4	0.3/0.2

[a]Ballottement followed a series of tone trials.

sity" of a vibroacoustic stimulus have resulted in more questions than answers. For example, Table 14.2 which includes the initial fetal response to a variety of stimuli for three groups of term fetuses, illustrates that a vibroacoustic stimulus with an airborne sound component of only 64 dB elicited a greater magnitude and frequency of fetal responses compared to an airborne noise of 110 dB (the study is reported later in this chapter; Kisilevsky & Muir, 1991). This finding indicates that sound alone can not account for differential responding among stimuli. More intriguing, however, is a study (Kisilevsky & Muir, unpublished) that failed to show fetal responding with one vibrator "judged" by adult subjects to be 50% more intense than a second vibrator that elicited responding. Undoubtedly, the vibroacoustic characteristics essential to eliciting a response and the salient features that control the magnitude of the response need to be identified before the intensity issue can be resolved.

It should be noted that Yao and colleagues (1990) determined intensity using an accelerometer that measured the velocity of a vibrating surface and found that maternal perceptions of movements increased with increasing intensity but that the occurrence of FHR accelerations did not change. Given that maternal perceptions may not be accurate (Kisilevsky et al., 1991), these results need to be replicated using ultrasound observations.

Stimulus Modality

As noted earlier, the results of a fetal study in which stimulus selection was partially based on neonatal behavior raised the issue of the continuity of fetal-newborn responses to sensory stimulation. The question was addressed in both the auditory and tactile modalities. Three parallel studies were conducted using the "same" stimulus materials and the "same" habituation procedure to test the "same" subjects twice, first as term fetuses and next as 1–4 day old newborns.[1] The stimuli included two 110-dB airborne sounds (a 2,000-Hz pure tone and a complex noise), a vibroacoustic stimulus, and a tactile ballottement[2] (Kisilevsky & Muir, 1991). Looking again at Table 14.2 which includes the results of the fetal studies, it can be seen that on the first stimulus trial/trial-block a greater magnitude of FHR acceleration and more movements were elicited by a vibrator compared to an airborne noise, and responding on pure tone trials could not be differentiated from spontaneous activity observed on control trials. The same pattern of responding was found for the neonates, suggesting a continuity of fetal and newborn behavior in response to similar, though not identical, stimulus materials.

Incorporated into Table 14.2 are the responses elicited by the first ballottement, which was preceded by a series of tone trials; the magnitude and frequency of responses to ballottement were similar to those elicited by a complex airborne sound. This finding was unexpected because the general consensus from a number of studies was that physical stimulation did not elicit fetal responding (e.g., Druzin et al., 1985; Richardson, Campbell, Carmichael, & Patrick, 1981; Visser, Zeelenberg, de Vries, & Dawes, 1983). One factor that may account for the apparent discrepancy between these results and earlier studies is the time course over which responding was measured. In this study, responding was measured over 20 sec from stimulus onset, whereas other studies used time periods of 20–90 min. If the response occurs in about half of the fetuses (58% in this study) and is short lived, then measurements over minutes may not be sensitive enough to detect responding.

Although, at first glance, comparison of response rates among the four stimuli might suggest that single modality stimuli elicit less responding than multimodal stimuli, this may or may not be the case. The finding that a vibroacoustic stimulus elicits more responding than a complex noise has been reported before (e.g., Grimwade et al., 1971). However, except for the intensity of the two airborne sounds, the stimuli were not equated. Furthermore, the ballottement occurred following repeated sound stimuli, which may have influenced responding. Indeed, an order effect was observed when touch followed sound. Fetal responding was significantly

---

[1]Because the fetus was housed in a liquid environment within the maternal abdomen and the neonate existed independently in air, the stimuli, procedures, and response measures used to examine fetal and subsequent newborn behavior in this study could not be identical. Necessary adaptations in stimulus delivery and response measurements in the two environments led to procedural modifications. (For a discussion of adaptations, see Kisilevsky & Muir, 1991.)

[2]Ballottement is a manual vibration of the fetus produced by the researcher gently rocking the mother's abdomen from side-to-side.

lower when the initial vibroacoustic stimulus was preceded by sound than when the initial stimulus was not preceded by sound, replicating a previous finding with newborn infants (Kisilevsky & Muir, 1984). Before any firm conclusions can be drawn, the stimuli need to be equated and ballottement needs to be examined without pretreatment.

Repeated Stimulation (Habituation)

In addition to the modality issue, responses to repeated stimulation were examined in the three parallel studies (Kisilevsky & Muir, 1991) using a classical habituation paradigm (i.e., response decrement to a repeating stimulus, followed by response recovery to a novel stimulus, and subsequent response recovery to the original repeating stimulus following the novel stimulus; Groves & Thompson, 1970; Thompson & Spencer, 1966). One group of term fetuses received eight 2.5-sec trials of the complex noise followed by two 2.5-sec trials of the novel vibration followed by two 2.5-sec trials of the re-presented complex noise. A second group received a vibration-noise-vibration pattern. And, a third group received a tone-ballottement-tone pattern of stimulation. Others had reported finding habituation of movement response, but not FHR acceleration, to a repeated vibroacoustic stimulus (Leader, Baillie, Martin, & Vermeulen, 1982; Madison et al., 1986) and response decrement of FHR acceleration to a repeated airborne complex sound (Lecanuet et al., 1986) and to a pure tone (Dwornicka, Jasienska, Smolarz, & Wawryk, 1964). To extend our understanding of the process underlying response decrement, two specific questions were addressed. First, could habituation of FHR acceleration and/or movement responses be demonstrated to an airborne sound stimulus? And second, could habituation of FHR acceleration be demonstrated to a repeated vibroacoustic stimulus? A peak FHR acceleration response was obtained for each subject on each trial by subtracting the maximum FHR within 20 sec of stimulus onset from the FHR at stimulus onset (for a description of the manual and computer techniques involved see Coleman, Kisilevsky, & Muir, 1993). Movement was scored within 5 sec of stimulation. Figure 14.2, which contains the fetal responses for the group that received the noise-vibration-noise pattern, clearly shows classical habituation of an FHR acceleration response elicited by a complex airborne sound. This finding is important because it illustrates the potential for using a habituation procedure for measuring central nervous system (CNS) functioning and for distinguishing between selective adaptation and retention of memory models of habituation in the fetus. Decrement of an FHR acceleration response to a repeated vibroacoustic stimulus was not demonstrated. Furthermore, in contrast to others (e.g., Kuhlman, Burns, Depp, & Sebbagha, 1988; Leader et al., 1982; Madison et al., 1986), movement

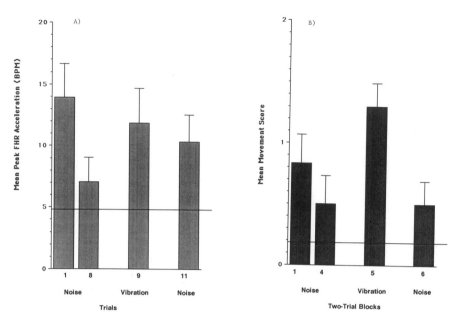

FIG. 14.2.   (A) Mean peak FHR acceleration (bpm) and (B) mean movement scores as a function of a repeating noise, a novel vibration, and the re-presented noise stimulus. Vertical lines represent standard error of the mean (SEM). The horizontal lines represent the mean response on no-stimulus control trials.

response decrement to repeated vibroacoustic stimulation was not demonstrated. The failure to replicate others may have occurred because a comparatively longer interstimulus interval (i.e., 1 min vs. 10–20 sec) and fewer trials (i.e., 8 vs. 10–50) were used. The first factor is known to bring about more rapid response decline (Thompson & Spencer, 1966). However, the minimum interstimulus interval was limited because both FHR and movement responses were measured and FHR does not always return to baseline within 20 sec of stimulation (Kisilevsky et al., 1989).

The studies just presented explicitly demonstrate that fetal responding is influenced by stimulus variables. Stimulus intensity, modality, and number of presentations determine the threshold for a response, the initial response magnitude, and response decline over repeated trials.

SUBJECT VARIABLES

Little is known about the subject variables that influence fetal response to acoustic and vibroacoustic stimuli. This section includes studies in two areas that are beginning to be examined—gestational age and risk status.

Gestational Age

As a first step in a research program to describe the maturation of fetal behavior elicited by sound and vibration, a study of FHR and movement responses to a vibroacoustic stimulus from 23 to 36 weeks gestational age was conducted using a sequential design (mixed cross-sectional and longitudinal methods; Kisilevsky, Muir, & Low, 1992). No-stimulus control trials were included instead of state control because they could be used across gestational ages. Although there is clear evidence that fetal states are distinguishable from 36 weeks gestation to term (Nijhuis, Prechtl, Martin, & Bots, 1982) and that state modulates responsiveness to weak stimuli (e.g., Schmidt et al., 1985), as fetuses get younger in age, states as defined by Nijhuis et al. (1982) become less determinate. Therefore, subjects received a series of three stimulus and three no-stimulus control trials intermixed and randomly presented. A vibroacoustic stimulus rather than an airborne sound was selected because previous studies in this laboratory had shown responding on an average of 92% of vibroacoustic trials compared to about 60% of airborne noise trials. Moreover, for this normative study, a standard commercial vibrator (Allied Traders) used in previous studies rather than an artificial larynx—probably the most commonly used vibroacoustic stimulus—was employed because of questions of the safety of the artificial larynx with preterm fetuses (Gerhardt, 1989) as well as reports that it induced tachycardia (Gagnon, Hunse, & Patrick, 1988), disorganized fetal state (Visser, Mulder, Wit, Mulder, & Prechtl, 1989), increased baseline FHR, and produced unusual FHR patterns (Thomas et al., 1989). As previously reported by others (e.g., Birnholz & Benacerraf, 1983), it was found that reliable stimulus driven movements appeared by 26 weeks, preceding the onset of reliable cardiac accelerations, which were not observed until 29 weeks. Furthermore, as expected (e.g., Crade & Lovett, 1988; Gagnon et al., 1988), developmental functions, illustrated in Fig. 14.3, also varied depending on the response measured. Figure 14.3 shows that with advancing gestation, movement responses increased in a gradual, continuous fashion. In contrast, FHR acceleration responses showed a discontinuous pattern with a rather abrupt change from no response to a relatively mature response between 29 and 31 weeks. It should be noted that the results were the same for both the average magnitude of the responses over trials and the percentage of subjects responding.

Surprisingly, when FHR change at 1-sec intervals for 20 sec following stimulus onset rather than the peak FHR change in those 20 sec was examined, a more complex maturational profile for cardiac responses was revealed. At 26–28 weeks, there was a small FHR deceleration observed in 9/12 fetuses ($M = 2.6$ bpm). Although one might be quite skeptical of this result because FHR variability is in the range of 3–6 bpm, there are at least

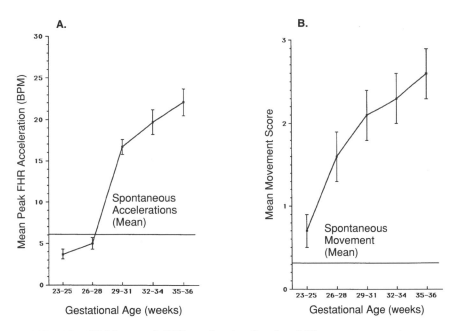

FIG. 14.3.   (A) Mean peak FHR acceleration (bpm) and (B) mean movement score elicited by a vibroacoustic stimulus as a function of gestational age. Vertical lines represent SEM.

three reasons why it should be taken seriously. It has been replicated in a separate group of high-risk fetuses (Kisilevsky, Muir, & Low, 1990a); it appears at a time in gestation when spontaneous decelerations are the most common FHR change (Wheeler & Murrills, 1978); and small decelerations have been reported in response to low-intensity auditory stimuli at term (Lecanuet, Granier-Deferre, Jacquet, & Busnel, 1992). At present there is no definitive explanation to account for this result. The change may occur because of a simple shift in the locus of control in the autonomic nervous system or a shift in the effectiveness of the stimulus, reflecting an increase in vibroacoustic sensitivity. Alternatively, given the multimodal nature of the stimulus, the mechanisms underlying the shift may be much more complex, involving individual or parallel changes in the auditory and tactile systems or interactions between the two. In addition to the developmental picture, these results suggest that FHR and body movement response measures are independently controlled.

Undoubtedly, the description of the maturation of FHR and movement responses to one vibroacoustic stimulus is only a beginning. To more fully understand fetal sensory development additional studies are needed to replicate the observation of an initial cardiac deceleration response, to untangle the loci of developmental trends and determine the mechanisms underlying the response, and to differentiate between the maturation of sensory and response systems.

Risk Status

Studies designed to systematically compare differential responding in low- and high-risk fetuses are just beginning. For example, a study of the maturation of fetal responses using the same age fetuses, the same vibroacoustic stimulus, and the same procedure detailed earlier is in progress employing high-risk fetuses. In the study, fetuses were designated high-risk because their mothers were in a hospital and threatening preterm delivery. Preliminary data analyses of the responses of a sample of 36 high-risk hospitalized fetuses, regardless of outcome, compared with a sample of 55 nonhospitalized healthy fetuses (from the maturation study) suggest that the behavior of the high-risk fetuses may be less mature (Kisilevsky, Muir, & Low, 1990b). The latency to a FHR acceleration response was delayed in the hospitalized group. Furthermore, as shown in Fig. 14.4, the magnitude of the cardiac acceleration over 1-sec intervals from time of stimulus onset in the 32–34 week low-risk, nonhospitalized fetuses was greater than for the high-risk hospitalized group. The magnitude of the hospitalized group was similar to that found in the 29–31 week nonhospitalized group rather than to nonhospitalized

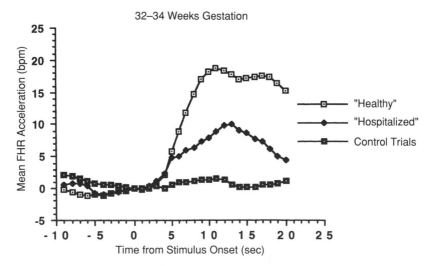

FIG. 14.4.   Mean FHR acceleration (bpm) on the first vibration trial as a function of time from stimulus onset (seconds) for healthy nonhospitalized and high-risk hospitalized fetuses at 32–34 weeks gestational age. Mean FHR acceleration (bpm) on the first no-stimulus control trial is also displayed.

agemates. Of course, a larger sample is required before any firm conclusion can be drawn. Nevertheless, these findings indicate the potential to differentiate the healthy from the compromised fetus using responses to sensory stimulation.

SUMMARY

The studies presented in this chapter are helping to provide a more complete picture of the influence of stimulus and subject variables on human fetal responses to sound and vibration. For example, it was demonstrated that the intensity of an airborne sound stimulus determines whether a response will be elicited as well as the magnitude of the response; it was shown that a multimodal vibroacoustic stimulus elicits a greater magnitude of FHR acceleration and more movements than either a unimodal acoustic (airborne noise) or a unimodal tactile stimulus (ballottement); classical habituation of a FHR acceleration response elicited by a complex airborne sound was illustrated; and maturation of responses to a vibroacoustic stimulus were described in a healthy population. Additionally, a number of questions for future research were identified. For example, the influence of the intensity of a vibroacoustic stimulus is a very complex problem that needs to be untangled; differential responding to unimodal versus multimodal stimuli needs to be explored using equivalent probes; and maturation of responses in low- and high-risk fetal populations needs to be compared. Clearly, a solid foundation of normative data is being laid from which to examine theoretical issues concerning fetal perception, attention (cognition), neurological organization, and the importance of prenatal experience on postnatal development. Furthermore, the results of these kinds of studies have the potential for immediate clinical application: (a) in developing tests for use in the assessment of fetal well-being, providing normative descriptions of perceptual behavior in the viable fetus, and (b) in determining optimal care in neonatal intensive care units with respect to tactile and auditory stimulation/exposure.

ACKNOWLEDGMENTS

The research reported in this chapter was conducted in collaboration with Dr. D. W. Muir, Professor, Department of Psychology, and Dr. J. A. Low, Professor, Department of Obstetrics and Gynaecology, Queen's University, Kingston, Ontario. The work was supported by Natural Sciences and Engineering Research Council of Canada, Hospital for Sick Children Foundation and Queen's University Advisory Committee grants. Statistical consultation was provided by Queen's University STAT LAB. Dr. Kisilevsky is supported by an Ontario Ministry of Health Career Scientist Award.

REFERENCES

Arulkumaran, S., Anandakumar, C., Wong, Y. C., & Ratnam, S. S. (1989). Evaluation of maternal perception of sound-provoked fetal movement as a test of antenatal fetal health. *Obstetrics and Gynecology, 73*, 182–186.

Bench, R. J., & Vass, A. (1970). Fetal audiometry. *Lancet, 1*, 91–92.

Benzaquen, S., Gagnon, R., Hunse, C., & Foreman, J. (1990). The intrauterine sound environment of the human fetus during labor. *American Journal of Obstetrics and Gynecology, 163*, 484–490.

Birnholz, J. C., & Benacerraf, B. R. (1983). The development of human fetal hearing. *Science, 222*, 516–518.

Coleman, G. E., Kisilevsky, B. S., & Muir, D. W. (1993). FHR digitizer: A hypercard tool for scoring fetal heart rate records. *Behavior Research Methods, Instruments, & Computers, 25*, 479–482.

Crade, M., & Lovett, S. (1988). Fetal response to sound stimulation: Preliminary report exploring use of sound stimulation in routine obstetrical ultrasound examinations. *Journal of Ultrasound Medicine, 7*, 499–503.

Druzin, M. L., Gratacos, J., Paul, R. H., Broussard, P., McCart, D., & Smith, M. (1985). Antepartum fetal heart rate testing: XII. The effect of manual manipulation of the fetus on the nonstress test. *American Journal of Obstetrics and Gynecology, 151*, 61–64.

Dwornicka, B., Jasienska, A., Smolarz, W., & Wawryk, R. (1964). Attempt of determining the fetal reaction to acoustic stimulation. *Acta Otolaryngologica, 57*, 571–574.

Gagnon, R., Hunse, C., & Patrick, J. (1988). Fetal responses to vibratory acoustic stimulation: Influence of basal heart rate. *American Journal of Obstetrics and Gynecology, 159*, 835–839.

Gelman, S. R., Wood, S., Spellacy, W. N., & Abrams, R. M. (1982). Fetal movements in response to sound stimulation. *American Journal of Obstetrics and Gynecology, 143*, 484–485.

Gerhardt, K. J. (1989). Characteristics of the fetal sheep sound environment. *Seminars in Perinatology, 13*, 362–370.

Grimwade, J. C., Walker, D. W., Bartlett, M., Gordon, S., & Wood, C. (1971). Human fetal heart rate change and movement in response to sound and vibration. *American Journal of Obstetrics and Gynecology, 109*, 86–90.

Groves, P. M., & Thompson, R. F. (1970). Habituation: A dual-process theory. *Psychological Review, 77*, 419–450.

Iggo, A. (1982). Cutaneous sensory mechanisms. In H. B. Barlow & J. D. Mollon (Eds.), *The senses* (pp. 369–408). New York: Cambridge University Press.

Kearsley, R. B. (1973). The newborn's response to auditory stimulation: A demonstration of orienting and defensive behaviour. *Child Development, 44*, 582–590.

Kisilevsky, B. S., Killen, H., Muir, D. W., & Low, J. A. (1991). Maternal and ultrasound measurements of elicited fetal movements: A methodologic consideration. *Obstetrics and Gynecology, 77,* 889–892.

Kisilevsky, B. S., Kilpatrick, K. L., & Low, J. A. (1993). Vibroacoustic induced fetal movement: Two stimuli and two methods of scoring. *Obstetrics and Gynecology, 81,* 174–177.

Kisilevsky, B. S., & Muir, D. W. (1984). Neonatal habituation and dishabituation to tactile stimulation during sleep. *Developmental Psychology, 20,* 367–373.

Kisilevsky, B. S., & Muir, D. W. (1991). Human fetal and subsequent newborn responses to sound and vibration. *Infant Behaviour and Development, 14,* 1–26.

Kisilevsky, B. S., Muir, D. W., & Low, J. A. (1989). Human fetal responses to sound as a function of stimulus intensity. *Obstetrics and Gynecology, 73,* 971–976.

Kisilevsky, B. S., Muir, D. W., & Low, J. A. (1990a, February). *Comparison of responses elicited by a vibroacoustic stimulus in "healthy" and "hospitalized" human preterm fetuses.* Poster presented at the 2nd International Conference on Sound and Vibration in Pregnancy, Gainesville, FL.

Kisilevsky, B. S., Muir, D. W., & Low, J. A. (1990b). Maturation of responses elicited by a vibroacoustic stimulus in a group of high-risk fetuses. *Maternal-Child Nursing Journal, 19,* 239–250.

Kisilevsky, B. S., Muir, D. W., & Low, J. A. (1992). Maturation of human fetal responses to vibroacoustic stimulation. *Child Development, 63,* 1497–1508.

Kisilevsky, B. S., Stack, D. A., & Muir, D. W. (1991). Fetal and infant response to tactile stimulation. In M. J. S. Weiss & P. R. Zelazo (Eds.), *Newborn attention: Biological constraints and the influence of experience* (pp. 63–98). Norwood, NJ: Ablex.

Kuhlman, K. A., Burns, K. A., Depp, R., & Sebbagha, R. E. (1988). Ultrasound imaging of normal fetal response to external vibratory acoustic stimulation. *American Journal of Obstetrics and Gynecology, 158,* 47–51.

Leader, L. R., Baillie, P., Martin, B., & Vermeulen, E. (1982). Fetal habituation in high risk pregnancies. *British Journal of Obstetrics and Gynaecology, 89,* 441–446.

Lecanuet, J. P., Granier-Deferre, C., & Busnel, M. C. (1988). Fetal cardiac and motor responses to octave-band noises as a function of central frequency, intensity, and heart rate variability. *Early Human Development, 18,* 81–93.

Lecanuet, J. P., Granier-Deferre, C., Cohen, H., Le Houezec, R., & Busnel, M. C. (1986). Fetal responses to acoustic stimulation depend on heart rate variability pattern, stimulus intensity and repetition. *Early Human Development, 13,* 269–283.

Lecanuet, J. P., Granier-Deferre, C., Jacquet, A. Y., & Busnel, M. C. (1992). Decelerative cardiac responsiveness to acoustical stimulation in the near term fetus. *The Quarterly Journal of Experimental Psychology, 44B,* 279–303.

Levarie, S., & Rudolph, N. (1978). Can newborn infants distinguish between tone and noise? *Perceptual and Motor Skills, 47,* 1123–1126.

Madison, L. S., Adubato, S. A., Madison, J. K., Nelson, R. W., Anderson, J. C., Erickson, J., Kuss, L., & Goodlin, R. C. (1986). Fetal response decrement: True habituation? *Developmental and Behavioral Pediatrics, 7,* 14–20.

Nijhuis, J. G., Prechtl, H. F. R., Martin, C. B., & Bots, R. S. G. M. (1982). Are there behavioural states in the human fetus? *Early Human Development, 6,* 177–195.

Nymen, M., & Westgren, M. (1989). Maternal perception of sound-provoked fetal movements in low-risk pregnancies during third trimester. *British Journal of Obstetrics and Gynaecology, 96,* 566–567.

Patrick, J. (1984). A reply to Jensen. *American Journal of Obstetrics and Gynecology, 149,* 918–919.

Patrick, J., Campbell, K., Carmichael, L., Natale, R., & Richardson, B. (1982). Patterns of gross fetal body movements over 24-hour observation intervals during the last 10 weeks of pregnancy. *American Journal of Obstetrics and Gynecology, 142,* 363–371.

Pickles, J. O. (1982). *An introduction to the physiology of hearing.* Toronto: Academic Press.

Richards, D. S., Frentzen, B., Gerhardt, K. J., McCann, M. E., & Abrams, R. M. (1992). Sound levels in the human uterus. *Obstetrics and Gynecology, 80,* 186–190.

Richardson, B., Campbell, K., Carmichael, L., & Patrick, J. (1981). Effects of external physical stimulation on fetuses near term. *American Journal of Obstetrics and Gynecology, 139,* 344–352.

Schmidt, W., Boos, R., Gnirs, J., Auer, L., & Schulze, S. (1985). Fetal behavioral states and controlled sound stimulation. *Early Human Development, 12,* 145–153.

Smith, C. V., Satt, B., Phelan, J. P., & Paul, R. H. (1990). Intrauterine sound levels: Intrapartum assessment with an intrauterine microphone. *American Journal of Perinatology, 7,* 312–315.

Thomas, R. L., Johnson, T. R. B., Besinger, R. E., Rafkin, D., Treanor, C., & Strobino, D. (1989). Preterm and term fetal cardiac and movement responses to vibratory acoustic stimulation. *American Journal of Obstetrics and Gynecology, 161,* 141–145.

Thompson, F. T., & Spencer, W. A. (1966). Habituation: A model phenomenon for the study of neuronal substrates of behavior. *Psychological Review, 73,* 16–43.

Turkewitz, G., Birch, H. G., & Cooper, K. K. (1972). Responsiveness to simple and complex auditory stimuli in the human newborn. *Developmental Psychobiology, 5,* 7–19.

Visser, G. H. A., Mulder, H. H., Wit, H. P., Mulder, E. J. H., & Prechtl, H. F. R. (1989). Disturbed fetal behaviour following vibro-acoustic stimulation. In G. Gennser, K. Marsal, N. Svenningsen, & K. Lindstrom (Eds.), *Fetal and neonatal physiological measurements III* (pp. 355–358). Malmoe, Sweden: Flenhags Tryckeri.

Visser, G. H. A., Zeelenberg, H. J., de Vries, J. I. P., & Dawes, G. G. (1983). External physical stimulation of the human fetus during episodes of low heart rate variation. *American Journal of Obstetrics and Gynecology, 145,* 579–584.

Wheeler, T., & Murrills, A. (1978). Patterns of fetal heart rate during normal pregnancy. *British Journal of Obstetrics and Gynaecology, 85,* 18–27.

Yao, Q. W., Jakobsson, J., Nyman, M., Rabaeus, H., Till, O., & Westgren, M. (1990). Fetal responses to different intensity levels of vibroacoustic stimulation. *Obstetrics and Gynecology, 75,* 206–209.

Part V

FETAL EXPERIENCE: BASIC STUDIES

15

Embryonic Sensory Experience and Intersensory Development in Precocial Birds

Robert Lickliter
Virginia Polytechnic Institute and State University

Developmental analysis of behavior can be characterized as consisting of two major strategies or approaches, normative assessment and experimental manipulation (Gottlieb, 1983; Miller, 1981; Petrinovich, 1981). The first strategy, normative assessment, involves the collection of baseline data, derived from naturalistic observation across a range of typically occurring developmental contexts. In its most general sense, this initial stage of developmental analysis attempts to describe what the developing organism "does" and the environmental/stimulative conditions under which its behaviors are seen. This normative baseline serves to both illuminate the range of behaviors and developmental outcomes characteristic of the organism–context interaction process and sensitize investigators to the experiential and stimulative history of the developing individual. This critical starting point for the developmental analysis of behavior can then be followed by the employment of a second strategy, experimental manipulation. In its most general sense, this approach involves the use of experiential modification or manipulation designed to uncover the conditions, experiences, and events necessary and sufficient for normal development to occur. In other words, this mode of developmental analysis attempts to identify the factors, processes, and mechanisms that actually contribute to the development of normal or species-typical patterns of behavior.

Historically, most work concerned with fetal behavior has been relatively normative or descriptive in nature and often has not attempted to directly address the specific processes and mechanisms that contribute to the development of fetal behavior (but see Carmichael, 1926; Gottlieb, 1968; Hamburger, 1963; Herrick & Coghill, 1915; Kuo, 1939; Oppenheim, 1974). However, as many of the contributions to this volume make clear, in recent years the study of fetal behavior has begun to move more and more from the necessary and important descriptive step of developmental analysis to the next step of attempting to discover and articulate the processes and mechanisms that underlie the behaviors associated with the prenatal period.

In this light, the nature and mechanisms of intersensory development during the prenatal period have emerged as a topic of growing interest over the last several years (Gottlieb, Tomlinson, & Radell, 1989; Lickliter, 1990a, 1990b, 1994; Lickliter & Stoumbos, 1991; Radell & Gottlieb, 1992). All sensory systems begin to develop prenatally and in some precocial species are structurally mature before birth (Gottlieb, 1971a). Importantly, onset of function within the various sensory modalities appears to proceed in an invariant pattern among vertebrate species, including humans. This temporal sequence of onset of sensory function (tactile → vestibular → chemical → auditory → visual) appears to hold whether the young of a particular species are born in a precocial or altricial condition (Alberts, 1984; Gottlieb, 1971a).

The fact that the sensory systems do not become functional at the same time in development raises the interesting question of how sensory systems and their respective stimulative histories might influence one another, especially during the prenatal period. In particular, because sensory systems develop at different rates, competition between them is likely to undergo marked changes during individual ontogeny. With this in mind, Turkewitz and Kenny (1982, 1985) proposed a theory of early perceptual development that centers around the role of developmental limitations of sensory experience. Turkewitz and Kenny argued that sensory limitations during early development both reduce available stimulation and mediate the timing of the introduction of stimulation, thereby reducing the amount of competition between maturing sensory modalities. From this perspective, limitations on sensory experience during early development are not handicaps or deficiencies to be overcome by the fetus or infant, but rather provide an important source of structure and order to help determine the nature of early intersensory relationships. In particular, limitations of sensory input were viewed by Turkewitz and Kenny as a key mechanism by which the quantity and/or quality of sensory stimulation available to the young organism is reduced at sensitive stages of perinatal development. If this is indeed the case, then altering the timing of onset of a sensory system during prenatal development should result in changes in the nature of perinatal intersensory relationships.

One avenue for advancing our understanding of the nature of this aspect of early perceptual organization is the identification of appropriate animal models that allow the systematic manipulation of early intersensory interaction. Because of the experimental limitations inherent in working with human subjects, the use of animal models has served and will continue to serve as a fundamental source for unpacking how asynchronous sensory development might influence perceptual development during the perinatal period (see Foreman & Altaha, 1991; Gottlieb et al., 1989; Kenny & Turkewitz, 1986; Lickliter, 1990a, 1990b, 1994; Radell & Gottlieb, 1992; Symons & Tees, 1990). One obvious requirement for any animal model used to examine prenatal sensory/perceptual organization is the ability to easily alter the time when particular forms of sensory experience are present and available to the developing embryo or fetus. Because their prenatal development takes place in ovo rather than in utero, birds are obviously more accessible to these types of embryonic manipulations than are mammalian species. In addition, precocial birds' auditory systems begin functioning embryonically, overlapping with the later onset of visual capability (Freeman & Vince, 1974; Gottlieb, 1971a). Although the precocial avian embryo is responsive to visual stimulation prenatally (Heaton, 1973), the embryo would not ordinarily experience patterned visual stimulation until after hatching from the egg. It is possible, however, to provide the precocial avian embryo with altered patterns of auditory and visual stimulation by the relatively simple experimental procedure of removing the shell and inner shell membrane over the air space at the large end of the egg several days prior to hatching, thereby exposing the head of the embryo. The technique of removing part of the shell to allow direct observation and manipulation of the avian embryo was first described by Kuo (1932) and has been used by a number of behavioral embryologists over the course of the last 60 years (see Oppenheim, Levin, & Harth, 1973). The avian embryo's bill normally penetrates the air space several days prior to hatching, and the embryo becomes capable of pulmonary respiration at this time (Freeman & Vince, 1974); the embryo's head can be exposed following this event without negatively affecting the bird's hatchability, survivability, or species-typical behavior (Gottlieb, 1971b, 1988; Heaton & Galleher, 1981).

Bobwhite quail (*Colinus virginianus*) chicks are particularly well suited to this kind of manipulation and thus lend themselves to the investigation of early intersensory development. Like many other precocial birds, quail chicks show a strong attraction to their maternal call and are capable of discriminating between it and similar conspecific and non-conspecific vocalizations in the period immediately after hatching (Heaton & Galleher,

1981; Heaton, Miller, & Goodwin, 1978). This species-specific auditory responsiveness provides a useful and reliable probe for assessing the impact of both altered auditory and visual experience on chicks' normal auditory functioning. In addition, unlike most other precocial birds, bobwhite quail synchronize their hatching with that of their broodmates; this hatching synchrony appears to depend, at least in part, on the embryo's prenatal exposure to auditory stimulation from neighboring embryos of their clutch (Vince, 1973), indicating a high degree of sensitivity to the stimulative aspects of the prenatal auditory environment on the part of the bobwhite embryo and providing an example of the regulation of embryonic behavior by prenatal sensory experience.

NORMATIVE PATTERNS OF PERINATAL SENSORY DOMINANCE

The fact that the quail chick's auditory system has had more prenatal experience at the time of hatching than has its visual system suggests that the quail hatchling's auditory system may be more fully developed and functional than its visual system in the days following hatching (Freeman & Vince, 1974; Gottlieb, 1971a, 1973). In other words, in part because of its earlier development and experiential precedence, the auditory system could be more structurally and functionally differentiated at hatching and thus should have an initial advantage when auditory and visual input compete for the hatchling's attention. Recent evidence supports the existence of such a functional "cue hierarchy" and sets the stage for further investigation of the prenatal factors and mechanisms underlying early perceptual organization.

For example, a study by Lickliter and Virkar (1989) examined the interaction between naturally occurring maternal auditory and visual stimulation in the control of social preferences in bobwhite quail hatchlings in the days immediately following hatching. Results obtained from simultaneous choice tests revealed a hierarchy in the functional priority of the auditory and visual systems of normally reared chicks. At 24 and 48 hr of postnatal age, differential responsiveness was found to depend on the auditory component of maternal stimulation. In other words, chicks consistently directed their social preferences towards the bobwhite maternal call at both 24 and 48 hr following hatching. At 72 and 96 hr of age, combined maternal auditory and visual stimulation was found necessary to direct chicks' social preferences. That is, chicks required both a hen and the maternal call to respond preferentially. However, even at these later ages the auditory modality remained dominant over the visual modality in eliciting responsiveness to the maternal hen. Specifically, chicks consistently responded to the maternal call in preference to maternal visual cues throughout the first 96 hr following hatching. In addition, chicks did not respond to species-specific visual cues when presented without auditory cues at any of the ages tested (Lickliter & Virkar, 1989). A similar pattern of early auditory dominance has also been reported for other precocial animal infants, including domestic chicks (Gottlieb, 1971b), ducklings (Johnston & Gottlieb, 1985; Gottlieb, 1973), and humans (Lewkowicz, 1988).

As discussed earlier, two related prenatal conditions exist that could serve to foster this early sensory dominance of the auditory system: (a) the earlier development and function of the auditory system when compared to the visual system, and (b) the longer stimulation history of the auditory system when compared to the visual system. As a first step in examining whether the timing of prenatal sensory experience does indeed impact postnatal intersensory functioning, my laboratory undertook a series of experiments concerned with the effects of unusually early visual experience on early perceptual organization. Specifically, the influence of prenatal visual stimulation on postnatal auditory, visual, and audiovisual functioning in bobwhite quail chicks was assessed (see Lickliter, 1993).

INTERSENSORY EFFECTS OF PRENATAL VISUAL EXPERIENCE

Turkewitz and Kenny (1985) proposed that differences in the functional relationship between sensory systems (i.e., dominance hierarchies) could stem from differences in the time of onset of the various systems in relation to each other. In this scenario, accelerating the onset of function of the visual system so that it becomes experienced prenatally should potentially alter the initial prepotence of the auditory system during early postnatal development. To test this notion, a set of studies was conducted in which bobwhite quail embryos were provided visual stimulation with a temporally patterned light (15-W light pulsed at 3 cycles per second) during the last 24–36 hr of incubation by removing the upper portions of the egg shell and exposing their heads as described earlier. As a result of this manipulation, the prenatal stimulation histories of the auditory and visual modalities were made to coincide during the late stages of the incubation period. In other words, bobwhite embryos received both normal auditory experience and abnormally early visual experience prior to hatching, thereby altering the typical prenatal pattern of reduced competition between the emerging auditory and visual systems. Following hatching, chicks were tested in simultaneous choice tests between auditory and visual features of a bobwhite hen versus auditory and visual features of hens of other species. Results were compared with those obtained from normal quail hatchlings, which show a strong auditory preference for the bobwhite maternal call but do not initially exhibit a preference for visual features of the bobwhite hen (Lickliter, 1994; Lickliter & Virkar, 1989).

The results of this work (Lickliter, 1990a, 1990b, 1994) revealed that when embryos receive unusually early (prenatal) visual experience, they subsequently exhibit postnatal auditory and visual preferences different from normal, unstimulated chicks. For example, quail chicks that experienced prenatal patterned visual stimulation showed a marked decline in auditory responsiveness to the bobwhite maternal call during the period immediately following hatching. Specifically, prenatally stimulated chicks failed to respond to maternal auditory cues when presented alone (without maternal visual cues) by 24 hr following hatching. This result stands in contrast to those obtained from control chicks, who continue to respond to auditory cues until some 72 hr following hatching. Interestingly, whereas auditory responsiveness to the maternal call declined rapidly following hatching, intersensory functioning appeared accelerated by the experience of premature visual experience. That is, birds that received prenatal visual experience as embryos required combined auditory and visual maternal cues to direct their social preferences as early as 24 hr following hatching (Lickliter, 1990a). In contrast, normally hatched chicks readily directed their social preferences on the basis of maternal auditory cues alone at both 24 and 48 hr following hatching, but eventually required combined auditory and visual cues by 72 hr of age (Lickliter & Virkar, 1989). Thus, hatchlings that received patterned visual stimulation as embryos demonstrated perceptual preferences at 24 hr of age comparable to those seen in unstimulated hatchlings at 72 hr of age. These results underscore the dynamic nature of early perceptual organization and suggest that the sequential onset of functioning of the sensory systems and the resulting reduction of competition between emerging modalities are important sources of perceptual organization in the perinatal period (Turkewitz & Kenny, 1982). In particular, these results suggest that the restricted visual experience of normally hatched embryos contributes to their species-typical pattern of perinatal perceptual organization.

EXPERIMENTAL ACCELERATION OF VISUAL RESPONSIVENESS

To further examine the role of asynchronous sensory system onset as a regulator of early intersensory relationships, several other related experiments utilizing the early visual experience procedure were undertaken (Lickliter, 1990b). In this work, prenatally visually stimulated chicks were tested postnatally in simultaneous choice tests with auditory and visual cues; however, the testing situation was arranged so that the auditory cues presented did not allow the basis for a choice to be made. Specifically, chicks were presented with identical bobwhite maternal calls paired with a stuffed bobwhite hen on one side of the testing arena and a stuffed scaled quail hen on the other side of the testing arena. This configuration required chicks to choose on the basis of available visual cues provided by the adult hen replicas in order to demonstrate a species-specific maternal preference, as the auditory cues present in the test (identical maternal calls) did not afford a basis for decision.

The results of this study revealed that prenatally visually stimulated chicks utilize species-specific visual cues to direct their social preferences as early as 24 hr following hatching (Lickliter, 1990b). In contrast, normally hatched chicks do not utilize visual cues at either 24 or 48 hr of age, but do use species-specific maternal visual cues by 72 hr following hatching (Lickliter & Virkar, 1989). These results indicate that prenatal visual experience accelerated the use of visual information in the early postnatal period. In other words, one result of an increase in prenatal visual stimulation is that subsequent behavior is somehow reorganized to utilize the earlier than normal visual information; prenatally stimulated chicks appear more "visually oriented" than normally hatched controls (see also Lickliter, 1994). This does not mean, however, that auditory information is unnecessary or ignored during the perinatal period. Bobwhite chicks do not direct their social preferences on the basis of visual cues alone during the first 4 days following hatching, whether or not they have received prenatal visual experience (Lickliter, 1990a; Lickliter & Virkar, 1989).

PRENATAL VISUAL EXPERIENCE AND PRENATAL AUDITORY INTERFERENCE

As discussed earlier, the auditory system of precocial birds and mammals is functional during the later stages of prenatal development. Furthermore, the embryos of a number of avian and mammalian species are capable of learning their parents' vocalizations before birth or hatching (DeCasper & Fifer, 1980; Gottlieb, 1988; Impekoven, 1976). Interestingly, if precocial duck embryos are exposed to prenatal visual stimulation concurrently with prenatal exposure to a maternal call, they do not learn the individually distinctive auditory features of that maternal call (Gottlieb et al., 1989). Such intersensory interference is likely the result, at least in part, of simultaneous auditory and visual stimulation during the prenatal period. Simultaneous sensory stimulation increases experiential competition between the auditory and visual modalites when both are still undergoing rapid maturation, thereby potentially overtaxing the immature attentional capacities of the embryo.

To further examine this notion, a recent set of experiments has examined the relationship between prenatal auditory learning and the timing of intersensory function (Lickliter & Hellewell, 1992). In this study, the ability of bobwhite embryos and hatchlings to learn an individual bobwhite maternal call was assessed. To our surprise, embryos demonstrated clearer evidence of early auditory learning than did older, more mature hatchlings. That is, embryos could learn an individual bobwhite maternal call and remember that familiar call for at least 24 hr following exposure. In contrast, group-reared chicks exposed postnatally to an individual maternal call did not demonstrate a preference for that familiar call over an unfamiliar bobwhite maternal call 24 hr following exposure.

One possible explanation for this rather surprising difference in performance between bobwhite embryos and hatchlings is that the more complex environment of the bobwhite hatchling somehow serves to disrupt or interfere with early auditory learning. To assess this possibility, we reared hatchlings under conditions of reduced visual and social experience during their postnatal exposure to an individual maternal call. Unlike group-reared hatchlings, these isolation-reared chicks did exhibit a significant preference for the familiar maternal call 24 hr following exposure. This result suggests that the perceptual and social complexity of postnatal rearing conditions somehow interferes with the young chick's early auditory learning.

Further support for this interference effect was provided by the finding that embryos also failed to exhibit a preference for an individual maternal call when the call was paired with patterned visual stimulation during the period prior to hatching. In other words, intersensory interference seemed to occur when the auditory and visual systems were concurrently stimulated in the embryo. This finding paralleled the negative results obtained from group-reared hatchlings and suggests that either (a) increasing the complexity of the prenatal environment by providing visual experience in the egg or (b) hatching into the more visually and socially complex postnatal environment can effectively distract the embryo and hatchling, thereby interfering with the development of a preference for an individual maternal call. Taken together, the results of the Lickliter and Hellewell (1992) study and the Gottlieb et al. (1989) study support the idea that limitation of visual experience during the prenatal period serves to reduce competition between the emerging auditory and visual modalities and thus contributes to the prenatal auditory learning seen in a variety of precocial animal infants. Failure to demonstrate prenatal auditory learning occurred only when the auditory and visual systems were concurrently stimulated prenatally.

The studies just reviewed suggest that the precocial avian embryo is not competent at attending to simultaneous sensory stimulation; it appears that the complexity and/or amount of stimulation present when immature sensory systems are stimulated simultaneously can, at least under some conditions, effectively overwhelm the embryo's attentional capabilities. Of course, the notion of attentional interference remains speculative at the present time, and additional research is currently underway in our laboratory to further examine this "embryonic attention" hypothesis. Interestingly, this hypothesis does fit nicely with the idea of the importance of limitation of sensory input to early intersensory development initially proposed by Turkewitz and Kenny (1982, 1985). From this perspective, sensory limitation during prenatal development may help to provide the embryo with a relatively simple, orderly world that does not overly tax its immature attentional abilities. This "constraints by design" notion provides a possible insight into how stable and reliable perceptual outcomes within a species are achieved during early development.

STRUCTURED ORGANISMS AND STRUCTURED ENVIRONMENTS

Of course, limitation of sensory input does not stem only from the limited functioning of the embryo's immature sensory systems. Limitation of sensory input is also regulated and achieved by the buffered, protected nature of the prenatal environment. All avian and mammalian embryos or fetuses are constrained within the buffered and relatively less variable stimulative system of the egg or uterus; as a result, sensory stimulation involving light, sound, temperature, and chemical cues is typically attenuated prior to reaching the developing embryo or fetus. It is important to stress that I am not suggesting that the avian or mammalian embryo does not receive an array of sensory stimulation prenatally. On the contrary, there is a wealth of data presented in this volume to document that embryos and fetuses receive ongoing sensory stimulation prenatally. In addition, avian and mammalian embryos are known to be responsive to a variety of tactile, acoustic, and chemosensory cues prior to birth or hatching (e.g., Bradley & Mistretta, 1975; Gottlieb, 1973, 1988; Lickliter & Stoumbos, 1992; Radell & Gottlieb, 1992; Smotherman & Robinson, 1987, 1992, and chapters 2 and 16, this volume). I am simply pointing out that by the very design of the egg or uterus, the developing embryo resides in a relatively simplified environment, and this simplified environment can contribute to the development and organization of early perceptual capabilities. In this view, both limited sensory capacities and a constrained developmental context combine to provide constraints that minimize the

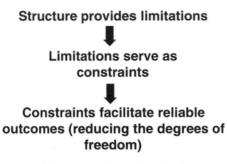

Structure provides limitations

Limitations serve as constraints

Constraints facilitate reliable outcomes (reducing the degrees of freedom)

FIG. 15.1.   Consequences of the structured organism/environment complex for developmental outcomes.

simultaneous or concurrent presentation of multiple sources of information to the developing embryo or fetus. As a result, the ongoing demands placed on the embryo's allocation of attention are effectively controlled or attenuated during sensitive stages of the prenatal period. Said another way, the order and constraint typically supplied by the sequential onset of sensory function prenatally and the simplified nature of the prenatal environment combine to reduce the possible degrees of freedom contributing to early perceptual organization (Fig. 15.1).

In this view, the asynchronous but orderly functional emergence of the various sensory modalities in concert with the sequestered milieu of the egg or uterus serve as both restrictive and ordering mechanisms, which reduce the amount and the timing of competition between rapidly maturing sensory systems. This condition provides a reliable order and structure to prenatal sensory experience and reduces the attentional demands placed on the developing embryo or fetus (see Campbell & Bickhard, 1992, Gottlieb, 1991, and Oyama, 1993, for recent discussions of the roles of constraints in development).

CONCLUSIONS AND FUTURE DIRECTIONS

As stated at the beginning of this chapter, the study of fetal behavior is rapidly maturing from primarily descriptive studies to those concerned with explanation. As the various chapters of this volume attest, substantial insights are being made into the various regulatory processes and mechanisms underlying the emergence of fetal capacities during the prenatal period. In this light, the discussion of the studies considered in this chapter has argued that the emergence of early perceptual organization is constrained and guided by features both of the organism's characteristics and of its developmental context. In the case of precocial birds, the order and constraint of the onset of prenatal sensory system function and the relatively closed system of the avian egg appear to provide a stable framework within which the embryo's species-typical patterns of intersensory relationships can take form and mature.

Much remains to be addressed in the study of early intersensory functioning, and the work reviewed here is merely a first step in attempting to understand the conditions under which specific experiential factors can facilitate or interfere with perinatal intersensory development. Although the "early exposure" paradigm employed in the studies reviewed in this chapter has proven to be a useful addition to more traditional sensory deprivation studies in the investigation of the effects of altered developmental histories on intersensory development, future work will need to expand on this theme and include a wider array of behavioral and physiological probes aimed at assessing the arousal, attentional, experiential, and motivational features contributing to perinatal intersensory development. For example, the nature of the relationship between the amount, type, and modality of prenatal sensory stimulation remains unclear at the present time. Is the overall amount of stimulation present in the prenatal environment the most critical experiential factor in determining subsequent intrasensory and intersensory effects? In other words, are the reported effects of unusually early visual experience discussed in this chapter primarily the result of increased amounts of prenatal stimulation, regardless of what type of stimulation or what modality of stimulation is provided the embryo? Alternatively, are embryos sensitive to the type of prenatal sensory stimulation provided, as has recently been demonstrated for hatchlings (McBride & Lickliter, 1994)? In a similar vein, is the modality of prenatal stimulation influential in determining the nature of subsequent intersensory relationships? These and related questions concerning the relationship between arousal and attentional mechanisms remain largely unexplored at present. Although it is certainly clear that prenatal sensory experience can dramatically affect early perceptual organization, the research reviewed here is only a first step in the difficult task of empirically assessing and cataloging the "experience" of such experience.

In any case, the ability to better define and manipulate the structure of both the developing fetus and its specific developmental context will undoubtedly lead to the reformulation of many traditional notions regarding the factors and relationships contributing to early behavioral and physiological development. As this chapter and the others of this volume suggest, emerging technological and methodological advances will likely challenge developmentalists to consider ever more complex, dynamic, and hierarchically based notions about the processes and mechanisms associated with fetal behavior development. In particular, students of fetal psychobiology will likely provide developmental science with increasingly sophisticated and precise models of the developmental pathways and trajectories that make up the fascinating process of behavioral development.

ACKNOWLEDGMENT

The research reported here was supported by National Institute of Mental Health Grant MH48949 awarded to Robert Lickliter.

REFERENCES

Alberts, J. R. (1984). Sensory-perceptual development in the Norway rat: A view toward comparative studies. In R. Kail & N. S. Spear (Eds.), *Comparative perspectives on memory development* (pp. 65–101). Hillsdale, NJ: Lawrence Erlbaum Associates.

Bradley, R. M., & Mistretta, C. M. (1975). Fetal sensory receptors. *Physiological Reviews, 55,* 352–382.

Campbell, R. L., & Bickhard, M. H. (1992). Types of constraints on development: An interactivist approach. *Developmental Review, 12,* 311–338.

Carmichael, L. (1926). The development of behavior in vertebrates experimentally removed from the influence of external stimulation. *Psychological Review, 33,* 51–58.

DeCasper, A. J., & Fifer, W. P. (1980). Of human bonding: Newborns prefer their mothers' voices. *Science, 208,* 1174–1176.

Foreman, N., & Altaha, M. (1991). The development of exploration and spontaneous alteration in hooded rat pups: Effects of unusually early eyelid opening. *Developmental Psychobiology, 24,* 521–537.

Freeman, B. M., & Vince, M. A. (1974). *Development of the avian embryo.* London: Chapman & Hall.

Gottlieb, G. (1968). Prenatal behavior of birds. *Quarterly Review of Biology, 43,* 148–174.

Gottlieb, G. (1971a). Ontogenesis of sensory function in birds and mammals. In E. Tobach, L. Aronson, & E. Shaw (Eds.), *The biopsychology of development* (pp. 67–128). New York: Academic Press.

Gottlieb, G. (1971b). *Development of species identification in birds.* Chicago: University of Chicago Press.

Gottlieb, G. (1973). Neglected developmental variables in the study of species identification in birds. *Psychological Bulletin, 79,* 362–372.

Gottlieb, G. (1983). The psychobiological approach to developmental issues. In M. Haith & J. Campos (Eds.), *Handbook of child psychology: Infancy and developmental psychobiology* (Vol. 2, pp. 1–26). New York: John Wiley.

Gottlieb, G. (1988). Development of species identification in ducklings: XV. Individual auditory recognition. *Developmental Psychobiology, 21,* 509–522.

Gottlieb, G. (1991). Experiental canalization of behavioral development: Theory. *Developmental Psychology, 27,* 35–39.

Gottlieb, G., Tomlinson, W. T., & Radell, P. L. (1989). Developmental intersensory interference: Premature visual experience suppresses auditory learning in ducklings. *Infant Behavior and Development, 12*, 1–12.

Hamburger, V. (1963). Some aspects of the embryology of behavior. *Quarterly Review of Biology, 38*, 342–365.

Heaton, M. B. (1973). Early visual function in bobwhite and japanese quail embryos as reflected by pupillary reflex. *Journal of Comparative and Physiological Psychology, 84*, 134–139.

Heaton, M. B., & Galleher, E. (1981). Prenatal auditory discrimination in the bobwhite quail. *Behavioral and Neural Biology, 31*, 242–246.

Heaton, M. B., Miller, D. B., & Goodwin, D. G. (1978). Species-specific auditory discrimination in bobwhite quail neonates. *Developmental Psychobiology, 11*, 13–21.

Herrick, C. J., & Coghill, G. E. (1915). The development of the reflex mechanisms in *Amblystoma*. *Journal of Comparative Neurology, 25*, 65–85.

Impekoven, M. (1976). Responses of laughing gull chicks (*Larus atricilla*) to parental attraction and alarm calls, and effects of prenatal auditory experience on the responsiveness to such calls. *Behaviour, 61*, 250–278.

Johnston, T. D., & Gottlieb, G. (1985). Development of visually controlled maternal preferences in Peking ducklings. *Developmental Psychobiology, 18*, 23–36.

Kenny, P., & Turkewitz, G. (1986). Effects of unusually early visual stimulation on the development of homing behavior in the rat pup. *Developmental Psychobiology, 19*, 57–66.

Kuo, Z.-Y. (1932). Ontogeny of embryonic behavior in aves. I. The chronology and general nature of the behavior of the chick embryo. *Journal of Experimental Zoology, 61*, 395–430.

Kuo, Z.-Y. (1939). Studies in physiology of the embryonic nervous system: Experimental evidence on the controversy over the reflex theory in development. *Journal of Comparative Neurology, 70*, 437–459.

Lewkowicz, D. J. (1988). Sensory dominance in infants: 1. Six month old infants' response to auditory-visual compounds. *Developmental Psychology, 24*, 155–171.

Lickliter, R. (1990a). Premature visual stimulation accelerates intersensory functioning in bobwhite quail neonates. *Developmental Psychobiology, 23*, 15–27.

Lickliter, R. (1990b). Premature visual experience facilitates visual responsiveness in bobwhite quail neonates. *Infant Behavior and Development, 13*, 487–496.

Lickliter, R. (1993). Timing and the development of perinatal perceptual organization. In G. Turkewitz & D. Devenny (Eds.), *Developmental time and timing* (pp. 105–123). Hillsdale, NJ: Lawrence Erlbaum Associates.

Lickliter, R. (1994). Prenatal visual experience alters postnatal sensory dominance hierarchy in bobwhite quail chicks. *Infant Behavior and Development, 17*, 185–193.

Lickliter, R., & Hellewell, T. B. (1992). Contextual determinants of auditory learning in bobwhite quail embryos and hatchlings. *Developmental Psychobiology, 25*, 17–24.

Lickliter, R., & Stoumbos, J. (1991). Enhanced prenatal auditory experience facilitates postnatal visual responsiveness in bobwhite quail chicks. *Journal of Comparative Psychology, 105*, 89–94.

Lickliter, R., & Stoumbos, J. (1992). Modification of prenatal auditory experience alters postnatal auditory preferences of bobwhite quail chicks. *Quarterly Journal of Experimental Psychology, 44B,* 199–214.

Lickliter, R., & Virkar, P. (1989). Intersensory functioning in bobwhite quail chicks: Early sensory dominance. *Developmental Psychobiology, 22,* 651–667.

McBride, T., & Lickliter, R. (1994). Specific postnatal auditory stimulation interferes with species-typical visual responsiveness in bobwhite quail chicks. *Developmental Psychobiology, 27,* 169–183.

Miller, D. B. (1981). Conceptual strategies in behavioral development: Normal development and plasticity. In K. Immelmann, G. W. Barlow, L. Petrinovich, & M. Main (Eds.), *Behavioral development* (pp. 58–82). New York: Cambridge University Press.

Oppenheim, R. W. (1974). The ontogeny of behavior in the chick embryo. In D. S. Lehrman, J. Rosenblatt, R. A. Hinde, & E. Shaw (Eds.), *Advances in the study of behavior* (Vol. 5., pp. 133–172). New York: Academic Press.

Oppenheim, R. W., Levin, H. L., & Harth, M. S. (1973). An investigation of various egg-opening techniques for use in avian behavioral embryology. *Developmental Psychobiology, 6,* 53–68.

Oyama, S. (1993). Constraints and development. *Netherlands Journal of Zoology, 43,* 6–16.

Petrinovich, L. (1981). A method for the study of development. In K. Immelmann, G. W Barlow, L. Petrinovich, & M. Main (Eds.), *Behavioral development* (pp. 83–130). New York: Cambridge University Press.

Radell, P. L., & Gottlieb, G. (1992). Developmental intersensory interference: Augmented prenatal sensory experience interferes with auditory learning in duck embryos. *Developmental Psychology, 28,* 795–803.

Smotherman, W. P., & Robinson, S. R. (1987). Psychobiology of fetal experience in the rat. In N. A. Krasnegor, E. M. Blass, M. A. Hofer, & W. P. Smotherman (Eds.), *Perinatal development: A psychobiological perspective* (pp. 39–60). New York: Academic Press.

Smotherman, W. P., & Robinson, S. R. (1992). Habituation in the rat fetus. *Quarterly Journal of Experimental Psychology, 44B,* 215–230.

Symons, L. A., & Tees, R. C. (1990). An examination of the intramodal and intermodal behavioral consequences of long-term vibrissae removal in the rat. *Developmental Psychobiology, 23,* 849–867.

Turkewitz, G., & Kenny, P. A. (1982). Limitations on input as a basis for neural organization and perceptual development: A preliminary theoretical statement. *Developmental Psychobiology, 15,* 357–368.

Turkewitz, G., & Kenny, P. A. (1985). The role of developmental limitation of sensory input on sensory/perceptual organization. *Journal of Developmental and Behavioral Pediatrics, 6,* 302–306.

Vince, M. A. (1973). Some environmental effects on the activity and development of the avian embryo. In G. Gottlieb (Ed.), *Behavioral embryology* (pp. 285–323). New York: Academic Press.

16

Habituation and Classical Conditioning in the Rat Fetus: Opioid Involvements

Scott R. Robinson
William P. Smotherman
Binghamton University

There is abundant evidence that fetal rats can modify their behavior and responsiveness to sensory stimuli as a function of experience. Repeated infusion of a lemon odor solution into the fetus's mouth results in diminished behavioral and cardiac responsiveness (habituation). Pairing a chemosensory infusion with LiCl injection suppresses fetal activity upon representation of the taste/odor cue (conditioned aversion). Pairing a chemosensory stimulus with another treatment that elevates motor activity results in increased activity upon representation of the stimulus (conditioned activation). These findings have confirmed that altricial fetuses exhibit basic forms of learning during the prenatal period. Most recently, experiments have suggested that the endogenous opioid system of the fetus and neonate may play a role in facilitating or interfering with early learning. Intraoral infusion of a small volume of milk, for example, results in elevated activity at the kappa subclass of opioid receptors. Opioid activity produced by pharmacological treatment or sensory manipulation has the effect of reducing fetal responsiveness to cutaneous stimulation of the perioral region; perioral cutaneous responsiveness thus can be used as a behavioral bioassay of opioid activity in the fetus. If milk infusion is paired with a chemosensory stimulus (sucrose) or an oral tactile stimulus (artificial nipple), the fetus will exhibit reduced responsiveness in this bioassay upon reexposure to the sucrose or nipple alone. Although opioids are demonstrably involved in mediating both the unconditioned response (evoked by milk) and conditioned response (evoked by sucrose or nipple after pairings with milk), the conditioned response involves activity in the mu opioid system, not the kappa system, suggesting that early learning promotes interactions between different opioid systems. The results of learning studies conducted with fetuses, which lack experience with milk or other suckling stimuli, have implications for understanding the sensory determinants and underlying neurobiology of behavior in the late prenatal period and during the first suckling episode after birth.

FETAL CHEMOSENSORY EXPERIENCE

Much of mammalian behavior is regulated by chemical stimuli that activate the olfactory, gustatory, or trigeminal systems. This is particularly true in young altricial mammals, which lack functional visual or acoustic senses and depend heavily on chemosensory cues in postnatal maternal–infant interactions, recognition of parents, siblings, and other kin, and the development of ingestive behavior and early dietary preferences. Most importantly, chemosensation plays crucial roles in suckling behavior and learning that occurs in the context of suckling. Odor cues on or around the nipple are important for many neonatal mammals to find and attach to the nipple (Blass, 1990); in humans, maternal breast odors facilitate recognition of the mother by the infant (Porter, 1991). Aromatic chemicals present in food or drink, such as garlic or alcohol, can be transferred to mother's milk and thereby transmitted to the breast-fed human infant, which can alter infant behavior at the nipple (Mennella & Beauchamp, 1991). Odors or tastes associated with suckling, or that are present in milk, provide the basis for learning in the neonate, which has been shown to influence adult food preferences, mate choice, and sexual behavior in rats (Galef & Henderson, 1972; Fillion & Blass, 1986).

The observation that the newborn can detect taste and odor stimuli and learn contingencies associated with suckling implies that chemosensation and the capacity to learn develop before birth. The past decade has seen rapid progress in the empirical study of fetal sensory and learning abilities. For obvious technical and ethical reasons, experimental investigation of behavioral responses to chemosensory stimuli and prenatal learning has been conducted primarily with animal subjects. Techniques that permit direct manipulation and visual observation of fetal rats and other rodents have provided a window for viewing the prenatal origins of behavior (Smotherman & Robinson, 1991a). Experiments have documented the temporal and spatial organization of nonevoked motor activity (Robinson & Smotherman, 1988), the prenatal expression of organized behavioral patterns in response to chemosensory stimulation (Robinson &

Smotherman, 1992a), and the capacity to modify responses as a function of prenatal sensory experience (Robinson & Smotherman, 1991; Smotherman & Robinson, 1987). The recognition of behavioral competence in the newborn thus is expanding its frame of reference to incorporate new findings about behavior, sensation, and learning in the fetus.

Study of learning in the fetus traces trajectories of behavioral development to their logical origins—in the prenatal period (Smotherman & Robinson, 1990). The fetus is exposed to various chemical agents that are transported across the placenta to diffuse into fetal circulation or amniotic fluid and thereby gain access to fetal chemosensory receptors (Beaconsfield, Birdwood, & Beaconsfield, 1980; Maruniak, Silver, & Moulton, 1983). But the fetus is unlikely ever to experience discrete, temporally delimited chemical stimulation in utero, ensuring that responses can be assessed to the first exposure of the fetus to various sensory manipulations. Measurement of the behavioral outcomes of sensory manipulations effectively integrates across many neural functions, including detection and processing of sensory information, acquisition, retention, and retrieval of stored information, generation of central commands for stimulus-specific behavioral responses, and control of organized motor behavior. Experimental investigation of fetal learning thus provides a method for assessing the integrated output of the central nervous system during prenatal development. Finally, practical information concerning the behavioral capacities of human infants born prematurely may be obtained from experimental study of the fetus. Fetal learning thus is not a curiosity, but an active area of research in the fields of developmental psychobiology, neurobiology, and child development.

LEARNING BY THE FETUS

Learning encompasses any long-lasting change in behavior that results from prior exposure to a sensory stimulus or configuration of stimuli. Various forms of learning have been characterized that appear to reflect increasing levels of stimulus complexity or central nervous system processing. Habituation may represent one of the simplest forms of learning, which is shared by virtually all animals (Thompson & Spencer, 1966). Habituation involves a decrement in behavioral or physiological response that occurs over a series of presentations of the same stimulus and is not due to receptor adaptation or motor fatigue. Several studies have documented waning responsiveness to repeated sensory stimulation in human fetuses. For example, heart rate decelerations (bradycardia) to acoustic or vibrotactile stimuli diminish over a series of trials (Leader, Baillie, Martin, & Vermeulen, 1982). However, less is known about whether such response decrements are central or peripheral effects. One approach for distinguishing habituation from other forms of response decrement is to present a novel stimulus after responsiveness to an original stimulus has waned: Vigorous responding to the second stimulus can rule out motor fatigue (if the responses are similar) and sensory adaptation (if the stimuli are similar) as possible influences. A more powerful approach is provided by dishabituation: Presentation of a novel stimulus after response waning can reinstate responsiveness to the original stimulus (Groves & Thompson, 1970). A few studies of human fetuses have reported fetal responding to a second stimulus and dishabituation (Kisilevsky & Muir, 1991; Madison et al., 1986), suggesting that human fetuses may exhibit habituation during the third trimester of gestation.

Habituation to chemosensory stimulation is beyond the scope of human studies, but has been demonstrated in experiments conducted with fetal rats (Smotherman & Robinson, 1992a). Data from rat fetuses have indicated that heart rate and motor activity can vary independently, suggesting the absence of cardiosomatic coupling before birth. Changes in heart rate and motor behavior thus can provide separate measures of responsiveness in fetal subjects (Smotherman, Robinson, Hepper, Ronca, & Alberts, 1991). On the last few days of the 21.5-day gestation, rat fetuses exhibit a pronounced increase in motor activity and bradycardia when a lemon odor solution is infused into the fetus's mouth. Over a series of nine lemon infusions, both motor and cardiac responses diminish nearly to baseline levels. Presentation of a second taste/odor solution—mint—after the last lemon trial is effective in reinstating responsiveness to lemon. Dishabituation is evident at an interval (2 min) that is insufficient to promote spontaneous recovery of fetal responsiveness. The decrement in fetal response to lemon infusions therefore is a centrally mediated effect, indicative of true habituation.

Prenatal exposure to chemosensory stimuli also can produce lasting changes in fetal responsiveness. Sensitization effects may result from one or many presentations of a stimulus in utero, without the need of reinforcing stimuli. Several experiments have demonstrated that exposure to a chemosensory fluid that is injected into the amniotic fluid that surrounds the fetus is sufficient to establish a preference for the same chemosensory stimulus after birth. For instance, adult rats that had received a single intra-amniotic injection of apple juice on day 20 of gestation (E20) preferred apple juice over a control solution (maple) in a two-bottle choice test (Smotherman, 1982a). Learning through prenatal exposure would appear to be a robust effect, for exposure to aversive substances, such as alcohol (6% ethanol solution), on E21 is sufficient to eliminate aversion to alcohol odor 8 days after birth (Chotro & Molina, 1990). The ability to instill preferences or reduce aversions to chemosensory stimuli through prenatal exposure stands in contrast to many studies of learning in young postnatal animals. In studies of learning after birth, subjects in control groups that receive presentations of individual stimulus elements (e.g., the conditioned stimulus without contingent stimulation) typically do not exhibit altered sensory responsiveness. It is unclear at present whether prenatal exposure learning is the result of mere presentation of a novel stimulus before birth, or whether the preference is established through adventitious pairing of the stimulus with an unrecognized reinforcer in utero.

Although reinforcing stimuli are not necessary for prenatal learning to occur, a number of studies have documented that fetuses have the capacity to associate independent stimulus events. Most experimental demonstrations of associative learning in the fetus have employed a conditioned aversion paradigm. Fetuses are exposed to a novel odor stimulus (the conditioned stimulus or CS) that is followed immediately by ip injection of lithium chloride. In adult rats, a single pairing of LiCl with a tastant or odorant results in reduced intake or avoidance of the CS (García, Hankins, & Rusiniak, 1974). Fetuses prepared on E20 retain information from the contingent presentation of apple juice and LiCl well into the postnatal period; rat pups conditioned in utero avoid nipples of lactating females that are painted with apple juice (Stickrod, Kimble, & Smotherman, 1982a), require more time to traverse a runway suffused with apple odor to gain access to their mother (Smotherman, 1982b), and spend less time over shavings scented with apple juice (Stickrod, Kimble, & Smotherman 1982b). Fetal rats that receive an odor–LiCl pairing on E17 exhibit changes in motor activity upon reexposure to the odor CS as fetuses on E19 (Smotherman & Robinson, 1985). Experiments such as these, which represent a form of classical conditioning, have firmly established that the fetus is capable of associative learning during the prenatal period.

FETAL LEARNING IN AN ECOLOGICAL CONTEXT

Although effective, the first demonstrations of fetal learning employed paradigms that involved somewhat arbitrary and artificial stimuli that were not clearly related to contingencies that the fetus or neonate might experience in its life history. These experimental approaches more recently have given way to paradigms employing stimuli of ecological relevance to the fetus or neonate. Hepper (1988), for example, has reported that introducing novel food items into the diet of pregnant rats can expose the fetus to specific chemosensory compounds (such as the aromatic sulfur compounds in garlic) that are transported across the placenta and gain access to fetal chemosensory receptors. Rat pups that are exposed in utero to garlic via maternal diet express a preference for the odor of garlic after birth. Cross-fostering to mothers that had no exposure to the garlic diet had no effect on the amount of time spent by pups over the garlic odor, suggesting that prenatal experience with garlic compounds was responsible for the garlic preferences expressed by pups.

Although on the surface it appears that prenatal exposure learning can occur in the absence of reinforcement, fetuses may experience conditions in utero that function like reinforcing stimuli. Hypoxia, which can occur under conditions of normal intrauterine development, is an example of a prenatal event that can support classical conditioning in the fetus. Under natural circumstances, hypoxia can occur when the umbilical cord becomes twisted or is otherwise occluded (Mann, 1986). Transient hypoxic episodes, induced by clamping the umbilical cord, evoke stereotypic behavioral responses in rodent fetuses (Robinson & Smotherman, 1992b), and can alter subsequent responsiveness to chemosensory stimuli present at the time of umbilical cord compression (Robinson & Smotherman, 1991). Changes in responsiveness to an odor present in the amniotic fluid can be conditioned by pairing the odor cue with the onset of hypoxia (resulting in an odor aversion, Hepper, 1991, or cessation of cord compression (resulting in an odor preference, Hepper, 1993). These experimental findings suggest that events that occur just before or at the time of birth can function as reinforcers to support classical conditioning.

Learning that occurs during the few hours before and after birth appears to play an important role in the natural history of the rat. During parturition, the mother engages in self-grooming and licking that have the effect of depositing amniotic fluid on her ventrum and nipples. The chemosensory properties of amniotic fluid, or of specific constituents of the fluid, serve to direct the first nipple attachment of the newborn rat (Pedersen & Blass, 1982). Subsequent to the initial attachment, other chemosensory cues regulate nipple attachment, including pup saliva that is deposited on nipples during suckling. The influence of amniotic fluid and pup saliva on nipple attachment may be attributed to exposure learning or conditioning that occurs around the time of birth.

The simple sulfur compound dimethyl disulfide (DMDS) is one component of pup saliva that is effective in directing nipple attachment in pups with suckling experience (Pedersen & Blass, 1981). Because DMDS is produced in the salivary glands of the newborn, it may be present in utero. Other sulfur compounds have been identified in the composition of milk and can be introduced into amniotic fluid via maternal circulation and transport across the placenta. Moreover, carbon disulfide (CS_2) is a constituent of the breath of rats that facilitates social transmission of dietary information in juvenile and adult rats (Galef, Mason, Preti, & Bean, 1988). An intriguing possibility suggested by these experimental findings is that simple chemical odorants that are present in body fluids or tissues, such as these sulfur-based compounds, may promote learning about food-related stimuli in the adult feeding or neonatal suckling situations. The reinforcing properties of such compounds may be related to their ability to engage different neurochemical systems of the fetus or pup. Brief exposure of the E21 rat fetus to DMDS, for instance, results in enhanced activity in the endogenous opioid system (Smotherman & Robinson, 1992b).

FETAL OPIOID SYSTEM: EFFECTS ON BEHAVIOR AND SENSORY RESPONSIVENESS

Since the discovery of endorphins in the 1970s, the endogenous opioid system has been found to encompass a number of classes of receptors and their associated ligands (Kosterlitz, 1991). Multiple classes of receptors have been identified and related to different biochemical, physiological and behavioral functions in the rat. In vitro studies have indicated that receptors for two opioid systems—the mu and kappa systems—are present in the brain and spinal cord during the prenatal period. The presence of precursor molecules, opioid peptides, and receptors of both the kappa and mu systems by midgestation (Leslie & Loughlin, 1993) suggests that these opioid systems are functional and may influence behavior in the fetus.

Initial investigations of the effects of opioids on fetal behavior administered opioid drugs, such as morphine, to pregnant rats and recorded changes in motor activity in fetal subjects (Kirby, 1981). More recent studies have administered selective opioid agonists and antagonists directly to individual fetal subjects and assessed effects on sensory responsiveness. Because conventional behavioral indices of opioid activity are impractical to employ with fetal subjects, several alternative behavioral bioassays have been developed based on neuroethological analysis of simple action patterns in the rat fetus (Smotherman & Robinson, 1992c, 1992d). One behavioral bioassay that has proven particularly sensitive to opioid manipulations is the facial wiping response evoked by perioral cutaneous stimulation (Smotherman & Robinson, 1992c). The stimulus in this bioassay is presented by applying a stiff bristle (von Frey filament) near the corner of the fetus's mouth. On E20 and E21, 70–80% of untreated fetal subjects respond to the perioral probe by performing one or more wiping strokes in which the forepaw is moved from ear to nose in contact with the face. Administration of mu or kappa opioid agonists, such as morphine, DAMGO (selective for mu receptors), or U50,488 (selective for kappa receptors) results in dose-dependent decreases in facial wiping expressed in this bioassay. The effects of opioid agonists can be blocked if subjects are treated with receptor-specific antagonists, such as ß-funaltrexamine HCl (FNA) or [Cys^2, Tyr^3, Orn^5, Pen^7]-amide (CTOP) for mu receptors, or nor-binaltorphimine diHCl (BNI) for kappa receptors, prior to agonist administration (Smotherman, Moody, Spear, & Robinson, 1993; Smotherman, Simonik, Andersen, & Robinson 1993). The effect of agonist and antagonist drugs on fetal responsiveness, as measured in the bioassay of perioral cutaneous sensitivity, indicates that the mu and kappa opioid systems are sufficiently mature to mediate changes in behavior in the late prenatal period.

The ability to produce behavioral effects with opioid drugs is evidence for one dimension of functionality around the time of birth, but implies little about the role of the endogenous opioid system in the regulation of fetal or neonatal behavior. Certain stimulus manipulations that mimic features of the postnatal environment are effective in evoking activity in the fetal opioid system. For instance, a single 20-μl infusion of milk into the mouth of the E21 fetus nearly eliminates the facial wiping response as expressed in the bioassay. The milk-induced reduction in fetal responsiveness is opioid-mediated and can be blocked by pretreatment with naloxone or the kappa-selective antagonist BNI (Smotherman & Robinson, 1992c). Reduced responsiveness is most pronounced when the perioral probe is applied 1 min after infusion, is still evident at 3 min, and dissipates approximately 5 min after exposure to milk. The finding that milk promotes activity in the kappa opioid system has been replicated in subsequent experiments with the bioassay of perioral sensitivity (Robinson, Moody, Spear, & Smotherman, 1993) and implicated in other metrics of fetal behavior (Smotherman & Robinson, 1992d). Exposure to milk has been reported to promote opioid activity in newborn rats delivered by caesarean section and tested before contact with the mother (Blass, Jackson, & Smotherman, 1991), and milk sucrose, corn oil, or other sapid solutions promote opioid-like behavioral effects in older rat pups (Blass & Fitzgerald, 1988; Shide & Blass, 1989, 1991); activation of the endogenous opioid system has been inferred from experiments with human infants (Blass, 1990). However, mono- or disaccharide solutions, lipids, or other chemosensory stimuli do not appear to affect opioid activity in the fetus. Apart from milk, only one other chemical stimulus—DMDS—has been found to evoke an opioid response, and like milk, this simple sulfur compound promotes activity in the kappa system (Smotherman & Robinson, 1992b). The ability of milk or DMDS to engage the endogenous opioid system of the fetus is evident upon the fetus's first exposure to these stimuli, indicating that suckling or specific chemosensory experience is not necessary for the expression of sensory-evoked opioid activity. Moreover, milk continues to evoke opioid activity after a series of infusions, suggesting that this form of fetal responsiveness does not quickly habituate.

Less information is available about the influence of endogenous opioids on fetal behavior in the absence of eliciting stimuli. Administration of naloxone to unmanipulated rat fetuses has modest effects on overall motor activity on E21, but not E20 (Smotherman & Robinson, 1992c). Similarly, BNI but not FNA or CTOP produces a slight increase in motor activity on E21, suggesting that the kappa opioid system exhibits spontaneous activity near term in the fetal rat. Studies of chemosensory habituation to repeated lemon infusions also have implied endogenous opioid activity in the E21 fetus. The expression of facial wiping quickly wanes in control subjects over a series of lemon infusions, and pretreatment with naloxone or BNI has little effect on the initial responsiveness of fetuses or the rapidity of response waning. Opioid blockade also does not affect the responsiveness of fetuses to a novel chemosensory or tactile stimulus presented 1 min after the infusion series. Pretreating fetal subjects with naloxone or BNI results in a significant increase in facial wiping upon representation of the original lemon stimulus. Moreover, novel chemosensory and tactile stimuli are both effective in reinstating responsiveness to lemon, suggesting that blockade of endogenous opioid activity facilitates dishabituation. Pretreatment with FNA or CTOP, however, does not appear to influence initial responsiveness, habituation, or dishabituation. Habituation is thought to represent a central process that regulates attention to novel and familiar stimulation (Groves & Thompson, 1970; Thompson & Spencer, 1966). Because fetuses are less attentive to changes in sensory stimulation as a result of endogenous opioid activity, the kappa opioid system may play a role in regulating selective attention and stimulus processing in the near-term fetus.

CLASSICAL CONDITIONING IN THE FETUS

In many respects, information about the learning abilities of the fetus has been guided by technologies and experimental procedures available to investigators. Nearly all earlier studies of associative learning, for example, employed experimental designs that involved exposing the fetus to one or more training trials at one gestational age and evaluating the effects of conditioning later in gestation or after birth (Smotherman & Robinson, 1987). This strategy, although sufficient to document that learning can occur, introduces confounds that limit the types of conclusions that may be drawn from data obtained in developing animals. One assumption that is implicit in studies of adult learning is that the behavioral repertoire of the subject changes little between the time of training and testing. Changes in behavior that are expressed upon reexposure to the CS therefore may be concluded to be the result of learning. Such an assumption is unwarranted in studies of developmental learning, because training and testing are superimposed on sensory, motor, and central neural systems that are

rapidly differentiating, with the consequence that the behavioral repertoire can change dramatically over the span of a few days. Many of the
experimental confounds that are intrinsic to developmental study may be
circumvented by employing a conditioning paradigm in which training
and testing are implemented at one age within a single experimental
session.

The conditioned activation of fetal behavior provides an example of
how associative learning may be investigated in a single-session paradigm
(Smotherman & Robinson, 1991b). Experimental subjects receive a series of
four paired infusions of a CS (sucrose) followed immediately by infusion
of lemon (the unconditional stimulus, US), which evokes an increase in
overall motor activity. This classical conditioning procedure results in an
increase in fetal activity upon representation of sucrose 6 min after the last
training trial. Various control groups represented within the same pregnancy confirm that the change in fetal response to sucrose is not a result of
sensitization effects due to repeated exposures to the CS alone, residual
effects of repeated presentation of the US, or nonassociative effects as
indicated by explicitly unpaired presentations of the CS and US. Because
training and testing are conducted at a single gestational age, it is unlikely
that changes in the behavioral repertoire contribute to the behavioral
activation expressed by fetuses exposed to CS–US pairings. Changes in
fetal motor activity therefore reflect associative learning of the contingency
between CS and US presentations during training. Because it avoids confounds that arise from training and testing subjects at different ages, the
single-session paradigm for classical conditioning represents an advance
in the ability to study age-related changes in learning capacities during the
prenatal period. It also offers the possibility of investigating neural mechanisms that subserve sensory and learning processes in the fetus through
administration of neuroactive substances at the time of training or testing.

CONDITIONED OPIOID ACTIVITY: A MODEL OF THE
FIRST SUCKLING EPISODE

A number of studies have implicated different neurotransmitter or
neuromodulator systems in the expression of learning early in development. Of particular interest is the endogenous opioid system, which appears to play a role in the reinforcing effects of milk. Milk has been shown
to support both classical conditioning (Johanson & Teicher, 1980; Brake,
1981) and appetitive learning (Johanson & Hall, 1979) in neonatal rats in
experiments conducted only a few days after birth. Exogenous administration of morphine during exposure to a novel odor can produce conditioning effects similar to milk, with low doses promoting a preference for the

odor (Kehoe, 1988). Similar experiments with selective agonists suggest that pharmacological activation of kappa opioid receptors results in conditioned odor preferences in 3-day-old rat pups, but conditioned aversions for the odor in 7-day-old and adult rats (Barr, 1993). Although the critical experiment, in which naloxone is administered to block the reinforcing effects of milk, apparently has not been conducted in rat neonates, circumstantial evidence suggests that milk engages the endogenous opioid system, which functions to reinforce learning in the neonate (Shide & Blass, 1991). Opioid activity also can be expressed as part of the conditioned response. After a novel odor is paired with an injection of morphine, reexposure to the odor results in diminished sensory responsiveness (increased latency to withdraw a paw from a heated surface), which is reversible with naloxone. Associative learning supported by pharmacological activation of the opioid system during training thus can promote conditioned opioid activity at the time of testing (Kehoe & Blass, 1989).

The functional relationship between milk, opioid activity, and learning recently has been explored in more detail in a series of experiments conducted with E20 rat fetuses (Arnold, Robinson, Spear, & Smotherman, 1993; Robinson, Arnold, Spear, & Smotherman 1993). These experiments have employed a single-session conditioning paradigm to determine whether pairings of milk with tactile or chemosensory cues can support classical conditioning in the fetus. Following a research strategy that has proven successful in studies of learning in neonatal subjects (e.g., Johanson & Terry, 1988), stimuli and response measures were selected to be developmentally appropriate for the behavioral capacities of fetuses. Specifically, the CS in these experiments was an artificial nipple, fashioned from soft vinyl in the approximate dimensions of a nipple from a lactating rat, which was presented to the fetus by gently touching the nipple to the external aperture of the mouth. Rat fetuses are responsive to the artificial nipple, exhibiting a variety of specific motor patterns including mouthing, licking, forelimb treadling and oral grasping of the nipple (Robinson et al., 1992). Fetal subjects are conditioned in a series of three training trials, in which the nipple (CS) is presented for a brief period and immediately followed by milk infusion (US). Fetuses exposed to nipple–milk pairings during training and reexposed to the nipple alone during testing exhibit reduced responsiveness in the bioassay of perioral cutaneous sensitivity (Fig. 16.1). No reduction in perioral responsiveness is evident among fetuses in control groups that are exposed during training trials to the nipple alone (CS sensitization controls), milk alone (US sensitization controls), or the artificial nipple several minutes after each milk infusion (unpaired exposure controls). The same pattern of results has been obtained from experiments employing a chemosensory CS (sucrose) paired with milk. These experimental findings indicate that presentation of the CS

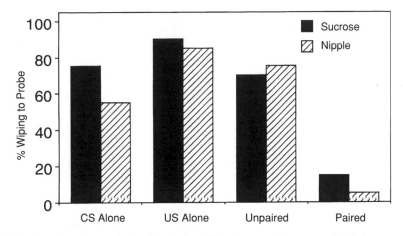

FIG. 16.1.   Experimental stimuli in fetal conditioning experiments consisted of presentation of an artificial nipple or intraoral infusion of sucrose as the conditioned stimulus (CS) and intraoral infusion of milk as the unconditioned stimulus (US). Different groups of fetal subjects were exposed to the CS alone, US alone, unpaired presentations of the US and CS, or paired presentations of the CS and US in a series of three conditioning trials separated by 5-min intervals. At min 18, all subjects were reexposed to the CS, and 1 min later were exposed to a perioral tactile stimulus to assess cutaneous sensitivity. This figure depicts the percentage of fetal subjects that exhibited a facial wiping response in the bioassay after reexposure to the sucrose or artificial nipple (CS).

during testing does not in itself alter fetal responsiveness in the bioassay, and confirms that contingent presentations of the artificial nipple (or sucrose) and milk can support classical conditioning of sensory responsiveness in the rat fetus.

A single milk infusion promotes opioid activity that reduces fetal responsiveness in the bioassay, and reexposure to the artificial nipple after nipple–milk pairings elicits a conditioned response that is expressed as altered cutaneous sensitivity. Reexposure to the nipple therefore may evoke a conditioned increase in activity within the endogenous opioid system. The hypothesis of conditioned opioid activity has been tested by administering naloxone after the series of training trials and before reexposure to the CS. Fetuses that experienced unpaired presentations of milk and the nipple exhibit high levels of facial wiping in the bioassay after reexposure to the nipple, regardless of naloxone treatment. Fetuses that receive a control injection of saline after nipple–milk pairings exhibit reduced responsiveness during testing, but the responsiveness of naloxone-treated subjects remains high, indicating that blockade of opioid activity before testing eliminates the expression of conditioned changes in fetal cutaneous sensitivity (Fig. 16.2). Administration of selective opioid antagonists before testing has confirmed that contingent presentations of the nipple and milk support the classical conditioning of opioid activity in the fetus. However, the CS–evoked reduction in fetal responsiveness is blocked with FNA or CTOP, not BNI, suggesting that the conditioned opioid response involves activity at mu, not kappa, opioid receptors (Fig. 16.2). The mu opioid system, which does not play a role in the initial responsiveness of fetuses after milk infusion, comes to be accessed by the artificial nipple after its association with milk.

Attachment to the nipple is one of the first critical actions that the newborn rat must perform. The opportunity to attach to the nipple and engage in sucking behavior, whether nutritive or nonnutritive, can serve as an effective reinforcer in both classical and instrumental learning paradigms applied to infant mammals (Amsel, Burdette, & Letz, 1976; Kenny & Blass, 1977). Furthermore, learning that takes place in the context of suckling appears to influence the development of nipple preferences in neonates, dietary preferences and kin recognition in juveniles, and reproductive behavior in adult rats. The ability of milk to engage the endogenous opioid system has been suggested as an important aspect of the reinforcing properties of milk (Shide & Blass, 1991). The experimental demonstration that pairing an artificial nipple with milk results in condi-

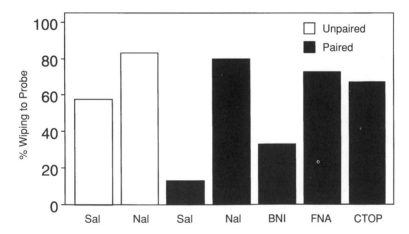

FIG. 16.2.   Fetuses were exposed to the artificial nipple (CS) and milk infusion (US) in a series of three unpaired or paired presentations during training. Subjects were reexposed to the CS 10 min later. To assess opioid activity after reexposure to the CS, subjects in unpaired or paired groups received an ip injection of saline (Sal), naloxone (Nal), ß-funaltrexamine (FNA) or CTOP (both mu antagonists), or nor-binaltorphimine (BNI, a kappa antagonist) 5 min before representation of the CS. The figure depicts the percentage of fetal subjects that exhibited a facial wiping response in the bioassay, which was administered 1 min after CS reexposure. Naloxone and the two mu antagonists were effective in reversing the effects of conditioning and reinstating facial wiping responses to the perioral cutaneous stimulus.

tioned opioid activity in the rat fetus, which lacks experience with milk, the nipple, or other suckling stimuli, provides further support for the pivotal role of opioids in early learning. Specifically, opioid conditioning in the fetus suggests that stimuli associated with milk during suckling can quickly come to engage opioid activity in advance of milk letdown in neonatal rats after only a few experiences at the nipple. Conditioned opioid activity evoked by the nipple or other suckling stimuli has been postulated as an important regulator of the sequence and timing of behavioral responses expressed by newborns during a suckling episode (Smotherman & Robinson, 1992e).

OPIOID INVOLVEMENT IN LEARNING AT THE NIPPLE

Through much of the recent history of research on the endogenous opioid system, opioids have been associated with subjective constructs such as the regulation of central affect or the perception of pleasant or painful qualities of a stimulus. It is clear from studies of fetal and neonatal animals that opioids also influence various forms of learning, including habituation, classical conditioning and appetitive learning (Kehoe, 1988; Smotherman & Robinson, 1993). Both the mu and kappa opioid systems attain a peak in receptor density in the perinatal period. Moreover, the endogenous opioid system can be engaged by a number of stimuli that are present in the environment of the newborn, such as milk, DMDS, and placental tissue (Kristal, 1991), and through association with these stimuli may be activated by other features of the suckling situation, such as the tactile or olfactory characteristics of the nipple. The numerous examples of interaction between ecologically relevant stimuli and endogenous opioid activity imply that opioids have functional significance in the early development of behavior.

One of the commonalities in the behavioral effects of opioids in the fetus is the change in behavioral organization and responsiveness associated with opioid activity. Organizational changes promoted by milk or opioid treatment resemble transitions between conventional behavioral states (Smotherman & Robinson, 1992e; Robinson & Smotherman, 1992c), which are associated with differences in the processing of sensory information and motor output. The learning process also has the effect of reducing the degrees of freedom in both sensory and behavioral domains: A few stimuli come to evoke specific behavioral responses. Particularly in young animals, behavioral development often proceeds by stabilizing many behavioral variables, which facilitates organized change in the few remaining variables (Golani & Fentress, 1985). It may be parsimonious to conceive of the reinforcing properties of opioid activity as a neurochemical mechanism for altering the way infants interact with their sensory environment. For instance, kappa opioid activity effected by pharmacological treatment does not uniformly suppress fetal motor activity and sensory responsiveness. Rather, kappa activity results in increased organization in motor activity, reduced responsiveness to perioral cutaneous stimuli, and increased responsiveness to intraoral chemosensory cues (Smotherman & Robinson, 1992d). Similarly, peripheral administration of mu-agonist drugs has little effect on fetal motor behavior and simultaneously reduces responsiveness to some cutaneous stimuli (e.g., perioral tactile probe; Smotherman, Simonik, Andersen, & Robinson, 1993) while increasing responsiveness to others (e.g., artificial nipple; Robinson et al., 1992). Opioid activity thus may facilitate learning by introducing sensory and behavioral stability in young animals that are surrounded by novel stimuli—the proverbial "blooming, buzzing confusion" referred to by William James (1890/1952). By redirecting and focusing responsiveness to a subset of available stimuli, activation of the endogenous opioid system may serve as an ontogenetic adaptation that promotes selective attention and facilitates learning early in development.

FUTURE DIRECTIONS

The empirical findings presented in this chapter are part of an ongoing program of research into the prenatal origins of motor behavior, sensory responsiveness, and learning. Experiments examining conditioned changes in the endogenous opioid system of the fetus have united several different lines of research in our laboratory and will serve as foci for further investigation. Learning experiments with fetal rats have corroborated that chemical senses develop and begin to exhibit function earlier than other sensory modalities (such as vision and audition), raising the question of whether presentation of stimuli in a chemosensory modality offers advantages for the investigation of prenatal sensory and learning capacities. The study of learning in neonatal animals has undergone a steady transformation from the use of artificial stimuli (such as electric shock and injection of illness-inducing chemicals) to contingencies that are relevant to the ecology of the developing mammal (such as odor cues and intraoral infusion of milk). Future investigation of learning in the fetus may also profit from the selection of unconditioned and conditioned stimuli that mimic environmental features that are important to the fetus or to the newborn. Much of the learning in the neonate appears to occur in settings, such as suckling, that affect the endogenous opioid system. Further studies will explore the role of opioid activity in regulating responsiveness to sensory stimuli and promoting learning in developing animals. Neurobiological substrates of learning typically are studied in animals that have relatively simple nervous systems, such as invertebrates. Investigation of learning in rodent fetuses may provide an analogous simple system for understanding the neural basis for learning and memory, but one that has more direct applicability for behavior in adult mammals. Ultimately, the broad aims of this basic research are to provide insights or suggest hypotheses that are relevant for the human fetus, premature infant, and full-term newborn. We expect that experimental study of fetal learning and behavioral plasticity will serve as a proving ground for potential therapies aimed at improving the health and development of premature infants and other infants at risk.

ACKNOWLEDGMENTS

The fetal research reported in this chapter was supported by National Institutes of Health grants HD 16102 to WPS and HD 28231 and HD 28014 to WPS and SRR.

REFERENCES

Amsel, A., Burdette, D. R., & Letz, R. (1976). Appetitive learning, patterned alternation, and extinction in 10-d-old rats with non-lactating suckling as reward. *Nature, 262*, 816–818.

Arnold, H. M., Robinson, S. R., Spear, N. E., & Smotherman, W. P. (1993). Conditioned opioid activity in the rat fetus. *Behavioral Neuroscience, 107*, 963–969.

Barr, G. A. (1993). Reinforcing properties of opiates during early development. In R. P. Hammer, Jr. (Ed.), *The neurobiology of opiates* (pp. 63–83). Boca Raton, FL: CRC Press.

Beaconsfield, P., Birdwood, G., & Beaconsfield, R. (1980, August). The placenta. *Scientific American, 243*, 80-89.

Blass, E. M. (1990). Suckling: Determinants, changes, mechanisms, and lasting impressions. *Developmental Psychology, 26*, 520–533.

Blass, E. M., & Fitzgerald, E. (1988). Milk-induced analgesia and comforting in 10-day-old rats: Opioid mediation. *Pharmacology Biochemistry & Behavior, 29*, 9–13.

Blass, E. M., Jackson, A. M., & Smotherman, W. P. (1991). Milk-induced opioid-mediated antinociception in rats at the time of cesarean delivery. *Behavioral Neuroscience, 105*, 677–686.

Brake, S. C. (1981). Suckling infant rats learn a preference for a novel olfactory stimulus paired with milk delivery. *Science, 211,* 506–508.

Chotro, M. G., & Molina, J. C. (1990). Acute ethanol contamination of the amniotic fluid during gestational day 21: Postnatal changes in alcohol responsiveness in rats. *Developmental Psychobiology, 23,* 535–547.

Fillion, T. J., & Blass, E. M. (1986). Infantile experience with suckling odors determines adult sexual behavior in male rats. *Science, 231,* 729–731.

Galef, B. G., & Henderson, P. W. (1972). Mother's milk: A determinant of the feeding preferences of weaning rat pups. *Journal of Comparative and Physiological Psychology, 78,* 213–219.

Galef, B. G., Jr., Mason, J. R., Preti, G., & Bean, N. J. (1988). Carbon disulfide: A semiochemical mediating socially-induced diet choice in rats. *Physiology & Behavior, 42,* 119–124.

García, J., Hankins, W. G., & Rusiniak, K. W. (1974). Behavioral regulation of milieu interne in man and rat. *Science, 185,* 824–831.

Golani, I., & Fentress, J. C. (1985). Early ontogeny of face grooming in mice. *Developmental Psychobiology, 18,* 529–544.

Groves, P. M., & Thompson, R. F. (1970). Habituation: A dual-process theory. *Psychological Review, 77,* 419–450.

Hepper, P. (1988). Adaptive fetal learning: Prenatal exposure to garlic affects postnatal preferences. *Animal Behaviour, 36,* 935–936.

Hepper, P. (1991). Transient hypoxia episodes: A mechanism to support associative fetal learning. *Animal Behaviour, 41,* 477–480.

Hepper, P. (1993). In utero release from a single transient hypoxic episode: A positive reinforcer? *Physiology & Behavior, 53,* 309–311.

James, W. (1952) *Principles of psychology.* Chicago: Encyclopaedia Britannica Press. (Original work published 1952)

Johanson, I. B., & Hall, W. G. (1979). Appetitive learning in 1-day-old rat pups. *Science, 205,* 419–421.

Johanson, I. B., & Teicher, M. H. (1980). Classical conditioning of an odor preference in 3-day-old rats. *Behavioral and Neural Biology, 29,* 132–136.

Johanson, I. B., & Terry, L. M. (1988). Learning in infancy: A mechanism for behavioral change during development. In E. M. Blass, (Ed.), *Handbook of behavioral neurobiology: Vol. 9. Developmental psychobiology and behavioral ecology* (pp. 245–281). New York: Plenum Press.

Kehoe, P. (1988). Opioids, behavior, and learning in mammalian development. In E. M. Blass, (Ed.), *Handbook of behavioral neurobiology, Vol. 9. Developmental psychobiology and behavioral ecology* (pp. 309–346). New York: Plenum Press.

Kehoe, P., & Blass, E. M. (1989). Conditioned opioid release in ten-day-old rats. *Behavioral Neuroscience, 103,* 423–428.

Kenny, J. T., & Blass, E. M. (1977). Suckling as incentive to instrumental learning in preweanling rats. *Science, 196,* 898–899.

Kirby, M. L. (1981). Effects of morphine and naloxone on spontaneous activity of fetal rats. *Experimental Neurology, 73,* 430–439.

Kisilevsky, B. S., & Muir, D. W. (1991). Human fetal and subsequent newborn responses to sound and vibration. *Infant Behavior and Development, 14,* 1–26.

Kosterlitz, H. W. (1991). Opioid receptor subtypes: Past, present and future. In O. F. X. Almeida & T. S. Shippenberg (Eds.), *Neurobiology of opioids* (pp. 3–9). Berlin: Springer-Verlag.

Kristal, M. B. (1991). Enhancement of opioid-mediated analgesia: A solution to the enigma of placentophagia. *Neuroscience & Biobehavioral Reviews, 15*, 425–435.

Leader, L. R., Baillie, P., Martin, B., & Vermeulen, E. (1982). The assessment and significance of habituation to a repeated stimulus by the human fetus. *Early Human Development, 7*, 211–219.

Leslie, F. M., & Loughlin, S. E. (1993). Ontogeny and plasticity of opioid systems. In R. P. Hammer, Jr. (Ed.), *The neurobiology of opiates* (pp. 85–123). Boca Raton, FL: CRC Press.

Madison, L. S., Adubato, S. A., Madison, J. K., Nelson, R. M., Anderson, J. C., Erickson, J., Kuss, L. M., & Goodlin, R. C. (1986). Fetal response decrement: True habituation? *Developmental and Behavioral Pediatrics, 7*, 14–20.

Mann, L. I. (1986). Pregnancy events and brain damage. *American Journal of Obstetrics and Gynecology, 155*, 6–9.

Maruniak, J. A., Silver, W. L., & Moulton, D. G. (1983). Olfactory receptors respond to blood-borne odorants. *Brain Research, 265*, 312–316.

Mennella, J. A., & Beauchamp, G. K. (1991). Maternal diet alters the sensory qualities of human milk and the nursling's behavior. *Pediatrics, 88*, 737–744.

Pedersen, P. E., & Blass, E. M. (1981). Olfactory control over suckling in albino rats. In R. N. Aslin, J. R. Alberts, & M. R. Petersen (Eds.), *The development of perception: Psychobiological perspectives* (pp. 359–381). New York: Academic Press.

Pedersen, P. E., & Blass, E. M. (1982). Prenatal and postnatal determinants of the 1st suckling episode in albino rats. *Developmental Psychobiology , 15*, 349–355.

Porter, R. H. (1991). Mutual mother-infant recognition in humans. In P. G. Hepper (Ed.), *Kin recognition* (pp. 413–432). Cambridge: Cambridge University Press.

Robinson, S. R., Arnold, H. M., Spear, N. E., & Smotherman, W. P. (1993). Experience with milk and an artificial nipple promotes conditioned opioid activity in the rat fetus. *Developmental Psychobiology, 26*, 375–387.

Robinson, S. R., Hoeltzel, T. C. M., Cooke, K. M., Umphress, S. M., Smotherman, W. P., & Murrish, D. E. (1992). Oral capture and grasping of an artificial nipple by rat fetuses. *Developmental Psychobiology, 25*, 543–555.

Robinson, S. R., Moody, C. A., Spear, L. P., & Smotherman, W. P. (1993). Effects of dopamine and kappa opioid receptors on fetal responsiveness to perioral stimuli. *Developmental Psychobiology, 26*, 37–50.

Robinson, S. R., & Smotherman, W. P. (1988). Chance and chunks in the ontogeny of fetal behavior. In W. P. Smotherman & S. R. Robinson (Eds.), *Behavior of the fetus*, (pp. 95–115). Caldwell, NJ: Telford Press.

Robinson, S. R., & Smotherman, W. P. (1991). Fetal learning: Implications for the development of kin recognition. In P. G. Hepper (Ed.), *Kin recognition* (pp. 308–334). Cambridge: Cambridge University Press.

Robinson, S. R., & Smotherman, W. P. (1992a). Fundamental motor patterns of the mammalian fetus. *Journal of Neurobiology, 23*, 1574–1600.

Robinson, S. R., & Smotherman, W. P. (1992b). Behavioral response of altricial and precocial rodent fetuses to acute umbilical cord compression. *Behavioral and Neural Biology, 57*, 93–102.

Robinson, S. R., & Smotherman, W. P. (1992c). The emergence of behavioral regulation during fetal development. *Annals of the New York Academy of Science, 662,* 53–83.

Shide, D. J., & Blass, E. M. (1989). Opioid-like effects of intraoral corn oil and polycose on stress reactions in 10-day-old rats. *Behavioral Neuroscience, 103,* 1168–1175.

Shide, D. J., & Blass, E. M. (1991). Opioid mediation of odor preferences induced by sugar and fat in 6-day-old rats. *Physiology & Behavior, 50,* 961–966.

Smotherman, W. P. (1982a). In utero chemosensory experience alters taste preferences and corticosterone responsiveness. *Behavioral and Neural Biology, 36,* 61–68.

Smotherman, W. P. (1982b). Odor aversion learning by the rat fetus. *Physiology & Behavior, 29,* 769–771.

Smotherman, W. P., Moody, C. A., Spear, L. P., & Robinson, S. R. (1993). Fetal behavior and the endogenous opioid system: D1 dopamine receptor interactions with the kappa opioid system. *Physiology & Behavior, 53,* 191–197.

Smotherman, W. P., & Robinson, S. R. (1985). The rat fetus in its environment: Behavioral adjustments to novel, familiar, aversive and conditioned stimuli presented in utero. *Behavioral Neuroscience, 99,* 521–530.

Smotherman, W. P., & Robinson, S. R. (1987). Psychobiology of fetal experience in the rat. In N. A. Krasnegor, E. M. Blass, M. A. Hofer, & W. P. Smotherman (Eds.), *Perinatal development: A psychobiological perspective* (pp. 39–60). Orlando, FL: Academic Press.

Smotherman, W. P., & Robinson, S. R. (1990). The prenatal origins of behavioral organization. *Psychological Science, 1,* 97–106.

Smotherman, W. P., & Robinson, S. R. (1991a). Accessibility of the rat fetus for psychobiological investigation. In H. N. Shair, M. A. Hofer, & G. Barr (Eds.), *Developmental psychobiology: Current methodology and conceptual issues,* (pp. 148–164). New York: Oxford University Press.

Smotherman, W. P., & Robinson, S. R. (1991b). Conditioned activation of fetal behavior. *Physiology & Behavior, 50,* 73–77.

Smotherman, W. P., & Robinson, S. R. (1992a). Habituation in the rat fetus. *Quarterly Journal of Experimental Psychology, 44B,* 215–230.

Smotherman, W. P., & Robinson, S. R. (1992b). Dimethyl disulfide mimics the effects of milk on fetal behavior and responsiveness to cutaneous stimuli. *Physiology & Behavior, 52,* 761–765.

Smotherman, W. P., & Robinson, S. R. (1992c). Kappa opioid mediation of fetal responses to milk. *Behavioral Neuroscience, 106,* 396–407.

Smotherman, W. P., & Robinson, S. R. (1992d). Opioid control of the fetal stretch response: Implications for the first suckling episode. *Behavioral Neuroscience, 106,* 866–873.

Smotherman, W. P., & Robinson, S. R. (1992e). Prenatal experience with milk: Fetal behavior and endogenous opioid systems. *Neuroscience & Biobehavioral Reviews, 16,* 351–364.

Smotherman, W. P., & Robinson, S. R. (1993). Habituation to chemosensory stimuli in the rat fetus: Effects of endogenous kappa opioid activity. *Behavioral Neuroscience, 107,* 611–617.

Smotherman, W. P., Robinson, S. R., Hepper, P. G., Ronca, A. E., & Alberts, J. R.

(1991). Heart rate response of the rat fetus and neonate to a chemosensory stimulus. *Physiology & Behavior, 50,* 47–52.

Smotherman, W. P., Simonik, D. K., Andersen, S. L., & Robinson, S. R. (1993). Mu and kappa opioid systems modulate responses to cutaneous perioral stimulation in the fetal rat. *Physiology & Behavior, 53,* 751–756.

Stickrod, G., Kimble, D. P., & Smotherman, W. P. (1982a). In utero taste/odor aversion conditioning in the rat. *Physiology & Behavior, 28,* 5–7.

Stickrod, G., Kimble, D. P., & Smotherman, W. P. (1982b). Met-enkephalin effects on associations formed in utero. *Peptides, 3,* 881–883.

Thompson, R. F., & Spencer, W. A. (1966). Habituation: A model phenomenon for the study of neuronal substrates of behavior. *Psychological Review, 73,* 16–43.

17

Transmission of Sound and Vibration to the Fetus

Robert M. Abrams
Kenneth J. Gerhardt
Aemil J. M. Peters
University of Florida

The 24th week of gestation marks the beginning of human fetal auditory responsiveness (Bernard & Sontag, 1947; Crade & Lovett, 1988). It is during the subsequent 15 weeks that sound exposure may have a pronounced effect on fetal behavior and central nervous system maturation. For example, speech perception and voice recognition in the newborn may result directly from repetitive, prosodic components of maternal speech heard by the fetus prenatally (Fifer & Moon, 1988). On the other hand, intense noises, as can be produced by vibrators and loudspeakers against the maternal abdomen, evoke unusual changes in fetal behavioral state and fetal movements that persist long after a very brief stimulus (Gelman, Wood, Spellacy, & Abrams, 1982; Visser, Mulder, Wit, & Prechtl, 1989). Periods of high-intensity airborne noise exposure in sheep increase the latencies in the fetal auditory brainstem response, suggesting some shift in the auditory threshold (Griffiths, Pierson, Gerhardt, Abrams, & Peters, 1994). Concerns about long-term fetal exposure to noise and vibration have been raised (Abrams & Wasserman, 1991; Gerhardt, 1990).

The degree to which auditory experiences shape fetal behavior or modify fetal maturation in positive and negative ways depends, in great measure, on the characteristics of the sound stimulus. These characteristics are defined by the duration and magnitude of acoustic signals in the maternal environment, by the spectral features of these signals in the amniotic fluid, by the "protection" offered to the fetus by reason of its fluid-filled external meatus and middle ear (Gerhardt et al., 1992), and by the competency of the cochlea (Griffiths et al., 1994). Because only a limited amount of information can be gleaned from human experimentation, investigators have turned to the sheep because similarities in body weight and abdominal dimension during pregnancy result in acoustic transmission characteristics (Armitage, Baldwin, & Vince, 1980; Gerhardt, 1990; Gerhardt, Abrams, Kovaz, Gomez, & Conlon, 1988) comparable to humans (Nyman et al., 1991; Richards, Frentzen, Gerhardt, McCann, & Abrams, 1992). In the following account, largely derived from our own experiments in sheep at the University of Florida, we discuss several features of the acoustic environment in which the fetus develops.

THE NOISE FLOOR

The composite of sounds and vibrations within the uterus results from sources outside the mother and from sources inside the mother, including maternal respiratory, cardiovascular, intestinal, and laryngeal activity, and physical movements (Armitage et al., 1980; Benzaquen, Gagnon, Hunse, & Foreman, 1990; Gerhardt, Abrams, & Oliver, 1990; Querleu,

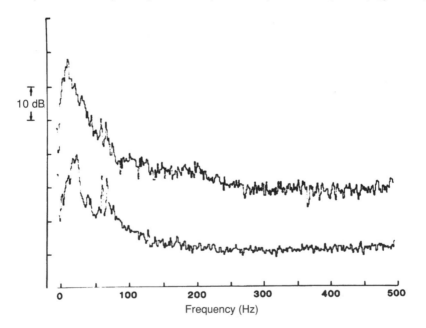

FIG. 17.1.   Two spectra of the internal noise levels in a pregnant ewe before (upper trace) and after (lower trace) death of ewe and fetus. Data were collected using a high-pass filter set at 60 Hz. From Gerhardt et al. (1990). Reprinted by permission.

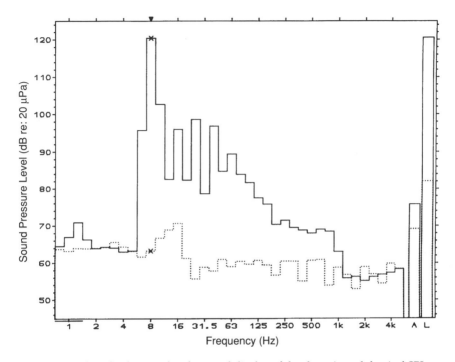

FIG. 17.2.   One-third-octave band spectral display of the sheep intraabdominal SPL during vibration at 8 Hz with a shaker on the abdominal wall (solid line). Dashed line represents the noise floor in the corresponding frequency bands without stimulation. From Peters, Abrams, Gerhardt, and Burchfield (1991). Reprinted by permission.

Renard, Versyp, Paris-Debrue, & Crepin, 1988; Vince, Armitage, Baldwin, & Toner, 1982), as well as fetal umbilical arterial pulsations (unpublished observations). This composite is dominated by frequencies below 500 Hz (Gerhardt, 1989) (Fig. 17.1). In order to measure the level of these sounds accurately, specially designed microphones are necessary. Sound pressures in fluids cannot be measured with microphones normally used to measure pressures in air, because an impedance mismatch prevents calibration to a recognized reference standard that is constant over frequency. Electric noise from the hydrophone (which is related to its sensitivity and dynamic range; the higher the maximum pressure that can be recorded, the higher the noise floor), together with the inherent background acoustical noise (e.g., in the laboratory), constitute the *noise floor*. Miniaturization of hydrophones necessary for intrauterine implantation results in a less than optimal sensitivity and, therefore, increased noise. Bruel and Kjaer model 8103 hydrophones with noise floor levels in ⅓-octave bands of 55–65 dB (re 20 μPa) were used in our studies. This particular hydrophone can be calibrated and referenced to standards, has a flat frequency response from 0.1 Hz to 20 kHz (±1 dB), and is almost optimal for recording sound pressures induced by vibroacoustic devices such as the electronic artificial larynx (EAL). Custom-built hydrophones such as those used by Benzaquen et al. (1990) allow studies over a wider dynamic range for noise floor purposes, revealing levels of ±40 dB above 500 Hz.

The noise floor varies slightly with frequency. Higher sound pressure levels (SPLs; 70–80 dB), which can be noted in the lower frequency range (<50 Hz), result mainly from vibrations normally present in buildings. This raised noise floor is present in intraabdominal recordings in both living and dead animals that are not isolated from building vibrations. The appearance of "peaks" in the low-frequency range results from a falloff in SPL produced by a filter adjusted to cut off below 60 Hz (Fig. 17.1). Without this filter, energy below 60 Hz would be even greater than the energy present at 60 Hz. Reduction in low-frequency noise (up to ~10 dB) can be achieved by placement of animals on a rack separated from the concrete floor by a heavy steel plate resting on several layers of carpet liner (Peters, Abrams, Gerhardt, & Burchfield, 1991). A spectrum recorded from a preparation placed in this rack is illustrated in Fig. 17.2.

HOW SOUNDS REACH THE FETUS: VIBRATORS

Mechanical Coupling of Vibrators to the Body

Obstetricians, as a professional group, have done the most to publicize the fact that vibratory mechanical forces applied to the abdomen of pregnant women are easily transmitted to the fetus. Usually the stimulation results in fetal movements and cardioacceleration (Richards, 1990; Visser et al., 1989). Acoustic stimulation tests have been introduced in clinical practice for antenatal and intrapartum surveillance (Gagnon, 1989). The electronic artificial larynx (EAL), which is commonly used for these obstetrical examinations, produces high sound pressure levels in the uterus (Gerhardt et al., 1988; Nyman et al., 1991; Peters, Abrams, Gerhardt, & Longmate, 1991). Vibromechanical devices such as the EAL were designed to propagate sound pressure more efficiently through tissue and fluid than through air (Oliver, 1989). This fact is documented both in humans (Nyman et al., 1991) and in sheep (Gerhardt et al., 1988), where there were intrauterine SPLs in the vicinity of the fetal ear of 129 and 135 dB, respectively. The EAL has a fundamental frequency of 86 Hz and multiple harmonics that are the result of complex vibration of the diaphragm (Fig. 17.3). Vibrating sources, including the EAL and mechanical shakers, produce distorted signals that are rich in high frequencies when driven at high levels (harmonic distortion). For example, a shaker driven by a subaudible pure tone (e.g., 10 Hz) produces harmonics at higher frequencies that may be of sufficient level to

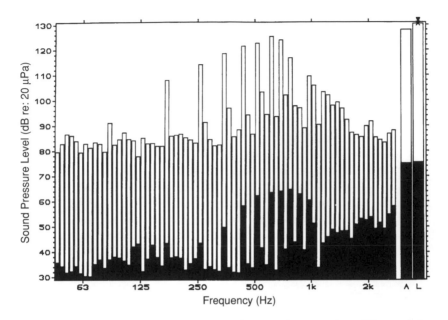

FIG. 17.3.   One-twelfth-octave band spectra of an EAL. Open envelope: SPL recorded with an intraabdominal hydrophone. Solid envelope: SPL recorded in air, not in contact with the skin. All SPL values refer to 20 μPa.

stimulate hearing (>20 Hz in humans). Figure 17.2 illustrates this phenomenon and draws attention to the fact that contact of the body with vibrating objects at the workplace could result in significant rises in intrauterine sound pressures. Whole-body vibration exposure can occur in the operation of over-the-road trucks and buses, heavy construction and farming equipment, and during operation of machines in manufacturing (Wasserman, 1990). Even vibroacoustic devices used at home (e.g., a belt vibrator used for weight reduction) can produce intrauterine SPLs that exceed 130 dB (Fig. 17.4) and that contain series of harmonics with an SPL well above the intrauterine noise floor. Vibrating structures with subaudible fundamental frequencies, once coupled to the abdomen, may therefore produce high intrauterine SPLs at both the subaudible fundamental frequencies and audible harmonic components.

In the context of fetal response, it is important to note the potentially serious consequences that result when the frequency of abdominal vibration exposure is at the body's natural resonant frequency of the abdomen and its contents. Spinal disorders in humans may result from prolonged exposure to resonant frequencies (Wasserman, 1990). Abdominal resonance, which occurs between 6 and 18 Hz in pregnant sheep (Peters, Abrams, Gerhardt, Burchfield, & Wasserman, 1992) (Fig. 17.5), theoretically provides optimal conditions for structural weakening and damage.

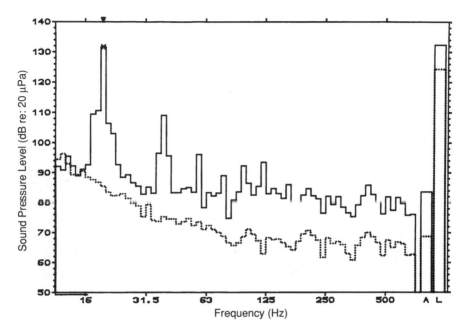

FIG. 17.4. Solid line: One-twelfth-octave band spectral display in sheep of intraabdominal SPL during vibration with a belt vibrator used in weight reduction. Dashed line: The noise floor in the corresponding frequency bands without stimulation.

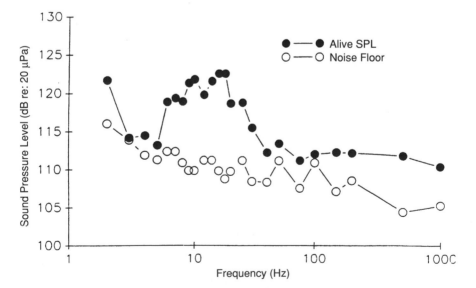

FIG. 17.5. Mean intrauterine SPL ($n = 4$) recorded in ⅓-octave bands during application of a shaker with a constant dynamic force on the skin surface at several frequencies between 2 Hz and 1 kHz; •, SPL in alive, pregnant sheep; ◯, noise floor level in corresponding frequencies without stimulation. From Peters et al. (1992). Reprinted by permission.

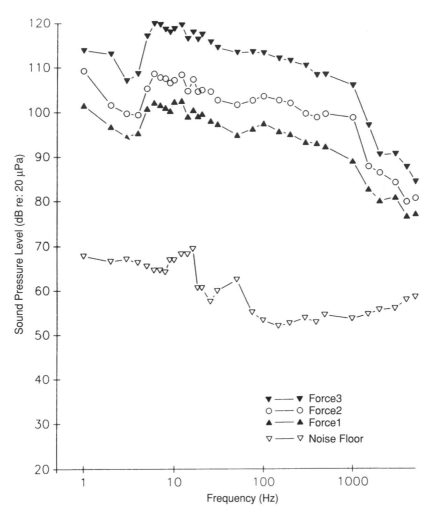

FIG. 17.6. Mean intraabdominal SPL ($n = 5$) recorded in ⅓-octave bands during application of a shaker with a constant static force at several frequencies between 1 Hz and 5 kHz. Three different dynamic forces were used during sinusoidal stimulation: ▲, 0.07 N; ○, 0.14 N; and ▼, 0.42 N. Reprinted from Peters, Abrams, Gerhardt, and Burchfield (1991), with permission.

Although there is as yet no good epidemiologic evidence of a relationship between vibration and poor fetal outcome, long-term exposure may impact on behavioral or more subtle functional development of the fetus manifested only later after birth.

There are many other interesting features of the vibroacoustic environment in which the fetus develops. The SPL, at any given position in the abdominal cavity and uterus, is highly dependent on the distance between

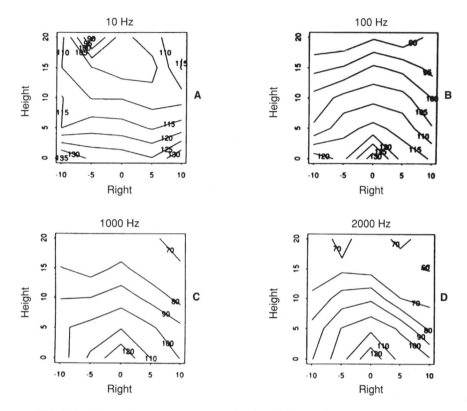

FIG. 17.7. Isosound pressure contours for four different frequencies; a–d, cross-sectional plane through the point of vibroacoustic stimulation (reference point, 0). From Peters, Abrams, Gerhardt, and Longmate (1991). Reprinted by permission.

the vibration and the target. This dependency was first shown by Gerhardt et al. (1988) by moving an EAL in ever-increasing concentric circles from a fixed intrauterine hydrophone. Increasing the radius by 3 in resulted in a 20-dB drop in SPL.

Intrauterine SPL is intimately determined by the coupling between the vibrator and the body. Increasing the applied dynamic force of the vibrator increases the generated intraabdominal SPL (Peters, Abrams, Gerhardt, & Burchfield, 1991) (Fig. 17.6). Surprisingly, altering the actuator head size between 2 and 32 cm^2 with dynamic force maintained constant did not meaningfully affect SPL across frequencies between 1 and 5,000 Hz. The static force applied to the vibrator and the frequency of the vibration had earlier been determined to be important factors determining the frequency response of intraabdominal SPL (Graham, Peters, Abrams, Gerhardt, & Burchfield, 1991).

Perhaps the most interesting and important study, one of a series published by Peters (Peters, Abrams, Gerhardt, & Longmate, 1991), was a three-dimensional analysis of sound and vibration frequency responses in the sheep abdomen. Sinusoidal stimulation was provided with a mechanical vibrator placed on the anterior abdominal wall just posterior to the umbilicus. A hydrophone was placed at 45 intraabdominal locations within a space measuring $20 \times 20 \times 20$ cm centered over the mechanical oscillator. Pure tones of 10, 100, 1,000, and 2,000 Hz were used to stimulate the abdominal wall. As anticipated, intraabdominal SPL was negatively correlated with distance between hydrophone and the vibrator, and negatively correlated with frequency of vibration. Of great interest was the distribution of isosound pressure contours, as a function of frequency, in cross-sectional and parasagittal maps. The shapes of the isopressure contours revealed important differences in the signal transmission of varying frequencies through the abdomen. The contours produced by 10 Hz were fairly flat in all directions, whereas the contours produced by 2,000 Hz were decidedly curved (Fig. 17.7). In terms of achieving a reproducible vibroacoustic signal, and thus a consistent fetal response, the exact position of the fetal head with reference to the actuator head of the vibrator must be known.

Airborne Signals Reaching the Surface of the Body

The first investigators to attempt to measure the intrauterine sound environment in pregnant women were impressed with the high attenuation of external sounds (Bench, 1968; Walker, Grimwade, & Wood, 1971). It has since been recognized by Gerhardt (1990; Fig. 17.8) that failure to take into full account the impedance mismatch between uterine tissue and fluids and the implanted rubber-covered condenser microphones were responsible for these high attenuation values. Armitage et al. (1980), Vince et al. (1982), and their colleagues from Cambridge were the first to note the rich and varied intrauterine sound environment of sheep, and to describe the effects of some sounds produced outside the mother. Gerhardt et al. (1990) confirmed these general findings in sheep and drew attention to hydrophone position as an important variable in SPL level (Table 17.1). The sound pressure recorded at different locations within the amnion, with respect to the sound source, varied from 6 to 15 dB, depending mainly on stimulus frequency. Above 0.25 kHz, sound attenuation increased at a rate of 6 dB per octave. For 4.0 kHz, sound attenuation averaged 20 dB.

Several investigators have called attention to the relatively low levels of sound attenuation in lower regions of the audible spectrum (data from humans and sheep have been summarized graphically, Gerhardt et al., 1990; Fig. 17.8). Careful measurements with attention to level of the stimulus showed an actual enhancement of SPL at low frequencies (<250 Hz) in

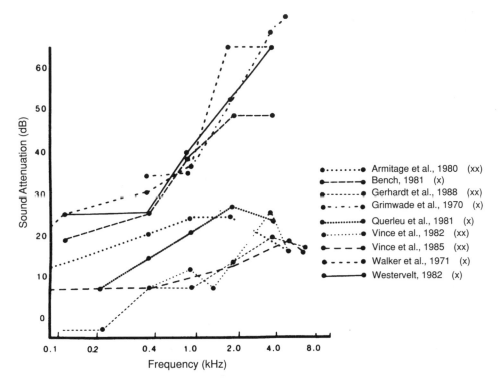

FIG. 17.8. Sound attenuation in humans and sheep: x, microphone recordings; xx, hydrophone recordings. From Gerhardt et al. (1990). Reprinted by permission.

TABLE 17.1
Average Sound Attenuation in Decibels for Broadband Noise, Pure Tones, and Music (Low-Pass Filtered)

Animal	Broadband noise Toward	Away	1.0 kHz Pure Tone Toward	Away	10.0 kHz Pure Tone Toward	Away	Music Toward	Away
O-21	0	3.5	9.5	13.5	—	—	-2.0	2.5
O-30	-0.75	0	16.5	—	—	—	—	—
O-15	3.0	9.0	—	12.8	—	—	—	4.7
B-114	12.5	12.5	2.0	3.5	15.0	25.0	5.5	—
B-104	4.8	9.2	0.5	10.0	16.0	8.0	-6.0	-7.0
B-121	5.0	6.0	2.5	—	8.0	3.5	—	3.5
B-134	9.5	19.5	16.0	23.0	16.0	30.0	0.3	—
Average	4.9	8.5	7.8	12.6	13.7	16.6	-0.6	0.9
Grand average	6.7		10.0		15.2		0.2	

Note. Signal levels exceeded 80 dB. Repeated measurements of various musical pieces and for the two positions of the ewe are reported. "Toward" and "Away" refer to the relation in the uterus of the hydrophone with respect to the speakers. From Gerhardt et al. (1990). Reprinted by permission.

the uterus of some animals (Gerhardt et al., 1990; Vince et al., 1982). This enhancement does not appear to be dependent on the position of the hydrophone within the abdomen (Peters, Gerhardt, Abrams, & Longmate, 1993).

The most extensive investigation of the transmission of airborne sound is that of Peters, Abrams, Gerhardt, & Griffiths (1993), who extended the range of frequencies of the stimulus over all possible full-frequency ranges of audition in a fetus (50–20,000 Hz). Surprisingly, sound attenuation varied inversely as a function of stimulus level at low frequencies (50–125 Hz) and at high frequencies (7,000–20,000 Hz; Fig. 17.9).

Peters, Gerhardt, Abrams, & Longmate (1993) measured airborne-induced sound pressures at 45 locations in a 20 × 20 × 20 array in the sheep abdomen. Overall differences in isosound pressure contours were observed when results were compared with the three-dimensional intraabdominal contours created with vibrators (Peters, Abrams, Gerhardt, & Longmate, 1991). Sound attenuation values, which confirmed earlier reports (Gerhardt et al., 1990; Richards et al., 1992; Vince et al., 1982), tended to be maximal toward the center of the cube for frequencies greater

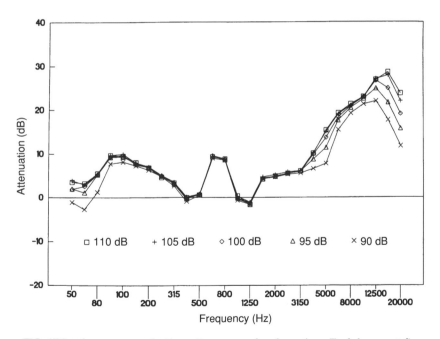

FIG. 17.9. Average sound attenuation curves for sheep (*n* = 5) abdomen at five different stimulating levels: 90, 95, 100, 105, and 110 dB SPL (dB re 20 μPa) Spectra were analyzed with ⅓-octave bands. From Peters, Abrams, Gerhardt, & Griffiths (1993). Reprinted by permission.

than 1,000 Hz, indicating a wrap-around effect of airborne sound, rather than a direct straight-line transmission of sounds through the torso as noted with vibrators.

These most recent data suggest that the distribution of sound within the uterus is strongly related to the origin of the sound source (airborne vs. vibratory) and that therefore the pressure variations within the uterus, and thus fetal hearing, may be strongly different depending on which type of stimulus the fetus is exposed.

THE SOUND ISOLATION OF THE FETUS

Assessment of the intrauterine fetal sound environment—a composite of ambient sounds outside the mother and sounds created by her—is an important step in understanding what might or might not be a true fetal stimulus capable of eliciting or modifying fetal behavior. But even though the peripheral sensory mechanisms and central pathways are formed and connected in both late gestation human and sheep fetuses, some sound isolation may be expected because of the attenuation of sound by tissues and fluids surrounding the fetus and by the fluid-filled fetal external ear canal and the middle ear chamber containing mesenchyme and fluid. The mechanical aspects of the ear and the conduction of sound into the cochlea are affected because ossicular motion is damped by these fluids. The pathways taken by acoustic pressures from fluids and tissues surrounding the fetal head to the fetal inner ear are not yet defined.

In order to estimate the degree to which the fetus is "isolated" globally from environmental sound, Gerhardt et al. (1992), recorded cochlear microphonics (CMs) in response to ⅓-octave band noises (0.125–2.0 kHz) delivered through a loudspeaker on one side of a pregnant sheep. After delivery, CMs were measured again from lambs placed in the same sound field. The CM is an alternating electrical potential generated at the level of the sensory cells within the cochlea. This bioelectric potential mimics the amplitude and frequency of the acoustic signal over a range that includes the main frequencies required for perception of both speech and music. Thus, as the signal amplitude increases, so does the amplitude of the CM. By comparing the sound pressure levels necessary to produce equal electrical outputs from the cochlea of the fetus and, later, after it has been delivered and time permitted for the fluids of the outer and middle ears to drain, estimates of fetal sound isolation can be made. Figure 17.10 illustrates the difference in SPL necessary to evoke equal CM amplitudes from fetus and newborn. Fetal sound isolation ranged from 11 dB for 125 Hz to 45 dB for 2,000 Hz.

The fetus is well protected from exogenous sounds with frequency

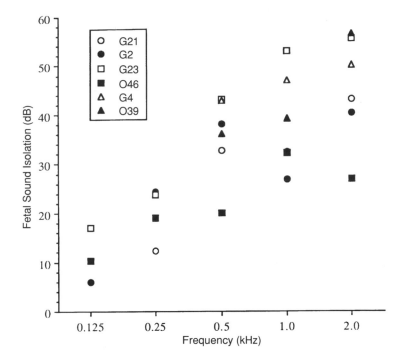

FIG. 17.10.   Fetal sound isolation. The average differences between the SPLs in decibels necessary to produce equal cochlear microphonic functions for each frequency recorded from the fetus and the newborn. From Gerhardt et al. (1992). Reprinted by permission.

content above 250 Hz. The protection would be equivalent to the protection derived from most personal hearing protectors. However, low frequencies (250 Hz and below) penetrate easily to the fetal inner ear with little reduction in sound pressure. Because of this, fetal hearing may be adversely affected by intense, low-frequency exposures to the mother.

EFFECTS OF EXOGENOUS NOISE OF FETAL HEARING

The extent to which exogenous sounds penetrate the uterus and stimulate fetal hearing can be estimated by evaluating temporary and/or permanent changes in function of the auditory system. One technique for testing is the auditory brainstem response (ABR). Woods, Plessinger, and Mack (1984) were the first to record this response from in utero fetal sheep.

The ABR is a minute, stimulus-locked, bioelectric potential evoked with either clicks or tone bursts with brief durations. The response is extracted from the ongoing fetal electrocorticogram using response averaging, differential amplification, and filtering. It is considered an early auditory potential, occurring within 10 ms after stimulus onset. The ABR is characterized in human hearing by five vertex-positive peaks corresponding to synchronous discharges from nuclei and fiber tracts beginning with the acoustic nerve and ending in the brainstem. The ABR threshold and latencies of the positive peaks provide methods for assessing hearing sensitivity.

In a fetal sheep experiment (Griffiths et al., 1994), ABRs were elicited with clicks and tone bursts delivered to the fetal skull with a bone vibrator (Radiometer, B70A) commonly used for audiologic assessment in humans. Following a 16 hr noise exposure (broadband noise, 120 dB SPL) delivered to the pregnant ewe through loudspeakers, there was a significant shift in the latencies of the ABR peaks. In addition, ABR thresholds were elevated following the noise exposure, and returned to nearly preexposure levels by 24–48 hr postexposure.

SUMMARY

Important differences in intrauterine sound transmission exist between airborne and direct mechanical application of sound and vibration to the abdominal segment of the mother. The importance of frequency in transmission of sound from maternal environment to fetal cochlea has been documented with uterine hydrophones and with electrodes on a fetal round window. The fetus is isolated from environmental sounds by reason of tissue and fluid attenuation and by some conduction loss through fluid-filled chambers in the ear. A temporary shift in fetal hearing sensitivity can be induced by exposure to intense noise in the maternal environment, although this isolation is considerably less for sounds with frequency content below 250 Hz.

REFERENCES

Abrams, R. M., & Wasserman, D. E. (1991). Occupational vibration during pregnancy. *American Journal of Obstetrics Gynecology, 164*, 1152.

Armitage, S. E., Baldwin, B. A., & Vince, M. A. (1980). The fetal sound environment of sheep. *Science, 208*, 1173–1174.

Bench, R. J. (1968). Sound transmission to the human foetus through the maternal abdominal wall. *Journal of Genetic Psychology, 113*, 85.

Benzaquen, S., Gagnon, R., Hunse, C., & Foreman, J. (1990). The intrauterine sound environment of the human fetus during labor. *American Journal of Obstetrics and Gynecology, 163*, 484–490.

Bernard, J., & Sontag, L. W. (1947). Fetal reactivity to tonal stimulation: A preliminary report. *Journal of Genetic Psychology, 70,* 205–210.

Crade, M., & Lovett, S. (1988). Fetal response to sound stimulation: Preliminary report exploring use of sound stimulation in routine obstetrical ultrasound examinations. *Journal of Ultrasound Medicine, 1,* 499–503.

Fifer, W. P., & Moon, C. (1988). Auditory experience in the fetus. In W. P. Smotherman, & S. R. Robinson (Eds.), *Behavior of the fetus* (pp. 175–226). Caldwell, NJ: Telford Press.

Gagnon, R. (1989). Stimulation of human fetuses with sound and vibration. *Seminars in Perinatology, 13,* 393–402.

Gelman, S. R., Wood, S. A., Spellacy, W. M., & Abrams, R. M. (1982). Fetal movements in response to sound stimulation. *American Journal of Obstetrics and Gynecology, 143,* 484–485.

Gerhardt, K. J. (1989). Characteristics of the fetal sheep sound environment. *Seminars in Perinatology, 13,* 362–370.

Gerhardt, K. J. (1990). Prenatal and perinatal risks of hearing loss. *Seminars in Perinatology, 14,* 299–304.

Gerhardt, K. J., Abrams, R. M., Kovaz, B. M., Gomez, K. J., & Conlon M. (1988). Intrauterine noise levels in pregnant ewes produced by sound applied to the abdomen. *American Journal of Obstetrics and Gynecology, 159,* 228–232.

Gerhardt, K. J., Abrams, R. M., & Oliver, C. C. (1990). Sound environment of the fetal sheep. *American Journal of Obstetrics and Gynecology, 162,* 282–287.

Gerhardt, K. J., Otto, R., Abrams, R. M., Colle, J., Burchfield, D. J., & Peters, A. J. M. (1992). Cochlear microphonics recorded from fetal and newborn sheep. *American Journal of Otolaryngology, 13*(4), 226–233.

Graham, E. M., Peters, A. J. M., Abrams, R. M., Gerhardt, K. J., & Burchfield, D. J. (1991). Intraabdominal sound levels during vibroacoustic stimulation. *American Journal of Obstetrics and Gynecology, 164,* 1140–1144.

Griffiths, S. K., Pierson, L. L., Gerhardt, K. J., Abrams, R. M., & Peters, A. J. M. (1994). Noise induced hearing loss in fetal sheep. *Hearing Research, 74,* 221–230.

Grimwade, J. C., Walker, D. W., & Wood, C. (1970). Sensory stimulation of the human foetus. *Australian Journal of Meutal Retardation, 2,* 63–64.

Nyman, M., Arulkumaran, S., Hsu, T. S., Ratnam, S. S., Till, O., & Westgren M. (1991). Vibroacoustic stimulation and intrauterine sound pressure levels. *Obstetrics and Gynecology, 78,* 803–806.

Oliver, C. C. (1989). Sound and vibration transmission in tissues. *Seminars in Perinatology, 13,* 354–361.

Peters, A. J. M., Abrams, R. M., Gerhardt, K. J., & Burchfield, D. J. (1991). Vibration of the abdomen in non-pregnant sheep: Effect of dynamic force and surface area of vibrator. *Journal of Low Frequency Noise and Vibration, 10,* 92–99.

Peters, A. J. M., Abrams, R. M., Gerhardt, K. J., Burchfield, D. J., & Wasserman, D. E. (1992). Resonance of the pregnant sheep uterus. *Journal of Low Frequency Noise and Vibration, 11*(1), 1–6.

Peters, A. J. M., Abrams, R. M., Gerhardt, K. J., & Griffiths, S. K. (1993). Transmission of airborne sound from 50-20,000 Hz into the abdomen of sheep. *Journal of Low Frequency Noise and Vibration, 12*(1), 16–24.

Peters, A. J. M., Abrams, R. M., Gerhardt, K. J., & Longmate, J. A. (1991). Three dimensional sound and vibration frequency responses of the sheep abdomen. *Journal of Low Frequency Noise and Vibration, 10,* 100–111.

Peters, A. J. M., Gerhardt, K. J., Abrams, R. M., & Longmate, J. A. (1993). Three-dimensional intraabdominal sound pressures in sheep produced by airborne stimuli. *American Journal of Obstetrics and Gynecology, 169,* 1304–1315.

Querleu, D., Renard, X., Versyp, F., Paris-Debrue, L., & Crepin, G. (1988). Fetal hearing. *European Journal of Obstetrics and Gynecology Reproductive Biology, 29,* 191–212.

Richards, D. S. (1990). The fetal vibroacoustic stimulation test: an update. *Seminars in Perinatology, 14,* 305–310.

Richards, D. S., Frentzen, B., Gerhardt, K. J., McCann, M. E., & Abrams, R. M. (1992). Sound levels in the human uterus. *Obstetrics and Gynecology, 80*(2), 186–190.

Vince, M. A., Armitage, S. E., Baldwin, B. A., & Toner, J. N. (1982). The sound environment of the foetal sheep. *Behavior, 81,* 296–315.

Vince, M. A., Billing, A. E., Baldwin, B. A., Toner, J. N., & Weller, C. (1985). Maternal vocalisations and other sound in the fetal lamb's sound environment. *Early Human Development, 11,* 179–190.

Visser, G. H. A., Mulder, H. H., Wit, H. P., & Prechtl, H. J. R. (1989). Vibroacoustic stimulation of the human fetus: Effect on behavioral state organization. *Early Human Development, 19,* 285–296.

Walker, D., Grimwade, J., & Wood, C. (1971). Intrauterine noise: A component of the fetal environment. *American Journal of Obstetrics and Gynecology, 109,* 91.

Wasserman, D. E. (1990). Vibration: Principles, measurements and health standards. *Seminars in Perinatology, 14,* 311–321.

Westervelt, P. J. (1982). Prenatal effects of exposure to high-level noise (Report of Working group 85). In *Committee on Hearing, Bioacoustics, and Biomechanics. Assembly of Behavioral and Social Sciences, National Research Council.* Washington, DC: National Academy Press.

Woods, J. R., Plessinger, M. A., & Mack, C. E. (1984). Fetal auditory brainstem evoked response (ABR). *Pediatric Research, 18,* 83–85.

18

Maternal Contributions to Fetal Experience and the Transition from Prenatal to Postnatal Life

April E. Ronca
Jeffrey R. Alberts
Indiana University

Historically, the expectant mother has been advised to keep herself cheerful, listen to good music, and frequent art galleries. Indeed, it was suggested "that if a woman about to become a mother plays the piano every day, her baby will be born a Victor Herbert" (Nathan & Mencken, 1921, p. 109), and that a tearful mother is likely to produce a mournful child (Shakespeare, *Henry VI* (3), Act IV, Scene iv).

Clearly, the purveyors of such edicts were asserting that the pregnant mother's behavior and mood exert formative influences on the fetus. This view is echoed by some contemporary pundits who urge expectant parents to advance their baby's intellectual and social development through prenatal communication and learning. Such claims and assertions have survived without empirical support.

Historically, the scientific community has taken a different stance. The pregnant mother has been viewed as a vehicle for the fetus and as a conduit for its nutrition and waste removal. It was assumed that, while inside the mother's body, the fetus lives in total isolation, utterly insulated and buffered from the fluctuations and exigencies of the outside world (Bichat, 1827; Preyer, 1937; Reynolds, 1962; Windle, 1940).

More recently, however, the scientific community has demonstrated admirable ability to change attitude; empirical findings of fetal experience

331

in utero have generated widespread interest and excitement. There is now general consensus that considerable sensory input impinges upon the fetus in utero, and that the mother's behavior and physiology make significant contributions to prenatal sensory experience (Fifer & Moon, chapter 19, this volume; Fifer & Moon, 1988; Hofer, 1981; Ronca, Lamkin & Alberts, 1993; Schaal, Orgeur, & Rognon, chapter 12, this volume; Vince, Billing, Baldwin, Toner, & Weller, 1985).

The time has come for precise, empirical studies of maternal contributions to fetal experience. The present chapter describes the forms of stimulation produced by the mother that impinge upon the fetus in utero, the ability of the fetus to detect and respond to maternally produced stimuli, and the role of perinatal sensory experience in the fetus's transition from prenatal to postnatal life. These issues are central to understanding the epigenetic contributions of prenatal sensory experience to early development, or, in other words, the ways in which prenatal stimulation may promote, facilitate, regulate, or trigger developmental pathways during early life (Oyama, 1985).

A major thesis of this chapter is that in order to understand prenatal sensory experience it is essential to consider the environment within which the fetus develops, for the two are inextricably linked. Our approach is based on principles of behavioral ecology and provides a useful framework for understanding experiential contributions to psychobiological development (Alberts & Cramer, 1988).

PRENATAL SENSORY FUNCTION

In order to appreciate the fetus's ability to detect intrauterine sensory events, it is essential to ask whether sensory function begins before birth, and if so, for which modalities. The answer depends, in part, on the species under consideration. In birds and mammals, the developmental emergence of sensory function follows a stereotyped sequence (Gottlieb, 1971). Figure 18.1 shows the developmental emergence of cutaneous, vestibular, auditory and visual function for the Norway rat (*Rattus norvegicus*) and the human. Onset of sensory function is plotted in relation to postconceptional age and birth date. The sequential emergence of the modalities is the same for both species, although birth occurs at relatively different points in the sequence. In the human, the functional onset of each modality occurs before birth. In the Norway rat, however, onset of function in the cutaneous and vestibular systems is prenatal, whereas auditory and visual sensitivity emerges well after birth. This comparison reveals that, in contrast to the human, the Norway rat is born at a relatively less advanced stage of sensory development. Yet, for both species, senses positioned early in the

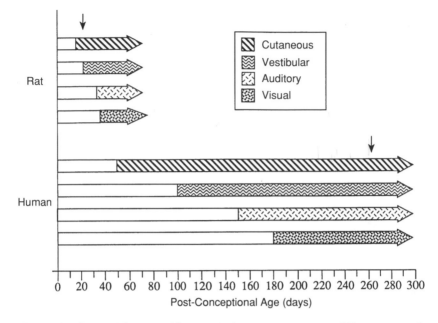

FIG. 18.1.   Sequential onsets of function in four sensory systems of Norway rat and human in relation to conception and the event of birth. The inverted arrow depicts each organism's birthdate. For each species, the horizontal arrows represent (top to bottom) onset of function for cutaneous, vestibular, auditory, and visual sensitivity. From Alberts (1984). Adapted by permission.

sequence begin to operate prenatally; that is, cutaneous and vestibular (Fig. 18.1) as well as chemical and thermal (not shown; see Alberts, 1984).

To the extent that the cutaneous and vestibular systems of fetuses are activated by stimulation that occurs within the natural context of the uterus, input to these modalities forms the basis for the earliest sensory experiences. One implication of this finding is that mammalian fetuses share a common sequence of experience during early development, not merely common environmental conditions. In other words, the same systems begin to function in the same sequence, and correspondingly, similar sensory inputs may be available within the uterine environment. Hence, we expect that rats share with humans (and other mammalian species) common prenatal sensory experiences (for further discussion, see Alberts & Ronca, 1993).

Early sensory experience is essential to the development of sensory systems and behavior. Formative effects of intramodal stimulation on the development of behavior and its neural substrate are well documented (Blakemore & Cooper, 1970; Wiesel & Hubel, 1963). Recent studies have shown that premature function in one modality can influence rates of functional maturation in other modalities as well (Kenny & Turkewitz, 1986; Lickliter, chapter 15, this volume). Taken together, these results suggest that early sensory function is regulated by both intramodal and intermodal stimulation, a conclusion that attains even greater significance when placed within the broader developmental and comparative frameworks discussed earlier.

THE NATURE OF PRENATAL SENSORY EXPERIENCE

Fetal sensory systems, when grossly immature, are capable of transducing sensory information (Alberts, 1984; Bradley & Mistretta, 1975; Gottlieb, 1971). Sensory-evoked reflex action has been observed in fetuses of many species (Coghill, 1929; Hamburger, 1963; Hooker, 1952; Kuo, 1932; Narayanan, Fox, & Hamburger, 1971). For instance, Hooker (1952) elicited rooting-like responses to tactile stimulation of the cheek in human fetuses. Smotherman and Robinson (1988a) documented motoric responses to tactile and chemosensory stimuli in rat fetuses. We have found cardiac responses in fetal rats to tactile, vestibular, and chemosensory stimuli (Ronca & Alberts, 1990, 1994; Smotherman, Robinson, Ronca, Alberts, & Hepper, 1991). Input to prenatal sensory systems can also recruit species-typical action patterns normally observed postnatally, such as facial wiping to noxious stimuli, and the stretch response to milk infusion in rats (Smotherman & Robinson, 1987).

As researchers have continued to examine fetal capabilities for stimulus processing, they have uncovered additional abilities and aspects of stimulus control over behavior. For instance, fetuses habituate to repeated presentations of a sensory stimulus (Lecanuet, Granier-Deferre, & Busnel, chapter 13, this volume, also Leader, chapter 21, this volume; Smotherman & Robinson, 1992). Newly born mammals recognize and discriminate sensory cues that were previously introduced into the prenatal environment (Hepper, 1988; Pedersen & Blass, 1982; Smotherman, 1982). Prenatal exposure to stimulation can modify postnatal responsiveness to the same stimulus (Vince, 1979; Vince, Armitage, Shillito-Walser, & Reader, 1982). Prenatal stimuli can acquire control over postnatal behaviors, such as suckling onset (Pederson & Blass, 1982).

Functionally, it has been suggested that prenatal sensory experience may form the basis for kin recognition (Hepper, 1987), promote mother–infant bonding (DeCasper & Fifer, 1980), facilitate learning (Parry, 1972), and mediate essential postnatal behaviors (Pederson & Blass, 1982).

It is within the area of ecologically relevant forms of prenatal stimulation that we focus our subsequent discussion. Investigators have begun to expand their analyses of sensory-evoked fetal responses to stimu.. ᴕᴕᴕᴕ normally occur within the uterine environment. There is evidence for newborn responses to sensory cues that are typically present in utero, including maternal speech (DeCasper & Fifer, 1980; DeCasper & Spence, 1986), and chemical constituents of the amniotic fluid (Hepper, 1987; Pedersen & Blass, 1982). We discuss next our own studies of fetal sensory experience in rats, which emphasize stimuli produced by the mother's behavior and physiology.

MATERNAL STIMULATION OF THE FETUS DURING GESTATION, LABOR AND DELIVERY

Of all the forms of stimulation with maternal origins that are present in utero, the prenatal acoustic environment has been the most extensively studied. The uterine cavity receives transmissions of the mother's vocalizations (Armitage, Baldwin, & Vince, 1980; DeCasper & Fifer, 1980; Vince et al., 1985), as well as sounds generated from maternal physiological processes, including vascular activity, breathing, eating, drinking, swallowing, and borborygmi, that is, the audible by-products of digestion (Henschall, 1972; Vince et al., 1985; Walker, Grimwade, & Wood, 1971). The fetal environment clearly contains an impressive array of sounds that vary in pitch, loudness, and pattern (Fifer & Moon, 1988).

Maternal behavior and physiology produce other forms of stimulation that may also impinge on the fetus in utero. The mother's physical activities can pressure, accelerate, and vibrate the fetus (Bradley & Mistretta, 1975; Hofer, 1981; Previc, 1991; Ronca et al., 1993). During parturition, the fetus is squeezed, pitched, and turned by the contracting uterus, compressed through the birth canal, and delivered into a cold extrauterine environment. Just as the human fetus can detect and process the acoustic stimuli associated with maternal vocalization, so might cutaneous, vestibular, and thermal stimuli from maternal sources be perceptible to prenatal offspring. If this is true, then stimuli that arise from maternal behavior and physiology are likely to produce some sensory experiences common to all mammals.

FETAL STIMULATION DURING GESTATION

Studies of maternal contributions to fetal sensation in both the chemical and the acoustic domains have generally relied on the postnatal expression of prenatal sensory experience (DeCasper & Fifer, 1980; Pederson & Blass, 1982; Smotherman, 1982; Vince, 1979; Vince et al., 1982), thereby providing

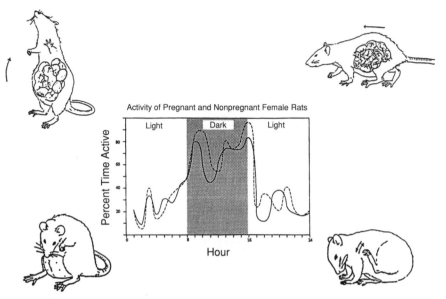

FIG. 18.2.   Behavioral activities of rat dams that stimulate fetuses in utero. Top: Rearing
(left) and locomotion (right) with a cut-away view of fetuses in utero. Bottom: Abdominal grooming (left) and hindlimb scratching (right). Center: Twenty-four hour activity
profiles of late-pregnant (———) and nonpregnant (– – –) rats across 8-hr light
(unshaded) and dark (shaded) portions of the circadian cycle. From Alberts and Ronca
(1993). Reprinted by permission.

no direct evidence for fetal perception of in-utero sensory events. An
alternate strategy is to directly measure the immediate reactions of the
fetus to stimuli normally present during gestation and birth. This approach requires knowledge of the prenatal sensory environment. We have
adopted such an approach and have used a prior descriptive analysis of
maternal behavior during gestation, labor, and delivery in the Norway rat
(Ronca et al., 1993).

Early reports, based on direct observation and time sampling, suggested that late pregnant female rats are lethargic and inactive (Rosenblatt
& Lehrman, 1963; Weisner & Sheard, 1933). In a recent study using time-
lapse videography, continuous behavioral profiles of pregnant females
were compiled over the final week of their 3-week gestation period (Ronca
et al., 1993). Behaviors that are prevalent in the dams' repertoire were
measured, including exploratory behavior, grooming, nest-building, and
feeding and drinking. Figure 18.2 (center) illustrates the percentage of
overall activity displayed by pregnant and nonpregnant females across a
24-hr period on day 20 of the 22-day gestation period. Pregnant dams were
as active as nonpregnant females until the day prior to parturition, sug-

gesting that the amount of activity displayed by the late gestation rat is more than ample to produce repeated, significant stimulations of fetuses in utero.

Figure 18.2 also depicts some of the behaviors that are prevalent in the dams' behavioral repertoire that can generate forces and stimuli within the uterus. Forward locomotion and rearing (top row) expose fetuses in utero to linear and angular acceleration. Grooming behaviors (bottom row) vibrate and compress fetuses in utero.

Quantitative analysis of the rat dam's behavior has shown that fetuses in utero may receive (each day) more than 100 linear accelerations associated with maternal locomotion, approximately 300 angular accelerations associated with rearing, about 10 min of mechanical pressure arising from abdominal grooming, and 125 episodes of vibration associated with hindlimb scratching (Ronca et al., 1993). These results support the view that maternal activities impose upon fetuses specific forms of stimulation, namely, linear acceleration, angular acceleration, mechanical pressure, and vibration. To the extent that these stimulations are transmitted in utero, maternal activities are potentially responsible for hundreds of fetal sensory inputs in a single day. This analysis raises the possibility that specific behaviors of pregnant mothers of other mammalian species, including humans, may stimulate the fetus in utero.

However, additional studies are necessary to determine whether sensory by-products of the mother's behavior actually reach the fetus in utero. In a study currently underway, we are making in-situ recordings of intrauterine pressure (IUP) in rat dams to determine the contributions of particular maternal activities to the fetal sensory environment. In this study, a single conceptus is replaced with a saline-filled latex balloon connected to a pressure transducer. Ongoing measurements of uterine activity are made and the mother's behavior is captured on videotape. During playback of the videotape, maternal activities are scored and matched to intrauterine pressure changes.

Our preliminary results support the view that maternal actions are transmitted to the fetus in utero. Figure 18.3 illustrates intrauterine pressure (IUP) signals during the behavior sequence of a late pregnant rat in which an initial period of behavioral quiescence is followed by a bout of grooming. These signals represent the net pressure on the uterine balloon, that is, ongoing uterine activity, contributions from maternal behavior, and contributions from nonmaternal sources, such as the movement of adjacent siblings. During the dam's quiescence, the signal consists of slow, regular increases in pressure. The periodicity of this initial signal is consistent with the interpretation that it arises from rhythmic activity of the uterus, that is, "contractures" (Nathanielsz, chapter 20, this volume). In

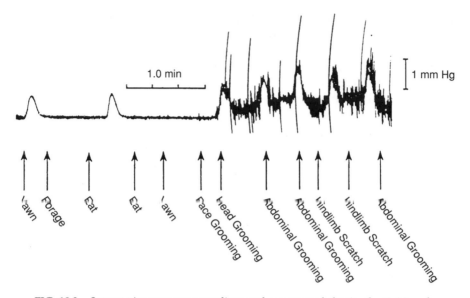

FIG. 18.3.   Intrauterine pressure recordings and concurrent behavioral activities of a
late pregnant rat. Pressure, 1 division per mm Hg; chart speed, 20 s/cm. From Alberts
and Ronca (1993). Reprinted by permission.

contrast, intrauterine pressure changes coupled with the grooming bout
appeared as high-frequency, irregular activity.

GESTATIONAL CHANGES IN THE FETAL
ENVIRONMENT

An important question that arises from discussion of the sensory environment in utero is, How do maternally produced stimuli present themselves
to the fetus in utero? In mammals, the uterine environment undergoes
systematic changes during pregnancy. Early in gestation, the fetus floats
within a fluid-filled amniotic sac, which provides offspring with the opportunity for symmetrical growth and movement and may buffer the
impact of extrinsic stimuli (Bradley & Mistretta, 1975). During the final
days of gestation, the amount of amniotic fluid declines precipitously
while fetal growth continues (Smotherman & Robinson, 1988; Tam &
Chan, 1977). As a result, the fetus becomes progressively more tightly
encased within the uterine sheath, and the effects of extrauterine stimuli
are altered. For instance, physical stimuli generated by the mother's behavior and physiology would influence fetal sensory receptors most directly, and provide maximally intense input during the interval
immediately preceding parturition.

FETAL STIMULATION ASSOCIATED WITH LABOR
AND DELIVERY

It has been noted that the mother's labor contractions squeeze the fetus with such force that the baby's head is molded into new and different shapes (Dawes, 1968). There is reason to expect that the fetus's experience of the powerful forces present during labor and delivery may be significant in the adaptive adjustments required to change from a fetus to an infant. For example, compression of the fetus' head during labor contributes to the massive release of adrenal and extraadrenal catecholamines that accompanies birth (Lagercrantz & Slotkin, 1986).

We can turn to laboratory studies for more precise and controlled analyses of labor and delivery. In the rat, the onset of labor begins about 6 hr in advance of delivery. In-situ measurements of IUP suggest that during labor, the rat fetus is exposed to contractions exceeding 15 mm Hg pressure (Fuchs, 1969). Accelerative forces on the fetus may provide an additional sensory component to uterine contractions.

The parturient rat dam shows two behaviorally distinct types of uterine contractions (Dollinger, Holloway, & Denenberg, 1980). During a lordosis contraction, the dam lies on her ventrum and elongates her body. Vertical contractions appear as a series of rapid, bilateral abdominal lifts. Peristaltic waves of the uteri, first described by Rosenblatt and Lehrman (1963), appear as quick rotary movements along the abdomen. It is not known at this time whether a different pattern of afferent input accompanies each contraction type; however, a single litter of pups is exposed to an average of 150 behaviorally discernible uterine contractions during prebirth labor (Ronca et al., 1993). Most (75%) of the contractions were concentrated in the hour preceding the delivery of the first pup; the remainder of contractions occurred during the intervals between pup deliveries.

Importantly, the onset of partus occurs after the diminution of the amniotic fluid's protective buffer, thereby exposing the fetus more directly to the impact of labor contractions and to a sizable increment in cutaneous stimulation. Novel patterns of afferent input impinge on fetal sensory receptors and their innervations as well.

Upon delivery from the birth canal, the newborn is bombarded with novel and intense stimuli. In the rat, the dam's behavior is the predominant source of postpartum stimuli (Rosenblatt & Lehrman, 1963; Ronca et al., 1993). When a pup begins to emerge from the birth canal, the dam often grasps the newborn with her teeth and extracts it from her vagina. She licks and handles the newborn, and removes its birth membranes. As the dam moves on to the next birth, previous newborns may be ignored for long periods and exposed to room temperature, which is more than 10° C cooler than intrauterine temperature (Ronca & Alberts, unpublished observa-

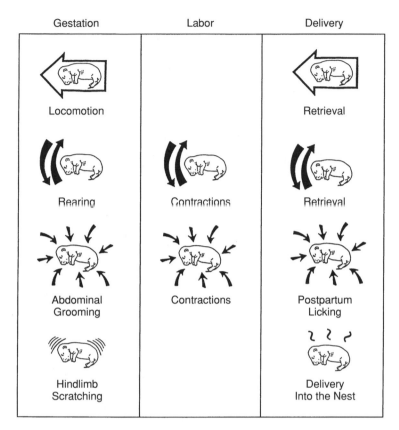

FIG. 18.4.   Iconographic chronology of stimuli across the perinatal period in the rat. From Ronca et al. (1993). Adapted by permission.

tion). Newborn pups may be deprived of the mother's warmth for over an hour while the parturition process continues (Ronca et al., 1993). Thermographic imaging techniques reveal that the newborn's surface temperature declines to ambient temperature within minutes of delivery into the nest (Alberts, Ronca, & Blumberg, 1992). These pups may be additionally exposed to harsh physical treatment as the dam sits, lies, and stands on them during subsequent deliveries.

Figure 18.4 presents an iconographic summary of these results. Linear acceleration is produced when the dam locomotes during gestation or retrieves newborn offspring. Angular acceleration is produced when the pregnant dam rears, circles, or self-grooms, possibly during labor contractions, and during postpartum retrieval by the dam. Pressure is associated with abdominal grooming prior to birth, uterine contractions, compression under the dam's body weight during lordosis contractions, and during postpartum licking. Vibration is produced by the dam's scratching, and cooling is associated with the newborn's arrival into the nest. Although our studies focus on the Norway rat, it is important to emphasize that analogous sensory inputs may arise from maternal behavior and physiology in any mammalian species.

THE FETUS'S ABILITY TO PERCEIVE MATERNAL STIMULATION

In order to determine whether sensory input produced by the mother during gestation, labor, and delivery influence prenatal behavior, development, or physiology, it is essential to determine whether the fetus is sensitive to the specific forms and levels of stimulation that are present in utero. There is now much empirical work that shows that the human fetus can detect auditory stimuli that are transmitted in utero (Fifer & Moon, 1988; Fifer & Moon, chapter 19, this volume; Lecanuet et al., chapter 13, this volume). However, virtually nothing is known of the fetus' ability to detect maternally generated cutaneous, vestibular, and thermal stimuli.

In a recent study, we found that fetal rats can detect and respond to simulations of the sensory forces produced by the dam (Ronca & Alberts, 1994). Using procedures for the direct observation of fetal rats (Narayanan et al, 1971; Smotherman, Richards, & Robinson, 1983), a spinal transection was administered to a rat dam on gestational day (GD) 21. The uterus was delivered from the abdomen into a warm saline bath, and a single pup was released from the uterus and amniotic sac (umbilical connections to the mother were preserved). The test pup was placed in a small egg-shaped cup in order to control the fetus's position within the water bath, buffer the subject fetus from its littermates, and prevent tension on the umbilical cord. Because we previously found that heart rate (HR) is a reliable measure of stimulus detection in fetal rats (Ronca & Alberts, 1990; Smotherman et al., 1991), HR was employed in this study. Each subject was fitted with a pair of fine (42 gauge) electrocardiogram (EKG) electrodes, then given a 5-min adaptation period prior to the onset of testing. Interbeat intervals (IBIs; in milliseconds) were collected via microcomputer for 30 sec, followed by delivery of a 5-sec stimulus to the subject fetus. The IBIs were measured for 60 sec following stimulus onset. For purposes of data analysis, IBIs were apportioned into 5-sec bins and converted to HR (beats per minute, bpm).

Subjects were presented with tactile, vestibular, or thermal stimuli designed to approximate sensory input normally present during gestation, labor and delivery in the rat (Fig. 18.4). These were:

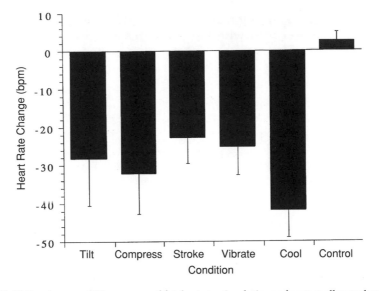

FIG. 18.5.   Average HR response of fetal rats to simulations of maternally produced stimuli. Group responses are plotted as the deviation from prestimulus baseline, for the first 30 sec following stimulus onset. Stimulus duration was 5 sec. (Tilt, $n = 12$; compress, $n = 11$; stroke, $n = 10$; vibrate, $n = 10$; cool, $n = 11$, control, $n = 12$.)

1. Angular acceleration, produced by tilting pups 70° from a lateral to head-up position, to mimic rearing of the pregnant dam.

2. Mechanical pressure, applied by compressing pups under an inflated balloon at an intensity of 15 mm Hg to simulate labor contractions.

3. Rapid stroking, produced using a set of artificial latex tongues mounted on a small motor to mimic postpartum licking.

4. Vibration, produced by applying a small motor to the egg-shaped cup containing the fetus, to approximate vibratory stimulation associated with the dam's hindlimb scratching.

5. Cooling, from 37.5°C (approximate intrauterine temperature) to 25°C (room temperature), in order to mimic the thermal effects of birth. Cooling was accomplished by infusing cooled water into the cup, followed by replacement of the heated water. To control for tactile effects of water movement during stimulation, a control group was infused with heated water only.

Figure 18.5 illustrates the average HR response of groups of pups receiving each form of stimulation. During the first 30-sec poststimulus interval, large cardiac decelerations were observed in each group. In each case, HR responses were accompanied by behavioral responses consisting of head, forelimb, hindlimb, and trunk movements. Fetuses in the thermal control condition showed neither HR or behavioral responses. These results suggest that the fetal rat can detect and respond to stimuli produced by the mother.

ON THE FUNCTIONAL SIGNIFICANCE OF MATERNAL STIMULATION

Throughout much of this chapter, we have implied that stimuli arising from the mother's behavior and physiology can have significant functional consequences for the fetus and newborn. Having reviewed the bases for such maternal stimulation as well as the fetus' ability to experience cues of maternal origin, we briefly consider some of the possible consequences of these experiences.

First, and very generally, we should recognize the general principle that sensory systems respond to stimulation prior to their full, functional maturation. Furthermore, such induced activity of sensory systems has been found to affect the development and subsequent function of these systems (see Alberts, 1984; Gottlieb, 1971). Most of the research supporting these important principles was conducted on visual and auditory systems (both relatively late-developing modalities; see Fig. 18.1), but all evidence indicates that these are basic and general rules. Hence, it is reasonable to posit that tactile and vestibular stimuli activate the corresponding sensory systems in the fetus around the time of onset of function, and thereby regulate sensory system maturation. Because fetuses tend to display motoric activation in response to suprathreshold stimuli (Smotherman & Robinson, 1988a; 1988b), we also suggest that prenatal stimulation, such as uterine contractions, provides afferent stimulation to the fetus and thereby induces arousal.

Prenatal stimulation may augment morphological and behavioral development by provoking fetal respiratory behavior, swallowing, and movement. Fetal respiratory behavior moves fluid through the lungs, stimulating pulmonary development and the neuromuscular action associated with breathing prior to the onset of postnatal respiration (Liggins, 1982). Tongue movements associated with fetal swallowing are required for normal development of the palate (Walker & Quarles, 1962). Depressed motor activity is associated with numerous morphological anomalies, including contractures of the joints, lung hypoplasia, facial anomalies, and growth retardation (Drachman & Sokoloff, 1966; Moessinger, 1983). Thus, there may be a developmental requirement for sensory-evoked behavior.

Stimulation associated with labor and delivery may assist the fetus's transition to postnatal life. At birth, the newborn must adapt quickly to the loss of the maternal life support system. Cardiovascular, thermoregulatory, and endocrine functions must conform to meet postnatal needs.

However, the most essential and immediate neonatal requirement is the onset of independent respiration. Contractions of the uterus prior to birth and postpartum stimulation derived from the sensory environment may play a key role in the newborn's adaptation to the postnatal environment. A massive surge of catecholamines, derived from the adrenal medulla and extraadrenal chromaffin tissue, accompanies the birth process and may prepare the infant to exist outside of the womb (Lagercrantz & Bistoletti, 1977; Lagercrantz & Slotkin, 1986). Catecholamine release, triggered mostly by hypoxic episodes during labor (Silver & Edwards, 1980), may protect the fetus from the debilitating effects of birth asphyxia (Lagercrantz & Slotkin, 1986; Seidler & Slotkin, 1985), promote the absorption of fetal lung liquid (Oliver, 1981), increase the volume of air inspired by the newborn (Boon, Milner, & Hopkin, 1981), and improve neurological adaptation for several days postpartum (Otamiri, Berg, Ledin, Leijon, & Lagercrantz, 1991).

There exist in the literature some examples of possible effects of early stimulation that are not evident until much later in development. One of these may be related to the fetus's experience of thermal stimuli around the event of parturition. The experience of cutaneous cooling, which often occurs with birth, is known to delay the postpartum rise in serum testosterone in newborn male rats (Matuszczyk, Silverin, & Larsson, 1990); one consequence of altering the timing of such hormonal responses can be seen later in life, during sexual behavior, when longer latencies to penile insertion are associated with cooling in infancy (Roffi, Chami, Corbier, & Edwards, 1987).

SENSORY MEDIATION OF THE FETUS' TRANSITION TO EXTRAUTERINE LIFE

The role of sensory factors in promoting the newborn's successful adaptation to the conditions of the postnatal world is discussed only anecdotally in textbooks of obstetrics and gynecology (James & Adamsons, 1989; Taylor, 1976). The majority of healthy human infants begin to breathe within a few minutes of being born, prior to occlusion of the umbilical cord (Page, Villee, & Villee, 1981), although postpartum breathing can presumably be induced with a slap on the newborn's rump or soles of its feet (James & Adamsons, 1989).

There is considerable debate among physiologists over identifying the critical stimulus for the onset of postnatal respiration in mammals. Possible candidates are removal of an inhibitory placental factor (Adamson, Kuipers, & Olson, 1991), cutaneous cooling (Dawes, 1968; Gluckman, Gunn, & Johnston, 1983), or mechanical stimulation of the skin (Condorelli

& Scarpelli, 1975; Scarpelli, Condorelli, & Cosmi, 1977). However, the actual biological levels of stimulation to which animals are normally exposed during labor and delivery are generally not known, and thus have not been employed in studies of postpartum respiration. Moreover, the orientation of these physiological analyses tends not to emphasize the sensory-perceptual factors that may induce or mediate the events that start the newborn's pulmonary respiration.

In a recent study we examined the role of sensory factors in the transition from umbilical to pulmonary respiration. We employed the simulations of somatic and thermal stimuli to which the fetal rat is normally exposed during labor and delivery, as described earlier. In this study, a rat dam was administered a spinal transection and a single fetus was placed in the egg-shaped capsule, as described earlier, with the exception that the capsule was positioned above the water bath in order to permit the fetus to breathe air. Air temperature was maintained at 37.5°C to simulate intrauterine temperature, unless otherwise indicated. Fetuses received one of four different treatments:

1. Mechanical stimulation to mimic labor contractions (a latex balloon was used to apply 15 compressions, each calibrated to produce 15 mm Hg pressure for 20 sec duration at the rate of 1/min).
2. Stroking with a foam brush to mimic the mother's postpartum licking.
3. Cooling of air temperature to 26°C to approximate the temperature of the nest at birth.
4. Umbilical cord occlusion using a microvascular clamp.

Subjects in a control group were externalized into warmed air (37.5°C) only. Subjects in the first three conditions and the control condition were fetuses (i.e., umbilical circulation to the dam remained intact throughout the test). These subjects were given the opportunity to breathe air, but were not required to do so. In contrast, fetuses in the fourth condition, which received umbilical cord occlusion, were required to initiate pulmonary respiration, because breathing was necessary for their continued survival. We videotaped each subject for 1 hr postpartum and, during playback of the videotapes, scored respiratory frequency.

Fetuses externalized from the uterus into cool air, as well as those in the control group, respired infrequently, but were still respiring at the end of the 1-hr test. Pups that received umbilical cord occlusion also breathed infrequently; however, none of these pups were breathing at the end of the test. In contrast, pups that received simulated uterine contractions showed a dramatic rise in respiratory rate, which persisted over the 1-hr test, even though stimulation was discontinued 15 min into the test interval. In a follow-up study, we found that compression completely reversed the 100% attrition rate produced by cord occlusion. Finally, stroking was as effective as compression in facilitating respiratory behavior, suggesting that cutaneous activation (rather than direct compression of the chest and lungs) may be an essential element in the onset of pulmonary respiration at birth.

We see these results as a preliminary affirmation of a distinct perspective: Fetal sensory-perceptual experience may play a vital role in the maintenance of behavior during gestation and in the successful transition from uterine existence to early postnatal life.

SUMMARY, CONCLUSIONS, AND FUTURE DIRECTIONS

Numerous implications can be derived from the perspective that we have developed in this chapter. We have noted the broad, evolutionary conservation of basic sequences of sensory maturation. Our appreciation of mammalian development can be enhanced by recognizing that the invariant sequence of sensory maturation (much of it occurring in utero) gives all mammals a common experiential foundation in early life. To the extent that early experience plays significant formative roles in the development of the central nervous system, endocrine system, and behavior, we can envision a science of early development with a richer domain for understanding the bases of species similarities and differences. Such a perspective will sharpen our ability to recognize the developmental origins of species differences as a particular mode of differentiation.

These kinds of considerations, of course, are particularly helpful for providing a common biological framework within which to examine human development. In addition, they help make animal models more accessible to the human condition, because it is easier to specify the bases of similarities and differences. Finally, we believe that a fuller appreciation of the factors that contribute to the full epigenesis of human development will inevitably illuminate the origins of certain forms of pathology, particularly those that involve divergence from typical sequences, timing, or pathways of development.

ACKNOWLEDGMENT

The research reported in this chapter was supported by National Institutes for Mental Health grant MH46485 to Jeffrey Alberts and April Ronca. We wish to acknowledge Mick Armbruster and Karen Cabell for technical assistance.

REFERENCES

Adamson, S. L., Kuipers, I. M., & Olsen, D. M. (1991). Umbilical cord occlusion stimulates breathing independent of blood gases and pH. *Journal of Applied Physiology, 70,* 1796–1809.

Alberts, J. R. (1984). Sensory-perceptual development in the Norway rat: A view toward comparative studies. In R. Kail & N. S. Spear (Eds.), *Comparative perspectives on memory development* (pp. 65–102). Hillsdale, NJ: Lawrence Erlbaum Associates.

Alberts, J. R., & Cramer, C. P. (1988). Ecology and experience: Sources of means and meaning of developmental change. In E. M. Blass (Ed.), *Handbook of behavioral neurobiology, Vol. 9, Developmental psychobiology and behavioral ecology* (pp. 1–40). New York: Plenum Press.

Alberts, J. R., & Ronca, A. E. (1993). Fetal experience revealed by rats: Psychobiological insights. *Early Human Development, 35,* 153–166.

Alberts, J. R., Ronca, A. E., & Blumberg, M. S. (1992). Thermal imaging rat pups upon delivery into the nest. *Abstracts of the International Society of Developmental Psychobiology, 25,* p. 10.

Armitage, S. E., Baldwin, B. A., & Vince, M. A. (1980). The fetal sound environment of sheep. *Science, 208,* 1173–1174.

Bichat, M. F. X. (1827). *Physiological researches upon life and death.* Boston: Richardson and Lord.

Blakemore, C., & Cooper, G. F. (1970). Development of the brain depends on the visual environment. *Nature, 228,* 477–478.

Boon, A. W., Milner, A. D., & Hopkin, I. E. (1981). Lung volumes and lung mechanics in babies born vaginally and by elective and emergency caesarean section. *Journal of Pediatrics, 98,* 812–815.

Bradley, R. M., & Mistretta, C. M. (1975). Fetal sensory receptors. *Physiological Reviews, 55,* 352–382.

Coghill, G. E. (1929). *Anatomy and the problem of behavior.* Cambridge, England: Cambridge University Press.

Condorelli, S., & Scarpelli, E. M. (1975). Somatic respiratory reflex and onset of regular breathing movements in the lamb fetus in utero. *Pediatric Research, 9,* 879–884.

Dawes, G. S. (1968). *Foetal and neonatal physiology: A comparative study of the changes at birth.* Chicago: Year Book Medical Publishers.

DeCasper, A. J., & Fifer, W. P. (1980). Of human bonding: Newborns prefer their mothers' voices. *Science, 208,* 1174–1176.

DeCasper, A .J., & Spence, M. J. (1986). Prenatal maternal speech influences newborns' perception of speech sounds. *Infant Behavior and Development, 9,* 133–150.

Dollinger, M. J., Holloway, W. R., & Denenberg, V. H. (1980). Parturition in the rat (*Rattus norvegicus*): Normative aspects and the temporal patterning of behaviors. *Behavioural Processes, 5,* 21–37.

Drachman, D. B., & Sokolov, L. (1966). The role of movement in embryonic joint development. *Developmental Biology, 14,* 401–420.

Fifer, W. P., & Moon, C. (1988). Auditory experience in the fetus. In W. P. Smotherman & S. R. Robinson (Eds.), *Behavior of the fetus* (pp. 175–188). Caldwell, NJ: Telford Press.

Fuchs, A. R. (1969). Uterine activity in late pregnancy and during parturition in the rat. *Biology of Reproduction, 1,* 344–353.

Gluckman, P. D., Gunn, T. R., & Johnston, B. M. (1983). The effects of cooling on breathing and shivering in unanesthaetized fetal lamb in utero. *Journal of Physiology (London), 343,* 495–506.

Gottlieb, G. (1971). Ontogenesis of sensory function in birds and mammals. In E. Tobach, L. R. Aronson, & E. Shaw (Eds.), *The biopsychology of development* (pp. 67–128). New York: Academic Press.

Hamburger, V. (1963). Some aspects of the embryology of behavior. *Quarterly Review of Biology, 38,* 342–365.

Henschall, W. R. (1972). Intrauterine sound levels. *Journal of Obstetrics and Gynecology, 112,* 577–579.

Hepper, P. G. (1987). The amniotic fluid: An important priming role in kin recognition. Animal *Behavior, 35,* 1343–1346.

Hepper, P. G. (1988). Adaptive fetal learning: Prenatal exposure to garlic affects postnatal preferences. *Animal Behavior, 36,* 935–936.

Hofer, M. A. (1981). *The roots of human behavior: An introduction to the psychobiology of early human development.* San Francisco: W. H. Freeman.

Hooker, D. (1952). *The prenatal origin of behavior.* 18th Porter Lecture Series. Lawrence, KS: University of Kansas Press.

James, L. S., & Adamsons, K. (1989). The neonate and resuscitation. In J. R. Scott, P. J. DiSaia, C. B. Hammond, & W. N. Spellacy (Eds.), *Danforth's obstetrics and gynecology* (pp. 675–690). Philadelphia: Lippincott.

Kenny, P. A., & Turkewitz, G. (1986). Effects of unusually early visual stimulation on the development of homing behavior in the rat pup. *Developmental Psychobiology, 19,* 57–66.

Kuo, Z. Y. (1932). Ontogeny of embryonic behavior in Aves: I. The chronology and general nature of the behavior of the chick embryo. *Journal of Experimental Zoology, 61,* 395–430.

Lagercrantz, H., & Bistoletti, P. (1977). Catecholamine release in the newborn. *Pediatric Research, 11,* 889–893.

Lagercrantz, H., & Slotkin, T. A., (1986). The "stress" of being born. *Scientific American, 254,* 100–107.

Liggins, G. C. (1982). The fetus and birth. In C. R. Austin & R. V. Short (Eds.), *Reproduction in mammals, Book 2: Embryonic and fetal development* (pp. 114–141). New York: Cambridge University Press.

Matuszczyk, J. V., Silverin, B., & Larsson, K. (1990). Influence of environmental events immediately after birth on postnatal testosterone secretion and adult sexual behavior in the male rat. *Hormones & Behavior, 24,* 450–458.

Moessinger, A. C. (1983). Fetal akinesia deformation sequence: An animal model. *Pediatrics, 72,* 857–863.

Narayanan, C. H., Fox, M. W., & Hamburger, V. (1971). Prenatal development of spontaneous and evoked activity in the rat. *Behavior, 40,* 100–134.

Nathan, G. J., & Mencken, H. L. (1921). *The American credo* (p. 109). New York: Alfred A. Knopf.

Oliver, R. E. (1981). Of labour and the lungs. *Archives of Disease in Childhood, 56,* 659–662.

Otamiri, G., Berg, G., Ledin, T., Leijon, I., & Lagercrantz, H. (1991). Delayed neurological adaptation in infants delivered by elective cesarean section and the relation to catecholamine levels. *Early Human Development, 26,* 51–60.

Oyama, S. (1985). *The ontogeny of information: Developmental systems and information.* New York: Cambridge University Press.

Page, E. W., Villee, C. A., & Villee, D. B. (1981). *Human reproduction: Essentials of reproductive and perinatal medicine.* Philadelphia: W. B. Saunders.

Parry, M. H. (1972). Infants' responses to novelty in familiar and unfamiliar settings. *Child Development, 43,* 233–237.

Pedersen, P. E., & Blass, E. M. (1982). Prenatal and postnatal determinants of the first suckling episode in albino rats. *Developmental Psychobiology, 15,* 349–355.

Previc, F. (1991). A general theory concerning the prenatal origins of cerebral lateralization in humans. *Psychological Review, 98,* 299–334.

Preyer, W. (1937). Embryonic motility and sensitivity [Specielle physiologie des embryo], trans. G. E. Coghill & W. K. Legner. *Monographs of the Society for Research in Child Development, 2,* 1–115.

Reynolds, S. R. M. (1962). Nature of fetal adaptation to the uterine environment: A problem of sensory deprivation. *American Journal of Obstetrics and Gynecology, 83,* 800–808.

Roffi, J., Chami, F., Corbier, P., & Edwards, D. A. (1987). Influence of the environmental temperature on the post-partum testosterone surge in the rat. *Acta Endocrinologica (Copenhagen), 115,* 478–482.

Ronca, A. E., & Alberts, J. R. (1990). Heart rate development and sensory-evoked cardiac responses in perinatal rats. *Physiology & Behavior, 47,* 1075–1082.

Ronca, A. E., & Alberts, J. R. (1994). Sensory stimuli associated with gestation and parturition evoke cardiac and behavioral responses in fetal rats. *Psychobiology 55,* 270–282.

Ronca, A. E., Lamkin, C. A., & Alberts, J. R. (1993). Maternal contributions to sensory experience in the fetal and newborn rat (*Rattus norvegicus*). *Journal of Comparative Psychology, 107,* 61–74.

Rosenblatt, J. S., & Lehrman, D. S. (1963). Maternal behavior in the laboratory rat. In H. L. Rheingold (Ed.), *Maternal behavior in mammals* (pp. 8–57). New York: Wiley.

Scarpelli, E. M., Condorelli, S., & Cosmi, E. V. (1977). Cutaneous stimulation and generation of breathing in the fetus. *Pediatric Research, 11,* 24–28.

Seidler, F., & Slotkin, T. A. (1985). Adrenomedullary function in the neonatal rat: Responses to acute hypoxia. *Journal of Physiology, 358,* 1–16.

Silver, M., & Edwards, A. V. (1980). The development of the sympatho-adrenal system with an assessment of the role of the adrenal medulla in the fetus and newborn. In H. Parvez & S. Parvez (Eds.), *Biogenic amines in development* (pp. 147–212). New York: Elsevier Biomedical Press.

Smotherman, W. P. (1982). Odor aversion learning by the rat fetus. *Physiology & Behavior, 29,* 769–771.

Smotherman, W. P., Richards, L. A., & Robinson, S. R. (1983). Techniques for observing fetal behavior in-utero: A comparison of chemomyelotomy and spinal transection. *Developmental Psychobiology, 17,* 661–674.

Smotherman, W. P., & Robinson, S. R. (1987). Prenatal expression of species-typical action patterns in the rat fetus (*Rattus norvegicus*). *Journal of Comparative Psychology, 101,* 190–196.

Smotherman, W. P., & Robinson, S. R. (1988a). Behavior of rat fetuses following chemical or tactile stimulation. *Behavioral Neuroscience, 102,* 24–34.

Smotherman, W. P., & Robinson, S. R. (1988b). The uterus as environment: The ecology of fetal behavior. In E. M. Blass (Ed.), *Handbook of behavioral neurobiology: Vol. 9. Developmental psychobiology and behavioral ecology* (pp. 149–196). New York: Plenum Press.

Smotherman, W. P., & Robinson, S. R. (1992). Habituation in the rat fetus. *Quarterly Journal of Experimental Psychology, 44B(3/4),* 215–230.

Smotherman, W. P., Robinson, S. R., Ronca, A. E., Alberts, J. R., & Hepper, P. (1991). Heart rate responses of the rat fetus and neonate to a chemosensory stimulus. *Physiology & Behavior, 50,* 47–52.

Tam, P. P. L., & Chan, S. T. H. (1977). Changes in the composition of maternal plasma, fetal plasma and fetal extraembryonic fluid during gestation in the rat. *Journal of Reproduction and Fertility, 51,* 41–51.

Taylor, E. S. (1976). *Beck's obstetrical practice and fetal medicine* (10th ed.). Baltimore, MD: Williams & Wilkins.

Vince, M. A. (1979). Postnatal effects of prenatal sound stimulation in the guinea pig. *Animal Behavior, 27,* 908–918.

Vince, M. A., Armitage, S. E., Shillito-Walser, E. S., & Reader, M. (1982). Postnatal consequences of prenatal sound stimulation in the sheep. *Behavior, 81,* 128–139.

Vince, M. A., Billing, B. A., Baldwin, B. A., Toner, J. N., & Weller, C. (1985). Maternal vocalisations and other sound in the fetal lamb's sound environment. *Early Human Development, 11,* 179–190.

Walker, B. E., & Quarles, J. (1962). Palate development in mouse foetuses after tongue removal. *Archives of Oral Biology, 21,* 405–412.

Walker, D., Grimwade, J., & Wood, C. (1971). Intrauterine noise: A component of the fetal environment. *American Journal of Obstetrics and Gynecology, 109,* 91–95.

Weisner, B. P., & Sheard, N. M. (1933). *Maternal behavior in the rat.* London: Oliver and Boyd.

Wiesel, T. N., & Hubel, D. H. (1963). Single-cell responses in striate cortex of kittens deprived of vision in one eye. *Journal of Neurophysiology, 26,* 1003–1017.

Windle, W. F. (1940). *Physiology of the fetus. Origin and extent of function in fetal life.* Philadelphia: W. B. Saunders.

19

The Effects of Fetal Experience with Sound

William P. Fifer
Columbia University

Chris M. Moon
Pacific Lutheran University

The study of early sensory stimulation and its role in shaping the sensory, perceptual, and learning capabilities of the infant brain has focused predominantly on the effects of postnatal experience. However, results from animal research, progress in the field of newborn perception, and the development of human fetal monitoring techniques have allowed us to more closely examine the short- and long-term effects of fetal experience. This chapter deals with a small piece of the puzzle concerning the role of environmental events in the sensory and perceptual development of the perinate. Specifically, what are the immediate and enduring effects of fetal experience with sound, and how does fetal experience with sounds affect the developing brain?

As is evident from other contributions to this volume, there are several issues that need to be addressed. We must be able to assess the capabilities of a rapidly maturing system in a constantly changing and often hidden environment. We need to study how these capacities change, both with time and further experience. We also have to monitor individual traits and states that will modulate the effects of this experience. This is a complex, but by no means novel, set of circumstances for a psychobiological research agenda. Unraveling these complexities will not only further our understanding of fetal behavior, but also may lead to more sensitive clinical measures of fetal well-being.

This chapter is divided into three parts: first, a brief review of the

351

studies in our laboratory describing the effects of fetal experience on later newborn behavior; second, the results of our investigations into cardiorespiratory responses of the newborn to speech sound stimulation; and third, a summary of our findings regarding the fetal response to auditory stimulation.

NEWBORN RESPONSE TO VOICES

Contingent Sucking Responses

Several laboratories have confirmed that newborns and infants will clearly orient to speech sounds and will respond differentially to their own mother's voice. DeCasper and Fifer (1980) showed that newborns less than 3 days of age would change the pattern and timing of their sucking patterns in order to hear recordings of their own mother's voice over other female voices. Contingent sucking paradigms have been subsequently used by DeCasper and his colleagues to study learning capacities in newborns (DeCasper & Carstens, 1981), the effect of prenatal stimulation with specific speech sounds on postnatal behavior (DeCasper & Spence, 1986), and the cognitive processes underlying the discrimination and preferences for sounds experienced in utero (DeCasper & Sigafoos, 1983; DeCasper & Spence, 1991; Spence & DeCasper, 1987). In our laboratory, using contingent sucking as the dependent measure and syllables as discriminative stimuli, a series of experiments was carried out to investigate factors underlying the newborn preference for the maternal voice (Fifer & Moon, 1989; Moon, Cooper & Fifer, 1993; Moon & Fifer, 1990a).

In one study, newborns less than 72 hr of age learned to suck more often to a stimulus paired with mother's voice than to one paired with a period of silence. Briefly, newborns were given a nonnutritive nipple (which was connected to a pressure transducer) to suck on, and were then presented (over headphones) with the following recorded sounds. A 4-sec presentation of "pat–pat–pat" was alternated with the same length recording of "pst–pst–pst." For half of the infants, if they sucked during "pat" the syllable recording would stop and a recording of mother's voice would be presented. The voice would remain on for as long as the sucking burst lasted. When the sucking burst ended, the syllable alternation (in random order) would begin again. If the infant sucked during "pst" a period of silence would occur for the duration of the burst (see Fig. 19.1). Syllable voice pairings were reversed for the other half of the infants. The sessions lasted 18 min. By the final third of the session, infants were sucking significantly more often to the syllables paired with the maternal voice.

These results showed that newborns could discriminate between two

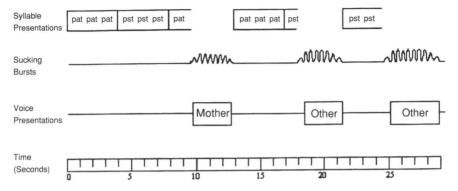

FIG 19.1.   A 30-sec example of a syllable/sucking/voice contingency. A 4-sec presentation of one syllable alternates with a 4-sec presentation of the other syllable until the infant initiates a sucking burst. When this happens, the syllables stop and one of the voices is presented for as long as the sucking burst continues. In this example, /pat/ was the signal for mother, and /pst/ was the signal for other female voice.

syllables, could learn to associate the syllables with either voice or silence in a rapid fashion (less than 18 min) and found mother's voice more reinforcing than periods of silence. A second study used the same syllables as signals, but with other female voices (a different stranger's voice for each infant) versus silence as the reinforcers. Again, the infants learned to suck more often to the signal predicting voices than to periods of silence. This finding served to replicate the results of the first study and showed that female strangers' voices are powerful reinforcers. This result also afforded a more cost-effective procedure to ask more questions regarding specific syllable discrimination capabilities of the newborn, that is, recordings of mother's voice are not required as a reinforcer when discrimination of syllables is being investigated (Moon, Bever, & Fifer, 1992). The final experiment in this series replicated the finding that newborns prefer their own mother's voice. With the same syllable pairs used as signals, newborns learned to suck more often to the signal for the maternal voice than for the signal predicting the stranger's voice (the voice of the previous subject's mother).

Another set of studies was designed to investigate speech cues that underlie the neonatal preference for mother's voice. If this preference is the result of fetal experience with mother's voice, then the newborn's memory and perhaps preference for this "in utero experience" should be strong. Using a procedure similar to that previously described, Moon and Fifer (1990a) presented newborn infants with the choice of hearing their own mother's voice or a filtered version of her voice. By sucking differentially to two different syllable signals (in this case "ah" vs. "ee"), newborns could turn on a recording of their mother's voice engaged in adult-to-adult conversation or the same recording filtered in such a way as to mimic a womblike version. This intrauterine version was lowpass filtered at 1,000 Hz, with "in utero" heartbeat sounds presented in the background. Neonates learned within 18 min to suck more often to the signal paired with the filtered version of the voice. In order to rule out the heart sounds as the salient feature of this recording, the experiment was repeated but with the heartbeat sounds eliminated from the filtered recording. Again, newborns chose to suck more often to the signal predicting the "in utero" or filtered version of their own mother's voice (Moon & Fifer, 1990b).

In another study we addressed the question, what is it about the voices that the perinate is remembering? Moon, Cooper, and Fifer (1993) presented 16 newborns with female voices either conversing in the language that they heard in utero or another language. Eight infants, who were born to monolingual Spanish speakers, were presented with one of several pairs of female voices conversing either in Spanish or in English. Eight infants born to monolingual English speakers were presented with the same recordings. The results showed that newborns responded to the language that they heard in utero. It is possible that this preference may have been partially shaped by postnatal experience during the first hours after birth. However, it is more likely that the newborns were responding to some general property of the native language they heard in utero. That is, the infants may be showing a preference for an intonation pattern characteristic of their mothers' native language.

There are limitations to this contingent sucking method. Infants must be at least 24 hr old and need to maintain an awake state for at least 18 min. This is clearly not possible with all infants, particularly with preterm or at-risk infants. Furthermore, the contingent sucking paradigms is not a viable alternative in investigations of fetal responsiveness. However, cardiorespiratory reactivity provides a rich source of psychophysiological correlates of attention and information processing.

Cardiorespiratory Responses

Heart rate change has been used extensively as a measure of attention in infants. However, there have been very few reports of decelerative changes in heart rate to auditory stimulation, that is, a pattern typically associated with the so-called "orienting" response (Berg & Berg, 1987). A change in respiration following stimulation, another component of an attentional response, has been largely ignored in studies of newborn attention. Furthermore, the response of the infant has yet to be systematically investigated during sleep—a state in which the newborn infant spends much of his or her time, and a time in which sensory system development may be strongly affected by external input. We have investigated neonatal heart rate and respiratory changes to speech sound stimulation during quiet sleep.

Healthy, vaginally delivered, full-term newborns between 24 and 48 hr old born at Columbia Presbyterian Babies Hospital served as subjects. Heart rate and respiration signals were collected via electrodes placed on the baby's chest. Digitized speech sounds were presented through a speaker placed 10 cm above the infant's head. The speech stimulus consisted of alternations of the synthesized vowel sounds "ah" and "ee." During stimulus trials, the vowel sounds were presented for 10-sec periods at 65 dB. During sham trials, no sounds were presented. There was a variable intertrial interval of at least 20 sec.

Data collection began after the infant had spent at least 3 min in quiet sleep, as defined by absence of rapid eye movements (REMs) and body movements, and regular respiration. A baseline period of 30 sec was followed by 10 stimuli and 10 sham trials presented in a pseudo-random order. Two experimenters were present throughout the session. One monitored the baby's state and code-recorded any body movements, REMs, and so forth. The other controlled the voice presentation. The testing session lasted approximately 15 min. For the purposes of analyzing respiration responses to the speech stimuli, the interval between breaths was computed for the 10-sec period prior to stimulus presentation, the 10 sec during the stimulus or sham, and the 10 sec postpresentation. These periods are referred to as baseline, stimulus, and post. The onset response is computed by subtracting the mean breath-to-breath interval during the stimulus period from that of the baseline period, and the offset response was defined as the post minus the stimulus periods.

There was a significant offset response reflected in a change in breath-to-breath intervals during the speech stimuli (see Fig. 19.2). Nine of the 10 infants decreased their time between breaths when the speech stimulus terminated. In other words, infants had a higher respiration rate during the 10 sec after termination of the stimulus. There was no significant onset response in respiration. No significant differences were found for sham onset or offset responses.

The heart rate change was analyzed after averaging heart rate in 5-sec epochs beginning 5 sec before each stimulus until 5 sec after stimulus offset. The onset response was computed by subtracting the average heart rate during the first 5-sec stimulus epoch from the 5-sec baseline epoch. The offset response was defined as the 5-sec epoch poststimulus minus the final 5-sec epoch during stimulus presentation.

There was a significant onset response to the speech stimuli. Nine of the 10 infants had a decrease in heart rate during the first 5 sec of stimulus presentation, although the heart rate change was less than 1 beat per minute (bpm) when averaged across trials (see Fig. 19.3). No significant differences were found for either the offset response or the sham trials. There were no trial effects for either the respiration or the heart rate responses.

We concluded that newborn infants show a reliable cardiorespiratory change to speech sound stimulation. It has been suggested that heart rate accelerations are a component of a defensive response, whereas heart rate decelerations are indicative of an orienting or attentional response (Clarkson & Berg, 1983; Graham, Anthony, & Zeigler, 1983; Pomerleau-Malcuit & Clifton, 1973). Whether this response qualifies as a "true" orienting response is arguable, given both the small magnitude of the response and the fact that it occurred during sleep. Regardless of designation, this attentional response, manifested by a change in heart rate, can be used to more systematically explore the effects of sensory input during sleep. Sensory stimulation during this period of development is having a significant sculpting effect on the developing brain (Leon, 1992: Rubel, 1985), and the perinate spends most of this time asleep. Recent electro-physiological evidence has confirmed that speech sounds presented to newborns will elicit auditory evoked potentials during sleep (Kurtzberg, Stapells, & Wallace, 1988). In fact, long latency evoked responses in young infants are enhanced in the associative auditory cortex during quiet sleep

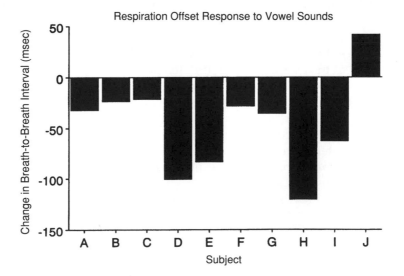

FIG. 19.2.   Respiration offset response to vowel sounds. The change in breath-to-breath interval is presented in milliseconds. A negative score indicates a decrease in breath-to-breath interval following stimulus offset. Therefore, 9 of the 10 infants increased their breathing rate when the stimulus was turned off.

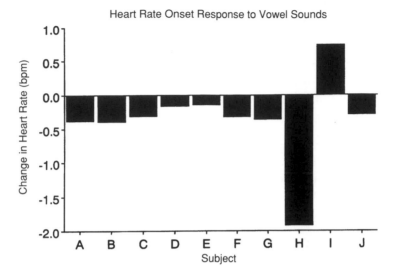

FIG. 19.3.   Heart rate onset response to vowel sounds. The change in infant heart rate during stimulation is presented in beats per minute. A negative score indicates a decrease in the heart rate from baseline. Nine of the 10 infants showed a lower heart rate during the first 5 sec of the stimulus.

(Duclaux, Challamel, Collet, Roullet-Solignac, & Revoli, 1991), and a functional hemispheric asymmetry in this temporal speech area may already exist in the fetus (Chi, Dooling, & Gilles, 1977).

FETAL RESPONSE TO SOUND

Heart Rate Change to Syllables

Fetal response to sound and vibratory stimuli has been studied for many years (see Abrams, Gerhardt, & Peters, chapter 17; Gagnon, chapter 8; Leader, chapter 21; Hepper, chapter 22; Kisilvsky, chapter 14; and Lecanuet, Granier-Deferre, & Bushnel, chapter 13, this volume). Historically, the research on fetal response to sound has focused on investigating the response to high-intensity stimulation, that is, the vibroacoustic stimulation used in clinical tests of fetal reactivity. Depending on the intensity, duration, and state in which the stimulus is presented (see Gagnon, chapter 8; Leader, chapter 21; and Kisilevsky, chapter 14; this volume), the response appears to range from transient heart rate changes that rapidly habituate, to prolonged alterations in state changes and bladder emptying (Zimmer, Chao, Guy, Marks, & Fifer, 1993; Divon et al., 1985). However, response to a more naturally occurring source of stimulation, voices, has only recently received attention. Lecanuet has reported that in the term fetus, sound stimuli of low intensity and low frequency evoke a decelerative heart rate response (Lecanuet, Granier-Deferre, & Busnel, 1989). These observations are consistent with studies of infants where the direction of heart rate change was dependent on the type of sound stimulus (Berg & Berg, 1987). Loud sounds were typically associated with heart rate accelerations, whereas low-intensity stimuli induced mainly heart rate decelerations.

External sounds, including speech sounds, are minimally masked by background uterine noise and are transmitted in utero with relatively little attenuation (see Abrams, Gerhardt, & Peters, chapter 17, this volume). Morphological and anatomical studies of the human cochlea, as well as studies of auditory brainstem evoked potentials, have shown that the fetus is capable of responding to sound as early as 25–26 weeks gestation (Birnholz & Benacerraf, 1983; Pujol, Lavigne-Rebillard, & Uziel, 1990). In addition, premature infants show reliable auditory evoked responses to speech sound stimuli (Kurtzberg, Hilpert, Kreuzer, & Vaughan, 1984). The aim of our study was to evaluate the heart rate responses to speech stimuli in the premature fetus at 26–34 weeks gestation (Zimmer, Fifer, Kim, Rey, Chao, & Myers, 1993).

Forty-one healthy women with normal singleton pregnancies at 26–34 weeks gestation were enrolled in the study. All subjects were healthy at delivery. Tests were performed in a quiet room with mothers leaning backward in a half-sitting position. Mothers did not wear headphones, and therefore were also aware of the sound stimuli. Stimuli were synthesized male voices used in the newborn study (Fifer & Moon, 1989), repeated pairs of "ee" alternating with "ah" and played at either 100, 105, or 110 dB. These sounds have been shown to be clearly transmitted in utero (Querleu, Renard, Boutteville, & Crepin, 1989). The speaker was located 1 cm above the maternal abdomen, over the fetal head.

The stimuli were delivered during periods of either low (<6 bpm amplitude range) or high (>6 bpm amplitude range) fetal heart rate variability. Ten fetuses received stimulation in both heart rate variability states. Stimulation was not performed during periods of fetal movements. Each fetus received between 5–15 stimulations, during both high- and low-variability states if possible, depending on the quality of heart rate signal acquisition and the amount of fetal movement. Presentations of the stimuli were at least 1 min apart. In cases with prolonged fetal movements or loss of the fetal heart rate signal, the intertrial interval could last several minutes.

The analog output from the fetal heart rate monitor was digitized at 10 samples per second, data were excluded if they differed by more than 8 bpm from the previous data point, and trials were rejected if the percent-

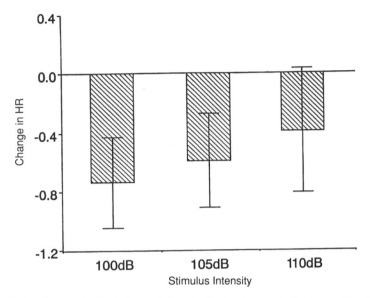

FIG. 19.4.   Average (±SEM) change in heart rate (bpm) from the last 5 sec of baseline to the 5 sec of the stimulus period at each intensity level (Zimmer, Fifer, Kim, Rey, Chao, & Myers, 1993). Adapted by permission.

age of heart rate artifact within any 5-sec period exceeded 15%. The mean and standard deviation (SD) of the accepted values were computed in 5-sec epochs beginning 20 sec before each stimulus and ending 5 sec after the offset of the stimulus. Repeated measures analysis of variance was used to test for heart rate changes between consecutive 5-sec epochs. Prior to these analyses, heart rates for each fetus were averaged across trials for periods of both high and low variability.

Changes in fetal heart rate (FHR) from the 5 sec of baseline to the 5 sec of stimulation are presented in Fig. 19.4. For the 20 subjects recorded during periods of low heart rate variability, there was, overall, a significant decrease in heart rate across trials, $p = .011$. The interaction between changes in heart rate and intensity level of the stimulus was not significant. There was a decrease in heart rate in 15 fetuses and an increase in 5 fetuses. There were no significant changes in FHR across control epochs. No significant changes were observed in heart rate from stimulation to the poststimulus period. For the subjects recorded during high heart rate variability, there were no significant changes in heart rate to either sound stimulation or its termination, that is, stimulus offset.

The standard deviation (SD) of heart rate increased from baseline during the stimulus in the low-variability state for both intensity levels of the stimulus (see Fig. 19.5). No changes in SD were found during the control periods. There was a significant decrease in SD, returning to approximately baseline levels during the poststimulus period (see Fig. 17.6). There was no difference in this pattern of response as a function of intensity of stimulus. For presentations during periods of high variability, there was a marginally significant increase in SD during stimulation and no change to stimulus offset.

We concluded that the preterm fetus (26–34 weeks gestation) is capable of responding to speech stimuli. There was a significant decrease in FHR with sound stimulation during periods of low variability, and no significant change during periods of high heart rate variability. In addition, in the periods of low variability there was a significant increase in the SD of FHR during stimulation, and a significant decrease in response to stimulus offset. No such changes were seen across control periods. During periods of high variability there was a trend toward an increase SD of FHR during stimulation, but no changes in FHR. In summary, during periods with low-variability heart rate patterns, the defining condition for the fetal equivalent of quiet sleep (Nijhuis, 1986), significant changes in the cardiovascular response to auditory stimuli were observed in preterm fetuses. These results are in agreement with Lecanuet et al. (1989), and may indicate a state-dependent sensory response.

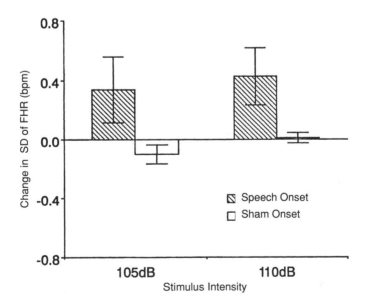

FIG. 19.5. The cross-hatched bars show the average (±SEM) change in standard deviation from the last 5 sec of baseline to the 5 sec of the stimulus period at both 105 and 110 dB. Open bars show the same changes for control epochs.

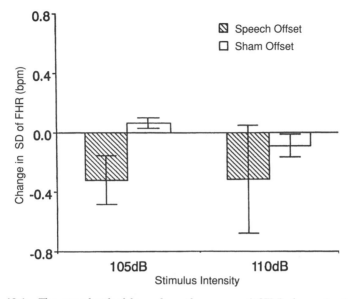

FIG. 19.6.   The cross-hatched bars show the average (±SEM) change in standard deviation for the experimental epochs (i.e., first 5 sec after stimulus offset minus the 5 sec of the stimulus period) at both 105 dB and 110 dB. Open bars show the same changes for control epochs (i.e., the third 5-sec period of the baseline minus the second 5 sec period of baseline).

Heart Rate Change to Mother's Voice

There is an extensive literature describing fetal heart rate changes to external sources of auditory stimulation (see Lecanuet, Granier-Deferre, 7 Busnel, chapter 13, this volume). We investigated whether the mother's naturally occurring speech would elicit a fetal attentional response. That is, when the mother is actually speaking, does the fetus respond with a change in heart rate?

Forty-five healthy women with normal singleton pregnancies at 36–40 weeks gestation participated in this study at Columbia Presbyterian Medical Center. Heart rate data was collected using a commercial fetal heart rate monitor. The analog output from this monitor was digitized and stored on a computer that also recorded onset and offset of stimuli.

In the first condition, mothers repeated a 10-sec rehearsed phrase of adult-directed speech, at least six times. These trials were alternated randomly with "sham trials" consisting of 10 sec of silence. In a second condition, mothers were asked to repeat a 10-sec rehearsed phrase of adult-directed speech at least five times. These trials were alternated randomly with "whisper trials" in which mothers whispered the same phrases.

In both experiments, data were collected in fetal state 1F (Nijhuis, 1986), the fetal analog to quiet sleep. This state is characterized by the relative absence of body movements and beat-to-beat heart rate changes of less than 6 bpm. Mothers were cued to speak at the beginning and end of each trial. The intertrial interval was a minimum of 30 sec.

In condition 1, artifact-free data were collected from 10 near-term fetuses and analyzed. Fetal heart rate was averaged across 5-sec epochs. Fetuses showed a significant heart rate decrease from baseline during the last 5 sec of the periods in which mothers were speaking (Fig. 19.7). No heart rate change was observed during the sham trials.

In condition 2, data from 15 near-term fetuses were analyzed as just described. Fetuses showed a significant heart rate decrease from baseline during the last 5 sec of the periods in which mothers were speaking (Fig. 19.8). There were no significant changes in heart rate during the whisper trials.

We concluded that in both experiments, fetuses consistently responded with a heart rate decrease during maternal speech. During periods of whispering, in which fetuses received similar vestibular and tactile stimulation from maternal breathing movements, no response was detected. These data provide evidence for a fetal heart rate change to a salient, naturally occurring stimulus during quiet sleep. We believe this early experience is shaping the developing auditory system and later newborn perceptual preferences.

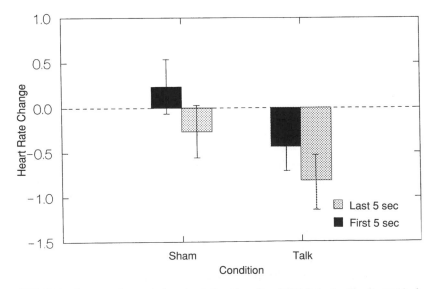

FIG 19.7.   Average change in heart rate from baseline (±SEM) during the first 5 (dark bars) and last 5 sec of stimulation (light bars) for both talk and sham trials.

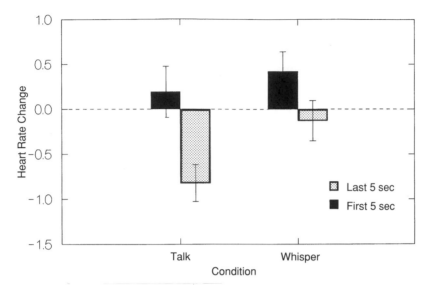

FIG. 19.8.   Average change in heart rate from baseline (±SEM) during the first 5 (dark bars) and last 5 sec of stimulation (light bars) for both talk and whisper trials.

In our current series of studies we are investigating the state-dependent effect of naturally occurring voice stimulation on both heart rate and breathing activity in the fetus (Masakowski & Fifer, 1994). The cardiorespiratory response may prove to be a particularly effective psychophysiological measure for understanding the effect of voice on the developing fetus.

DISCUSSION

The investigation of the perinatal response to maternal voice may serve as a model for how very early experience shapes the developing brain and behavior of the fetus. The mother's voice is a naturally occurring and salient stimulus during a critical time period in which there is significant development in virtually all areas of the brain. There appear to be immediate as well as enduring effects of this stimulation. Consequently, the response to voice may offer a unique probe for studying behavioral, cognitive, and autonomic capacities from the fetal through the newborn period.

Several key issues remain to be more fully addressed in the future. We believe the role of sleep state in modulating the immediate and enduring effects of sensory stimulation is a particularly important area for further inquiry. The impression left by a data-poor literature is that the perinate often uses sleep to "tune out" stimulation. The implication, using an adult model of sensory thresholds during sleep, is that the effects of most sensory stimulation on the central nervous system are minimal. The data presented in this chapter, and elsewhere in this volume, argue strongly for more creative and systematic research into the sleep-dependent effects of stimulation on the brain and behavior of the developing fetus.

Another important area for future research is the development of the autonomic nervous system (ANS) and its capacity to respond to environmental stimulation. Improved technology now enables more accurate and noninvasive collection of fetal respiration and heart rate for psychophysiological research. However, little is known either about the capacity of the system to respond at different points in time, or about how the topography of the autonomic response changes as the underlying physiological systems develop. Specifically, when can the fetal ANS first respond to a sound? When will the system differentially respond, for example, to a voice versus a loud noise? Will the response difference be in amplitude, direction, duration, or latency? How will the state-dependent nature of the autonomic response evolve during this period as the organization and nature of sleep are also changing?

A final research issue warranting future attention centers on the application of fetal behavioral research to understanding the "unnatural" experience with sound and voices encountered by the fetal newborn—the premature infant. First, does the deprivation of in utero stimulation and premature experience with extraordinary sensory input of the neonatal intensive care unit (NICU) directly lead to unique long-term deficits? How does the severely premature infant respond to voice and sound in different sleep states and at different conceptional and postnatal ages? The response to voice and sound may offer a more sensitive probe of premature infant well-being and, ultimately, aid in the design of the optimal ex utero environment of the fetal newborn.

ACKNOWLEDGMENTS

This research has been supported by National Institutes of Health grants HD13063, HD22817, and HD20102. The authors also thank Manveet Saluja and Theresa Jinks for their help in preparing the manuscript.

REFERENCES

Berg, W. K., & Berg, K. M. (1987). Psychophysiological development in infancy: State, startle, and attention. In J. Osofsky (Ed.), *Handbook of infant development* (2nd ed., pp. 238–317). New York: Wiley.

Birnholz, J. C., & Benacerraf, B. R. (1983). The development of human fetal hearing. *Science, 222,* 516–518.

Chi, J. G., Dooling, E. C., & Gilles, F. H. (1977). Left-right asymmetries of the temporal speech area of the human fetus. *Archives of Neurology, 34,* 346–348.

Clarkson, M. G., & Berg, W. K. (1983). Cardiac orienting and vowel discrimination in newborns: Crucial stimulus parameters. *Child Development, 54,* 162–171.

DeCasper, A. J., & Carstens, A. A. (1981). Contingencies of stimulation: Effects on learning and emotion in neonates. *Infant Behavior and Development, 4,* 19–35.

DeCasper, A. J., & Fifer, W. P. (1980). Of human bonding: Newborns prefer their mothers' voices. *Science, 208,* 1174–1176.

DeCasper, A. J., & Sigafoos, A. D. (1983). The intrauterine heartbeat: A potent reinforcer for newborns. *Infant Behavior and Development, 6,* 19–25.

DeCasper, A. J., & Spence, M. J. (1986). Prenatal maternal speech influences newborns' perception of speech sounds. *Infant Behavior and Development, 9,* 133–150.

DeCasper, A. J., & Spence, M. J. (1991). Auditorily mediated behavior during the perinatal period: A cognitive view. In M. J. Salomon Weiss & P. R. Zelazo (Eds.), *Newborn attention: Biological constraints and the influence of experience* (pp. 142–176). Norwood, NJ: Ablex.

Divon, M. Y., Platt, L. D., Cantrell, C. J., Smith, C. V., Yeh, S. Y. Y., & Paul, R. H. (1985). Evoked fetal startle response: A possible intrauterine neurological examination. *American Journal of Obstetrics and Gynecology, 153,* 454–456.

Duclaux, R., Challamel, M. J., Collet, L., Roullet-Solignac, I., & Revoli, M. (1991). Hemispheric asymmetry of late auditory evoked response induced by pitch changes in infants: Influence of sleep stages. *Brain Research, 566,* 152–158.

Fifer, W. P., & Moon, C. (1989). Psychobiology of newborn auditory preferences. *Seminars in Perinatology, 13(5),* 430–433.

Graham, F. K., Anthony, B. J., & Zeigler, B. L. (1983). The orienting response and developmental processes. In D. Siddle (Ed.), *Orienting and habituation: Perspectives in human research* (pp. 371–430). UK: Wiley, Sussex.

Kurtzberg, D., Hilpert, P. L., Kreuzer, J. A., & Vaughan, H. G., Jr. (1984). Differential maturation of cortical auditory evoked potentials to speech sounds in normal fullterm and very low-birthweight infants. *Developmental Medicine and Child Neurology, 26,* 466–475.

Kurtzberg, D., Stapells, D. R., & Wallace, I. F. (1988). Event related potential assessment of auditory system integrity: Implications for language development. In P. M. Vietz & H. G. Vaughan (Eds.), *Early identification of infants with developmental disability* (pp. 160–180). Philadelphia: Grune and Stratton.

Lecanuet, J., Granier-Deferre, C., & Busnel, M. (1989). Differential fetal auuditory reactiveness as a function of stimulus characteristics and state. *Seminars in Perinatology, 13(5),* 421–429.

Leon, M. (1992). The neurobiology of filial learning. *Annual Review of Psychology, 43,* 377–98.

Masakowski, Y., & Fifer, W. P. (1994, June). *The effects of maternal speech on fetal behavior.* Presented at the International Conference on Infant Studies, Paris.

Moon, C., Bever, T. G., & Fifer, W. P. (1992). Canonical and non-canonical syllable discrimination by two-day-old infants. *Journal of Child Language, 19,* 1–17.

Moon, C., Cooper, R. P., & Fifer, W. P. (1993). Two-day-olds prefer their native language. *Infant Behavior and Development, 16(4),* 495–500.

Moon, C., & Fifer, W. (1990a). Syllables as signals for 2-day-old infants. *Infant Behavior and Development, 13,* 377–390.

Moon, C., & Fifer, W. P. (1990b, April). *Newborns prefer a prenatal version of mother's voice.* Presented at biannual meeting of International Society of Infant Studies, Montreal.

Nijhuis, J. G. (1986). Behavioural states: Concomitants, clinical implications and the assessment of the condition of the nervous system. *European Journal of Obstetrics and Gynecology and Reproductive Biology, 21,* 301–308.

Pomerleau-Malcuit, A., & Clifton, R. K. (1973). Neonatal heart-rate response to tactile, auditory, and vestibular stimulation in different states. *Child Development, 44,* 485–496.

Pujol, R., Lavigne-Rebillard, M., & Uziel, A. (1990). Physiological correlates of development of human cochlea. *Seminars in Perinatology, 14,* 275–280.

Querleu, D., Renard, X., Boutteville, C., & Crepin, G. (1989). Hearing by the human fetus? *Seminars in Perinatology, 13(5),* 409–420.

Rubel, E. W. (1985). Auditory system development. In N. A. Krasnegor & G. Gottlieb (Eds.), *Measurement of audition and vision in the first year of postnatal life* (pp. 53–86). Norwood, NJ: Ablex.

Spence, M. J., & DeCasper, A. J. (1987). Prenatal experience with low-frequency maternal-voice sounds influences neonatal perception of maternal voice samples. *Infant Behavior and Development, 16,* 133–142.

Zimmer, E. Z., Chao, C. R., Guy, G. P., Marks, F., & Fifer, W. P. (1993). Vibroacoustic stimulation evokes human fetal micturition. *Obstetrics and Gynecology, 81(2),* 178–180.

Zimmer, E. Z., Fifer, W. P., Kim, Y., Rey, H. R., Chao, C. R., & Myers, M. M. (1993). Response of the premature fetus to stimulation by speech sounds. *Early Human Development, 33,* 207–215.

Part VI

CLINICAL EVALUATION OF
PERINATAL EXPERIENCE

20

The Effects of Myometrial Activity During the Last Third of Gestation on Fetal Behavior

Peter W. Nathanielsz
Cornell University

During development the fetus is exposed to two major categories of influence. First there is the set of genetic instructions encoded in the nucleus. This program for development, collectively called *nature*, is then modified by the effects of surrounding environmental influences on the embryo and the fetus. Collectively these environmental influences are called *nurture*. In the last 15 years, it has become clear that one major aspect of the environment that influences fetal behavioral development is the level and pattern of contractility of the myometrium. This influence has been most extensively investigated in late gestation, and this review covers investigations conducted in the last third of pregnancy. Myometrial activity does affect uterine blood flow, and it is likely that there may be effects of myometrial activity on the developing embryo and early fetus. The potential effects of myometrial activity on the fetus during these early periods of development have not been studied. The metabolic demands of the early embryo and early fetus are not as great as those of the late, near-term fetus, and therefore, small changes in oxygen and nutrient delivery may not exert as major effects on fetal development in early pregnancy as they have the potential to exert in late pregnancy. Firm information on the possible effect of myometrial activity in early pregnancy awaits appropriately designed experiments. The purpose of this chapter is to review the effects of myometrial activity on fetal neurophysiological, neuroendocrinological, and behavioral development during the last third of pregnancy.

CHARACTERISTICS OF MYOMETRIAL ACTIVITY THROUGHOUT PREGNANCY

In all species studied to date, the myometrium is active throughout pregnancy. Studies of myometrial activity in pregnant sheep (Jansen et al., 1979), monkeys (Taylor, Martin, Nathanielsz, & Seron-Ferre, 1983), baboons (Morgan et al., 1992), pigs (Taverne, 1982), dogs (van der Weyden et al., 1989), and many other species throughout pregnancy utilizing electromyographic (EMG) and intraamniotic pressure (IAP) measurements have demonstrated the occurrence of regular epochs of activity lasting more than 3 min and generating only small changes in IAP. These epochs of activity, *contractures*, are clearly differentiated from the short (lasting less than 1 min) and efficient (generating greater changes in IAP) contractions of labor and delivery. In sheep contractures occur at roughly 40-min intervals, whereas in nonhuman primates they appear to occur slightly more frequently. Contracture activity can easily be distinguished from contraction activity by the application of power spectral analysis to either myometrial EMG or IAP recordings as shown in Fig. 20.1. Figure 20.1 demonstrates the power spectra of contracture activity and contraction activity in pregnant sheep. Similar patterns are demonstrated in both the rhesus monkey (Hsu, Figueroa, Honnebier, Wentworth, & Nathanielsz, 1989) and baboon (Morgan et al., 1992).

Effects of Myometrial Activity on Fetal Brain Growth and Development

Throughout this review data presented apply to the sheep unless otherwise stated. The developing sheep brain shows two major rapid phases of growth of brain tissue. The first, due to multiplication of neural cells, occurs at 40–80 days gestation. The second, at around 100–140 days gestation, is due predominantly to multiplication of glial cells and subsequently myelination (McIntosh, Baghurst, Potter, & Hetzel, 1979). The developmental mechanisms discussed in this chapter relate to the second period of growth and development. During this period, synaptogenesis is occurring and important neuronal interconnections are being established. Experimental studies have shown that electrical activity within neuronal networks will alter the organization of neuronal networks (Nelson, Yu, Fields, & Neale, 1989). Thus, altered afferent input into the developing brain may well play an important role in maturation of brain structure and function.

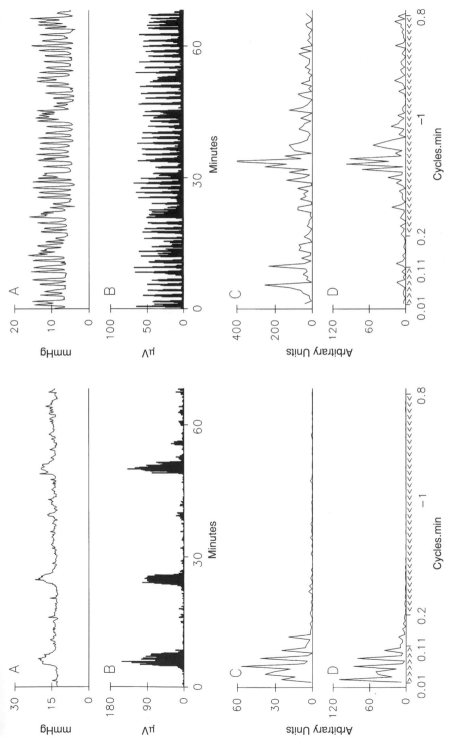

FIG. 20.1. Power spectral analysis of (left) contracture activity and (right) contraction activity in a pregnant sheep: (A) intrauterine pressure recording, (B) myometrial electromyogram, (C) power spectral analysis of intrauterine pressure recording, and (D) power spectral analysis of electromyogram.

As we demonstrate, myometrial activity does indeed alter such input to the developing brain.

Effects of Hormones on Fetal Brain Growth and Development

Many endocrine, paracrine, and autocrine factors influence the development of the brain. Myometrial activity has been shown to alter secretion of some of these regulating factors. This change in fetal endocrine function produced as a result of myometrial activity may be both a cause and an effect of fetal brain maturation. The effects of glucocorticoids on protein synthesis, cell growth, and mitosis have been extensively examined in vitro and in vivo. Rat pups to which corticosterone has been administered at birth demonstrate a transient inhibition of dendritic formation within the cerebral cortex and decreases in the lateral length of the dendritic tree (Schapiro, 1968). In addition, cortisol induces enzymes that are of considerable importance in both myelin formation, such as glial-specific alpha-glycerol phosphate (De Vellis & Inglish, 1968) and tryptophan hydrolase (Azmita & McEwen, 1969). Thyroid hormones also play an important role in maturing the fetal brain (Pelt, 1972). Thus, any effect of myometrial activity on the release of these hormones may alter fetal brain development permanently. It is particularly important to remember that there are critical periods in brain development that must occur for normal activity and development to proceed. Thus, if newborn rats are handled daily it appears that later in life they have improved abilities in novel environments (Levine, 1970).

EFFECT OF MYOMETRIAL ACTIVITY ON FETAL OXYGENATION

Contractures of the uterus are accompanied by a fall in fetal PO_2 (Jansen et al., 1979), which probably results from a decrease in uterine and umbilical blood flow. Similar changes in fetal oxygenation are obtained when contractures are induced artificially by the administration of oxytocin to the pregnant ewe (Woudstra, Kim, Aarnoudse, & Nathanielsz, 1991). This change in fetal oxygenation is accompanied by altered fetal behavioral state as reflected by fetal electrocorticogram and fetal breathing movements. At the present time it is uncertain whether these 15%–30% decreases in fetal blood oxygen content are reflected by a decrease in cerebral oxygen consumption. However, the changes in neuronal function observed during contractures may well represent a compensatory response to the decreased oxygen availability. Experiments in which fetal arterial

PO_2 has been decreased in the absence of contractures clearly show that the fetus can sense small changes in PO_2 and respond appropriately by modifying its behavioral activity and endocrine secretion.

SENSORY STIMULATION OF THE FETUS BY CONTRACTURES

In late pregnancy there is insufficient amniotic fluid to completely surround the fetus. This can be clearly seen by examination of the fetus in the uterus with either ultrasound or nuclear magnetic resonance techniques (Kay & Mattison, 1986). The relative decrease in the amount of amniotic fluid in relation to fetal surface area results in the fetus being in contact with uterine wall at several locations. This contact between the fetus and the uterine wall can easily be seen at laparotomy in late pregnancy. Upon opening the abdomen of the pregnant animal or woman in late pregnancy, the outline of various fetal body parts can be seen through the uterine wall. This could only occur if these parts of the body are in contact with the uterine wall. As a result of this contact, when the uterus contracts in late gestation the fetus is squeezed (Nathanielsz, Bailey, Poore, Thorburn, & Harding, 1980). The degree of this squeeze varies with the intensity and the exact location of each individual contracture. Recordings in pregnant sheep in which a multiple array of electrodes has been placed around the uterus clearly show that during a contracture the majority, but not all, of the uterine wall is active (Harding et al., 1982). Thus the direct influence of each individual contracture on the fetus will be determined by several factors. The most important of these is the exact portions of the fetus that are in contact with the uterus as the fetus moves within the uterine cavity, the amount of amniotic fluid in relation to uterine and fetal volume, and the exact location of the areas of the uterus that are contracted and the areas of the uterus that are relaxed.

Very sensitive measurements of fetal dimensions can be made by the placement of transit-time ultrasound crystals across various fetal dimensions (Nathanielsz et al., 1980). Using this technique we have shown (Fig. 20.2) that during a contracture the chest wall diameters of the fetal sheep decrease by up to 30% (Nathanielsz et al., 1980). In addition, due to the squeeze exerted by the myometrium, the pressure rises within various compartments of the fetus. This has been determined by recording intracranial pressure and intrathoracic pressure (Walker & Harding, 1986).

Behavioral state is generally evaluated in fetal sheep by recording fetal electrocorticogram (ECOG), fetal electrooculogram (EOG), and fetal skeletal muscle activity, in particular fetal nuchal muscle activity. The evaluation of fetal ECOG has, until recently, in general been made only in relation

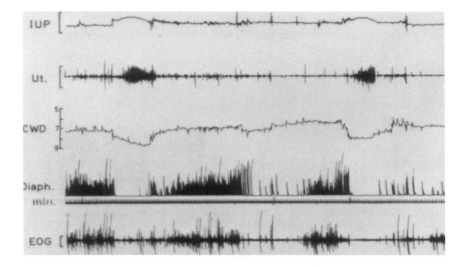

FIG. 20.2.   Relationship of intrauterine pressure (IUP), uterine EMG (Ut.), and chest wall diameter (CWD) with diaphragmatic EMG (Diaph.) and EOG at 137 days gestational age. CWD is distance, in centimeters, between bilaterally placed transducers in the midaxillary line at the level of the seventh intercostal space. From Nathanielsz et al. (1980). Reprinted by permission.

to changes in the amplitude of ECOG, which has been divided into low voltage (LV) and high voltage (HV). Newer techniques are now being introduced to look at the waveform spectrum of the ECOG. Until these more sophisticated methods have been placed on a firmer basis it is probably wise to avoid such terms as *quiet sleep* and the *awake state* in fetal sheep. However, the occurrence of rapid eye movements during some of the low voltage activity does enable the investigator to determine some periods of activity as rapid eye movement sleep (REM) when characteristic REM EOG patterns exist. However, it should be noted that LV ECOG activity does occur in the absence of REM. To obtain a complete picture of fetal behavioral variability and the transitions between various states, it will be necessary to evaluate the exact spectral analysis of different types of LV activity and associate the various spectra with other variables such as skeletal muscle activity. In the last 30 days of fetal life, contractures are associated with a switch from LV to HV ECOG and a cessation of fetal breathing movements (Nathanielsz et al., 1980). Late in gestation 60% of contractures are associated with changes in fetal breathing movements. Over 90% of the changes involve a cessation of fetal breathing movements. Raising fetal intracranial pressure will produce changes in fetal behavior similar to those observed during a contracture (Lye, Wlodek, & Challis, 1985).

EFFECTS OF CONTRACTURES ON FETAL
PITUITARY ADRENAL FUNCTION

Oxytocin administered as a single intravenous bolus to the pregnant ewe produces a contracture that is accompanied by a decrease in fetal arterial PO_2 and a rise in fetal plasma adrenocorticotropin (ACTH; Woudstra et al., 1991; Lye et al., 1985). In order to determine the respective roles played by the fall in fetal PO_2 and the potential stimulation of the fetus as a result of being squeezed during oxytocin-induced contractures, studies have been conducted in which oxytocin has been administered to the ewe to induce a contracture while at the same time preventing the fall in fetal PO_2 by the administration of oxygen to the ewe via a tracheal tube. In this situation there was no rise in fetal ACTH during oxytocin-induced contractures (Woudstra et al., 1991; Fig. 20.3). The conclusion from this study is that the fall in fetal PO_2 is a necessary component of the input to the fetal brain that results in the change of activity of the fetal pituitary adrenal axis. However, it is not possible to conclude that the sensory stimulation to the fetus

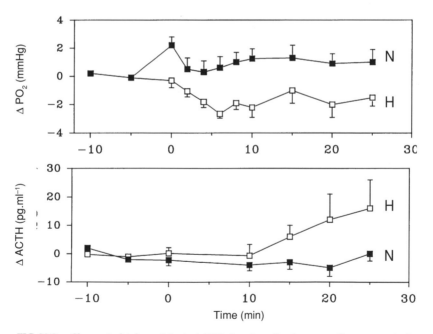

FIG. 20.3.   Change in fetal carotid arterial PO_2 from baseline (average of two preoxytocin injection values) and change in fetal carotid arterial ACTH before and after 70 mU oxytocin administration to the maternal jugular vein at time 0 over 5 sec, when oxygen was administered to the ewe via a tracheal catheter to maintain fetal oxygen (N, ■) and when no oxygen was administered (H, ▫).

as a result of the squeeze produced by the contracture is unimportant. The sensory stimulation may be necessary but insufficient to stimulate the pituitary adrenal axis. Further studies are required to elucidate the interaction of the fall in fetal PO_2 with the sensory stimulation of the fetus as a result of this squeeze produced by the contracture. The fact that increased intracranial pressure alone can alter fetal behavioral state is shown by the studies of Walker and Harding, who demonstrated that a rise in intracranial pressure produced by infusion of small amounts of saline into the extradural space produced a decrease in fetal breathing and switch from LV to HV ECOG in fetal sheep (Walker & Harding, 1986). The techniques used by these investigators would also have produced areas of ischemia of the fetal cerebral cortex, which may have constituted a hypoxic stimulus. It will therefore be of interest to observe the effects of contractures unaccompanied by a change in fetal oxygenation on fetal behavioral variables. To date no study such as that described to separate the effects of hypoxemia and physical stimulation on fetal adrenal function has been performed in relation to fetal behavior.

EFFECTS OF LONG-TERM ALTERATION OF MYOMETRIAL ACTIVITY ON FETAL BEHAVIORAL DEVELOPMENT

In order to investigate the possibility that alteration of myometrial activity at critical periods of development may affect the structural and functional development of the brain, Sadowsky and co-workers have conducted studies on the effects of increasing contracture activity for several days (Sadowsky, Martel, Jenkins, Poore, Cabalum, & Nathanielsz, 1992; Sadowsky, Martel, Cabalum, Poore, & Nathanielsz, 1992). Unfortunately, at present, no experimental techniques exist that enable us to abolish contractures completely. The prostaglandin synthase inhibitor indomethacin does have a powerful effect in reducing contracture myometrial activity. However, indomethacin will cross the placenta and markedly modify fetal prostaglandin production. Changes in fetal prostaglandin production have been shown to have direct effects on fetal brain function as reflected by fetal breathing (Wallen et al., 1986). For this reason, experiments to date have been limited to observing effects of increased contracture activity on fetal brain and behavioral development.

Now that it has been established that individual contractures are accompanied by changes in fetal behavioral state, it is necessary to ask the question, Does long-term alteration of contracture patterns also alter the development of fetal pituitary adrenal function? Sadowsky et al. studied long-term effects of pulsing the pregnant ewe with oxytocin for 5 min every 30 min for 6 days to determine the effect the increased contracture frequency produced on fetal adrenal function and fetal ECOG. Control ewes received pulses of saline. These studies were conducted beginning at 127.8 ± 1.5 days gestational age (dGA). At this stage of development the fetal ECOG is showing several features of maturation. The most marked feature is the increased amplitude of HV ECOG (Figs. 20.4–20.6). The amplitude of fetal HV ECOG increased in both groups, but the rate of increase was faster in the fetuses of ewes receiving oxytocin (Fig. 20.7) (Sadowsky, Martel, Cabalum, Poore, & Nathanielsz, 1992). There were no differences in the amounts of time the fetus spent in HV or LV when the two groups of fetuses were compared. Spectral analysis was not used to subdivide different types of HV or LV. Figure 20.7 demonstrates that increased contracture activity is associated with a increase in the rate at which the amplitude of HV ECOG activity increases. The interpretation of this finding is that increased contracture activity modifies the density of synaptic and dendritic formation within the cerebral cortex. Whether this altered structural development will affect long-term fetal brain function remains to be determined.

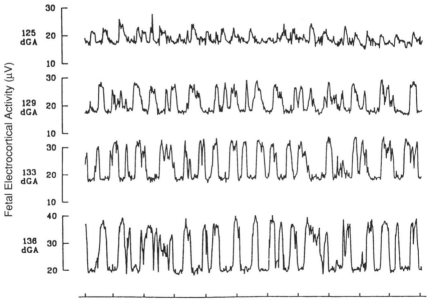

Time in Hours

FIG. 20.4.   Maturation of the fetal electrocorticogram of one control animal between 125 and 136 days gestational age showing the normal development of high-voltage and low-voltage electrocorticogram epochs with increasing gestational age. From Sadowsky, Martel, Jenkins, Poore, Cabalum, and Nathanielsz (1992). Reprinted by permission.

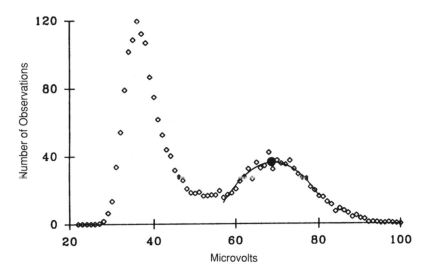

FIG. 20.5. Electrocorticogram of one fetal sheep plotted as time (minutes) spent per day as a function of electrocorticogram amplitude (microvolts) for each day over the gestational age period 126–133 days. Quadratic inflection point for high-voltage fetal electrocorticogram for each day is indicated (solid circle). From Sadowsky, Martel, Jenkins, Poore, Cabalum, and Nathanielsz (1992). Reprinted by permission.

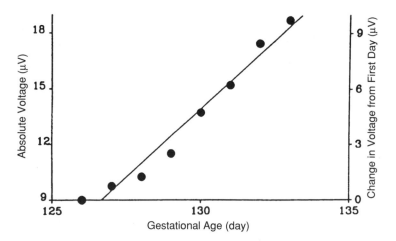

FIG. 20.6. Regression analysis of quadratic inflection point (voltage) of high-voltage fetal electrocorticogram regressed on gestational age (days) for one sheep. Rate of maturation (slope of regression) of high-voltage fetal electrocorticogram for this animal was $1.14\,\mu V\,day^{-1}$. From Sadowsky, Martel, Jenkins, Poore, Cabalum, and Nathanielsz (1992). Reprinted by permission.

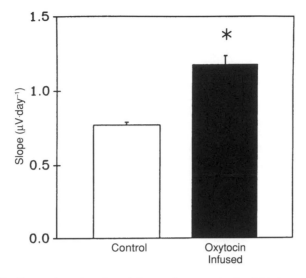

FIG. 20.7. Rate of maturation (slope of regression) of high-voltage fetal electrocorticogram (V day^{-1}) for oxytocin-infused and control ewes (mean ± SEM); *$p<.05$. From Sadowsky, Martel, Jenkins, Poore, Cabalum, and Nathanielsz (1992). Reprinted by permission.

In similar studies also begun around 128 days of gestation when total myometrial activity was increased to 160% of baseline by the administration of oxytocin intravenously for 5 min out of every 30 min to the pregnant ewe, by day 4 of oxytocin administration fetal plasma cortisol was significantly elevated above the fetal plasma cortisol concentrations in the fetuses of control ewes (Wallen et al., 1986). Adrenocorticotropin was not found to be elevated in fetal carotid arterial plasma in either group. The failure to observe a rise in ACTH may reflect the inability of the sampling regime utilized to demonstrate changes in the pulsatile release of ACTH. Alternatively, changes in fetal neural activity may alter other features of the fetal pituitary adrenal axis. Fetal splanchnic nerve function modifies the fetal adrenal response to ACTH in hypoxemia (Myers, Robertshaw, & Nathanielsz, 1990). Thus, a prolonged alteration of incoming influences to the fetal brain may affect fetal adrenal function via mechanisms other than circulating plasma ACTH concentrations.

Recent studies have also shown that altered myometrial contracture patterns can alter fetal neuroendocrine responses to stress. We evaluated the effect of approximately 5 weeks of increased contracture activity produced by administration of 600 μU min^{-1} kg^{-1} of oxytocin via the maternal jugular vein of pregnant sheep as a 5-min pulse every 20 min, starting at 97 ± 1 dGA. Hypotension was induced at 133 ± 1 dGA by slow infusion of nitroprusside (100 μg min^{-1}) to the fetus to lower fetal arterial blood pressure 50% for 10 min. Fetuses subjected to long-term increases in myometrial activity had a smaller ACTH and cortisol response to the hypertensive challenge than fetuses of control ewes with pulses of saline (Owiny, Sadowsky, & Nathanielsz, 1993). Using a similar paradigm we demonstrated a normal fetal ACTH response to hypoxemia but reduced cortisol response in fetuses of ewes pulsed with oxytocin compared with fetuses of controls pulsed with saline (Owiny, Jenkins, Sadowsky, & Nathanielsz, 1993). This observation is very similar to the effect observed following splanchnic nerve section (Myers et al., 1990), suggesting that alteration of contracture patterns over a large proposition of gestation may influence the fetal neural mechanisms that respond to hypoxemia via the splanchnic nerve.

SUMMARY AND CONCLUSIONS

Observations by several groups of investigators have demonstrated that contractures constitute a physiologically significant feature of the intra-uterine environment in late gestation. Contractures will alter both the oxygenation of the fetal brain and the sensory input to the brain at critical times of development in late gestation. Some of these changes in input are very subtle. However, the brain has been clearly demonstrated to be able to detect these alterations in sensory input. Future work will be necessary to determine the physiological, and potential pathological, significance of any consequent alterations in neuronal function produced by alterations in myometrial contractility. This remains a fertile and interesting area of study in our attempts to evaluate the relative importance of nature and nurture on fetal brain development.

ACKNOWLEDGMENTS

The work presented in this review was supported by the National Institute of Child Health and Human Development (NICHD), HD 28014. I would like to thank my many colleagues in the Laboratory for Pregnancy and Newborn Research and my secretary Karen Moore for her assistance with the manuscript.

REFERENCES

Azmita, E. C., Jr., & McEwen, B. S. (1969). Corticosterone regulation of tryptophan hydroxylase in midbrain of the rat. *Science, 166,* 1274–1276.
De Vellis, J., & Inglish D. (1968). Hormonal control of glycerol phosphate dehydro-genase in the rat brain. *Journal of Neurochemistry, 15,* 1061–1070.

Harding, R., Poore, E. R., Bailey, A., Thorburn, G. D., Jansen, C. A. M., & Nathanielsz, P. W. (1982). Electromyographic activity of the nonpregnant sheep uterus. *American Journal of Obstetrics and Gynecology, 142,* 448–457.

Hsu, H. W., Figueroa, J. P., Honnebier, M. B. O. M., Wentworth, R., & Nathanielsz, P. W. (1989). Power spectrum analysis of myometrial electromyogram and intrauterine pressure changes in the pregnant rhesus monkey in late gestation. *American Journal of Obstetrics and Gynecology, 161,* 467–473.

Jansen, C. A. M., Krane, E. J., Thomas, A. L., Beck, N. F. G., Lowe, K. C., Joyce, P., Parr, M., & Nathanielsz, P. W. (1979). Continuous variability of fetal PO_2 in the chronically catheterized fetal sheep. *American Journal of Obstetrics and Gynecology, 134,* 776–783.

Kay, H. H., & Mattison, D. R. (1986). Nuclear magnetic resonance spectroscopy and imaging in perinatal medicine. In P. W. Nathanielsz (Ed.), *Animal models in fetal medicine* (Vol. 5, pp. 269–323). Ithaca, NY: Perinatology Press.

Levine, S. (1970). The pituitary-adrenal system and the developing brain. In D. deWied & J. A. W. M. Weijnen (Eds.), *Progress in brain research, Vol. 32, Pituitary, adrenal, and brain* (pp. 79–85). Amsterdam: Elsevier.

Lye, S. J., Wlodek, M. E., & Challis, J. R. G. (1985). Possible role of uterine contractions in the short-term fluctuations of plasma ACTH concentrations in fetal sheep. *Journal of Endocrinology, 106,* R9–11.

McIntosh, G. H., Baghurst, K. I., Potter, B. J., & Hetzel, B. S. (1979). Foetal brain developing in the sheep. *Neuropathology of Applied Neurobiology, 5,* 103–114.

Morgan, M. A., Silavin, S. L., Wentworth, R. A., Figueroa, J. P., Honnebier, B. O. M., Fishburne, J. I., Jr., & Nathanielsz, P. W. (1992). Different patterns of myometrial activity and 24h rhythms in myometrial contractility in the gravid baboon during the second half of pregnancy. *Biology of Reproduction, 46,* 1158–1164.

Myers, D. A., Robertshaw, R., & Nathanielsz, P. W. (1990). Effect of bilateral splanchnic nerve section on adrenal function in the ovine fetus. *Endocrinology, 127,* 2328–2335.

Nathanielsz, P. W., Bailey, A., Poore, E. R., Thorburn, G. D., & Harding, R. (1980). The relationship between myometrial activity and sleep state and breathing in fetal sheep throughout the last third of gestation. *American Journal of Obstetrics and Gynecology, 138,* 653–659.

Nelson, P. G., Yu, C., Fields, R. D., & Neale, E. A. (1989). Synaptic connections in vitro: Modulation of number and efficacy by electrical activity. *Science, 244,* 585–587.

Owiny, J. R., Jenkins, S. L., Sadowsky, D., & Nathanielsz, P. W. (1993). Effect of pulsatile oxytocin administration to pregnant sheep from 100 days gestation on fetal response to short-term hypoxemia. *Society for Gynecologic Investigation,* March 31–April 2, Toronto, Canada. (Abstract no. P32.)

Owiny, J. R., Sadowsky, D., & Nathanielsz, P. W. (1993). Effect of pulsatile oxytocin administration to pregnant sheep from 100 days gestation on fetal response to hypotension. *Society for Gynecologic Investigation,* March 31–April 2, Toronto, Canada. (Abstract No. S7.)

Pelt, F. L. (1972). *The effects of neonatal treatment with methylthiouracil and triiodothyronine on physical and behavioural development.* Unpublished doctoral dissertation, Bronder-Offset, NV, Rotterdam.

Sadowsky, D. W., Martel, J., Cabalum, T., Poore, M. G., & Nathanielsz, P. W. (1992).

Oxytocin given in a pulsatile manner to the ewe at 120 to 140 days' gestational age increases fetal sheep plasma cortisol. *American Journal of Obstetrics and Gynecology, 166,* 200–205.

Sadowsky, D. W., Martel, J. K., Jenkins, S. L., Poore, M. G., Cabalum, T., & Nathanielsz, P. W. (1992). Pulsatile oxytocin administered to ewes at 120 to 140 days gestational age increases the rate of maturation of the fetal electrocorticogram and nuchal activity. *Journal of Developmental Physiology, 17,* 175–181.

Schapiro, S. (1968). Some physiological, biochemical and behavioral consequences of neonatal hormone administration: Cortisol and thyroxine. *General and Comparative Endocrinology, 10,* 214–228.

Taverne, M. A. M. (1982). Myometrial activity during pregnancy and parturition in the pig. In D. J. A. Cole & G. R. Foxcroft (Eds.), *Control of pig reproduction* (pp. 419–436). London: Butterworths.

Taylor, N. F., Martin, M. C., Nathanielsz, P. W., & Seron-Ferre, M. (1983). The fetus determines circadian oscillation of myometrial electromyographic activity in the pregnant rhesus monkey. *American Journal of Obstetrics and Gynecology, 146,* 557–567.

van der Weyden, G. C., Taverne, M. A. M., Dieleman, S. J., Wurth, Y., Bevers, M. M., & van Oord, H. A. (1989). Physiological aspects of pregnancy and parturition in dogs. *Journal of Reproduction and Fertility, Supplement, 39,* 211–224.

Walker, D. W., & Harding, R. (1986). The effects of raising intracranial pressure on breathing movements, eye movements and electrocortical activity in fetal sheep. *Journal of Developmental Physiology, 8,* 105–116.

Wallen, L. D., Murai, D. T., Clyman, R. I., Lee, C. H., Mauray, F. E., & Kitterman, J. A. (1986). Regulation of breathing movements in fetal sheep by prostaglandin E2. *Journal of Applied Physiology, 60,* 526–531.

Woudstra, B., Kim, C., Aarnoudse, J., & Nathanielsz, P. W. (1991). Myometrial contracture-related increases in plasma adrenocorticotropin in fetal sheep in the last third of gestation are abolished by maintaining fetal normoxemia. *Endocrinology, 129(4),* 1709–1713.

21

The Potential Value of Habituation in the Prenate

Leo R. Leader
University of New South Wales, Sydney, Australia

This chapter looks at the way fetal well-being is currently being assessed. It raises the question of fetal compensatory mechanisms under stress and questions the value of testing under basal conditions. The possible clinical value of using habituation to repeated vibroacoustic stimuli are outlined. It covers the history of habituation and its relationship to altered function of the central nervous system (CNS) as well as the different ways of measuring it. It outlines how factors such as gestational age, drugs, decreased O_2 tension, and cigarette smoking affect habituation. It also examines the differences in habituation patterns seen in both high-risk fetuses and those with Down syndrome and their possible predictive value. The question of the safety of its use is also discussed. In this chapter the terms *fetus* and *prenate* are used interchangeably to try to emphasize the continuity between prenatal life and life after birth.

One of the major challenges facing clinicians dealing with "high–risk" pregnancies, such as those complicated by intrauterine growth retardation (IUGR) or severe hypertension, is determining the optimal time for delivery not only to try to avoid any risk of serious perinatal complications but also to reduce the possibility of minimal brain damage. It has been shown that the incidence of minor neurological dysfunction (MND) was 16% in normal infants and up to 40% in preterm infants born small for gestational age (SGA; Hadders-Algra & Towen, 1990).

MANAGEMENT OF HIGH-RISK PREGNANCIES

In the management of these high-risk pregnancies, provided the clinical situation does not pose a serious threat to the mother, the pregnancy is usually allowed to continue to achieve the maximal maturity. These prenates are monitored by asking the mother to record fetal movements, measuring the variability of fetal heart rate (cardiotocograph; CTG), or a combination of observations in a biophysical profile using real-time ultrasound. Many units are using Doppler flow velocity waveforms to assess fetal well-being.

Delivery is usually indicated if one or more of these tests are abnormal, as there is a strong association between abnormal results and perinatal complications such as asphyxia, acidosis, and admission to special care units. Most of these observations are made with the fetus at rest.

RESERVE MECHANISMS

Most physiological systems have compensatory mechanisms that begin to function only when the organism is stressed or finds itself under suboptimal conditions. In human prenates, it has been shown using Doppler flow velocity studies that in the presence of hypoxia, the resistance index in the carotid vessels falls to preserve the blood flow to the fetal brain. This is associated with an increase in the resistance in the umbilical vessels (Arias & Retto, 1988). Thus a test performed under resting conditions may be of only limited predictive value, as these reserve mechanisms may be functioning and give an apparently normal test (e.g., in adults, a resting electrocardiograph [EKG] may be normal but a stress EKG may show marked abnormalities).

EFFECT OF STRESS

To test the limits of any system, it needs to be challenged or stimulated. Selye (1976) described the general adaptation syndrome (GAS), which outlines a tripartite physiological–behavioral response to stress:

1. An alarm reaction.
2. A stage of resistance (adaptation) during which the organism's defense mechanisms are mobilized and symptoms are alleviated.
3. Should the stress situation continue beyond the organism's finite level of "adaptation energy," exhaustion occurs and changes will be detectable under resting conditions.

Stimulation

Stimulation can be used in two ways: (a) By measuring the response to a single stimulus, or (b) by observing the decrease in response to repeated stimulation, that is, habituation.

A test that elicits a behavioral response will provide more information, as it involves both sensory and motor responses that require a higher degree of neuronal involvement. This is supported by the observation that although anencephalic fetuses may have normal movement activity and resting CTG recordings, they do not show a response to vibroacoustic stimulation (VAS) (Leader, Baillie, Martin, & Vermeulen, 1982a; Ohel, Brikenfeld, Rabinowitz, & Sadowsky, 1986), nor do they habituate (Brackbill, 1971).

This is also the rationale for the increasing use being made of CTG changes following transabdominal VAS to assess fetal well-being.

Ideal Prenatal Test

Currently used measures outlined earlier are indirect and assess general well-being, which has only an indirect relationship to cortical function, the ultimate arbiter of excellence in humans. Translated into more practical terms, the ideal test of well-being in the prenate should provide a precise measure of central nervous system (CNS) integrity. Habituation may be such a test.

HABITUATION

Habituation is the decrease leading to cessation of a behavioral response that occurs when an initially novel stimulus is presented repeatedly (Thompson & Glansman, 1966). Although habituation is remarkably simple, it is one of the most widespread forms of learning (Buckwald & Humphrey, 1973; Kandel, 1979; Stevensson & Siddle, 1983). Overt activity reflects only a minor part of the information processing by the central nervous system. In an environment of constant sensory stimulation, this ability to ignore meaningless stimuli is essential for the efficient functioning and survival of the organism.

There is good evidence that a normal habituation pattern reflects an intact and fully functioning central nervous system (Jeffrey & Cohen, 1971; Lewis, 1971; Madison, Adubato, Madison, Nelson, Anderson, Erickson, Kuss, & Goodlin, 1986a; Wyers, Peek, & Hertz, 1973).

It is not known which part of the CNS controls habituation, but there are data to suggest that the cerebral cortex is essential for normal habituation (Leader & Bennett, 1995).

PRENATAL OBSERVATION OF HABITUATION

Peiper (1925) first noted cessation of the fright response to repeated sound using an automotive horn sounded near the maternal abdomen. Fleischer (1955) noted habituation of fetal movements to repeated sound stimulation. Leader et al. (1982a, 1982b) examined habituation of the fetal movement response to repeated VAS. Habituation of the blink-startle response was described by Birnholz and Benacerraf (1983). Madison et al. (1986) also demonstrated habituation of the fetal movement response to repeated vibroacoustic stimulation. Similar observations were made by others (Kuhlman, Burns, Depp, & Sabbagha, 1988; Shalev, Weiner, & Serr, 1989). More recently, Hepper and Shahidullah (1992) noted prenatal habituation of the movement response to repeated stimulation using sine waves with a frequency of either of 250 or 500 Hz. They have refined the response by establishing the intensity at which each individual fetus responds and using that intensity to demonstrate habituation. Smotherman and Robinson (1992) also recently demonstrated habituation of the heart rate and movement response to repeated chemosensory stimuli in fetal rats using infusions of a lemon solution onto the fetal tongue.

HABITUATION AND ALTERED CNS FUNCTION

According to Lewis (1971), a normal habituation pattern reflects an intact CNS. Deviations from normal central nervous system function have altered habituation in that brain damage produces a reduction of behavioral response habituation (Holloway & Parsons, 1971). Schizophrenics have different habituation patterns compared to normals (Gruzelier & Venables, 1972), as do patients suffering dementia due to cortical atrophy and Parkinson's disease.

Hyperactive children have impaired habituation to visual, tactile, and auditory stimuli (Hutt & Hutt, 1964; Tizard, 1968). Autistic children do not show normal behavioural and electroencephalographic habituation (Hutt, Hutt, Lee & Dunstead, 1965). Different habituation patterns have been found between children with Down's syndrome and normal controls (Dustman & Callner, 1979). Anencephalic infants also fail to habituate (Brackbill, 1971).

In animal studies, drugs known to effect the central nervous system such as amphetamines (Davis et al., 1975), lysergic acid diethylamide (Key, 1961), and barbiturates and chlordiazepoxide (Lader & Wing, 1969) alter habituation.

FETAL HABITUATION

In the studies outlined next, a broad-spectrum vibroacoustic stimulus generated by a Ronson's electric toothbrush was used. The fetal movement response was assessed by a modified Hewlett-Packard cardiotocograph, real-time ultrasound watched by an independent observer, and maternal observation.

The toothbrush was placed on the maternal abdomen over the prenate's head and a 5-sec stimulus was applied approximately every 20 sec. Movement that occurred either during the stimulus or within 2.5 sec of its cessation was regarded as a response. Movement after that time was regarded as spontaneous. If there was spontaneous movement when the stimulus was due, it was withheld until the movement ceased.

Lack of response to 5 consecutive stimuli indicated habituation, and the number of stimuli required to produce habituation was recorded. These criteria were similar to those described in the newborn infant by Brackbill, Kane, Manniello, and Adamson (1974) and Madison et al. (1986) in human fetuses. It has been suggested that the probability of five consecutive observation periods without any fetal movement would occur by chance in less than 5% of the time.

PATIENT SELECTION

Normal Range

To establish a normal range, 40 subjects who had a normal uncomplicated antenatal, intrapartum, and neonatal course and were delivered of infants thought to be in optimal condition were used as controls (Michaelis, Rooschuz, & Dopfer, 1980). These subjects were determined retrospectively.

The optimality concept was suggested by Prechtl (1980) and places the emphasis in finding the best possible conditions rather than on normality, abnormality, or pathology. An optimal condition is more restrictive and is not synonymous with normality. It is more narrowly defined; for example, a teenage patient having her first baby may well be considered normal but would not be considered optimal because of the well-known increased mortality rates compared to a patient in her twenties having her second or third baby. Figure 21.1 shows that 37 of the 40 patients studied habituated after between 10 and 50 stimuli, and 34 (85%) habituated in 40 or less. This is similar to a previous study in which normal neonates took between 20

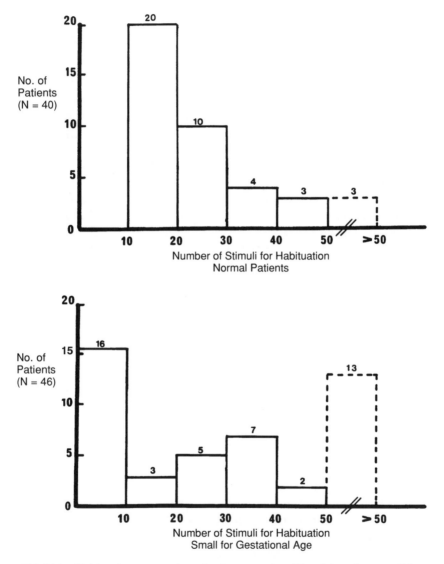

FIG. 21.1.   Habituation patterns in optimal prenates ($n = 40$) and those born small for gestational age ($n = 46$). Dash line indicates prenates that fail to habituate by 50 stimuli.

and 37 stimuli to habituate to a broad-spectrum sound stimulus (Eisenberg, Coursin, & Rupp, 1966).

High-Risk Pregnancies

The optimal group was then compared to 46 patients whose infants had birth weights below the 10th percentile for the local population and were classified as SGA (Fig. 21.1). In that group, 8 failed to show any response to stimulation, 4 habituated between 1 and 9, 17 were in the normal range, and 13 failed to habituate after 50 stimuli. Similar habituation patterns were seen in a further 38 who had decreased growth velocity as assessed by serial ultrasound observations of their biparietal diameters and in 28 patients who had meconium staining of the amniotic fluid, as well as in a further 28 prenates who had normal growth on their serial ultrasound biparietal diameters. This was a mixed group consisting of some normal pregnancies and some complicated by hypertension, antepartum hemorrhage, and decreased fetal movements. This suggests that in some at-risk pregnancies, the presence of normal fetal growth may not mean that all is well. There were very highly significant differences between the optimal control group and the high-risk groups.

HABITUATION PATTERNS

Leader et al. (1982a, 1982b) were able to identify four different patterns of response:

1. Normal habituators, who take between 10 and 50 stimuli.
2. Nonresponders, a group that failed to respond to stimulation.
3. Fast habituators, who habituated between one and nine stimuli.
4. Slow habituators, who were still responding after 50 stimuli.

That study included five patients whose infants had major CNS abnormalities, four anencephalics, and one microcephalic. All five infants failed to respond to stimulation.

Dishabituation

Dishabituation classically refers to the recovery of a habituated response to the original stimulus following the presentation of a novel stimulus. This process is very important as it differentiates between neural or receptor fatigue and habituation. In the study just outlined, dishabituation was demonstrated using a second mechanical vibrator and was noted in 83% of normal patients. Dishabituation has also been demonstrated by Madison et al. (1986) and more recently by Hepper and Shahidullah (1992). Smotherman and Robinson (1992), in studies in fetal rats, also demonstrated dishabituation.

FACTORS EFFECTING HUMAN PRENATAL HABITUATION

Gestational Age

Twenty-seven nonsmoking subjects were studied at two weekly intervals from approximately 22 weeks of gestation to determine at what age the human prenate first responded and habituated (Leader et al., 1982a). At 23–24 weeks, only 7% of fetuses responded. By 27–28 weeks, 89% of them responded. The onset of the response occurred earlier in females than males. There were 75% of the 12 females responding by 25–26 weeks, compared to only 33% of the 15 males. All females responded by the 28th week, whereas 80% of the males responded by then. By 30 weeks, all fetuses responded. This is in keeping with known neurophysiological data that female infants mature earlier than males (Singer, Westphal, & Niswander, 1968).

The blink-startle response to a VAS was first noted at 24–25 weeks and was consistently present after 28 weeks (Birnholz & Benacerraf, 1983). Similar observations have since been made by others (Hepper, 1992; Kuhlman & Depp, 1988).

Effect of Repetition

Fifteen subjects who had normal pregnancies and had reached more than 36 weeks of gestation were tested on two successive days. Fourteen of them required fewer stimuli for habituation. The sign test in this group is significantly negative ($p = .035$). The only fetus who showed no decrease was found to have meconium staining of the amniotic fluid when his mother went into labor. Infants tested after intervals of 3–4 days showed no consistent habituation pattern and a sign test was not significant. This seems to indicate some evidence of fetal memory that lasts for 24 hr. When tested after 72 hr there was no evidence of such an effect.

Cigarette Smoking

Eight subjects were tested more than 1½ hr after their last cigarette. All 10 had a normal habituation pattern (10 –50 stimuli). When the same individuals were tested 3–7 days later, less than 1½ hr after smoking, seven had an abnormal habituation pattern (<9 or >50 stimuli). The remaining subject, who smoked 40 cigarettes a day, required 6 hr before fetal habituation returned to normal (Leader, 1987). More recently, Hepper (1992) showed that prenates whose mothers smoke require a greater intensity of stimulus to evoke a response compared to those mothers who don't smoke.

In addition, a further study examined the effects of smoking. Thirteen nonsmoking subjects who were more than 36 weeks pregnant were tested for habituation. They remained recumbent on their left sides on the examination couch. After a 30-min break, they were retested for habituation, and the test was repeated for the third time after a further 20-min break. Nine smokers, all of whom had refrained from smoking for 6 hr, were tested using a similar protocol. It differed, however, in that mothers were asked to smoke two cigarettes at the end of their second trial.

Figure 21.2 shows that there was a progressive decrease in the number of stimuli required for habituation after the third trial. Smokers took significantly longer to habituate than the nonsmokers ($p = .006$).

Effects of Drugs

Following the observation that patients on sedatives tended to have an abnormal habituation pattern, nine normal subjects who were more than 36 weeks of pregnant were recruited. They consented to take phenobarbitone 30 mg every 8 hrs for 3 days. The test was then repeated after 4–5 days. Where possible a third test was done on the 7th or 8th day.

A group of 14 subjects with similar characteristics acted as controls and were tested at approximately the same intervals. However, they did not receive any barbiturates.

In the nine fetuses whose mothers took barbiturates, all nine had a normal habituation pattern before commencing any drugs. When the test was repeated on day 4, only three had a normal pattern. Seven of the 13 when tested on day 4 or 5 failed to habituate by 50 stimuli. When they were tested afterward when they had stopped the sedatives, their habituation pattern returned to normal once again.

The control group showed no change in their habituation pattern. The controls differed significantly from the drug group comparing day 4 alone or together with day 5 ($p < .05$).

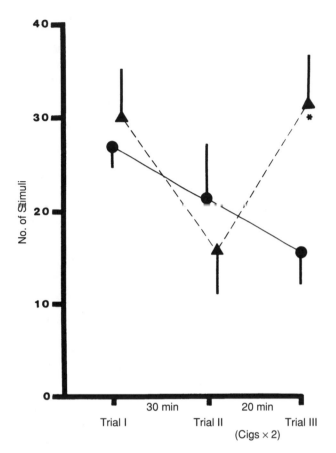

FIG. 21.2.   Habituation rates in prenates of 9 mothers who smoked and 13 who did not. Smokers had two cigarettes in the 20 min between trials 2 and 3. Significant differences: *p = .006, smokers trial 2 versus trial 3; p = .02, trial 3 smokers versus nonsmokers. Key: ▲ = smokers; ● = nonsmokers.

Alterations in Inspired Maternal Oxygen

Thirty-three nonsmoking normal subjects who were more than 36 weeks pregnant were recruited (Leader & Baillie, 1988). Ten subjects were initially tested for habituation while breathing room air, and the test was repeated the following day at approximately the same time of day while breathing 12% oxygen. A second group of eight prenates was tested while their mothers were breathing 12% oxygen on the first day and repeated the next day while mothers were breathing room air. There was a third group of five subjects tested in room air on the first day and retested the following day while breathing air through the same apparatus used to deliver the 12% oxygen.

All 10 subjects while mothers were breathing air on the 1st day had a normal habituation pattern compared to only 1 when tested breathing 12% oxygen. In the group who had 12% oxygen the 1st day only one had a normal pattern and seven had abnormal patterns. When tested the following day breathing room air, seven out of the eight had normal habituation patterns. In the controls, no significant differences were seen in subjects when they breathed air through the same apparatus. It is thus clear that altering the amount of inspired oxygen effects the habituation pattern on a temporary basis. Breathing 12% oxygen is the equivalent of living at 13,000 ft above sea level and reduces the maternal PAO_2 from 99 mm Hg to 44 mm Hg. The arterial saturation, however, only falls to 86%.

Down Syndrome and Response Latencies

Hepper and Shahidullah (1992) reported two cases of Down syndrome, of whom one failed to habituate and the other took longer to habituate than controls. They also determined the time from the onset of the stimulus to the initiation of movement. Normal prenates show a progressive decrease in latency over trials. One of the Down prenates who failed to show any change in its response latency died shortly after birth, although there was no detectable difference between the two antenatally.

Effect of State on Fetal Habituation

Until recently it was widely believed that the fetus had little capacity to respond to external stimulation, and if it did, the responsiveness was dependent on fetal behavioral state (Prechtl, 1985; Schmidt, Boos, Gnirs, Auer, & Schulze, 1985). Those studies failed to take into account, however, the type of stimulus, its intensity, how it was delivered, and the effects of repetition (habituation). It was also suggested that the decreased responsiveness seen in infants was not habituation but a change in state (Hutt, Von Bernuth, Lenard, & Prechtl, 1968). More recent studies clearly demonstrated that fetal responsiveness increases as the intensity and frequency increases (Gagnon, 1989; Kisilevsky, Muir, & Low, 1989; Lecanuet, Granier-Deferre, & Busnel, 1989; Yao, Jakobsson, & Nyman, 1990) and is of increased duration (Pietrantoni et al., 1991). These studies demonstrate that if the stimulus is strong enough it will override the effect of state.

ANIMAL STUDIES

Habituation in Fetal Sheep

Because of the suggestion that fetal responsiveness to auditory stimulation was state dependent, an animal model was established using fetal sheep (Leader, Stevens, & Lumbers, 1988). The fetus was stimulated using a mechanical vibrator attached to the maternal abdomen. That study also showed quite clearly that fetuses responded to stimulation and habituated during both high-voltage (HV) and low-voltage (LV) electrocortical activity. Although they took 13 stimuli in HV compared to 23 in LV, these differences were not statistically significant. Similar observations were made in human fetuses (Shalev, Weiner, & Serr, 1990).

Hypoxia

A further study was done examine the effects of maternal hypoxia on fetal habituation (Leader, Smith, Lumbers, & Stevens, 1989). Hypoxia was induced by placing a bag over the ewe's head and altering the amount of inspired O_2 to 9% + 3% CO_2. This reduced the fetal PO_2 from a mean of 18 mm Hg before stimulation to approximately 10 mm Hg during the stimulation. Hypoxic fetuses habituated far more rapidly than controls (2.4 ± 1.3 vs. 16.7 ± 2.7 stimuli, respectively, $p < .01$) Habituation was tested while infusing a solution of noradrenaline directly into the fetus to produce levels of noradrenaline consistent with those seen during hypoxia. During the noradrenaline infusion, fetuses habituated significantly more rapidly than controls (4.6 ± 0.8 and $14.5 + 2.3$ stimuli, respectively, $p < .001$).

Effect of Alcohol

Alcohol was infused into the pregnant ewe to produce blood levels in the fetus before stimulation of approximately 80 to 90 mg per 100 ml. This resulted in more rapid habituation (7.25 ± 1.28 stimuli) compared to the control experiment preceding alcohol (21.5 ± 3.57) and after alcohol (17.5 ± 5.83).

Fetal alcohol infusion was associated with a significant decrease in spontaneous fetal movements. The most likely explanation for this response is that it is due to catecholamine release that occurs after small amounts of alcohol (Leader, Smith, & Lumbers, 1990).

Prenatal Heart Rate Habituation

Habituation of the fetal heart rate response to sound stimulation was described by Goodlin and Lowe (1974) and to vibroacoustic stimulation by

Leader, Baillie, Martin, and Molteno (1984), but no real clinical application was made of this observation.

METHOD

Following a 10-min control CTG, the fetus was stimulated for 5 sec using a vibroacoustic stimulator (Corometrics Medical Systems, model 146, CT). This produced an intrauterine sound level of 90 dB (Arulkumaran, Talbert, Chua, Anandakumar, & Ratnam, 1992). The fetal state was measured before and after each stimulus. The fetal heart rate changes were measured until it returned to the baseline for 2 min. At this point, the fetus was stimulated again and the same response was measured. The stimulus was then repeated for the third time.

Specially developed computer software allowed the mean heart rate prior to stimulation to be calculated, as well as the changes at 1 min after stimulation.

RESULTS

There were 79 tests in 30 prenates born to mothers from optimal pregnancies (Leader et al., 1982b) and 37 high-risk patients whose hypertension was sufficiently severe to warrant medication, or those with suspected intrauterine growth retardation who delivered SGA infants (below the 10th percentile).

Figure 21.3 shows that in optimal pregnancies there is a significant decrease in the change in heart rate between the first and second stimuli ($p < .01$) as well as between the second and third stimuli ($p < .01$). In the high-risk groups, not only is the initial response significantly less ($p < .001$) but there is no habituation of the changes in fetal heart rate at 1 min after the next two stimuli.

Table 21.1 shows the percentage change in fetal heart rate from the prestimulus level compared to the level at 1 min after stimulation with each of the three stimuli. Results are presented as mean ± SEM. In optimal pregnancies there was a significant decrease in the percentage change between the first and second stimulus ($p < .01$) and between the second and third stimulus ($p < .01$). In the high-risk pregnancies, the percentage change after the first stimulus was significantly less than the optimal group ($p < .001$) and there was no habituation of the percentage change after the second and third stimuli. Calculating the percentage change in

396   LEADER

heart rate excludes the possibility that the decrease in the heart rate change seen is the result of an increase of the prestimulus heart rate.

Recently, Goldkrand and Litvak (1991) also demonstrated habituation heart rate changes after VAS in prenates. Human fetuses between 28 and 43 weeks of gestation were given a 1-sec VAS every minute for 20 min and were classified into four patterns. That study showed that 67.5% of fetuses who did not habituate antenatally had a complication either in labor or in the nursery, compared to only 6.4% of fetuses who did.

Safety of Vibroacoustic Stimulation

The safety of using VAS has recently been questioned by Visser, Mulder, Wit, Mulder, and Prechtl (1989). They observed that stimulation with an electronic artificial larynx (EAL) induces excessive fetal movements, a prolonged tachycardia, and nonphysiological state changes—that is, many fetuses spent more time in state 4F or in an episode nonclassifiable because of an atypical heart rate tracing.

Our own experience has been quite different, perhaps because of the experimental design, in that the fetus is only stimulated once the heart rate has returned to its baseline. The mean time for the fetal heart rate to return to its baseline after the first stimulus was 5.8 min (range 0.5–15 min), after

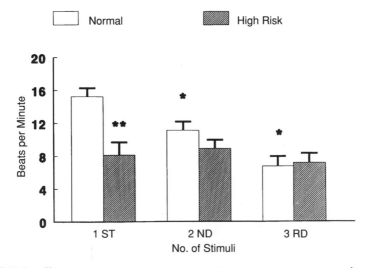

FIG. 21.3.   Change in heart rate from the prestimulus level to the rate at 1 min after each of the three stimuli in both the optimal ($n = 79$) and high-risk ($n = 37$) groups. Results are expressed as means ± SEM. Groups were tested using Student's t test (paired and unpaired as appropriate with a Bonferroni correction). *$p < .01$. ** $p < .001$.

TABLE 21.1
Percentage Change in Heart Rate After Stimulation

	First Stimulus	Second Stimulus	Third Stimulus
Optimal	11.6 ± .79	8.43 ± .82	5.15 ± .84
High Risk	6.28 ±1.2	6.78 ± .8	5.47 ± .88

the second stimulus 4.49 min (range 0.5–18 min), and after the third stimulus 3.13 min (range 0.5–10 min).

Sound Levels

When measured in air, the EAL had a sound pressure level of 105 dB at a distance of 5 cm from the vibrating membrane. When the EAL was tested in pregnant ewes by means of a hydrophone implanted within the uterus the sound level was even higher (135 dB) (Gerhardt, 1989). The overall sound pressure level produced by the stimulus used was 74 dB and has been previously described (Leader et al., 1982a). Its frequencies also differ from the EAL.

Does Vibroacoustic Stimulation Affect Fetal State?

Because of the concern expressed by others on the effects of VAS on fetal state, two sets of experiments were done. Fetal state was determined according to the accepted criteria (Nijhuis, Prechtl, Martin, & Bots, 1982).

State 1F is usually associated with low heart rate variability and no eye or body movements. State 2F is associated with higher heart rate variability, accelerations, and the presence of eye and body movements. State 3F is usually associated with low heart rate variability but also the presence of fetal eye movements. State 4F is associated with prolonged accelerations, eye and excessive body movements.

In the first experiment only a cardiotocograph was used to determine fetal state according to the heart rate variability. This was similar to the method reported by others (Lecanuet, Granier-Deferre, Cohen, Le Houezec, & Busnel, 1986). The fetus was stimulated three times as described in the section on heart rate habituation.

Table 21.2 shows the heart rate variability before and after each of the three stimuli in 90 tests. Percentages are shown in parentheses. As can be seen from the table, fetal stimulation was associated with a change in fetal state but the changes were short-lived. The incidence of LV and HV did not differ significantly from each other before each of the three stimuli. There was also a decrease in the frequency of LV after stimulation. Although 15%

TABLE 21.2
Changes in Heart Rate Variability Associated with Stimulation

	First Stimulus		Second Stimulus		Third Stimulus	
	Before	After	Before	After	Before	After
HV	70(78)	72(80)	77(85)	63(70)	60(82)	63(88)
LV	20(22)	7(8)	12(13)	7 (8)	12(13)	4(5)
LV to HV	0	3(3)	0	2 (2)	0	2(3)
HV to LV	0	2(2)	0	4 (4)	0	2(3)
VR	0	4(4)	1(1)	14(15)	2 (3)	2(3)

Note. HV, high variability; LV, low variability; VR, very reactive prolonged accelerations.

of fetuses scored as very reactive (similar to state 4) after the second stimulus, most of these fetuses reverted to either LV or HV over the 10 min before the third stimulus. Only 3% had very reactive tracings after the third stimulus. This may represent another form of habituation to the stimulus.

In the second set of experiments, the effects of two different vibroacoustic stimuli and a sham stimulus were assessed on fetal state. The VAS used were the Ronson's electric toothbrush (Leader et al., 1982a) and the Corometrics acoustic stimulator. Fetal state was assessed using two real-time ultrasound scanners and a cardiotocograph as described Nijhuis et al. (1982). There was approximately 60 hr of observation in nine patients. After a 30-min control period, three 5-sec VAS were applied and the changes in fetal state were observed for 30 min after each stimulus.

This study also found that although there were some changes in fetal state, these were short-lived, and fetuses who were regarded to have changed to state 4 reverted back to either state 1 or 2 before the next stimulus was due (Leader, Fawcus, & Clark, 1992). The tachycardias and atypical patterns described as frequent by Visser et al. (1989) were not seen. This difference in findings from those of Visser et al. is likely to be due to the intensity and frequency of their stimulus.

Visser et al. (1989) also expressed concern that the changes in heart rate may be due to sudden release of catecholamines and may be harmful in severely growth-retarded fetuses and lead to intracranial bleeding. Using our less intense stimulus, we have found that these fetuses if severely affected do not respond to stimulation (Leader et al., 1984). In addition, Fisk et al. (1991) demonstrated that in the human fetus VAS is not associated with a rise in adrenaline or noradrenaline.

Ohel, Horowitz, Linder, and Schmer (1989) showed that neonatal auditory function is normal following intrapartum VAS, and Nyman, Barr, and

Westgren (1992) also showed that VAS does not have an adverse effect on infant development.

PREDICTIVE VALUE OF HABITUATION

Lewis (1971) found that the rate of visual habituation at 1 year of age was significantly related to learning tasks and IQ at 44 months of age. More recent studies have also shown that performance on habituation tasks has been predictive of later cognitive function (Bornstein, 1989; Rose & Wallace, 1985).

Further evidence to support the habituation as having predictive value was provided by Leader et al. (1984), who found that infants who had normal intrauterine fetal movement habituation patterns scored significantly higher on the Griffiths Mental Developmental Scale at 1 year of age compared with those who had abnormal intrauterine habituation patterns. In a further study of fetal movement habituation that confirmed our original observations, fetal movement habituation was found to be clearly associated with postnatal behaviour using the Brazelton Scale after birth (Madison, Madison, & Adubato, 1986). At 4 months of age, using the Bayley Scales of Infant Development, faster habituators were found to have significantly higher mental development score. Fast habituators probably represent the group in a stage of resistance described by Selye in his general adaptation syndrome (discussed earlier). Supporting this theory is the observation that fetuses who show a mixed heart rate pattern of accelerations and decelerations (which may reflect mild stress) in labor have a superior developmental outcome compared to those fetuses who have either a normal or markedly abnormal heart rate tracing in labor (Toomey, Emory, & Savoir, 1987).

CONCLUSION

Fetal habituation shows promise as a measure of central nervous system function. It is affected by smoking, sedative drugs, and decreased O_2 but not significantly by fetal state using vibroacoustic stimuli. There are significant differences between normal and high-risk pregnancies complicated by conditions that are frequently associated with increased neurological damage. It may be possible to identify those prenates that are at risk and reduce their risk by earlier delivery. The stimulus used in the studies outlined in this chapter did not results in long-term alterations in fetal behavioral state. Habituation can also be used as a technique to study the possible effects of drugs such as alcohol, caffeine, and antihypertensive agents in the antenatal period.

FUTURE RESEARCH QUESTIONS

1. What is the Most Effective Way to Stimulate the Fetus?

Although it appears that using an intense broad-spectrum vibroacoustic stimulus produces the most reliable responses, this employs a fixed intensity. Titrating the intensity level for each individual may offer an additional measure of sensitivity and provide more information. There also needs to be a determination of which type of stimulus, its duration, and how frequently it should be repeated.

2. What is the Best Response to Measure?

At present habituation of both the fetal movement and heart rate response have been used. The heart rate change is easier to quantitate but may be less sensitive. Techniques need to be developed to quantitate the fetal movement response so that it can be measured more accurately and then compared to the heart rate changes. Response latency shows promise as one way of quantifying the fetal movement response.

3. What is the Long-Term Predictive Value of Prenatal Habituation?

Once the best method for measuring habituation has been determined, then follow-up studies need to be undertaken to determine how prenatal central nervous system function relates to long-term development.

4. Which Part of the Central Nervous System is Responsible for a Normal Habituation Pattern?

The controlling mechanism for habituation has yet to be determined. There is some evidence that suggests a normal cerebral cortex is essential for a normal habituation pattern. It may be possible to study this in appropriate animal models.

5. Should the Endpoint Against Which Prenatal Tests are Measured Include a Determination of Optimality?

At present, most studies of antenatal fetal well-being use morbidity as the endpoint against which they compare their predictive values. Because of the difficulty in finding suitable endpoints, investigators tend to use a wide variety of measures. It may be better to assess a test's ability to predict not only morbidity but optimality as well. It may be easier to select more uniform criteria that will enable researchers to more easily compare their results.

REFERENCES

Arias, F., & Retto, H. (1988). The use of Doppler waveform analysis in the evaluation of the high risk fetus. *Obstetrics and Gynecology Clinics of North America, 15,* 265–281.

Arulkumaran, S., Talbert, D., Chua, T. S., Anandakumar, C., & Ratnam, S. S. (1992) In utero sound levels when vibroacoustic stimulation is applied to the maternal abdomen: An assessment of the possibility of cochlear damage in the fetus. *British Journal of Obstetrics and Gynaecology, 99,* 43–45.

Birnholz, J. C., & Benacerraf, B. R. (1983). The development of human fetal hearing. *Science, 222,* 516–518.

Bornstein, M. H. (1989). Attention in infancy and the prediction of cognitive capacities in childhood. *Seminars in Perinatology, 13,* 450–457.

Brackbill, Y. (1971). The role of the cortex in orienting. Orienting reflex in an anencephalic human infant. *Developmental Psychobiology, 5,* 195–201.

Brackbill, Y., Kane, J., Manniello, R. L., & Adamson, D. (1974). Obstetric premedication and infant outcome. *American Journal of Obstetrics & Gynecology 118,* 377–384.

Buckwald, J. S., & Humphrey, G. L. (1973). An analysis of habituation in specific sensory systems. In E. Stellar & J. Sprague (Eds.), *Progress in physiological psychology* (Vol. 5, pp. 1–75). New York: Academic Press.

Davis, M., Svensson, T. H., & Aghajanian, G. K. (1975). Effects of D- and L-amphetamine on habituation and sensitisation of the acoustic startle response in rats. *Psychopharmacology, 43,* 1–11.

Dustman, R. E., & Callner, D. A. (1979). Cortical evoked responses and response decrement in non-retarded and Down's syndrome individuals. *American Journal of Mental Deficiency, 83,* 391–396.

Eisenberg, R., Coursin, D. B., & Rupp, N. R. (1966). Habituation to an acoustic pattern as an index of differences among human neonates. *Journal of Auditory Research, 6,* 239–248.

Fleischer, K. (1955). Untersuchungen zur Entwickling der Innenohrfunktion (interuterine Kindsbewegungen nag Schallreizen) [Investigations into the development of inner ear function (Intrauterine fetal movements following sound stimuli)]. *Zeitschrift fuer Laryngologie, Rhinologic, und Otologien, 34,* 733–740.

Fisk, N. M., Nicolaidis, P. K., Arulkumaran, S., Weg, M. W., Tannirandorn, Y., Nicolini, U., Parkes, M. J., & Rodeck, C. (1991). Vibroacoustic stimulation is not associated with sudden catecholamine release. *Early Human Development, 25,* 11–17.

Gagnon, R. (1989). Stimulation of human fetuses with sound and vibration. *Seminars in Perinatology, 13,* 393–402.

Gerhardt, K. J. (1989). Characteristics of the fetal sheep sound environment. *Seminars in Perinatology, 13,* 362–365.

Goldkrand, J. W., & Litvack, B. L. (1991). Demonstration of fetal habituation and patterns of fetal heart rate response to vibroacoustic stimulation in normal and high-risk pregnancies. *Journal of Perinatology, 11,* 25–29.

Goodlin. R. C., & Lowe, E. W. (1974). Multiphasic fetal monitoring. A preliminary evaluation. *American Journal of Obstetrics & Gynecology, 119,* 341–357.

Gruzelier, J. H., & Venables, P. H. (1972). Skin conductance orienting activity in a heterogeneous sample of schizophrenics. *Journal of Nerve and Mental Disease, 155,* 277–287.

Hadders-Algra, M., & Touwen, B. C. L. (1990). Body measurements, neurological and behavioural development in six-year-old children born preterm and/or small for gestational age. *Early Human Development, 22,* 1–13.

Hepper, P. (1992). An interface between psychology and medicine; The antenatal detection of handicap. In R. Klimek (Ed.), *Pre- and perinatal psycho-medicine* (pp. 133–138). Cracow, Poland: DWN Dream.

Hepper, P., & Shahidullah, S. (1992). Habituation in normal and Down's syndrome fetuses. *Quarterly Journal of Experimental Psychology, 44B,* 305–317.

Holloway, F. A., & Parsons, O. A. (1971). Habituation of the orienting response in brain damaged patients. *Psychophysiology, 8,* 623–634.

Hutt, S. J., & Hutt, C. (1964). Hyperactivity in a group of epileptic (and some non-epileptic) brain damaged children. *Epilepsia, 5,* 334–351.

Hutt, S .J., Hutt, C., Lee, D., & Dunstead, C. (1965). A behavioural and electroencephalographic study of autistic children. *Journal of Psychiatric Research, 3,* 181–197.

Hutt, C., Von Bernuth, H., Lenard, H. G., & Prechtl, H. F. R. (1968). Habituation in relation to state in the human neonate. *Nature, 220,* 618–620.

Jeffrey, W. E., & Cohen, L. B. (1971). Habituation in the human infant. In H. W. Reese (Ed.), *Advances in child development and behaviour* (Vol. 6, pp. 63–97). New York: Academic Press.

Kandel, E. R. (1979). Small system of neurones. *Scientific American, 241,* 67–76.

Key, B. J. (1961). Effects of chlorpromazine and lysergic acid diethylamide on the role of habituation of the arousal response. *Nature (London), 190,* 275–277.

Kisilevsky, B. S., Muir, D. W., & Low, J. A. (1989). Human fetal responses as a function of stimulus intensity. *Obstetrics and Gynecology, 73,* 971–976.

Kuhlman, K. A., Burns, K. A., Depp, R., & Sabbagha, R. E. (1988). Ultrasonic Imaging of normal fetal response to external vibratory acoustic stimulation. *American Journal of Obstetrics and Gynecology, 158,* 47–51.

Kuhlman, K. A., & Depp, R. (1988). Acoustic stimulation testing. *Obstetrics and Gynecology Clinics of North America, 15,* 303–319.

Lader, M. J., & Wing, L. (1965). Comparative bioassay of chlordiazepoxide and amylobarbitone sodium therapies in patients with anxiety states using physiological and clinical measures. *Journal of Neurology Neurosurgery & Psychiatry, 28,* 414–424.

Leader, L. R. (1987). The effects of cigarette smoking and maternal hypoxia on fetal habituation. In K. Maeda (Ed.), *The fetus as a patient* (pp. 83–88). Amsterdam: Elsevier.

Leader, L. R., & Baillie, P. (1988). The changes in fetal habituation patterns due to a decrease in inspired maternal oxygen. *British Journal of Obstetrics & Gynaecology, 89,* 441–446.

Leader, L. R., Baillie, P., Martin, B., & Molteno, C . (1984). Fetal responses to vibrotactile stimuli: A possible predictor of fetal and neonatal outcome. *Australian & New Zealand Journal of Obstetrics & Gynaecology, 24,* 251–256.

Leader, L. R., Baillie, P., Martin, B., & Vermeulen, E. (1982a). The assessment and significance of habituation to a repeated stimulus by the human fetus. *Early Human Development, 7,* 211–219.

Leader, L. R., Baillie, P., Martin, B., & Vermeulen, E. (1982b). Fetal habituation in high risk pregnancies. *British Journal of Obstetrics & Gynaecology, 89,* 441–446.

Leader, L. R., & Bennett, M. J. (1995). Fetal habituation and its clinical application. In M. I. Levine, R. J. Lilford, M. J. Bennett, & J. Punt (Eds.), *Fetal & neonatal neurology & neurosurgery* (pp. 45–60). London: Churchill Livingstone.

Leader, L. R., Fawcus, S., & Clark, I. (1992, April). The effect of repeated vibroacoustic stimulation on fetal behavioural state. Presented at the annual meeting of the Royal Australian College of Obstetricians and Gynaecologists, Melbourne.

Leader, L. R., Smith, F. G., & Lumbers, E. R. (1990). The effect of ethanol on habituation and the cardiovascular response to stimulation in fetal sheep. *European Journal of Obstetrics and Gynecology, 36,* 87–95.

Leader, L. R., Smith, F. G., Lumbers, E. R., & Stevens, A. D. (1989). The effect of hypoxia and catecholamines on the habituation rates of chronically catheterised ovine fetuses. *Biology of the Neonate, 56,* 218–221.

Leader, L. R., Stevens, A. D., & Lumbers, E. R. (1988). Measurement of fetal responses to vibroacoustic stimuli. Habituation in fetal sheep. *Biology of the Neonate 53,* 73–85.

Lecanuet, J. P., Granier-Deferre, C., & Busnel, M. C. (1989). Differential fetal auditory reactiveness as a function of stimulus characteristics. *Seminars in Perinatology, 13,* 393–402.

Lecanuet, J. P., Granier-Deferre, C., Cohen, H., Le Houezec, R., & Busnel, M. C. (1986). Fetal responses to acoustic stimulation depend on heart rate variability pattern, stimulus intensity and repetition. *Early Human Development, 13,* 269–283.

Lewis, M. (1971). Individual differences in the measurement of early cognitive growth. Exceptional infant 2. In J. Hellmuth (Ed.), *Studies in abnormalities* (pp. 172–210). New York: Brunner Mazel.

Madison, L. S., Adubato, S. A., Madison, J. K., Nelson, B. M., Anderson, J. C., Erickson, J., Kuss, L. M., & Goodlin, R. C. (1986). Fetal Response decrement: True habituation? *Developmental & Behavioural Pediatrics, 87,* 14–20.

Madison, L. S., Madison, J. K., & Adubato, S. A. (1986). Infant behaviour and development in relation to fetal movement and habituation. *Child Development, 57,* 1475–1482.

Michaelis, R., Rooschuz, B., & Dopfer, R. (1980). Prenatal original of spastic hemiparesis. *Early Human Development, 4,* 243–255.

Nijhuis, J. G., Prechtl, H. F. R., Martin, C. B., Jr., & Bots, R. S. G. M. (1982). Are these behavioural states in the human fetus? *Early Human Development, 6,* 177–195.

Nyman, M., Barr, M., & Westgren, M. (1992). A four year follow-up of hearing and development in children exposed in utero to vibroacoustic stimulation. *British Journal of Obstetrics and Gynaecology, 99,* 685–688.

Ohel, G., Birkenfeld, A., Rabinowitz, R., & Sadovsky, E. (1986). Fetal response to vibratory acoustic stimulation in periods of low heart rate reactivity and low activity. *American Journal of Obstetrics & Gynecology, 154,* 619–621.

Ohel, G., Horowitz, E., Linder, N., & Sohmer, H. (1989). Neonatal auditory acuity following in utero vibratory acoustic stimulation. *American Journal of Obstetrics & Gynecology, 157,* 440–441.

Peiper, A. (1925). Sinnesesempfindungen des kindes vor seiner Geburt [Sensory Perceptions of Children Before Birth]. *Monatschrift fuer Kinderheilkunde, 29,* 236–241.

Pietrantoni, M., Angel, J., Parsons, M. T., McClain, L., Arango, H. A., & Spellacy, W. (1991). Human fetal response to vibroacoustic stimulation as a function of stimulus duration. *Obstetrics and Gynecology, 78,* 807–810.

Prechtl, H. F. R. (1980). The optimality concept. *Early Human Development, 4,* 201–203.

Prechtl, H. F. R. (1985). Ultrasound studies of human fetal behaviour. *Early Human Development, 12,* 91–98.

Rose, S. A., & Wallace, I. F. (1985). Visual recognition memory: A predictor of later cognitive functioning in preterms. *Child Development, 56,* 843–852

Schmidt, W., Boos, R., Gnirs, J., Auer, I., & Schulze, S. (1985). Fetal behavioural states and controlled sound stimulation. *Early Human Development, 12,* 145–153.

Selye, H. (1976). Forty years of stress research: Principal remaining problems and misconceptions. *Canadian Medical Association Journal, 115,* 53–56.

Shalev, E., Bennett, M. J., Megory, E., Wallace, R. M., & Zuckerman, H. (1989). Fetal habituation to repeated sound stimulation. *Israeli Journal of Medical Sciences 25,* 77–80.

Shalev, E., Weiner, E., & Serr, D. M. (1990). Fetal habituation to sound stimulus in various behavioural states. *Gynecological and Obstetrical Investigation, 29,* 115–117.

Singer, J. E., Westphal, M., & Niswander, K. R. (1968). Sex differences in the incidence of neonatal abnormalities and abnormal performance in early childhood. *Child Development, 39,* 103–112.

Smotherman, W. P., & Robinson, S. R. (1992). Habituation in the rat fetus. *Quarterly Journal of Experimental Psychology, 44B,* 215–230.

Stevenson, D., & Siddle, D. (1983). Theories of habituation. In D. Siddle (Ed.), *Orienting and habituation: Perspectives in human research* (pp. 183–236). New York: Wiley.

Thompson, R. F., & Glansman, D. L. (1966). Neural and behavioural mechanisms of habituation and sensitisation. In T. J. Tighe & R. N. Leaton (Eds.), *Habituation* (pp. 49–93). Hillsdale, NJ: Lawrence Erlbaum Associates.

Tizard, B. (1968). Habituation of EEG and skin potential changes in normal and severely sub-normal children. *American Journal of Mental Deficiency, 73,* 16–43.

Toomey, K., Emory, E. K., & Savoir, T. (1987, March). *Prediction from intrapartum fetal heart rate to four month infant development.* Paper presented at Biennial Meeting for Society for Research in Child Development.

Visser, G. H. A., Mulder, H. H., Wit, H. P., Mulder, E. J. H., & Prechtl, H. F. R. (1989). Vibroacoustic stimulation of the human fetus: Effect on behavioural state organisation. *Early Human Development, 19,* 285–296.

Wyers, E. J., Peek, H. V. S., & Herz, M. J. (1973). Behavioural habituation in invertebrates. In H. V. S. Peek & M. J. Herz (Eds.), *Habituation. Physiological substrates* (Vol. 2, pp. 1–57). New York: Academic Press

Yao, Q. W., Jakobsson, J., & Nyman, M. (1990). Fetal responses to different intensity levels of vibroacoustic stimulation. *Obstetrics and Gynecology, 75,* 206–209.

22

The Behavior of the Fetus as an Indicator of Neural Functioning

Peter G. Hepper
Queen's University of Belfast, Northern Ireland, U.K.

The fact that the fetus exhibits behavior and responds to external stimuli means that its nervous system is, to some extent, functioning. Thus observations of the behavior of the fetus can be used to inform regarding the development, functioning, and integrity of the developing individual's neural system. This chapter considers how examination of the behavior of the fetus can be used to elucidate certain aspects of neural system development and, moreover, can be used to indicate the presence and severity of abnormalities in the fetus's nervous system.

The study of fetal behavior is obviously important in and of itself to describe the ontogenesis of behavior, but behavioral observations may also be used to elucidate the development of central nervous system functioning. The behavior of the fetus at any particular age can be related to the current structural status of the nervous system to provide information on the role of these structures in behavior. Longitudinal studies observing behavior at different ages during gestation can document the relationship between behavioral and neural maturation to examine how changes in particular neural structures affect behavior and how changes in behavior affect particular neural structures. Given the evidence that has shown that the development of the nervous system is influenced by experiential factors (e.g., Blakemore & Cooper, 1970; Greenough, 1975, 1986), the study of the behavior of the fetus can provide information on the interaction between experiential and genetic factors in the formation and functioning of the nervous system. The detailed description of the behavior of the fetus can be used to build a picture of "normal" fetal behavior and thus neural system functioning (see also contributions by Arduini, Rizzo, & Romanini, chapter 16; James, Pillai, & Smoleniec, chapter 7; and Nijhuis, chapter 5, in this volume). This description can then be used to provide a standard against which the performance of the fetus can be compared and can enable abnormalities in behavior to be identified. Such behavioral abnormalities may enable the identification of concomitant abnormalities in the individual's nervous system.

The following discussion has two main aims. The first is to exemplify how observation of the behavior of the fetus can be used to examine the development of its nervous system. The second is to show how the analysis of the behavior of the fetus may be used in the identification of abnormalities of neural system functioning. It is not intended to comprehensively review the literature relating to the these points but rather to present illustrative cases of the use of fetal behavior as an indicator of neural functioning.

FETAL HANDEDNESS AND CEREBRAL LATERALIZATION

Humans exhibit a marked hand preference: The vast majority, approximately 90%, exhibit a preference for their right hand, whereas the remaining 10% prefer their left hand (Porac & Coren, 1981). Similar laterality of function has been found during examination of role of the left and right cortical hemispheres (Kitterle, 1991). The most pronounced example is, perhaps, the apparent localization of language abilities in the left cerebral hemisphere. Although the relationship between handedness and lateralization of language is unclear (Bryden & Steenhuis, 1991), almost all right handers are left-hemisphere dominant for speech (Segalowitz & Bryden, 1983). The exhibition of behavioral and cerebral laterality of function implies there are differences in the neural structure of the two hemispheres that control these behaviors and roles (Geschwind & Galaburda, 1987). An understanding of the developmental origins of these behavioral asymmetries may enable the differences in neural structure underlying them to be elucidated. Identification of when a lateralized behavior first commences may enable investigation of hemispheric structure at that time to identify differences in neural structure that may be responsible for these behaviors.

Although handedness per se only becomes apparent during infancy as the infant's motor abilities develop (Harris & Carlson, 1988), early indications of handedness or motor bias have been sought in the newborn by examining head position preferences. Newborns have been observed to lie with their head turned to the right and show a preference for turning their

TABLE 22.1
Number of Individuals Observed Sucking Either Their Left or Right
Thumb at Three Different Gestational Ages.

	Gestational Age			
	15–21	28–34	36-term	Total
Right thumb	71	88	93	252
Left thumb	10	4	8	22
Total				274

Note. From Hepper, Shahidullah, and White (1991). Reprinted by permission of Elsevier Science Ireland Ltd.

head right after first having it held in the mid-line position (Dooling, Chi, & Gilles, 1983; Goodwin & Michel, 1981; Harris, 1983). This would suggest that handedness, or a right-sided bias, is present at birth, however, the developmental origins of this ability are unknown.

In a recent study (Hepper, Shahidullah, & White, 1991) the origins of handedness in the prenatal period were examined. One of the many behaviors exhibited by the fetus, which can be clearly detected by ultrasound observation, is that of thumb sucking, that is, the fetus's thumb is present in its mouth (DeVries, Visser, & Prechtl, 1982; Hepper, 1990). The high resolution of modern ultrasound machines clearly enables the presence of the thumb in the mouth to be identified, especially when viewed in the median (sagittal) plane. The particular thumb, left or right, being sucked can easily be determined by tracing back from the hand up the arm to the shoulder and then observing its relation to the heart. If a right-sided bias is present during the prenatal period, then a preference for sucking the right thumb may be observed.

Of 274 instances of thumb sucking (about 5% of all fetal observations of the head region report evidence of thumb sucking; thus thumb-sucking behavior, although common, is not frequently observed), from 274 separate pregnancies, 252 fetuses were observed to be sucking their right thumb (see Table 22.1). This preference was present from as early as 15 weeks of gestational age. Eight fetuses (12–14 weeks of gestational age) were observed sucking their thumbs prior to 15 weeks of gestational age. Seven were observed sucking their right thumb and one the left. Longitudinal observations performed on 20 fetuses revealed that fetuses maintained the preference for their right, or left, thumb throughout pregnancy.

However, the preference of the fetus for sucking a particular thumb did correlate highly with the head-turning preference of the newborn. If an individual showed a preference for sucking its right thumb as a fetus, then when, as a newborn, it was laid in a supine position with its head held in the mid-line, it was found to turn its head to the right (23 of 28 fetuses).

Similarly, fetuses who sucked their left thumb were observed to turn their head to the left when head position preferences were examined in the newborn period (three of four fetuses). Most recently, preliminary investigations of the grasping behavior of 15–18-month-olds reveals that the thumb, left or right, sucked as a fetus is predictive of the hand that will be used to grasp a ball suspended in front of the infant when sitting up.

This study indicates that a behavioral asymmetry, expressed by thumb sucking, is present before birth and possibly from as early as 12 weeks of gestational age. This obviously has implications for theories regarding the developmental origins of laterality. Given the early evidence of lateralized behavior, 12–15 weeks of gestational age, genetic models (Annett, 1985) rather than neuropathological or familial (Bakan, Dibb, & Reed, 1973; Satz, 1973) may provide the most appropriate explanation, although asymmetric cleavage of the embryo (Boklage, 1980) may also play a role in the origins of this behavior.

The results also have implications for neural development more generally. Laterality of function and cerebral lateralization are well-established phenomena of the mature nervous system The results of this study suggest that lateralization of the nervous system is present very early during development. Asymmetries in the planum temporale have been observed in adults (Geschwind & Levitsky, 1968), in neonates (Witelson & Paille, 1973), and in the fetus during late gestation (Chi, Dooling, & Gilles, 1977). The early exhibition of a behavioral asymmetry is suggestive of the fact that asymmetries in neural structure would also be present during the first trimester. It has been argued that hemispheric cerebral lateralization leads to the exhibition of handedness (Best, 1988; Harris, 1983). Applied to the results just reported, this would suggest that brain lateralization is present before the observation of a preference for sucking a particular thumb, that is, before 12–15 weeks of gestational age. Alternatively, it could be speculated that an initial preference for the right thumb is caused by advanced right-sided neuromuscular development. It is known that stimulation can influence brain organization (Blakemore & Cooper, 1970; Greenough, 1975, 1986), and it may be that sucking the right thumb differentially stimulates the left and right brain hemispheres and this begins the development of hemispheric specialization and subsequent laterality of function. This remains to be resolved.

The study is illustrative of how observation of the behavior of the fetus can inform regarding the developmental status of its nervous system. Observation of a behavior of the fetus, thumb sucking, reveals that a prominent facet of adult behavior, laterality of function, is present early during development. This observation combined with information regarding the structural status of the fetal nervous system will enable inferences to be drawn regarding the development of the fetal nervous system in general and the role of various neural structures in the exhibition of handedness in particular.

ABNORMAL BEHAVIOR AND ABNORMAL NEURAL FUNCTIONING

The behavior of the developing fetus can be argued to represent the functioning and integrity of its nervous system (Hepper, 1990; Leader & Bennett, 1988). Therefore observation of the behavior of the fetus provides a means of assessing neural dysfunction. To behave "normally" requires an intact and fully functioning neural system. If the individual's neural system is not fully integrated or is not functioning normally, then this may be reflected in the behavior of the individual. Thus, by the observation of the behavior of the fetus it is possible to enable the well-being of the fetus to be determined. Moreover, because fetal behavior is to a certain extent infinitely variable, quantitative and qualitative measures of fetal behavior afford the opportunity of determining the severity and extent of dysfunction. The more severely affected the nervous system is, the greater the observed differences in behavior from those with an intact nervous system.

The fetus exhibits a wide range of behaviors (DeVries et al., 1982), commencing around 7.5 weeks of gestational age with slow flexions and extensions of the vertebral column and passive movements of the limbs (DeVries et al., 1982). The diversity of fetal movements increases rapidly over the next 3–4 weeks, and over 20 different movement patterns have been identified (DeVries et al., 1982). Moreover, as the fetus matures, the movements of the fetus become more coordinated and regular, presumably as a result of increased maturation and integration of the neural system. The exhibition of this diverse repertoire of behaviors enables the construction of a picture of normal fetal behavior from which abnormalities in behavior can be identified.

Two examples of the use of behavioral observations in the fetus to assess neural integrity are presented next. The first uses the spontaneous behavior of the fetus, that is, behavior emitted under its own internal volition, and the second uses elicited behavior, that is, behavior emitted in response to external stimulation.

Spontaneous Behavior and Spontaneous Abortion

Approximately 15–20% of recognized human pregnancies end in spontaneous abortion (Warburton & Strobino, 1987), with the majority occurring during the first trimester (Boué, Phillippe, Giroud, & Boué, 1976; Warburton

& Frazer, 1964). Spontaneous abortions have been attributed to two main causes: either as a result of some maternal factor, such as cervical incompetence or maternal disease, or as a result of a fetal problem. Morphological abnormalities have been observed in a large proportion of spontaneous abortuses (Fantel, Shepard, Vadheim-Roth, Stephens, & Coleman, 1980; Poland, Miller, Harris, & Livingston, 1981). In these latter cases where fetal abnormalities are present, given the close relationship between behavior and neural integrity, it may be expected that the behavior of these fetuses would show differences from fetuses who did not undergo a spontaneous abortion or who were aborted due to a maternal factor.

A recent study (Shahidullah & Hepper, 1992) examined the behavior of fetuses who later spontaneously aborted during the first trimester to determine whether their behavior differed from that of normal fetuses.

In this study 121 singleton fetuses, all of whom exhibited a heartbeat within the normal range (Achiron, Tadmor, & Mashiach, 1991) and were appropriately grown for gestational age at 7–8 weeks of gestation, were observed at 10 weeks of gestational age using ultrasound. Three behaviors were observed: startles (number), isolated arm movements (number), and general body movements (number and duration).

In the 2 weeks following the observations performed at 10 weeks of gestational age, 5 of the 121 fetuses underwent a spontaneous abortion. The results of the behavioral observations conducted on the fetuses who continued to term and the five who underwent a spontaneous abortion are reported in Table 22.2.

Observation of this table reveals that three of the five fetuses that spontaneously aborted exhibited behavioral patterns that differed from those observed in fetuses that continued to term. On all four measures that were recorded, the number of startles, general movements, and isolated arm movements and the duration of general movements, 2 of these fetuses exhibited behavior outside the range of behavior exhibited by the 116 fetuses that continued to term. For the third fetus only general body movements were found to be in the normal range.

Although postmortem information was unavailable on any of the fetuses who underwent a spontaneous abortion, the following is offered as a working hypothesis. The three fetuses who aborted and exhibited abnormal behavior had concomitant abnormalities of their nervous system, hence their subsequent abortion. The two fetuses who aborted but did not exhibit abnormalities in their behavior may have had an intact neural system and their abortion was due to some maternal cause. Although more work is needed to confirm these specific hypotheses, the results do indicate that the behavior of the fetus at early gestations may provide information regarding the status of the individual's nervous system.

TABLE 22.2

Number (Mean, Standard Deviation, and Range) of Startles, Isolated Arm Movements, and General Body Movements Exhibited, and the Percent of Recording Time That General Movements Were Observed, by Fetuses at 10 Weeks of Age Who Continued to Term and by Fetuses Who Spontaneously Aborted by 12 Weeks of Age

Fetuses	Number of Startles	Number of Isolated Arm Movements	Number of General Body Movements	Percent of Time in General Body Movements
Normal (n = 116)				
Mean	11.51	7.41	19.11	11.2
SD	3.47	2.26	4.47	3.9
Range	5–21	3–12	9–30	6.4–23.2
Fetuses undergoing spontaneous abortion (n = 5)				
Fetus 1	30	2	34	32.4
Fetus 2	4	2	11	5.6
Fetus 3	22	18	41	37.2
Fetus 4	13	8	17	10.6
Fetus 5	9	7	23	13.4

Note. From Shahidullah and Hepper (1992). Reprinted by permission of Elsevier Science Ireland Ltd.

Habituation and the Severity of Abnormality

One feature of abnormalities of the nervous system is their variable nature. Similar handicapping conditions may result in a very severe effect on behavior in some, whereas in others very little effect may be observed. For example, trisomy 21 may result in different degrees of effect on different individuals, even though the underlying causation is the same. Although current biomedical technology can detect the presence of Down syndrome, it is unable to determine how severely the individual will be affected. Unlike biomedical techniques for the detection of, for example, trisomy 21, where analysis of the individual's cells reveals the presence or absence of a third 21st chromosome, the behavior of the fetus is not bimodally distributed but rather forms a continuum. The number of individual movements in a particular observation period may vary from 0 to n. This diversity of behavior thus affords the opportunity of assessing the severity of any nervous system effect.

In an attempt to gain more information on the condition of the fetus's nervous system, attention has turned to ability of the fetus to habituate (see also contributions by Kisilevsky, chapter 14, and Leader, chapter 21, in this volume). Habituation is defined as the decrement in response to repeated stimulation and is reflective of central nervous system functioning (Jeffrey & Cohen, 1971; Thompson & Spencer, 1966). The first study of habituation in the fetus was presented by Peiper (1925), who reported a decrease in fetal movements after repeated presentation of a stimulus (a car horn) sounded in close proximity to the fetus. Since then, a number of studies have demonstrated habituation (e.g., Bennett, 1984; Granier-Deferre, Lecanuet, Cohen, & Busnel, 1983; Leader, Baille, Martin, & Vermeulen, 1982a, 1982b)

Hepper and Shahidullah (1992) examined the response of normal ($n = 10$) and Down's syndrome ($n = 2$, Fetus A and B) fetuses to a repeated auditory stimulus, measuring the number of trials to habituate and the latency to respond on each trial. This latter measure had not previously been applied to investigations of the fetus. The aim of the experiment was to see if performance on a habituation task would enable the differentiation of "normal" fetuses from those with Down's syndrome and would discriminate between fetuses with Down's syndrome.

Very briefly, the procedure used consisted of three stages. In stage 1 a series of 250-Hz tones of 2 sec duration and 5 sec interstimulus interval (ISI) were presented to the fetus until no response was observed from the fetus on five successive trials. A response was defined as a movement of the arms or upper body of the fetus within 4.5 sec of the onset of the stimulus. After the fetus ceased to respond to the 250-Hz tone, stage 2 commenced and the fetus was presented with a series of 500-Hz tones (2

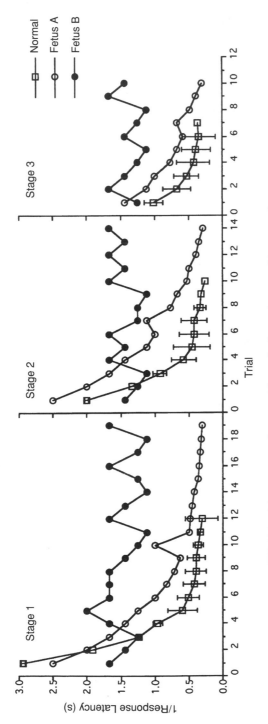

FIG. 22.1. Mean response latency with standard error for normal fetuses and response latency for Down syndrome fetuses (fetus A and fetus B) on each stage of testing. Fetus B received 30 stimulus presentations on each stage, but the number of trials presented is limited to the last response of fetus A during each stage of testing. The pattern of responding on the trials not shown here for fetus B did not differ from those shown. From Hepper and Shahidullah (1992). Reprinted by permission. Copyright by the Experimental Psychology Society.

413

sec duration and 5 sec ISI) until no response was observed on five consecutive trials. The 250-Hz tone was then re-presented (stage 3) and continued until the fetus exhibited no response (the absence of movement within 4.5 sec of stimulus onset) on five consecutive trials.

The results were considered representative of true habituation if the fetus (a) after a number of stimulus presentation ceased to respond to the first stimulus, (b) on presentation of the new stimulus re-commenced responding, (c) habituated its response to this stimulus, (d) on re-presentation of the original stimulus re-commenced responding, and (e) habituated faster (fewer number of trials) to the second presentation of the original stimulus. Observation of Fig. 22.1 reveals this to be the case for all of the normal fetuses and for one of the Down syndrome fetuses. The results of the latency to respond to the stimulus are presented in Fig. 22.1. The response latency exhibited by normal fetuses increased after repeated presentation of the stimulus but recovered following presentation of the new stimulus at the start of stage 2 and stage 3. The decrement in response latency exhibited by the two Down syndrome fetuses differed both from the normal fetuses and from each other. Both Down syndrome fetuses exhibited quicker response latencies than the normal fetuses. One, fetus B, did not habituate and evidenced no increase in latency with repeated stimulus presentation. The other, fetus A, did habituate but at a much slower rate than the normal fetuses. The decrement in response latency exhibited by the two Down syndrome fetuses also differed from one another. Fetus B died soon after birth, although there were no significant obstetric or physical differences observed between the two fetuses before birth that would suggest increased probability of mortality in fetus B. Although the incidence of neonatal mortality in Down syndrome is very low, the significant point is that a behavioral measure discriminated between the two fetuses although genetic or other measures did not.

The results of this study indicate that performance on an habituation task may enable the detection not only of the presence of an abnormality but also of how severe it is. One goal of obstetric practice is the prediction of fetal well-being; the analysis of the behavior of the fetus offers the opportunity of evaluating both the presence and severity of neural system dysfunction.

CONCLUDING REMARKS

The aim of this chapter has been to illustrate that behavioral observations of the fetus can be used to gain an understanding of the development of the human fetal nervous system and can be used to assess the condition of the fetal nervous system. There is no doubt that behavioral observations can inform regarding neural system functioning and integrity, and have a crucial role in documenting the ontogenesis of neural system functioning. Inferences regarding the functioning of the nervous system rely on the accurate documentation of the behavior of the fetus, and it is essential that descriptions of all aspects of the behavior of the fetus are undertaken objectively in order to achieve a greater understanding of prenatal neural functioning and of the role of this in the subsequent development of the nervous system.

The small numbers of subjects in the studies discussed reveal one of the major problems in obtaining data for behavioral analysis of abnormalities. Genetic events or spontaneous abortion, compared to normal uncomplicated pregnancies, are rare and difficult to predict. They do serve an important indication that behavioral indices can be used to detect abnormalities of central nervous system functioning, and there is now a need for concerted and coordinated effort using similar methodologies for large-scale studies to examine the usefulness of behavioral monitoring in a clinical setting. There is now little doubt that behavioral observations have the potential to provide extensive information on the functioning of the nervous system, and one of the greatest challenges facing researchers in this area is to realize this potential and develop its clinical value.

ACKNOWLEDGMENTS

I thank Norman Krasnegor and Jean-Pierre Lecanuet for their invitation to present this work at the Fetal Behaviour Conference in Paris, September 1992. I also thank the National Institute for Child Health & Development, U. S. A., and CNRS, France, for their support of the conference. This work is supported by grants from the Medical Research Council, U.K. and the Wellcome Trust.

REFERENCES

Achiron, R., Tadmor, O., & Mashiach, S. (1991). Heart rate as a predictor of first-trimester spontaneous abortion after ultrasound-proven viability. *Obstetrics & Gynecology, 78*, 330–334.

Annett, M. (1985). *Left, right, hand and brain: The right shift theory.* Hillsdale, NJ: Lawrence Erlbaum Associates.

Bakan, P., Dibb, G., & Reed, P. (1973). Handedness and birth stress. *Neuropsychologia, 11*, 363–366.

Bennett, M. J. (1984). The assessment of fetal well-being. In M. J. Bennett (Ed.), *Ultrasound in perinatal care* (pp. 117–126). London: Wiley.

Best, C. T. (1988). The emergence of cerebral asymmetries in early human development: A literature review and neuroembryological model. In D. F. Molfese & S. J. Segalowitz (Eds.), *Brain lateralization in children* (pp. 5–34). New York: Guilford.

Blakemore, C., & Cooper, G. F. (1970). Development of brain depends on the visual environment. *Nature, 228*, 477–478.

Boklage, C. E. (1980). The sinistral blastocyst: An embryonic perspective on the development of brain function asymmetries. In J. Herron (Ed.), *Neuropsychology of left-handedness* (pp. 115–137). New York: Academic Press.

Boué, J., Philippe, E., Giroud, A., & Boué, A. (1976). Phenotypic expression of lethal chromosomal anomalies in human abortuses. *Teratology, 14*, 3.

Bryden, M. P., & Steenhuis, R. E. (1991). Issues in the assessment of handedness. In F. L. Kitterle (Ed.), *Cerebral laterality* (pp. 35–51). Hillsdale, NJ: Lawrence Erlbaum Associates.

Chi, J. G., Dooling, E. C., & Gilles, F. H. (1977). Gyral development of the human brain. *Journal of Neurology, 1*, 86–93.

DeVries, J. I. P., Visser, G. H. A., & Prechtl, H. F. R. (1982). The emergence of fetal behaviour: 1. Qualitative aspects. *Early Human Development, 7*, 301–322.

Dooling, E. C., Chi, J. G., & Gilles, F. H. (1983). Telencephalic development: Changing gyral patterns. In F. H. Gilles, A. Leviton, & E. C. Dooling (Eds.), *The developing human brain: Growth and epidemiologic neuropathy* (pp. 94–104). Boston: J. Wright.

Fantel, A. G., Shepard, T. H., Vadheim-Roth, C., Stephens, T .D., & Coleman, C. (1980). *Human embryonic and fetal death.* New York: Academic Press.

Geschwind, N., & Galaburda, A. S. (1987). *Cerebral lateralization.* Cambridge, MA: MIT Press.

Geschwind, N., & Levitsky, W. (1968). Human brain: Left right asymmetries in temporal speech region. *Science, 161*, 186–187.

Goodwin, R. S., & Michel, G. F. (1981). Head orientation position during birth and in infant neonatal period, and hand preference at nineteen weeks. *Child Development, 52*, 819–826.

Granier-Deferre, C., Lecanuet, J. P., Cohen, H., & Busnel, M. C. (1983). Preliminary evidence on fetal auditory habituation. In G. Rossi (Ed.), *Noise as a public health problem* (Vol. 1, pp. 561–572). Milan, Italy: Edizioni Tecniche.

Greenough, W. T. (1975). Experimental modification of the developing brain. *American Scientist, 63*, 37–46.

Greenough, W. T. (1986). What's special about development? Thoughts on the bases of experience-sensitive synaptic plasticity. In W. T. Greenough & J. M. Juraska (Eds.), *Developmental neuropsychology* (pp. 387–407). New York: Academic Press.

Harris, L. J. (1983). Laterality of function in the infant: Historical and contemporary trends in theory and research. In G. Young, S. J. Segalowitz, C. M. Corter, & S. E. Trehub (Eds.), *Manual specialisation and the developing brain* (pp. 177–247). New York: Academic Press.

Harris, L. J., & Carlson, D. F. (1988). Pathological left-handedness: An analysis of theories and evidence. In D. F. Molfese & S. J. Segalowitz (Eds.), *Brain lateralization in children* (pp. 289–372). New York: Guilford.

Hepper, P. G. (1990). Fetal behaviour. A potential diagnostic tool. *Midwifery, 6*, 193–200.

Hepper, P. G., & Shahidullah, S. (1992). Habituation in normal and Down syndrome fetuses. *Quarterly Journal of Experimental Psychology, 44B*, 305–317.

Hepper, P. G., Shahidullah, S., & White, R. (1991). Handedness in the human fetus. *Neuropsychologia, 29*, 1107–1111.

Jeffrey, W. E., & Cohen, L. B. (1971). Habituation in the human infant. *Advances in Child Development & Behavior, 6*, 63–97.

Kitterle, F. L. (Ed.). (1991). *Cerebral laterality.* Hillsdale, NJ: Lawrence Erlbaum Associates.

Leader, L. R., Baille, P., Martin, B., & Vermeulen, E. (1982a). The assessment and significance of habituation to a repeated stimulus by the human foetus. *Early Human Development, 7*, 211–219.

Leader, L. R., Baille, P., Martin, B., & Vermeulen, E. (1982b). Foetal habituation in high risk pregnancies. *British Journal of Obstetrics and Gynaecology, 89*, 441–446.

Leader, L. R., & Bennett, M. J. (1988). Fetal habituation. In M. I. Levene, M. J. Bennett, & J. Punt (Eds.), *Fetal and neonatal neurology and neurosurgery* (pp. 59–70). Edinburgh, Scotland: Churchill.

Peiper, A. (1925). Sinnesempfindungen des Kindes vor seiner geburt [The sensory awareness of the child before birth]. *Monatsschrift fur Kinderheilkunde, 29*, 237–241.

Poland, B. J., Miller, J. R., Harris, M., & Livingston, J. (1981). Spontaneous abortion. A study of 1961 women and their conceptuses. *Acta Obstetrica et Gynaecologica Scandinavica, Supplement, 102*, 1.

Porac, C., & Coren, S. (1981). *Lateral preferences and human behavior.* New York: Springer-Verlag.

Satz, P. (1973). Left handedness and early brain insult: An explanation. *Neuropsychologia, 11*, 115–117.

Segalowitz, S. J., & Bryden, M. P. (1983). Individual differences in hemisperic representation of language. In S. J. Segalowitz (Ed.), *Language functions and brain organization* (pp. 341–372). New York: Academic Press.

Shahidullah, S., & Hepper, P. G. (1992). Abnormal fetal behaviour in first trimester spontaneous abortion. *European Journal of Obstetrics & Gynecology and Reproductive Biology, 45*, 181–184.

Thompson, R. F., & Spencer, W. A. (1966). Habituation: A model for the study of neuronal substrates of behavior. *Psychological Review, 73*, 16–43.

Warburton, D., & Frazer, F. C. (1964). Spontaneous abortion risks in man: Data from reproductive histories collected in a medical genetics unit. *American Journal of Human Genetics, 16*, 1.

Warburton, D., & Strobino, B. (1987). *Spontaneous and recurrent abortion.* Oxford: Blackwell.

Witelson, S. F., & Paille, W. (1973). Left hemisphere specialisation for language in the newborn: Neuroanatomical evidence of asymmetry. *Brain, 96*, 641–646.

23

Fetal Alcohol Learning Resulting from Alcohol Contamination of the Prenatal Environment

Juan Carlos Molina
María Gabriela Chotro
Héctor Daniel Domínguez
*Instituto de Investigación Médica Mercedes y Martín Ferreyra,
Córdoba, Argentina*

This chapter is based on studies that intend to analyze fetal experience with alcohol in terms of its effects and mechanisms leading to changes in postnatal recognition and acceptance patterns of this agent. Previous fetal research concerned with sensory and learning capabilities of the organism proximal to birth encouraged and oriented such an analysis (Smotherman & Robinson, 1987, 1988). A second factor that encouraged these studies relates to an increasing knowledge about alcohol responsiveness during early postnatal development (Domínguez, Bocco, Chotro, Spear, & Molina, 1993; Hunt, Molina, Rajachandran, Spear, & Spear, 1993; Molina & Chotro, 1989a, 1989b; Molina, Hoffmann, & Spear, 1986).

Before analyzing the studies conducted with fetuses, it seems prudent to summarize briefly the capabilities of the neonate relative to recognition and learning about alcohol. Infantile responsiveness to alcohol is then examined as a function of two alternative techniques that involve fetal exposure to alcohol in an altricial mammal. The first technique is basically defined by alcohol contamination of the amniotic fluid prior to birth. This manipulation is sufficient to alter neonatal responsiveness to alcohol chemosensory cues. The strategy seems better interpreted in terms of associative learning comprising fetal perception of such cues paired with consequences derived from cesarean and/or perinatal manipulations. The second strategy is defined by experimental, chronic maternal alcohol intoxication during the last days of pregnancy. This experience profoundly affects reactivity to ethanol odor and consumption of the drug when the offspring are tested after birth. The common denominator in both techniques is the observation that the near-term fetus is capable of acquiring alcohol-related information that will later affect interactions between the organism and the drug.

RESPONSIVENESS TO ALCOHOL'S ATTRIBUTES AS A FUNCTION OF EARLY EXPERIENCES WITH THE DRUG

In the human species, experience with alcohol can take place during infancy. Following maternal intake, this relatively simple molecular compound diffuses into breast milk and is incorporated by the neonate through suckling (Abel, 1984; Binkiewicz, Robinson, & Senior, 1978; Little, Anderson, Ervin, Worthington-Roberts, & Clarren, 1989; Mennella & Beauchamp, 1991). Alcohol-containing beverages can be accidentally consumed by the infant or even deliberately administered by parents who seek sedative effects upon the child or who are not aware of its potential dangers and merely follow alcohol-related sociocultural habits (Buteler, 1989; Croce, 1977; Quiroga de García, 1979).

Any of these infantile experiences with alcohol implies that the organism establishes contact with one or more sensory and/or postabsorptive effects of the drug.

Studies performed in altricial mammals indicate that different alcohol attributes are processed by the infant animal and alter subsequent recognition and acceptance patterns of the drug or of nonethanol cues that were originally paired with alcohol's postabsorptive effects. Preweanling rats consume more alcohol after being briefly exposed to ethanol odor (Molina, Serwatka, & Spear, 1984). Alcohol chemosensory processing in infant rats also has been demonstrated through appetitive and aversive conditioning procedures where alcohol odor and/or taste act as conditioned stimuli (Molina, Hoffmann & Spear, 1986; Molina, Serwatka, Spear, & Spear, 1985). Early memories related to alcohol orosensory cues are retained over a considerable time span and modulate adult alcohol intake as assessed through chronic preference tests (Molina, Serwatka, & Spear, 1986).

Infant animals also seem capable of processing different alcohol attributes that derive from its postabsorptive effects. Acute alcohol intoxication during early development can represent:

1. An unconditioned stimulus that promotes aversions to novel sensory cues (Hunt, Molina, Spear, & Spear, 1990).
2. An interoceptive context capable of retrieving memories acquired under a similar context (Hunt et al., 1990).
3. A factor that also promotes alcohol orosensory processing due to salivary and respiratory nonmetabolic elimination of the drug and/or hematogenic stimulation of olfactory receptors (Molina & Chotro, 1989a, 1989b; Molina, Chotro, & Spear, 1989).

THE NEAR-TERM FETUS ACUTELY EXPOSED TO ALCOHOL IN THE AMNIOTIC FLUID: EFFECTS ON NEONATAL RESPONSIVENESS TO ALCOHOL

An approach based on alcohol pharmacokinetics during pregnancy indicates that there exists a rapid bidirectional transfer of the drug between the mother and the fetus. Following maternal ethanol consumption, the drug is detected in the placenta, the umbilical cord vein, and fetal tissue and plasma, as well as in the amniotic fluid (Abel, 1984; Szeto, 1989).

Is there evidence suggesting that during fetal life, memories are acquired relative to some of the drug's properties? The prolific work of fetal neuroethologists certainly endorses this possibility. Physiological and anatomical studies suggest that certain olfactory subsystems are already functional in the rat and mouse near-term fetus (Coppola & O'Connell, 1989; Pedersen, Stewart, Greer, & Shepherd, 1983). During the last days of gestation, the rat fetus responds with specific behavioral patterns to chemosensory cues such as mint, citral, lemon, and cyclohexanone (Smotherman & Robinson, 1990). Contamination of the amniotic fluid with apple juice has been found to promote increased consumption of this stimulus during adulthood due to the specificity of the stimulation performed in utero (Smotherman, 1982a). Furthermore, chemosensory conditioned aversions are acquired even during gestational day 17 (Smotherman, 1982b; Smotherman & Robinson, 1985, 1987, 1988; Stickrod, Kimble, & Smotherman, 1982). Taken as a whole, these studies show the capability of the fetal organism in terms of processing salient chemosensory cues present in the prenatal environment and of retaining this information over a considerable time span. It is possible then that the unborn organism will be capable of acquiring information about alcohol attributes when this psychopharmacological agent contaminates the prenatal milieu.

A recent series of studies has analyzed neonatal responsiveness to alcohol's sensory cues as a function of acute fetal experience with the drug. In this experimental situation, near-term rat fetuses were exposed to a mild alcohol solution (6% v/v) administered into the amniotic fluid 10 min prior to cesarean delivery. This brief exposure to alcohol was sufficient to modify autonomic responses elicited by alcohol odor during the first hours of postnatal life. The odorant induced stable and relatively low cardiac decelerations in pups that were prenatally exposed to saline or an alcohol-free lemon extract. Prenatal experience with alcohol promoted significantly stronger bradycardiac patterns that lasted throughout most of the testing procedure (Chotro & Molina, 1992). Heart rate decelerations caused by salient stimuli have been reported in both cesarean and vaginally delivered pups (Ronca & Alberts, 1990). Changes in heart rate seem to represent a component of the orienting response to relevant stimuli (Emory & Toomey, 1988). These earlier data suggest that the fetus had acquired information about alcohol sensory cues that were later expressed as changes in the cardiovascular component of the orienting response toward alcohol odor.

Acute administration of alcohol into the amniotic fluid was sufficient to modify later cardiac responsiveness to ethanol odor. Is this prenatal manipulation able to affect the infant's alcohol olfactory and intake acceptance patterns? This issue has been addressed by employing prenatal manipulations similar to those used in the study just described and postnatal techniques previously used to examine infant's capabilities of recognizing alcohol derived cues (Molina, Serwatka, & Spear, 1984; Molina, Hoffman, & Spear 1986; Molina, Serwatka, Spear, & Spear, 1985). During gestational day 21 (GD 21), alcohol, lemon, or saline was administered in the amniotic fluid 10 min prior to performing a cesarean section. During postnatal day 8 (PD 8), pups representative of the three prenatal treatments were tested in an olfactory preference test. One section of the apparatus was scented with alcohol odor, whereas the alternative one was defined by ambient lemon odor. Subjects prenatally exposed to alcohol spent significantly greater time over the alcohol odor when compared to the odor preference data for the lemon- or saline-treated animals. Lemon-pretreated infants spent less time over the alcohol odor and hence more time over the alternative lemon-scented section of the apparatus. In other words, olfactory preferences were differentially affected by the nature of the prenatal experience.

The same pups that received the odor preference assessment were later tested (PD 9) to assess alcohol intake. A mild alcohol solution (6% v/v) was infused intraorally through an implanted cheek cannula (Hoffmann, Molina, Kucharski, & Spear, 1987; Molina, Hoffmann, & Spear, 1986). Cumulative percentage body weight gains during the infusion procedure were recorded in a consumption test that lasted 30 min. Lemon and saline prenatal treatments lead to similar intake scores across the entire test. Of major importance for this study was the finding that prenatal alcohol exposure resulted in significantly higher intake scores relative to those observed in the control treatments (Chotro & Molina, 1990). When coupling the results attained in both assessments (olfactory preference and alcohol intake tests), it appears that sensory information experienced prior to birth can affect the infants predisposition to accept alcohol after birth.

It could be argued that the effects derived from alcohol contamination of the amniotic fluid were promoted by alcohol's toxic and/or teratogenic properties rather than by fetal exposure to alcohol-derived sensory cues. Two factors argue against this possibility. As previously observed, animals that experienced a nontoxic stimulus such as lemon during prenatal life subsequently showed an enhanced preference toward lemon odor. A similar result was obtained whenever alcohol contaminated the amniotic fluid: Subjects exposed to this stimulus showed an enhanced alcohol olfactory preference later in life (Chotro & Molina, 1990). Furthermore, gas chromatographic head-space analysis of ethanol concentrations in fetal blood and the amniotic fluid strongly argues against fetal alcohol intoxication in the preceding experiments (Chotro, Córdoba, & Molina, 1991; Hachenberg & Schmidt, 1985). Indeed, even when using an alcohol solution three times more concentrated than the one employed in these experiments and leaving the fetuses in utero 30 rather than 10 min after exposure, fetal blood alcohol levels are practically undetectable. On the contrary, high and persistent alcohol levels are registered in the amniotic fluid.

The sensory experience with alcohol in utero is also capable of modulating subsequent learning about alcohol's sensory attributes. As is the case with a variety of chemosensory cues (methyl, Miller, Molina, & Spear, 1990; lemon, Rudy & Cheatle, 1978; citral, Fillion & Blass, 1986; etc.), infant rats readily associate alcohol odor with appetitive or aversive reinforcers (Hunt et al., 1990; Molina et al., 1985; Molina & Chotro, 1989a, 1989b). Conditioned alcohol olfactory preferences are obtained in infants exposed to paired presentations of alcohol odor and intraoral infusions of a sweet tastant such as sucrose. The magnitude of the response toward alcohol odor is intimately related to the concentration of the sucrose solution employed as a reinforcer. Further, intraamniotic incorporation of ethanol prior to delivery significantly augments the magnitude of the appetitive conditioned response toward ethanol odor that is attained with different sucrose concentrations (Chotro, Córdoba, & Molina, 1991).

Prenatal alcohol treatment not only interacts with learning defined by the association between alcohol odor and an appetitive reinforcer such as sucrose. The prenatal experience with alcohol appears also capable of modulating aversive infantile conditioning toward ethanol chemosensory cues. As previously stated, nonmetabolic routes of alcohol elimination provide means for determining alcohol orosensory processing during the drug's postabsorptive state (Molina et al., 1989; Molina & Chotro, 1989a,

1989b). Infants treated with a mild dose of alcohol that also experience footshock during peak levels of blood alcohol later avoid the odor of alcohol in a two-way odor locational test (alcohol vs. lemon olfactory test; Molina & Chotro, 1989b) and an assessment of alcohol intake. This aversive profile is markedly attenuated in organisms that experienced alcohol in the amniotic fluid 10 min before cesarean delivery (Chotro, Córdoba, & Molina, 1991).

The results reported in the present section indicate that the fetus can acquire information about alcohol's sensory cues and express the memory of the prenatal experience in terms of:

1. Changes in the cardiac component of the orienting response toward alcohol odor.
2. An enhanced consumption of an alcohol solution.
3. An enhanced alcohol odor preference.
4. A potentiated learned response toward alcohol odor when this cue is postnatally paired with an appetitive reinforcer such as sucrose.
5. An inhibitory effect upon the aversive learned response to alcohol odor when this cue is postnatally paired with an aversive event such as footshock.

Are all these effects derived exclusively from sensory preexposure mechanisms? In other words, was prenatal alcohol sensory exposure by itself the factor that promoted all these changes in alcohol responsiveness later in life?

AN ASSOCIATIVE ANALYSIS OF THE EFFECTS DERIVED FROM ACUTE ALCOHOL CHEMOSENSORY CONTAMINATION OF THE PRENATAL ENVIRONMENT

As previously demonstrated, the near-term rat fetus has the capacity to associate chemosensory cues with certain reinforcers (Smotherman, 1982b; Stickrod et al., 1982). In all the previously described experiments, chemosensory contamination of the uterine environment was carried out in close temporal proximity to cesarean delivery procedures. The following experiments suggest that chemosensory cues present in the amniotic fluid are likely to be associated with the consequences of cesarean delivery and/or neonatal tactile stimulation. As a function of this association, it appears that the organism acquires a conditioned response to sensory cues, such as those derived from alcohol, which later modify responsiveness to similar cues.

Neonatal motor responsiveness to the odor of alcohol or lemon was found to be affected not only by the sensory nature of the stimulus that contaminated the amniotic fluid, but also by the delay existing between onset of this contamination and birth induction via cesarean delivery. In a first experiment the amniotic fluid of 21-day-old fetuses was contaminated 10 or 40 min prior to cesarean delivery with either an alcohol or a lemon solution. After delivery, the organisms were evaluated in terms of overall motor activity when the testing environment was scented with either alcohol or lemon odor. This testing device consisted of a hollow spherical plastic chamber equipped with touch-sensitive electrodes that were activated as a function of fetal–electrode interactions. Neonates that experienced either alcohol or lemon in the amniotic fluid 40 min prior to birth induction failed to exhibit differential alcohol or lemon olfactory-induced motor activity. Pups pretreated with these chemosensory cues 10 min prior to birth exhibited a dramatically different response profile. Alcohol odor induced significantly higher activity relative to lemon odor in those subjects pretreated with alcohol 10 min prior to delivery. The opposite was observed when lemon was present prior to delivery. Furthermore, alcohol or lemon administered 10 min prior to cesarean delivery resulted in significantly higher motor responsiveness to the odor of such stimuli when compared to that recorded in pups were exposed to similar cues but 40 min before birth (Molina & Chotro, 1991). If these results were exclusively related to prenatal preexposure effects, differential responsiveness to neonatal odorants as a function of prenatal treatments should have been expected independently from the delay existing between sensory exposure and cesarean delivery. Another experiment also argues against a preexposure mechanism as the sole process underlying these effects. Fetuses were exposed sequentially to both chemosensory cues, that is, lemon 40 min prior to delivery followed by alcohol (10 min prior to birth), or the same stimuli with the sequence reversed. These two groups later were evaluated as neonates in terms of motor activity elicited by alcohol or lemon odor. Differential responsiveness to alcohol and lemon appeared to be related to the sequence of chemosensory administration. The stimulus presented closer to birth induction elicited a higher rate of activity (Molina & Chotro, 1990).

It is important to note that these experiments do not demonstrate conclusively that fetuses form an association between the chemosensory stimulus and the consequences derived from birth induction. Adequate control of the temporal contiguity factor (delay between prenatal sensory experience and cesarean delivery) is far from achieved, because even with the 40-min delay procedure the stimuli might still be present in the uterine environment prior to birth. Nevertheless, it is important to note that prior conditioning studies in immature rats suggest that duration of the conditioned stimulus negatively correlates with the strength of the association that involves this stimulus and a given reinforcer (Rudy & Cheatle, 1978, 1983). This observation seems to favor the associative hypothesis under consideration.

This associative hypothesis gained support in additional studies. Fetuses received an intraamniotic administration of an alcohol solution (0, 6 or 18% v/v), either 3, 10, or 30 min prior to birth. One hour prior to neonatal assessments of motor activity induced by alcohol ambient odor, subjects received either no further postnatal experience with alcohol odor or unreinforced exposure to the alcohol cue (7.5 or 15 min). The test consisted of a short adaptation session to the apparatus (3 min) followed by presentation of ethanol odor during an equivalent amount of time. Under these circumstances, extensive pilot work indicated that neonates with no prenatal experience with alcohol showed strong decrements in activity when alcohol odor was presented relative to the corresponding unscented adaptation phase of the test. This relative decrement was observed in the majority of the groups under analysis. There were two clear exceptions: Animals that experienced alcohol (6 or 18% v/v) in the amniotic fluid 10 min prior to birth and had no further postnatal experience with ethanol odor prior to test performance (Fig. 23.1).

Once again it appears that in this exposure situation, contamination of the amniotic fluid is a necessary but not a sufficient condition to establish patterns of alcohol responsiveness different from the ones observed in subjects lacking exposure to alcohol. A critical interaction between different factors appears responsible for generating a memory that will later affect such responsiveness. Onset of the sensory stimulation provided through contamination of the amniotic fluid relative to cesarean delivery is one of the factors comprising this interaction. As was the case in previous experiments, a 10-min delay appeared optimal to induce higher reactivity toward ethanol.

If these results are interpreted in an associative framework defined by optimal contingency between alcohol as a conditioned stimulus (CS) and cesarean delivery and/or perinatal manipulation as an unconditioned stimulus, then it should be expected that postnatal reexposure to the CS should decrease the magnitude of the hypothetical learned response (extinction effect). This appears to be the case. A 7.5- or 15-min unreinforced postnatal exposure to alcohol odor completely changed the response profile of groups that experienced alcohol 10 min prior to birth but were not subjected to further experience with this cue. The associative hypothesis suggests that this change in the effect of the alcohol odor cue through

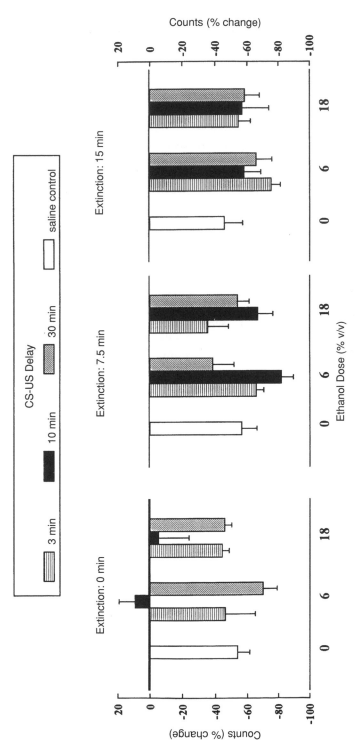

FIG. 23.1. Percentage changes in motor activity relative to baseline performance as a function of the solution administered prenatally (EtOH dose: 0, 6, or 18% v/v), delay between administration and delivery (3, 10, or 30 min), and postnatal extinction procedures (0, 7.5, or 15 min). Data corresponding to saline controls in the different extinction conditions were collapsed across the temporal delay factor. Vertical lines represent standard errors of the means. From Domínguez, Chotro, and Molina (1993). Reprinted by permission of Academic Press, Inc.

postnatal reexposure represents an extinction effect. This same effect was later observed in an alcohol intake test. Pups experienced alcohol or saline in the amniotic fluid 10 min before birth. During PD 11 an alcohol intake test similar to those previously described was performed. One hour prior to testing procedures, half of the animals in each prenatal treatment were exposed to either an unscented chamber or a similar chamber containing the alcohol odor. These exposures were 7.5 min in duration. Prenatal experience with the drug promoted heightened ingestion relative to corresponding saline controls. This intake pattern was partially reversed whenever alcohol odor was presented prior to testing procedures (Fig. 23.2; Chotro, Domínguez, & Molina, 1991; Domínguez, Chotro, & Molina, 1993).

Which consequences derived from fetal to neonatal life passage might act as an unconditioned event? Hypoxia, hypercapnia, acidosis, hypothermia, abrupt decompression, and context change all seem to represent powerful factors that could be associated with sensory cues present in the aminiotic fluid. Tactile manipulations of the perinate during and immediately after birth should not be disregarded as activating stimuli with reinforcement capacity (Hall, 1987; Hofer, 1987; Leon et al., 1987; Leon, Wilson, & Guthrie, 1991; Sullivan & Wilson, 1991). An experiment related to this issue seems to suggest that postnatal re-creation of the contingency between alcohol's sensory cues and tactile stimulation can potentiate re-

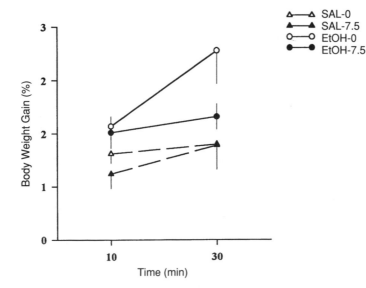

FIG. 23.2.   Intake (percentage of body weight gain) of a 6% v/v alcohol solution as a function of prenatal manipulations (saline or ethanol in the amniotic fluid), postnatal extinction procedure (0 or 7.5 min), and time of assessment (0–10 min or 10–30 min). Vertical lines represent standard errors of the means. From Dominguez, Chotro, and Molina (1993). Reprinted by permission of Academic Press, Inc.

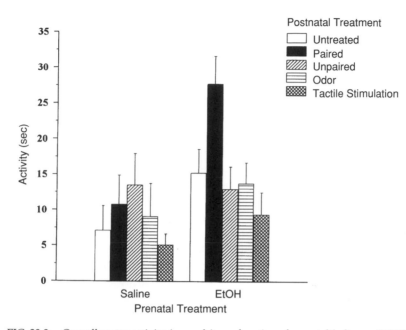

FIG. 23.3. Overall motor activity (seconds) as a function of prenatal (saline or EtOH) and postnatal treatments (untreated, paired presentation of alcohol odor and tactile stimulation, unpaired presentation of similar stimuli, only olfactory stimulation, or only tactile stimulation). The results represent scores attained during the first minute of the test. Vertical lines represent standard errors of the means.

sponsiveness to alcohol odor. Fetuses that received saline or alcohol in utero were later exposed to one of five neonatal treatments after cesarean delivery: no further stimulation, only tactile stimulation, only ambient ethanol odor, both stimuli explicitly unpaired, or both events explicitly paired. Tactile stimulation consisted in rostral stroking of the neonates. This stimulation was performed replicating the one used when aspiring nostrils and mouths after cesarean section, which served to avoid bronchial and alveolar incorporation of the amniotic fluid. Direct observation of the perinates indicated that this procedure was highly activating. Pups exposed to alcohol in utero that were later subjected to pairings between alcohol odor and tactile stimulation similar to the one performed after cesarean delivery exhibited significantly higher activity scores than did pertinent controls (Domínguez & Molina, 1991). In this experiment, duration of overall motor activity elicited by alcohol odor was recorded with video techniques when pups were placed in a spherical hollow device similar to the one employed in previous experiments (Fig. 23.3; Molina & Chotro, 1991).

This pattern of results indicates one more circumstance in which exposure to the sensory characteristics of alcohol in utero interacts with later experience that involves ethanol's sensory cues. Interestingly, this later experience is defined by contingent presentations between alcohol odor and tactile stimulation similar to the one performed immediately after delivery. This later source of stimulation acts as an activating stimulus that might represent one relevant biological event capable of reinforcing previously perceived cues. Tactile stimulation of the neonate establishes neural and behavioral conditioned responses to olfactory events, which in turn are extinguished by subsequent unreinforced exposure to similar chemosensory stimuli (Sullivan & Wilson, 1991). The later results, in combination with the observed inhibitory effects through postnatal reexposure to alcohol odor (Dominguez, Chotro, & Molina, 1993), suggest that associations as those reported by Sullivan and Wilson (1991) can occur during the passage from fetal to neonatal life. This suggestion implies that tactile stimulation of the perinate could be viewed as a reinforcer capable of being associated with cues perceived prior to delivery. Obviously, this in no way eliminates the possibility that other perinatal events related to cesarean or vaginal birth constitute unconditioned stimuli capable of supporting associative learning.

MATERNAL ADMINISTRATION OF ALCOHOL DURING THE LAST DAYS OF PREGNANCY ALSO AFFECTS ALCOHOL RESPONSIVENESS OF THE PROGENY

The fetal studies reported in this chapter clearly indicate that proximal to birth the organism detects alcohol in the amniotic fluid. Under specific conditions, the perinatal experience with the odor of alcohol is evident with autonomic, motor activity, and alcohol preference indices. The use of this strategy of acute exposure progressively guided our research to investigate potential associative learning established through the contingency of chemosensory perception and consequences derived from the transition from fetal to neonatal life.

When alcohol administration during pregnancy is maintained until delivery, enhanced ethanol intake has been described in the progeny (Bond & DiGiusto, 1976). Is it possible that fetal learning about alcohol-related cues mediate such an effect? First experimental steps have been taken in regard to the preceding question. Aside from the results obtained with the acute alcohol contamination technique (earlier in this chapter), two basic considerations guided the investigative approach: (a) presence of alcohol in the fetal environment following maternal intoxication (Smotherman et al., 1986; Szeto, 1989), and (b) fetal processing of nonbiological chemosensory cues, a phenomenon that has been observed to occur as early as GD 17 (Smotherman & Robinson, 1985).

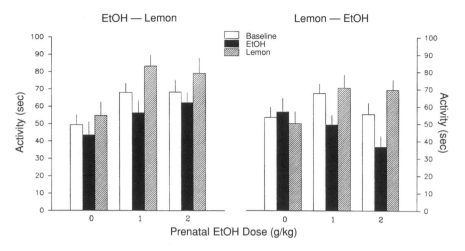

FIG. 23.4. Overall duration of motor activity (seconds) as a function of maternal administration of alcohol (0, 1, or 2 g/kg), phases of the assessment procedure (unscented baseline or phases scented with EtOH or lemon odors), and sequence of presentation of lemon and alcohol ambient odorants (EtOH–lemon or lemon–EtOH). Vertical lines represent standard errors of the means.

During GD 17–20 pregnant females received one daily intragastric administration of 0, 1, or 2 g alcohol per kilogram of body weight. Following these treatments, cesarean-delivered offspring (GD 21) were placed in a clear Plexiglas chamber and exposed to an unscented air stream or air streams scented with alcohol or lemon. The scented streams were counterbalanced in terms of order of presentation within each prenatal treatment (lemon followed by ethanol odor or vice versa). Hyperactivity in pups prenatally exposed to alcohol, a widely encountered teratological effect of the drug, was evident in these tests (Abel, 1984; U.S. Department of Health and Human Services, 1990). Pups exposed to alcohol prenatally that received the olfactory test sequence alcohol–lemon showed significantly higher motor baseline activity relative to control subjects. This same difference is observed in both odor-defined tests. This is not the case when testing procedures followed the opposite sequence (lemon–alcohol). A significant dose-dependent inhibition of the behavior of the neonate was recorded during alcohol odor presentation. Interestingly, this inhibition was expressed despite the overall hyperactive effect induced by the prenatal administration of the 1- and 2-g/kg alcohol doses Fig. (23.4; Chotro, Domínguez, & Molina, 1992).

It appeared that pups exposed to alcohol prenatally showed differential responding to alcohol ambient odor. This response was more clearly observed when neonatal odor stimulation was first performed with a novel cue such as lemon. Attentional deficits have also been commonly reported in organisms that suffer alcohol's teratogenic effects (U.S. Depart-

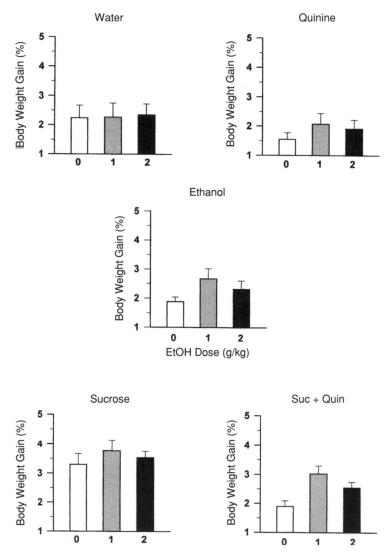

FIG. 23.5.   Consumption scores (percent body weight gains) as a function of maternal administration of alcohol (0, 1, or 2 g/kg) and the nature of the solution infused during the test (water, quinine at 0.0001 M, ethanol at 6% v/v, sucrose at 0.1 M, and a configuration of sucrose and quinine using similar concentrations as those independently described). Vertical lines represent standard errors of the means.

ment of Health and Human Services, 1990). It could be possible that retrieval of an acquired memory under this attentional deficit requires prior experience with novel sensory cues leading to perceptual sharpening.

At PD 15 similar prenatal treatments were evaluated in terms of their effects on consumption of palatable substances (water, quinine, sucrose, alcohol, and a solution containing sucrose and quinine). The later solution was included because neural and behavioral studies indicate that it strongly correlates with the taste of alcohol (Di Lorenzo, Kiefer, Rice, & García 1986; Kiefer, Morrow, & Metzler, 1988). The gustatory properties of certain solutions clearly affected consumption scores of pups on PD 15.

As expected, sucrose was the stimulus that promoted the highest intake scores and quinine the lowest ones. The prenatal status of the pups failed to affect water, sucrose or quinine intake (Fig. 23.5). Prenatal treatment significantly affected consumption of the alcohol solution and of the sucrose–quinine solution. Animals prenatally exposed to the 1-g/kg alcohol dose consumed significantly more of these last two solutions when compared to the 0-g/kg prenatally treated pups. Pups prenatally exposed to the highest alcohol dose (2 g/kg) consumed intermediate amounts relative to the remaining groups (0 and 1 g/kg). Is it possible that such a nonmonotic function obeys to teratological effects accrued in utero? Can we expect that what was learned about alcohol is later subjected to retention, retrieval, and/or expression deficits caused by central nervous system dysfunction when employing a 2-g/kg alcohol dose? Notice that pups prenatally treated with the 1-g/kg alcohol dose exhibited significantly higher ingestion of the sucrose–quinine configuration when compared with subjects with no alcohol experience in utero (0 g/kg). As observed, this solution seems to share palatability attributes of alcohol (Di Lorenzo et al., 1986; Kiefer et al., 1988). It is difficult to conceive that olfactory cues are present in such solution (sucrose concentration 0.1 M and quinine concentration 0.0001 M). Olfactory rather than gustatory perception participates in chemosensory processing achieved proximal to birth (Smotherman, 1982b; Smotherman & Robinson, 1990). Therefore, is retrieval of this information dependent on transfer across sensory modalities, a phenomenon frequently reported in immature organisms (Almli, 1984; Molina, Hoffman, Serawatka, & Spear, 1991)? Can this transfer be affected by teratogenic properties of high alcohol doses administered during late gestation?

SUMMARY AND CONCLUDING COMMENTS

Across the different experiments summarized in this chapter, it seems possible to extract one common principle. Simply stated, the near-term fetus acquires information about alcohol when this drug contaminates the prenatal environment. Both acute ethanol contamination of the amniotic fluid during GD 21 and chronic maternal intragastric alcohol intubation (GD 17–20) lead to enhanced postnatal consumption of the drug by the neonate. Although the two exposure techniques produce similar patterns of results, the data in no way argue in favor of a common mechanism responsible for the effect. In this respect it is also interesting to note that behavioral responsiveness to alcohol olfactory cues in these two exposure paradigms had opposite effects: Relative to pertinent controls, experimental subjects exposed to alcohol via contamination of the amniotic fluid evidenced higher activity in the presence of alcohol odor, whereas the opposite outcome was registered in fetuses exposed to alcohol through maternal exposure. In the acute situation, an associative process determined by non-alcohol-derived events seems to play an important role in the establishment of postnatal responsiveness to the drug. This situation appears free of toxic and/or teratogenic properties induced by ethanol administration. This is not the case in the alternative strategy, because evidence of behavioral teratogenic effects (hyperactivity) was recorded (Chotro, Domínguez, & Molina, 1992). The results attained with chronic exposure are difficult to interpret through an associative mechanism that involves birth induction as a critical event. In this model, the fetus is probably subjected not only to the presence of alcohol in the amniotic context but also to a wide spectrum of nonsensory effects induced by toxic effects in mother and fetuses. As previously discussed, very early in ontogeny the animal seems capable of responding to postabsorptive effects of the drug and to other abrupt changes in its environment triggered by the presence of alcohol in maternal circulation. Relative to the former aspect (processing of alcohol's postabsorptive effects) we still ignore how the fetus reacts to factors such as the drug's reinforcing capabilities, which in turn are likely to be modulated through maternal reactivity to the drug or its metabolites.

It appears that fetal experience with alcohol during late gestation can modulate subsequent responsiveness to certain attributes of the drug. Progressive knowledge about the circumstances and mechanisms that determine fetal learning about alcohol as well as its interaction with subsequent experience with the drug represents a challenge aimed at understanding the development of alcohol intake patterns.

ACKNOWLEDGMENTS

This work was supported by grants from Consejo de Investigaciones Científicas y Tecnológicas de la Provincia de Córdoba (CONICOR, 1989–1992), Consejo Nacional de Investigaciones Científicas y Técnicas (CONICET, 1992), and Fundación Antorchas awarded to J. C Molina and by an institutional grant from Perez Companc awarded to the Institute Ferreyra. The authors express their gratitude to Marcelo Fernando Lopez for his technical support.

REFERENCES

Abel, E. L. (1984). *Fetal alcohol syndrome and fetal alcohol effects.* New York: Plenum.

Almli, C. R. (1984). Early brain damage and time course of behavioral dysfunction: Parallels with neural maturation. In S. Finger & C. R. Almli (Eds.), *Early brain damage: Vol. 2. Neurobiology and Behavior* (pp. 99–116). San Diego: Academic Press.

Binkiewicz, A., Robinson, M. J., & Senior, B. (1978). Pseudo-Cushing syndrome caused by alcohol in breast milk. *Journal of Pediatrics, 93,* 965–967.

Bond, N. W., & DiGiusto, E. L. (1976). Effects of prenatal alcohol consumption on open-field behavior and alcohol preference in rats. *Psychopharmacologia, 46,* 163–165.

Buteler, R. (1989, September). *Intoxicación alcohólica aguda en niños* [Acute alcohol intoxication in children]. Paper presented at IV Curso Nacional de Actualización sobre Alcoholismo, Córdoba, Argentina.

Chotro, M. G., Córdoba, N. E., & Molina, J. C. (1991). Acute prenatal experience with alcohol in the amniotic fluid: Interactions with aversive and appetitive alcohol orosensory learning in the rat pup. *Developmental Psychobiology, 24,* 431–451.

Chotro, M. G., Domínguez, H. D., & Molina, J. C. (1991, September). *Aprendizaje perinatal con alcohol: Incidencia de la duración de la droga en líquido amniótico, contigüidad con el nacimiento y reexposicion postnatal* [Perinatal learning with alcohol: Effects of duration of the drug in the amniotic fluid, contiguity with birth and postnatal reexposure]. Paper presented at the Asociación Argentina de Ciencias del Comportamiento, Córdoba, Argentina.

Chotro, M. G., Domínguez, H. D., & Molina, J. C. (1992, November). Contaminación etílica del contexto prenatal durante los últimos dias gestacionales: Efectos sobre la discriminación sensorial del alcohol en la rata [Ethanol contamination of the prenatal context during the last gestational days: Effects upon alcohol's sensory discrimination]. Paper presented at the XXIV Annual Meeting of the Sociedad Argentina de Farmacologia Experimental, Buenos Aires, Argentina.

Chotro, M. G., & Molina, J. C. (1990). Acute ethanol contamination of the amniotic fluid during gestational day 21: Postnatal changes in alcohol responsiveness in rats. *Developmental Psychobiology, 23,* 535–547.

Chotro, M. G., & Molina, J. C. (1992). Bradycardiac responses elicited by alcohol odor in rat neonates: Influence of in utero experience in ethanol. *Psychopharmacology, 106,* 491–496.

Coppola, D. M., & O'Connell, R. J. (1989, November). *Perinatal olfaction in the mouse: Developmental morphology of the vomeronasal channel in preliminary 2-deoxyglucose studies in utero.* Paper presented at the Eleventh Annual Meeting of the Association of Chemoreception Sciences (AChemS XI), Sarasota, FL.

Croce, P. (1977). El alcohol y los niños. In Secretaría de Medicina Sanitaria (Ed.), *Alcohol y Alcoholismo.* Buenos Aires, Argentina. Sector Educación para la Salud.

Di Lorenzo, P., Kiefer, S., Rice, A., & García, J. (1986). Neural and behavioral responsivity to ethil alcohol as a tastant. *Brain Research Bulletin, 3,* 55–61.

Domínguez, H. D., Bocco, G. C., Chotro, M. G., Spear, N. E., & Molina, J. C. (1993). Operant responding controlled by milk or milk contaminated with alcohol as positive reinforcers in infant rats. *Pharmacology, Biochemistry and Behavior, 44,* 403–409.

Domínguez, H. D., Chotro, M. G., & Molina, J. C. (1993). Alcohol in the amniotic fluid prior to cesarean delivery: Effects of subsequent exposure to alcohol odor upon alcohol responsiveness. *Behavioral and Neural Biology, 60,* 129–138.

Domínguez, H. D., & Molina, J. C. (1991, September). *Reactivacion de memorias perinatales de orden asociativo en la rata* [Reactivation of associative memories in the perinatal rat]. Paper presented at the Asociación Argentina de Ciencias del Comportamiento, Córdoba, Argentina.

Emory, E. K., & Toomey, K. A. (1988). Environmental stimulation and human fetal responsivity in late pregnancy. In W. P. Smotherman & S. R. Robinson (Eds.), *Behavior of the fetus* (pp. 141–161). Caldwell, NJ: Telford.

Fillion, T., & Blass, E. M. (1986). Infantile experience with suckling odors determines adult sexual behavior in male rats. *Science, 231,* 729–731.

Hachenberg, H., & Schmidt, A. P. (1985). *Gas chromatographic head-space analysis.* New York: Wiley.

Hall, W. G. (1987). Early motivation, reward, learning, and their neural basis: Developmental revelations and simplifications. In N. A. Krasnegor, E. M. Blass, M. A. Hofer, & W. P. Smotherman (Eds.), *Perinatal development: A psychobiological perspective* (pp. 251–274). Orlando, FL: Academic Press.

Hofer, M. A. (1987). Shaping forces within early social relationships. In N. A. Krasnegor, E. M. Blass, M. A. Hofer, & W. P. Smotherman (Eds.), *Perinatal development: A psychobiological perspective.* Orlando, FL: Academic Press.

Hoffmann, H., Molina, J. C., Kucharski, D., & Spear, N. E. (1987). Further examination of ontogenic limitations on conditioned taste aversions. *Developmental Psychobiology, 20,* 455–463.

Hunt, P. S., Molina, J. C., Rajachandran, L., Spear, L. P., & Spear, N. E. (1993). Chronic administration of alcohol in the developing rat: Expression of functional tolerance and alcohol olfactory aversions. *Behavioral and Neural Biology, 59,* 87–99.

Hunt, P. S., Molina, J. C., Spear, L. P., & Spear, N. E. (1990). Ethanol-mediated taste aversions and state-dependency in preweanling (16-day old) rats. *Behavioral and Neural Biology, 54,* 300–322.

Kiefer, S., Morrow, N., & Metzler, C. (1988). Alcohol aversion generalization in rats: Specific disruption of taste and odor cues with gustatory neocortex or olfactory bulb ablations. *Behavioral Neuroscience, 5,* 733–739.

Leon, M., Coopersmith, R., Lee, S., Sullivan, R., Wilson, D., & Woo, C. C. (1987). Neural and behavioral plasticity induce by early olfactory learning. In N. A. Krasnegor, E. M. Blass, M. A. Hofer, & W. P. Smotherman (Eds.), *Perinatal development: A psychobiological perspective* (pp. 145–167). Orlando, FL: Academic Press.

Leon, M., Wilson, D. A., & Guthrie, K. M. (1991). Plasticity in the developing olfactory system. In J. L. Davis & H. Eichenbaum (Eds.), *Olfaction: A model system for computational neuroscience.* Cambridge, MA: MIT Press.

Little, R. E., Anderson, K. W., Ervin, C. H., Worthington-Roberts, B., & Clarren, S. K. (1989). Maternal alcohol use during breast-feeding and infant mental and motor development at 1 year. *New England Journal of Medicine, 321,* 425–430.

Mennella, J. A., & Beauchamp, G. K. (1991). The transfer of alcohol to human milk. Effects on flavor and the infant's behavior. *New England Journal of Medicine, 325,* 981–985.

Miller, J., Molina, J. C., & Spear, N. E. (1990). Ontogenetic differences in the expression of odor-aversion learning in 4- and 8-day-old rats. *Developmental Psychobiology, 23,* 319–330.

Molina, J. C., & Chotro, M. G. (1989a). Acute alcohol intoxication paired with appetitive reinforcement: Effects upon ethanol intake in infant rats. *Behavioral and Neural Biology, 51,* 326–345.

Molina, J. C., & Chotro, M. G. (1989b). Acute alcohol intoxication paired with aversive reinforcement: Ethanol odor as a conditioned reinforcer in rat pups. *Behavioral and Neural Biology, 52,* 1–19.

Molina, J. C., & Chotro, M. G. (1991). Association between chemosensory stimuli and cesarean delivery in rat fetuses: Neonatal presentation of similar stimuli increases motor activity. *Behavioral and Neural Biology, 55,* 42–60.

Molina, J. C., Chotro, M. G., & Spear, N. E. (1989). Early (preweanling) recognition of alcohol's orosensory cues resulting from acute ethanol intoxication. *Behavioral and Neural Biology, 51,* 307–325.

Molina, J. C., Hoffman, H., Serwatka, J., & Spear, N. E. (1991). Establishing intermodal equivalence in preweanling and adult rats. *Journal of Experimental Psychology: Animal Behavior Processes, 17,* 433–447.

Molina, J. C., Hoffmann, H., & Spear, N. E. (1986). Conditioning of aversion to alcohol orosensory cues in 5- and 10-day rats: Subsequent reduction in alcohol ingestion. *Developmental Psychobiology, 19,* 175–183.

Molina, J. C., Serwatka, J., & Spear, N. E. (1984). Changes in alcohol intake resulting from prior experience with alcohol odor in young rats. *Pharmacology, Biochemistry and Behavior, 21,* 387–391.

Molina, J. C., Serwatka, J., & Spear, N. E. (1986). Alcohol drinking patterns of young adult rats as a function of infantile aversive experiences with alcohol odor. *Behavioral and Neural Biology, 46,* 257–271.

Molina, J. C., Serwatka, J., Spear, L. P., & Spear, N. E. (1985). Differential ethanol olfactory experiences affect ethanol ingestion in preweanling but not in older rats. *Behavioral and Neural Biology, 44,* 90–100.

Pedersen, P. E., Stewart, W. B., Greer, C. A., & Sheperd, G. M. (1983). Evidence for olfactory function in utero. *Science, 221,* 478–480.

Quiroga de García, S. (1979). El alcoholismo en la infancia [Alcoholism in infancy]. *Psicodeia, 33,* 192–196.

Ronca, A. E., & Alberts, J. R. (1990). Heart rate development and sensory-evoked cardiac responses in perinatal rats. *Physiology and Behavior, 47,* 1075–1082.

Rudy, J., & Cheatle, M. (1978). A role of conditioned stimulus duration in toxiphobia conditioning. *Journal of Experimental Psychology: Animal Behavior Processes, 4,* 399–411.

Rudy, J., & Cheatle, M. (1983). Odor aversion learning by rats following LiCl exposure: Ontogenetic influences. *Developmental Psychobiology, 16,* 13–22.

Smotherman, W. P. (1982a). In utero chemosensory experience alters taste preferences and corticosterone responsiveness. *Behavioral and Neural Biology, 37*, 284–301.

Smotherman, W. P. (1982b). Odor aversion learning by the rat fetus. *Physiology and Behavior, 29*, 769–771.

Smotherman, W. P., & Robinson, S. R. (1985). The rat fetus and its environment: Behavioral adjustments to novel, familiar, aversive and conditioned stimuli presented in utero. *Behavioral Neuroscience, 99*, 521–530.

Smotherman, W. P., & Robinson, S. R. (1987). Psychobiology of fetal experience in the rat. In N. A. Krasnegor, E. M. Grass, M. A. Hofer, & W. P. Smotherman (Eds.), *Perinatal development: A psychobiological perspective* (pp. 39–60). Orlando, FL: Academic Press.

Smotherman, W. P., & Robinson, S. R. (1988). *Behavior of the fetus.* Caldwell, NJ: Telford.

Smotherman, W. P., & Robinson, S. R. (1990). Rat fetuses respond to chemical stimuli in gas phase. *Physiology & Behavior, 47*, 863–868.

Smotherman, W. P., Woodruff, K. S., Robinson, S. R., Del Real, C., Barron, S., & Riley, E. P. (1986). Spontaneous fetal behavior after maternal exposure to ethanol. *Pharmacology, Biochemistry and Behavior, 24*, 165–170.

Stickrod, G., Kimble, D. P., & Smotherman, W. P. (1982). In utero taste/odor aversion conditioning in the rat. *Physiology and Behavior, 28*, 5–7.

Sullivan, R. M., & Wilson, D. A. (1991). Neural correlates of conditioned odor avoidance in infant rats. *Behavioral Neuroscience, 105*, 307–312.

Szeto, H. H. (1989). Maternal-fetal pharmacokinetics and fetal dose-response relationships. *Annals of the New York Academy of Sciences, 562*, 42–55.

U.S. Department of Health and Human Services. (1990). *Alcohol and Health.* Seventh special report to the U.S. Congress, Rockville, MD.

24

The Preterm Infant: A Model for the Study of Fetal Brain Expectation

Heidelise Als
Harvard Medical School
Children's Hospital, Boston

From the very first days of the child's development his activities acquire a meaning of their own in a system of social behavior, and being directed towards a definite purpose, are refracted through the prism of the child's environment....
—L. S. Vygotsky (1978, p. 30)

The focus of this chapter is the discussion of the study of the behavioral individuality of preterm infants in terms of the developmental trajectories of such infants and the effects of the extrauterine environment on this development, in order to elucidate the specificity of the brain's expectation for sensory input. The dynamic interplay of human fetal brain development, environment, and behavior is outlined, and inferences are drawn from data presented regarding healthy preterm behavioral and neurophysiological functioning, as well as from data regarding the impact of environmental and care modification for preterm behavioral and neurophysiological functioning.

THE PRETERM MODEL FOR THE STUDY OF BRAIN ENVIRONMENT INTERACTION

Over the past two decades there has been a marked increase in the survival of low-birth-weight infants (LBW: < 2,500 g) both in this country and abroad (Hack, Fanaroff, & Merkatz, 1979). Of the 3.7 million live births annually in the United States, approximately 400,000 (10.8%) are LBW and

439

born more than 4 weeks too early. This is an increase of 15% from 1981 (U.S. Department of Health, 1993). Approximately 41,000 (1.1%) are of very low birth weight (VLBW) and born more than 12 weeks too early (Behrman, 1985; Bernbaum & Hoffman-Williamson, 1986). For infants with birth weights between 750 and 1,000 g, born 14–16 weeks too early, survival is now likely (>50%), and for infants with birthweights between 1,000 and 1,250 g, born 12–14 weeks too early, it is now probable. More than 95% of moderately premature infants, born about 8–12 weeks too early, will live if cared for in high-risk pregnancy identification and newborn intensive care unit (NICU) perinatal referral centers, providing an extensive opportunity and responsibility for the study of the specificity of brain development and environment interaction.

Preterm infants are developing in extrauterine settings at a time when their brains are growing more rapidly than at any other time in their life span (McLennan, Gilles, & Neff, 1983). As humans, they are neurodevelopmentally expecting three securely inherited, evolutionarily promised environments in support of their appropriate development, namely, their mother's uterus, their parents' bodies, and their family's and community's social group (Hofer, 1987). Yet they have removed themselves from these environments at a possibly vulnerable phase of brain development and are furthermore in need of care only available in the specialized, medical technological environments of newborn intensive and special care units (NICUs and SCNs). Preterm infants in these unexpected, yet medically necessary, environments have been shown to be at high risk for organ impairments, especially very low birth weight and very immature infants for whom the most devastating of these risks include such medical conditions as chronic lung disease or bronchopulmonary dysplasia (BPD); Avery et al., 1987; O'Brodovich & Mellins, 1985) intraventricular hemorrhage (IVH; Volpe, 1989a, 1989b) retinopathy of prematurity (ROP; Gong, Van Heuven, Berlanga, & Escobedo, 1989), and necrotizing enterocolitis (NEC; Kliegman & Walsh, 1987). Even in the more stable low-birth-weight infant, whose organs may be spared such dramatic impairment, the mismatch of brain expectation for the womb environment and the demands of the intensive or special care unit may present significant challenges, influencing the infant's neuropsychological, psychoemotional and psychosocial development (Als, 1992; Hunt, Cooper, & Tooley, 1988; McCormick, Brooks-Gunn, Workman-Daniels, Turner, & Peckman, 1992). Parental disruption of the expected emotional and physical pregnancy stages in preparation of appropriately nurturing the child is accompanied by at times physical and often significant emotional trauma for the parent and further adds to the challenge (Als, 1986, 1992; Cupoli, Gagan, Watkins, & Bell, 1986; Klaus & Kennel, 1982; Klaus, 1982; Minde, Whitelaw, Brown, &

Fitzhardinge, 1983; Minde, Morton, Manning, & Hines, 1980; Minde et al., 1978). Thus, the preterm infant presents an experiment of nature to study the specificity of the developing brain's expectation for coregulatory input in various domains.

It used to be thought that the brain of the less than 32 week preterm infant was so immature that it did not matter what the sensory input to the brain was. This, however, has to be questioned, given that even the medically healthy preterm infant with only transient need for respiratory support and at low danger for the development of lung disease and intraventricular hemorrhage does not appear to be spared the later developmental challenges of specific learning disability, consistently lower intelligence quotients, executive function and attention deficit disorder, lower threshold to fatiguability influencing many activities of daily living, distractibility, impulsivity, concentration difficulties, visual motor impairment, spatial processing disturbances, language comprehension, and speech problems, as well as emotional vulnerability and difficulties with self-regulation and self-esteem (Als, Duffy, McAnulty, & Badian, 1989; Chaudhari, Kulkarni, Pajnigar, Pandit, & Deshmukh, 1991; Duffy, Als, & McAnulty, 1990; Hunt, Tooley, & Cooper, 1992; Hunt, Tooley, & Harvin, 1982; Largo, Molinari, Kundu, Lipp, & Duc, 1990; Oberklaid, Sewall, Sanson, & Prior, 1991; Sostek, 1992; Waber, McCormick, & Workman-Daniels, 1992). Even medically low-risk preterm infants appear to frequently show significant school performance deficits and have increased need for special education services (Sostek, 1992). These issues are even more accentuated when parental impairment and social circumstances are exacerbating the child's developmental vulnerabilities (Liaw & Brooks-Gunn, 1993). From these findings, it appears that preterm infants, even those who are medically at low risk, are largely unprepared for the postbirth adjustments they are required to make, and their development in the extrauterine environment leads to different and potentially maladaptive developmental trajectories.

BRAIN–ENVIRONMENT INTERACTION

The observation that neurodevelopmental impairment is present in preterm infants spared the more massive insults of intracranial hemorrhage or known hypoxemic anoxic events forces one to consider that the environment may influence the development of the immature brain in additional ways, namely, through the various senses of the organism—the visual, auditory, cutaneous, tactile, somasthetic, kinesthetic, olfactory, and gustatory senses. It is postulated that the interplay of sensory information and experience in the womb forms species-appropriate ontogenetic integration patterns whereas extra utero it may form unexpected challenges, leading to malfunction or distortion of brain development and therewith of function (Duffy, Mower, Jensen, & Als, 1984). A look at the complexity and rapidity of fetal brain development, as evidenced by the work of Finlay and Miller (1993), Gilles, Leviton, and Dooling (1983), Marín-Padilla (1993), Rakic (1991), and Rakic, Suñer, and Williams (1991), among others, makes this postulation plausible.

Premature activation of cortical pathways may actively inhibit later differentiations and interfere with appropriate development and sculpting, especially of cross-modal connection systems implicated in complex mental processing and attentional regulation (Cornell & Gottfried, 1976; Duffy et al., 1984, 1990; Linn, Horowitz, Buddin, Leake, & Fox, 1985; Turkewitz & Kenny, 1985).

In the full-term child, axonal and dendritic proliferation and the massive increase in outer layer cortical cell growth and differentiation leading to the enormous gyri and sulci formation of the human brain, as Fig. 24.1 shows (Cowan, 1979), occur in an environment of mother-mediated protection from environmental perturbations, with a steady supply of nutrients, temperature control, and the multiple regulating systems, including those of chronobiological rhythms, afforded by the intrauterine environment (Reppert & Rivkees, 1989). In contrast, for the preterm infant, these are absent and substituted by inputs from the very differently organized NICU environment. There is increasing evidence that the NICU environment involves sensory overload and stands in stark sensory mismatch to the developing nervous system's expectation for inputs necessary for normal brain development (Freud, 1991; Gottfried & Gaiter, 1985; Wolke, 1987). It has been shown that prolonged diffuse sleep states, crying (Hansen & Okken, 1979; Martin, Okken, & Rubin, 1979), supine positioning (Martin, Herrell, Rubin, & Fanaroff, 1979), routine and excessive handling (Danford, Miske, Headley, & Nelson, 1983; Long, Philip, & Lucey, 1980; Murdoch & Darlow, 1984; Norris, Campbell, & Brenkert, 1982), ambient noise (Long, Lucey, & Philip, 1980), lack of opportunity for nonnutritive sucking (Anderson, Burroughs, & Measel, 1983; Burroughs, Asonye, Anderson-Shanklin, & Vidyasagar, 1978; Field et al., 1982), and poorly timed social and caregiving interactions (Gorski, Hole, Leonard, & Martin, 1983) have adverse developmental effects, presumably mediated through brain developmental changes. What are the effects for the nervous system to move too early from the relative equilibrium of the intrauterine aquatic econiche of the mother to the extrauterine terrestrial environment of the NICU, skipping, as it were, the on-parent body phase of the mammalian full-term newborn and being thrust into an entirely different social group than expected?

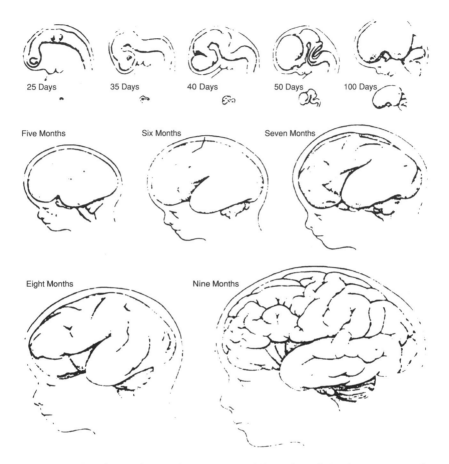

25 Days   35 Days   40 Days   50 Days   100 Days

Five Months   Six Months   Seven Months

Eight Months   Nine Months

FIG. 24.1. Developing human brain is viewed from the side in this sequence of drawings, which show a succession of embryonic and fetal stages. The drawings in the main sequence (bottom) are all reproduced at the same scale: approximately four-fifths life-size. The first five embryonic stages are also shown enlarged to an arbitrary common size to clarify their structural details (top). The three main parts of the brain (the forebrain, the midbrain, and the hindbrain) originate as prominent swellings at the head end of the neural tube. In human beings the cerebral hemispheres eventually overgrow the midbrain and the hindbrain and also partly obscure the cerebellum. The characteristic convolutions and invaginations of the brain's surface do not begin to appear until about the middle of the pregnancy. Assuming that the fully developed human brain contains on the order of 100 billion neurons and that virtually no new neurons are added after birth, it can be calculated that neurons must be generated in the developing brain at an average rate of more than 250,000 per minute. From Cowan (1979). Copyright (1979) by Scientific American, Inc. Reprinted by permission.

THE STUDY OF MEDICALLY HEALTHY PRETERM
INFANTS

In order to estimate the effects of the extrauterine environment on the brain development of the preterm infant, a sample of 160 medically healthy infants spanning the gestational age range at birth from 26 to 41 weeks was studied neurobehaviorally and neurophysiologically (Als, Duffy, & McAnulty, 1988a, 1988b; Duffy et al., 1990). All infants were selected to be appropriate for gestational age (AGA) in weight at birth; free of significant medical, genetic, or neurologic problems for the mother as well as the infant; without documented social hardships; and without family history of substance abuse. None of the infants had perinatal asphyxia at birth, intraventricular hemorrhage (IVH), bronchopulmonary dysplasia (BPD), seizures, hydrocephalus, persistent retinopathy of prematurity (ROP), or necrotizing enterocolitis (NEC). All were singletons. By 1 week postterm, all infants were at home with their families. All were considered normal by both family and pediatrician. They were studied at 2 weeks postterm, regardless of their gestational age at birth. Of the 160 infants evaluated neurobehaviorally, 64 were born between 26 and 32 weeks, referred to as PPTs (very early preterms or prepreterms); 48 were born between 33 and 37 weeks, referred to as PTs (middle preterms); and 48 were born between 38 and 41 weeks, referred to as FTs (full-terms). Of the 160 infants, 135 were also evaluated neurophysiologically: 55 PPTs, 43 PTs, and 37 FTs. Neurobehaviorally, all infants were studied with the Assessment of Preterm Infants' Behavior (APIB; Als, Lester, Tronick, & Brazelton, 1982a, 1982b), by examiners blind to the infant's gestational age at birth. The APIB was developed to quantify not only the infant's skill repertoire, but primarily the modulation of response to controlled environmental input (Als, 1983, 1985; Als & Brazelton, 1981; Als & Duffy, 1983) along five subsystems of functioning, the autonomic, motor, state, attentional, and self-regulatory systems, additionally quantifying the degree of facilitation necessary to reestablish subsystem balance. The assessment attempts to quantify the differences between, for instance, the infant who demonstrates alertness and shows visual following to animate and inanimate stimuli, but only with great cost to respiration and visceral functioning, compared to the infant who does so with alacrity and ease, requiring little to no support. The differential cost to the infant in handling and responding to the maneuvers of the examination is a key feature of the assessment, estimating the infant's executive function capacity. The results indicate that the six system variables show strong differences between FTs, PTs, and PPTs, with the strongest differences between FTs and the two PT groups together, and fewer, yet significant, differences also between the PTs and PPTs, as Fig. 24.2 shows (Duffy et al., 1990). The PPTs were consistently the

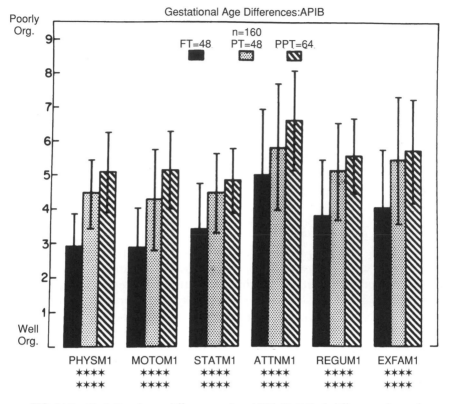

FIG. 24.2. Gestational age difference using APIB. Statistical difference shown by
****$p < .00001$.

most reactive, hypersensitive, and disorganized, the PTs took the middle
position, and the FTs were the most well modulated and well differentiated.

The neurophysiological evaluation by quantified electroencephalo–
graphic (EEG) study with topographic mapping (qEEG) (Duffy, Bartels, &
Burchfiel, 1981; Duffy, Burchfiel, & Lombroso, 1979), performed on the
same day as the neurobehavioral study, involved spectral analysis of EEG
in sleep (BTA, baby tracé alternant), defined according to the usual criteria
(Dreyfus-Brisac et al., 1957; Lombroso, 1981); alert processing (BAP, Baby
alert processing), defined as full interactive alertness with bright,
shiny-eyed appearance, attention focused on the source of stimulation,
appearing to process information actively; and awake nonprocessing (BNP,
Baby not processing), defined as noninteractive wakefulness, with eyes
open or half open, with a glazed or dull look, giving the impression of little
involvement, or, if focused, seeming to look through, rather than at, the
examiner. It furthermore involved photic evoked response study in sleep

to strobe, as a measure known to be sensitive to neonatal maturation (Engel & Benson, 1968; Laget et al., 1977; Watanabe, Iwase, & Hara, 1972; Whyte, Pearce, & Taylor, 1987). Signs of active sleep were absent.

Group comparisons of qEEG data were performed using significance probability mapping (SPM) (Duffy et al., 1981). For each state and each electrode, among-group analysis of variance was performed and the resultant F statistic imaged. This F-SPM process resulted in topographic maps of among-group differences, one map for each study condition or state. From F-SPMs, templates were formed by eliminating regions not reaching a desired level of statistical significance. These templates were placed over each subject's data, and the values beneath the templates were summated so as to form numerical features. Such features reflect the contribution of each subject to the corresponding among-group difference and are used for subsequent statistical evaluation (Duffy, Denckla, Bartels, Sandini, & Kiessling, 1980). This established neurophysiological technique served as the means to reduce the large number of variables produced by the multielectrode mapping study. Analysis of variance (ANOVA) was performed on the resultant electrophysiological parameters by gestational age group following assessment and correction for normality where indicated. Linear and polynomial regression were then used in order to estimate the nature of the relation between each electrophysiological variable and gestational age. Multivariate stepwise regression was performed for the behavioral as well as the neurophysiological variables in a forward manner in order to assess the interrelation among variables and gestational age. Path analysis (Duncan, 1966; Wright, 1921, 1960) was used to investigate the influence of postnatal complications (PEDCO) on the relation of the behavioral and the electrophysiological outcome measures with gestational age. This technique allowed the calculation of partial effects of an independent variable in the presence of one or more intervening variables. Using techniques of multiple regression, coefficients representing both a direct effect for the independent variable and the indirect effects through the intervening variable, PEDCO, were calculated. The dependent variables were the behavioral variables from the APIB and the electrophysiological variables. Gestational age at birth was the independent variable.

Results for the ANOVA among the three gestational age (GA) groupings are shown in Table 24.1 for the six APIB system summary scores of the 135 infants for whom neurophysiological data were complete (Duffy et al., 1990). Linear regression against gestational age at birth was significant for all six APIB variables. In every instance, direction of change indicated lower (better) scores for the later born infants. Polynomial regression against gestational age at birth showed the first-order linear term to be the

TABLE 24.1
Analysis of Variance on APIB System Scores

APIB System Variables	Gestational Age Groups (mean)[a]			Significance Test	Pairwise Comparisons[b]		
	FT (n = 37)	PT (n = 43)	PPT (n = 55)	F (df = 2,132)	FT/PT	FT/PPT	PT/PPT
PHYSM1	2.94	4.57	5.24	53.47****	***	***	**
MOTOM1	2.80	4.44	5.25	42.42****	***	***	*
STATM1	3.26	4.67	4.91	24.13****	***	***	—
ATTNM1	4.51	6.06	6.79	21.77****	***	***	—
REGUM1	3.45	5.37	5.67	36.08****	***	***	—
EXFAM1	3.61	5.68	5.87	24.83****	***	***	—
PEDCO1	152.43	99.72	69.66	143.64****	***	***	***

Note. Variable abbreviations: PHYSM1, autonomic organization; MOTOM1, motoric organization; STATM1, state organization; ATTNM1, attentional organization; REGUM1, regulatory organization; EXFAM1, examiner facilitation; PEDCO1, Postnatal Complication Scale score. From Duffy et al. (1990). Reprinted with permission.
[a]FT, full term, 38–41 weeks; PT, preterm, 33–37 weeks; PPT, prepreterm, 26–32 weeks.
[b]Not significant.
*$p < .05$. **$p < .02$. ***$p < .01$. ****$p < .001$. *****$p < .00005$.

best descriptor of the regression for three summary scores, namely, state organization (STATM1), attentional organization (ATTNM1), and regulatory organization (REGUM1). The second-order polynomial was the best descriptor for the remaining three—autonomic organization (PHYSM1), motor organization (MOTOM1), and examiner facilitation (EXFAM1).

Postnatal complication scores (PEDCO1), as would be expected, also differed across gestational age groupings by ANOVA ($p < .00005$), with higher scores for FTs and lower for PTs and PPTs (see Table 24.1). Path analysis, performed as already outlined, with the postnatal complications score (PEDCO1) as the single intervening variable between gestational age and all dependent variables, showed, as can be seen in Table 24.2, PHYSM1 and MOTOM1 to have a highly significant direct effect. REGUM1 showed a much weaker direct effect, and the remaining variables, STATM1, ATTNM1, and EXFAM1, did not show significant direct effects.

Figure 24.3 shows the results of the F-SPM qEEG analysis among the three gestational age groupings. Seventeen operationally independent regions of among-group difference were delineated, 6 from EEG data (three from BAP, one from BNP, two from BTA) and 11 from evoked potential data (BVR). The frontal region was implicated for 12 of the 17 F-SPMs. Involvement was largely symmetrical for 10, more right-sided for 6, and more left-sided for 1 F-SPM. All results were in the direction of lower amplitudes for earlier born infants. Path analysis, performed for the

TABLE 24.2
Path Analysis to Behavioral Measures and to Electrophysiological
Measures from Gestational Age via Postnatal Complications

Variable Name	Direct Effect P_{13}	Indirect Effect $P_{23} \times P_{12}$	Correlation r
Behavioral Measures			
PHYSM1	−.39****	−.24	−.63****
MOTOM1	−.43****	−.13	−.56****
STATM1	−.20	−.28	−.48****
ATTNM1	−.23	−.24	−.47****
REGUM1	−.27*	−.24	−.50****
EXFAM1	−.16	−.26	−.42****
Electrophysiological Measures			
BAPDELTA	.25	−.02	.23**
BAPTHETA	.23	−.04	.19
BAPALPHA	.33**	−.09	.22*
BNPDELTA	.17	.07	.24**
BTATHETA	.06	.14	.20*
BTAALPHA	.20	.07	.27***
BVR60	.00	−.26	−.26***
BVR108	−.14	−.10	−.25**
BVR236	.19	.15	.35****
BVR276	.27*	.08	.34****
BVR420	−.08	−.13	−.21*
BVR568	−.15	−.05	−.20*
BVR1132	.05	.13	.18
BVR1252	−.04	.02	−.02
BVR1368	.21	.09	.30***
BVR1448	.27*	.07	.34****
BVR1488	.32**	.06	.38****

Note. N = 135. Behavioral variable abbreviations: PHYSM1, autonomic organization; MOTOM1, motoric organization; STATM1, state organization; ATTNM1, attentional organization; REGUM1, regulatory organization; EXFAM1, examiner facilitation.

*p < .05. **p < .02. ***p < .01. ****p < .001.

17 regions using PEDCO1 as the intervening variable, as Table 24.2 shows, indicates that four continued to show significant gestational age effects, all four involving the frontal region and the right hemisphere.

These results confirm previous findings (Als et al., 1988a, 1988b; Ferrari, Grosoli, Fontana, & Cavazzuti, 1983; Sell, Luick, Poisson, & Hill, 1980) that full-term and preterm infants differ neurobehaviorally even when selected to be medically healthy and studied at comparable age points after expected date of confinement, with the full-term infants showing better autonomic, motoric, state, attentional, and self-regulatory organization and needing less facilitation than either preterm group. Analysis of quantified EEG data with topographic mapping revealed extensive regional electrophysiological differences among gestational age groups, with across-the-board amplitude reduction and differential frontal lobe vulnerability. Although all infants were selected to represent optimal medical health, the subtle unavoidable complications of being born prematurely

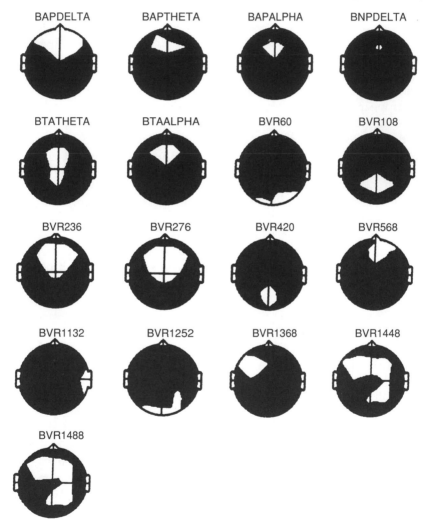

FIG. 24.3.   Regional topographic differences among the three gestational age groups as shown by qEEG F-SPM templates. From Duffy et al. (1990). Reprinted by permission.

nevertheless appear to influence brain function to some extent. For the behavioral data, autonomic (PHYSM1), motor (MOTOM1), and self-regulation organization (REGUM1) were uninfluenced, yet state and attentional organization were affected by postnatal complications. For the neurophysiological data, 4 of the 17 features, all strongly frontal and right hemispheric features, were uninfluenced by postnatal complications: the alpha feature in alert processing (BAPALPHA) continued to show a strong effect, as did the visual evoked response of the 1,488-msec epoch (BVR1488). The visual evoked responses at 276 msec (BVR276) and 1,448 msec (BVR1448) showed weaker but significant direct effects. All others were significantly influenced.

The implication of these findings is that, despite selection of optimal health, there are medical complications associated with premature birth that appear to explain some of the behavioral and many of the electro-physiological findings. State organization (STATM1) assesses the infant's ability to move from sleep to focused, animated alertness and to robust crying in response to a series of graded stimuli without disturbance of motor or autonomic control. Attentional organization (ATTNM1) mea-sures the robustness and animation of optimal alertness. Poor state and attention scores are seen in infants who are difficult to bring to alertness, move from sleep into uncontrolled crying, and show much stress with state transition, or can only muster strained alertness, diffuse protest, and diffuse sleep. These are the infants who require much examiner facilitation for state maintenance (EXFAM1). It has been shown that such newborns are likely to exhibit attentional difficulties and distractibility in later in-fancy, even in the face of normal cognition (Als, Duffy, & McAnulty, in press). It is of interest that these three variables were most influenced by postnatal medical factors, and that one of them, the attentional measure, also showed the strongest correlations with more qEEG features than any other behavioral variable (Duffy et al., 1990). Clinical experience with older children indicates that difficulty in concentrating and problems with attention and distraction are the most common subtle neurologic residua after recovery from even very mild encephalopathy. This is supported, for example, by Black, Blumer, Wellner, Jeffries, and Walker (1970), who reported irritability, short attention span, and hyperkinesis as the most common sequelae of even very mild closed head injury. Similarly, mild reduction of clinical EEG background voltages may be seen as subtle residua of anoxic encephalopathy, toxic or metabolic derangements, or seizures. Thus, the finding of slight but statistically significant reduction of EEG spectral content as the legacy of postnatal medical complications is quite understandable.

Prominent regional involvement specific to the frontal area, as identi-fied by qEEG (see Fig. 24.2), is of interest given the known association of attentional disorders with frontal dysfunction (Denckla, 1978; Pontius, 1973, 1974). The frontal lobe may be relatively more sensitive to subtle insult than other regions. Because the path analysis model may not be complete, it is not certain that these residual features are demonstrating primarily gestational age effects. It may be that other toxic factors not yet considered could explain these apparently residual effects. Postmortem studies have shown many instances of hypoxic damage "imprinted" upon the fetal brain weeks to months before delivery (Duffy et al., 1990). However, it seems warranted to wonder whether the simple fact of premature extrauterine experience may in and of itself have important consequences, as has been reviewed by Duffy et al. (Duffy et al., 1984). Thus, the extrauterine multisensory experience prior to term may trigger sensitive periods at a time when the preterm infant cannot appropriately incorporate such sensory influences, thereby inducing altered subsequent neural development. Preliminary results from follow-up at 8 years corrected age of the infants studied appear to indicate that the earliest born group (PPTs) shows a high number of children who exhibit extraordinary within child cognitive processing domain variability. Figure 24.4 shows the example of a PPT child's performance profile on a number of the neuropsychological subtests (Als, Duffy, & McAnulty, in preparation-b). Although this child showed a verbal and performance IQ both at 115, one standard deviation above the mean for age, this child had great difficulty in the classroom. The subtest profile indicates extraordinarily high performance on several subtests—for example, Similarities (WISC–R) and Gestalt Closure (K–ABC) were three standard deviations above the mean, in the very superior, gifted range—whereas other subtests showed performance at or below one standard deviation below the mean for age in the dull normal to borderline range, such as Arithmetic (WISC–R), Matrix Analogies (K–ABC), and the Rey-Osterreith Complex Figure Test - Recall condition. Subdomain discrepancy with valleys of disability is typical for children with brain lesions. Yet such children do not show the extraordinary peaks of excellence seen in the presumably focally brain-intact, yet very early born preterm. This performance picture may indeed indicate brain reorganization rather than lesion, due to very early difference in brain–environment interaction, which may have differentially accentuated the development of certain brain systems ready to take advantage of the extrauterine challenge while inhibiting other brain systems that expected intrauterine inputs for several more months.

The next question then becomes, can careful environmental management for the early born preterm infant reduce such effects and if so, can such reduction be achieved through the minimization of subtle but cumulative noxious events or more directly through active support to differentiated brain function?

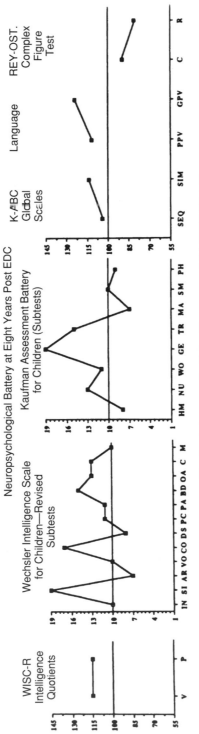

FIG. 24.4. Test profile of early born, medically healthy preterm child. WISC-R Intelligence Quotients: V, Verbal IQ; P, Performance IQ. WISC-R Subtests: IN, Information; SI, Similarities; AR, Arithmetic; VO, Vocabulary; CO, Coding; DS, Digit Span; PC, Picture Completion; PA, Picture Arrangement; BD, Block Design; OA, Object Assembly; C, Coding; M, Mazes. Kaufman Assessment Battery for Children (K-ABC) Subtests: HM, Hand Movements; NU, Number Recall; WO, Word Order; GE, Gestalt Closure; TR, Triangles; MA, Matrix Analogies; SM, Similarities; PH, Photo Series. K-ABC Global Scales: SEQ, Sequential Processing; SIM, Simultaneous Processing. Language PPV, Peabody Picture Vocabulary Test–Revised; GPV, Gardner One Word Picture Vocabulary Test–Revised. Rey-Osterreith Complex Figure: C, Copy; R, Recall.

MODIFICATION OF THE EXTRAUTERINE
ENVIRONMENT FOR THE PRETERM INFANT

In the formulation of brain development outlined, it is hypothesized that it is feasible to estimate the expectation of the fetal brain for sensory input by observing the extrauterine fetal infant's behavior. The question to be tested becomes whether interpreting the infant's behavior as actively engaged in patching across the mismatch of expected and available opportunities for interaction, and seeking to construct an NICU environment supportive of behavioral development, puts one in a position to better meet the fetal brain's expectations and therewith to reduce some of the developmental sequelae.

The approach suggested postulates that the infant's own behavior provides the best information base from which to estimate the infant's current expectations, infer what the infant appears to attempt to accomplish and what strategies the infant uses, and, on the basis of this information, estimate what supports might be currently useful in furthering the infant's competencies and supporting overall neurobehavioral organization in the face of necessary medical and nursing procedures. The infant is seen as continuously and actively self-constructing (Fischer & Rose, 1994), and the task of care is that of collaborating with the infant, keeping in mind the brain's evolved expectation for a complex of multisensory inputs and experiences while acknowledging that, by virtue of the transition from the intra- to extrauterine environment, various brain systems have been irreversibly triggered to function differently than they did in the womb environment, as the aquatic fetus becomes a terrestrial preterm with all that this habitat shift entails (Alberts & Cramer, 1988). Thus, the formulation and design of support for a prematurely born infant is conceptually based in a combination of knowledge of fetal developmental progression, of full-term developmental functioning as the biological blueprint and aiming point inherent in the fetus's makeup, yet modified by the altered environment–fetus transaction, and of the individual-specific strategies employed by each infant. The dilemma posed by the lack of a biological model of best care, given the artifactual nature of survival of the preterm due to medical technology, paired with the inherent individuality of development, highlights the opportunity that the behavior of the infant may offer as a base for inference of appropriate environment and care (Als, 1982).

It has been shown that even the earliest born and most fragile of infants display reliably observable behaviors, in the form of autonomic and visceral responses such as respiration patterns, color fluctuations, spitting, gagging, hiccupping, bowel movement strains, and so on; in the form of movement patterns, postures and tone of trunk, extremities and face, such as finger splays, arching, and grimacing; and in the form of levels of awakeness, referred to as *states*, such as sleeping, wakefulness, and aroused upset (Als, 1983, 1984; Als et al., 1982a). This makes possible the development of an approach geared to the interpretation of such behaviors as evidence of stress experienced or of competence and goal strivings displayed, thus providing a base for staff training in ways to reduce observed stress and support behavioral competence and goal strivings (Als, 1992; Als & Gibes, 1986). This approach to environmental support and care is increasingly widely advocated (Becker, Grunwald, Moorman, & Stuhr, 1993; Grunwald & Becker, 1990; Lawhon, 1986; Lawhon & Melzar, 1991; VandenBerg, 1990a, 1990b; VandenBerg & Franck, 1990; Wolke, 1987) and has been preliminarily tested

Studies with High-Risk Preterm Infants

There are currently three published studies that document beneficial effects of such an individualized approach to care for the very low birth weight ventilated preterm infant. Als et al. (Als, Lawhon, Brown, Gibes, Duffy, McAnulty, & Blickman, 1986) found improved medical outcome in terms of shorter stays on the respirator, in supplemental oxygen and on gavage feedings, improved behavioral outcome at 2 weeks corrected age as assessed with the APIB (Als et al., 1982a, 1982b), and at 9 months in terms of Bayley Scale scores and behavioral regulation assessed in a videotaped play paradigm (Kangaroo-Box Paradigm) (Als & Berger, 1986; Als et al., in press). Becker et al. (Becker, Grunwald, Moorman, & Stuhr, 1991; Becker et al., 1993; Grunwald & Becker, 1990) found significantly lower scores of morbidity in the first 4 weeks of hospitalization, as measured with the Minde Daily Morbidity scale (Minde et al., 1983); they found significantly earlier onset of oral feedings, better average daily weight gains, shorter hospital stays, and improved overall behavioral functioning at discharge, as measured with the NBAS (Brazelton, 1984).

Long-term outcome assessed for the Als et al. study at 18 months and 3 and 7 years continues to show consistently the developmental advantage of the experimental group over the control group (Als, Duffy, & McAnulty, in preparation-a). The longitudinal data available at age 7 years from this study preliminarily show much improved performance of the experimental group on a number of the neuropsychological measures. Figure 24.5a shows an example of the performance profile of a child from the control group. Figure 24.5b shows that of a child from the experimental group, indicating considerable improvement in performance and showing the islands of extraordinary excellence of the early born preterm for the experimental group child, despite this study population's severe initial illness and ventilator dependency.

NEUROPSYCHOLOGICAL BATTERY AT SEVEN YEARS POST EDC

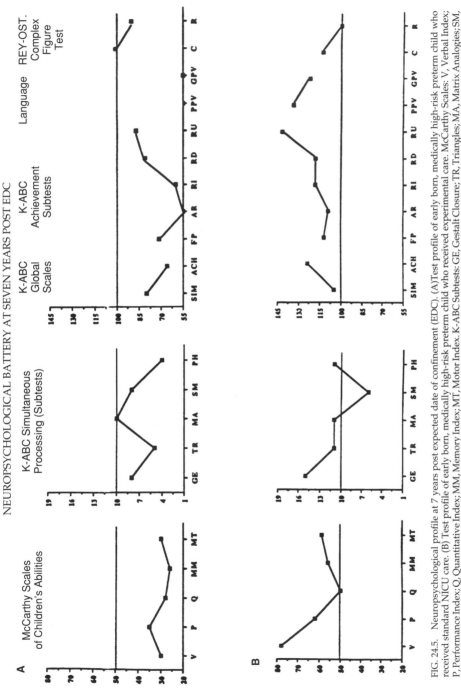

FIG. 24.5. Neuropsychological profile at 7 years post expected date of confinement (EDC). (A)Test profile of early born, medically high-risk preterm child who received standard NICU care. (B) Test profile of early born, medically high-risk preterm child who received experimental care. McCarthy Scales: V, Verbal Index; P, Performance Index; Q, Quantitative Index; MM, Memory Index; MT, Motor Index. K-ABC Subtests: GE, Gestalt Closure; TR, Triangles; MA, Matrix Analogies; SM, Similarities; PH, Photo Series. K-ABC Global Scales: SIM, Simultaneous Processing; ACH, Achievement. K-ABC Achievement Subtests: FP, Faces and Places; AR, Arithmetic; RI, Riddles; RD, Reading/Decoding; RU, Reading/Understanding; Language: PPV, Peabody Picture Vocabulary Test–Revised; GPV, Gardner One Word Picture Vocabulary Test–Revised. Rey-Osterreith Complex Figure Test: C, Coding; R, Recall.

456   ALS

A modified replication study (Als, Lawhon, Duffy, McAnulty, Gibes-Grossman, & Blickman, 1994) utilized random assignment of infants, weighing < 1,251 g, born before 30 weeks gestational age, intubated within the first 3 hr after delivery and requiring mechanical ventilation for at least 24 of the first 48 hr. Eighteen control and 20 experimental group infants met these criteria. For this study, a group of nurses was especially educated and trained in the approach to utilizing systematic behavioral observation for improvement of individualized caregiving. Staffing was structured in such a way that for the experimental group infants, at least one shift in a 24-hr day was covered by a specially behaviorally educated nurse. Formal behavioral observations began within the first 24 hr and were repeated every 10 days until discharge from the nursery. Again the observations provided the basis for support to the primary teams for individualization of developmental care for the experimental group infants and their families. Control group infants were identified to the NICU staff within 2 weeks before discharge so as not to influence and bias their staffing and care in any way. The experimental group infants showed significant reduction in hospitalization length, age at discharge, improved weight gain to 2 weeks after due date, reduced rate of IVH, and reduced severity of chronic lung disease, as well as reduced hospital charges. They also showed improved developmental outcomes at 2 weeks and 9 months corrected age. Systematic electrophysiological group differences by quantified EEG (qEEG) with topographic mapping (Duffy et al., 1979) were also found at 2 weeks postterm, implicating a large central region of brain function difference, as well as a frontal right and an occipital right hemispheric region. When the infants with intraventricular hemorrhages were excluded from the analyses, the right frontal and right occipital regions still showed significant between-group differences, indicating that the experimental approach may have supported and protected development in these regions (Als et al., 1994).

In a further study (Als, Lawhon, Melzar, Duffy, McAnulty, & Blickman, in preparation), the integration of this individualized approach into the NICU was tested by assignment of experimental group high-risk infants to specially trained care teams supported on an ongoing basis by two developmental specialists, who, however, did not conduct serial behavioral observations. Preliminary analysis of outcome again showed reduction in number of days on the ventilator and in need of gavage tube feedings, decreased length of hospitalization, and improved weight gain, as well as improved developmental outcome at 2 weeks and 9 months after due date, yet no decrease in incidence of IVH or severity of chronic lung disease. The IVH effects may well depend on developmental support in the acute first few hours of admission, when systematic feedback may be differentially productive.

A current multicenter study involving four different NICUs focuses on

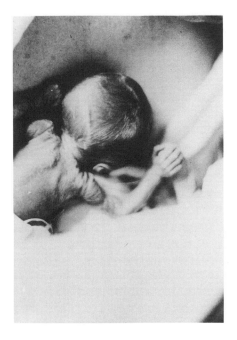

FIG. 24.6.   Day 3 of 25-week preterm intubated infant held and cared for in skin-to-skin contact with the mother. From Als (1992). Reprinted by permission from Ablex Publishing Company.

ventilator-dependent high-risk preterms born at ≤28 weeks gestation and compares inborn versus transported infants, and nurseries employing primary care nursing versus conventionally scheduled nursing. Preliminary results validate the effectiveness of the developmental care model in terms of significant reduction in morbidity in various domains and in reduction of length of hospital stay. Developmental outcome, as measured with the APIB and Prechtl examinations (Prechtl, 1977), also shows significant improvement. Furthermore, preliminary analysis of the assessment of family functioning shows the experimental group parents significantly more differentiated and effective in the understanding of their infants as individuals and themselves as parents (Als & Gilkerson, 1989–1994).

These studies provide consistent evidence that the developmental approach to care for the very low birth weight, very high-risk preterm infant holds promise for the improvement of brain function and developmental outcome of such children. Figures 24.6, 24.7 and 24.8 (Als, 1992) show images of individualized developmental care in the NICU. The overriding principle for the experimental treatment is its developmental process orientation. Prescriptive approaches and protocol-based care, although taught more readily and more traditional in health care delivery, are typically not sensitive to the goals of enhancing and supporting develop-

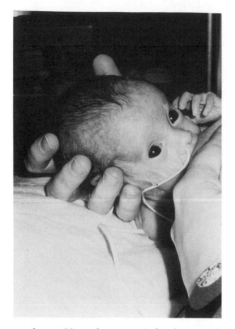

FIG. 24.7.   Shiny-eyed, now 30-week preterm infant born at 25 weeks, nippling on the breast while gavage feeding. From Als (1992). Reprinted with permission from Ablex Publishing Company.

ment individually and nurturing infants and parents on a joint and mutually supportive developmental path. The approach to care used is based on ongoing observation of each infant, and considers the contribution, competence, and goals of the infant as well as those of the parents. Its formulation involves collaboration of the parents, nursing care team, primary physician, and relevant therapist(s) supported by developmental professionals. It always attempts to consider the comprehensive functioning of infant and parents (Als, 1992).

Studies with Medically Healthy Preterm Infants

The neurodevelopmental improvements obtained in the very high-risk ventilated preterm infant attributable to the individualized developmental environment and care approach in the NICU may be mediated by the reduction in focal insult to the brain due to the reduction in ventilation, decreased severity of chronic lung disease, improved weight gain, and, in one study (Als et al., 1994), reduction of intraventricular hemorrhage. These results do not allow assessment of effectiveness in modification of preterm cortical brain system development per se in the absence of prevention or reduction of focal lesions. In order to test the efficacy of the neurodevelopmental care approach in supporting brain system development in the unlesioned brain, a sample of medically healthy low-risk preterm infants free of known focal and suspected lesions has been studied preliminarily in order to evaluate the feasibility of the hypothesis (Buehler, Als, Duffy, McAnulty, & Liederman, in press).

Thirty-two consecutively born preterm singleton inborn infants, cared for in a 16-bed level II special care nursery (SCN), were randomly assigned to an experimental and a control group. They were < 34 weeks gestational age at birth, of appropriate birthweight for gestational age, with uneventful labor and delivery histories, not requiring mechanical ventilation for more than 24 hr, genetically and neurologically intact, and had healthy mothers. The experimental group received individualized developmental care with formal observation of the infant within the first 24 hr and every

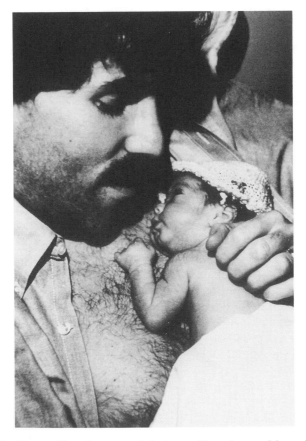

FIG. 24.8.   Former 25-week preterm infant, now 32 weeks, cared for and relaxing in skin-to-skin contact with the father. From Als (1992). Reprinted with permission from Ablex Publishing Company.

seventh day thereafter, and with ongoing support by a developmental psychologist to family and primary care team. In terms of 80 medical and demographic background variables assessed, experimental and control groups were comparable on all but four: Experimental group infants, in the first 24 hr, had slightly higher requirements for medical procedures, as measured with the NTISS score (Gray, Richardson, McCormick, Workman-Daniels, & Goldman, 1992) [7.5 {2.31} vs. 6.13 {2.03}; $p < .08$], and more required transient oxygen on day 2 (5/16 vs. 0/16; $p < .02$), making outcome in favor of the experimental group more conservative; control group mothers had more prior abortions [1.6 (1.6) vs. 0.6 (0.6); $p < .04$], and more were of lower socioeconomic status (5/16 vs. 1/16; $p < .10$), confounding outcome in favor of the experimental group. Therefore, analysis of covariance was performed on all outcome measures using number of abortions and social class as covariates. The neurobehavioral outcome evaluation performed at 2 weeks postterm, using the Prechtl Neurological Evaluation of the Fullterm Newborn Infant (Prechtl, 1977) and the Assessment of Preterm Infants' Behavior (APIB) (Als et al., 1982a, 1982b), showed a range of significant differences. Of the 12 Prechtl variables measured, 4 showed improvement, namely, postural control, tone, reactivity, and the summary score. Furthermore, the experimental group showed significantly better overall modulation on three of six APIB systems measured, namely, the autonomic system, the state system, and the attentional system. The experimental group also showed improved functioning on 7 of 25 specific behavioral measures, including capacity to deal with position change, degree of normal reflex performance, autonomic stability, overall motoric maturity, decrease in extensor overflow movements and postures, state regulation, and overall behavioral and interactive competence.

Electrophysiological results, from the 2 week postterm assessment with quantified evoked potentials with topographic mapping (Duffy et al., 1979), of a subsample of the first 12 control and 12 experimental group infants compared to 12 full term comparison group infants have so far been analyzed and preliminarily reported (Buehler et al., in press). All activation conditions (auditory evoked potentials in awake to speech, nonspeech, and clicks, and visual evoked potentials in quiet sleep and in active sleep to strobe) showed significant differences, yielding a total of 41 significant differences out of the 70 regions tested (58.6%). Of these 41, 18 (41%) involved the frontal lobe.

The overrepresentation of the frontal lobe is of particular interest because, as outlined earlier, the frontal lobe is implicated in attention deficit disorder and cognitive processes involving executive function and integrative planning (Denckla, 1991, 1993; Siwek & Pandya, 1991; Yeterian & Pandya, 1991; Zametkin et al., 1990). The neurophysiological measures showed a high proportion of significant correlations with state and attentional measures. Furthermore, the time after 600 ms, the late latency period, showed the highest proportion (69%) of significant correlations. Late latencies are interpreted to reflect cortical processing. Comparison with healthy full-term controls indicated deficit in cortical organization of the control preterm group and acceleration of cortical organization for the experimental preterm group. These results are encouraging in view of the attentional and higher order learning disability findings reviewed earlier for the low-risk preterm population at school age. They are also corroborated by the earlier reported findings of preterm–fullterm spectral power and visual evoked response differences with lower spectral amplitudes for healthy earlier born infants and lower positive and negative peaks observed in the preterm visual evoked response (Duffy et al., 1990). As pointed out, cortical regions revealing the greatest differences across the groups involved predominantly frontal lobe, secondarily right hemisphere areas. Furthermore, major frontal and right hemispheric differences persisted even after path analysis took into account the effects of relatively minor complications associated with prematurity in the healthy preterms studied.

SUMMARY

The studies outlined suggest that intrauterine and extrauterine environments may differentially influence brain development. Provision of coregulatory, neurodevelopmental support and care for the preterm infant understood as biologically evolved in a neuroregulatory family system may enhance neurobehavioral, neuroelectrophysiological, and family functioning not only for high-risk, but also for medically quite healthy preterm infants.

As Marín-Padilla (1993) concluded, during the perinatal period from 24 weeks gestation to the time of fullterm birth, the human cortex appears particularly vulnerable because its neurons are undergoing significant structural and functional transformations in response to incoming fibers. To achieve its complex structural and functional organization, the cerebral cortex must be subject to significant developmental constraints. Disruptions through injury or violation in evolved expectancy of input may well result in disturbance of the cortex's anatomical and neurochemical integrity and therewith challenge the normal developmental constraints of the still growing cortex. Thus, the neurofunctional differences observed in the preterm infants studied may represent secondary modification and readaptation to locally disturbed cortical development. The differential vulnerability of the frontal lobe system is of particular importance in designing preventive and ameliorative brain nurturing environments and care provision. The frontal lobe in the human is the most species-specific lobe of the brain, most recently evolved, most complexly organized and critically important for complex planning and communication, apparently necessary to foresee and predict outcome without trial and error action sequences. It inhibits impulsive stimulus reactions and supports reflective analysis of complex, multidimensional open-ended situations; supports delay of gratification and suspension of judgment and action while affording sustained inquiry in the face of ambiguity and uncertainty; and diffuses pressure toward solutions, while maintaining initiative and goal orientation, supporting decision power and prioritizing. This uniquely human species survival organ of the cortex appears to be simultaneously the most easily damaged or altered. In the good-enough full-term situation, it appears to be nurtured in the social–emotional communicative matrix of good-enough parenting in good-enough social groups. In violated situations, it requires special attention for preventive and ameliorative care. Several investigators demonstrated the important role of frontal lobe functioning in the development of self-regulatory behavior (Dawson, Panagiotides, Klinger, & Hill, 1992) and in the regulation of cognitive development (Case, 1992). Others (Davidson, 1992; Davidson & Fox, 1989; Fox, 1991; Fox & Bell, 1990) documented individual stability in frontal system asymmetry, showed its implication for temperament and processing of emotional content in infants, and examined its limits in containing emotional stress and showed its shift-over and recruitment of temporal lobe activation when overtaxed (Sidorova & Kostyunina, 1993), perhaps suggestive of the lower emotional thresholds to react with upset and frustration observed in those with poor frontal lobe functioning.

Social contexts evolved in the course of human phylogeny are surprisingly fine-tuned in specificity to provide good-enough environments for the human cortex to unfold, initially intrauterinely, then extrauterinely, adequate in assuring the continuation of human evolution. With the advances in medical technology, that is, material culture, even very immature nervous systems exist and develop outside the womb. However, the social contexts of traditional special care nurseries bring with them less than adequate support for immature nervous systems and their neurobiologically necessary and expected nurturance by their social systems, leading to maladaptions and disabilities, yet also to accelerations and extraordinary abilities. Detailed observation of the behavior of the fetus displaced from the uterus into the NICU provides the opportunities to estimate and infer appropriate environmental and social contexts sufficiently astute in order to support the highly sensitive and vulnerable nervous systems in their developmental progressions.

The studies reported indicate that an individualized, behavioral-developmental approach to care, emphasizing from early on the infant's own strengths and apparent developmental goals and instituting supports for self-regulatory competence and achievement of these goals, improves outcome not only medically but also behaviorally and neurophysiologically. The results indicate that increase in support to behavioral self-regulation improves developmental outcome, perhaps by preventing active inhibition of CNS pathways due to inappropriate inputs during a highly sensitive period of brain development. Developmentally appropriate care may thus be associated with improved cortical and specifically frontal lobe development. It appears that in order to improve medical and developmental outcome for preterm infants, structuring of environment and care can be productively based on the astute observation of the individual infant's current behavior and the interpretation of behavior in a framework of regulatory efforts towards self-set goals of continued differentiation and self-construction. The results support the formulation of highly specific brain expectations during early development. Longitudinal outcome studies as well as studies of continuity of neurodevelopmental support after NICU discharge and of support to focally and to diffusely altered developing brains will provide further avenues for the better understanding of fetal development as well as for improved care.

ACKNOWLEDGMENTS

This work was supported by grant GO-08720110 from the National Institute of Disability and Rehabilitation Research; HO-24590003 from the Office of Special Education Research, U.S. Department of Education; the Merck Family Fund; and by grant P30 HD18655-12 from the National Institutes of Health, to J. J. Volpe. The author thanks particularly her collaborator F. H. Duffy for his expertise regarding the brain's function and development.

REFERENCES

Alberts, J. R., & Cramer, C. P. (1988). Ecology and experience: Sources of means and meaning of developmental change. In E. M. Blass (Ed.), *Handbook of behavioral neurobiology: Developmental psychobiology and behavioral ecology* (pp. 1–40). New York: Plenum.

Als, H. (1982). Towards a synactive theory of development: Promise for the assessment of infant individuality. *Infant Mental Health Journal, 3,* 229–243.

Als, H. (1983). Infant individuality: Assessing patterns of very early development.

In J. Call, E. Galenson, & R. L. Tyson (Eds.), *Frontiers of infant psychiatry* (pp. 363–378). New York: Basic.

Als, H. (1984). *A manual for the naturalistic observation of the newborn (preterm and fullterm)* (rev. ed.). Revision. Boston: The Children's Hospital.

Als, H. (1985). Patterns of infant behavior: Analogues of later organizational difficulties? In F. H. Duffy & N. Geschwind (Eds.), *Dyslexia: A neuroscientific approach to clinical evaluation* (pp. 67–92). Boston: Little, Brown.

Als, H. (1986). A synactive model of neonatal behavioral organization: Framework for the assessment and support of the neurobehavioral development of the premature infant and his parents in the environment of the neonatal intensive care unit. In J. K. Sweeney (Ed.), The high-risk neonate: Developmental therapy perspectives. *Physical and Occupational Therapy in Pediatrics, 6*(3/4), 3–55.

Als, H. (1992). Individualized, family-focused developmental care for the very low birthweight preterm infant in the NICU. In S. L. Friedman & M. D. Sigman (Eds.), *Advances in applied developmental psychology* (pp. 341–388). Norwood, NJ: Ablex.

Als, H., & Berger, A. (1986). *Manual and scoring system for the assessment of infants' behavior: Kangaroo-Box paradigm.* Boston Children's Hospital. (Unpublished manual.)

Als, H., & Brazelton, T. B. (1981). A new model of assessing the behavioral organization in preterm and fullterm infants: Two case studies. *Journal of the American Academy of Child Psychiatry, 20,* 239–269.

Als, H., & Duffy, F. H. (1983). The behavior of the premature infant: A theoretical framework for a systematic assessment. In T. B. Brazelton & B. M. Lester (Eds.), *New approaches to developmental screening of infants* (pp. 153–174). New York: Elsevier, North Holland.

Als, H., Duffy, F. H., & McAnulty, G. B. (1988a). Behavioral differences between preterm and fullterm newborns as measured with the A.P.I.B. system scores: I. *Infant Behavior and Development, 11,* 305–318.

Als, H., Duffy, F. H., & McAnulty, G. B. (1988b). The A.P.I.B.: An assessment of functional competence in preterm and fullterm newborns regardless of gestational age at birth: II. *Infant Behavior and Development, 11,* 319–331.

Als, H., Duffy, F. H., & McAnulty, G. B. (in preparation-a). *Longterm effects to 3 and 7 years post term of very early individualized developmental care in the NICU.*

Als, H., Duffy, F. H., & McAnulty, G. B. (in preparation-b). *The silent handicap of prematurity: Learning disabled yet gifted.*

Als, H., Duffy, F. H., & McAnulty, G. B. (in press). Neurobehavioral competence in healthy preterm and fullterm infants: Newborn period to 9 months. *Developmental Psychology.*

Als, H., Duffy, F. H., McAnulty, G., & Badian, N. (1989). Continuity of neurobehavioral functioning in preterm and full-term newborns. In M. H. Bornstein & N. A. Krasnegor (Eds.), *Stability and continuity in mental development* (pp. 3–28). Hillsdale, NJ: Lawrence Erlbaum Associates.

Als, H., & Gibes, R. (1986). *Newborn individualized developmental care and assessment program (NIDCAP).* Children's Hospital. (Unpublished training guide.)

Als, H., & Gilkerson, L. (1989–1994). *National collaborative research institute for early childhood intervention: Family-focused developmental care and intervention for the very low birthweight preterm infant at high risk for severe medical complication and develop-*

mental disabilities. Children's Hospital, Boston, U.S. Department of Education, OSERS, EEPCD.

Als, H., Lawhon, G., Brown, E., Gibes, R., Duffy, F. H., McAnulty, G. B., & Blickman, J. G. (1986). Individualized behavioral and environmental care for the very low birth weight preterm infant at high risk for bronchopulmonary dysplasia: Neonatal intensive care unit and developmental outcome. *Pediatrics, 78,* 1123–1132.

Als, H., Lawhon, G., Duffy, F. H., McAnulty, G. B., Gibes-Grossman, R., & Blickman, J. G. (1994). Individualized developmental care for the very low birthweight preterm infant: Medical and neurofunctional effects. *Journal of the American Medical Association, 272,* 853–858.

Als, H., Lawhon, G., Melzar, A., Duffy, F. H., McAnulty, G. B., & Blickman, J. G. (in preparation). *Individualized behavioral and developmental care for the VLBW preterm infant at high risk for bronchopulmonary dysplasia and intraventricular hemorrhage. Study 3: A clinical model.*

Als, H., Lester, B. M., Tronick, E. Z., & Brazelton, T. B. (1982a). Manual for the assessment of preterm infants' behavior (APIB). In H. E. Fitzgerald, B. M. Lester, & M. W. Yogman (Eds.), *Theory and research in behavioral pediatrics* (pp. 65–132). New York: Plenum.

Als, H., Lester, B. M., Tronick, E. Z., & Brazelton, T. B. (1982b). Towards a research instrument for the assessment of preterm infants' behavior. In H. E. Fitzgerald, B. M. Lester, & M. W. Yogman (Eds.), *Theory and research in behavioral pediatrics* (pp. 35–63). New York: Plenum.

Anderson, G. C., Burroughs, A. K., & Measel, C. P. (1983). Non-nutritive sucking opportunities: A safe and effective treatment for preterm neonates. In T. Field & A. Sostek (Eds.), *Infants born at risk* (pp. 129–147). New York: Grune and Stratton.

Avery, M. E., Tooley, W. H., Keller, J. B., Hurd, S. S., Bryan, H., Cotton, R. B., Epstein, M. F., Fitzhardinge, P. M., Hansen, C. B., Hansen, T. N., Hodson, A., James, L. S., Kitterman, J. A., Nielsen, H. C., Poirier, T. A., Truog, W. E., & Wiung, J. T. (1987). Is chronic lung disease in low birth weight infants preventable? A survey of eight centers. *Pediatrics, 79,* 26–30.

Becker, P. T., Grunwald, P. C., Moorman, J., & Stuhr, S. (1991). Outcomes of developmentally supportive nursing care for very low birthweight infants. *Nursing Research, 40,* 150–155.

Becker, P. T., Grunwald, P. C., Moorman, J., & Stuhr, S. (1993). Effects of developmental care on behavioral organization in very-low-birth-weight infants. *Nursing Research, 42,* 214–220.

Behrman, R. (1985). Preventing low birth weight: A pediatric perspective. *Journal of Pediatrics, 107,* 842–854.

Bernbaum, J., & Hoffman-Williamson, M. (1986). Following the NICU graduate. *Contemporary Pediatrics 3,* 22–37.

Black, P., Blumer, D., Wellner, A., Jeffries, J. J., & Walker, A. E. (1970). An interdisciplinary study of head trauma in children. In C. R. Angle & E. A. Bering (Eds.), *Physical trauma as an etiological agent* (pp. 287–290). Washington, DC: U.S. Department of Health, Education, and Welfare, U.S. Printing Office.

Brazelton, T. B. (1984). *Neonatal Behavioral Assessment Scale* (2nd ed.). Philadelphia: Spastics International Medical Publications, Lippincott.

Buehler, D. M., Als, H., Duffy, F. H., McAnulty, G. B., & Liederman, J. (in press). Effectiveness of individualized developmental care for low risk preterm infants: Behavioral and electrophysiological evidence. *Pediatrics.*

Burroughs, A. K., Asonye, U. O., Anderson-Shanklin, G. C., & Vidyasagar, D. (1978). The effect of non-nutritive sucking on transcutaneous oxygen tension in non-crying preterm neonates. *Research in Nursing and Health, 1,* 69–75.

Case, R. (1992). The role of the frontal lobes in the regulation of cognitive development. *Brain and Cognition, 20,* 51–73.

Chaudhari, S., Kulkarni, S., Pajnigar, F., Pandit, A. N., & Deshmukh, S. (1991). A longitudinal follow up of development of preterm infants. *Indian Pediatrics, 28,* 873–880.

Cornell, E. H., & Gottfried, A. W. (1976). Intervention with premature human infants. *Child Development, 47,* 32–39.

Cowan, W. M. (1979). The development of the brain. *Scientific American, 241,* 113–113.

Cupoli, J. M., Gagan, R. J., Watkins, A. H., & Bell, S. F. (1986). The shapes of grief. *Journal of Perinatology, 6,* 123–126.

Danford, D. A., Miske, S., Headley, J., & Nelson, R. M. (1983). Effects of routine care procedures on transcutaneous oxygen in neonates: A quantitative approach. *Archives of Disease in Childhood, 58,* 20–23.

Davidson, R. J. (1992). Anterior cerebral asymmetry and the nature of emotion. *Brain and Cognition, 20,* 125–151.

Davidson, R. J., & Fox, N. A. (1989). Frontal brain assymmetry predicts infants' response to maternal separation. *Journal of Abnormal Psychology, 98,* 127–131.

Dawson, G., Panagiotides, H., Klinger, L. G., & Hill, D. (1992). The role of frontal lobe functioning in the development of infant self-regulatory behavior. *Brain and Cognition, 20,* 152–175.

Denckla, M. B. (1978). Minimal brain dysfunction. In J. Chall & A. Mirsky (Eds.), *77th Yearbook of the National Society for the Study of Education: Education and the brain* (pp. 223–268). Chicago: University of Chicago Press.

Denckla, M. B. (1991). Attention deficit hyperactivity disorder-residual type. *Journal of Child Neurology, 6,* S44–50.

Denckla, M. B. (1993). The child with developmental disabilities grown up: Adult residua of childhood disorders. *Neurologic Clinics, 11,* 105–125.

Dreyfus-Brisac, C., Fischgold, H., Samson-Dollfus, D., Sainte-Anne Dargassies, S., Monod, N., & Blanc, C. (1957). Veille, sommeil, reactivité sensorielle chez le premature, le nouveau-né et le nourrison. *Electroencephalography and Clinical Neurophysiology, 6,* (Suppl.), 418–440.

Duffy, F., Bartels, P., & Burchfiel, J. (1981). Significance probability mapping: An aid in the topographic analysis of brain electrical activity. *Electroencephalography and Clinical Neurophysiology, 51,* 455–462.

Duffy, F. H., Als, H., & McAnulty, G. B. (1990). Behavioral and electrophysiological evidence for gestational age effects in healthy preterm and fullterm infants studied two weeks after expected due date. *Child Development, 61,* 1271–1286.

Duffy, F. H., Burchfiel, J. L., & Lombroso, C. T. (1979). Brain electrical activity mapping (BEAM): A method for extending the clinical utility of EEG and evoked potential data. *Annals of Neurology, 5,* 309–321.

Duffy, F. H., Denckla, M. B., Bartels, P., Sandini, G., & Kiessling, L. S. (1980). Dyslexia: Automated diagnosis by computerized classification of brain electrical activity. *Annals of Neurology, 7,* 421–428.

Duffy, F. H., Mower, G. D., Jensen, F., & Als, H. (1984). Neural plasticity: A new frontier for infant development. In H. E. Fitzgerald, B. M. Lester, & M. W. Yogman (Eds.), *Theory and research in behavioral pediatrics* (pp. 67–96). New York: Plenum.

Duncan, O. D. (1966). Path analysis: Sociological examples. *American Journal of Sociology, 72,* 1–16.

Engel, R., & Benson, R. C. (1968). Estimate of conceptional age by evoked response activity. *Biologia Neonatorum, 12,* 201–213.

Ferrari, F., Grosoli, M. V., Fontana, G., & Cavazzuti, G. B. (1983). Neurobehavioral comparison of low-risk preterm and fullterm infants at term conceptual age. *Developmental Medicine and Child Neurology, 25,* 450–458.

Field, T. M., Ignatoff, E., Stringer, S., Brennan, J., Greenberg, R., Widmayer, S., & Anderson, G. C. (1982). Non-nutritive sucking during tube feedings: Effects on preterm neonates in an intensive care unit. *Pediatrics, 70*(3), 381–384.

Finlay, B. L., & Miller, B. (1993). Regressive events in early cortical maturation: Their significance for the outcome of early brain damage. In A. M. Galaburda (Ed.), *Dyslexia and Development* (pp. 1–21). Cambridge, MA: Harvard University Press.

Fischer, K. W., & Rose, S. T. (1994). Dynamic development of coordination of components in brain and behavior: A framework for theory and research. In G. Dawson & K. W. Fischer (Eds.), *Human behavior and the developing brain* (pp. 3–66). New York: Guilford.

Fox, N. A. (1991). If it's not left, it's right. *American Psychologist, 46,* 863–872.

Fox, N. A., & Bell, M. (1990). Electrophysiological indices of frontal lobe development: Relations for cognitive and affective behavior in human infants over the first year of life. *Annals of the New York Academy of Sciences, 608,* 677–698.

Freud, W. E. (1991). Das "Whose Baby" Syndrom. Ein Beitrag zum psychodynamischen Verständnis der Perinatologie [The "Whose Baby" Syndrome. A contribution to the psychodynamic understanding of perinatology]. In M. Stauger, F. Conrad, & G. Haselbacher (Eds.), *Psychosomatische Gynäkologie und Geburtshilfe* (pp. 123–137). Berlin: Springer-Verlag.

Gilles, F. H., Leviton, A., & Dooling, E. C. (1983). *The developing human brain.* Boston: John Wright.

Gong, A. K., Van Heuven, W. A. J., Berlanga, M., & Escobedo, M. B. (1989). Severe retinopathy in convalescent preterm infants with mild or regressing retinopathy of prematurity. *Pediatrics, 83,* 422–425.

Gorski, P. A., Hole, W. T., Leonard, C. H., & Martin, J. A. (1983). Direct computer recording of premature infants and nursery care: Distress following two interventions. *Pediatrics, 72,* 198–202.

Gottfried, A. W., & Gaiter, J. L. (1985). *Infant stress under intensive care.* Baltimore, MD: University Park Press.

Gray, J. E., Richardson, D. K., McCormick, M. C., Workman-Daniels, K., & Goldman, D. A. (1992). Neonatal therapeutic intervention scoring system: A therapy-based severity-of-illness index. *Pediatrics, 90,* 561–567.

Grunwald, P. C., & Becker, P. T. (1990). Developmental enhancement: Implementing a program for the NICU. *Neonatal Network, 9*(6), 29–45.

Hack, M., Fanaroff, A., & Merkatz, I. (1979). The low-birth weight infant—Evolution of a changing outlook. *New England Journal of Medicine, 301,* 1162–1165.

Hansen, N., & Okkcn, Λ. (1979). Continuous TcPO2 monitoring in healthy and sick newborn infants during and after feeding. *Birth Defects: Original Article Series, Vol. XV, 4,* 503–508.

Hofer, M. A. (1987). Early social relationships: A psychobiologist's view. *Child Development, 58,* 633–647.

Hunt, J. V., Cooper, B. A. B., & Tooley, W. H. (1988). Very low birth weight infants at 8 and 11 years of age: Role of neonatal illness and family status. *Pediatrics, 82,* 596–603.

Hunt, J. V., Tooley, W. H., & Cooper, B. A. B. (1992). Further investigations of intellectual status at age 8 years: 1. Long-term consequences into adulthood: 2. Neonatal predictors. In S. L. Friedman & M. D. Sigman (Eds.), *Advances in applied developmental psychology: Vol. 6. The psychological developmental of low birthweight children* (pp. 315–337). Norwood, NJ: Ablex.

Hunt, J. V., Tooley, W. H., & Harvin, D. (1982). Learning disabilities in children with birthweights < 1,500 grams. *Seminars in Perinatology, 6,* 280–287.

Klaus, M., & Kennel, J. H. (1982). *Parent-infant bonding.* St. Louis, MO: Mosby.

Klaus, M. H. (1982). Application of recent findings to clinical care. In M. H. Klaus & M. O. Robertson (Eds.), *Birth, interaction, and attachment* (pp. 129–134). Johnson and Johnson Pediatric Roundtable. Skillman, NJ.

Kliegman, R. M., & Walsh, M. C. (1987). Neonatal necrotizing enterocolitis: Pathogenesis, classification, and spectrum of illness. *Current Problems in Pediatrics, 17,* 213–288.

Laget, P., Flores-Guevara, R., D'Allest, A. M., Ostre, C., Raimbault, J., & Mariani, J. (1977). La maturation des potentiales evoques chez l'enfant normal. *Electroencephalography and Clinical Neurophysiology, 43,* 732–744.

Largo, R. M., Molinari, L., Kundu, S., Lipp, A., & Duc, G. (1990). Intellectual outcome, speech and school performance in high risk preterm children with birth weight appropriate for gestational age. *European Journal of Pediatrics, 149,* 845–850.

Lawhon, G. (1986). Management of stress in premature infants. In D. J. Angelini, C. M. Whelan Knapp, & R. M. Gibes (Eds.), *Perinatal neonatal nursing: A clinical handbook* (pp. 319–328). Boston: Blackwell.

Lawhon, G., & Melzar, A. (1991). Developmentally supportive interventions. In J. P. Cloherty & A. R. Stark (Eds.), *Manual of neonatal care* (pp. 581–584). Boston: Little, Brown.

Liaw, F. R., & Brooks-Gunn, J. (1993). Patterns of low-weight children's cognitive development. *Developmental Psychology, 29,* 1024–1035.

Linn, P. L., Horowitz, F. D., Buddin, B. J., Leake, J. C., & Fox, H. A. (1985). Stimulation in the NICU: Is more necessarily better? *Clinics in Perinatology, 12,* 407–422.

Lombroso, C. T. (1981). Normal and abnormal EEGs in fullterm neonates. In C. E. Henry (Ed.), *Current Clinical Neurophysiology* (pp. 83–150). Holland: Elsevier North Holland.

Long, J. G., Lucey, J. F., & Philip, A. G. S. (1980). Noise and hypoxemia in the intensive care nursery. *Pediatrics, 65,* 143–145.

Long, J. G., Philip, A. G. S., & Lucey, J. F. (1980). Excessive handling as a cause of hypoxemia. *Pediatrics, 65*(2), 203–207.

Marín-Padilla, M. (1993). Pathogenesis of late-acquired leptomeningeal heterotopias and secondary cortical alterations: A golgi study. In A. M. Galaburda (Eds.), *Dyslexia and development* (pp. 64–89). Cambridge, MA: Harvard University Press.

Martin, R. J., Herrell, N., Rubin, D., & Fanaroff, A. (1979). Effect of supine and prone positions on arterial oxygen tension in the preterm infant. *Pediatrics, 63,* 528–531.

Martin, R. J., Okken, A., & Rubin, D. (1979). Arterial oxygen tension during active and quiet sleep in the normal neonate. *Journal of Pediatrics, 94,* 271–274.

McCormick, M. C., Brooks-Gunn, J., Workman-Daniels, K., Turner, J., & Peckman, G. J. (1992). The health and developmental status of very low-birthweight children at school age. *Journal of the American Medical Association, 267*(16), 2204–2208.

McLennan, J. E., Gilles, F. H., & Neff, R. (1983). A model of growth of the human fetal brain. In F. H. Gilles, A. Leviton, & D. C. Dooling (Eds.), *The developing human brain* (pp. 43–59). Boston: John Wright.

Minde, K., Whitelaw, A., Brown, J., & Fitzhardinge, P. (1983). Effect of neonatal complications in premature infants on early parent-child interactions. *Developmental Medicine and Child Neurology 25,* 763–777.

Minde, K. K., Morton, P., Manning, D., & Hines, B. (1980). Some determinants of mother-infant interaction in the premature nursery. *Journal of the American Academy of Child Psychiatry, 19,* 1-21.

Minde, K. K., Trehub, S., Carter, C., Boukydis, C., Celhoffer, L., & Morton, P. (1978). Mother-child relationships in the premature nursery: An observation study. *Pediatrics, 61,* 373–379.

Murdoch, D. R., & Darlow, B. A. (1984). Handling during neonatal intensive care. *Archives of Disease in Childhood, 29,* 957–961.

Norris, S., Campbell, & Brenkert, S. (1982). Nursing procedures and alterations in transcutaneous oxygen tension in premature infants. *Nursing Research, 31,* 330–336.

Oberklaid, F., Sewall, J., Sanson, A., & Prior, M. (1991). Temperament and behavior of preterm infants: A six-year follow-up. *Pediatrics, 87,* 854–861.

O'Brodovich, H., & Mellins, R. (1985). Bronchopulmonary dysplasia. Unresolved neonatal acute lung injury. *American Review of Respiratory Disease, 132,* 694–709.

Pontius, A. A. (1973). Dysfunction patterns analagous to frontal lobe system and caudate nucleus syndromes in some groups of minimal brain dysfunction. *Journal of the American Medical Women's Association, 28,* 285–292.

Pontius, A. A. (1974). Basis for a neurological test of frontal lobe system functioning up to adolescence—A form analysis of action expressed in narratives. *Adolescence, 9,* 221–232.

Prechtl, H. F. R. (1977). *The neurological examination of the fullterm newborn infant* (2nd ed.). Philadelphia: Lippincott.

Rakic, P. (1991). Experimental manipulation of cerebral cortical areas in primates. *Philosophical Translations. Royal Society of London, 331,* 291–294.

Rakic, P., Suñer, I., & Williams, R. W. (1991). A novel cytoarchitectonic area induced experimentally within the primate visual cortex. *Proceedings. National Academy of Sciences, 88,* 2083–2087.

Reppert, S. M., & Rivkees, S. A. (1989). Development of human circadian rhythms: Implications for health and disease. In S. M. Reppert (Eds.), *Development of circadian rhythmicity and photoperiodism in mammals* (pp. 245–259). Ithaca, NY: Perinatology Press.

Sell, E. J., Luick, A., Poisson, S. S., & Hill, S. (1980). Outcome of very low birthweight (VLBW) infants. I. Neonatal behavior of 188 infants. *Journal of Developmental and Behavioral Pediatrics, 1,* 78–85.

Sidorova, O. A., & Kostyunina, M. B. (1993). The participation of cortical areas of the brain in processes of the perception and reproduction of emotional states of man. *Neuroscience and Behavioral Physiology, 23,* 135–141.

Siwek, D. F., & Pandya, D. N. (1991). Prefrontal projections to the mediodorsal nucleus of the thalamus in the rhesus monkey. *Journal of Comparative Neurology, 312,* 509-524.

Sostek, A. M. (1992). Prematurity as well as intraventricular hemorrhage influence developmental outcome at 5 years. In S. L. Friedman & M. D. Sigman (Eds.), *Advances in applied developmental psychology, Volume 6. The psychological development of low birthweight children* (pp. 259–274). Norwood, NJ: Ablex.

Turkewitz, G., & Kenny, P. A. (1985). The role of developmental limitations of sensory input on sensory/perceptual organization. *Journal of Developmental and Behavioral Pediatrics, 6,* 302–306.

U.S. Department of Health, Education and Welfare, Public Health Service, National Center for Health Statistics. (1993). Births, marriages, divorces and deaths. *Monthly Vital Statistics Report, 42,* 6-42.

VandenBerg, K. A. (1990a). Nippling management of the sick neonate in the NICU: The disorganized feeder. *Neonatal Network, 9*(1), 9–16.

VandenBerg, K. A. (1990b). Behaviorally supportive care for the extremely premature infant. In L. P. Gunderson & C. Kenner (Eds.), *Care of the 24–25 week gestational age infant (small baby protocol)* (pp. 129–157). Petaluma, CA: Neonatal Network.

VandenBerg, K. A., & Franck, L. S. (1990). Behavioral issues for infants with BPD. In C. Lund (Eds.), *BPD: Strategies for total patient care* (pp. 113–152). Petaluma, CA: Neonatal Network.

Volpe, J. J. (1989a). Intraventricular hemorrhage in the premature infant—Current concepts: Part I. *Annals of Neurology, 25*(1), 3–11.

Volpe, J. J. (1989b). Intraventricular hemorrhage in the premature infant—Current concepts. Part II. *Annals of Neurology, 25*(2), 109–116.

Vygotsky, L. S. (1930). *Tool and symbol in child development.* In M. Cole, V. John-Steiner, S. Scribner, & E. Souberman (Eds.), *Mind in society: The development of higher psychological processes* (pp. 19–30). Cambridge, MA: Harvard University Press.

Waber, D. P., McCormick, M. C., & Workman-Daniels, K. (1992, February). *Neurobehavioral outcomes in very low birthweight, low birthweight, and normal birthweight children with and without medical complications.* Abstract presented at the International Neuropsychological Society 21st Annual Meeting, Galveston, Texas.

Watanabe, K., Iwase, K., & Hara, K. (1972). Maturation of visual evoked responses in low-weight infants. *Developmental Medicine and Child Neurology, 14,* 425–435.

Whyte, H. E., Pearce, J. M., & Taylor, M. J. (1987). Changes in the VEP in preterm neonates with arousal states, as assessed by EEG monitoring. *Electroencephalography and Clinical Neurophysiology, 68,* 223–225.

Wolke, D. (1987). Environmental and developmental neonatology. *Journal of Reproductive and Infant Psychology, 5,* 17–42.

Wright, S. (1921). Correlation and causation. *Journal of Agricultural Research, 20,* 557–585.

Wright, S. (1960). Path coefficients and path regressions: Alternative or complementary concepts? *Biometrics, 16,* 189–202.

Yeterian, E., & Pandya, D. N. (1991). Prefronto-striatal connections in relation to cortical architectonic organization in rhesus monkey. *Journal of Comparative Neurology, 312,* 43–67.

Zametkin, A. J., Nordahl, T. E., Gross, M., King, A. C., Semple, W. E., Rumsey, J., Hamburger, S., & Cohen, R. N. (1990). Cerebral glucose metabolism in adults with hyperactivity of childhood onset. *New England Journal of Medicine, 323,* 1361–1366.

Author Index

Subject Index